'One of the great puzzles of modernity invc
change the very systems that spawn them.
City brings together a diverse array of idea
opments from autonomous vehicles, drone:
omies and predictive policing, are changing the way we behave and the
regulations we are inventing to contain them. This is the first book to
provide an integrated picture of the new landscape of urban artificial intelligences, one that we will all need to navigate on the road to the future.
Essential reading for all who are attempting to understand the critical
challenges of AI.'

Michael Batty, *Bartlett Professor of Planning,*
University College London

'The advent of generative AI and deep learning algorithms has undercut
and transcended the concept and technical practice of the so-called smart
city. With *Artificial Intelligence and the City* the shift from smart ontologies to AI logics of the urban is explored across multiple case studies, from
urban drones to autonomous vehicles in the city. A timely and important
intervention.'

Louise Amoore, *Professor of Political Geography,*
Durham University

'Artificial intelligence is transforming the socio-technical characteristics of
cities under late modernity. This vital collection of essays presents multiple
vantage points from which to reflect on emerging articulations between AI
and urban space.'

Matthew Gandy, *Professor of Geography,*
University of Cambridge

'By departing from the polemic that typifies explorations of artificial intelligences, this book is a well-structured and thoughtfully curated volume
on the interrelationships between AI and cities. This welcome departure
from smart urbanism explores the textures of urban AI at varying scales
and geographic contexts, and offers the reader many stories of caution and
hope by exploring, not only how the city is influenced by autonomous
vehicles, robotics, platforms and algorithms, but also how it reframes and
reorders these socio-technical relations.'

Nancy Odendaal, *Professor in City Planning,*
University of Cape Town

ARTIFICIAL INTELLIGENCE AND THE CITY

This book explores in theory and practice how artificial intelligence (AI) intersects with and alters the city. Drawing upon a range of urban disciplines and case studies, the chapters reveal the multitude of repercussions that AI is having on urban society, urban infrastructure, urban governance, urban planning and urban sustainability.

Contributors also examine how the city, far from being a passive recipient of new technologies, is influencing and reframing AI through subtle processes of co-constitution. The book advances three main contributions and arguments:

- First, it provides empirical evidence of the emergence of a post-smart trajectory for cities in which new material and decision-making capabilities are being assembled through multiple AIs.
- Second, it stresses the importance of understanding the mutually constitutive relations between the new experiences enabled by AI technology and the urban context.
- Third, it engages with the concepts required to clarify the opaque relations that exist between AI and the city, as well as how to make sense of these relations from a theoretical perspective.

Artificial Intelligence and the City offers a state-of-the-art analysis and review of AI urbanism, from its roots to its global emergence. It cuts across several disciplines and will be a useful resource for undergraduates and postgraduates in the fields of urban studies, urban planning, geography, architecture, urban design, science and technology studies, sociology and politics.

Federico Cugurullo is Assistant Professor in Smart and Sustainable Urbanism at Trinity College Dublin.

Federico Caprotti is Professor of Human Geography at the University of Exeter, UK.

Matthew Cook is Professor of Innovation at the Open University, UK.

Andrew Karvonen is Professor of Urban Design and Planning at Lund University, Sweden.

Pauline McGuirk is Senior Professor in Urban Geography at the University of Wollongong, Australia.

Simon Marvin is Professor of Urban Geography at the University of Sheffield's Urban Institute, UK.

ARTIFICIAL INTELLIGENCE AND THE CITY

Urbanistic Perspectives on AI

Edited by Federico Cugurullo, Federico Caprotti, Matthew Cook, Andrew Karvonen, Pauline McGuirk and Simon Marvin

Routledge
Taylor & Francis Group

LONDON AND NEW YORK

Designed cover image: Eleonora Casetta

First published 2024
by Routledge
4 Park Square, Milton Park, Abingdon, Oxon OX14 4RN

and by Routledge
605 Third Avenue, New York, NY 10158

Routledge is an imprint of the Taylor & Francis Group, an informa business

British Library Cataloguing-in-Publication Data
A catalogue record for this book is available from the British Library

ISBN: 978-1-032-43147-5 (hbk)
ISBN: 978-1-032-43146-8 (pbk)
ISBN: 978-1-003-36587-7 (ebk)

DOI: 10.4324/9781003365877

Typeset in Sabon
by SPi Technologies India Pvt Ltd (Straive)

CONTENTS

FIGURES

TABLES

EDITORS

Federico Cugurullo is Assistant Professor in Smart and Sustainable Urbanism at Trinity College Dublin. His current research explores how artificial intelligence is impacting urban governance and planning, thereby influencing the sustainability of cities. He is the author of *Frankenstein Urbanism* (Routledge 2021) and a co-editor of *Inside Smart Cities* (Routledge 2019).

Federico Caprotti is Professor of Human Geography at the University of Exeter. His main interests are in the urban future and how digital and other infrastructures can be understood in visions for urban development in both the global North and South. He has led research projects on smart and eco-urbanism, and on the off-grid city, in Europe, China and South Africa.

Matthew Cook is Professor of Innovation at the Open University in the United Kingdom. His research interests are in technological change and urban development, with particular reference to the governance of urban and regional infrastructures and digitalization. He leads the Open University's Future Urban Environments research team.

Andrew Karvonen is Professor of Urban Design and Planning at Lund University in Sweden. He conducts sociotechnical research on urban development processes related to infrastructure networks, urban laboratories and experiments, and smart cities and digitalization. He is a co-editor of *Smart and Sustainable Cities? Pipedreams, Practicalities and Possibilities* (Routledge 2021).

Pauline McGuirk is Senior Professor in Urban Geography and Director of the Australian Centre for Culture, Environment, Society and Space (ACCESS) at the University of Wollongong, Australia. Her research focuses on critical studies of urban governance, its changing geographies, practices and politics, with a current focus on innovation. She is a Fellow of the Academy of Social Sciences, Australia.

Simon Marvin is Professor of Urban Geography and former Director of The Urban Institute at the University of Sheffield, UK. He is the author and a co-editor of several books, including *Urban Operating Systems* with Andres Luque-Ayala (MIT Press 2020).

CONTRIBUTORS

Sarah Barns is a practitioner, researcher and Industry Fellow at the Queensland University of Technology, whose work engages with a range of civic governance and design implications of digital transformation in public spaces. She is the author of *Platform Urbanism: Negotiating Platform Ecosystems in Connected Cities* (Palgrave, 2020).

David Bissell is Professor of Human Geography at the University of Melbourne. He is a cultural geographer who undertakes qualitative research on mobile lives and technological futures. His current and recent projects explore the impact of digital on-demand mobile work on cities; how automation is changing workplaces; and how households respond to mobile work practices.

Silvio Carta is an architect, chartered building engineer and Associate Professor at the University of Hertfordshire. His work focuses on the application of technology and computational design to improve the physical environment and encourage positive societal change. Silvio is the author of *Big Data, Code and the Discrete City* (Routledge 2019) and *Machine Learning and the City* (Wiley 2022).

Bei Chen is a former journalist working in China and currently a PhD student in the Department of Urban Studies and Planning at the University of Sheffield. Her research programme focuses on the socio-political dimensions of China's AI, robotics, and automation visions, policies and experimental practices in urban contexts.

Dean Curran is an Associate Professor of Sociology at the University of Calgary. His research areas include risk, economic sociology, social theory and inequalities. He has publications in the *British Journal of Sociology*, *Antipode*, *Urban Studies* and a (2016) book with Palgrave Macmillan, *Risk, Power and Inequality in the 21st Century*.

Vincent J. Del Casino Jr. is Professor of Urban and Regional Planning at San José State University. He has published articles in the *Annals of the American Association of Geographers*, *Progress in Human Geography*, *Social and Cultural Geography*, *Antipode: a Journal of Radical Geography* and *Transactions of the Institute of British Geographers*, to name a few.

Robyn Dowling is Professor and Dean of the School of Architecture, Design and Planning, University of Sydney. Her current research is concerned with the ways in which urban governance and urban life are responding to climate change and technological disruptions.

Philip Garboden is the HCRC Professor in Affordable Housing Economics, Policy, and Planning in the Department of Urban and Regional Planning at the University of Hawai'i Economic Research Organization. He holds a PhD in Sociology, a Master's in Public Policy and an MSE in Applied Math from Johns Hopkins.

Zongtian Guo is a doctoral student in smart city studies at Trinity College Dublin's Department of Geography. His PhD project looks at how urban AI is applied in Guangzhou (China) to meet citizens' needs.

Debbie Hopkins is an Associate Professor in Human Geography at the University of Oxford. She conducts research which examines climate breakdown, mobile work and technologies and automations across passenger and freight transport. From 2022 to 2025, Debbie will lead an ESRC-funded project on working lives in the UK trucking sector.

Anna Jackman is a Lecturer in Human Geography and the University of Reading. Anna's research explores technological visibilities, volumes, relations and futures. Through the lens of the drone, Anna interrogates the unmanning of everyday, urban and military life. Anna acted as Specialist Advisor for the 2019 Science and Technology Committee Inquiry into 'Commercial and recreational drone use in the UK.'

Eva Kassens-Noor is a Professor and Chair of the Institute of Transport Planning and Traffic Engineering in the Civil and Environmental Engineering Department at TU Darmstadt. She is an Adjunct at Michigan State University.

Her interests are mobility behaviours for, during and despite of extreme events and urban transformations.

Weiqiang Lin is Associate Professor at the Department of Geography, National University of Singapore. He is a cultural geographer interested in mobility infrastructures. His recent research includes the production of air-spaces in Southeast Asia; framings of air logistics in Singapore and China; and labour and automation in Asia's international airports.

Casey R. Lynch is Assistant Professor of Digitalization and Society at the University of Twente, Netherlands. He has published articles in the *Annals of the American Association of Geographers*, *Antipode* and *Urban Geography*, among others. His research interests include the politics and ethics of techno-capitalism and emerging digital technologies, imaginaries of urban futures, geographic thought and critical social theory.

Adam Moore is a PhD candidate at the University of Melbourne. They are a cultural geographer and urban planner who researches the socio-technical relationships that shape and sustain digital infrastructures and their publics. Their current research examines the working lives and practices of coopera-tive platform labour.

Cian O'Donovan is a Senior Research Fellow at University College London's Department of Science and Technology Studies. He researches the impacts of digital transformation on social care, asking who benefits from forms of innovation, who pays and who decides. He is the principal investigator of the Empowering Future Care Workforces project.

Davide Pisu is an architect and a Post-doctoral Fellow at the University of Cagliari. The focus of his academic works is on the relationship between design and morphology and the normative realm. His work has been pub-lished in many journals including *Architectural Theory Review* and the *Journal of Architecture*.

Stephen Potter is Emeritus Professor of Transport Strategy at the Open University, where he played a key role in developing the University's links with the Milton Keynes Low Carbon and Smart City programmes. His research is focused on the human and institutional aspects of transport innovation.

Eva Rosen is an Associate Professor at the McCourt School of Public Policy. She holds a PhD in Sociology and Social Policy from Harvard University and is the author of *The Voucher Promise: "Section 8" and the Fate of an American Neighborhood*.

Aaron Shapiro is Assistant Professor of Technology Studies in the Department of Communication at the University of North Carolina, Chapel Hill. His book *Design, Control, Predict: Logistical Governance in the Smart City* was published in 2020 by the University of Minnesota Press.

Alistair Sisson is a Postdoctoral Research Fellow in the School of Geography and Sustainable Communities, University of Wollongong. His work spans housing, stigma, gentrification, urban development and urban governance.

Alan Smart is a Professor Emeritus in the Department of Anthropology and Archaeology at the University of Calgary. His research interests include political economy, urban anthropology, borders, smart cities and posthumanism. He is the author of *Making Room: Squatter Clearance in Hong Kong, The Shek Kip Mei Myth: Squatters, Fires, and Colonial Rule* and *Posthumanism: Anthropological Perspectives* (co-author Josephine Smart).

Luca Staricco is an Associate Professor in Spatial Planning at Politecnico di Torino. His main research fields are related to interactions between mobility and land use, coordination of spatial and transport planning, transit-oriented development, sustainable mobility, liveability of urban spaces and regional and urban resilience.

Jack Stilgoe is a Professor of Science and Technology Policy at University College London, where he researches the governance of emerging technologies. He was the principal investigator of the ESRC Driverless Futures project (2019–2021). He works with Government and research funders to develop frameworks and practices for responsible innovation.

Shanti Sumartojo is Associate Professor of Design Research in the Emerging Technologies Research Lab in the Faculty of Art Design and Architecture at Monash University. With a strong commitment to interdisciplinary and collaborative scholarship, she researches how people experience and understand design and technology in their surroundings.

Miriam E. Sweeney is an Associate Professor at the University of Alabama in the School of Library and Information Studies. Her research explores the intersections of identity, design and dataveillance in AI voice assistants, digital assistants and chatbot interfaces using critical cultural perspectives.

Miguel Valdez is a Lecturer in Technology and Innovation Management and a member of the Future Urban Environments team at the Open University. His research explores how various publics as well as civic, industrial and governmental bodies use urban experiments to make sense of innovative technologies and collectively negotiate the future of their city.

Elisabetta Vitale Brovarone is an Assistant Professor in Spatial Planning at Politecnico di Torino. Her research focuses on mobility, land use–transport interaction, and accessibility, governance and local development in metropolitan, rural and mountain areas. On these topics, she has authored several publications, had professional experiences and taken part in international research projects.

Aidan While is Co-director of the Urban Institute and Senior Lecturer in the Department of Urban Studies and Planning at the University of Sheffield. Aidan's research interests include environmentalism, land-use regulation and urban technologies. His research has increasingly focused on the emerging role of automation, robotics and AI in reshaping cities and ecology.

Si Jie Ivin Yeo is a DPhil student in the School of Geography and the Environment, University of Oxford. He is an urban and cultural geographer interested in the transformative capabilities of smart and digital technologies, everyday well-being in urban green and blue spaces, and the nature of post-human life.

Yawei Zhao is a lecturer in the Department of Geography at the University of Manchester. Her research focuses on the intersection of migration, digital technologies and urbanization. Her most recent work concerns emerging AI technologies and the multi-scalar expansion of governance platforms.

1

INTRODUCING AI INTO URBAN STUDIES

Federico Cugurullo, Federico Caprotti, Matthew Cook, Andrew Karvonen, Pauline McGuirk and Simon Marvin

Introduction: the dawn of AI urbanism

Innovation in artificial intelligence (AI) is transforming cities in unprecedented ways. Robots are increasingly managing key urban services, performing jobs that were once the exclusive domain of humans and maintaining the infrastructure of cities (Lynch et al., 2022; Macrorie et al., 2021). Self-driving cars are reshaping urban transport systems, thereby triggering new mobilities that impact the design of the built environment (Cugurullo et al. 2021; Dowling and McGuirk, 2022). City brains and digital platforms are gradually reengineering the practice of urban governance by operating entire urban systems that range from health to transport and from security to ecosystems (Caprotti and Liu, 2020; Curran and Smart, 2021; Marvin et al., 2022). Meanwhile, through mobile apps and personal computers, invisible software agents are sifting and sorting urban lives, for instance, deciding which residents to quarantine and which residents qualify for a mortgage (Kitchin, 2020; Lee and Floridi, 2021). In essence, the advent of AI introduces multiple non-biological intelligences that act upon and within cities. For the first time in history, the control of the city is not determined exclusively by humans. It is also influenced by AIs whose logics and actions sometimes diverge significantly from ours (Cugurullo, 2021; Russell, 2019). We are witnessing the beginning of a new and uncertain urban era, replete with risks and opportunities.

In different spaces and through diverse modalities, AIs and urban systems are converging at a rapid pace (Amoore, 2023; Son et al., 2023; While et al., 2021; Yigitcanlar et al., 2023). The urban changes associated with AI are challenging to describe and analyse in theoretical and empirical terms. There

DOI: 10.4324/9781003365877-1

are many different types of AI being applied in heterogeneous urban spaces, unleashing a transformative force of rare impetus. These AIs are *urban* in the sense that they operate primarily in urban environments and, in order to function, they need resources and infrastructures, such as Big Data, electrical grids and server farms, that are urban in nature. We refer to this polymorphous agglomeration of AIs, comprising robots, autonomous vehicles, city brains and software agents, as *urban artificial intelligences* or simply *urban AI* (see also Cugurullo, 2020; Luusua et al., 2023). Moreover, we note that the diffusion of urban AI in the life, governance and planning of cities is generating a distinct kind of urbanism which we term *AI urbanism*. Here, the configuration of urban systems, the form of the built environment and, more broadly, the experiences of urban residents are morphing into something markedly distinct from past iterations and in ways that are only partially understood.

The emergence of AI urbanism is neither a linear nor an atemporal process, but rather a multiform and geographically sensitive phenomenon influenced by previous urbanisms, that is destabilizing the material and immaterial fabric of cities. In this book, while we argue that the use of AI technologies in the management of urban services and infrastructures is connected to well-known practices of smart urbanism (see Coletta et al., 2019; Karvonen et al., 2019; Willis and Aurigi, 2020), we also claim that the emergence of AI in cities is a turning point at which *smart* is theoretically and empirically insufficient to explain the urban transformations generated by AI. Urban AI would not be able to function without common smart technologies, such as sensors and the repositories of Big Data that they generate. At the same time, however, urban AI embodies technologies, capabilities and operations which go well beyond traditional smart-city initiatives. For example, the ability to extract concepts and to reason, and the power to decide and act autonomously in real-life environments without human supervision, situates AI and its numerous urban incarnations in theoretical and empirical grounds which diverge from smart urbanism and, thus, require close scrutiny and debate (Cugurullo, 2020).

Drawing upon a range of urban disciplines and over 20 international case studies, the aim of this book is to explore in theory and practice how AI intersects with and alters the city. The chapters reveal a multitude of repercussions that AI is having on urban society, urban infrastructure, urban governance, urban planning and urban sustainability. At the same time, this collection aims to examine how the city, far from being a passive recipient of new technologies, is influencing and reframing AI through subtle processes of co-constitution and co-determination. The focus on AI is specific in the sense that we seek to explicitly look beyond the literature on smart urbanism, by synthesizing new empirical data on AI and its hitherto overlooked urban dimensions and presenting novel concepts and theories about AI urbanism.

Our focus is also broad since we take into account multiple types of AI and urban scales from the individual citizen to the single building and from entire cities to regional and international urban networks.

Overall, we advance three main contributions and arguments in the book. First, we discuss the emergence of a post-smart trajectory for cities in which new material and decision-making capabilities are being assembled through multiple AIs. In so doing, we inquire into the distinctiveness and implications of novel AI logics in the urban context. Second, we stress the importance of understanding the mutually constitutive relations between the new experiences enabled by AI technology and the urban context. We question how AI shapes urban life and places and how the urban condition shapes AI in turn. Third, we engage with the concepts required to clarify the often opaque relations that exist between AI and the city, as well as how to make sense of these relations from a theoretical perspective. In essence, this collection provides a state-of-the-art review of AI urbanism, from its historical roots to its contemporary global emergence, in an attempt to develop the empirical and theoretical foundations for the next generation of urban socio-technical studies.

In the following sections, we unpack the connections between AI and the urban by clarifying the concept of *urban AI* and illustrating its most prominent incarnations, namely autonomous vehicles, urban robots, city brains and urban software agents. We then explain how the emergence of urban AI is contributing to the formation of a new type of urbanism which we call *AI urbanism*. We note how AI urbanism derives from but also extends well beyond smart urbanism, along three main axes: function, presence and agency. We discuss the similarities and differences underpinning *AI* and *smart* urbanism and, after stressing the problematic implications of human–machine interactions in the making and governance of cities, we call on urban researchers and stakeholders to scrutinize the critical intersections between urban development and the development of artificial intelligences.

Making sense of AI from an urbanistic perspective

AI is now one of the dominant forces that is transforming our planet and lives, and yet its meaning and manifestations are elusive (Crawford, 2021). As Greenfield (2018) notes, AI is an obscure and esoteric set of technologies in the sense that the intricate mechanics and thought processes of artificial intelligences are usually understood only by a small group of experts with specialized knowledge in computer science and engineering. This epistemological complexity is exacerbated by the fact that neither a single type of AI nor a universal blueprint to build one exists (Bostrom, 2017; Cave et al., 2020). The field of AI is thus difficult to navigate, especially from the perspective of the social sciences and humanities. To address this issue, we propose a threefold approach to make sense of AI. In this section, we begin by acknowledging the wide range of AI technologies that are present in the world. We then summarize the core characteristics of AI across its multiple incarnations and, finally, provide examples to make them visible (and therefore easier to understand) by focusing on how they manifest themselves in real-life urban spaces.

The first step in making sense of AI is to talk about artificial *intelligences* and avoid the conceptual trap of singular nouns. A singular noun refers to (and thus makes us think about) a clearly delineated person, place or thing. Specifically in relation to the subject of our inquiry, the term *AI*, as a singular noun, is misleading since it implies the existence of a singular technology possessing a singular type of intelligence. In reality, this is far from being the case. There are many different artificial intelligences manifesting diverse types and degrees of intelligence (Russell and Norvig, 2016; Samoili et al., 2020). A useful analogy here is offered by a widely recognized form of intelligence: *biological intelligence*. We know that there is an extraordinary variety of intelligent life forms on Earth, ranging from mammals to insects, and human intelligence represents only a fraction of this variety. In science, we do not generalize biological intelligence and instead acknowledge the cognitive and behavioural differences as well as the similarities that exist among species. This same logic applies to AI. We understand AI as a complex cosmos comprising a myriad of diverse non-biological intelligences whose cognition and behaviour varies significantly from case to case.

The second step is to identify and characterize the most common traits that are shared among different AIs. These traits include (a) the quality of being artificial, (b) the capacity for learning, (c) the ability to extract concepts, (d) the power to manage uncertainty and (e) the capability to act rationally and (f) autonomously. All AIs are considered to be artificial, in the sense that their development is not the outcome of a natural process such as the formation of the human brain, whose current morphology is the byproduct of thousands of years of evolution (Bruner, 2021; Galway-Witham and Stringer, 2018). In contrast, AI is either human-made or, as Bostrom (2017) notes, created by machines through technological processes that are relatively fast. The assembly of a simple robot, for instance, takes less than five minutes, while algorithms can be created in a matter of hours (Rubenstein et al., 2014; Sherry and Thompson, 2021).

In terms of key capabilities, AIs can learn and develop knowledge *directly* by sensing a given environment using sensors such as cameras and microphones, and *indirectly* by being fed large data sets (Russell and Norvig, 2016). AIs can then make sense of the information that they acquire by extracting concepts from it (Bostrom, 2017). This capacity is a mark of their intelligence since it shows the ability to find meanings and recognize ideas in what is being observed. Examples include AI-driven cars that are capable of understanding that the colour red in a traffic light means that they must stop, and service robots operating in a restaurant that can distinguish customers from inanimate objects and then comprehend that it is a good idea to attend to the customers. It is also important to note that AIs can, as a result of learning, devise new rule sets that take us beyond previously existing human-centred logics. As Bostrom (2017) remarks, it would be dangerous to always assume an affinity between the logics developed by biological and non-biological intelligences.

Ultimately concepts lead to actions and most AIs are designed to act in chaotic and uncertain situations in which some information might be missing or unclear (Kanal and Lemmer, 2014). Their actions are considered to be rational inasmuch as they are 'based on reasons' which determine what is right or wrong and inform their behaviour (Lupia et al., 2000: 7; Russell and Norvig, 2016). This assumes the presence of a moral order underpinning the actions of AIs. However, the field of AI ethics remains underdeveloped, especially in practical terms. AI moral guidelines are often incoherent and ignored by the private sector actors that are supposed to implement them (Munn, 2022). As a result, there is a problematic lack of clarity regarding the moral compass behind AIs' actions, particularly in contexts in which AI systems operate with humans out of the loop. When humans do not steer the actions of an AI or supervise its behaviour, that AI can be said to be *autonomous* because it is exercising intelligence in an independent manner (Cugurullo, 2020; Levesque, 2017).

The urban is the space where AIs become most prominently visible and materially situated in the physical landscape. It is the locus where their actions occur and where their behaviours are materialized. AI is intrinsically linked to urbanity, for three interconnected reasons. First, AI requires physical environments to act upon, and these are frequently urban. Autonomous cars, for example, operate on public roads in urban settlements. Similarly, service robots function in shops and restaurants located in urban environments. Even the actions of the most ethereal AIs have an inevitable material dimension, like in the case of algorithms that calculate the market value of a property or predict the location of a crime. Second, AI is an *agent* (Russell and Norvig, 2016). As such, it acts and, by nature, it engages in a plethora of activities. Urban settlements encapsulate an increasing proportion and range of activities on our planet (Balland et al., 2020; Elmqvist et al., 2021; Kaddar et al., 2022). Therefore, whether an AI is poised to participate in a social activity, engage in an economic transaction, influence a political process or contribute to global environmental changes, it is compelled to interact with urban systems. Third, the development of AI depends on urban development. Most AIs currently develop their intelligence through processes of *machine learning* whereby they are 'set loose on vast fields of data' to learn from them (Greenfield, 2018: 220). As Lee (2018: 14) points out, 'there's no data like more data.' The more data an AI is exposed to, the more and faster its intelligence grows. As the primary location of manifold human activity, urban spaces are massive generators of data, and it is thus in the urban realm that AI has the greatest opportunity to learn and evolve.

In terms of quality, the urban generates the fine-grain data most useful for machine learning. It is *real-life data* which differs substantially from datasets that are carefully curated and cleaned by computer scientists and then stored digitally. In urban spaces, instead, AI learns *in the wild* and has the possibility to contemplate actually existing social, political, economic, cultural and environmental phenomena as they unfold in real time in the real world. In terms of quantity, cities in particular offer the largest sources of data. Cities, as urban spaces with high population densities, host an unparalleled concentration of human activities that fuel intense processes of consumption, social interaction, mobility and intellectual exchange (Balland et al., 2020; Moran et al., 2018). There are few limits to what can happen in a large city, which is an ideal condition for machine learning and its limitless thirst for knowledge. In China, for example, AI companies are building a competitive advantage by using dense cities as a playground for machine learning (Lee, 2018). In essence, the contemporary city is the microcosm through which AI observes and learns about the entire world.

The connection between the urban and AI makes the latter visible in four distinct forms which, in turn, can be understood as four main types of urban AI. The first one is represented by *autonomous vehicles* (AVs). These are terrestrial devices built for transporting persons or things, which are driven by an AI. They are characterized by different vehicle types including autonomous cars, trucks and buses, as well as by diverse public and private ownership models and service types, such as car-sharing, mass transport and mobility-as-a-service (Acheampong et al., 2021; Nikitas et al., 2021). The urbanity of AVs is evident from a spatial perspective since this type of urban AI necessitates urban spaces to fulfil its main function: transportation. Most pointedly, autonomous cars operate on public roads predominantly in urban environments where the quality of road infrastructure tends to be higher (and thus easier to sense and navigate for an AI) than in rural areas, and where it is more common to find fast and reliable communication networks. Cities, in particular, are at the centre of AV innovation and related disruptions (see Figure 1.1). It is in cities that companies like Waymo and Tesla are testing their autonomous cars (Dowling and McGuirk, 2022). It is in cities that car-sharing services and mobility-as-a-service initiatives abound and drive the deployment of fully autonomous fleets à la Uber (Schaller, 2021). It is across cities that autonomous trucks are employed to sustain the logistics of urban economies. And it is in the city that human road users (ranging from drivers to pedestrians and from cyclists to people with disabilities) and AVs are struggling to share the same spaces and ultimately competing to preserve their own mobility (Gaio and Cugurullo, 2023; Talebian and Mishra, 2022).

FIGURE 1.1   An autonomous car operating in Hong Kong.
Source: © Shutterstock/Yu Chun Christopher Wong.

Urban robots represent a second type of urban AI. Similar to AVs, robots have an evident physical presence, but unlike vehicles, they do not have an empty interior to accommodate passengers or cargo and do not operate exclusively within the field of transportation. Instead, urban robots come in many different shapes and their influence cuts across a plethora of urban domains. There are robots whose design mimics the general features of the human body including limbs, eyes and an erect posture, with *androids* being almost indistinguishable from humans (Mara and Appel, 2015; Müller et al., 2021). Other robots, such as *drones,* do not have an anthropomorphic appearance, while *nanobots* are so small that they are almost undetectable (Jackman, 2022; Toumey, 2013). Overall, urban robots are infiltrating core sectors of cities, including security, education, retail and hospitality, and their role in the maintenance of urban infrastructure is increasing (Macrorie et al., 2021; Tiddi et al., 2020; Valdez and Cook, 2023; While et al., 2021). In so doing, robots are in continuous interaction with the principal inhabitants of the built environment: humans. *Service robots,* for instance, populate everyday urban spaces and are designed to assist humans on *the frontline* (Pozharliev et al., 2021; Wirtz et al., 2018). This position involves direct and often face-to-face interactions, as in the case of robot waiters that are deployed to understand and accommodate a client's needs (see Figure 1.2). The proliferation of service robots, however,

FIGURE 1.2   A robot waiter serving food at a restaurant in Chennai (India).

Source: © Getty Images/Arun Sankar.

does not necessarily imply cooperation. De facto urban robots are a 'new class' of intelligent machines whose labour frequently comes at the expense of a human's job, and it is important to remember that 'few employment fields are immune' (Bissell and Del Casino, 2017: 436; Del Casino, 2016: 847). From this perspective, urban robots are replacing rather than supporting their human counterparts.

A third type of urban AI is the *city brain*. City brains are *large-scale* urban AIs inasmuch as their agency extends to large portions of urban territory, infrastructure and the public sector (Cugurullo, 2021; Zhang et al., 2019). While in the case of AVs and urban robots, AI is animating a car or a drone, in the case of city brains what is being controlled by AI are buildings, telecommunication networks and even entire cities. This type of urban AI is materially and geographically more extensive but also elusive when compared to the previous types. It does not reside in a single material artefact. Instead, it is located within a digital platform, infused through the urban fabric, where AI acts like a brain and controls different parts of the city in a way that resembles a human brain in control of different parts of the human body. Due to their existence inside digital platforms, city brains can be understood as an extension of *platform urbanism* (Barns, 2019; Caprotti et al., 2022; Caprotti and Liu, 2020; Hodson et al., 2020). Because of its hybrid physical and digital nature, platform urbanism is challenging to map and so are city brains (Fields et al., 2020; van der Graaf and Ballon, 2019). To further complicate matters geographically, city brains have *actuators* which bridge digital and physical spaces. These are material components through which city brains penetrate the real world, such as CCTV cameras that a city brain uses as eyes to observe what is happening in the city (Curran and Smart, 2021). However, more than just a neutral observer, a city brain acts on the city and influences its governance by attempting to predict the future and enacts adaptations to respond to future conditions including, for example, anticipated traffic congestions or concentration of demand for emergency services (Cugurullo, 2021; Zhang et al., 2019). This is essentially what Brayne (2017) defines as the shift from *reactive* to *proactive* approaches to urban governance, whereby the unprecedented computational power of AI is exploited to calculate large amounts of future possibilities, and then enable certain urban futures while suppressing others (Luque-Ayala and Marvin, 2020).

Urban software agents are a fourth type of urban AI which captures a seemingly invisible yet highly impactful dimension of AI in urban contexts. While the other types of urban AI are physically embodied and possess material actuators allowing them to act tangibly on cities, urban software agents are immaterial. Examples include computer programs that use algorithms to determine which individuals or families qualify for a home mortgage or insurance policy, contact-tracing apps that identify individuals to be quarantined, AI chatbots that create social bonds with humans and digital assistants such as Alexa and Siri that respond to voice commands and execute domestic tasks (Kitchin, 2020; Lee and Floridi, 2021; O'Neil, 2016; Strengers and Kennedy, 2021). Using Waze, a popular navigation map app, as an example, Fisher (2022: 75) notes that these aethereal AIs have a *spatiality* since they change 'how space is known, experienced, and acted upon.' Urban software agents are more prolific than one might imagine and their immateriality belies their profound influence on the daily lives of urban residents. From a geographical perspective, the location of many urban software agents shows how AI is entering our private spaces, including our homes, and becoming part of our everyday life. In the shape of software agents, AI is always with us, whether talking through a speech synthesizer sitting on the kitchen counter or simply operating our smartphones silently. The intimacy of this AI tech implies that, willingly or not, we are constantly sharing personal information with AI systems (Zuboff, 2019). These are systems that, XAI (Explainable Artificial Intelligence) scholars warn us, only few experts in computer science and engineers comprehend. Yet, as Zuboff (2019: v) remarks, these AIs are growing in popularity, assimilating unprecedented quantities of behavioural data and contributing to the formation of a system of surveillance 'that asserts dominance over society' (Baum et al., 2022; Langer et al., 2021).

From smart to AI urbanism

The four types of urban AI described above serve as the organizational scaffolding for this book and provide a means to classify the current evolution of urbanism from *smart* to *AI*. In Part I of the book, *Autonomous Vehicles and Mobility*, the authors examine the impact that vehicles driven by AI are having on cities and the social, political and economic dynamics through which such vehicles are accommodated and integrated into the city. In Part II, *Urban Robots and Robotic Spaces*, the contributors illuminate the presence and role of robots in a variety of urban domains, as well as the diversity of urban spaces altered by robotics. The authors in Part III of the book explore *City Brains and Urban Platforms* and highlight the operation and influence of large-scale AI control systems intended to manage vast portions, aspects and domains of the city, which underpin everyday life. In the final part (Part IV), *Urban Software Agents and Algorithms*, the authors focus on immaterial AIs and consider the implications of digital assistants, computer programs and seemingly neutral machinic procedures for urban living, design and governance.

Overall, the book draws on over 20 case studies based on empirical research. We use these case studies to illustrate the emergence of *urban AI* defined as a class of material and immaterial artificial intelligences that operate most intensely in urban spaces and that depend on urban resources, as they mediate urban services and influence urban sectors, by means of their capacity to understand manifold spheres of urban life and act on them in an autonomous manner (see Figure 1.3). In addition, we emphasize how the proliferation of urban AI across urban spaces and sectors is generating what we term *AI urbanism*: a novel urbanism that derives from smart urbanism but also departs both empirically and theoretically from traditional smart-city projects and trajectories. More specifically, we identify a series of points of connection and departure along three axes, namely *function*, *presence* and *agency*, captured in Figure 1.4.

First, there is a notable difference between the function of technologies employed in smart cities versus the function of artificial intelligences in AI urbanism. The technologies in smart cities are used to count and calculate urban metabolic processes. This involves quantifying specific phenomena, such as household energy consumption and neighbourhood crime rates by collating and analysing *Big Data* (Bhati et al., 2017; Catlett et al., 2019; Kitchin and McArdle, 2016). In contrast, urban AI produces an account of urban phenomena by collecting and analysing data to explain why and how certain things occur in cities. Urban AIs extract patterns and concepts from large datasets and follow seemingly objective and unbiased logics to produce predictions of urban futures yet to come. This is particularly evident in the case of urban software agents like *Palantir*, a predictive policing system

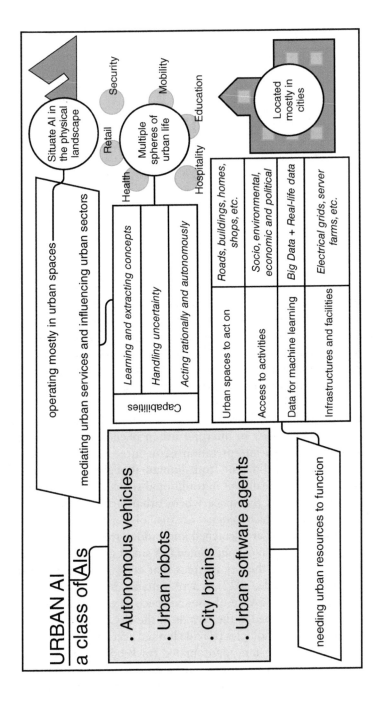

FIGURE 1.3   Urban AI.
Source: authors' original.

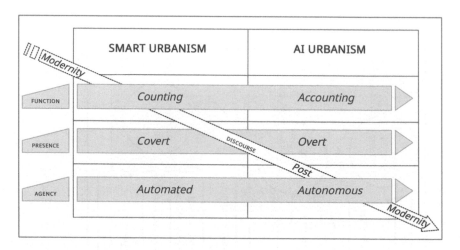

FIGURE 1.4 Comparing smart and AI urbanism.

Source: authors' original.

whose function is to explain why some urban residents are more likely to commit a crime and to foresee where unlawful activities will cluster within a given city (McDaniel and Pease, 2021; Richardson et al., 2019). In essence, along the *function* axis, we observe an evolution in the role and purpose of technology from performing calculations on enormous sets of quantitative data to providing an account of the urban condition. AI uses Big Data to produce explanatory and interpretative models akin to narratives. These models are not comprehensive stories analogous to human storytelling, but they denote AI's novel capacity to interpret urban phenomena, rather than simply quantifying them. An interpretation is, in turn, a sign of thinking. Although rudimentary and different from human thought processes, such manifestations of thinking are absent in traditional smart city technologies.

The second axis concerns the space where urban artificial intelligences function. While smart-city technologies are usually installed in confined spaces or infrastructures that are detached and hidden from humans, urban AIs are more visible sociotechnical phenomena. A smart grid, for example, is located below the surface of the city in areas that are inaccessible to urban residents (Quitzow and Rohde, 2022), where it manages the distribution of energy services. Citizens are aware of the existence of this technology but cannot see it because it is buried in the bowels of the city, away from human perception. Other smart technologies provide limited accessibility and visibility. In urban transport, for instance, automated track-bound metro systems and personal rapid transport networks can be accessed by passengers, but only in specially built guideways that are often underground and devoid of other vehicles and, above all, of pedestrians (Cugurullo, 2021). This is not the case in AI urbanism. Autonomous vehicles traverse public roads, operating next to pedestrians and sharing the same space with traditional vehicles and cyclists (Brovarone et al., 2021; Martens et al., 2022). Many robots work on the frontline in environments such as shops, restaurants and airports, where they are constantly encountering and interfacing with humans (Lin et al., 2022; Sumartojo et al., 2022). Even software agents can make their presence visible by animating the apps in our omnipresent smartphones. Overall, this describes an evolution of the *presence* of technology from being covert in smart urbanism to becoming overt in AI urbanism.

Third, we observe notable differences with respect to *agency*. In smart urbanism, technologies are programmed to repeat the same actions over and over. They are *automated* technologies in the sense that they follow 'repetitive processes' which are 'constant and automatic' (Bourdieu, 2018: 17). These processes are programmed by human engineers and computer scientists and the machine is compelled to abide by them. A smart sensor, for example, automatically switches on the light every time a movement is detected. Similarly, an automated tram follows a prescribed route and is bound to fixed tracks from which it cannot escape. In essence, when it comes to automation, 'there is no room for variations or improvisation' (Cugurullo, 2021: 161). In contrast, urban AIs are becoming more and more autonomous. Our observation resonates with the notion of *autonomous technology* developed by Langdon Winner (1978: 16), whereby 'technology governs its own course.' At the end of the third axis, machines decide the course of their actions. They make important decisions de facto engaging with ethical conundrums about what is right or wrong on a logical course of action derived from machine learning and then act accordingly, with little or no human supervision. An autonomous vehicle, for instance, determines its own route which is constantly changing *on the run* as unexpected factors, such as traffic jams and accidents, come into play. In this context rich in uncertainty, autonomous technologies introduce new ethical dilemmas, especially in situations where harms to humans are unavoidable (Awad et al., 2018; Hagendorff, 2020; Kaker et al., 2020). Autonomy is not a concern in smart cities where decision-making and ethical decisions remain firmly in the hands of humans.

Cutting across these three main axes, we begin to notice the emergence of a fourth axis which encapsulates the dominant *discourse* underpinning smart urbanism and AI urbanism. The grand narrative that fueled the genesis of smart cities was based upon a modernist ideal of control (Cugurullo, 2018; Datta, 2015) whereby technology was understood as an instrument in the hands of humans, designed and employed to fulfil human dreams and visions in an anthropocentric manner (Berman, 1983; Boyer, 1986; Cugurullo, 2021). Nowadays, in the practice of AI urbanism, some of the core principles of modernity no longer hold. In particular, AI urbanism pushes beyond the modernist ideal of control by ceding agency to autonomous technologies that take initiative instead of following human instructions. Urban artificial intelligences cannot be conceptualized as tools completely in the hands of humans and in the service of human visions, given that they have the capacity to develop their own narratives and to act autonomously in the pursuit of emergent futures. The modernist logic of control applied in the case of smart cities where technology was confined and contained in specific spaces, but it is not pertinent in an urban context in which multiple AIs increasingly roam free as autonomous agents. Modernist ideals of control are gradually falling apart, along a trajectory towards *post-modernity* which we understand as the faltering of the tenets, assumptions and promises of modernity (Harvey, 1989). More specifically, we see in the advent of an emergent urbanism shaped by co-constitutive human/AI relations a condition in which modernist promises of centralized and anthropocentric control are broken by dispersed forms of control that are more-than-human in nature. This post-modern age of AI upends the central role of humans as the sole builders and governors of cities, spreads power and control across uncharted digital platforms and opens up urban development to new post-human conditions.

Conclusions: transcending smart urbanism in the age of AI

The urban trends that we have discussed in this chapter indicate that, with the advent of AI in cities, practices and theories of urban development, governance and design are transcending what for decades has been known as *smart urbanism*. The transition to AI urbanism has begun, but its empirical and theoretical implications remain to be seen. The future that lies ahead is unknown, though it is unlikely to be spatially homogeneous, as different cities are experimenting with AI technologies in ways that reflect their specific geography, history and political economy. We already see the emergence of new master-planned urban settlements such as The Line in Saudi Arabia, where AI is being rolled out to have complete control over urban governance and a single AI system is intended to monitor the life of every urban resident (Batty, 2022). In other places, AI is being implemented through small-scale urban experiments to manage buildings and districts autonomously, which suggests that AI's impacts will be felt differentially *within* as well as across urban geographies (Aguilar et al., 2021; Marvin et al., 2022). Overall, the comprehensive and piecemeal applications of AI serve as two ends on a broad spectrum of trajectories of AI urbanism. However, one common denominator in AI urbanism is clear: a more-than-human component that is redefining the urban experience, as artificial and biological intelligences collide and collude in the making and governance of cities.

These collisions and collusions of humans and urban AIs will be significant regardless of the scale. Some urbanists, for example, ponder the genesis of *autonomous cities* where 'diverse artificial intelligences, from service robots to digital platforms, perform urban activities that have traditionally been human activities' (Allam, 2021; Cugurullo, 2021: 17). Even if such fully autonomous cities do not become a reality around the world, there will still be a myriad of small-scale human–AI interactions whose impact on the everyday life of cities and urban residents will be largely invisible but profound. For example, one can imagine the devastating consequences of a declined mortgage application assessed by an AI on a family struggling to find shelter during a housing crisis. Such an example is not the work of science fiction. As this book shows, similar episodes are rapidly emerging as the new normal for everyday life in many cities. The enormous and multifaceted impact of AI urbanism, and its problematic and progressive possibilities, requires sustained scrutiny, research and critique. AI technologies have been introduced into the city and they are here to stay. Their form, function and impacts will be variable and co-constituted by existing urban contexts. Now is the time to introduce AI into urban studies, to understand empirically and theoretically the intersection between the development of artificial intelligences and the development of cities in the decades to come.

References

Acheampong, R. A., Cugurullo, F., Gueriau, M., & Dusparic, I. (2021). Can autonomous vehicles enable sustainable mobility in future cities? Insights and policy challenges from user preferences over different urban transport options. *Cities*, 112, 103134.

Aguilar, J., Garces-Jimenez, A., R-Moreno, M. D., & García, R. (2021). A systematic literature review on the use of artificial intelligence in energy self-management in smart buildings. *Renewable and Sustainable Energy Reviews*, 151, 111530.

Allam, Z. (2021). Big data, artificial intelligence and the rise of autonomous smart cities. In Allam, Z. (Ed.), *The rise of autonomous smart cities*. Palgrave Macmillan, Cham, 7–30.

Amoore, L. (2023). Machine learning political orders. *Review of International Studies*, 49(1), 20–36.

Awad, E., Dsouza, S., Kim, R., Schulz, J., Henrich, J., Shariff, A., … Rahwan, I. (2018). The moral machine experiment. *Nature*, 563(7729), 59–64.

Balland, P. A., Jara-Figueroa, C., Petralia, S. G., Steijn, M., Rigby, D. L., & Hidalgo, C. A. (2020). Complex economic activities concentrate in large cities. *Nature Human Behaviour*, 4(3), 248–254.

Barns, S. (2019). *Platform urbanism: Negotiating platform ecosystems in connected cities*. Springer Nature, Berlin.

Batty, M. (2022). The Linear City: Illustrating the logic of spatial equilibrium. *Computational Urban Science*, 2(1), 1–17.

Baum, K., Mantel, S., Schmidt, E., & Speith, T. (2022). From responsibility to reason-giving explainable artificial intelligence. *Philosophy & Technology*, 35(1), 1–30.

Berman, M. (1983). *All that is solid melts into air: The experience of modernity*. Verso, London.

Bhati, A., Hansen, M., & Chan, C. M. (2017). Energy conservation through smart homes in a smart city: A lesson for Singapore households. *Energy Policy*, 104, 230–239.

Bissell, D., & Del Casino, V. J. (2017). Whither labor geography and the rise of the robots? *Social & Cultural Geography*, 18(3), 435–442.

Bostrom, N. (2017). *Superintelligence*. Oxford University Press, Oxford.

Bourdieu, P. (2018). *On the state: Lectures at the Collège de France, 1989–1992*. John Wiley & Sons.

Boyer, M. C. (1986). *Dreaming the rational city: The myth of American city planning*. MIT Press, Cambridge.

Brayne, S. (2017). Big data surveillance: The case of policing. *American Sociological Review*, 82(5), 977–1008.

Brovarone, E. V., Scudellari, J., & Staricco, L. (2021). Planning the transition to autonomous driving: A policy pathway towards urban liveability. *Cities*, 108, 102996.

Bruner, E. (2021). Evolving human brains: Paleoneurology and the fate of Middle Pleistocene. *Journal of Archaeological Method and Theory*, 28(1), 76–94.

Caprotti, F., Chang, I., Catherine, C., & Joss, S. (2022). Beyond the smart city: A typology of platform urbanism. *Urban Transformations*, 4(1), 1–21.

Caprotti, F., & Liu, D. (2020). Platform urbanism and the Chinese smart city: The co-production and territorialisation of Hangzhou City Brain. *GeoJournal*, 87, 1–15.

Catlett, C., Cesario, E., Talia, D., & Vinci, A. (2019). Spatio-temporal crime predictions in smart cities: A data-driven approach and experiments. *Pervasive and Mobile Computing*, 53, 62–74.

Cave, S., Dihal, K., & Dillon, S., (eds.). (2020). *AI narratives: A history of imaginative thinking about intelligent machines*. Oxford University Press, Oxford.

Coletta, C., Evans, L., Heaphy, L., & Kitchin, R. (Eds.). (2019). *Creating smart cities*. Routledge, London and New York.

Crawford, K. (2021). *Atlas of AI: Power, politics, and the planetary costs of artificial intelligence*. Yale University Press, New Haven and London.

Cugurullo, F. (2018). The origin of the smart city imaginary: From the dawn of modernity to the eclipse of reason. In Linder, C. & Meissner, M. (Eds.) *The Routledge companion to urban imaginaries*. Routledge, London, 113–124.

Cugurullo, F. (2020). Urban artificial intelligence: From automation to autonomy in the smart city. *Frontiers in Sustainable Cities*, 2, 38.

Cugurullo, F. (2021). *Frankenstein urbanism: Eco, smart and autonomous cities, artificial intelligence and the end of the city*. Routledge, London and New York.

Cugurullo, F., Acheampong, R. A., Gueriau, M., & Dusparic, I. (2021). The transition to autonomous cars, the redesign of cities and the future of urban sustainability. *Urban Geography*, 42(6), 833–859.

Curran, D., & Smart, A. (2021). Data-driven governance, smart urbanism and risk-class inequalities: Security and social credit in China. *Urban Studies*, 58(3), 487–506.

Datta, A. (2015). A 100 smart cities, a 100 utopias. *Dialogues in Human Geography*, 5(1), 49–53.

Del Casino Jr, V. J. (2016). Social geographies II: Robots. *Progress in Human Geography*, 40(6), 846–855.

Dowling, R., & MᶜGuirk, P. (2022). Autonomous vehicle experiments and the city. *Urban Geography*, 43(3), 409–426.

Elmqvist, T., Andersson, E., McPhearson, T., Bai, X., Bettencourt, L., Brondizio, E., ... & Van Der Leeuw, S. (2021). Urbanization in and for the Anthropocene. *Urban Sustainability*, 1(1), 1–6.

Fields, D., Bissell, D., & Macrorie, R. (2020). Platform methods: Studying platform urbanism outside the black box. *Urban Geography*, 41(3), 462–468.

Fisher, E. (2022). Do algorithms have a right to the city? Waze and algorithmic spatiality. *Cultural Studies*, 36(1), 74–95.

Gaio, A., & Cugurullo, F. (2023). Cyclists and autonomous vehicles at odds: Can the transport oppression cycle be broken in the era of artificial intelligence? *AI & Society*, 38(3), 1223–1237.

Galway-Witham, J., & Stringer, C. (2018). How did Homo sapiens evolve? *Science*, 360(6395), 1296–1298.

Greenfield, A. (2018). *Radical technologies: The design of everyday life*. Verso Books, London.

Hagendorff, T. (2020). The ethics of AI ethics: An evaluation of guidelines. *Minds and Machines*, 30(1), 99–120.

Harvey, D. (1989). *The condition of postmodernity: An enquiry into the origins of cultural change*. Wiley-Blackwell, London.

Hodson, M., Kasmire, J., McMeekin, A., Stehlin, J. G., & Ward, K. (Eds.). (2020). *Urban platforms and the future city: Transformations in infrastructure, governance, knowledge and everyday life*. Routledge, London.

Jackman, A. (2022). Domestic drone futures. *Political Geography*, 97, 102653.

Kaddar, M., Barak, N., Hoop, M., Kirchberg, V., & de Shalit, A. (2022). The artistic spirit of cities: How cities influence artists' agency. *Cities*, 130, 103843.

Kaker, S. A., Evans, J., Cugurullo, F., Cook, M., & Petrova, S. (2020). Expanding cities: Living, planning and governing uncertainty. In Scoones, I. & Stirling, A. (Eds.), *The politics of uncertainty*. Routledge, London, 85–98.

Kanal, L. N., and Lemmer, J. F. (Eds.). (2014). *Uncertainty in artificial intelligence*. Elsevier, Amsterdam.

Karvonen, A., Cugurullo, F., & Caprotti, F. (2019). *Inside smart cities*. Routledge, London and New York.

Kitchin, R. (2020). Civil liberties or public health, or civil liberties and public health? Using surveillance technologies to tackle the spread of COVID-19. *Space and Polity*, 24(3), 362–381.

Kitchin, R., & McArdle, G. (2016). What makes Big Data, Big Data? Exploring the ontological characteristics of 26 datasets. *Big Data & Society*, 3(1), 2053951716631130.

Langer, M., Oster, D., Speith, T., Hermanns, H., Kästner, L., Schmidt, E., ... Baum, K. (2021). What do we want from Explainable Artificial Intelligence (XAI)?–A stakeholder perspective on XAI and a conceptual model guiding interdisciplinary XAI research. *Artificial Intelligence*, 296, 103473.

Lee, K. F. (2018). *AI superpowers: China, Silicon Valley, and the new world order*. Houghton Mifflin, Boston.

Lee, M. S. A., & Floridi, L. (2021). Algorithmic fairness in mortgage lending: From absolute conditions to relational trade-offs. *Minds and Machines*, 31(1), 165–191.

Levesque, H. J. (2017). *Common sense, the turing test, and the quest for real AI: Reflections on natural and artificial intelligence*. MIT Press, Cambridge.

Lin, W., Adey, P., & Harris, T. (2022). Dispositions towards automation: Capital, technology, and labour relations in aeromobilities. *Dialogues in Human Geography*, 20438206221121652.

Lynch, C. R., Bissell, D., House-Peters, L. A., & Del Casino Jr, V. J. (2022). Robotics, affective displacement, and the automation of care. *Annals of the American Association of Geographers*, 112(3), 684–691.

Lupia, A., McCubbins, M. D., & Popkin, S. L. (Eds.). (2000). *Elements of reason: Cognition, choice, and the bounds of rationality.* Cambridge University Press, Cambridge.

Luque-Ayala, A., & Marvin, S. (2020). *Urban operating systems: Producing the computational city.* MIT Press, Cambridge.

Luusua, A., Ylipulli, J., Foth, M., & Aurigi, A. (2023). Urban AI: Understanding the emerging role of artificial intelligence in smart cities. *AI and Society*, 8, 1039–1044.

Macrorie, R., Marvin, S., & While, A. (2021). Robotics and automation in the city: A research agenda. *Urban Geography*, 42(2), 197–217.

Mara, M., & Appel, M. (2015). Effects of lateral head tilt on user perceptions of humanoid and android robots. *Computers in Human Behavior*, 44, 326–334.

Martens, K., Beyazit, E., Henenson, E., Thomopoulos, N., Milakis, D., Mladenović, M., … Negulescu, M. (2022). Autonomous and Connected Transport as Part of an Inclusive Transport System: WG2: Social Challenges.

Marvin, S., While, A., Chen, B., & Kovacic, M. (2022). Urban AI in China: Social control or hyper-capitalist development in the post-smart city? *Frontiers in Sustainable Cities*, 155, 1–11.

McDaniel, J. L., & Pease, K. (Eds.). (2021). *Predictive policing and artificial intelligence.* Routledge, London.

Munn, L. (2022). The uselessness of AI ethics. *AI and Ethics*, 3, 869–877.

Moran, D., Kanemoto, K., Jiborn, M., Wood, R., Többen, J., & Seto, K. C. (2018). Carbon footprints of 13 000 cities. *Environmental Research Letters*, 13(6), 064041.

Müller, B. C., Gao, X., Nijssen, S. R., & Damen, T. G. (2021). I, robot: How human appearance and mind attribution relate to the perceived danger of robots. *International Journal of Social Robotics*, 13(4), 691–701.

Nikitas, A., Thomopoulos, N., & Milakis, D. (2021). The environmental and resource dimensions of automated transport: A nexus for enabling vehicle automation to support sustainable urban mobility. *Annual Review of Environment and Resources*, 46, 167–192.

O'Neil, C. (2016). *Weapons of math destruction: How Big Data increases inequality and threatens democracy.* Penguin, London.

Pozharliev, R., De Angelis, M., Rossi, D., Romani, S., Verbeke, W., & Cherubino, P. (2021). Attachment styles moderate customer responses to frontline service robots: Evidence from affective, attitudinal, and behavioral measures. *Psychology & Marketing*, 38(5), 881–895.

Quitzow, L., & Rohde, F. (2022). Imagining the smart city through smart grids? Urban energy futures between technological experimentation and the imagined low-carbon city. *Urban Studies*, 59(2), 341–359.

Richardson, R., Schultz, J. M., & Crawford, K. (2019). Dirty data, bad predictions: How civil rights violations impact police data, predictive policing systems, and justice. *NYUL Review Online*, 94, 15.

Rubenstein, M., Ahler, C., Hoff, N., Cabrera, A., & Nagpal, R. (2014). Kilobot: A low cost robot with scalable operations designed for collective behaviors. *Robotics and Autonomous Systems*, 62(7), 966–975.

Russell, S. (2019). *Human compatible: Artificial intelligence and the problem of control*. Penguin, London.

Russell, S. J., & Norvig, P. (2016). *Artificial intelligence: A modern approach*. Pearson Education Limited, Harlow.

Samoili, S., Lopez Cobo, M., Gomez Gutierrez, E., De Prato, G., Martinez-Plumed, F., & Delipetrev, B. (2020). AI WATCH. Defining Artificial Intelligence, EUR 30117 EN, Publications Office of the European Union, doi:10.2760/382730, JRC118163.

Schaller, B. (2021). Can sharing a ride make for less traffic? Evidence from Uber and Lyft and implications for cities. *Transport Policy*, 102, 1–10.

Sherry, Y., & Thompson, N. C. (2021). How fast do algorithms improve? *Proceedings of the IEEE*, 109(11), 1768–1777.

Son, T. H., Weedon, Z., Yigitcanlar, T., Sanchez, T., Corchado, J. M., & Mehmood, R. (2023). Algorithmic urban planning for smart and sustainable development: Systematic review of the literature. *Sustainable Cities and Society*, 104562, 1–43.

Strengers, Y., & Kennedy, J. (2021). *The smart wife: Why Siri, Alexa, and other smart home devices need a feminist reboot*. MIT Press, Cambridge.

Sumartojo, S., Lundberg, R., Kulić, D., Tian, L., Carreno-Medrano, P., Mintrom, M., ... & Allen, A. (2022). The robotic production of spatiality: Predictability, partitioning, and connection. *Transactions of the Institute of British Geographers*, 48(1), 56–68.

Talebian, A., & Mishra, S. (2022). Unfolding the state of the adoption of connected autonomous trucks by the commercial fleet owner industry. *Transportation Research Part E: Logistics and Transportation Review*, 158, 102616.

Tiddi, I., Bastianelli, E., Daga, E., d'Aquin, M., & Motta, E. (2020). Robot–city interaction: Mapping the research landscape—a survey of the interactions between robots and modern cities. *International Journal of Social Robotics*, 12(2), 299–324.

Toumey, C. (2013). Nanobots today. *Nature Nanotechnology*, 8(7), 475–476.

van der Graaf, S., & Ballon, P. (2019). Navigating platform urbanism. *Technological Forecasting and Social Change*, 142, 364–372.

Valdez, M., & Cook, M. (2023). Humans, robots and artificial intelligences reconfiguring urban life in a crisis. *Frontiers in Sustainable Cities*, 5, 27.

While, A. H., Marvin, S., & Kovacic, M. (2021). Urban robotic experimentation: San Francisco. Tokyo and Dubai, *Urban Studies*, 58(4), 769–786.

Willis, K. S., & Aurigi, A. (Eds.). (2020). *The Routledge companion to smart cities*. Routledge, London and New York.

Winner, L. (1978). *Autonomous technology: Technics-out-of-control as a theme in political thought*. MIT Press, Cambridge.

Wirtz, J., Patterson, P. G., Kunz, W. H., Gruber, T., Lu, V. N., Paluch, S., & Martins, A. (2018). Brave new world: Service robots in the frontline. *Journal of Service Management*, 29, 907–931.

Yigitcanlar, T., Agdas, D., & Degirmenci, K. (2023). Artificial intelligence in local governments: Perceptions of city managers on prospects, constraints and choices. *AI & Society*, 38, 1135–1150.

Zhang, J., Hua, X. S., Huang, J., Shen, X., Chen, J., Zhou, Q., et al. (2019). City brain: Practice of large-scale artificial intelligence in the real world. *IET Smart Cities* 1, 28–37.

Zuboff, S. (2019). *The age of surveillance capitalism: The fight for a human future at the new frontier of power*. Profile books, London.

PART I

Autonomous vehicles and mobility

2

REINFORCING AND REFRACTING AUTOMOBILITY

Urban experimentation with autonomous vehicles

Robyn Dowling, Pauline McGuirk and Alistair Sisson

Introduction

Over the past decade, driverless vehicles have quickly moved from an imagined future to a present condition. In cities and regions across the world, driverless metros are multiplying, alongside automation of freight systems and trucking (Hopkins and Schwanen, 2018a), mining vehicles (Ellem, 2016) and the focus of our chapter: autonomous passenger vehicles or driverless cars (Hopkins and Schwanen, 2018b). While the widespread presence of fully autonomous vehicles (AVs[1]) remains a distant possibility, such vehicles, and their constituent political–economic ecosystems, have begun to attract the critical attention of urban geographers. This includes (inter alia): consideration of the challenges they pose to transport infrastructure, regulation, insurance and liability (see Bissell, 2018; Stone et al., 2018); their intersection with urban material infrastructures such as building design, parking requirements and urban form (see Cugurullo et al., 2021; Hopkins and Schwanen, 2018b); and the mappings of the city produced by their data (Alvarez León, 2019). In this chapter, we contribute to this emergent research through the lens of artificial intelligence. As Cugurullo (2021) has outlined, AVs are a prevalent manifestation of urban artificial intelligence, in at least three ways. The operation of AVs involves, first, sensing the surrounding environment, second, learning about cities through data such as that found on maps and, third, assembling and employing this information to propel the vehicle; all without significant human action. Simultaneously, however, AVs embed one of the key limits of current urban artificial intelligence as defined by Batty (2018): patterns of behaviour and infrastructures that are idiosyncratic rather than routine.

In this chapter, we consider the implications of autonomous passenger vehicles for city form and life through an analysis of 'actually existing' AVs in

DOI: 10.4324/9781003365877-3

cities, and, in particular, the AVs traversing cities and regions in increasing numbers, principally (although not exclusively) in several hundred 'real world' trials. While they include tests of technologies such as cameras, sensors and vehicles, these trials are also events that are being shaped by and are shaping the material, political and economic fabric of cities. Through these trials, and the anticipatory gestures they invoke, cities of the present and future are being calibrated: the fit of existing urban infrastructures, economies and socialities to AVs is being assessed and, simultaneously, new infrastructure, economies and socialities are being preconfigured (and materialized) to fit AVs. The trials, therefore, offer unique insight into how future cities in which AVs are prevalent are being prefigured, by whom, and to what ends and, by implication, the shape of cities and urban mobility configured by AI. Echoing Barns' (2021) recent thoughts on urban data and artificial intelligence, our argument suggests that recourse to past socio-economic patterns defines many of these trials and their effects.

In the next section, we outline the concept of urban experimentation and explain how it enables us to understand the various ways that AV experiments can reshape cities politically and materially. Our discussion works through the broad elements of automobility as recently dissected by Mattioli et al. (2020): political economies of provision, forms of mobility and urban materialities, imaginaries and infrastructures. We draw on critical urban scholarship on experimentation to frame our subsequent analysis of current AV trials, emphasizing the importance of spatial and institutional contexts of the urban to the political and material potentialities of AV experiments. The transformative potential of AV experiments is, in short, an effect of *how, by whom* and *to what ends* they are being conducted (Cugurullo, 2020). Our conclusion includes a reflection on the implications for governance.

The AV experiments discussed in this chapter differ in terms of what is being tested (infrastructure, technology, regulations, socio-cultural dimensions), the actors involved, the basis of claims to political authority, and the sense in which they rely upon or invoke urban materialities, capacities or imaginaries. Together, these variables allow us to consider the extent to which experimentation is confined to exploring socio-technical 'fixes' to enable the city fabric to accommodate driverless vehicles or enact a more transformational impulse, in which experimenting with driverless vehicles is connected to other political projects such as sustainable mobility or fracturing automobility.[2]

In section three we discuss two forms of AV experimentation which are reinforcing cultures of individualized automobility – namely, on-road trials and test beds – through predominantly corporate constellations of actors vested in the reproduction of existing urban automobility infrastructures. In the fourth section, we discuss two types of AV experiments which have greater potential to transform existing forms of automobility: precinct trials and AV Living Labs. While these experiments do not depart from it radically, they envisage and preconfigure collective or shared forms of automobility, to either supplement existing forms of collective transport or as part of a wider shift towards more sustainable or 'smart' mobility and urban development. Yet, despite these differences among AV experiments – between those that are reinforcing automobility and those that are refracting it – their embeddedness within existing sites of urban politics and power and logics of urban development mean that there is little 'disruption' occurring. As we discuss in the conclusion of this chapter, these 'actually existing' AV experiments are largely motivated by urban entrepreneurialism, economic competitiveness and 'smart city' objectives that risk reproducing the inequalities of existing infrastructures and cultures of automobility.

Urban experimentation and autonomous vehicles

While AVs are far from widespread, AV *experimentation* is remaking urban mobility in various and significant ways. Through experiments, technologies and practices are introduced 'in order to purposively reshape [social and] material realities' (den Hartog et al., 2018). Moreover, legitimation is sought, claims to authority pursued, and publics engaged or persuaded (Bulkeley et al., 2016; Karvonen et al., 2014; Evans, 2016). That is, socio-technical experiments do political and material work. Mobility experimentation is frequently urban; current thinking on urban experimentation emphasizes that the urban, as a socio-political–material space, is a distinctly favourable environment for experimentation (though not exclusively: see Lovell et al., 2018). Crucial challenges such as obdurate infrastructures or carbon-intensive practices are amassed in cities, along with a concentration of actors developing responses. Regarding transport, cities are where critical challenges are most pronounced and where markets for new forms of mobility are located.

Drawing on work that identifies the recursive dynamics that unfold between the urban and experimentation (Torrens et al., 2019: 213), we are interested in tracing how the urban is materially, institutionally and politically woven through, and reconstituted by, practices of experimentation. Following Edwards and Bulkeley (2018), we see experimentation as a disposition and practice that is altering the politics, epistemologies and ontologies, and materialities of cities. Experimentation, in other words, is a political process; political outcomes are open, contingent on context, especially in terms of the actors enrolled, and the intent and logics that condition experimentation.

AV trials are urban in the testing of interactions of vehicles and technologies with urban infrastructures (streets, buildings, sensors, Wi-Fi), urban socio-natures (humans, animals, topographies, surfaces) and urban regulation (of driving, licensing, liability). In this respect, cities offer complex challenges to be addressed and resolved, such that, just as smart city experiments or living labs alter the material fabric of the city as they test it (Cardullo et al., 2018), so too do AV experiments. In testing the digital infrastructural requirements of AVs, the city is materially altered, with infrastructures potentially established and mobility futures 'preconfigured.' Institutional path dependencies are also being created as organizational visions and governance relationships are consolidated and become difficult to dislodge. More than just a container for experiments, the urban also encapsulates process and imaginary, and it is also in this sense that AV experimentation is urban. For the city to be a 'truth spot' that grounds the production of knowledge, it needs to be imagined in specific ways (Gieryn, 2006). Socio-technical experiments like AV trials, in short, constitute imaginaries, materialities and institutional geographies of the urban.

While the importance of context to the politics of experimentation is recognized, the links between context and experiment are only just beginning to be explored (see Torrens et al., 2019). Savini and Bertolini argue for explicit recognition of the influence of institutional context and spatial conditions on the paths that niche experiments may take, identifying transformation as just one of four possible paths. Niches may also become marginalized, disappear or be assimilated – 'transformative potential is co-opted by existing networks of actors aiming to legitimise an established institutional order' (Savini and Bertolini, 2019: 842). The political outcomes of experiments are therefore contingent rather than predetermined. Moreover, when experimentation encounters the 'realpolitik of neoliberal urbanism' (Calvet and Castán Broto, 2016: 107), even a transformative intent may not translate into progressive transformation. In Masdar City, for example, diverse public and private interests collided with the intent of the experiment to achieve smart sustainability, such that transformative potential was not achieved (Cugurullo, 2016, 2020; Cardullo et al., 2018). Likewise, the shaping of smart city experiments in Austin, Texas, by existing governance regimes and political interests saw experimentation undergird entrepreneurial forms of governance (Levenda, 2019; see also van Houdt and Schinkel, 2019). Specifically in relation to mobility, Laurent and Tironi's (2015) examination of Renault's testing of car-sharing technologies and institutions in a small town in France documents multiple political outcomes. In testing 'the development of technical devices needed to turn an ordinary car into a vehicle ready to be included in a car sharing system' (Laurent and Tironi, 2015: 218), relations between public and private organizations in the delivery of transport solutions were recalibrated, to the principal, but not exclusive, benefit of the automobile industry. Experiments' political outcomes and their impact on urban governance are therefore contingently realized and recursively shaped by their contexts.

Given that the actors, intent and outcomes of urban experiments are determined in practice and in context, we now explore the configuration, materiality and politics of different AV trials. In many instances, the cultural dominance of private automobility in transport planning and in the design of cities (Mattioli et al., 2020; Urry, 2004) carries over into the framing, politics and materiality of AVs trials. In other words, the institutional composition, governance arrangements and infrastructural requirements of an AV trial emerge in the context of the societal, political and material embeddedness of automobility. Within such a context, mobility futures envisaged remain dominated by the private vehicle and are likely to cement existing patterns of automobility and the institutional and material relationships that underpin them. However, new forms of mobility that exceed automobility are also being imagined, and different political–economic assemblages enacted, that may forge alternative mobility futures.

Reinforcing urban automobility

AV trials conducted by existing automobile manufacturers and technology companies tend not to challenge car dependency but instead augment it technologically. While the government is not absent from such trials (regulatory approval is a precondition for much of this work), these are corporate driven-experiments which are more likely to transform urban mobility in ways that are vested with corporate interests and strategic purposes (Bulkeley and Castán Broto 2013: 373). They assemble an expanded yet largely private array of actors and, through the mobilization of material, knowledge, regulatory and institutional and governance resources, develop the capacity to shape an automated future in their own interests, reaffirming or even extending the dominance of the car and, by implication, automobility. Rather than being transformative, these are forms of experimentation that can be understood as part of the orchestration of the power and agency to govern mobility in ways that reaffirm the dominance of existing interests.

On-road trials are one such form of corporate-driven AV experiments that are reinforcing urban automobility. On-road trials involve the driving of an autonomous vehicle on an existing road – primarily automobiles rather than shared passenger vehicles – to assess the robustness of the vehicle and its systems in an existing, dynamic, real-world situation. Equally importantly, these are simultaneously data collection exercises. Since 2009, *Google's* AV spinoff *Waymo* has collected data from over 20 million miles of on-road autonomous driving to inform their ongoing development (Waymo, 2020).

The politics of on-road trials converge around the reproduction of urban automobility. They are principally used to secure the position of existing automotive businesses in an era of rapid technological change and associated disruption to business models. Household names such as *General Motors*, *Volkswagen* and *Volvo* have laid out company plans for an autonomous future and, through activities such as on-road trials, are establishing themselves as leaders in the development of autonomous driving systems. On-road trials are also used by new transport entrants, particularly technology companies, to establish authority and develop futures in their own image. Uber's trialling in cities such as Pittsburgh is well known, as is *Google's Waymo* in

California, Texas and Arizona, and *Baidu*'s in China and California. Technology companies with an application focus on vehicles, such as *Aptiv* (founded following mobility technology company *Delphi*'s acquisition of startup *NuTomony*), are undertaking trials as well. Importantly, despite the disruption that these actors purport to lead, these are also futures in which the automobile remains central. On-road trials using existing vehicles (cars) and infrastructures (roads), with established actors seeking to maintain authority and new actors seeking to obtain it, present city futures in which individualized automobility continues to reign, though in automated ways (Figure 2.1).

AVs are also trialled in 'test beds': environments designed for the specific purpose of vehicle testing, such as purpose-built test tracks quarantined from everyday urban mobility. Test beds are deliberately isolated from the messy materialities, socialities and institutional landscape of the city. They instead simulate urban conditions, creating, where possible, a controlled environment or 'in vitro' experiment (see Hopkins and Schwanen, 2018b). Purpose-built test beds model simulated built environments or staged interventions for testing purposes (e.g. pedestrians running in front of an AV). So while many are not urban in location (indeed many are in rural or remote locations), their

FIGURE 2.1 A Waymo AV during an on-road trial near Google's Silicon Valley headquarters in 2018.

Source: zombieite.

intent is to replicate and laboritize the urban and identify learnings to apply to real-world urban conditions. The actors involved in these experimental sites are varied and multi-sectoral; some are owned and operated by automotive manufacturers, like *Volvo*'s facility outside Gothenburg in Sweden, while others, especially in the United States, have emerged out of partnerships between governments, universities and the private sector, such as the University of Michigan Mobility Transformation Center's *Mcity* (Figure 2.2).

Test beds have become sites that anticipate and seek to preconfigure urban futures – political–economic futures as well as mobility futures. While governments are involved in test beds to a greater extent than in on-road trials, it is not necessarily for the purpose of public or collective transport. Test beds have become central components of the economic development strategies of city authorities and local businesses. *Mcity*, for example, located on 12 hectares of former automotive industrial heartland, has stated aspirations to re-establish the university and the state as the centre of a post-industrial, automated, automotive sector. Similarly, the 200-hectare *Willow Run* test bed in Ypsilanti, Michigan, operated by the American Center for Mobility (ACM), has begun developing and testing AV technology in a former *Ford* and *General Motors* factory complex. The ACM positions this development as 'expanding the region's business incubation and acceleration capabilities' (ACM, 2018: no page). Test beds thus become urban through their

FIGURE 2.2   University of Michigan's MCity test facility.

Source: University of Michigan.

enrolment into urban economies and political aspirations, with the city providing governance support, and acting as a promoter as well as a regulator (Aoyama and Alvarez Leon, 2021). Here, the "scientific mission" of AV testing can obscure political and economic agendas (Cugurullo, 2020) which are reinforcing the dominance of private automobility.

Refracting urban automobility

Not all AV experiments reinforce the current paradigm of private automobility; there are some that more closely reflect the history of 'public' transport. By this we mean a set of actors and framings whose concern is the crafting of mobility that is not just individual but collective, and through which broader social equity aspirations may be achieved. A claim to the legitimacy of alternative automated mobility futures is also made through the work of public engagement and public persuasion, both materially and rhetorically (Karvonen and van Heur, 2014). Such experiments are more often state-led rather than corporate-led, though with significant public–private partnerships and governance arrangements in evidence, and place-based. The narrative of mobility is reframed, and futures in which mobility is more thoroughly transformed are preconfigured: not merely automated but shared, networked to mass-transit systems and available on-demand.

Precinct trials are one such form of AV experiment that are preconfiguring alternative mobility futures. Geographically bounded but with an expansive approach to mobility, precinct trials model the opportunities to disrupt hegemonic urban automobility that are created by automation. They primarily experiment with 'first and last mile' passenger mobility, focusing on travel to and from public transit stops (e.g. rail or bus) or parking stations or to-the-door freight delivery from wider distribution networks. They are dominated by *shared* AV trials, most commonly electric autonomous shuttle buses on short, low-speed fixed routes, usually contained within a business park, university campus or innovation precinct. The trials test vehicle technology and communications, hard infrastructure and the design of subsidiary infrastructure in place (such as bus stops and other signage).

Not unlike precinct trials, AV Living Labs involve testing technical, legal and societal aspects of implementing AVs in porous, complex and dense urban environments. They often do so via multiple trials, including autonomous passenger shuttles, automated urban deliveries, remote teleoperation demonstrations and high-fidelity simulator trials testing interactions between regular and automated vehicles. While most cities thus far have focused on trialling a particular suite of technologies, some, such as Singapore (at One North and Jurong West districts), Dubai and London (across the borough of Greenwich; see Hopkins and Schwanenen, 2018b), have positioned themselves as providing comprehensive real-world testbed facilities for multiple modes of AV and automated transport futures, preconfiguring a deeply transformed mobility regime.

In both precinct trials and AV Living Labs, the performance of vehicle automation is just one component of a multi-dimensional testing regime, alongside on-road and pedestrian traffic interaction with the vehicles, and pedestrian and driver responses to route signage and road markings. Some also test on-demand hailing of the buses via customized smartphone apps. Formal evaluations of public attitudes towards AVs are often included, addressing aspects such as shared driverless shuttles' perceived safety, comfort, speed and convenience, public acceptance and willingness to use. These trials are centrally testing resistance to the disruption of "sticky" cultural, aesthetic and affective relationships with driving (Pink et al., 2018).

Both AV Living Labs and precinct trials typically involve multi-sectoral consortia that combine diverse kinds of expertise and capacities, including technological, regulatory and institutional. Three key sets of actors are discernable: providers of automation hardware and software (e.g. *Navvya*, *EasyMile*); university or specialized government agency partners that supply expertise, logistics support and/or funding; and sites of formal, legal authority, since new and/or modified regulatory and insurance frameworks in which AV can legally operate are essential in these precincts. In sum, state rather than non-state actors characterize AV Living Labs and precinct trials, albeit in partnership with emergent transport businesses, shaping facilitative governance arrangements to facilitate and advance these forms of trials. The role of city governments is not limited only to promotion and regulation but extends to mediation and data catalysis as well (Aoyama and Alvarez Leon, 2021).

The multi-sectoral institutional structure of AV Living Labs and precinct trials, and their connection to specialized government agencies and broader strategic agendas, makes them less likely to see private car-based culture prioritized. Against the hegemony of individualized automobility, precinct trials seek to extend shared travel and integrate it within wider systems of public transit, giving them the *potential* to reframe the narrative of city mobility (Karvonen et al., 2014). They not only augment the capacity and catchment of public transit networks (often in a context of sustained under-investment in mass transit infrastructures), but they also align with wider aspirations to shift the modal mix away from private cars and towards a more socially and environmentally sustainable one.

AV Living Labs pursue more extensive urban mobility transformations than precinct trials, which, given their spatial and juridical confinement (e.g. university campuses or innovation districts), prompt questions about scalability beyond the boundaries of the precinct, and whether political–economic interests will similarly align to realize these mobility futures in the wider urban context (Hannon et al., 2016; Haque and Brakewood, 2020; Nesheli et al., 2021). For Living Labs, automated mobility is one element of a broader 'smart city' vision of the urban future, with automated mobilities across shared and individualized passenger transit, and automated freight and delivery at its spine. AV Living Labs set out to demonstrate holistically – and thus preconfigure – how the automated mobility city might emerge. As such, they have the potential to be deeply transformative, both in terms of the social and environmental outcomes they preconfigure and in terms of how they rework political–economic opportunities, relations of authority and governance capacity.

Like their counterparts, smart city Living Labs, AV Living Labs also seek to harness AV innovation to wider goals of innovative governance and economic development. The United Kingdom's *GATEway project* (Greenwich Automated Transport Environment) for instance, seeks to produce 'exploitable knowledge of the systems required for the effective validation, deployment, management and integration of automated transport within the smart city environment' (GATEway project, 2022a: no page) and 'capitalise on the consortium strengths to position UK PLC at the forefront of the global marketplace encouraging inward investment and job creation' (GATEway project, 2022b: no page). Thus, as with the test beds discussed in the previous section, AV Living Labs (and precinct trials) are not governed by 'pure' scientific objectives but bound up with the politics of urban economic development (Cugurullo, 2020). Governing to shape a multi-faceted AV innovation ecosystem is seen as a pathway to positioning the city favourably in the emergent global complex of hardware, software and knowledge industries emerging around AV (Figure 2.3).

FIGURE 2.3 A driverless shuttle in Greenwich, UK, running as part of the GATEway project in 2017.

Source: citytransportinfo.

Conclusion

In testing autonomous transport, the lineaments of present and future cities – their mobility, materiality and governance arrangements – are writ large. We have illustrated the ways in which differentiated conditions of possibility emerge from AV trials for contesting and reconfiguring, or re-embedding the city's 'automobility' materially and politically. Especially interesting here are the ways in which the label 'experiment' enables new sets of actors and expertise to be authorized in the city and lays the foundation for new regulatory norms and governance practices (see Späth and Knieling, 2020). Different political outcomes result from the actor constellations driving the different experiments, combining with different infrastructures and materials of mobility. Each preconfigures socio-material futures, mobility infrastructures and regulatory frameworks.

Two possible futures are being imagined: one, constituted through on-road trials and test beds, in which private, individualized car-based cultures remain prioritized; the other, constituted through precinct trials and AV living labs, in which alternative futures of collective and perhaps more sustainable mobility are more visible. On-road trials are most tightly tethered to hegemonic automobility, experimenting with and altering vehicle technologies while leaving intact the city fabric – especially roads and the interaction of vehicle and pedestrian infrastructures currently in place. In test beds, testing in environments that are beyond the urban allows calibration of technology, data and related regulatory frameworks necessary to underpin the widespread adoption of AV mobility in any place. As urban simulacra, they provide key data and learnings to be translated to other cities and suggest the new urban materialities required to accommodate AVs. As such, on-road trials and test beds are likely to further entrench infrastructural obduracies and their facilitation of automobility, especially in prioritizing the ability of all streets to accommodate AVs. They involve an expanded array of actors empowered to govern (including automated vehicle manufacturers, software companies and tech firms), and the resources and legitimacy they mobilize are reshaping the city to 'fit' automated mobility.

Precinct trials and AV Living Labs, in contrast, are beginning to stake a claim for alternative mobility infrastructures. Here, experimentation has a dual focus on technologies of vehicle automation as well as its broader infrastructural affordances, not least due to greater state involvement than with corporate-led on-road trials and test beds. In the case of AV Living Labs, the wider affordances of urban robotics are also considered, especially through the Internet of Things that may constitute future urban environments The narrative of mobility is reframed and futures in which mobility is more thoroughly transformed are preconfigured: not merely automated but shared, networked to mass-transit systems and available on-demand. In precinct and

AV living lab trials the complex socio-material character of cities is critical to the experimentation. Moreover, it is in these trials that the material transformations of existing cities to meet an anticipated automated future are occurring, such as the introduction of the digital skin of sensing capabilities required for automation (Rabari and Storper, 2015). A claim to the legitimacy of alternative automated mobility futures is also made through the work of public engagement and public persuasion, both materially and rhetorically (Karvonen and van Heur, 2014). It may be that such living labs are more akin to classic 'niches' that nurture future visions beyond the hegemony of automobility. These forms of experimentation open up wider questions about the appropriate roles of governments in shaping alternative trajectories of AVs and about the forms of governance needed to underpin these alternatives.

To date, however, the vision of the city underpinning and/or constituted through all these experiments is narrow. Unlike experimentation's more traditional trope of fostering the emergence of something new (see Kullman, 2013), these urban experiments are tied to, rather than disruptive of, city politics and power. With the exception of on-road trials, all are strongly embedded in broader logics of urban development that position cities as economically competitive, as pivots in ecosystems of innovation or as integral components of smart city discourses and practices (see Clark, 2020). In testing some parameters and not others (such as social justice considerations; see Bissell et al., 2020), they are continuing the lock-in characteristics of urban automobility, especially its uneven development. Furthermore, the significance of cities' situatedness and context is underappreciated: the places where experiments are occurring tend to simply 'stand in' for a generic urban – narrowly construed and abstracted primarily from the cities of the Global North, connected to private rather than public or smaller-scale forms of mobility and dependent on affluence. The potential of AV to transform mobility in cities otherwise, particularly cities of the Global South, is, essentially, conceptually denied (though see – Pink et al., 2021).

As we stated at the outset, AVs are useful objects for thinking through cities and artificial intelligence. Using our analysis of AVs, we make some final observations on the potential urbanisms being crafted through AI experimentation. Our finding from the experiments examined in this chapter is that the prospects for AI challenging automobility remain slight. Again echoing Barns' analysis of the use of urban Big Data (2021), AVs are an instance of future cities being produced through recourse to past patterns, with limited prospects for change. We have also shown, however, that this is not exclusively a function of the application of artificial intelligence. Rather, the entanglement of data, sensing and learning with diverse constellations of actors, materialities, rationales, contexts, scale, scope and relation to 'the urban' mean that some experiments have more transformative potential than others. As AV technology and trial aspirations further develop, and as the complexity of this recursivity deepens, in-depth, comparative analysis of key cases and their contexts will be crucial.

Notes

1 There is debate about the accuracy of the term 'autonomous'. AVs are autonomous in the sense that they have no human driver. Yet, as highly connected nodes in an Internet of Things, they are not autonomous. We follow the widespread acceptance of the term nonetheless and use it here.
2 For further discussion of the methods involved in examining and categorizing AV experiments, see Dowling & McGuirk (2022).

References

Alvarez León, L. F. (2019). Counter-mapping the spaces of autonomous driving, *Cartographic Perspectives*, 2019(92), 10–23.

American Centre for Mobility (ACM) (2018). *Locate at ACM Willow Run*. Available at: https://www.acmwillowrun.org/locate-at-acm. [Accessed 19/01/2023].

Aoyama, Y., & Alvarez Leon, L. F. (2021). Urban governance and autonomous vehicles. *Cities*, 119, 103410, 1–10.

Barns, S. (2021). Out of the loop? On the radical and the routine in urban big data. *Urban Studies*, 58(15), 3203–3320.

Batty, M. (2018). Artificial intelligence and smart cities. *Environment and Planning B*, 45(1), 3–6.

Bissell, D. (2018). Automation interrupted: How autonomous vehicle accidents transform the material politics of automation. *Political Geography*, 65, 57–66.

Bissell, D., Birtchnell, T., Elliott, A., & Hsu, E. L. (2020). Autonomous automobilities: The social impacts of driverless vehicles. *Current Sociology*, 68(1), 116–134.

Bulkeley, H., & Castán Broto, V. (2013). Government by experiment? Global cities and the governing of climate change. *Transactions of the Institute of British Geographers*, 38(3), 361–375.

Bulkeley, H., McGuirk, P., & Dowling, R. (2016). Making a smart city for the smart grid? The urban material politics of biquitous smart electricity networks. *Environment and Planning A*, 48(9), 1709–1726.

Calvet, M. S., & Castán Broto, V. (2016). Green enclaves, neoliberalism and the constitution of the experimental city in Santiago de Chile. In Evans, J., Karvonen, A., & Raven, R. (Eds.), *The Experimental City*. Routledge, London, 107–122.

Cardullo, P., Kitchin, R., & Di Feliciantonio, C. (2018). Living labs and vacancy in the neoliberal city, *Cities*, 73, 44–50.

Clark, J. (2020). *Uneven Innovation: The Work of Smart Cities*. Columbia University Press, New York.

Cugurullo, F. (2016). Frankenstein cities: (de)composed urbanism and experimental eco-cities. In Evans, J., Karvonen, A., & Raven, R. (Eds.), *The Experimental City*, Routledge, London, 195–205.

Cugurullo, F. (2020). Urban artificial intelligence: From automation to autonomy in the smart city. *Frontiers in Sustainable Cities*, 2(38), 1–14.

Cugurullo, F. (2021). *Frankenstein Urbanism: Eco, Smart and Autonomous Cities, Artificial Intelligence and the End of the City*. Routledge, London.

Cugurullo, F., Acheampong, R. A., Gueriau, M., & Dusparic, I. (2021). The transition to autonomous cars, the redesign of cities and the future of urban sustainability. *Urban Geography*, 42(6), 833–859.

Den Hartog, H., Sengers, F., Xu, Y., Xie, L., Jiang, P., & de Jong, M. (2018). Low-carbon promises and realities: Lessons from three socio-technical experiments in Shanghai. *Journal of Cleaner Production*, 181, 692–702.

Dowling, R., & McGuirk, P. (2022). Autonomous vehicle experiments and the city. *Urban Geography*, 43(3), 409–426.

Edwards, G. A. S., & Bulkeley, H. (2018). Heterotopia and the urban politics of climate change experimentation. *Environment and Planning D: Society and Space*, 36(2), 350–369.

Ellem, B. (2016). Geographies of the labour process: automation and the spatiality of mining. *Work, Employment and Society*, 30(6), 932–948.

Evans, J. (2016). Trials and tribulations: problematizing the city through/as urban experimentation. *Geography Compass*, 10(10), 429–443.

GATEway project (2022a). *About*. Available at: https://gateway-project.org.uk/about/ [Accessed 19/01/2023].

GATEway project (2022b). *Driverless Cars*. Available at: https://www.digitalgreenwich.com/driverless-cars/ [Accessed 19/01/2023].

Gieryn, T. F. (2006). City as truth-spot: Laboratories and field-sites in urban studies. *Social Studies of Science*, 36(1), 5–38.

Hannon, E., McKerracher, C., Orlandi, I., & Ramkumar, S. (2016). *An integrated perspective on the future of mobility* (Sustainability & Resource Productivity Report: October). McKinsey & Company. Available at: http://www.mckinsey.com/business-functions/sustainability-and-resource-productivity/our-insights/an-integrated-perspective-on-the-future-of-mobility. [Accessed 19/01/2023].

Haque, A. M., & Brakewood, C. (2020). A synthesis and comparison of American automated shuttle pilot projects. *Case Studies on Transport Policy*, 8(3), 928–937.

Hopkins, D., & Schwanen, T. (2018a). Governing the Race to Automation. In Marsden, G. and Reardon, L. (Eds.), *Governance of the Smart Mobility Transition*. Emerald Publishing Limited, Bingley, 65–84.

Hopkins, D., & Schwanen, T. (2018b). Experimentation with vehicle automation. In Jenkins. K. E. H. and Hopkins, D. (Eds.), *Transitions in Energy Efficiency and Demand*. Taylor and Francis, Abingdon, 72–93.

Karvonen, A., Evans, J., & van Heur, B. (2014). The politics of urban experiments: radical change or business as usual? In Mike Hodson & Simon Marvin (Eds.), *After Sustainable Cities?*. Routledge, London, 104–116.

Karvonen, A., & van Heur, B. (2014). Urban laboratories: experiments in reworking cities. *International Journal of Urban and Regional Research*, 38(2), 379–392.

Kullman, K. (2013). Geographies of experiment/experimental geographies: A rough guide. *Geography Compass*, 7(12), 879–894.

Laurent, B., & Tironi, M. (2015). A field test and its displacements. Accounting for an experimental mode of industrial innovation. *CoDesign*, 11(3–4), 208–221.

Levenda, A. M. (2019). Mobilizing smart grid experiments: Policy mobilities and urban energy governance. *Environment and Planning C: Politics and Space*, 37(4), 634–651.

Lovell, H., Hann, V., & Watson, P. (2018). Rural laboratories and experiment at the fringes: A case study of a smart grid on Bruny Island, Australia. *Energy Research & Social Science*, 36, 146–155.

Mattioli, G., Roberts, C., Steinberger, J. K., & Brown, A. (2020). The political economy of car dependence: A systems of provision approach. *Energy Research &
Social Science*, 66, 1–18.

Nesheli, M. M., Li, L., Palm, M., & Shalaby, A. (2021). Driverless shuttle pilots:
Lessons for automated transit technology deployment. *Case Studies on Transport
Policy*, 9(2), 723–742.

Pink, S., Fors, V., & Glöss, M. (2018). The contingent futures of the mobile present:
automation as possibility. *Mobilities*, 13(5), 1–17.

Pink, S., Gomes, A., Zilse, R., Lucena, R., Pinto, J., Porto, A., ... Duarte De Oliveira,
M. (2021). Automated and connected? Smartphones and automobility through
the global south. *Applied Mobilities*, 6(1), 54–70.

Rabari, C., & Storper, M. (2015). The digital skin of cities: urban theory and research
in the age of the sensored and metered citbiquitous computinging and big data,
Cambridge Journal of Regions, Economy and Society, 8(1), 27–42.

Savini, F., & Bertolini, L. (2019). Urban experimentation as a politics of niches.
Environment and Planning A: Economy and Space, 51(4), 831–848.

Späth, P., & Knieling, J. (2020). How EU-funded Smart City experiments influence
modes of planning for mobility: observations from Hamburg. *Urban Transform*,
2(2), 1–17.

Stone, J., Ashmore, D., Scheurer, J., Legacy, C., & Curtis, C. (2018). Planning for
disruptive transport technologies: How prepared are australian transport agencies?. In Marsden, G. & Reardon, L. (Eds.), *Governance of the Smart Mobility
Transition*. Emerald Publishing Limited, Bingley, 123–137.

Torrens, J., Schot, J., Raven, R., & Johnstone, P. (2019). Seedbeds, harbours, and battle-
grounds: on the origins of favourable environments for urban experimentation with
sustainability. *Environmental Innovation and Societal Transitions*, 31, 211–232.

Urry, J. (2004). The 'system' of automobility. *Theory Culture & Society*, 21(4–5),
25–39.

van Houdt, F., & Schinkel, W. (2019). Laboratory Rotterdam. Logics of
Exceptionalism in the Governing of Urban Populations. In Scholten, P., Crul, M.,
& van de Laar, P. (Eds.), *Coming to Terms with Superdiversity: The Case of
Rotterdam*. Springer International Publishing, New York, 133–151.

Waymo (2020). Safety Report. Available at: https://storage.googleapis.com/sdc-prod/
v1/safety-report/2020-09-22-safety-report.pdf [Accessed 19-01-2023].

3

TRIALS AND TRIBULATIONS

Who learns what from urban experiments with self-driving vehicles?

Jack Stilgoe and Cian O'Donovan

Introduction: olympian dreams and concrete realities

> I sometimes felt that the government's enthusiasm for making this country a testbed for driverless technology would give us all the benefits that Christmas Island got from being a testbed for nuclear weapons. You get all the pain, but you don't necessarily get much of the gain.[1]
>
> – *Former UK Department for Transport civil servant*

An orange and white pod, described by one engineer as resembling a giant toaster, is making slow circuits of London's Olympic Park on a sunny September morning. The shell of the vehicle is the same as those that ferry passengers from a car park to a terminal in a dedicated concrete lane at Heathrow Airport. Here, the 2019 version has upgraded software, radar, lidar, GPS and other sensors to aid its omniscience and now it is driving itself without rails. But the pods are still being defended, by a team of hi-vis-wearing marshalls. Although there's no driver sitting with the four passengers in the POD, an engineer is stewarding proceedings on her tablet-based control interface, walking among the marshalls behind. Inside, there's an onboard safety steward. The presence of the steward is contributing to the under-whelming experience of the public passengers who have been offered a ride by marshalls along the way. The passengers seem nonplussed. At only 4 miles per hour, with frequent juddering halts interrupting progress, they'd likely have been quicker walking.

A new automation control system means the pod can leave the physical rails of Heathrow behind. But the vehicle is still far from roadworthy. That's

DOI: 10.4324/9781003365877-4

why it's in the car-free Olympic Park, where transport bylaws and legal exceptions offer a simpler regulatory route to delivery compared with open highways. It's also the reason why the marshalls have been given a strict brief. Their job is to notify pedestrians and cyclists that the pod is approaching and, if necessary, encourage them away from the vehicle. If an "obstacle" cannot be removed, they must notify the safety steward. In the event of an emergency, the marshalls are required to assist the first responder (the safety steward riding in the pod) and a designated incident manager. The brief, like the formation the marshalls take up on the pathways, is defensive. Self-driving vehicles represent a high-profile test case for the use of artificial intelligence in the wild, with software in control of high-stakes and high-momentum hardware through unpredictable environments. But if this 'trial' is an experiment, it's a strange one, because it's designed at all costs not to fail. Given this is supposed to be a 'driverless,' 'autonomous' vehicle, there are a surprising number of people involved.

The trial is part of a £4 million research and development consortium of public and private transport players. Private-sector engineers, including some of the team behind the original airport vehicles, are producing data and technical knowledge. Legal and insurance experts are building case studies for the industry. University transport studies researchers are interviewing participants on their experiences and attitudes. And public sector authorities are building relationships with all of the above. On one day during the trial, a team of cybersecurity researchers arrived and attempted to break-in to the pod's systems. On another, a toy rat was attached to a remote control car in an attempt to play havoc with the pod's sensors. The sight of a robotic car in a public place is undeniably interesting to many different groups, but it's not clear what's at stake or for whom.

Interviews with some of the partners involved in the project suggested that learning was taking place, but it was happening behind the scenes. Asked about what the tests were really testing, one consultant involved in managing the project responded,

> So, yeah, what am I allowed to say about that? I think it would be different if we were stood at a bar (laughs). So, of course, I know what [the project] is supposed to be doing. The vehicles are supposed to be able to operate amongst people in a pedestrianised area, and I think they also need to be able to operate on roads in some way… a university with six months and a few thousand pounds can make a vehicle drive itself… The real research is around how they work: are they up for 24/7 operation? Do they work on these kinds of narrow roads where they're very busy? Do they work on these kinds of roundabouts, and, given all that stuff, do people like them, will they get on them, and so on and so forth?
>
> *(Interviewee A)*

As the project developed, it became clear that even these modest ambitions for "real research" would need moderating. A collaborator on the same project explained that the need to deliver a public demonstration had overtaken the initial research aims. 'We said that we'd do it... so we need to do it. What are we really testing?... It's quite difficult to test the actual use case. Ideally, we want to be able to test the technology' but, he went on, 'The challenge for us is that, given the technology constraints, we couldn't really deliver a trial which matched an obvious use case. So it's a fairly contrived route for the pods.' (Interviewee B). The question of whether large numbers of people would actually use the technology was complicated by the technology's inability to cope with large numbers of people.

According to this interviewee,

> there's been little interest from [the funders] in the outcomes of our project... I'm astonished, if I'm quite honest – the amount of money that's being put in – at how little interest there is from [the funders] to pull together the findings and the learnings across their investments.
>
> *(Interviewee B)*

His colleague suspected that funders and policymakers were more interested in keeping up appearances:

> I think they're all trying to say on a worldwide stage, 'Look. Look what we've done! How fantastic it is!' So, I think a project that learns a lot and doesn't show something with lots of video, and people at it, and, you know, press coverage, and such, is not all that interesting... they're looking for that message to the world, 'Hey, we are the best place to come and try and test these sorts of things.'
>
> *(Interviewee A)*

In this chapter, we consider what cities might learn from public tests of self-driving vehicle technologies. We draw on research conducted as part of two projects *Driverless Futures?* and SCALINGS. These projects involved more than 50 interviews with innovators and stakeholders in the US, UK and elsewhere in Europe, public surveys in the UK and US, British public dialogue exercises and a series of technographic observations in the US and UK with organizations developing and testing the technology. Our engagement with self-driving vehicles starts from our position as researchers in Science and Technology Studies, so while we share the interest in emerging 'smart' cities, urban artificial intelligence (Cugurullo, 2020) and urban robotics (While et al., 2021) that originates in geography and planning, our analysis has followed technological promises into urban contexts rather than starting in the city. As we argue below, a major issue with innovators' claims about self-driving vehicles is that they are intentionally dislocated – disconnected from particular places. In seeking to understand how technological promises might come down to earth, the city has become a vital site for analysis.

As Science and Technology Studies (STS) scholars, we are particularly interested in experimentation and the claims that innovators make about experiments. In this chapter, by focussing on experimentation, we investigate how public trials of the technology are framed by technology companies and the policymakers who support them. We see that 'trials' are more about public persuasion than technological testing. A constructive response to such urban testbeds might therefore be to ask for more experimentation, not less. Our aim in this chapter is not to reject experiments as useless, or unethical, although there are reasons to be concerned about both the productivity and morality of such things. Instead, we argue that a democratic engagement with experimentation as a way of opening technological black boxes could offer new possibilities for governance.

Innovation and urban experimentation

The characterization of technologies and technological progress in terms of experimentation has a long history among evangelists and analysts as well as critics of particular technological schemes. The language of trials, experimentation and laboratories invite both positive associations with future-making and concerns about uncertainties, unintended consequences and consent if citizens are unwilling or unwitting experimental subjects. The definitional politics of experimentation demand closer analysis, and we can build on two key insights from science and technology studies. The first point is that much innovative activity we might consider experimental is not publicly acknowledged as such. It is often in innovators' interests to pretend that a technology's effects are well-known. STS scholars (e.g. Krohn and Weingart, 1987) have highlighted the uncertainties and hidden experimentality of nuclear energy, and they have analysed public responses to corporate experiments with social media where ethical questions were not asked in advance (Boyd, 2016). For innovators, to be explicitly experimental is to admit both uncertainty and ethical ambiguity.

The second insight from STS is that much activity that might be badged an 'experiment' is not very experimental, in the sense of it being closed to the possibility of surprise (Gross, 2021). Public 'tests' of a technology are often so controlled, and the possibility of failure so constrained, that they resemble performances or demonstrations rather than trials (Collins, 1988). Where new modes of governance are tried, including experiments in deliberative democracy (Laurent, 2011), policymakers often delimit the possibility of surprise or impact as a way to maintain control. The deployment, at least discursively, of the language of experiments and laboratories as a mode of urban development (Karvonen and van Heur, 2014) demands critical analysis in these terms. Experiments, rather than being a way of opening up urban governance, may just be a new discourse for control. AV trials do, however, present an opportunity for democratization, because they are at least partly public. There is an interesting reversal of the trend observed by Paul Leonardi (Leonardi, 2010), in which automotive testing became increasingly detached from the real world as computer simulation improved. Now, simulated possibilities of self-driving need to be exposed to the real world in order to test whether they are practically workable. Engels et al. (2019: 3) analyse the new enthusiasm for 'test beds,' which

> re-interpret what is meant by "laboratory" in that they do not test technologies in a separate space prior to use within society. "Living" labs rather test new sociotechnical arrangements by tentatively adopting the very technologies in question "as if" the involved technologies had been found safe and had entered the market already.

Or, to use Linnet Taylor's phrase, 'the experimentation taking place does not aim to test technology using people, but to test people using technology' (Taylor, 2021: 1902). Employed in this way, the idea of the testbed leapfrogs considerations that, as social scientists, we would regard as vital to do with the assessment, uptake and scaling of technology, in order to assert, via a proof-of-concept, the inevitability of an innovation. In this way, testbeds and 'living labs' become not just experiments but ways of performing innovation (Laurent and Tironi, 2015) to a public that is imagined as sceptical. This mode of persuasion becomes particularly important in the case of artificial intelligence, where innovators are likely to shift attention to systems' performance – what AI is able to do – rather than the processes through which it systems are created or operate – how and why AI works – because of a combination of technical opacity and corporate secrecy (Burrell, 2016).

Cugurullo (2018) uses the allegory of Frankenstein to critique current approaches to 'smart city' urban development that look to privatize experimentation and innovate for innovation's sake. We should remember Langdon Winner's (Winner, 1977) question: 'what, after all, is Frankenstein's problem?' It is not, says Winner, that the experiment is performed, but that the doctor takes no care for the creature nor the wider meaning of his experiment. Perhaps, rather than demanding less experimentation, we should instead be asking experimenters to "love your monsters" (Latour, 2004), to take greater care of their creations in the context of their environments (see also Cugurullo, 2021). AVs could be an opportunity for a more careful model of experimentation in which, rather than innovation happening *to* citizens, it happens *for* them and possibly *with* them. In the UK, at least, the approach has been to foreground experimentation as a new approach to technology policy.

Laboratory as policy

British policy on AVs reflects a desire to capture both the imagined social benefits of the technology – safety, accessibility, efficiency and more besides – and as a slice of an imagined economic dividend. The concern over the nation's performance in what policymakers see as a global 'race' to develop the technology is palpable. But the UK's policy approach reflects a neurosis that the country is no longer a manufacturing superpower, nor does it play host to the sort of giant technology companies that have come to dominate AI infrastructures. Its bet is therefore that it can be a laboratory for imported or homegrown novelty. In 2015, the Council for Science and Technology, a senior advisory body, recommended the establishment of a 'real-world lab' within the UK.[2] At the same time, the Government published a code of practice for testing AVs that attempted to free up would-be innovators to conduct tests. A 2017 Act of Parliament sought to 'ensure the next wave of self-driving technology is invented, designed and operated safely in the UK.' In the years since, a series of projects supported by a new Centre for Connected and Autonomous Vehicles (CCAV) within the Government have put prototype technologies in public places and a handful of start-up companies have been given permission to test self-driving systems on public roads (see Hopkins and Schwanen, 2018 for further policy analysis).

The impact of this policy shift towards real-world demonstrations can be seen on the ground, inside British robotics labs, where engineers and others come together to test machines, infrastructures, safety systems and public acceptability. Analysis of CCAV-funded projects at one of the UK's largest public robotics labs shows a diversity of expertise being brought to bear. A logic of experimentation informed the lab's research and design of driverless vehicles (Michalec et al., 2021), but capabilities to steer the research were kept firmly in the hands of the automotive industry. Researchers on the ground were empowered to accelerate innovation, but could not steer, raising the question of where the direction of the UK's innovation for AVs is being charted.

The UK's AV trial projects have in most cases included some narrowly framed contributions from social science, asking questions to do with user acceptance (Stilgoe and Cohen, 2021). In addition, some have been studied by social scientists who are able to ask, at one stage removed, what the purposes and politics of such trials are (e.g. McDowell-Naylor, 2018; Wu, 2022). The conclusion from scholars such as Marres (2020) is that because of the cautious, sanitized performance of such trials, nothing much is being learnt. As experiments have transgressed the lab's boundaries to be closer to the public, in living labs, testbeds and on public roads, the technological contingencies are often hidden (Engels et al., 2019; Marres, 2020; (Paddeu et al., 2020).

The ifs and buts of autonomous vehicles

The trial of the pods in the Olympic Park and others like it are symptoms of a pattern that characterizes AV innovation and policy. The narrative of a self-driving future extends the idea of 'autonomy' far beyond its narrow engineering sense (Tennant and Stilgoe, 2021). The story told by innovators is of direct substitutability between human and machine drivers, giving the impression of always-and-everywhere autonomy, able to plug-and-play in urban environments. This narrative serves multiple purposes: it is 'disruptive' while also being comfortable; it suggests the possibility of rapid innovation; and, crucially, it also maintains that the future is in tech companies' hands rather than depending upon others, such as regulators or infrastructure providers. Urban trials typically seek to enact the narrative, by emphasizing the 'autonomy' of vehicles rather than the connectivity on which they actually depend. For urban policymakers, however, such a narrative is unhelpful because it seeks to strip the technology of context. If cities are to make good decisions about self-driving technologies, they need to understand the technologies' limits, the conditions that allow for their safe and smooth operation, their infrastructural needs and their likely relationships with other actors (Stilgoe, 2017).

Close observation of the development of AVs reveals a collection of ifs and buts that define the technology (see Tennant and Stilgoe, 2021 for more detail). As well as the people that protect AVs in trial situations (including safety drivers and remote operators able to take over during technological wobbles), most vehicles depend on some form of a digital high-definition map. While most rely on cameras and lidar sensors to observe the world, developers admit that smart infrastructure communicating directly with the world would improve the operation of their systems. And, though they may not admit it, the successful operation of any road user, robotic or otherwise, depends on the cooperation of others. AVs have trouble with unpredictable pedestrians, but their systems are built to see pedestrians just as they see other objects they might encounter, as passive threats rather than active agents with whom they have mutual relationships. These ifs and buts – connections, conditions and relationships – that define 'autonomous' vehicles are rarely foregrounded in trial situations, even though they are precisely the things that would be useful for people wishing to assess the potential for the technology to make a positive difference within (parts of) a city.

The UK has seen a strategic attempt to deliver on the early ambition to build a "real-world lab." An organization called Zenzic has smartened up a set of existing infrastructures and rebranded it as 'Testbed UK.' In London, the Smart Mobility Living Lab (SMLL) forms part of the network. Described in one presentation as offering an AV test of everything 'from the nursery slopes to the black run,' the SMLL argument has been that London should be a laboratory not because it is well-suited to AVs but precisely because it is a hard case. An appreciation for geographical contingency hints at a recognition that AV systems are likely to vary between locations, but the more commonly deployed argument is a "Sinatra strategy" ('If I can make it there, I'll make it anywhere'), a logic that has also been used by companies testing in Arctic Norway (Ryghaug et al., 2022). This narrative, in which any issue can be resolved through the gathering of more data, can be seen as an attempt to escape from the attachments that actually define the technology (Tennant and Stilgoe, 2021). So if we take a definition of urban experiments as 'political acts of defining and creating niches, by influencing both the social norms and physical spaces in which new social practices (can) emerge and thrive' (Savini and Bertolini, 2019: 832), 'autonomous' vehicles are an odd fit.

For all the talk, however, the SMLL is making life easy for AVs. It is serving up 15 miles of monitored urban roads, "instrumenting" the environment with connected infrastructure, offering a high-definition digital map of the whole testbed, controlling public access to certain areas and blanketing the area with a 5G network to enable constant communication (Naqvi, 2021). It claims to be a 'living lab,' putting innovation to the test, but, as Naqvi (2021) identifies, it is not clear how anything would fail its tests. As with other technologies of AI, innovators are, most of the time, able to reconfigure 'failure' as just one more argument for more data.

The 'lab' is clearly more an instrument of industrial strategy than of technology assessment. A 2020 innovation report from CCAV uses variations of the phrase *world-leading* 33 times in framing UK self-driving vehicle innovation over only 12 pages.[3] Zenzic's *UK Connected and Automated Mobility Roadmap*, produced in 2019, takes the same line. 'We are a world leader' is the concluding clause in its vision statement for 2030. It seems that the desire to perform and win on a world stage, to an audience never actually specified, is a central goal, rather than a productive spillover, of British AV policy. The UK policy of seeking to encourage and organize experimentation becomes clearer when compared with some of the approaches taken in other places.

Detached and dislocated experimentation

In the US, Federal and local governments have offered less direct funding, but have been even more enthusiastic, opening up their streets to AV testing with few constraints. As of 2022, Waymo, a company that began life as Google's self-driving car project, reports that its vehicles have driven 20 million 'autonomous driving miles' on public roads and 20 billion miles in simulation. In Phoenix, Arizona, thousands of customers have been driven by 'Waymo One,' a taxi service with nobody in the driver's seat. What began as a trial has become a de facto deployment of an AV system (in a limited area and only in favourable weather conditions). In 2022, Waymo began operating their cars in San Francisco, where another company, Cruise, has also started running self-driving cars with no backup driver, albeit only at night, when the roads are quieter. The electric car company Tesla is running a different sort of experiment. After charging some customers thousands of dollars to purchase 'full self-driving' as an optional extra, with the vague promise that the company would do its best, via software updates, to deliver such a feature, Tesla has allowed a subset to download a version – 'FSD Beta' – that enables users to help the company debug its software.

The results of these experiments are unclear. Waymo are growing in confidence and allowing users to record and publicly comment on their rides, but most of the data that would be of interest to cities is kept secret. One bureaucratic attempt at collaboration, designed by the California Department of Motor Vehicles, demands that AV companies report 'disengagements,' moments of switching between automated and manual mode. Though criticized by some because of a lack of clarity about what counts as disengagement, the initiative has at least allowed some form of external learning (Favarò et al., 2017; Sinha et al., 2021).[4]

One major analysis of AV trials around the world has explored and explained such tests according to their purposes, participants and the technologies involved (Dowling and McGuirk, 2022). This audit of what was, as of 2019, 135 AV trials concluded that, while some cities are playing more active roles in reshaping AV tests, many tests are not real tests at all, while the learning from others is intensely privatized. McAslan et al. (2021) start their analysis of US AV trials from the perspective of city governments and find a common disconnect between AV developers' and cities' aims, reducing the trials' value in informing local transport strategies.

As trials have proliferated, showing more interest in performance than learning, one could argue that the real lessons have come from the moments of unarguable technological failure. An early misadventure on the part of Uber resulted in the death of the first bystander from an AV (Macrae, 2021; Stilgoe, 2019). Uber's self-driving R&D arm subsequently became one of many loss-making operations to be acquired by a competitor. Other crashes involving Tesla (Stilgoe, 2018) have also been investigated and revealed not just the limits of the technology, but the governance challenges that lie ahead in rolling out safe and accountable mobility systems.

We should ask what all of these trials, tests and experiments add up to. Do they provide real-world evidence of the technology at work in diverse contexts? Do they show the range of companies and actors involved? Do they provide support for the idea that *the* technology is inevitable – a question of when, not if? Or does quantity have a quality of its own? Are these trials just a means of amassing data for machine learning or a way to impress the public and policymakers by, as Uber put it, 'crushing miles'?[5] If the experiments were genuinely collaborative ones, we (and the companies involved) might see them as a source of social learning, but their performative role in the 'race for autonomy' obscures the potential for reflection.

City authorities should recognize the paradox produced by the dominant narrative of autonomy that surrounds self-driving vehicle innovation. The technology will be defined not by its purported 'autonomy,' but by its attachments to a byzantine sociotechnical system that comprises infrastructures, sensors, safety drivers, data-labellers, emerging regulations, digital maps, other road users and more besides (Tennant and Stilgoe, 2021). The more the technologies develop, the clearer the attachments become. Social research with members of the public has revealed that non-experts recognize unavoidable attachments (Cugurullo et al., 2021; Stilgoe and Cohen, 2021), but these are downplayed by innovators. Companies developing technologies and testing them on local streets are more tied to particular places than they would care to admit, but their eyes are on the distant horizon.

The narrative of autonomy is a story of an artificial intelligence learning to drive like a human, but better, at which point the world is its oyster. The ambition, as with other AI technologies, is to develop a platform that can be sold as software with monopolistic rents. Given the excitement about these technologies, it remains perplexing that none has a clear route to market. For instance, even a cursory economic analysis shows the fragility of the assumptions underpinning proposed business models for 'robotaxis' (Nunes and Hernandez, 2020).

Many of the technological demonstrations are in principle rather than in practice, designed to give the impression that a truly self-driving car is either already with us or "just around the corner." The line connecting current AV experiments to urban futures is faint, and neither innovators nor national policymakers are doing much to help clarify it. Innovators are more interested in solving narrowly defined technical problems than in addressing complex social needs – ends that are necessarily defined by others. Even as an evaluation of roadworthiness, AV trials often reveal just how far their contexts are from a traditional driving test (see Stilgoe, 2021). While they may reveal little in terms of technological or mobility possibilities, these trials might at least demonstrate how claims to the relevance and proximity of the technology should be taken lightly.

For cities, the important political and economic issues will be to do with whether the technology merely follows the money, exacerbating existing economic and transport injustices, or whether it can be emancipatory for particular groups who currently have few mobility options. Cities will want to know whether the technology will be able to pay its own way, demand public subsidies or, as with other platform technologies, need to be supported by a data-hungry advertising model. Cities should ask whether the technology can be reconfigured for local needs or whether it has path dependencies that enforce a take-it-or-leave-it standard. Questions about users, business models, winners and losers seem to have been deliberately postponed until after the technology is shown to "work." But the reality is that systems are tightly constrained by what their engineers call 'operational design domains.' If they work within their own comfort zones, they may be incapacitated outside them. Diverse, variegated cities, may find that self-driving technologies suit only small areas. The problem may be that the potential benefits for road safety and opening up mobility access are greatest where the technical and economic challenge is hardest – in areas with poor infrastructure. The technologies are inextricably attached to their local environments but have little to say to local decision-makers wondering what the future of mobility looks like.

Conclusion: opening up experimentation

A year after we observed the orange and white pods navigating the footpaths of East London's Olympic Park, the consortium returned for a final week of trials. This time the fleet of pods came installed with a remote safety stewarding system. According to the project's promotional material, this freed up a seat in the pod resulting in 'a larger passenger capacity and achieved a world first in operations of an autonomous vehicle without a safety driver on board in a public environment.'

The strapline used on a summary video was clear about the intent and the achieved outcome of the trials which focussed on 'building regulatory and market confidence in autonomous pods.' This hints at the recognition of some attachments, even as it neglects others. Documents released in the project's final months emphasized prospective frameworks for verifying and validating emerging technologies in real-world settings. They pointed to the need for safety scenarios designed for testing amongst the public, not just in simulations, and cyber security reports emphasized the potential of future methodologies. Undoubtedly then, the trials produced *something*. However, much of what was being learnt, about the technology's limits and its likely relationships with others, did not fit the dominant narrative of innovation. Publicly, therefore, the narrative that what was needed was more of the same remained strong.

In the main, the knowledge produced through these trials is directed inwards towards consortia and industry interests, illustrating and occasionally strengthening relationships between players already in the AV sector. Outputs such as verification and validation frameworks provide justificatory arguments for ever more testing and ever more data gathering. But on their own, they do little to tell us why or how these technologies contribute to public life.

Where the expertise, interests and knowledge of the public were included in the trials they were constrained. Experiments designed to test trust are a case in point. Social scientists surveyed more than 300 of the pod's passengers throughout the project, investigating whether, for example, facing forwards or backwards, or riding with a safety steward made a difference to how much riders trusted the technology. These results are perhaps useful for future design iterations, but they reveal almost nothing about the trustworthiness or accountability of emerging transport infrastructures.

These trials, and policymakers' enthusiasm for staging them, have important ramifications for debates about the governance of AI in and by cities. First, by asserting control over the conditions and outcomes of public trials and framing the future deployment of technologies as inevitable, AV trials preclude the possibility of failure. Second, by foregrounding interactions and attachments between members of the public and a discrete technology such as the pods, they are bypassing meaningful public engagement at a systemic level. These issues pose risks to the governance of urban technological systems in the long term. Unreflexive trials, even though they are temporary, help cement their subjects in urban space. If the danger is that we sleepwalk into technological change (Winner, 2001), public trials can have a soporific effect, even though they hold the potential to alert their experimenters and others to important contingencies.

The lessons extend beyond governing the technology stack and into the city's political system. Trustworthiness, accountability and authority rest on the possibility of failure in experiments. In robotics, the trustworthiness and safety of autonomous systems are verified and validated against established and standardized knowledge in any given application domain such as city streets. But this kind of technological governance works only if someone is accountable for validating the veracity of the scientific (i.e. experimental) knowledge claims. Accountability in a broader political sense then rests on the vulnerability of political leaders to exposed failures of knowledge claims. In other words, the option of removing politicians from office is the quid pro quo demanded by citizens for allowing complex digital systems to play such a pervasive role in our lives. Experiments or trials that foreclose the possibility of failure entirely risk diminishing the trustworthiness of experts who build and maintain autonomous systems and the politicians who ultimately govern them on our behalf. In this sense, the most important revelation from urban experiments with AVs is the scale of the work still left to do. Opening up the testing of AV technologies to make them relevant to urban decision-making will require a radical expansion of experiments' framing, apparatuses and participants. In the UK and in many other places, cities are already notionally involved in AV testing, but they have so far been reluctant to reframe experimentation so that questions of failure, technological limits and other infrastructural dependencies become the focus. If the results of such tests are going to be relevant for urban policy, such experiments urgently need to become more experimental.

Acknowledgements

This research was supported by three funded projects: SCALINGS (Horizon 2020 grant 788359), Driverless Futures? (Economic and Social Research Council grant ES/S001832/1) and RAILS (Engineering and Physical Sciences Research Council grant EP/W011344/1). Thanks are due to our many collaborators on those projects, particularly Carlos Cuevas Garcia, Chris Tennant and Nuzhah Miah.

Notes

1 From an interview conducted as part of a podcast for the *Driverless Futures?* project.
2 In July 2015, the Council for Science and Technology wrote a letter to the Prime Minister on how the UK can get the greatest value from the autonomous and connected vehicles industry. See https://assets.publishing.service.gov.uk/government/uploads/system/uploads/attachment_data/file/459521/cst-15-1-driverless-vehicles.pdf.
3 See Centre for Connected and Autonomous Vehicles (2020). https://www.gov.uk/government/publications/connected-and-automated-vehicles-in-the-uk-2020-information-booklet.
4 The California DMV originally drafted regulations that demanded substantial collaboration between companies and the state on the terms and conduct of the social experiment. California announced in March 2017 their intention to relax these controls. Instead, they would put the onus on manufacturers to declare that their cars were safe and fully insured and trust that the legal system would work out questions of liability and unintended consequences. The threat of being sued is imagined to be the strongest lever.
5 Quote taken from 'I'm the operator,' *Wired* magazine, 8 March 2022, https://www.wired.com/story/uber-self-driving-car-fatal-crash/.

References

Boyd, D. (2016). Untangling research and practice: What Facebook's "emotional contagion" study teaches us, *Research Ethics*, 12(1), 4–13.
Burrell, J. (2016). How the machine "thinks": Understanding opacity in machine learning algorithms. *Big Data & Society*, 3(1), 2053951715622512.
Centre for Connected and Autonomous Vehicles (2020). *Information*. Available at: https://www.gov.uk/government/publications/connected-and-automated-vehicles-in-the-uk-2020-information-booklet [Accessed 19/01/2023].
Collins, H.M. (1988). Public experiments and displays of virtuosity: The core-set revisited, *Social Studies of Science*, 18(4), 725–748.
Cugurullo, F. (2018). Exposing smart cities and eco-cities: Frankenstein urbanism and the sustainability challenges of the experimental city', *Environment and Planning A: Economy and Space*, 50(1), 73–92.
Cugurullo, F. (2020). Urban artificial intelligence: From automation to autonomy in the smart city. *Frontiers in Sustainable Cities*, 2, 38.
Cugurullo, F. (2021). *Frankenstein Urbanism: Eco, Smart and Autonomous Cities, Artificial Intelligence and the End of the City*. Routledge, Abingdon and New York.

Cugurullo, F., Acheampong, R.A., Gueriau, M., & Dusparic, I. (2021). The transition to autonomous cars, the redesign of cities and the future of urban sustainability. *Urban Geography*, 42(6), 833–859.

Dowling, R., & McGuirk, P. (2022). Autonomous vehicle experiments and the city. *Urban Geography*, 43(3), 409–426.

Engels, F., Wentland, A. & Pfotenhauer, S.M. (2019). Testing future societies? Developing a framework for test beds and living labs as instruments of innovation governance. *Research Policy*, 48(9), 103826.

Favarò, F.M., Nader, N., Eurich, S.O., Tripp, M., & Varadaraju, N. (2017). Examining accident reports involving autonomous vehicles in California, *PLOS ONE*, 12(9), e0184952.

Gross, M. (2021). *Ignorance and Surprise: Science, Society, and Ecological Design*. MIT Press, Cambridge.

Hopkins, D., & Schwanen, T. (2018). Automated mobility transitions: Governing processes in the UK, *Sustainability*, 10(4), 956.

Karvonen, A., & van Heur, B. (2014). Urban laboratories: Experiments in reworking cities, *International Journal of Urban and Regional Research*, 38(2), 379–392.

Krohn, W., & Weingart, P. (1987). Commentary: Nuclear power as a social experiment—European political "Fall Out" from the Chernobyl Meltdown, *Science, Technology, & Human Values*, 12(2), 52–58.

Latour, B. (2004). *Love Your Monsters|The Breakthrough Institute*. Available at: https://thebreakthrough.org/journal/issue-2/love-your-monsters [Accessed 19/01/2023].

Laurent, B. (2011). Technologies of Democracy: Experiments and Demonstrations, *Science and Engineering Ethics*, 17(4), 649–666.

Laurent, B., & Tironi, M. (2015). A field test and its displacements. Accounting for an experimental mode of industrial innovation, *CoDesign*, 11(3–4), 208–221.

Leonardi, P.M. (2010). From road to lab to math: The co-evolution of technological, regulatory, and organizational innovations for automotive crash testing, *Social Studies of Science*, 40(2), 243–274.

Macrae, C. (2021). Learning from the failure of autonomous and intelligent systems: Accidents, safety, and sociotechnical sources of risk, *Risk Analysis*, 42(9), 1999–2025

Marres, N. (2020). Co-existence or displacement: Do street trials of intelligent vehicles test society? *The British Journal of Sociology*, 71(3), 537–555.

McAslan, D., Najar Arevalo, F., King, D.A., & Miller, T.R. (2021). Pilot project purgatory? Assessing automated vehicle pilot projects in US cities. *Humanities and Social Sciences Communications*, 8(1), 1–16.

McDowell-Naylor, D. (2018). *The Participatory, Communicative, and Organisational Dimensions of Public-Making: Public Engagement and The Development of Autonomous Vehicles in the United Kingdom*. PhD Thesis.

Michalec, O., O'Donovan, C., & Sobhani, M. (2021). What is robotics made of? The interdisciplinary politics of robotics research, *Humanities and Social Sciences Communications*, 8(1), 1–15.

Nunes, A., & Hernandez, K.D. (2020). Autonomous taxis & public health: High cost or high opportunity cost?, *Transportation Research Part A: Policy and Practice*, 138, 28–36.

Paddeu, D., Shergold, I., & Parkhurst, G. (2020). The social perspective on policy towards local shared autonomous vehicle services (LSAVS). *Transport Policy*, 98, 116–126.

Ryghaug, M., Haugland, B. T., Søraa, R.A., & Skjølsvold, T. M. (2022). Testing emergent technologies in the arctic: How attention to place contributes to visions of autonomous vehicles. *Science & Technology Studies*, 35(4), 4–21.

Savini, F., & Bertolini, L. (2019). Urban experimentation as a politics of niches, *Environment and Planning A: Economy and Space*, 51(4), 831–848.

Sinha, A., Vu, V., Chand, S., Wijayaratna, K., & Dixit, V. (2021). A crash injury model involving autonomous vehicle: Investigating of crash and disengagement reports. *Sustainability*, 13(14), 7938.

Stilgoe, J. (2017). Seeing like a Tesla: How can we anticipate self-driving worlds. *Glocalism: Journal of Culture, Politics and Innovation*, 3, 1–20.

Stilgoe, J. (2018). Machine learning, social learning and the governance of self-driving cars, *Social Studies of Science*, 48(1), 25–56.

Stilgoe, J. (2019). *Who's Driving Innovation?: New Technologies and the Collaborative State*. Springer Nature.

Stilgoe, J. (2021). How can we know a self-driving car is safe? *Ethics and Information Technology*, 23(4), 635–647.

Stilgoe, J. & Cohen, T. (2021). 'Rejecting acceptance: Learning from public dialogue on self-driving vehicles', *Science and Public Policy*, 48(6), 849–859.

Taylor, L. (2021). Exploitation as innovation: research ethics and the governance of experimentation in the urban living lab. *Regional Studies*, 55(12), 1902–1912.

Tennant, C., & Stilgoe, J. (2021). 'The attachments of "autonomous" vehicles', *Social Studies of Science*, 51(6), 846–870.

While, A.H., Marvin, S., & Kovacic, M. (2021). Urban robotic experimentation: San Francisco, Tokyo and Dubai, *Urban Studies*, 58(4), 769–786.

Winner, L. (2001). *Autonomous technology: technics-out-of-control as a theme in political thought*. 9. printing. MIT Press, Cambridge.

Wu, X. (2022). Fast forward: technography of the social integration of connected and automated vehicles into UK society. doi:10.7488/era/2320.

4

AUTONOMOUS LORRIES, ARTIFICIAL INTELLIGENCE AND URBAN (FREIGHT) MOBILITIES

Debbie Hopkins

Introduction

> The big thing is, without us being on the road, and that's all lorry drivers, they [the public] would be hungry, naked and homeless because we carry everything from bricks to food, clothes. Everything that you can buy in a shop is carried by a lorry.
>
> *(Lorry Driver L, 'Julia')*

The quote above is from an interview conducted in 2018 as part of a project on vehicle automation in the freight sector. It was said with frustration, by a lorry driver, who felt that the British public did not appreciate the work they did; that the public just wanted lorries – and their drivers – off the road. By 2021, the British public had become intimately aware of the role of lorries, and lorry drivers, in keeping society functioning. Empty shelves became a symbol of 2021 and were partly the result of the well-documented and highly publicized 'driver shortage' (Hopkins and Akyelken, 2022), Brexit, 'supply chain issues' and more. Freight mobilities are just one dimension of logistics, but perhaps where logistical *workers* are made visible (Cowen, 2014). At the same time, as Chua et al. (2018: 620) argue, innovations across the logistics sector, including processes of containerization and automation, 'have underpinned a reorganization of labor along the supply chain, with significant consequences for transportation and warehouse workers.' Whether the British public want lorries, their drivers or both off the roads is unclear, but vehicle automation has been loudly touted by public and private sector actors as one 'solution' to the 'problem' of freight mobilities in cities (and elsewhere). This chapter interrogates the ways that artificial intelligence (AI) – manifest

DOI: 10.4324/9781003365877-5

through vehicle automation – is proposed as both a problem and solution to urban challenges, while also questioning how the socio-materiality of the city might foreshadow what AI can become.

Lorries and cities sit uneasily together. Frictions emerge between imaginings of people-centred 'sustainable' cities and the (often large) vehicles that get goods in and waste out of cities. These lorries (also called 'trucks' outside of the UK or Heavy Goods Vehicles [HGVs]) – and, ostensibly, their drivers – are codified as dangerous and dirty, resulting in unsafe and polluted urban environments. A number of infrastructure changes and physical alterations to lorry design have been made to increase the driver's line of view and the visibility of other road users, yet fatalities and injuries continue. Since their inception in 1992, Euro standards have improved lorry emissions, yet they remain stubbornly reliant on fossil fuels. Despite efforts to instigate changes to limit lorry movements to the outer edges of cities (the 'suburbs') – itself with clear spatial politics – lorries remain a central feature of how "stuff" is moved in cities.

Urban transformation and the autonomous supply chain

Cities, as one urban form, are diverse in their material, social and economic configurations. Nonetheless, they are frequently pitted as 'saviours' or 'foes' for sustainable urban futures (Angelo and Wachsmuth, 2020). On the one hand, cities are presupposed as sustainability leaders, where new governance, ideas, practices and innovations are able to take hold amongst a population receptive to such progressive change. On the other, they are represented as the site of hyper-consumption, excess and disconnect from a supposedly distant "Nature." Such totalizing and homogenizing discourses have been strongly critiqued for their omission of the partial, heterogeneous and fragmented nature of urbanity. Responses to urban challenges, including but not limited to pollution and inequalities, have come in a variety of forms, but often relate to 'knowing the issue better' through increased tracking, monitoring and data-driven forms of surveillance, followed by often-technological solutions seeking to make for a better city, however understood, although often protecting vested interests and benefitting those in/with power. Both of these approaches are aided, and potentially accelerated, by AI. Nevertheless, discourses of smart urbanism, Luque-Ayala and Marvin (2019: 210) suggest, are 'deeply rooted in seductive and normative visions of the future where digital technology stands as the primary driver for change.' This dominant discourse is frequently led by corporate and political elites, with synergies and overlaps with sustainable urbanism (Long and Rice, 2019), often curtailing any radical potential for urban transformation (Cugurullo, 2020).

AI seeks to mimic and optimize human thought processes/processing through deep learning functions to solve complex problems. In the context of urban transport, AI is posited as a way to overcome a range of issues wherein a solution for one problem may further exacerbate another. This is particularly relevant for social groups and communities already disadvantaged by the dominant transport system. Since 'cities are full of routine behaviours' (Barns, 2021: 3203), AI proponents argue that these can be both tracked and understood through Big Data analytics. The movement of a lorry of bricks through a city to a building site or that of a refrigerated unit taking supplies to a supermarket, may be understood through this lens; as routinized and scheduled actions which can be optimized through data. Actually existing patterns of freight movement are already used to make sense of traffic flows, congestion levels and particulate matter (PM) readings as well as injury and fatality rates, all quantifiable metrics of urban life, but qualitatively experienced.

AI methods being adopted within transport research include Artificial Neural Networks (ANN), Genetic Algorithms (GA) and Fuzzy Logic Models (FLM), amongst others, (Abduljabbar et al., 2019) which all seek, in their different ways, to make sense of complexity by understanding and predicting patterns of travel behaviour. At the nexus of AI, urban mobilities and smart cities sits vehicle automation, Unmanned Aerial Vehicles (UAVs) and Mobility-as-a-Service (MaaS). The autonomous lorry has emerged within the broader shift to automating the transport system. This process includes changes to technologies, business models, practices, infrastructures, policies, insurance, financing and urban form, through the application of advanced automation (Lin, 2022). It includes public and private modes, and passenger and freight transport. As a low-profit-margin sector, with a largely fragmented and un-unionized workforce, innovations for the freight sector that offer cost-savings are particularly appealing to many managers and sectoral leaders (Sindi and Woodman, 2021). With salaries making up about a third of all operating costs for freight, reducing this by way of automation has gathered attention and built hype in some parts of the sector, but has also led to spatio-temporally fragmented expectations of automation. In sum, AI technologies have emerged in a variety of ways offering the potential to reconfigure and remake urban governance and urban life. Autonomous lorries are an important manifestation of this phenomenon as they contribute to the maintenance of an essential component of cities' metabolism, its supply chains.

The focus on automated lorries can be contextualized within a broader discussion of global supply chains and the increasingly visible supply chain crisis characterized by accelerated material flows, along with shortages of containers, pallets, ships and workers. Danyluk (2021: 2149) characterizes supply chain urbanism as 'efforts to remake urban space in the name of smooth, efficient circulation,' and describes the struggles over land, labour and environments, in the name of logistics. Rather than centring on individual cities, supply chain urbanism seeks to foreground the connections between places and people through logistics-oriented urbanization, contributing to a relational understanding of the production of urban space. This, then, offers a space for developing an understanding of the connections between places: how freight mobilities in cities – and lorries in cities – are part of a broader web of logistical infrastructures, vehicles, workers and technologies. A related theorization of labour, automation and supply chains in late capitalism comes from Weiqiang Lin (2022) who uses the idea of 'automated infrastructure' to interrogate the contours of a shift to 'virtualized transactions,' explained through the role(s) of advanced automation in logistics. This is particularly relevant here as it helps to uncover the changing configurations of working and conditions for workers. AI and automation have emerged in a variety of forms throughout and across the supply chain, often leading to the surveilling, disciplining and policing of workers. This includes tracking mobile workers spatially (through GPS) and temporally (through digital tachographs) (Hopkins, 2022; Levy, 2022), introducing autonomous robots for picking and sorting in warehouses and at ports, and the use of autonomous vehicles for off-road/private road conditions. Thus, while vehicle automation is not new, its increasing use *in* and its role in the production *of* urban logistical space warrants further attention.

Urban freight mobilities and autonomous lorries

While lorries are broadly considered to be incongruous with contemporary urban sustainability, there are presently few seemingly viable alternatives which can easily operate within current models of both urban form and built environment. Lorries do a variety of work in cities. They keep cities moving, while also keeping them congested; their mobilities are relational and contingent. The 'first/last mile' is a term frequently used in transport spheres. Rarely referring to a measured unit of distance, it is often a shorthand for the 'first/last portion' of a journey. In passenger transport, the last mile often refers to the piece between, for example, a train station and one's home. For freight, it often refers to the final stage, and with the massive growth in home delivery in the past decade (particularly through consumer-to-consumer trading and online shopping) 'last mile' is often used to denote the journey from its final depot to a household or shop (see Altenried, 2019 for an analysis of logistical urbanism). This is broadly thought to be the most carbon-intensive and financially expensive portion of a trip (per mile/kilometre). City logistical patterns take a number of forms: 1) to and from a 'hub' with another mode/vehicle doing the last mile, 2) to and from final destinations (which could be commercial or residential), 3) all freight movements within the city and 4) travelling through the city (without a destination in the city). Lorries feature in first/last mile mobilities as well as what is referred to as the 'middle-mile' which connects two distribution hubs, often connected by motorway/

highway roads. Thus, the use of lorries is not only limited to some routes/ roads but a dominant characteristic of transport systems within and beyond cities, connecting people, places, markets and economies but with (hyper) localized impacts and implications.

Lorries represent just one of many modes for freight mobilities in cities, but their use remains stubbornly locked in place. Responses to urban mobility challenges are often hamstrung by logics of continued automobility, where alternative business models, modes and regulations are restricted and sidelined. There are a number of measures which challenge the dominance of vehicular freight in cities, through these we can see what other futures are possible and the context through which AI Urbanism has manifested and grown. The first, Urban Consolidation Centres (UCCs), offer a spatial redevelopment of urban freight, through the use of lower-cost land on the edges of towns and cities used as a hub for large vehicles (lorries) to deposit their freight, for it then to be repackaged and delivered (the last mile) via electric vehicles (cars, vans or e-bikes) or cargobikes. Such an approach presents a way to reduce the number of large freight vehicles (i.e., lorries) entering cities while still accounting for the work they do to keep cities functioning. Since they allow for the adoption of non-fossil fuelled vehicles, UCCs are often part of low-emission urban imaginaries (e.g., Allen et al., 2012). Cargobikes, on the other hand, offer further digression from the dominant norm with a modal shift to active modes for urban cores, but also increasingly to suburbs. And there is a suggestion that cargobikes might be a faster (than motorized modes) option in some locations (Verlinghieri et al., 2021). The adoption of low/zero-emission zones in cities is going some way, if not the whole way to reduce the number of polluting freight vehicles (e.g., Browne et al., 2005). In addition to these zones, a variety of controls have been initiated to guide the mobilities of lorries in UK cities. The London Lorry Control Scheme, for example, presents a time restriction on the movements of lorries (over 18-tonne maximum gross weight) on some, but not all, London roads.

Emissions and pollutants are not the only hazards presented by freight vehicles in cities, however. Road safety emerges as an important dimension of freight mobilities, particularly relating to lorries. In the UK, between 2015 and 2020, the highest proportion of casualties that were fatal occurred in 2-vehicle accidents involving a lorry (6.1%, Department for Transport, 2021). In 2013, 12% of cyclist fatalities on EU roads involved a lorry (International Transport Forum, 2013) and in Norway, the number is as high as 20% nationally and 35% in cities (Pokorny et al., 2017). Mcdonald et al. (2021) also show the important role of freight transport mode in predicting road safety outcomes in the US, with lorries (or large commercial vehicles, in their words) being more likely to lead to severe injury and fatalities than smaller commercial vehicles (e.g., vans), potentially indicating the role mode shift could play in reducing fatalities and injuries. The International Road

Transport Union (IRU, 2017) also points out the broader safety issues associated with supply chains transport with issues for traffic and workplace safety, these include being hit by a moving (often reversing) vehicle, falling on or from a vehicle, vehicles (e.g., forklifts) turning over or being hit by objects from vehicles.

With questions of safety comes the allocation of responsibility and, more problematically, blame. Spinney et al. (2015) interrogate the relationship between cyclists and the (freight) driver-citizen. They point to the variety of safety technologies introduced in the past 10 years, including the installation of sensors, new mirror configurations and larger windows, designed to increase the amount of information available to the driver when they make decisions (i.e., to turn, merge, stop etc.). This is, in part, a reaction to what the authors call the 'blind spot excuse': 'a law firm specialising in cycling injury claims argues that "the blind spot excuse is routinely used by drivers of large vehicles when a vulnerable road user comes out of nowhere. For a commercially available [safety] system [...] to eliminate them all, it's exactly the sort of thing that will make the blind spot excuse a thing of the past ..."' (Spinney et al., 2015: 339). Such discourse has material implications for the imagining, design and construction of freight vehicle innovation. But more than this, the removal of the 'unsafe driver' becomes an important ideal around which support is built for driver*less* vehicles. Yet Pokorney et al. (2017) show multiple causes of collisions involving cyclists and lorry drivers: 1) truck turning right, 2) intersection movements/crossing and 3) low-speed manoeuvres of trucks. Each presents different actions of cyclists and drivers, infrastructures, weather conditions, speed limits and road maintenance, depicting a more complex picture in which the driver is but one component of an unsafe city mobility system. Urban design, zoning and the development, design and route of cycleways emerge as necessary areas for intervention too (see, for example, Pitera et al., 2017; Conway et al., 2016; Pivo et al., 1997).

AI has been recognized as a way to reduce road deaths, with the United Nations claiming that AI could halve road deaths by 2030 (United Nations, 2021). They suggest this can be achieved through the use of AI to collect and analysis of vehicle collision data and improve post-crash response, as well as enhancing road infrastructure, and inspiring regulatory innovation. These same actions have since become the foundations for the AI for Road Safety initiative (AI for Good, 2021) and connect to the work of the International Telecommunications Union (ITU, 2020: no page) – the UN agency for ICT – on AI for autonomous and assisted driving, which sees a central role as 'build(ing) the public trust in the future of AI-enabled safe mobility for all.' In positioning the driver as dangerous, discourses of vehicle automation gain traction. There is a relatively long history of vehicle modifications and related policies being launched first for freight vehicles before including passenger vehicles (i.e., mandatory seatbelts) and the same is now happening with the automation of driving tasks. Automated features are being integrated into lorries (see, Hopkins and Schwanen, 2021, for a discussion of the SAE levels of vehicle automation and automated features), largely under the guise of 'increased safety,' yet to date these largely relate to motorway driving – with features such as adaptive cruise control, lane assist and automatic braking working best at high speeds. Further, despite these claims to the contrary, there is still uncertainty about the contributions automation will make to increasing the safety of the transport system (Ghandriz et al., 2020).

Autonomous lorries

There have been multiple waves of experimentation with different forms of vehicle automation (see, for example, Hopkins and Schwanen, 2018), including for freight mobilities. Yet the 'rapid rollout of these technologies, across multiple locations and domains at once' (Lin, 2022: 471) brought about by the conditions of the pandemic – notably lockdowns and safety fears – has ushered a new age of 'machine-led' logistical or supply chain urbanism. The autonomous lorry does not exist in the imagination alone, both start-ups and incumbents are working to develop their technologies for testing on public roads. TuSimple (tusimple.com), for instance, is a US company established in 2015 with the mission of improving the 'safety and efficiency of the trucking industry' and 'creating a new standard for safety,' with benefits for their Autonomous Freight Network – an 'ecosystem' of 'autonomous trucks, digital mapped routes, strategically placed terminals… and autonomous operations monitoring system' (FleetOwner, 2020: no page) stated to be a reduced carbon footprint, via "aggressively" low-cost pricing and 99% reliability. TuSimple seeks to operate in the 'middle mile'; by and large using the motorway/highway networks to 'trunk' goods between terminals (Forbes, 2021). In late 2021, a TuSimple-technology truck completed an 80-mile route in Arizona without human intervention and with no human on board (FleetOwner, 2022a).

The European Truck Platooning Challenge was coordinated by the Dutch European Union presidency in 2016. This involved convoys of 'smart trucks' travelling to Rotterdam (Netherlands) from across Europe, seeking to test the institutional and operational challenges of truck platooning rather than the technologies per se (European Commission, 2016). In 2017, there was a flurry of media attention in the UK on the testing of convoys of 'driverless trucks' purportedly happening in 2018, following a £8.1m investment from the Department for Transport and Highways England for the 'Helm UK project'. In 2021, UK's Transport Research Laboratory reported that their consortium, which includes DHL, DAF, Millbrook Proving Ground, Costain and Ricardo, was testing autonomous platoons of lorries but that routes and roads included in the trials would not be disclosed for safety reasons

(MotorTransport, 2021), instead providing videos and photographs of pla-tooning lorries on their website. The final project report claims that while 'platooning systems are not yet commercially available... the prototype sys-tem HelmUK successfully and safely deployed on real roads demonstrated that the technological building blocks already exist' (Helm, 2022: 9). And, in specific reference to human drivers, argued that 'driver workload did increase slightly due to platooning, but only by a very small amount – overall, driver workload was not substantially impacted' (Helm, 2022: 6).

The Plus Safety Report (2020) published by Plus self-driving trucking company (plus.ai), describes their approach as 'safety-first,' and through the report put this into action, describing how they are building safety into their 'self-driving system' including system architecture, vehicle cybersecurity, daily operations, testing and validation. Plus present two steps to deploy-ment of a 'safe self-driving truck product': 1) developing a functional sys-tem and 2) proving it is safe. To justify this approach, they characterize truck driving as 'one of the most dangerous careers in the country, with accidents involving trucks resulting in nearly 5,000 fatalities and over 150,000 injuries in 2018' (Plus Safety Report, 2020: III). Thus, danger and safety are discursively employed to rationalize and prioritize an AI-centred mobility future.

Similar to broader narratives shared with passenger transport, is the senti-ment that roads are already highly dangerous and that this is the result of human error. But logistics company DFDS (n.d.) takes this further, to claim that driverless freight vehicles represent a new paradigm of liability and safety. Writing in an industry publication titled 'trucking's safer, self-driving future,' they state

> By the end of this decade, trucks powered by supercomputers will be haul-ing freight across the country on some of the safest roads in a century. Driver assistance technologies on commercial and passenger vehicles are more prevalent each year, creating the potential to reduce road crashes caused by human error. As artificial intelligence (AI) grows more power-ful, there won't be drivers operating some commercial vehicles running on major freight corridors.
>
> *(FleetOwner, 2021)*

Safety is not the only rationale however and AI is not limited to vehicle and supply chain automation; there are examples where it is being designed to 'make truckers' lives better'; Variant is a US trucking company using AI to manage their driver's routes (FleetOwner, 2022b). The company states that '(w)ithout truck drivers, there is no trucking. But our industry treats these hardworking professionals like expendable resources. We're out to change that. Permanently. And for the better' – appearing to contrast driverless futures put forward by driverless freight imaginaries. Variant differs in terms of its application of AI (routing over vehicle automation) but also its vision of freight futures, yet the problem framing has similarities and speaks to industry-wide challenges with driver recruitment and retention (Hopkins and Akyelken, 2022). This serves to represent the diversity of ways that AI is being proposed as a solution not only to logistical challenges but also to the reorganization of labour and the consequences for workers. These two forms – automation and AI-driven task allocation are not unconnected; and both serve to reproduce dominant logistical logics (Hopkins, 2022). By centring on routing, there are parallels with smart city data analytics and AI-informed traffic management, yet the discourse put forward by Variant articulates benefits for individual drivers when it is likely that such benefits would be accrued to the broader freight/transport system (in terms of reduced congestion, accurate arrival times).

In the final section of this chapter, I reflect upon interviews with lorry drivers in England (2017–2021), particularly building upon the themes developed so far around AI, autonomy and city logistics. This is done to illuminate the everyday experiences of lorry drivers and driver expectations of automation of the sector, which are often at odds with discourses of optimization, securitization and safety which are propagated by both industry and government to justify investment in AI and automation. This section will indicate how changes to volumes of information and the automation of *some* tasks relate to the becoming of safe(r) human–lorry drivers.

Becoming 'safe': the autonomous lorry driver

Academic and policy discussions of urban mobility largely centre on two dimensions: first, the volumes and flows of traffic and second, the associated pollutants and externalities including un/safety. Both of these are knowable through Big Data which then subsumes the role of responsible agent. Experiences of urban mobility are – rightly – focused on raising attention to those who are trying to exist in an automobile city, such as cyclists and pedestrians. But to understand the logics underpinning the push to automation, particularly for freight vehicles, it is useful to consider the context of driver's experiences.

Horrible, frightening, dangerous, terrifying, chaotic, difficult. All these words were used by lorry drivers to describe driving in London (England). Amongst the 28 lorry drivers I have interviewed, not one enjoyed driving into cities, most actively avoided it – itself a privilege only afforded to some drivers (usually those who had been driving longest and arguably were best prepared for driving in cities). London was singled out as a particularly challenging place to drive a lorry. But it is not just the infrastructure, the busy-ness, the potential consequences, but the combination of all of these, as well as the vehicle itself, the mirrors, the checks, as well as times of day, routes and loads. Being safe in the city is hard, the drivers would tell me.

> It really is [hard to drive in cities] because you've got to look everywhere all at once. Even on a standard truck you've got nowadays six mirrors and a lot of the ones that are regularly going into cities now also have cameras down the sides for looking out for cyclists. So, you've got that in a truck and then you've got a split second to go into a gap, for example, on a roundabout and before you set off, you have to check all six of these mirrors and any other cameras that you've got and you've got to do that in a split second. And it's easily possible that a cyclist could not appear in one mirror and then when you look in the other mirror, then it would have appeared in the mirror you've just looked in. So, there could be a cyclist very, very close to your vehicle and you've done all of your conscientious checks and you still can't see it. You're always going to be the one at fault because you're in the big vehicle and that's terrifying, it really is.
>
> *(Lorry Driver F, 'Nina')*

Nina reflects on the 'split second' decisions she is required to make. She talks about the multiple sources of information on-board modern lorries and the challenges of reconciling these on-the-move; reflecting the argument developed by Spinney et al. (2015). The increased information available to human drivers complexifies rather than simplifying the task at hand, with the potential to increase collisions. Speed of decision-making emerges as a key concern for AI, for instance, with Chowdhury and Sadek (2012: 6) arguing that 'AI tools can facilitate faster decision making by automating the decision-making process. Through data gathering and screening, processing, and decision making, AI can support faster solutions to complex problems' thus the increasing information available to human drivers in efforts to increase safety may progress intentions for AI-dependent futures through practices of informational abundance which overwhelm human drivers, but work to the sensibilities of autonomous mobile subjects.

Similarly, the predictability of other road users' mobilities was recognized as sometimes adding to the stresses experienced by lorry drivers, for Jack,

> It is chaotic. It's so busy and talking about road users, the only ones that really used to annoy me were the mopeds and the motorbikes in London. They would squeeze up the middle and they don't care how tight it is.
>
> *(Lorry Driver B, 'Jack')*

Again, the capacity for the autonomous system to predict and respond to these conditions represents a becoming for the autonomous lorry driver, where the human driver is deemed incapable. Such a claim would be, however, refuted by some. Josh, for instance, a driver trainer as well as a lorry driver himself, argued that 'Drivers, if they've been taught correctly, will always be safe anyway. It's only the people that want to be unsafe that will be unsafe' (Lorry Driver G, 'Josh').

For others, the issues facing human drivers arise from a lack of support, leading to unsafe infrastructures, policies and regulations: 'The trouble is these days the Government are not helping the lorry drivers to do their job. They moan about lorry drivers being in London, they moan about lorry drivers being out on the road' (Lorry Driver J, 'Mark'). Across these examples, we see contentions and contestations of driver experiences. Complexity comes through, and this complexity is used to underpin the development and deployment of AI systems for city transport. Micro-automations have already emerged in response to the complexity in the transport system and often to reduce the burden on drivers. Yet as the HelmUK project shows, driver workload is often increased through these micro-automations, however minimally. Thus, it could be argued, the human driver is being further stressed and overloaded in the process of developing innovations to create a safer (non/human) lorry driver.

Existing micro-automations take a variety of forms, including safety interventions which "read" infrastructural cues to understand what the human driver might be doing. One such cue is the painted lines which denote the edges of the road lanes. With sensors assessing the movement of the lorry, an alarm is triggered if the vehicle crosses a painted line without first *indicating* (indicating a move is a proxy for it being an intentional act). For drivers, these offer a 'back up' alarm to alert them to this 'unintended' move across lanes. But for many of the lorry drivers I spoke to, UK road infrastructure made this perhaps well-intentioned intervention frustrating:

> The system believes that you're possibly nodding off so you will either get a 'beep, beep, beep', which is incredibly annoying, or the system will override whatever is coming out of the radio and turn it to white noise. All very well and good but not when you're on roads which have lines painted all over them because of roadworks and stuff and every 15 seconds you get this god almighty earth-shattering noise come through the speaker system...
>
> *(Lorry Driver D, 'Harry')*

The operation of micro-automations may, then, lead to frustrations and irritations for drivers.

Discourses of urban transport automation have complex entanglements with questions of safety, particularly of the figure of the unsafe lorry driver. Lorry drivers' visions and expectations of fully autonomous freight systems, but also everyday experiences of partial automation, suggest that specific formulations of changes to volumes of information and partial automations may allow some drivers to 'become' safe(r) human drivers, but not others. For Peter, an autonomous truck – likely configured as part of an AI-enabled logistical system (and perhaps 'smart city') means that 'the role of the driver is still the same but the importance of what you're actually doing has changed.' He goes on to use the example of a manual lorry versus an automatic lorry – how the automation of one driving task frees the driver up for other tasks.

> If you've got an automatic truck, you can drive into the centre of London and you've got more time to look out for car drivers, cyclists, pedestrians if you're not having to change gear. You can concentrate more on the driving and your surrounds than on actually driving the truck and gear selection.
>
> *(Lorry Driver E, 'Peter')*

But other sociotechnologies produce more information, rather than reducing (human)tasks. This then suggests that configurations of driver skill, (micro-) automations, data, built environment, road users and regulations will influence the ways freight drivers experience their work in an AI-enabled transport system and this will evolve over time.

While the drivers' experiences of automation described above centred on automated features, this is not isolated from the imagined fully autonomous lorry. The logics of automation, safety and human error are being used as catalysts for public and private investment in innovation. In this way, the unsafe lorry driver character becomes an important actor in the development of advanced automation and within AI urbanism. By understanding the freight system as part of routine city behaviours – as part of urban metabolism, not contained within a fully knowable city limit, but as a primary urban function – the opportunities for fully autonomous freight and logistics are extended. But, following Barns (2021: 3208), there are questions about the limits to the capacity of Big Data as it 'visualises, replicates and reproduces that which is routine about existing cities, and uses these existing patterns to create agents that act autonomously on behalf of humans,' such limits include the potential for radical change away from the existing systems. Is a less polluting, less harmful urban freight system the one we – collectively – want? What opportunities are there to learn from partial automation to enact alternatives rather than reproducing the status quo?

Conclusion: AI and autonomous urban freight mobilities

> You hear about these driverless lorries now. I suppose eventually where we'd be in 2027, potentially these trucks could replace us drivers and as there's such a shortage for drivers, then yes but my argument is what

happens when they fail? Because like any computer, it fails at some point, it gets a glitch and it's not fool proof or you get a hacker that hacks into the system and can potentially run a lorry through Central London.

(Lorry Driver H, 'Lisa')

Lorry driver configurations are used in different ways to rationalize automation as a safer option to the unsafe human driver. The unsafe lorry driver is made up of 1) the relative size of the lorry to other urban road users, 2) the recklessness of the dangerous human driver and 3) the unsuitability of urban infrastructures. These are not only used independently but brought together to show how, where and why urban lorry-driving is unsafe. This then becomes a starting point for the development and integration of AI into urban freight. Dominant logics of vehicle automation and AI-driven logistical planning offer attempts to continue the idea of 'smooth' and 'efficient' supply chains across spatial scales (Danyluk, 2021), particularly within cities where congestion and collisions are prevalent. Where AI entities take the management and governance out of human hands (Cugurullo, 2020), the possibilities for reproducing 'just in time' ideologies appear.

AI and advanced automation, in their various guises, may both advance and/or prevent a radical rethinking of urban mobilities, limiting the options and potential for a different kind of mobility system, while also offering the potential for new and alternative logistical futures. Where the data produced through and by logistical operations more generally, and lorry drivers, in particular, goes is an open question; within the lorry, an increasing array of technologies exist to track, watch and monitor human driver's movements (i.e., through GPS), observance of driver's hours' regulations (i.e., digital tachograph), compliance with business, government and social rules (i.e., road- and driver-facing cameras). These produce a variety of forms of data, owned largely by private companies, but also potentially owned/accessed by tech companies and the government. In what ways might this data make the 'horrible, frightening, dangerous, terrifying, chaotic, difficult' city in a different form, produce alternative ways of becoming safe and enact forms of AI-enabled logistical urbanism?

Acknowledgements

The research informing this chapter was supported by the Research Councils United Kingdom (RCUK) Energy Programme [grant EP/K011790/1, 'Centre on Innovation and Energy Demand' (CIED)], the Chartered Institute of Logistics and Transport Seed Corn fund 2017–2018 ['Gender, Freight and Automation'] and the University of Oxford John Fell Fund [grant 171/306, 'Experimenting with Mobile Methods for Research with Mobile Freight Workers'].

References

Abduljabbar, R., Dia, H., Liyanage, S. & Bagolee, S.A. (2019). Applications of artificial intelligence in transport: An overview. *Sustainability*, 11(1), 189.

AI for Good (2021). *AI for Road Safety*. Available at: https://aiforgood.itu.int/about-ai-for-good/ai-ml-pre-standardization/ai4roadsafety/ [Accessed 19/01/2023].

Allen, J., Browne, M., Woodburn, A., & Leonardi, J. (2012). The role of urban consolidation centres in sustainable freight transport. *Transport Reviews*, 32(4), 473–490.

Altenried, M. (2019). On the last mile: logistical urbanism and the transformation of labour. *Work Organisation, Labour and Globalisation*, 13(1), 114–129.

Angelo, H., & Wachsmuth, D. (2020). Why does everyone think cities can save the planet? *Urban Studies*, 57(11), 2201–2221.

Barns, S. (2021). Out of the loop? On the radical and the routine in urban big data. *Urban Studies*, 58(15), 3203–3210.

Browne, M., Allen, J., & Anderson, S. (2005). Low emission zones: The likely effects on the freight transport sector. *International Journal of Logistics Research and Applications*, 8(4), 269–281.

Chowdhury, M., & Sadek, A. W. (2012). Advantages and limitations of artificial intelligence. *Artificial Intelligence Applications to Critical Transportation Issues*, 6(3), 360–375.

Chua, C., Danyluk, M., Cowen, D. & Khalili, L. (2018). Introduction: Turbulent Circulations: Building a critical engagement with logistics. *Environment and Planning D: Society and Space*, 36(4), 617–629.

Conway, A., Tavernier, N., Leal-Tavares, V., Gharamani, N., Chauvet, L., Chiu, M., & Bing Yeap, X. (2016). Freight in a bicycle-friendly city: Exploratory analysis with New York city open data. *Transportation Research Record*, 2547(1), 91–101.

Cowen, D. (2014). *The Deadly Life of Logistics: Mapping Violence in Global Trade*, University of Minnesota Press.

Cugurullo, F. (2020). Urban artificial intelligence: From automation to autonomy in the smart city. *Frontiers in Sustainable Cities*, 2, 38.

Danyluk, M. (2021). Supply-chain urbanism: Constructing and contesting the logistics city. *Annals of the American Association of Geographer*, 111(7), 2149–2164.

Department for Transport (2021). *Reported road casualties in Great Britain: pedal cycle factsheet, 2020, 30 September 2021*. Available at: https://www.gov.uk/government/statistics/reported-road-casualties-great-britain-pedal-cyclist-factsheet-2020/reported-road-casualties-in-great-britain-pedal-cycle-factsheet-2020 [Accessed 19/01/2023].

DFDS (n.d.). *The impact of self-driving trucks*. Available at: https://www.dfds.com/en/about/insights/newsletters/self-driving-trucks [Accessed 19/01/2023].

European Commission (2016). *Success of truck platooning challenge clears way for real-life convoys – Steve Phillips, CEDR*. Horizon: The EU Research and Innovation Magazine, April 11 2016. Available at: https://ec.europa.eu/research-and-innovation/en/horizon-magazine/success-truck-platooning-challenge-clears-way-real-life-convoys-steve-phillips-cedr [Accessed 19/01/2023].

FleetOwner (2020). *TuSimple launches first autonomous freight network*, July 1 2020. Available at: https://www.fleetowner.com/technology/autonomous-vehicles/article/21135592/tusimple-launches-first-autonomous-freight-network [Accessed 19/01/2023].

FleetOwner (2022a). *As excitement of self-driving trucks grows, fleets will soon have produces to choose from.* January 18 2022. Available at: https://www.fleetowner.com/technology/article/21213982/as-excitement-of-selfdriving-trucks-grows-fleets-will-soon-have-products-to-choose-from [Accessed 19/01/2023].

FleetOwner (2022b). *U.S. Xpress explores how Kodiak AVs can fit into its fleet,* April 8 2022. Available at: https://www.fleetowner.com/technology/article/21238451/us-xpress-explores-how-kodiak-avs-can-fit-into-its-fleet [Accessed 19/01/2023].

Forbes (2021). *The autonomous truck revolution is right around the corner,* May 11 2021, Available at: https://www.forbes.com/sites/stevebanker/2021/05/11/the-autonomous-truck-revolution-is-right-around-the-corner/?sh=5409f6d22c96 [Accessed 19/01/2023].

Ghandriz, T., Jacobson, B., Laine, L., & Hellgren, J. (2020). Impact of automated driving systems on road freight transport an electrified propulsion of heavy vehicles. *Transportation Research Part C: Emerging Technologies*, 115, 102610.

Helm (2022). *Helm UK Final Report,* 14 July 2022. Available at: https://trl.co.uk/uploads/trl/documents/HelmUK_Final-Report-_Accessible.pdf [Accessed 19/01/2023]

Hopkins, D. (2022). Buffering as Everyday Logistical Labour, *Roadsides,* 007: Logistics. DOI 10.26034/roadsides-202200708.

Hopkins, D., & Akyelken, N. (2022). MotherTruckers? Gendered work in logistics and freight, In Wright, T., Budd, L., & Ison, S. (Eds.), *Gender and Work in Transport*, Emerald Publishing.

Hopkins, D., & Schwanen, T. (2018). Governing the Race to Automation. In Marsden, G. & Reardon, L. (Eds.), *Governance of Smart Mobility.* Emerald, Bingley, UK.

Hopkins, D., & Schwanen, T. (2021). Talking about automated vehicles: What do levels of automation do? *Technology in Society,* 64, 101488.

International Road Transport Union [IRU] (2017). *Safe and efficient goods reception for road transport.* February 7 2017. Available at: https://www.iru.org/resources/iru-library/safe-and-efficient-goods-reception-road-freight?token=a7b80d9cd18b6e82dd2a1d6a854c36c1-1650549728-df6de072 [Accessed 19/01/2023]

International Telecommunications Union [ITU] (2020). *Focus group on AI for autonomous and assisted driving (FG-AI4AD).* Available at: https://www.itu.int/en/ITU-T/focusgroups/ai4ad/Pages/default.aspx [Accessed 19/01/2023]

International Transport Forum (2013). *Cycling, health and safety.* OECD Publishing, Paris.

Levy, K. (2022). *Data Driven: Truckers, Technology, and the New Workplace Surveillance.* Princeton University Press, Princeton NJ.

Lin, W. (2022). Automated infrastructure: COVID-19 and the shifting geographies of supply chain capitalism. *Progress in Human Geography,* 46(2), 463–483.

Long, J., & Rice, J. L. (2019). From sustainable urbanism to climate urbanism. *Urban Studies,* 56(5), 992–1008.

Luque-Ayala, A., & Marvin, S. (2019). Developing a critical understanding of smart urbanism, In Schwanen, T. & van Kempen, R. (Eds.), *Handbook of Urban Geography,* Edward Elgar, London.

Mcdonald, N., Lyons, T., Wang, J., Cherry, C., Azad, M., Parajuli, S., & Grembek, O. (2021). *Urban freight and road safety trends and innovative strategies.* CSCRS-R30. December 2021. Available at: https://www.roadsafety.unc.edu/wp-content/uploads/2021/12/CSCRS_urban-Freight_Report_12_9_21_508C.pdf [Accessed 19/01/2023].

MotorTransport (2021). *Motorway trials of autonomous HGV platoons resume.* July 9 2021. Available at: https://motortransport.co.uk/blog/2021/07/09/motorway-trials-of-autonomous-hgv-platoons-resume/ [Accessed 19/01/2023].

Pitera, K., Pokorny, P., Kristensen, T., & Bjørgen, A. (2017). The complexity of planning for goods delivery in a shared urban space: A case study involving cyclists and trucks. *European Transport Research Review*, 9, 46.

Pivo, G., Carlson, D., Kitchen, M., & Billen, D. (1997). *Learning from truckers: Moving goods in compact, livable urban areas*, Research Project T9903, Task 69. June 1997.

Plus Safety Report (2020). *The future of trucking, today.* October 2020. Available at: https://plus.ai/Plus_Safety_Report_2021.pdf [Accessed 19/01/2023].

Pokorny, P., Drescher, J., Pitera, K., & Jonsson, T. (2017). Accidents between freight vehicles and bicycles, with a focus on urban areas, World Conference on Transport Research 2016. *Transport Research Procedia*, 25, 999–1007.

Sindi, A., & Woodman, R. (2021). Implementing commercial autonomous road haulage in freight operations: An industry perspective. *Transportation Research Part A: Policy & Practice*, 152, 235–253.

Spinney, J., Kullman, K., & Golbuff, L. (2015). Driving the 'Starship Enterprise' through London: Constructing the im/moral driver-citizen through HGV safety technology. *Geoforum*, 64, 333–341.

United Nations (2021). *Artificial intelligence can help halve road death by 2030.* October 7 2021. Available at: https://news.un.org/en/story/2021/10/1102522 [Accessed 19/01/2023].

Verlinghieri, E., Itova, I., Collignon, N., & Aldred, R. (2021). *The promise of low-carbon freight: Benefits of cargo bikes in London.* August 2021. Available at: https://static1.squarespace.com/static/5d30896202a18c0001b49180/t/61091edc3acfda2f4af7d97f/1627987694676/The+Promise+of+Low-Carbon+Freight.pdf [Accessed 19/01/2023].

5

AN URBANISTIC TAKE ON AUTONOMOUS VEHICLES

Federico Cugurullo and Eva Kassens-Noor

Introduction: autonomous vehicles beyond transportation

Autonomous vehicles (AVs) are coming. This is happening particularly in cities where AVs are being increasingly employed as devices for land transport, which are fully driven by artificial intelligence (AI). The advent of AVs is taking place through different forms. We can observe the emergence of discourses and images that idealize this new type of autonomous urban transport (Kassens-Noor et al., 2021a; McCarroll and Cugurullo, 2022a). We can see urban experiments being implemented in precincts and testing facilities where AI-controlled cars and buses are trialled (Dowling and McGuirk, 2022). We can read policies drafted and released by a number of states to accelerate the diffusion of AVs (Cugurullo et al., 2021; McAslan et al., 2021). And we can also look at the actual technology as it operates on public roads, with companies like Waymo and Tesla competing in existing urban spaces to win what the media have termed *the self-driving race* (Hoeft, 2021).

In these images, experiments, policies and early technologies, the autonomous vehicle is mostly (re)presented as a means of transport: a device employed to carry people or cargo. Through this characterization, AVs are emerging largely as a matter of transportation with a focus on logistics. Their dominant role and function appear to be about moving someone or something from A to B; an autonomous truck, for instance, distributing commercial goods in a city or an autonomous car taking passengers to their desired location. The mainstream narrative pictures autonomous vehicles primarily as transport technologies that simply move things and people in space.

In contrast with this mainstream narrative, there is a growing critical literature that points out that AVs are more than just a matter of transportation.

DOI: 10.4324/9781003365877-6

Social scientists, in particular, stress that this emerging transport technology has a prominent social dimension (Cohen et al., 2020; Kassens-Noor et al., 2020; Milakis and Müller, 2021); that it is a matter of urban politics and governance (Aoyama and Leon, 2021; Cugurullo et al., 2021); that it is intrinsically linked to the design of the built environment (Duarte and Ratti, 2018); that it is has profound policy implications (Acheampong et al., 2021; Lundgren, 2021; Milakis et al., 2020); and that it is deeply influenced by the existing social, political and material realities of the city where its implementation takes place (Dowling and McGuirk, 2022). In this chapter, we build upon this strand of literature on AVs, to unpack and critically discuss the dimensions of the AV that exceed its transportation role. We do so by adopting an urbanistic perspective, in an attempt to show how what is generally portrayed as a simple vehicle is in reality a potent driver of urban change whose actual impact and repercussions can be properly understood only within the field of urbanism.

Autonomous vehicles and urbanism

There is a wide and profound connection between AVs and the urban. It is wide because vehicles driven by AI relate to a number of urban dimensions, including urban governance, urban planning, urban design and urban mobility. This connection is of course not unique to vehicles operated by AI. There is extensive academic literature demonstrating that vehicles, historically, regardless of who (or what) is driving them, have been intrinsically connected to the governance, planning and design of cities (Mumford, 1961; Sheller and Urry, 2000; Urry, 2004). There is also emerging literature which notes how the development of AI is influencing the development of cities (Cugurullo, 2020; Macrorie et al., 2021). In essence, the autonomous vehicle stands, conceptually and empirically, at the conjunction of these two themes, *vehicles* and *AI*, which are both prominent in the study of cities. Therefore, in this section, we draw on complementary strands of literature in urban studies, to unpack what we argue are the three main *urban* dimensions of AVs, which go beyond solely transportation. These are *data*, *design* and *environmental impact*.

Data

First, our intention is to portray the AV not just as a vehicle, but as a *source of data*. More specifically, we see AVs as *mobile data collectors* that traverse cities, capturing information about many urban activities, urban spaces and residents. This is due to the fact that, technologically speaking, AVs are designed and built to be able to collect as much data as possible in order to function in the chaos of the urban. There is thus a significant spatial dimension behind the processes of data collection carried out by AVs, as it is *in* and *from* urban spaces that AI gets the data necessary to operate an autonomous vehicle in a real-life environment (León, 2019; Mattern, 2017). Cities are spaces of uncertainty where many activities take place simultaneously and it is hard to predict what will happen next (Kaker et al., 2020). Transportation is a case in point: a jaywalker crossing a road, an unexpected protest with hundreds of people disrupting traffic or a lockdown that on short notice confines everyone at home. Humans manage to daily cope with the chaotic nature of cities and urban events, by collecting information on what happens around them and using this data to inform their decisions. AVs do exactly the same, although with different media and intensities. A human being has five senses capturing a variety of information, while an autonomous vehicle has cameras and a lidar system (Cugurullo, 2020). The sensorial apparatus varies in nature, size and scope, but the outcome is almost identical: the development of a *situational awareness* intended as the knowledge of what is happening in the city (Luque-Ayala and Marvin, 2020).

What is crucial to note is that AVs do not capture data in a selective manner, in the sense that they do not focus exclusively on matters of transportation. Intuitively one might think that an AV's arsenal of sensors would capture information related entirely to what the technology has been primarily built for: navigating urban spaces and transporting passengers and objects. In reality, however, AVs' cameras observe everything that is happening around them. They are mobile digital eyes constantly moving all around the city and harvesting data on a plethora of urban activities. In addition, AVs can sense what is happening *inside* them. This means that autonomous cars, for instance, can observe and understand what their passengers are doing, including privacy-sensitive information about time-use (McCarroll and Cugurullo, 2022a). Both the *outside* and *inside* data collected by AVs is not neutral and there is a politics to it. As many scholars have stressed, this is data that is often gathered without the consent of users and held under private rather than public ownership (Crawford, 2021; Sadowski, 2020; Zuboff, 2019). Particularly from a spatial perspective, what is somehow paradoxical to note is that AVs exploit public spaces to get data, 'often in the service of powerful actors such as corporations and states,' but neither the technology nor the data is open to public scrutiny (León, 2019: 11).

Furthermore, it is important to remember that AVs are interconnected urban AIs that do not work in isolation. They are linked to broader digital platforms and systems of information containing vast amounts of urban data. Waymo, for example, one of the largest autonomous driving technology development companies, is part of Alphabet (i.e. Google), while Zoox, an emerging company specialized in autonomous ride-hailing, is a subsidiary of Amazon. This type of connection should not be underestimated, since its key implication is that Waymo and Zoox AVs are, at the same time, feeding Google's and Amazon's platforms with the information collected on public roads and inside vehicles, and being fed with the enormous datasets already built by Google and Amazon. From an urbanistic perspective, this is a clear case of *platform urbanism* whereby information about the city and its inhabitants is absorbed and black-boxed by 'profit-driven digital platforms' (Barns, 2020; Caprotti et al., 2022; Fields et al., 2020: 462).

Urban design

The second urbanistic aspect of AVs that we want to emphasize is *urban design*. Here we seek to represent an AV not as a device for transporting persons or things but as a potent *space-shaper*, namely a medium to change the shape of cities and, more generally, urban spaces and infrastructures, with repercussions and ramifications extending to the use and function of space itself. There is a long-standing connection between the development of urban vehicles and the alteration of the design and function of the built environment. For example, Mumford (1961) notes that the design of the Baroque city was heavily influenced by the stagecoach whose rapid diffusion was incompatible with the crooked and narrow streets of the Medieval city. Modern stagecoaches required broad and straight roads to function at full speed and this is one of the reasons why, in early modern Europe, city plans evolved in a linear way in a blaze of axes (Benevolo, 1993). During the seventeenth century, in many European cities, buildings were positioned symmetrically along large and horizontal roads which replaced the curvy narrow alleys typical of Medieval urban design, allowing the transit of modern stagecoaches (Mumford, 1961). Similarly, in the Modernist city, early 1900s cars required highways, junctions and arterial roads, and their popularization led to the development of what Hall (2002: 295) terms 'the city on the highway'; not to mention the fact that automobiles, when static, needed what back then was an unusual type of urban space: parking spaces (Watkin, 2005).

Specifically in relation to AVs, similar dynamics of urban change are and will be taking place, and we expect the design of the built environment to morph as AI-driven cars grow popular (Gaio and Cugurullo, 2023). In theory, AVs are capable of communicating with each other and of travelling on public roads with a minimum safety distance from each other, like a modular train, in a travel mode commonly called *platooning* (Gong and Du, 2018). This means that, potentially, from an urban design perspective, public roads could be redesigned to be narrower since interconnected AVs would require less urban space to function. Similarly, there is a growing literature on shared autonomous vehicles (SAVs) that shows how, on the basis of computer simulations, a single SAV would be able to replace up to 11 conventional cars and 4 taxis, thereby substantially decreasing both traffic and car ownership in cities (Fagnant and Kockelman, 2018; Guériau et al., 2020; Maciejewski and Bischoff, 2018). In light of this hypothesis, it is fair to assume that cities could be redesigned in a less car-centric way, maximizing the production of green and public spaces (Cugurullo et al., 2021; Duarte and Ratti, 2018). However, the opposite scenario is equally plausible because, as Hawkins and Nurul Habib (2019: 69) stress, 'the decrease in travel disutility' that AVs will inevitably trigger is likely to prompt 'people to travel more frequently and across greater distances,' thus increasing the number of vehicles in urban regions.

From an urbanistic perspective, the way the function of an AV (as a shared or privately owned means of transport) influences the shape of the city, resonates with urban design theory and, in particular, with the centuries-old norm *form follows function* (Kassens-Noor and Hintze, 2020). This principle of design assumes that the evolution of the shape of the built environment is at least in part determined by the function or purpose of the built environment itself (Batty, 2018). What is interesting to note is that, in the case of AVs, we are not talking about a building, an infrastructure or a road whose function determines the shape of the city, but of a technology whose application moulds the urban space that it serves. However, the lens of urbanism makes us also note that AI-driven cars are not being dropped into a tabula rasa, and that pre-existing urban cultures, politics and political economies partly shape AV technologies and their deployment in cities (Acheampong and Cugurullo, 2019; Dowling and McGuirk, 2022; McCarroll and Cugurullo, 2022b; Sovacool and Griffiths, 2020).

Environmental impact

The third and final urban dimension of AVs that we want to unpack concerns the environment and its consumption. We see autonomous cars and trucks as *environmental drainers* whose production and diffusion, if left unchecked, can lead to the depletion of natural resources and ecosystems. From a historical perspective, this claim is not new. For many decades, urbanists have denounced the environmental damages that urban vehicles cause. Kenworthy and Laube (1996), for example, see an evident tension between cars and ecology. They remark that, historically, the popularization of automobiles has accelerated the physical growth of cities and the formation of arterial roads and highways that have taken up prime farmland and destroyed ecosystems (Kenworthy and Laube, 1996). Similarly, Register (1987) contends that the car is responsible for the proliferation of a *flat urbanism* characterized by miles of suburban areas that spread horizontally from the city centre, thus covering natural habitats in concrete and steel.

AVs are no exception. Like any conventional car, they require a flat built environment to operate and spaces of concrete that almost never are compatible with an ecological urbanism (Cugurullo, 2021). Particularly during their transition, AVs also require a well-maintained (or new) road infrastructure that can be easily read and interpreted by the AI operating the vehicle. In essence, AVs are connected to what Urry (2004) terms the *system of automobility* which, historically, has repeatedly led to the flattening and cleansing of the environment, so as to produce spaces where cars can easily function. We cannot know for sure whether AVs will entrench the system of automobility and reproduce a car-centric urbanism, especially considering that there are notable geographical variations in automobile dependence and land use across urban regions (Kenworthy, 2019). However, this is a possibility whose ecological risks should not be underestimated.

Moreover, the fact that AVs are not just vehicles, but *AI-driven* vehicles, adds an extra and novel environmental tension. Recent studies point out that AI is not an eco-friendly technology (Crawford, 2021; Dauvergne, 2022; Yigitcanlar and Cugurullo, 2020). From an environmental perspective, the creation of AI tech requires the extraction of critical materials and this is why Crawford (2021) defines AI as an *extractive technology* (Zhou et al., 2021). This is the same problem that, since the late 1990s, has emerged in smart urbanism: smart-city initiatives are based on the installation of smart technologies that, in turn, are based on intensive processes of extraction, with metallic ores such as coltan and cobalt often extracted in countries like Congo to the detriment of local ecosystems and societies (Nkulu et al., 2018; Van den Brink et al., 2020). As a result, studies in urban geography show that the formation of smart cities in one place frequently causes environmental degradation in another locality (Cugurullo, 2016; Kaika, 2017). From an urbanistic point of view, this line of critique resonates with the theory of *urban political ecology* and its emphasis on uneven metabolic processes of production and consumption, that perpetually connect and shape seemingly unrelated urban spaces (Keil, 2020; Swyngedouw and Heynen, 2003).

Conclusions: autonomous vehicles through the lens of urban theory

In this chapter, we have shown how the autonomous vehicle is a technology whose sphere of influence goes well beyond the field of transportation. There are strong connections between the production of AVs and the production of large urban datasets. There are direct correlations between the diffusion of AVs and the redesign of the built environment, and there are also deep metabolic relations between the creation of AVs and the consumption of natural resources. The urban is the common thread that cuts across all these links, and, in this final section, we draw upon urban theory to critically reflect on the main urban repercussions that AVs are likely to trigger in present and future cities. We believe that urban theory can be very useful to address questions about AVs and the future of transportation, whose answers cannot be found solely within the field of transportation research. At the same time, we also argue that the lens of urban theory can shed light on new questions about AVs and the future of cities: questions that have not been asked yet and that, as we will stress in the remainder of the chapter, are of crucial importance.

First, there is the question of data, which is essentially a question about the information that AVs generate and share via digital platforms and that they eventually have at their disposal when they operate in cities. This is an issue whose ramifications extend into many fields that are only tangentially connected to transportation, and ethics is a case in point. In a seminal study on AVs, entitled *The Moral Machine Experiment*, Awad et al. (2018: 59) ask the following question:

> Think of an autonomous vehicle that is about to crash, and cannot find a trajectory that would save everyone. Should it swerve onto one jaywalking teenager to spare its three elderly passengers?

The authors further complicate the experiment and its ethical questions by adding other hypothetical characters, such as *criminals*, *pregnant women* and *doctors*, to a set of possible car accident scenarios (see Awad et al., ibid). Should an autonomous car spare a jaywalker if she was pregnant? And in case of an accident in which the death of either the passenger or a bystander is inevitable, who should the AI behind the wheel prioritize sparing? A criminal or a doctor? These complex moral questions suggest a bigger critical question: *how would an AV know if a jaywalker or passenger were pregnant or had been legally convicted of a crime?* Urban theory and, more specifically literature on platform urbanism, can help us find an answer. As we saw in the previous section, urbanists have repeatedly emphasized the connections and flows of data that underpin digital platforms and we drew on these insights to characterize the AV as a mobile *data collector* linked to some of the biggest datasets ever built (Google and Amazon, for example). As these connections keep growing, and so does the amount of private information that we share on digital platforms (see Zuboff, 2019), it is not difficult to imagine how in the near future a Google AV will be part of the same data landscape associated with Gmail, Android, Drive and Search containing information of personal nature. It is important to remember that these platforms operate according to corporate interests to maximize economic gains and, going back to Awad et al. (2018)'s original question, we should then not expect them to aim for the public good.

Second, there is a profound question of space: how will AVs shape present and future cities? Urban design and planning theory can shed light on the future of the built environment in the era of autonomous transport. As we noted in the previous section, there is a long-standing connection between the material evolution of the built environment and the introduction of new transport technologies into cities. When it comes to AVs and urban design, the crux of the matter is the mode through which this emerging technology will be employed and, more specifically, whether it will follow traditional and unsustainable patterns of car ownership or alternative car-sharing schemes. In this context where the urban future is still open and full of possibilities, we need to realize that it is not simply a choice between different transport modes that matters but, above all, how that choice will be made (Kassens-Noor et al., 2021b). Urban theory can again be helpful since current studies indicate that the diffusion of AVs is being directed by the private sector: car manufacturers, in particular, which are releasing new transport technologies into largely unregulated urban environments that simply adapt to the rules of the market without questioning them (Cugurullo et al., 2021; Kaßens-Noor and Darcy, 2022). There is a strand of literature that acknowledges public reserve about AVs (and, more generally, about AI), including potential data leaks, cyber-attacks and glitches, but so far these concerns have not been incorporated into the urban policy process where corporate interests tend to reign supreme (Cugurullo and Acheampong, 2023; León, 2019). Urbanists have often lamented the lack of dissensus over the private interests that shape our cities and public spaces, seeing in it the symptoms of a dangerous apolitical condition (see Swyngedouw, 2018). We hear this lament as the wake-up call that cities need to politicize the advent of AVs. This technology has the power to reshape everybody's space, and its implementation should not be led by the car industry and its acolytes alone.

Last but not least, there is the pressing question of sustainability. Even if we were able to realize a hypothetical scenario in which AVs are shared and their diffusion help cities decrease their traffic levels and carbon footprint, there would be no escape from the crude truth that urban political ecology theory makes us face: any AI-driven car is part of international metabolic processes and supply chains whose socio-environmental impact is questionable at best. AI is a technology that needs critical materials at risk of supply constraints, environmental degradation and labour exploitation (Dauvergne, 2020). Moreover, AI is an agent that, although often described as *autonomous*, requires a substantial amount of *ghost work* in order to function on the ground: underpaid workers lacking employment protection who clean and classify the data that is eventually used by AI technologies such as AVs to make sense of the complexity of urban ecosystems (Gray and Suri, 2019). We are still far away from developing strategies capable of aligning the diffusion of AVs with the production of spaces of sustainability, but one thing is clear: a sustainable urbanism in its fullest sense will never be possible if the autonomous vehicle is seen and understood only as a means of transport.

References

Acheampong, R. A., & Cugurullo, F. (2019). Capturing the behavioural determinants behind the adoption of autonomous vehicles: Conceptual frameworks and measurement models to predict public transport, sharing and ownership trends of self-driving cars. *Transportation Research Part F: Traffic Psychology and Behaviour*, 62, 349–375.

Acheampong, R. A., Cugurullo, F., Gueriau, M., & Dusparic, I. (2021). Can autonomous vehicles enable sustainable mobility in future cities? Insights and policy challenges from user preferences over different urban transport options. *Cities*, 112, 103134.

Aoyama, Y., & Leon, L. F. A. (2021). Urban governance and autonomous vehicles. *Cities*, 119, 103410.

Awad, E., Dsouza, S., Kim, R., Schulz, J., Henrich, J., Shariff, A., … Rahwan, I. (2018). The moral machine experiment. *Nature*, 563(7729), 59–64.

Barns, S. (2020). *Platform Urbanism: Negotiating Platform Ecosystems in Connected Cities*. Springer, Berlin.

Batty, M. (2018). *Inventing Future Cities*. MIT Press, Cambridge.

Benevolo, L. (1993). *The European City*. Blackwell, London.

Caprotti, F., Chang, I., Catherine, C., & Joss, S. (2022). Beyond the smart city: a typology of platform urbanism. *Urban Transformations*, 4(1), 1–21.

Cohen, T., Stilgoe, J., Stares, S., Akyelken, N., Cavoli, C., Day, J., … Wigley, E. (2020). A constructive role for social science in the development of automated vehicles. *Transportation Research Interdisciplinary Perspectives*, 6, 100133.

Crawford, K. (2021). *Atlas of AI*. Yale University Press, New Haven.

Cugurullo, F. (2016). Urban eco-modernisation and the policy context of new eco-city projects: Where Masdar City fails and why. *Urban Studies*, 53(11), 2417–2433.

Cugurullo, F. (2020). Urban artificial intelligence: From automation to autonomy in the smart city. *Frontiers in Sustainable Cities*, 2, 38.

Cugurullo, F. (2021). *Frankenstein Urbanism: Eco, Smart and Autonomous Cities, Artificial Intelligence and the End of the City*. Routledge, Abingdon and New York.

Cugurullo, F., & Acheampong, R.A. (2023). Fear of AI: an inquiry into the adoption of autonomous cars in spite of fear, and a theoretical framework for the study of artificial intelligence technology acceptance. *AI & Society*. DOI:10.1007/s00146-022-01598-6.

Cugurullo, F., Acheampong, R. A., Gueriau, M., & Dusparic, I. (2021). The transition to autonomous cars, the redesign of cities and the future of urban sustainability. *Urban Geography*, 42(6), 833–859.

Dauvergne, P. (2020). *AI in the Wild: Sustainability in the Age of Artificial Intelligence*. MIT Press, Cambridge.

Dauvergne, P. (2022). Is artificial intelligence greening global supply chains? Exposing the political economy of environmental costs. *Review of International Political Economy*, 29(3), 696–718.

Dowling, R., & McGuirk, P. (2022). Autonomous vehicle experiments and the city. *Urban Geography*, 43(3), 409–426.

Duarte, F., & Ratti, C. (2018). The impact of autonomous vehicles on cities: A review. *Journal of Urban Technology*, 25(4), 3–18.

Fagnant, D. J., & Kockelman, K. M. (2018). Dynamic ride-sharing and fleet sizing for a system of shared autonomous vehicles in Austin, Texas. *Transportation*, 45(1), 143–158.

Fields, D., Bissell, D., & Macrorie, R. (2020). Platform methods: studying platform urbanism outside the black box. *Urban Geography*, 41(3), 462–468.

Gaio, A., & Cugurullo, F. (2023). Cyclists and autonomous vehicles at odds: Can the transport oppression cycle be broken in the era of artificial intelligence? *AI & Society*, 38(3), 1223–1237.

Gong, S., & Du, L. (2018). Cooperative platoon control for a mixed traffic flow including human drive vehicles and connected and autonomous vehicles. *Transportation Research Part B: Methodological*, 116, 25–61.

Gray, M. L., & Suri, S. (2019). *Ghost Work: How to Stop Silicon Valley from Building a New Global Underclass*. Houghton Mifflin Harcourt, Boston.

Guériau, M., Cugurullo, F., Acheampong, R. A., & Dusparic, I. (2020). Shared autonomous mobility on demand: A learning-based approach and its performance in the presence of traffic congestion. *IEEE Intelligent Transportation Systems Magazine*, 12(4), 208–218.

Hall, P. (2002). *Cities of Tomorrow*. Blackwell, London.

Hawkins, J., & Nurul Habib, K. (2019). Integrated models of land use and transportation for the autonomous vehicle revolution. *Transport Reviews*, 39(1), 66–83.

Hoeft, F. (2021). Fun to drive? The dynamics of car manufacturers' differentiation strategies. *Strategic Change*, 30(5), 489–500.

Kaika, M. (2017). 'Don't call me resilient again!': the New Urban Agenda as immunology... or... what happens when communities refuse to be vaccinated with 'smart cities' and indicators. *Environment and Urbanization*, 29(1), 89–102.

Keil, R. (2020). An urban political ecology for a world of cities. *Urban Studies*, 57(11), 2357–2370.

Kaker, S.A., Evans, J., Cugurullo, F., Cook, M., & Petrova, S. (2020). Expanding cities: Living, planning and governing uncertainty. In *The Politics of Uncertainty* Scoones, I. & Stirling, A., Eds. Routledge, London, pp. 85–98.

Kassens-Noor, E., Dake, D., Decaminada, T., Kotval-K, Z., Qu, T., Wilson, M., & Pentland, B. (2020). Sociomobility of the 21st century: Autonomous vehicles, planning, and the future city. *Transport Policy*, 99, 329–335.

Kassens-Noor, E., & Hintze, A. (2020). Cities of the future? The potential impact of artificial intelligence. *AI*, 1(2), 192–197.

Kassens-Noor, E., Wilson, M., & Yigitcanlar, T. (2021a). Where are autonomous vehicles taking us? *Journal of Urban Technology*, 28(3–4), 1–4.

Kassens-Noor, E., Wilson, M., Kotval-Karamchandani, Z., Cai, M., & Decaminada, T. (2021b). Living with autonomy: Public perceptions of an AI-mediated future. *Journal of Planning Education and Research*, 0739456X20984529.

Kaßens-Noor, E., & Darcy, C. H. (2022). Our autonomous future. *Journal of the American Planning Association*, 88(3), 429–432.

Kenworthy, J. R. (2019). Urban transport and eco-urbanism: a global comparative study of cities with a special focus on five larger Swedish urban regions. *Urban Science*, 3(1), 25.

Kenworthy, J. R., & Laube, F. B. (1996). Automobile dependence in cities: an international comparison of urban transport and land use patterns with implications for sustainability. *Environmental Impact Assessment Review*, 16(4–6), 279–308.

León, L. F. A. (2019). Counter-mapping the spaces of autonomous driving. *Cartographic Perspectives*, 92, 10–23.

Luque-Ayala, A., & Marvin, S. (2020). *Urban Operating Systems: Producing the Computational City*. MIT Press, Cambridge.

Lundgren, B. (2021). Safety requirements vs. crashing ethically: what matters most for policies on autonomous vehicles. *AI & Society*, 36(2), 405–415.

Maciejewski, M., & Bischoff, J. (2018). Congestion effects of autonomous taxi fleets. *Transport*, 33, 971–980.

Macrorie, R., Marvin, S., & While, A. (2021). Robotics and automation in the city: a research agenda. *Urban Geography*, 42(2), 197–217.

Mattern, S. (2017). Mapping's intelligent agents. *Places Journal*. DOI: 10.22269/170926.

McAslan, D., Gabriele, M., & Miller, T. R. (2021). Planning and policy directions for autonomous vehicles in Metropolitan Planning Organizations (MPOs) in the United States. *Journal of Urban Technology*, 28(3–4), 175–201.

McCarroll, C., & Cugurullo, F. (2022a). Social implications of autonomous vehicles: a focus on time. *AI & Society*, 37(2), 791–800.

McCarroll, C., & Cugurullo, F. (2022b). No city on the horizon: Autonomous cars, artificial intelligence, and the absence of urbanism. *Frontiers in Sustainable Cities*, 4, 184.

Milakis, D., Thomopoulos, N., & Van Wee, B. (2020). *Policy Implications of Autonomous Vehicles*. Academic Press, Cambridge.

Milakis, D., & Müller, S. (2021). The societal dimension of the automated vehicles transition: Towards a research agenda. *Cities*, 113, 103144.

Mumford, L. (1961). *The City in History: Its Origins, Its Transformations, and Its Prospects*. Brace & World, New York.

Nkulu, C.B.L., Casas, L., Haufroid, V., De Putter, T., Saenen, N.D., Kayembe-Kitenge, T., Obadia, P.M., Wa Mukoma, D.K., Lunda Ilunga, J.M., Nawrot, T.S., Luboya Numbi, O., Smolders, E., & Nemery, B. (2018). Sustainability of artisanal mining of cobalt in DR Congo. *Nature Sustainability*, 1(9), 495–504.

Register, R. (1987). *Ecocity Berkeley: Building Cities for a Healthy Future*. North Atlantic Books, Berkeley.

Sadowski, J. (2020). *Too Smart: How Digital Capitalism is Extracting Data, Controlling Our Lives, and Taking Over the World*. MIT Press, Cambridge.

Sheller, M., & Urry, J. (2000). The city and the car. *International Journal of Urban and Regional Research*, 24(4), 737–757.

Sovacool, B. K., & Griffiths, S. (2020). Culture and low-carbon energy transitions. *Nature Sustainability*, 3(9), 685–693.

Swyngedouw, E. (2018). *Promises of the Political: Insurgent Cities in a Post-political Environment*. MIT Press, Cambridge.

Swyngedouw, E., & Heynen, N.C. (2003). Urban political ecology, justice and the politics of scale. *Antipode*, 35(5), 898–918.

Urry, J. (2004). The 'system'of automobility. *Theory, Culture & Society*, 21(4–5), 25–39.

Watkin, D. (2005). *A History of Western Architecture*. Laurence King Publishing, London.

Van den Brink, S., Kleijn, R., Sprecher, B., & Tukker, A. (2020). Identifying supply risks by mapping the cobalt supply chain. *Resources, Conservation and Recycling*, 156, 104743.

Yigitcanlar, T., & Cugurullo, F. (2020). The sustainability of artificial intelligence: An urbanistic viewpoint from the lens of smart and sustainable cities. *Sustainability*, 12(20), 8548.

Zhou, L., Fan, H., & Ulrich, T. (2021). Editorial for Special Issue "Critical Metals in Hydrothermal Ores: Resources, Recovery, and Challenges". *Minerals*, 11(3), 299.

Zuboff, S. (2019). *The Age of Surveillance Capitalism: The Fight for a Human Future at the New Frontier of Power*. Profile Books, London.

6

A ROADMAP FOR THE SUSTAINABLE DEPLOYMENT OF AUTONOMOUS VEHICLES

Superblocks driving cars out of neighbourhoods

Elisabetta Vitale Brovarone and Luca Staricco

Introduction

Artificial Intelligence (AI) is bringing unprecedented potential into the urban scene and may have disruptive effects on cities and social practices. The emergence of AI in cities can potentially trigger radical changes, automating most routines in real time and autonomously managing unexpected events. Many cities around the world are installing sensors, telecommunication systems and computational cores, which allow the collection of near real-time data (Allam and Dhunny, 2019), making 'the invisible visible' (Barns, 2021: 3208) and providing an unprecedented amount of data. AI and machine learning can elaborate on such data, providing a deeper understanding of urban dynamics and improving urban efficiency and performance. However, besides techno-solutionist approaches that often dominate policy arenas, the emergence of AI in the management of cities, operating in an autonomous manner and somehow taking urban governance out of human control, is raising serious concerns. The salvific power of urban smartification, which is implicit in the smart city discourse, should not be taken for granted (Tulumello and Iapaolo, 2021), nor should its sustainability (Cugurullo, 2020). Furthermore, the post-human conditions and ethical dilemmas that are linked with AI (Cugurullo, 2021) raise the 'thorny ethical question of how a non-human intelligence comes to determine what is ideal for a human environment' (Cugurullo, 2020: 5). In essence, although AI has significant potential for urban efficiency and performance, a passive laissez-faire approach from public administrations can lead to undesired, unexpected and ungovernable outcomes. The deployment of autonomous vehicles (AVs), being a dominant manifestation of the emergence of AI in the management and development of cities, fully encapsulates these dilemmas.

DOI: 10.4324/9781003365877-7

The advent of autonomous driving is likely to produce significant changes in transport and mobility systems, as well as second and third-order effects on energy consumption, land use, location choices, social equity and the economy (Milakis, 2019; Zakharenko, 2016). However, when, how and to what extent these changes will take place is unclear, due to several dimensions of uncertainty. Although many cities are testing AVs on public roads, these vehicles are not yet fully autonomous, nor commercially viable (Bazilinskyy et al., 2019). Besides the optimism of the automotive industry, there is high uncertainty about when full automation (the so-called *Level 5*) will be commercially available and reach significant market penetration. The direction and intensity of the potential impacts of AVs on mobility choices and behaviours have been assessed by several scholars (Milakis and Müller, 2021). Positive effects are expected in terms of safety (Winkle, 2016), road capacity and parking spaces (Metz, 2018) and improved accessibility for those who cannot drive a car (Milakis et al., 2018; Zandieh and Acheampong, 2021). On the other hand, AVs are expected to have negative impacts on public transport and active mobility (Bahamonde-Birke et al., 2018; Botello et al., 2019), increased vehicle miles travelled, congestion and sprawl (Childress et al., 2015; Zakharenko, 2016).

The direction and intensity of the effects that AVs will generate are related to how public administrations will intervene in their diffusion. If left unconditionally to technology enthusiasts and to the market, the negative effects could overcome the positive ones and worsen the quality and liveability of cities (Grindsted et al., 2021). Public administrations need to deal with this challenge through dedicated planning and policies, in the short and medium terms (Vitale Brovarone et al., 2021). Nevertheless, public authorities are reluctant to take up this challenge, due to various factors, such as the high level of uncertainty of the transition process (Curtis et al., 2019), the long horizon – much longer than the timeframe of administrative and political offices, for instance – and the lack of sufficient "actionable" information to direct investments or planning priorities (Guerra, 2016).

This chapter summarizes the results of a research project aimed to address the issue of governing the transition to autonomous driving, defining a policy pathway towards urban liveability and sustainability.[1] The policy pathway, which is organized in policy packages towards a 30-year horizon, was developed through a collaborative backcasting approach. The process, which was applied to the case study of Turin (Italy), involved public and private actors and shed light on two very important issues. First is the power of anticipatory visions (Kinsley, 2012) and the importance of defining concrete propositions to govern the transition to autonomous driving (and AI urbanism more generally), beyond techno-determinism and towards desired urban futures. Second is the opportunity to ride the wave of the seductive power of technological innovation and AV deployment, rather than hinder it, in order to promote goals of liveability and reduction of vehicle traffic within urban neighbourhoods.

The chapter is organized as follows: the next section focuses on the importance of planning the transition to AVs and backcasting as an appropriate method to deal with the high level of uncertainty of this transition. The aims of the research and its methodology are then presented. Next, the vision for Turin in 2050 – in which vehicle circulation is regulated in a way that contributes positively to the liveability of the city – and the proposed policy pathway to achieve it are presented. The main findings are then discussed in terms of the power of anticipatory visions and concrete propositions in promoting urban liveability with AI.

Backcasting for planning the transition to AVs

Surveys in the USA (Guerra, 2016), Australia (Legacy et al., 2019) and Germany (Fraedrich et al., 2019) have shown that planners are often aware of the potential negative impacts of AVs, as well as of the key role urban and transport planning can play in governing the transition to AVs so as to minimize these impacts. Some authors have provided policy recommendations in this sense: integrate AVs in a high-quality multimodal transport system (Abe, 2021), enhance electric mobility (Legacy et al., 2019; Marletto, 2019), favour the use of shared services and MaaS[2] practices over private motorized mobility (Hasan and Van Hentenryck, 2021), support car-free areas (Basu and Ferreira, 2020) and prevent further sprawling processes (Simons and Arancibia, 2020).

Despite the consensus about the need to govern the transition to AVs, public authorities are often reluctant to take the lead and tend to adopt a "watch and wait" attitude (Cohen and Cavoli, 2019; Curtis et al., 2019). As a matter of fact, the transition to autonomous driving is still surrounded by many uncertainties (for example, in terms of timing, commercial viability and market penetration rates of AVs (Bazilinskyy et al., 2019), that planners are generally unprepared to address (Legacy et al., 2019). Future studies based on scenario analysis can help decision-makers face these high levels of uncertainty. They can be classified into three categories (Bibri, 2018):

- scenario planning studies, focused on identifying possible futures (what might happen?);
- forecasting studies, which try to assess probable futures (what is most likely to happen?);
- backcasting studies, focused on preferable futures (what we would prefer to happen?).

Most scenario-based researches on AVs belong to the first two categories, which try to explore and assess possible and probable evolutions of current conditions. The third category, backcasting, works in the opposite direction, from the future to the present, as it identifies desirable visions and then defines policy pathways to achieve them (Dreborg, 1996). The backcasting process is normally organized in a sequence of phases, pivoted around visioning and policy packaging (Nogués et al., 2020; Soria-Lara and Banister, 2018). The transition to AVs entails the conditions which, according to Dreborg (1996), make backcasting particularly appropriate (high level of uncertainty and complexity, need for major changes, important externalities and long time horizon). However, very few other applications of backcasting to AVs can be found in the literature. González-González et al. (2019) used backcasting to investigate whether the potential impacts of AV implementation can support or threaten a range of urban development policy goals. In another article, the same authors (2020) identified a set of three policy pathways, with eight policy packages (mainly related to the reuse and reallocation of parking and road space) for the next 20–30 years, that could better guide AV rollout in European cities. Moreover, Nogués et al. (2020) reported the third phase of that backcasting process, conducted through an expert survey to assess the policy packages defined in the previous phases.

Aims and method

A collaborative backcasting approach was used to define a policy pathway for steering the diffusion of AVs towards urban liveability in the case study of Turin. The pathway focuses on the use of road space in the city, concerning above all the regulation of circulation and parking of AVs in the urban road network. The process combined desk analysis, interviews, questionnaires and focus groups, with a mixed think-tank and participatory method (Staricco et al., 2020) and involved 69 expert stakeholders belonging to the public and private sectors. During the first phase (Staricco et al., 2019), three visions of Turin in 2050 were predefined by the research group and assessed through a focus group with expert stakeholders and in-depth semi-structured interviews and questionnaires. The result of this phase was the definition and selection of a vision for 2050, which is structured around six themes: road hierarchy; restriction of vehicle circulation; parking and pick-up/drop-off areas; local public transport; sharing (both motorized and non-motorized); active mobility (walking and cycling).

The policy packages defined in the second phase – which combined inputs from literature, case study analysis, interviews, questionnaires and a workshop – were geared towards this vision. During the interviews, representatives from automotive companies, providers of ICT and mobility services, research centres (in various fields, such as smart city and innovation, transport and mobility, real estate, consultancy, etc.), public administrations, trade, professionals and environmentalist citizens' associations, were asked to identify possible measures to reach the most desired vision. Their answers were then analysed and a list of 18 actions was defined, which set the ground for a backcasting workshop with 8 experts selected from the 69 stakeholders who were involved in the previous phases.[3] The participants discussed and distributed these actions along a 30-year timeline (from 2020 to 2050), adding some more measures. As a final result, 33 key actions, grouped around the six above-mentioned themes of the vision, were streamlined and distributed along the timeline.

Turin: an automobile city rebranding its identity

Turin is the chief town of the Piedmont region, in the north-western part of Italy and the fourth most populated Italian city, with around 850,000 inhabitants (1,760,000 in the Functional Urban Area). It is a very car-dependent city: the car ownership rate is 0.64 cars per inhabitant (the average rate in Europe is 0.54, ranging from 0.33 in Romania to 0.68 in Luxemburg), with a significant modal share of private motorized mobility (39%). Although it is one of the Italian cities with high air pollution, car circulation is poorly moderated. There is only one relatively small limited traffic zone (in the city centre), covering 2% of the municipal area and a few small 30 km/h zones. Alternatives to the car are underused: public transport, which consists of one metro line, 8 streetcar lines and around 90 bus lines, has a modal share of 24%, while cycling accounts for 4% and walking for 33%.

Since the beginning of the last century, the city developed a hyper-specialization in car manufacturing, hosting the headquarters and the first manufacturing plant of FIAT, the most renowned Italian car manufacturing company. FIAT shaped the city and its image for decades and attracted lots of workers. Then, since the 1970s, similar to other "one-company" cities which were subject to the crisis of Fordism, the city has suffered a dramatic downturn linked to the decline of the car industry. In the last decades, the city tried to diversify its economic structure and started to undertake a process of redefinition of its external and internal image (Colombino and Vanolo, 2017; Vanolo, 2015), grounded respectively on food excellence and the smart city discourse (Crivello, 2015; Vanolo, 2015). However, the 'car city' image and mindset are still deep-rooted in the local image and practices, and this is one of the causes of high car-dependency.

In view of the above, it can be assumed that if the diffusion of AVs is not governed with a clear urban future vision by the administration, and simply left to the market, it may result in particularly negative impacts. In 2018, Turin was the first municipality in Italy to launch a pilot project for testing

AVs in a real-life environment, aiming to bring the city to the forefront of the transition to AVs in Italy and position it as a smart city. The initiative was developed within the framework of the 'Smart Road' initiative, launched by the Italian Ministry of Infrastructure and Transport to accompany the digital transformation of roads and the deployment of AVs. The city has defined a 35-kilometre route through its street network and started the process of technological infrastructure adaptation of such a route, though this process was delayed due to the COVID-19 pandemic. The intention to be the first city in Italy to test AVs is part of a broader set of initiatives aimed at redefining the city's identity through a smart city perspective, with particular emphasis on smart mobility. Like many other cities across the globe, Turin is somehow seeking to redefine its local and global reputation by provincializing the smart city concept to its context and to become a recognized player in the urban innovation system (Burns et al., 2021; Karvonen et al., 2019).

The aim of the visioning and backcasting was to seize the momentum and bring to the attention of the city administration the opportunity to make a step forward and steer the diffusion of AVs towards a desired vision, defining and assessing short- and medium-term measures to be integrated into its transport and urban development policies and tools.

A superblock city vision for 2050

In the first phase of the backcasting process, the involved stakeholders had to select the most desirable among three different visions (Staricco et al., 2019, 2020). The three visions were drafted by the research team (urban and transport planners, transport engineers and sociologists), based on a review of scientific and grey literature and according to three scenarios, optimistic, pessimistic and neutral (Papa and Ferreira, 2018):

- optimistic scenario: a technology-centred 'strong deregulation' vision, assuming that the impacts of AVs will be largely positive and that AVs could freely circulate on the whole network;
- pessimistic scenario: a 'strong regulation' vision, assuming that the negative impacts of AVs will prevail unless their circulation is governed (in this case through a superblock approach);
- neutral scenario: a 'Business as Usual' vision, assuming that AVs will have neither positive nor negative impacts and entailing an inertial evolution of the current planning directions.[4]

The three visions were then validated by seven experts (politicians, managers and technicians in the mobility sector) and subsequently assessed by 51 stakeholders (Staricco et al., 2019), that were chosen so as to represent automotive companies involved in car manufacturing and sales, providers of ICT and mobility services, research centres, public administrations, environmentalist, people with disabilities, trade or professional associations, and trade unions. The 'strong regulation' vision turned out to be by and large the preferred one: 45 out of the 51 respondents chose it. Only one respondent preferred the 'strong deregulation' vision and five preferred the 'business as usual' vision. The respondents were asked to evaluate not only the vision as a whole, but a number of aspects (road network, parking, car circulation, public transport, active mobility, etc.). The preference for the strong regulation vision was independent of stakeholders' age, gender, profession, education and usual mode of transport.

The chosen vision is inspired by the superblock model, as a way to improve the quality and liveability of public spaces at the neighbourhood level and to reduce the modal share of private motorized vehicles. The superblock model traces back to neighbourhood unit principles and is based on the separation of 'access traffic' (car trips whose origins or destinations are located in the neighbourhood) from 'cut-through traffic' (car trips whose origins and destinations are both located outside the neighbourhood) which is discouraged inside superblocks and diverted to main thoroughfares outside them. In Europe, the most well-known example is Barcelona (Rueda, 2019; Scudellari et al., 2020). As well as Barcelona, the superblock model is well suited to Turin as a city characterized by a regular street pattern, which allows easy identification of the road hierarchy and the superblocks.

In the vision for Turin in 2050, all circulating vehicles are expected to be fully connected and autonomous (Level 5). The city is reorganized into superblocks, in order to reduce the circulation of private AVs (in particular inside residential neighbourhoods) and to promote the use of shared AVs, public transport and soft means of mobility. A main network of thoroughfares (with a speed limit of 50 km/h) is intended to support cut-through traffic; all the meshes of this network are re-thought as superblocks. Inside each superblock, only shared AVs or AVs belonging to the residents can circulate, at a maximum speed of 20 km/h. On-road parking is removed and partially replaced with platforms to facilitate boarding and alighting for AVs' passengers; multilevel parking facilities are provided around each superblock and intermodal parking facilities are provided at the terminals of public transport lines. The freed-up space (made free by removing parking and reducing motorized traffic inside the superblocks) is redesigned and repurposed, to support non-motorized mobility and multiple uses, for instance, enlarging pedestrian spaces and green areas, as the superblock model entails and optimistic scenarios assume (Cugurullo et al., 2021), although in this case, this is associated with strong political will, a predefined urban vision and the policy pathway to pursue it (Figure 6.1).

As far as public transport is concerned, streetcars run on reserved lanes on the thoroughfares of the main network and transport systems with exclusive right of way (metro and metropolitan railway) are provided at a higher

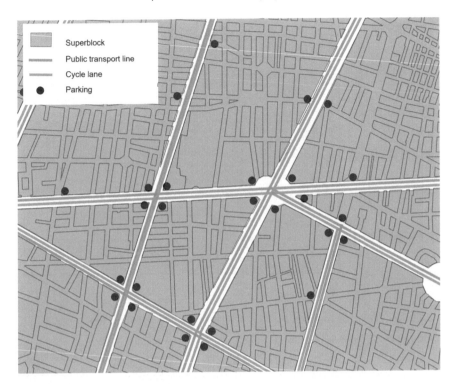

FIGURE 6.1 The organization of superblocks.

Source: authors' original.

frequency than that at present. Inside the superblocks, no public transport service is operated, except in the larger ones where autonomous shuttles are provided as feeders to the main lines. Car- and bike-sharing services are widely provided both on a peer-to-peer basis and by private companies. Cycle lanes are provided on all main roads and cyclists can freely circulate inside superblocks, where road space is organized as a shared space with priority given to walking. As a result, the modal split is assumed to result in a significant increase of all alternative modes to private motorized vehicles.

A policy pathway towards urban liveability

As mentioned previously, the policy pathway to support the public administration in steering the diffusion of AVs towards the 'superblock vision' is mainly focused on regulating AVs' circulation and parking and integrating them into the mobility system. The SUMPs[5] that the city of Turin has to develop each decade are set as milestones of the roadmap towards the vision (Figure 6.2).

	2020	2030	2040	2050
ACTIVE MOBILITY	Improved pedestrian areas in the superblocks and cycling network on the thoroughfares	Street experiments inside the superblocks gradually made permanent	Public (road) space structurally and permanently redesigned to prioritise active mobility	
SHARING	Sharing mobility enhanced (car, e-scooter, bike); ADAS on car sharing; AVs test on the main network	Sharing mobility enhanced (car, e-scooter, bike) and integrated with PT (MaaS); shared AVs on the main network	Integrated sharing facilities in the whole city (MaaS)	
PUBLIC TRANSPORT	Reorganization of the PT network, incentives and communication, test of AVs on the main network	Autonomous PT on the main network; integration with car sharing services (MaaS)	Autonomous PT on the main network, last mile shuttles in the largest superblocks	
PARKING	Less on-street parking for private cars, more for sharing, new multistorey and park&ride	On-street parking further reduced, additional multistorey and park&ride on the main network	No on-road parking; pick-up/drop-off platforms	
VEHICLE CIRCULATION	Speed limit set to 30 km/h inside the superblocks; further restriction to circulation in the central LTZ	No cut-through traffic inside the superblocks; 30 km/h zones turned into limited traffic zones	Speed limit 20 km/h; no cut-through traffic inside the superrblocks, only shared and residents' vehicles	
ROAD HIERARCHY	Road network organized in two levels: main and local; the meshes are the superblocks	V2I connection infrastructure on the main network, progressivley extended to inner roads	V2I connection on the whole road network	

FIGURE 6.2   The timeline and policy packages to reach the superblock vision.
Source: authors' original.

In the first decade (SUMP 2020–2030), actions are aimed at setting up the city and testing the technology, improving the liveability of neighbourhoods and getting people accustomed to the separation of access and cut-through traffic. The network of main thoroughfares and superblocks are defined and the areas inside the superblocks are set at 30 km/h zones. Cut-through traffic is also discouraged. Tests are made on the main network in which the technological infrastructure for vehicle-to-road connection is progressively provided. The local public transport system is reorganized according to the new structure of the road network, to channel the circulation of AVs outside the superblocks. On-road parking is reduced inside the 30 km/h zones, especially for private cars. The road space that is freed up is redesigned through light, low-cost tactical urbanism interventions, to improve its quality and attractiveness for social interaction and active mobility. On-road private parking is reduced, while lots for shared vehicles are increased. New park-and-ride facilities are built at the edges of the city and possible locations for new multi-storey car parks are identified. The offer of shared means of transport is reinforced (car, bike, moped, etc.) and advanced driver-assistance systems (ADAS) are installed on the car-sharing fleet. Pedestrian spaces are improved especially within the superblocks and the cycling network on the main road network. Incentives and communication campaigns support active mobility, sharing and public transport.

In SUMP 2030–2040, the provision of the vehicle-to-road connection infrastructure on the main road network is completed. Autonomous public transport services are made available on the main network and are coordinated with car-sharing services according to the MaaS paradigm. The promotion of alternatives to private automobility continues through incentives and communication campaigns. Vehicle-to-road connection infrastructures are progressively extended to the inner roads of the superblocks, and, starting with the city centre, 30km/h zones are turned into limited traffic zones where circulation is reserved for private cars owned by superblock residents and for shared cars and cut-through traffic is prohibited.[6] On-street parking is further reduced and additional multi-storey parking structures are built on the main road network. Street experiments for improving the quality and liveability of public spaces inside the superblocks are progressively extended and replaced by structural permanent interventions.

In SUMP 2040–2050, the reconfiguration of the city into superblocks is brought to completion. The vehicle-to-road connection infrastructure enables the prohibiting of cut-through traffic and circulation inside the superblocks is limited to shared vehicles and to residents' private vehicles, with a 20 km/h speed limit. All on-road parking spaces are removed inside the superblocks and partially replaced by pick-up/drop-off platforms. Public transport is concentrated on the main network and inside the larger superblocks, it is replaced by autonomous shuttles for last-mile trips. Like in the previous decades, the promotion of active mobility, sharing and public transport is carried on. The public (road) space inside the superblocks is structurally and permanently redesigned, to prioritize non-motorized modes and improve health, well-being and quality of life.

Governing AVs as a Trojan horse to reduce car traffic

The collaborative backcasting process allowed two main issues to emerge. On the one hand, it showed how the allure of high-tech can help bring non-digital goals and challenges to the forefront. On the other hand, it made evident how, contrary to what is currently the case, immediate action is needed to steer the transition to autonomous driving, rather than passively accommodating it.

Applying the superblock model to the entire urban area is certainly ambitious and rather radical in terms of social practices and spatial configuration. Notwithstanding, the vision was welcomed and positively evaluated by most stakeholders, regardless of their profession, age, education, preferred mode of transport, etc. Especially in an automobile-centred city like Turin, the superblock vision challenges habits and mindsets that are rather deep-rooted and such a broad consensus was unexpected by the research team. Not only did the vast majority of the interviewees rate it as the most desirable one, but it was approved without proposing alternative visions. Remarkably, the research raised a lot of interest in private companies in the automotive sector (not only car makers, but also components, testing, insurance and financing), who participated with enthusiasm and active engagement. While the first contact with the research was focused on AVs, attention gradually moved to the superblock vision, which pivoted around liveability goals and the restriction of private vehicle circulation inside neighbourhoods. Had the project been aimed at proposing the superblock vision regardless of AVs, it may well have gained less attention, participation and endorsement. The possibility of shaping more sustainable and liveable urban futures through the affordances of planning for AVs was not a priority of the research, which was aimed at limiting the negative impacts of AVs, but it gradually emerged as a very promising opportunity. The proposed policy packages are meant to cope with uncertainty in governing the transition, but at the same time, they promote a more sustainable mobility system and liveable urban environment even in the short-medium term, with human-driven cars. In a way, the technological innovation generated by AVs has been a Trojan horse bringing to the forefront the pros of traffic separation and reducing car traffic in neighbourhoods.

As noted previously, high levels of uncertainty surround AVs and the future of transport and mobility (Acheampong et al., 2021; Harb et al., 2021). With such an uncertain future, consensus-building among different actors about the measures and actions to implement may reveal particularly difficult. In this respect, the backcasting method can be very helpful: starting with a clear vision of the desired future can make it easier to think about the actions that should be put in place and define the possible pathway to reach that vision. In the case study presented in this chapter, although there was a large consensus about the vision, the allocation of actions on the timeline turned out to be quite complex for workshop participants. Especially during the final workshop, the stakeholders became aware of how long and complex it can be to define the pathway towards a long-time horizon with concrete actions referred to a real-life context. Most of the actions were set in the first decade of the timeline, suggesting the difficulty of dealing with long-term horizons. However, this made it equally evident that unless many actions are taken in the short term, it will not be possible to reach the desired vision. The process demonstrated how policy integration is much easier as a concept than in practice (Vigar, 2009). To implement the policy packages, planning processes and interventions in different sectors besides transport and across multiple scales must be coordinated (Aoyama and Alvarez Leon, 2021). An integrated policy framework relies on the agreement between planning sectors on the vision and development priorities. Furthermore, it entails the capacity for dialogue and collaboration among actors and sectors, which cannot be taken for granted. Awareness of the need to integrate different actions was already present in the interviews and questionnaires phase, but the final backcasting workshop made this need clear and evident, bringing together actors from different sectors and allowing them to dialogue and interact.

The need for immediate action and integration across different sectors also confirmed the essential importance of an active leading and coordination role by the local administration. In addition, the participation of representatives from different sectors was crucial in order to represent different aspects and grasp the multiplicity of actions needed to achieve the vision. However, willingness to take part in participatory processes cannot be taken for granted (nor can the willingness and ability to integrate different actors in planning and implementation), not least because not all cultural contexts have the same enthusiasm for such processes, due to administrative traditions, institutional, cultural and subjective factors (Enserink et al., 2007; Huxley et al., 2016). Furthermore, general knowledge of the topic can be a critical factor for stakeholder involvement. The project explicitly targeted experienced stakeholders in the field of mobility, although in-depth knowledge of AVs was not required in order to avoid limiting the sample too much. Nevertheless, the lack of knowledge of some of the participants raised some critical issues. In this respect, the involvement of private citizens proved very difficult, as general knowledge about AVs is very low, and involving a limited sample of private citizens would have raised problems of representativeness. In order to address this critical issue, citizens' associations involved in the process were considered representatives of citizens' opinions.

Besides the fact that involving stakeholders was quite complicated in general, the most reluctant actors were in fact those in the public administration, the intended recipients and activators of the policy pathway. The reasons for this reluctance and lack of involvement are manifold: for example, the difficulty in planning actions with long-time horizons beyond the terms of political office, but also frustration due to the daily need to cope with contingent problems and stringent bureaucratic apparatuses. Undoubtedly, this constituted a limitation of the project while also signalling that this aspect deserves to be considered in greater depth.

Conclusion

The research presented in this chapter showed how urban and transport planning can contribute to reducing the negative effects of the transition to AVs and to exploiting positive opportunities. The policy pathway proposed here is one of the possible ways in which the advent of this new technology can be actively steered towards a desired vision. However, public administrations are generally reluctant to lead this transition with a clear future vision. In the case of Turin, the city was mainly interested in being at the forefront of hosting innovation, but without any idea of the future beyond the technological aspects. Key factors of this passive approach are the great uncertainty and the lack of usable knowledge to act in the short and medium term (Legacy et al., 2019), but also a techno-enthusiasm (Schuelke-Leech et al., 2019) ignoring the socio-technical nature of transport systems (Milakis and Müller, 2021).

The policy pathway and the vision to which it is targeted aim at promoting alternatives to private automobility and making neighbourhoods more liveable. Even if the transition to AVs will take longer than assumed, this pathway can contribute to improving the sustainability of local urban transport systems. This research focused on how AVs circulation can be actively governed so as to benefit from their advantages and limit their shortcuts. Other very important issues should be considered, such as social acceptance, cybersecurity, pricing, land use regulation and laws, user preferences and equity issues. Moreover, while this research focused on the urban scale, measures to address the impacts of AVs at the metropolitan scale should also be explored. Finally, the acceptability of the proposed vision and policy pathway for residents should be considered. Since the involvement of private citizens in backcasting processes can be very difficult, other methods can be more suitable for a wider participative process. Overall, the research contributed to shedding light on the importance and possibility of planning the transition to autonomous driving beyond technology enthusiasm. This approach can be used also in other contexts, referring to different visions or technologies.

Notes

1 The main findings are presented in more detail in Staricco et al. (2019, 2020) and Vitale Brovarone et al. (2021).
2 MaaS is the acronym for Mobility as a Service, an emerging concept signifying a single platform which comprises multiple transport modes (public transport and shared cars, bicycles, e-scooters, etc.), payment options and technologies, catering for personalized and customized services (Liimatainen and Mladenović, 2021).
3 The stakeholders were selected so as to have representatives from all the above-mentioned categories.
4 A fourth 'critical' scenario could have been assumed, in which the transition to AVs is strongly questioned and challenged (see, on this issue, Legacy et al., 2019). This scenario was not considered, as the city of Turin was already committed to testing and promoting the introduction of AVs on its roads.
5 In Europe, the SUMP is the key planning tool to govern the urban mobility system. Moreover, the European guidelines for developing and implementing SUMPs recommend leading the transition towards connected and automated driving.
6 In the proposed vision, vehicle-to-road infrastructure is used also as a tool to govern the circulation of AVs, preventing or limiting their circulation inside the superblocks.

References

Abe, R. (2021). Preferences of urban rail users for first- and last-mile autonomous vehicles: Price and service elasticities of demand in a multimodal environment. *Transportation Research Part C: Emerging Technologies*, 126, 103105. DOI:10.1016/j.trc.2021.103105.

Acheampong, R. A., Cugurullo, F., Gueriau, M., & Dusparic, I. (2021). Can autonomous vehicles enable sustainable mobility in future cities? Insights and policy challenges from user preferences over different urban transport options. *Cities*, 112. DOI:10.1016/j.cities.2021.103134.

Allam, Z., & Dhunny, Z. A. (2019). On big data, artificial intelligence and smart cities. *Cities*, 89, 80–91.

Aoyama, Y., & Alvarez Leon, L. F. (2021). Urban governance and autonomous vehicles. *Cities*, 119, 103410. DOI:10.1016/j.cities.2021.103410.

Bahamonde-Birke, F. J., Kickhöfer, B., Heinrichs, D., & Kuhnimhof, T. (2018). A systemic view on autonomous vehicles. *DisP – The Planning Review*, 54(3), 12–25.

Barns, S. (2021). Out of the loop? On the radical and the routine in urban big data. *Urban Studies*, 58(15), 3203–3210.

Basu, R., & Ferreira, J. (2020). Planning car-lite neighborhoods: Examining long-term impacts of accessibility boosts on vehicle ownership. *Transportation Research Part D: Transport and Environment*, 86, 102394. DOI:10.1016/j.trd.2020.102394.

Bazilinskyy, P., Kyriakidis, M., Dodou, D., & de Winter, J. (2019). When will most cars be able to drive fully automatically? Projections of 18,970 survey respondents. *Transportation Research Part F: Traffic Psychology and Behaviour*, 64, 184–195.

Bibri, S. E. (2018). Backcasting in futures studies: A synthesized scholarly and planning approach to strategic smart sustainable city development. *European Journal of Futures Research*, 6(1), 13.

Botello, B., Buehler, R., Hankey, S., Mondschein, A., & Jiang, Z. (2019). Planning for walking and cycling in an autonomous-vehicle future. *Transportation Research Interdisciplinary Perspectives*, 1, 100012. DOI:10.1016/j.trip.2019.100012.

Burns, R., Fast, V., Levenda, A., & Miller, B. (2021). Smart cities: Between worlding and provincialising. *Urban Studies*, 58(3), 461–470.

Childress, S., Nichols, B., Charlton, B., & Coe, S. (2015). Using an activity-based model to explore the potential impacts of automated vehicles. *Transportation Research Record*, 2493(1), 99–106.

Cohen, T., & Cavoli, C. (2019). Automated vehicles: Exploring possible consequences of government (non)intervention for congestion and accessibility. *Transport Reviews*, 39(1), 129–151.

Colombino, A., & Vanolo, A. (2017). Turin and Lingotto: Resilience, forgetting and the reinvention of place. *European Planning Studies*, 25(1), 10–28.

Crivello, S. (2015). Urban policy mobilities: The case of turin as a smart city. *European Planning Studies*, 23(5), 909–921.

Cugurullo, F. (2020). Urban artificial intelligence: From automation to autonomy in the smart city. *Frontiers in Sustainable Cities*, 2, 38.

Cugurullo, F. (2021). *Frankenstein Urbanism: Eco, Smart and Autonomous Cities, Artificial Intelligence and the End of the City*. Routledge, Abingdon and New York

Cugurullo, F., Acheampong, R. A., Gueriau, M., & Dusparic, I. (2021). The transition to autonomous cars, the redesign of cities and the future of urban sustainability. *Urban Geography*, 42(6), 833–859.

Curtis, C., Stone, J., Legacy, C., & Ashmore, D. (2019). Governance of future urban mobility: A research agenda. *Urban Policy and Research*, 37(3), 393–404.

Dreborg, K. H. (1996). Essence of backcasting. *Futures*, 28(9), 813–828.

Enserink, B., Patel, M., Kranz, N., & Maestu, J. (2007). Cultural factors as co-determinants of participation in river basin management. *Ecology and Society*, 12(2).

Fraedrich, E., Heinrichs, D., Bahamonde-Birke, F. J., & Cyganski, R. (2019). Autonomous driving, the built environment and policy implications. *Transportation Research Part A: Policy and Practice*, 122, 162–172.

González-González, E., Nogués, S., & Stead, D. (2019). Automated vehicles and the city of tomorrow: A backcasting approach. *Cities*, 94, 153–160.

González-González, E., Nogués, S., & Stead, D. (2020). Parking futures: Preparing European cities for the advent of automated vehicles. *Land Use Policy*, 91, 104010. DOI:10.1016/j.landusepol.2019.05.029.

Grindsted, T. S., Christensen, T. H., Freudendal-Pedersen, M., Friis, F., & Hartmann-Petersen, K. (2021). The urban governance of autonomous vehicles – In love with AVs or critical sustainability risks to future mobility transitions. *Cities*, 103504. DOI:10.1016/j.cities.2021.103504.

Guerra, E. (2016). Planning for cars that drive themselves: Metropolitan planning organizations, regional transportation plans, and autonomous vehicles. *Journal of Planning Education and Research*, 36(2), 210–224.

Harb, M., Stathopoulos, A., Shiftan, Y., & Walker, J. L. (2021). What do we (Not) know about our future with automated vehicles? *Transportation Research Part C: Emerging Technologies*, 123, 102948. DOI:10.1016/j.trc.2020.102948

Hasan, M. H., & Van Hentenryck, P. (2021). The benefits of autonomous vehicles for community-based trip sharing. *Transportation Research Part C: Emerging Technologies*, 124, 102929. DOI:10.1016/j.trc.2020.102929

Huxley, K., Andrews, R., Downe, J., & Guarneros-Meza, V. (2016). Administrative traditions and citizen participation in public policy: A comparative study of France, Germany, the UK and Norway. *Policy & Politics*, 44(3), 383–402.

Karvonen, A., Cugurullo, F., & Caprotti, F. (Eds.). (2019). *Inside smart cities: Place, politics and urban innovation*. Routledge.

Kinsley, S. (2012). Futures in the making: Practices to anticipate 'Ubiquitous Computing'. *Environment and Planning A: Economy and Space*, 44(7), 1554–1569.

Legacy, C., Ashmore, D., Scheurer, J., Stone, J., & Curtis, C. (2019). Planning the driverless city. *Transport Reviews*, 39(1), 84–102.

Liimatainen, H., & Mladenović, M. N. (2021). Developing mobility as a service – user, operator and governance perspectives. *European Transport Research Review*, 13(1), 37.

Marletto, G. (2019). Who will drive the transition to self-driving? A socio-technical analysis of the future impact of automated vehicles. *Technological Forecasting and Social Change*, 139, 221–234.

Metz, D. (2018). Developing policy for urban autonomous vehicles: Impact on congestion. *Urban Science*, 2(2), 33.

Milakis, D. (2019). Long-term implications of automated vehicles: An introduction. *Transport Reviews*, 39(1), 1–8.

Milakis, D., Kroesen, M., & Van Wee, B. (2018). Implications of automated vehicles for accessibility and location choices: Evidence from an expert-based experiment. *Journal of Transport Geography*, 68, 142–148.

Milakis, D., & Müller, S. (2021). The societal dimension of the automated vehicles transition: Towards a research agenda. *Cities*, 113, 103144. DOI:10.1016/j.cities.2021.103144.

Nogués, S., González-González, E., & Cordera, R. (2020). New urban planning challenges under emerging autonomous mobility: Evaluating backcasting scenarios and policies through an expert survey. *Land Use Policy*, 95, 104652. DOI:10.1016/j.landusepol.2020.104652.

Papa, E., & Ferreira, A. (2018). Sustainable accessibility and the implementation of automated vehicles: Identifying critical decisions. *Urban Science*, 2(1), 5.

Rueda, S. (2019). Superblocks for the design of new cities and renovation of existing ones: Barcelona's case. In M. Nieuwenhuijsen & H. Khreis (Eds.), *Integrating Human Health into Urban and Transport Planning: A Framework* (pp. 135–153). Springer International Publishing.

Schuelke-Leech, B.-A., Jordan, S. R., & Barry, B. (2019). Regulating autonomy: An assessment of policy language for highly automated vehicles. *Review of Policy Research*, 36(4), 547–579.

Scudellari, J., Staricco, L., & Vitale Brovarone, E. (2020). Implementing the Supermanzana approach in Barcelona. Critical issues at local and urban level. *Journal of Urban Design*, 25(6), 675–696.

Simons, R. A., & Arancibia, A. (2020). Will driverless vehicle adoption cause more urban sprawl or prevent it? *Journal of Sustainable Real Estate*, 12(1), 51–68.

Soria-Lara, J. A., & Banister, D. (2018). Evaluating the impacts of transport backcasting scenarios with multi-criteria analysis. *Transportation Research Part A: Policy and Practice*, 110, 26–37.

Staricco, L., Rappazzo, V., Scudellari, J., & Vitale Brovarone, E. (2019). Toward policies to manage the impacts of autonomous vehicles on the city: A visioning exercise. *Sustainability*, 11(19), 5222.

Staricco, L., Vitale Brovarone, E., & Scudellari, J. (2020). Back from the future. A backcasting on autonomous vehicles in the real city. *TeMA – Journal of Land Use, Mobility and Environment*, 13(2), 209–228.

Tulumello, S., & Iapaolo, F. (2021). Policing the future, disrupting urban policy today. Predictive policing, smart city, and urban policy in Memphis (TN). *Urban Geography*, 43(3), 1–22. DOI:10.1080/02723638.2021.1887634.

Vanolo, A. (2015). The Fordist city and the creative city: Evolution and resilience in Turin, Italy. *City, Culture and Society*, 6(3), 69–74.

Vigar, G. (2009). Towards an integrated spatial planning? *European Planning Studies*, 17(11), 1571–1590.

Vitale Brovarone, E., Scudellari, J., & Staricco, L. (2021). Planning the transition to autonomous driving: A policy pathway towards urban liveability. *Cities*, 108, 102996. DOI:10.1016/j.cities.2020.102996.

Winkle, T. (2016). Safety benefits of automated vehicles: Extended findings from accident research for development, validation and testing. In M. Maurer, J. C. Gerdes, B. Lenz, & H. Winner (Eds.), *Autonomous Driving: Technical, Legal and Social Aspects* (pp. 335–364). Springer.

Zakharenko, R. (2016). Self-driving cars will change cities. *Regional Science and Urban Economics*, 61, 26–37.

Zandieh, R., & Acheampong, R. A. (2021). Mobility and healthy ageing in the city: Exploring opportunities and challenges of autonomous vehicles for older adults' outdoor mobility. *Cities*, 112, 103135. DOI:10.1016/j.cities.2021.103135.

PART II

Urban robots and robotic spaces

7

REGULATING AND MAKING SPACE FOR THE EXPANDED FIELD OF URBAN ROBOTICS

Aidan While

Introduction

There is growing interest in urban studies and robotics in understanding and anticipating the extended use of robots in the public realm of cities, both as a discrete activity of urban change and as part of the wider remaking of urban social life through artificial intelligence (AI) and automation (Bissell, 2018; Cugurullo, 2020, 2021; Del Casino et al., 2020, Elliott, 2018; Sumartojo et al., 2023; While et al., 2021). Robotic applications are increasingly being trialled on the streets and in the skies of cities with the potential for major spatial restructuring. Robots are coming to a city near us in various forms, serving a variety of purposes such as unmanned autonomous vehicles (on the ground and in the sky) and various police, security, delivery and service robots. Robots in the public realm – *urban robots* – will take many forms, becoming more ubiquitous but smaller and less visible. The rise of urban robotic applications is being facilitated by developments in robotics and AI, governmental interest in the potential benefits for urban management and policing (including the replacement of potentially unruly human labour) and the symbolic and economic development value of being at the cutting edge of future technology. In countries and cities around the world, urban space is being re-regulated for robotic trials and experiments and robots are increasingly supplementing, if not replacing, ideas of *smart* or low-carbon as the organizing principle for technology-enhanced future cities (While et al., 2021). Robotic technologies are becoming more commonplace and are entangled in 'making and remaking the structures, conditions and relations of everyday life' (Del Casino et al., 2020: 606).

There are many issues raised by roboticized urbanism for urban research, politics and policy. What do robots mean for the organization and public

DOI: 10.4324/9781003365877-9

life? What are the implications for urban design and infrastructure? How will robots and citizens co-evolve? Who or what will benefit most from urban robots? How will the potential benefits (for supporting independent living, addressing congestion, more effective use of urban space) be balanced with the potential disadvantages (such as increased surveillance and social control, increased control by technology firms)? This chapter addresses those issues explicitly and implicitly by focusing on the challenges in developing effective public regulatory frameworks for facilitating and regulating the extended application of robots in the public realm.

The point of departure is the following research question: *if individual free-doms and rights to the city are potentially challenged by robotics, what sorts of regulatory issues need to be addressed and how might that be achieved?* For example, a distinction is made between the current *first-wave* challenges of creating space to trial and develop emerging robotic technology and its poten-tial benefits in cities. This is primarily an issue of creating space for experimen-tation with the hardware and interfaces of urban robotics given the potential disruption and harm of robots for humans and prevailing uses and configura-tions of urban space. The first wave of urban robotics is contrasted with future waves of robotic operation and regulatory challenges which raise wider and more indirect questions about the role of robotics in the re-partitioning of urban space and the potential role of robots in social control, human restraint and wider processes of 'software sorting' as robotics become more embedded in AI (Cugurullo, 2020, 2021; Sumartojo et al., 2023). Acting now on address-ing these *second-wave* issues is, it is argued, of urgent importance because the first-wave opening of the city to robots will set in train trajectories and path-ways for robotic operation that might be difficult to reverse in the future. Central to the chapter is the need to better connect the material and immate-rial, visible and invisible, and the politics of urban robotic restructuring.

The chapter starts by setting out the idea of a first wave of urban robotic regulation, exploring the issues involved in opening cities to robotic trialling and experimentation. The chapter then moves on to critically examine the socio-spatial work that robots might do in the city and that maps on to the regulatory landscape and countervailing forces that might occlude or obscure the wider impact of urban robots. The issues raised are explored empirically through the example of San Francisco, which by a combination of factors has been ground zero for experiments in robotic regulation that encompass first- and second-wave concerns. The conclusions draw out the implications for future research, policy and practice.

First-wave urban robotic regulation: creating space for robots

In essence, a robot is any machine that operates at a distance from direct human control, either autonomously or with different degrees of human con-trol. Indeed, in engineering robotics tends to be classed as robotics and autonomous systems (RAS). *Urban robots* are defined as a remotely operating machine that exists in the public realm (as opposed to enclosed buildings) and the scope for urban robotics reflects advances in service and field robotics and AI that enables robots to operate and co-exist with humans in complex and unstructured environments (Royakkers and van Est, 2015; While et al., 2021). Innovation in these fields means more sophisticated forms of robotic mobility, environmental response and physical functionality, leading to novel applications with inherently spatial implications. Robots interact with the physical world via sensors and actuators, with autonomy extended increasingly by AI.

Urban robots and their capabilities will continue to evolve. Cities and urban life will co-evolve with them in the public and private realms. Whilst robots are being deployed in many domains, their prominence in urban spaces and cities reflects their potential to address challenges and maximize market and technological opportunities associated with mobility and driverless vehicles, logistics and last mile service delivery and large-scale policing, surveillance and people management. Robots have a particular appeal to governments because they can replace the unruliness of individualized human operation of machines (and reduce dependence on unruly human labour) or operate in ways or places that would be dangerous, inaccessible or costly for humans. This might be seen as an opportunity to transcend the limits of existing urban management, overcoming the sub-optimality of individualized collective human activity and providing new solutions to old and new problems of turbulence and threat in cities. It is becoming clear that 'robotic technology development is shifting and disrupting geographic imaginaries and everyday social, cultural, and ecological practices' (Del Casino et al., 2020: 605) in urban spaces and spaces and cities.

Within urban studies, there has been increased interest in the need for experimental urban sites for the testing, trialling and development of new technologies, and cities and urban contexts are actively constructed as active sites for trialling new technologies (Bulkeley et al., 2016; Caprotti and Cowley, 2017; Evans et al., 2016; Evans and Karvonen, 2014;). Central to these real-world testing sites is the question of how new products and services will mesh with humans and the existing configurations of urban environments. This is especially the case with urban robotics, where laboratory testing can only go so far in developing complex human–technology–infrastructure interactions. The problem for those seeking to develop urban robotic technologies is that urban robotics are potentially disruptive and dangerous, posing not insignificant challenges to the regulation of urban space (Tiddi et al., 2020). For example, in Arizona, the decision to open roads for driverless car experiments for economic development benefits led to attacks on automated vehicles following the death of a woman cyclist after a collision with a driverless Uber vehicle in the city of Tempe in 2018 (Greene, 2018; McCarroll and Cugurullo, 2022; Neuman, 2018). The development of urban robotics, therefore, requires governments and citizens to create opportunities for meaningful human–robotic interaction, requiring supportive changes in regulation, policy and culture to open-up spaces for experimentation and demonstration.

Research has explored the emergence of new spaces of urban robotic experimentation. Certainly, there is evidence that robotics researchers and firms have been putting pressure on urban governments to open up streets and skies for robotic applications that would otherwise be prevented by existing regulations (While et al., 2021). Making space for robotic applications can be complicated and challenging for governments given concerns about public safety and disruption, but numerous cities across the world are now involved in some form of experimentation with urban robotics. Increasingly new experimental sites are being floated in new cities oriented around robotics and AI, such as Neom in Saudi Arabia (Hassan, 2020) or the Toyota 'Woven City' in Japan (McCurry, 2020). Whilst robotic developers might want access to open environments, concerns about public safety, conflicts with other users, intellectual property, commercial competition and the need for supporting regulation inevitably mean that experimental spaces must be constrained and closed in various ways. Different levels or types of closure and openness might be required for different types of testing and technology readiness. Extensive comparative research on global trials and testing of autonomous vehicles in urban contexts led Dowling and M\u1d9cGuirk (2022) to develop an analytical typology of four forms of experimentation – on-road, test bed, precinct and living lab – each with differing relations to the city and differing potentials for political transformation. However, whatever the spatial location of robotic experimentation, the regulatory politics of this first wave of robotic development is mainly about public safety and infrastructural disruption, with regulation triggered by the need for changes in land-use planning and transportation and health and safety. An increasing number of cities are meeting that challenge of creating regulatory environments that open space for robotics.

The second wave of robotic regulation: privacy, surveillance and rights to the city

As urban robots move from experimental novelty to everyday reality, they raise a broader set of concerns for public debate and political regulation. The focus is not so much on the disruptive impact of robotics and more on the work they might perform in relation to social control and accountability when automated uses alter access to roads and sidewalks and reshape choices about how citizens move around; what Sumartojo et al. (2023) term a new 'partitioning' of urban space and infrastructure. This will work through the overt material politics of human safety and disruption but also the indirect, invisible and immaterial capabilities of urban robots to restrain, control and steer aspects of human life and access to infrastructure.

The re-partitioning of space and infrastructure access

Infrastructural reworkings of the city always have the potential to reshape social life and rework rights to the city in various intended and unintended ways. This is particularly the case when robots are linked to wider systems of automated urban management within the wider 'internet of robotic things' (Simoens et al., 2018). For example, a robot-controlled vehicle does not simply replace a human-driven car but opens opportunities to connecting private mobility to automated transport management systems, such as the City Brain in China (Caprotti and Liu, 2022; Curran and Smart, 2021), with the potential for enhanced differential pricing and access to road space and a new urban 'splintering' (Graham and Marvin, 2001) of infrastructure.

In principle, there are benefits to the automation of traffic flows in relation to efficient use of urban road space, the management of congestion and public safety. However, concerns are raised about the extent to which automated traffic management, telematics and access platforms, and autonomous vehicles might combine to reconfigure rights to the road. The issue of infrastructural shaping via autonomous vehicles is not solely about the reworking of urban space (in principle, urban space does not need to be reworked significantly and AVs might help rethink the public realm, which are generally beneficial), but about the affordances of an automated individualized transport system. Whilst potentially less worrying for socio-spatial inclusion and exclusion, research on drone delivery systems in Africa suggests that given the challenges in regulating Unmanned Autonomous Vehicles, their operation (either for delivery or for human mobility) in urban areas will require some form of corridor flight path and registration system (Lockhart et al., 2021). There are obvious appeals to service delivery companies to access the skies, but also for health and medical deliveries. However, questions are raised about what firms and organizations might gain privileged access to those corridors, how those corridors will link up with service hubs, and what that might mean for different interests and residents. Robotic reworking of power and control in the city as a new urban infrastructure is potentially always a reworking of relations of power and control, especially given the intersection between robotics and the extension of automated urban management.

The negative social impact of robotics on the public realm is perhaps most evident in their potential use for policing, surveillance and social control. As Shaw (2017) graphically outlines, the future of urban policing has the potential, at a relatively low cost, not only to vastly extend the reach of policing into areas where robots are less visible than human police but also to replace and extend police activities (see also Szocik and Abylkasymovam, 2021).

This includes the capability to track individuals more effectively than through CCTVs and the potential to intervene at a distance with weaponized robots, using technology developed in warfare. Indeed, robots have already killed individuals in civilian settings in the US by use of robot-wielded bombs (Glaser, 2016; Taft, 2016). The American Civil Liberties Union (ACLU) expressed human rights concerns about these events in the following way:

> It is easy to think up scenarios where weaponized robots might save the day, but such scenarios are likely to be rare—and meanwhile the potential for abuse and overuse is so significant that policymakers should closely monitor police departments' acquisition of and involvement with such machines.
>
> *(Stanley, 2016: no page)*

Again, what becomes important here is the co-evolution of robotics as a physical presence and the fact that all robots are in some form data-gathering machines (Elliott, 2018) which potentially pass power to technology firms involved in the development of the technology. Again, what becomes important here is the co-evolution of robotics as a physical presence, and the capacity of the policy or organiszation to process and sift through visual and textual using automated processing and AI. Cross-cutting all these issues is the fact that all robots are in some form data-gathering machines and that they potentially pass power to technology firms involved in the development of the technology.

Robots and software sorting

Robots cannot be separated from the wider data processing context in which they operate. What matters in the examples of urban re-partitioning and social control given in the previous section is the potential to combine the material functionality of robots with AI-enabled and algorithmic data processing and decision-making, including the extent to which robotic actions are shaped by biases and assumptions within automated interpretation and prediction systems. Thus, the idea of a discrete individual robots in the public realm is being supplemented by the notion of an Internet of Robotic Things (IoRT): 'a concept where sensor data from a variety of sources are fused, processed using local and distributed intelligence and used to control and manipulate objects in the physical world' (Simoens et al., 2018: 1). As Simoens et al. argue (2018: 1), 'in this cyber-physical perspective of the IoRT, sensor and data analytics technologies from the IoT are used to give robots a wider situational awareness that leads to better task execution.' Humans can also be integrated as sensors in the IoRT using electroencephalographic signals (Sudharsan & Deny, 2021).

Robotic technologies are, therefore, deeply embedded in what Elliott (2018: 25) calls a 'new protocological infrastructure' which 'collects, sorts, circulates and acts upon vast quantities of digital information. Robotic capacities depend on rapid and large-scale data processing, machine learning and decision-making algorithms which enable rationalisation of and response to dynamic material environments.' These insights are important in making the link between robot capabilities (including their data gathering and tracking capacity and their material capability to restrain and control), to extend the negative socio-spatial impacts of 'software sorting' (Graham, 2005) and predictive policing.

Seduction, side-tracking and capacity in urban robotic regulation

Robotics is fast joining (and in some cases transcending) the dominant tropes of the advanced, aspirational contemporary city around the world. Spatial imaginaries of creating exemplary smart or low-carbon (and ideally smart low-carbon) cities or neighbourhoods now have a robotic-automation narrative and, in some cases, robotics and automation are a dominant idea for cities of tomorrow. As with previous waves of future city development, the possibilities for building these futuristic visions should be treated with caution, but what they demonstrate is the use of robotics as a seductive trope of positive and aspirational urban futures. Robotic seduction is evident across the political spectrum. Thus Bastani (2019), for example, celebrates the emancipatory promise of robotics and automation in a manifesto for *Fully Luxury Automated Capitalism*. The argument is partly about taking control of a robot revolution that the author argues, will happen regardless, but it is a powerful example of the seductive power of the robotic imaginary. In addition to seduction, the politics of urban robotics can be side-tracked by arguments about progress, efficiency, public benefits and economic development or indeed by an overwhelming focus on issues of public safety and the material appearance of robots. It might be added that as their use becomes more widespread and habitual, public scrutiny of the work they do is likely to diminish. As Oravec (2022: 13) argues,

> people who question the expansion of the use of robotics in society can face strong opposition from robotics and AI advocates who preach their inevitability and try to defend their economic benefits, and who often assert that these entities "outclass" humans in some dimensions.

The final point to make in this section is that the current context for urban robotic regulation is fragmented. Making space for urban robotics in the public realm invariably requires changes in regulation or infrastructure that bring robotics into the public and political decision-making sphere. In many contexts around the world, that decision-making space is not open to (or not inviting of) in-depth interrogation of the wider implications of urban change, and that can include the difficulties for decision-makers and the public in grasping the full complexities of new technologies and their possible future implications. Moreover, in many cases, urban robotics is currently being rolled out through discrete urban initiatives which are often framed as experimental initiatives, often backed up with seductive, benign imaginaries, in a context of weak or non-existence national regulation. Particularly in areas of policing and security, police forces and other organizations may be given additional freedoms to operate robots that are determined in closed decision-making environments. There are questions about whether regulatory frameworks have the capacity and focus to engage systematically with the full implications of urban robotics.

Whether or not wider questions of robotic impact are debated depends on the extent to which there are effective public and political mechanisms for debate and regulation and appropriate structures of democratic oversight and accountability. Much of what is unfolding around urban robotics might be seen to be about robotics by stealth. The urban robot sits in a liminal space of accountability. It is in this context that the chapter now turns to the example of San Francisco in the USA to reflect on what might be required in future robotic regulation.

San Francisco: ground zero for urban robotic regulation

In many respects, San Francisco has emerged as an exemplary site of contestation and experimentation in urban robotic regulation (While et al., 2021). This reflects a range of factors, but particularly (a) the intersection of pressure to open the city for robotic applications from the vibrant ecosystems of technology firms and interests in the region; (b) the city's active urban politics of the public realm; and (c) public and political responses to high profile cases of unregulated or partially regulated urban robotic deployment in the city.

The rapid development of robotics activity in the San Francisco Bay Area of Northern California – with Silicon Valley at its heart – reflects those dynamics, with a proliferation of smaller firms seeking to develop a 'platform' of robotic service applications, alongside established high technology firms such as Amazon and Google. This vibrant ecosystem of innovation has led to pressure on municipalities across the Bay Area to open opportunities for robotic experimentation, with examples initially of robots being deployed without permission by start-up firms. Start-up firms and tech interests presented examples of other US cities such as Virginia (Idaho) and Washington DC that had passed legislation to facilitate the use of delivery robots, to argue for a more flexible approach in the Bay Area. Whilst robot application has been facilitated in several municipalities in California (While et al., 2021),

San Francisco is of particular interest to technology firms because of the complexity of its built environment when compared to suburban municipalities and the potential markets for robotic services in a dense urban area where existing platforms for service delivery (of food, for example, or Amazon deliveries) might be augmented or enhanced through robots. Indeed, new modes of service delivery have been the most visible example of robot application in the first wave of Northern Californian urban robotics. Moreover, in the US, it is possible for states and municipalities unilaterally to facilitate localized robotics experiments on roads and pavements. However, it is less easy for cities to create experimental airspaces for drones, as US commercial drone operations are approved on a case-by-case basis by the Federal Aircraft Authority, which has warned against the proliferation of city drone ordinances that might compromise public and air space safety (While et al., 2021).

The opportunities and pressures to open up San Francisco's streets to private-sector-led robots have intersected in several ways with the city's long-standing culture of political and public debate. Thus, the City of San Francisco authority banned street robots in 2017 following growing public and political concern about surveillance and control and the intrusion of unregulated experiments with street robots undertaken by small tech firms and tech entrepreneurs. The concern was specifically about the impact on pedestrians of the proliferation of 'six-wheeled [food delivery] boxes, roughly the size of beer coolers, ambling along city pavements, delivering food and other items' (Zaleski, 2017: no page) without regulation. This was in part an issue of the rights of pedestrians in a 'walkable city' but also reflected wider concerns about privacy and social control, which were brought to a head in a highly publicized case in 2017 when the San Francisco branch of the Society for the Protection of Cruelty to Animals used a robot to deter homeless people from pavements around its premises (Vincent, 2017). Subsequently, in 2019, San Francisco was the first US city to ban the use of facial recognition software by the police and other agencies within the City and the County (Conger et al., 2019).

Although the restrictive legislation of 2017 prohibited robotic experiments on San Francisco's streets, the City's Board of Supervisors has subsequently sought to find ways of supporting commercial robotic experiments through collaborative dialogue between different public and private interests. In December 2017, the regulation was changed to allow companies to apply for a permit to deploy up to three robots in designated zones of the city and permits restricted to a maximum of nine robots operating in total at any given time (City and County of San Francisco, 2017). San Francisco is divided into Residential, Neighbourhood Commercial, Downtown, Industrial and Mixed-Use zoning districts and the robots have been restricted to the industrial zones where there are fewer pedestrians. In mid-2018, the City and County of San Francisco established regulations and guidelines for the use and operation of autonomous delivery devices within the public right-of-way, which required coordinated action across transport regulation and land use planning (San Francisco Public Works, 2018).

San Francisco's experiments with robotic experimentation were subsequently extended in 2018 when the City of San Francisco established an Emerging Technology Open Working Group to develop a regulatory framework for delivery robots and other emerging urban robotic technologies, covering a broad range of topics, from data privacy and cybersecurity to what kind of legal body should be formed to deal with urban robot regulations. Participants included a wide range of stakeholders, from civic groups, such as Elder Care Alliance and San Francisco Council of District Merchants Associations, to companies such as Kiwi, Lyft, Marble and Microsoft, and to civil service offices at the City Council and San Francisco Airport. Topics included: how to define 'emerging technology'; issues of trust between government and companies; moving from reactive to proactive regulations; communication with the public; equitable benefits; accessibility and safety; and data sharing and privacy (City and County of San Francisco, 2019). Though prompted by sidewalk robots, the Group discussed a wide range of emerging technologies:

> It is important that there is a democratic process, and that the community is also involved that it's not just the policy makers or the big businesses making those decisions, that balance. I think what we're struggling with as a city is not only finding that balance but then, policy works slowly, right? And innovation does not, and it will not. How do we not just keep up, but kind of forecast? And support, and that's why with this emerging technology work group we really wanted not just city folks at the table or disability advocates, but we wanted academics and people in the tech sector to be at the table to help us, let's work on this together.
>
> *(Interview, Municipal Government Officer, October 2018,*
> *quoted in While et al., 2021)*

Emerging technology was defined by the City Administrator Naomi W. Kelly as those systems that 'are in development and have only been tested at market level on a limited basis; will have a measurable impact economically, socially, or morally in the next five to ten years; and do not fit within existing regulatory code' (Kelly, 2019: 10). Examples included drones, facial recognition system, biometrics, autonomous delivery robots and artificial intelligence, among others.

Specific recommendations in the final report of the Emerging Technology Open Group included: creating a central point of contact for companies and the public; improving communication with the community by informing technology companies of best practices for engaging local residents and businesses; a requirement to safety test and evaluate new technologies with clear evaluation criteria; to support responsive policy development in areas such as equity, accessibility, privacy and data ethics; and to foster smart forecasting through expert collaboration (City and County of San Francisco, 2019). The report focused particularly on the need to anticipate the impacts of emerging technologies:

> lack of trust between government and companies, regulations being reactive rather than proactive, the need for the City and companies to communicate with the public, equitable benefits, accessibility and safety, data sharing and privacy, and anticipated impacts on the city.
> *(City & County of San Francisco, 2019: 6)*

Critically, both the commercial and public agencies we interviewed frequently view stakeholder engagement as being key to the development of permitting processes. This form of 'collaborative governance' was designed to build community-centred cooperation between public, private and government actors with the aim to co-produce legislation, to ensure stakeholders' interests are represented in how the new technology is integrated into the city and the ways it interacts with the users. These principles have been harder to formulate in practice, in part because the rapid pace of robotic potential has made it difficult to maintain slower forms of regulatory oversight in relation to the expanded field of robotic application and the co-evolution of human–robotic relations but also because the work of the Emerging Technology Open Working Group has not translated into an appropriate regulatory framework across the city. This was graphically demonstrated in November 2022 when the city's Board of Supervisors gave local police the right to kill criminal suspects by weaponizing the city's 17 police robots if there was a sufficient threat to the public or police (Stokel-Walker, 2022). The public backlash and protests against the 'killer robots plan' led to the policy being reversed a month later pending further review but the idea has not been abandoned. San Francisco would be the first city in the USA to allow robots to use lethal force but there is pressure across the country to create those powers in the context of mass shootings by civilians. It might be noted that the creation of robotic capability within the police force itself had largely happened under the radar of public and political scrutiny.

San Francisco is, therefore, a fascinating example of what might be required and achieved with robotic regulation but also of the challenges in embedding appropriate regulation within the fast-moving context of urban robotization. Potentially worrying robotic applications such as police killer robots have been partially held in check by the city's culture of public resistance but that is unlikely to happen in many other urban contexts. Even in San Francisco, urban robotic regulation and accountability are struggling to keep pace with the expanded field of second-wave urban robotics.

Conclusions

This chapter has sought to connect concerns about the negative socio-spatial impact of the urban robotic revolution with the unfolding context for regulating robotic activity in the urban public realm. Central to the chapter is a reframing of the urban robotic regulation around the politics of robotic seduction and relations of what is explicit and implicit in grasping the potential socio-spatial role of robots. The paradox is that unlike many of the 'invisible' social-spatial impacts of AI, robots are a highly visible presence. For the most part (and especially at this early stage of urban robotics), robots can be seen, they must be navigated, they can be attacked and vandalized and they can cause physical harm to humans. This visibility should, in principle, stimulate public debate about the implications of robotic reworking of public space. However, the implications of robotics–city interactions – and especially the work that robots might do in cities and for whose benefit – are in many respects not so visible. Indeed, where it exists, public or political concern about creating space for robots has tended to focus on human safety and material nuisance, though often those concerns are muted by a fascination with the novelty and benignity of the robotic form and faith in its public benefits (Cugurullo and Acheampong, 2023). Very limited public or political attention is being given to issues of power, control and socio-spatial sorting. As Pasquale (2020) remarks, new 'laws of robotics' are needed to prevent the social injustice and even violence that he argues will result from robotic logics.

The argument is that foregrounding these relations of robotic (in)visibility is not something to be left to the future because urban robots are already starting to shape the future of cities and, moreover, decisions taken now about creating urban space for robots will be difficult to reconfigure in the future. As Oravec (2022: 22) argues,

> some people will continue to vent their frustrations toward robots and autonomous vehicles in violent acts or resistance or participate in forms of technological sabotage. However, many people will continue to adopt robotics and AI into their everyday routines, often with little awareness or concern about potential negative results.

More critical accounts are concerned about the potential loss of human agency and the centralization of non-accountable control as power is vested in machine learning and algorithms (Eubanks, 2018; Graham, 2005). The example of San Francisco demonstrates ways forward for urban robotic regulation but also highlights the challenges and difficulties in implementing and maintaining effective frameworks for urban robotic regulation. This chapter has provided a stimulus for more focused attention on the urgent need for regulation that can keep pace with the speed of change in urban robots in order to protect the public interest.

Acknowledgements

This chapter was supported by the ESRC project on 'Urban robotics as a new urban infrastructure' (ES/W010542/1).

References

Bastani, A. (2019). *Fully automated luxury communism*. Verso, London.

Bissell, D. (2018). Automation interrupted: How autonomous vehicle accidents transform the material politics of automation. *Political Geography*, 65, 57–66.

Bulkeley, H., Coenen, L., Frantzeskaki, N., Hartmann, C., Kronsell, A., Mai, L., Marvin, S., McCormick, K., van Steenbergen, F., & Voytenko Palgan, Y. (2016). Urban living labs: Governing urban sustainability transitions. *Current Opinion in Environmental Sustainability*, 22, 13–17.

Caprotti, F., & Cowley, R. (2017). Interrogating urban experiments. *Urban Geography*, 38(9), 1441–1450.

Caprotti, F., & Liu, D. (2022). Platform urbanism and the Chinese smart city: the co-production and territorialisation of Hangzhou City Brain. *GeoJournal*, 87(3), 1559–1573.

City and County of San Francisco (2017). *Board of Supervisors. Revised Legislative Digest, file No. 170599*. Available at: https://sfgov.legistar.com/View.ashx-?M=F&ID=5170963&GU ID=7D565EB3-E6B8-4F6C-B7B2-2D01CFE 6D99A [Accessed 19/01/2023].

City and County of San Francisco (2019). *Final Report of The Emerging Technology Open Working Group*. Available at: https://emergingtech.sfgov.org/sites/default/files/2019-01/ET_Report_FINAL.pdf [Accessed 19/01/2023].

Conger, K., Fausset, R., & Kovaleski, S.F. (2019). San Francisco bans facial recognition technology. *The New York Times*, 14 May. Available at: https://www.nytimes.com/2019/05/14/us/ facial-recognition-ban-san-francisco. html [Accessed 19/01/2023].

Cugurullo, F. (2020). Urban artificial intelligence: From *automation* to *autonomy* in the smart city. *Frontiers in Sustainable Cities*, 2, 38.

Cugurullo, F. (2021). *Frankenstein urbanism: eco, smart and autonomous cities, artificial intelligence and the end of the city*. Routledge, London.

Cugurullo, F., & Acheampong, R. A. (2023). Fear of AI: an inquiry into the adoption of autonomous cars in spite of fear, and a theoretical framework for the study of artificial intelligence technology acceptance. *AI & Society*, 1–16.

Curran, D., & Smart, A. (2021). Data-driven governance, smart urbanism and risk-class inequalities: Security and social credit in China. *Urban Studies*, 58(3), 487–506.

Del Casino, V.J., House-Peters, L., Crampton, J.W., & Gerhardt, H. (2020). The social life of robots: The politics of algorithms, governance, and sovereignty. *Antipode*, 52(3), 605–618.

Dowling, R., & MᶜGuirk, P. (2022). Autonomous vehicle experiments and the city. *Urban Geography*, 43(3), 409–426.

Elliott, A. (2018). Automated mobilities: From weaponized drones to killer bots. *Journal of Sociology*, 55(1), 20–36.

Eubanks, V. (2018). *Automating inequality: how high-tech tools profile, police, and punish the poor*. New York, St. Martin's Press.

Evans, J., & Karvonen, A. (2014). Give me a laboratory and I will lower your carbon footprint! Urban laboratories and the governance of low-carbon futures. *International Journal of Urban and Regional Research*, 38(2), 413–430.

Evans, J., Karvonen, A., & Raven, R. (Eds.) (2016). *The Experimental City*. Routledge, London.

Glaser, A. (2016). 11 police robots patrolling around the world. *Wired*. Available at: https://www.wired.com/2016/07/11-police-robots-patrolling-around-world/ [Accessed 19/01/2023].

Graham, S. (2005). Software-sorted geographies. *Progress in Human Geography*, 29(5), 562–580.

Graham, S., & Marvin, S. (2001). *Splintering urbanism: networked infrastructures, technological mobilities and the urban condition*. London, Routledge.

Greene, T. (2018). Anti-robot vigilantes in Arizona try to scare off Waymo's self-driving cars. *Artifical Intelligence*, 13 December. Available at: https://thenextweb.com/artificial-intelligence/ 2018/12/12/anti-robot-vigilantes-in-arizona-try-to-scare-off-waymos-self-driving-cars/ [Accessed 19/01/2023].

Hassan, O. (2020). Artificial Intelligence, Neom and Saudi Arabia's economic diversification from oil and gas. *The Political Quarterly*, 91, 222–227.

Kelly, N. M. (2019). *The final report of the emerging technology open working group*. City and County of San Francisco. Available at: https://emergingtech.sfgov.org/sites/default/files/2019-01/ET_Report_FINAL.pdf [Accessed 19/01/2023].

Lockhart, A., While, A., Marvin, S., Kovacic, M., Odendaal, N., & Alexander, C. (2021) Making space for drones: The contested reregulation of airspace in Tanzania and Rwanda. *Transactions of the Institute of British Geographers*, 46, 850–865.

McCarroll, C., & Cugurullo, F. (2022). No city on the horizon: Autonomous cars, artificial intelligence, and the absence of urbanism. *Frontiers in Sustainable Cities*, 4, 184.

McCurry, J. (2020). Toyota unveils plan to build 'city of the future' near Mount Fuji. *Guardian*, 7 January. Available at: https://www.theguardian.com/world/2020/jan/07/toyota-city-of-thefuture-japan-mount-fuji [Accessed 19/01/2023].

Neuman, S. (2018). Arizona governor helped make state 'Wild West' for driverless cars. *NPR*. Available at: https://www.npr.org/sections/thetwo-way/2018/03/20/595115055/arizona-governor-helped-make-state-wild-west-for-driverless-cars [Accessed 19/01/2023].

Oravec, J. A. (2022). *Good robot, bad robot: dark and creepy sides of robotics, automated vehicles, and AI*. Palgrave-Macmillan, New York.

Pasquale, F. (2020). *New laws of robotics*. Harvard University Press, Cambridge, MA.

Royakkers, L., & Van Est, R. (2015). *Just ordinary robots: automation from love to war*. London, CRC Press.

San Francisco Public Works (2018). *Autonomous Delivery Devices*. Available at: https://www.sfpublicworks.org/services/permits/autonomous-delivery-devices [Accessed 19/01/2023].

Shaw, I. (2017). *Policing the future city: Robotic being-in-the-world*. Antipode-Foundation.org, 19 May [Accessed 29 November 2021].

Simoens, P., Dragone, M., & Saffiotti, A. (2018). The Internet of Robotic Things: A review of concept, added value and applications. *International Journal of Advanced Robotic Systems*, 15(1), DOI: 1729881418759424.

Stanley, J. (2016). The use of killer robots by police *ACLU*. Available at: https://www.aclu.org/news/criminal-law-reform/use-killer-robots-police [Accessed 19/01/2023].

Stokel-Walker, C. (2022). San Francisco has reversed its killer robot plan. *Wired*, 7th December. Available at: https://www.wired.com/story/san-francisco-police-killer-robots-ban/ [Accessed 19/01/2023].

Sudharsan, R. R., & Deny, J. (2021). Brain–computer interface using electroencephalographic signals for the Internet of Robotic Things. In Anandan, R., Suseendran, G., Balamurugan, S., Mishra, A. & Balaganesh, D. (Eds.) *Human Communication Technology: Internet of Robotic Things and Ubiquitous Computing*. Wiley, London, 27–53.

Sumartojo, S., Lundberg, R., Kulić, D., Tian, L., Carreno-Medrano, P., & Mintrom, M. (2023). The robotic production of spatiality: Predictability, partitioning, and connection. *Transactions of the Institute of British Geographers*, 48, 56–68.

Szocik, K., & Abylkasymovam, R. (2021). Ethical Issues in police robots. the case of crowd control robots in a pandemic. *Journal of Applied Security Research*, 17, 530–545.

Taft, I. (2016). Police use of robot to kill Dallas suspect unprecedented, experts say. *Texas Tribune*. Available at: https://www.texastribune.org/2016/07/08/use-robot-kill-dallas-suspect-first-experts-say/ [Accessed 19/01/2023].

Tiddi, I., Bastianelli, E., Daga, E., d'Aquin, M., & Motta, E. (2020). Robot–city interaction: mapping the research landscape—a survey of the interactions between robots and modern cities. *International Journal of Social Robotics*, 12(2), 299–324.

Vincent, J. (2017). Animal shelter faces backlash after using robot to scare off homeless people. *The Verge*. Available at: https://www.theverge.com/2017/12/13/16771148/robot-security-guardscares-homeless-san-francisco [Accessed 19/01/2023].

While, A., Marvin, S., & Kovacic, M. (2021). Urban robotic experimentation: San Francisco, Tokyo and Dubai. *Urban Studies*, 58(4), 769–786.

Zaleski, A (2017). San Francisco to delivery robots: get off the damn sidewalk. *Citylab*, 19 May. Available at: https://www.citylab.com/life/2017/05/san-francisco-to-deliveryrobots-get-off-the-damn-sidewalk/527460/ [Accessed 19/01/2023].

8

EVERYDAY DRONING

Uneven experiences of drone-enabled AI urbanism

Anna Jackman

Introduction: the rise of everyday droning

In September 2021, global e-retailer Amazon announced a series of new products. At an event streamed to global audiences, Amazon articulated a future in which robots would become 'a core part of everyday home life' (Amazon, 2021: no page). They described a 'paradigm' of 'ambient intelligence,' one in which artificial intelligence (AI) is 'all around you,' learning and understanding your environment to 'help you when you need it, and recede into the background when you don't' (Amazon News, 2021: no page). This approach, Amazon continued, takes the 'complex science' of AI and 'makes it beautifully simple to use' (Amazon News, 2021: no page). In a bid to realize their unfolding vision of the AI-enabled home, Amazon launched a suite of domestic products. Designed to 'make customer lives better' and to 'deliver peace of mind,' these included *Astro*, the household robot assistant and home security provider, and *Alexa together*, a digital caregiving platform enabling remote assistance to ageing family members (Amazon News, 2021: no page). The announcement also featured details of Amazon's hotly anticipated *Always Home Cam*.

The Always Home Cam is an indoor, camera-equipped, autonomous home security drone. Pictured emerging from its charging dock (Figure 8.1), the drone is designed to provide a real-time view of a customer's home via a video stream to their smartphone. Alongside the persistence the system's name evokes, Amazon (through its subsidiary Ring) emphasizes the flexibility of the Always Home Cam as a system that can 'fly preset' courses, check appliances 'at a moment's notice,' and autonomously respond to a triggered

DOI: 10.4324/9781003365877-10

FIGURE 8.1   Always Home Cam.

Source: Ring.

house alarm to scan 'for intruders' (Vasani, 2021: no page; Ring, 2020: no page). Marketed as providing its users with 'every viewpoint around the home' (Ring, 2020: no page), the drone is touted with embedding 'ambient AI' through options like 'custom' detection and alerts 'allowing customers to teach the cameras to recognise things such as a car being parked in the drive' (Gibbs, 2021: no page). While the device remains presently accessible by invitation-only purchase, underscoring a wider eliteness of personal security drones (Jackman and Brickell, 2021), the Always Home Cam resonates with the wider dronification of domestic and urban airspace.

This chapter explores AI urbanism as it is enacted and enabled by the drone. AI urbanism refers to the embedding of AI in urban 'spaces, infrastructures, and technologies' (Yigitcanlar and Cugurullo, 2020: 2). The chapter offers a drone-focussed contribution to work exploring both AI's 'morphing' of urban spaces, governance and life (Cugurullo, 2020: 1, 2021; Kitchin, 2015; Lally, 2021) and the 'robotization of urban services' and securities (Macrorie et al., 2021: 5; Del Casino et al., 2020). It understands the drone as both a robotic actor that 'senses, thinks and acts' (Lynch, 2021: 1; see also Del Casino et al., 2020; While et al., 2021) and a technology increasingly permeating urban 'sociospatial realities and imaginaries' in significant ways (Del Casino, 2016: 846; Jackman and Jablonowski, 2021). Foregrounding the 'embodied' and 'everyday' nature of such technologies (Thomasen, 2020: 7; Pink and Sumartojo, 2018), the chapter adopts a feminist approach to interrogate the drone as it enters domestic airspace above, and within, urban homes, impacting both everyday life and bodies caught and dwelling in its midst.

Following the repeated assertion that we have entered a 'drone age' or 'zeitgeist' (Coley and Lockwood, 2015; Rothstein, 2015), an established literature interrogating the military drone along well-documented lines, from the drone's histories and networked infrastructure, to its implications on practices and understandings of warfighting, territory and sovereignty, has emerged (Asaro, 2013; Gregory, 2011a, 2011b; Hall Kindervater, 2017; Jackman, 2021; Shaw, 2016a; Wilcox, 2017; Williams, 2011). Further, in recognition that drones both comprise a diverse ecosystem (Jackman, 2019) and are increasingly deployed beyond the battlefield in diverse applications 'at home' (Kaplan and Miller, 2019: 419), scholars have extended such analysis to interrogate the drone across more multiple applications, contexts and users. Work focuses on the drone's growing mobilization by state actors such as police, in part due to their comparatively rapid adoption of small drones (Fish and Richardson, 2021). Scholars have explored the drone's 'transformation of how the aerial realm is lived as a context, object and perspective of policing' (Klauser, 2021a: 1; Klauser, 2021b), while foregrounding drone 'governance' that 'seeks to enlist all subjects' (Davies, 2019: 357).

In recognition of the drone's blurring of 'military and civilian, battleground and homefront' (Kaplan and Miller, 2019: 419; Shaw, 2016a; Wall, 2013, 2016), scholars have also mobilized the concept of 'everyday militarism,' referring to the ways in which 'military histories, logics, technologies, and practices become presences within the texture of the quotidian' (Richardson, 2020: 859). Here, they've explored both the 'wider robotic revolution in security' and the 'banal and everyday deployment of robots' by state and non-state actors (Del Casino et al., 2020: 608; Jackman and Brickell, 2021). In recognition of the drone's 'twin imperative to secure and profit' (Shaw, 2017a: 884), attention has also been drawn to the drone-commercialization of airspace. The concept of 'enclosure' is mobilized as a framework to engage critically the 'privatisation and securing of common (air)spaces,' and the uneven affordances enacted through this 'parcelling off' (Shaw, 2017a: 883, 2016a; see also Richardson, 2018; Crampton, 2016). Recognizing that commercial drone usage is variable, scholars have highlighted that drone visibilities are neither 'systematic' nor 'routine,' but rather 'novel, multisided and complex' (Pauschinger and Klauser, 2020: 443). Lastly, alongside exploring the more-than-military drone's visual 'capacities,' scholars have urged attention to 'their effects and affects' (Crampton, 2016: 137). In this vein, Richardson (2018: 79–80) outlines 'drone capitalism' as the drone's 'increasing entanglement in daily life,' with convenience afforded at the 'price of surveillance.'

While recognizing that drone scholarship is increasingly diverse, this chapter takes as its focus *drone-enabled AI urbanism* as approached through the lens of feminist geopolitics. A body of work 'redefining what counts' as (geo) political (Massaro and Williams, 2013: 567), feminist geopolitics foregrounds more diverse actors, acts, spaces and scales of geopolitical power, agency and experience (Hyndman, 2019; Sharp, 2020). Focussing on 'power as it unfolds,' it reflects on how security practices and their effects remain 'unevenly distributed' across lines of 'gender, race and sexuality' (Massaro and Williams, 2013: 567, 573) and are differently experienced at the 'finest' geopolitical scale of the body (Hyndman, 2019: 4). This chapter builds upon work bringing drone literatures into dialogue with feminist geopolitics through the articulation of the concept of 'everyday droning' (Jackman and Brickell, 2021). Here, we referred to the 'honing and homing of military technology and drone capitalism,' shifting attention to the 'growing range of non-state actors multiply mobilising, experiencing, and subject to the drone' (Jackman and Brickell, 2021:1, 2). Engaging work attentive to both the drone's shared 'promises of liberation from the burdens of human existence – from war to work' (Richardson, 2018: 79) and the 'complex ways in which civilian life is lived with, through and against' the 'domestic drone' (Bradley and Cerella, 2019: no page), this chapter interrogates the drone as it enters both airspace above, and domestic relations inside, the urban home. While cognizant that drones enact 'multiple logics and forms of visibility' (Pauschinger and Klauser, 2020: 462), it foregrounds commercial drone services, drawing attention to those 'favoured' and 'excluded' (Thomasen, 2020: 3) by such commercialized visions of dronified airspace.

Everyday droning: (in)securities and the drone home

In 2020, Sunflower Labs promoted their *Home Awareness System* at CES, a large annual US-based technology exhibition. Presented as the 'first fully autonomous residential drone,' the home security system features 'always-on activity sensors' disguised as 'attractive garden lights,' which, when triggered, deploy a drone around the property's perimeter in the detection of 'unusual activity' (Sunflower Labs, n.d.). While presently available to reserve (for a $999USD fee) with expected delivery in 2022 (Sunflower Labs, n.d.), the Sunflower systems' role as a 'techno-security-agent' patrolling domestic perimeters while cohabiting therein raises important questions around domestic and everyday life as it shifts in the drone age (Jackman and Brickell, 2021: 2). While recognizing the 'idealized' homes and privileged inhabitants pictured as ripe to afford drone protection,[1] adopting a feminist approach attentive to difference enables us to explore how this presentation of 'security' for one may mark insecurity for another (Jackman and Brickell, 2021: 10). After all, securitization – as 'processes through which spaces and subjectivities become targets of surveillance in the name of ensuring security' – acts on behalf of privileged populations, with 'uneven effects' (Williams and Massaro, 2013: 752). To this end, scholars of both the home and the drone have urged for attention to questions of 'protection' *for whom* (Brickell, 2012; Shaw, 2016a; Wall, 2016).

Here, it is important to understand how the home security drone sees. Just as scholars have observed that drones in the hands of police enable 'novel ways' of 'looking from above and below' (Klauser, 2021a: 1), so too do home security drones. Drone vision comprises both daylight cameras and 'more-than-visual' sensor payloads (Garrett and McCosker, 2017: 16; Jensen, 2020). For example, the Always Home Cam described in the introduction (Figure 8.1) is activated when it leaves the dock, only filming and recording video 'when in motion' (Amazon, 2021: no page). Conversely, Sunflower Labs' drone (Figure 8.2) does not encompass video cameras, rather functioning using 'a combination of motion and vibration sensors to detect activity' (Sunflower Labs, n.d.). The drone then sends a notification to the customer, providing a heat map of activity sites (Figure 8.3). The system is also described as seeking 'the best alert decisions' by drawing upon 'information from other smart home devices' (Sunflower Labs, n.d.).

In interrogating drone home security, we must then ask how is 'unusual behaviour' or 'activity' determined and what kinds of power relations may be enacted therein? (Jackman and Brickell, 2021). Recognizing the need to explore the co-productive role of AI technologies in (airspace) governance (Coletta and Kitchin, 2017), attention can be turned to the logics underpinning such versions and visions of drone-enabled AI urbanism.

Individuals have of course long been subject to 'coding and categorization' via their 'personal information' (Lyon, 2007). Such surveillant 'social sorting' is understood as a 'performance of power' that unevenly targets and subjugates particular communities and citizens, 'amplifying social inequalities' (Monahan, 2011: 495, 497). Understanding AI as a 'way of seeing, thinking, and approaching the world' that 'sorts and circumscribes what can be known,

FIGURE 8.2   Sunflower Labs drone.

Source: Sunflower Labs.

FIGURE 8.3   How the Always Home Cam (left) and Sunflower Labs drone (right) see.
Source: Ring and Sunflower Labs.

said, and subsequently acted upon' (Walker et al., 2021: 203), is useful to reflect on AI-enabled categorizations and designations of 'unusual' and 'risky' behaviour. Scholars have raised critical questions about the 'assumptions, biases' and 'values encoded' and embedded into such systems (Walker et al., 2021: 206; see also Del Casino et al., 2020). Citing issues of 'miscategorization' and the disproportionate impact of AI 'misidentification' upon 'people of colour, women, and young people' (Buolamwini and Gebru, 2018: 2), scholars have highlighted the ingrained biases of image recognition software-led determinations of behaviour and 'criminality' (West et al., 2019: 3). Thus, while AI continues to 'infiltrate every aspect of society,' it nonetheless remains discriminatory (Buolamwini and Gebru, 2018: 1). An exploration of AI urbanism thus necessitates attention to the 'imbrications' of such technologies 'with racial capitalism' (Schnepf, 2019: 749; see also Vasudevan and Smith, 2020) and the ways in which AI-enabled 'modes of classification figure racialized bodies' (Phan and Wark, 2021: 2) and enact 'white space' (Mirzoeff, 2020: 1).

Such questions remain pertinent given ongoing concerns that have engulfed Ring's wider home security products, including Ring's popular doorbell, 'detecting motion when people come to the property' and enabling users to 'see, hear and speak to visitors in real time from anywhere' (Ring, n.d.). Since Amazon purchased Ring in 2018, they have reportedly 'brokered over 1,800 partnerships' with US policing agencies 'who can request recorded video content from Ring users without a warrant' (Bridges, 2021: no page). In addition, Ring's 'Neigbors' app, one badged as a neighbourhood safety app, enables its millions of users to receive and share 'real-time, hyper-local safety updates' from both 'fellow neighbors and the public safety agencies that serve them' (Ring, n.d.). Participating public safety agencies are also able to 'ask the public for help with an active investigation' via a 'request for assistance' (Ring, n.d.).

We can unpack the 'extensions' that such forms of surveillance enact (Heilweil, 2020) in different ways. Helpful here is the concept of 'surveillance capitalism,' one referring to an economic order and logic which 'unilaterally claims human experience as free raw material for translation into behavioural data,' underpinning a 'new kind of marketplace for behavioural predictions' (Zuboff, 2019: 8). Citing examples such as police using a 'smart utility meter, iPhone, and Amazon Echo' to identify a murder suspect, Zuboff (2019) reflects on the growth of institutions 'seeking to access instrumentarian power.' The growth of 'surveillance-as-service' represents a wider determination to 'find a shortcut to certainty' (Zuboff, 2019: 387). Writing of its manifestation as predictive policing, Lally (2021: 3) observes that such 'algorithmic augmentations of policing' remain 'entangled within the inescapable presence of structural racism.' As such, in further understanding surveillance capitalism, we can think with work recognizing that our understandings of security can be 'fundamentally transformed if we begin at the scale of the individual body' and attend to the embodied 'ways geopolitical processes are experienced unevenly across differently situated populations' (Massaro and Williams, 2013: 570; see also Hyndman, 2003; Stewart, 2020). In this vein, it has been argued that Ring at once 'relies on infrastructural obfuscation to hide their infrastructures through urban camouflage,' while 'extending the industrial police-surveillant state' (Bridges, 2021: 830). Enacting a form of 'racialized algorithmic sorting' (Bridges, 2021: 832), such technologies act to perform 'ontological insecurity' wherein particular bodies are 'othered' and 'made out of place' (Browne, 2012: 72).

Lastly, in reflecting critically on the 'creation' of AI-enabled designations of 'criminality' 'increasingly woven into socio-spatial realities,' so too are we urged to recognize that such technologies are 'demonstrative of their own agencies' (Del Casino et al., 2020: 611). For example, Cugurullo (2021: 152) explores the 'ability of artificial intelligences to engage with ambivalent concepts like good and bad,' raising questions about the 'alignment of AI with human goals.' Here, Cugurullo (2021: 158) argues that the assumption that an 'AI learns a set of concepts' (e.g. 'good,' 'bad') invites a question of 'how' such concepts may come to 'be applied to variegated situations in which there are shares of grey between black and white.' Thus, in attending to the diversity, and co-constitution, of human and nonhuman agencies at play, it remains that in the 'evolving agency of technical systems' (Lynch and Del Casino, 2020: 383; see also Amoore, 2019, 2021) AI may emerge and (self-) learn to understand 'unusual behaviour' in different and distinct ways.

In collectively considering such 'corporate-owned, civilian-installed surveillance networks' (Bridges, 2021a: no page) we must therefore ask: What assumptions are embedded in drone-enabled AI urbanism's mobilization of racialized 'languages of threat,' 'alert' and 'activity'? (Crampton, 2016: 141; Wall, 2016: 1127). How are these forms of categorization enacted in and by such systems, to what end and through what kinds of (human and nonhuman) agencies and relations? And, who is 'consuming' such verticalized, militarized 'protective' services, and who is consumed and subsumed by them? (Jackman and Brickell, 2021: 10). While long understood that the 'sky is public' (Crampton, 2016: 140), drones have 'rendered public airspace physically accessible' in new ways (Thomasen, 2020: 14), their 'roboticized capitalism' both underpinned by diverse modes of categorization and prompting 'material, psychological and emotional' responses (Shaw, 2016b: 20) necessitating further attention.

Everyday droning: labour and care in the drone home

Robotic technologies are increasingly present in 'economic and social life' (Macrorie et al., 2021: 197). Attention is focused on their 'potentially profound' and 'conflictual' impact upon 'jobs and labour markets' (Bissell and Del Casino, 2017: 435; Lin, 2021: 2). It is argued that such technologies may produce 'new socio-spatial relations of production and consumption,' while reshaping urban relations and lives (Bissell and Del Casino, 2017: 436; Macrorie et al., 2021). Here, feminist work is instructive. Feminist scholars have mobilized the analytic of the 'everyday' as both a 'critical' lens and an 'entry point to understanding connections between the local and wider relations of power' (Dyck, 2005: 234, 236; Kaplan et al., 2020). Everyday life, and the spaces within which it takes place, is recognized as sites and scales of practising and corporeally experiencing politics (Tarrant and Marie Hall, 2020; Jackman and Brickell, 2021). In re-focusing attention from the 'global and grand' to the 'everyday' (Hyndman, 2007: 37), divisions between the 'public' arena of politics and the 'private' space of home are dismantled (Blunt and Dowling, 2006; Brickell, 2012). As such, the home and domestic life emerge as foundational loci of geopolitical power and process (Brickell, 2020; Carter and Woodyer, 2020).

In its foregrounding of 'everyday robo-deployments' (Del Casino et al., 2020: 608), this section considers the movement of drones inside the home. Following that 'social robots' are increasingly present and 'intervening in the spaces of everyday life' (Lynch, 2021: 1), it turns attention to 'dronified labour' in the home (Richardson, 2018). An example is helpful here. Akin to Astro (Amazon's robot assistant), technology giant Samsung in 2021 debuted 'Bot™ Handy,' a robot designed to 'help you work around the house' (Figure 8.4). Outlining a similar vision of 'AI as the core enabler, for your better tomorrow' (Tibken, 2021: no page), Samsung positioned 'Bot™ Handy' as an 'extension of you,' its 'advanced AI' enabling the robot to pick up and move

FIGURE 8.4 Samsung Bot™ Handy.

Source: Samsung.

'household items and objects, working as your trusted partner to help with house chores' (Samsung Newsroom, 2021: no page). Like other social robots, 'Bot™ Handy' has been anthropomorphized, 'animated' with eyes that blink and an appendage positioned like an arm (Cugurullo, 2020, 2021). The range of the robot's grip is emphasized, its dexterity enabling tasks from 'putting dirty dishes in a dishwasher to placing a flower in a vase' (Tibken, 2021: no page).

'Bot™ Handy' seeks to reshape home through 'altering the undertaking of domestic tasks' (Dodge and Kitchin, 2009: 1362). This desired 'reshaping' is underpinned by narratives of the easing of household labour, making domestic life more convenient and efficient by 'freeing up time' (Macrorie et al., 2021: 206) and releasing us from 'drudgery' (Phan, 2019: 12). This is echoed in the promotion of smart home technologies more widely (Lupton et al., 2021; West et al., 2019; Sinanan and Horst, 2021), with corporations emphasizing technological 'anticipations and responses to the needs of occupants' (Sadowski et al., 2021: 4), individualizing service while capturing 'troves of data' (Richardson, 2018: 85; Zuboff, 2019).

We too see these practices of innovation, and the logics underpinning them, emerging in the drone space. Alongside the rise of disinfection drones during the COVID-19 pandemic (Martins et al., 2021), visions of future homes served by cleaning drones are growing. The example described here is purposefully future-orientated. In foregrounding visions of drone-enabled AI urbanism in the future home, I follow Leszczynski (2016: 1691) who highlights that 'material projects of future-ing, i.e. of anticipating particular kinds of cities-to-come' shed important light on emergent socio-technical relations (see also Kinsley, 2012). After all, such imaginaries at once 'form an important part of the assemblage of robotic technologies' (Sumartojo et al., 2021: 99) and 'elevate some imagined futures above others' (Valdez et al., 2018: 3387; see also Luque-Ayala and Marvin, 2015). For example, forecasts by commercial outfits from insurers to property management alike anticipate 'multidrone households' (Comparethemarket.com, 2020: no page). As one such articulation describes of cleaning drones enabling 'sparkling homes': 'UV light drones could be programmed to sterilise surfaces, meaning that kitchen and bathroom surfaces would automatically be cleaned overnight, ready for the next day's use...likely resulting in healthier inhabitants' (Comparethemarket.com, 2020: no page). Here, the bio-political 'immunitary logic' that characterizes the military drone is domesticated; the drone home of the future is 'sparkling clean, sanitised and healthier because of its drone workforce' (Jackman and Brickell, 2021: 13). These 'anticipatory' forms (Anderson and Adey, 2012) position the drone as efficient, convenient and caring, while also poised to mitigate human failings of inattention (Jackman and Brickell, 2021: 13). In doing so, they raise questions about life, labour and care relations in the home.

In exploring these issues further, we can turn to wider work that, in interrogating the drone's 'softer, neoliberal side' (Parks, 2016: 227), explores how the 'promise' of drone capitalism 'comes at a price' (Richardson, 2018: 81). Of course, such drone systems remain geared to achieve 'particular ends (economic, security)' and are thus 'saturated with specific power relations' worthy of attention (Del Casino et al., 2020: 611). Recognizing that the home is 'increasingly in the sights and sites of capitalism' (Jackman and Brickell, 2021: 3), the remainder of this section explores the dronification of labour and care in the home. After all, while stories mount of 'robots, their role in society, and what they might do for or in place of humans' (Del Casino, 2016: 846), so too is there growing recognition of the home as an 'assemblage of technologies' that 'supports certain models of work' (Sadowski et al., 2021: 1; see also Lupton et al., 2021).

In exploration of shifting labour relations in the drone age, scholars have examined it as a 'productive' technology 'enclosing' airspace volumes and life within (Shaw, 2017a; Crampton, 2016). Extending attention to the gendered dimensions of 'droning' (Thomasen, 2018), scholars have argued that in its enclosure of home, the drone is positioned as a technology to 'unburden us' from a range of 'responsibilities and tasks' (Jackman and Brickell, 2021: 14). This 'unburdening' is enabled by the drone's 'accumulation of data' about us and our households, at once 'quantifying' routines, offering 'value to other actors,' and itself 'entailing labour' (Richardson, 2018: 86). In exploring such relations, scholars have mobilized Marxist thought. Marx argued that 'machines reduce costs, extend the amount of surplus value that can be extracted from labor, and help capital expand the workforce' (Del Casino, 2016: 847). The advent of robotics thus results in 'labour systems, the social relations of production, and types of work done' being 'co-constituted by machines' (Del Casino, 2016: 847; Shaw, 2016a). Turning to the home, McNally (2017: 1) notes that necessary labour time is the 'portion of the workday in which the worker makes value equivalent to what is needed for her own reproduction,' whereas 'surplus labor time is the remainder of the workday, where she makes additional value for capital.' In the case of the drone home, the drone 'not only releases the worker from a greater portion of necessary labor to enable more time for surplus labour, but it also commands social reproduction to produce surplus value' (Jackman and Brickell, 2021: 14).[2] The result of this is the 'devaluing of time to care, and by extension, the time-spaces of social reproduction,' with the embedded assumption that 'time and energy are more beneficially spent elsewhere on productive labour tasks rather than strengthening relational bonds through social reproductive work' (Jackman and Brickell, 2021: 14). In this vein, Sadowski et al. (2021: 1, 5) elucidate the twin concept of 'Big Mother' – a 'spinoff of Big Brother' to refer to 'a system that, under the guise of maternal care, seeks to manage, monitor and marketise domestic spaces and practices.' In recognition that 'social reproductive labor is geopolitical' (Vasudevan and Smith, 2020: 1164), emergent work is interested in how and to what end such devices render household activities as commodifiable (data).

Across such work on smart and dronified labour, scholars call for further attention to 'techno-affectivities' (Richardson, 2018: 91) and the embodied relations mobilized in dwelling together therein. Here, scholars have raised questions about robots 'staking out positions as caring subjects' (Del Casino, 2016: 852; see also Lynch, 2021) and their impact upon human experience and relations (Macrorie et al., 2021: 210; Yeo and Lin, 2019). Approaching home as an assemblage of human and nonhuman actors, we can thus ask – what kinds of caring relations does the domestic(ated) drone enact and engender? What kinds of agencies are at play when drones become 'our roommates' (Maalsen and Sadowski, 2019: 118)? In the visions of the future drone home outlined, the drone is centrally positioned as 'providing emotional, caring, and intimacy labours,' those most commonly falling to women (Sadowski et al., 2021: 9). Here, the drone potentially simultaneously interacts with 'humans in increasingly intimate ways' (Lynch, 2021: 1), while upholding particular visions of home and household labour that can reproduce gendered 'sameness' (Spigel in Sadowski et al., 2021: 9; see also Lupton et al., 2021). This may also act to exclude and 'obscure' other household configurations, inhabitants and labours (Sinanan and Horst, 2021; Phan, 2019). For example, alongside providing assistance, technologies also *require assistance* to 'dislodge from an obstacle' or 'open a door' (Thomasen, 2020: 33).

While the dronification of labour raises important questions around social reproduction and care, scholars of feminist geopolitics remind us that the 'micropolitical' and corporeal are not the 'be all and end all' of feminist inquiry (Dixon, 2014: 147). Here, attention is drawn to the diverse 'matter of the geopolitical' and the ways nonhuman actors 'negotiate and transform' geopolitical worlds (Dixon and Marston, 2011: 445; Meehan et al., 2013). After all, the future drone home also contains wider nonhuman intelligences, agencies and capacities, impacting relations in the home. Consider two examples. Drones are increasingly equipped with advanced navigation capacities, from 'sense and avoid' to 'intelligent flight.' Referring to the ability to 'lock onto and follow particular points, objects, and persons' (Jackman, 2019: 368), drones enlivened with 'intelligent flight' modes remind us of the 'multiplicity' of intelligence and its 'situation in and between spaces, bodies, objects, and technologies' (Lynch and Del Casino, 2020: 382; Yeo and Lin, 2019). How, then, might a 'more-than-human geopolitics' (Shaw, 2017b: 451) account for both agential drones and diverse forms of intelligence coming together in the home? Secondly, humans are not the only life in the home, animals are both 'interlocutors and actors' – '(re-)making urban space' and life (Oliver et al., 2021: 2, 3). Just as we should consider the 'physical intrusiveness' of the drone upon 'individuals occupying' urban space (Thomasen, 2020: 3), so too should we reflect on the drone's impacts on non-humans. Alongside growing numbers of videos of 'domestic' animals downing drones – demonstrating that drone power can be 'arrested, diverted or subverted' (Fish and Richardson, 2021: 11), researchers have shown that drones also prompt 'disturbances,' stresses and behavioural modifications in animal life (Duffy et al., 2018: 16; Mulero-Pázmány et al., 2017). How then might we more equitably unpack these 'more-than-human entanglements' (Bear and Holloway, 2019: 212)? Engaging (drone-enabled) AI urbanism thus requires further attention to shifting 'human-non-human relations, subjectivities, and potentialities' (Del Casino et al., 2020: 606) therein.

Conclusion

Robotics and AI bring with them both the 'transformation of cities and urban social life,' and the need for critical attention to the 'possibilities, realities and implications' with which such urbanisms are bound (While et al., 2021: 769, 770). In recognition that urban artificial intelligences comprise 'a number of incarnations across different scales' (Cugurullo, 2021: 158), this chapter draws attention to commercial 'ambient' drone technologies as a particular form of AI as it becomes part of built and domestic environments. In its discussion of ambient technologies, the chapter recognizes that the drone's 'domestication' remains 'born of militarized technologies and ways of knowing' (Schnepf, 2019: 749), while turning attention to particular commercialized and commodified drone 'instrumentalizations of air' (Klauser, 2021a: 12).

In its contribution to understanding the diverse impacts of urban robots as they 'reconfigure' everyday spaces and life (Del Casino, 2016; Yeo and Lin,

2019), the chapter foregrounds the generative and messy relations between drones and ambient environments of home. Adopting a feminist approach attentive to everyday life and its 'supposedly non-political spaces,' it traces AI's 'power as it unfolds' and is unevenly practised and experienced therein (Sharp, 2020: 2; Massaro and Williams, 2013: 567). After all, while often celebrated for its 'enriching capabilities or prospects,' AI urbanism remains bound to 'new territories of anxiety, danger, and violence' (Zuboff, 2019: 4), those with 'haunting' and unevenly distributed ramifications for surveillance subjects (Wall and Monahan, 2011: 240).

Contributing to critical projects interested in the 'who' and 'to what end' or urban AI experimentation (Cugurullo, 2021: 186), the chapter first examines drone-enabled home security systems operating above the home. Such technologies at once reveal the 'complex politics of vertical space' (Graham and Hewitt, 2012: 72) while seeking and 'implying security from insecurities below' (Adey, 2010: 58). Here, it highlights the importance of interrogating the drone's composition and amplification of 'social inequalities' (Thomasen, 2018: 309), asking: 'what sorts of subjectivities are made possible and/or closed off?' (Del Casino et al., 2020: 606). Second, the chapter heads inside the home. Building on work on 'drone capitalism' as it 'arrives in the home only to complicate the body' (Richardson, 2018: 93), it mobilizes the feminist analytic 'of the everyday' as an important political scale and texture (Kaplan et al., 2020: no page). It explores a 'reshaping and shifting' of both 'everyday activities' and 'power relations' (Del Casino et al., 2020: 606) through attention to practices and experiences of dronified labour, social reproduction and care in the drone home. While framed as easing or 'removing the inefficacies and biases of human labor,' it shares an interest in the ways that such technologies nonetheless 'impose their own encoded inequities' (Mattern, 2021: 3).

In closing the chapter, I wish to outline two areas for further consideration. First, I would like to reflect on the 'paradigm' described in the chapter's introduction, that of 'ambient AI.' The term has roots in 'ambient technology' and 'ambient intelligence,' namely visions in which devices are 'ubiquitous, interconnected and responsive' and 'fading into the background hum of our lives' (Palumbo, 2021: no page; see also McCullough, 2013). Ambience refers to how an environment senses and responds to our presence, with ambient technology as devices designed to blend with our homes, fitting with us rather than necessitating that we change our behavior to engage with technology. In a world of ambient intelligence, 'our environment is not a passive backdrop but an active agent in organizing daily lives' (Crang and Graham, 2007: 789). This reflection resonates with Allen's (2006: 441) work on 'privatised public space' which argues that power exceeds 'guards and gates' and is, instead, increasingly ambient. Referring to 'the character of an urban setting,' Allen's (2006: 445) notion of 'ambient power' highlights the ways ambience can seduce, prompt and limit 'movements and interactions.' In this vein, Barns (2021: 17) argues that digital services and devices are 'increasingly ambient and distributed,' with 'platform intermediation' ever more 'intricately part of our everyday environments.' Drawing on McCullough's (2013) work on the 'ambient commons,' Barns (2021: 129–130) reflects on approaching ambient platform urbanism in embodied and 'multisensory' ways that recognize alterations of both our 'senses of space and knowledges of the urban.' Thinking specifically with ambient power as it spatialized and experienced in and above the home, rendered visible are ambient technologies seeking to 'anticipate our lives' in ever more complex ways (Crang and Graham, 2007: 791). Ambient AI seeks to realize this vision in a particularly 'proactive' way in the home, 'suggesting and prompting' (Palumbo, 2021: no page). This is exemplified through innovations such as digital home assistant Alexa's 'Hunches' feature, one (following opt-in) which sees Alexa 'decide what to do around your home based on your habits' – from turning lights off to lowering the thermostat (Palumbo, 2021: no page). In unpacking ambient AI and its encroaching into more intimate spaces, then, we might reflect further both on shifting agencies and their 'ambient' qualities, and how ambient power may come to differently impact actors and relations in the home.

Second, I'd like to give pause to the recurrent framing of drones as *disruptive technology*' a commercial(ized) adage referring to technology 'changing the way things are done' (Cambridge Dictionary, no page). While part of a wider fetishization of drones as 'dreamlike, silver-bullet' technologies (Wall, 2013: 36), the drone can nonetheless also be *disrupted*. Videos of drone crashes are commonplace. From animals that attack, humans that hack and malware that spoofs (King, 2015; Holland Michel, 2019), multiple agencies – both human and nonhuman – can disrupt the drone's idealized functioning. Alongside 'home making,' we thus need to consider how the drone may engage in domestic 'unmaking' (Harris et al., 2020: 1292). After all, while the depictions of the drone home are vacated of the 'fleshy, messy and indeterminate stuff of everyday life' (Katz, 2001: 711), the reality is that life with 'smart domestic technologies' is 'far messier' (Lupton et al., 2021: 2). Here, attention is needed to the 'complex agencies' at play within 'systems of automation,' those which can contravene 'imaginaries of automated convenience' in 'interruptive' ways (Bissell, 2018: 57; see also Fish and Richardson, 2021). After all, the drone can feel like something that 'has not yet quite arrived: clumsy and incomplete, defined by its glitches and gaps in connection' (Richardson, 2018: 93; see also Del Casino et al., 2020).

Here, the use of the word 'glitch' is notable, as the term has been mobilized in feminist commentary on (urban) techno-futures. Scholars first note that when writing about techno-futures, our 'predominant orientation has been technodystopian' and 'technodeterministic' (Elwood, 2021: 211; McLean et al., 2019: 740). While it remains important to 'understand digital mediations of domination' they argue that we can 'theorize beyond these formulations' (Elwood, 2021: 211). Here, work has mobilized Legacy Russell's (2012) 'notion of the glitch,' one referring to 'an inherent characteristic of digital formations that expresses simultaneous potential for both error (malfunction, failure) and erratum (correction to a system)' (Leszczynski, 2020: 191). While the word 'glitch' commonly connotes 'error,' Russell (2012) re-frames it as an opportunity, a moment of stalling or interruption allowing us to 'choose our own adventure.' Leszczynski (2020: 191) argues that the glitch is theorized in 'the minor,' mobilizing a feminist attentiveness to the everyday ways in which people (mundanely, creatively, hopefully) intervene in and comprise digital space. How, for example, might drones be mobilized by/in service of different 'forms of local, placebased, and indigenous intelligences' that make up the city (Mattern, 2021: 12)? In some senses, we see the glitch 'declining second rank to common convention' (Russell, 2012) through the mobilization of drones for purposes exceeding the platforms' designs, from citizens hacking altitude ceilings to delegating dog walking to drones. After all, drones can 'participate in protest as well as policing, civil as well as state observation,' remaining bound to a 'complex atmospheric politics' (Kaplan, 2020: 51). Further investigations of 'drone power' and AI urbanism should thus attend to diverse forms of techno-disruption, raising critical questions of whose needs are prioritized and served, and interrogating the drone's multiple identities as 'protagonist and antagonist' (Fish and Richardson, 2021: 4, 18), at once discriminating, empowering and playful. Given that our urban futures remain unlikely to be 'robot free' (Del Casino et al., 2020: 615), there remain, as Jablonowski (2015) asserts, more 'drone stories' to tell.

Notes

1 This portrayal of a large, detached home represents only one form of home. While recognizing the variety of urban homes with varying politics and privileges (Blunt and Sheringham, 2019), 'luxury' high rises are increasingly envisioned as ripe for drone operation through their equipping of balconies with drone delivery landing stations (Jackman and Jablonowski, 2021). In recognition of the need for critique to exceed a focus on 'technological innovation' (Cugurullo, 2021: 193), attention is needed to the role of domestic drone security in enacting a 'cloaked co-presence' between wealthy urban homeowners and wider city inhabitants (Atkinson, 2016: 1302).
2 Social reproduction refers to 'the gendered biological, material, and care-based work required to reproduce households day-today, that is primarily undertaken by women' (Bakker 2007 in Jackman and Brickell, 2021: 12). The 'labour of social reproduction' is targeted by the drone as a 'future for capitalist expansion' (Huws, 2019: 122; Jackman and Brickell, 2021).

References

Adey, P. (2010). Vertical security in the megacity: Legibility, mobility and aerial politics, *Theory, Culture & Society*, 27(6), 51–67.

Allen, J. (2006). Ambient power: Berlin's Potsdamer Platz and the seductive logic of public spaces, *Urban Studies*, 43(2), 441–455.

Amazon (2021). *Amazon Devices & Services news—September 2021*. Available at: https://www.aboutamazon.com/news/devices/amazon-devices-services-news-september-2021 [Accessed 19/01/2023].

Amazon News (2021). *Introducing Amazon's latest devices and services*. Youtube. Available at: https://www.youtube.com/watch?v=ytDANg8A9AE&ab_channel=AmazonNews [Accessed 19/01/2023].

Amoore, L. (2019). Doubt and the algorithm: On the partial accounts of machine learning, *Theory, Culture & Society*, 36(6), 147–169.

Amoore, L. (2021). The deep border, *Political Geography*, 102547, DOI: 10.1016/j.polgeo.2021.102547.

Anderson, B., & Adey, P. (2012). Guest editorial. *Future Geographies, Environment and Planning A*, 44(7), 1529–1535.

Asaro, P.M. (2013). The labor of surveillance and bureaucratized killing: New subjectivities of military drone operators, *Social Semiotics*, 23(2), 196–224.

Atkinson, R. (2016). Limited exposure: Social concealment, mobility and engagement with public space by the super-rich in London. *Environment and Planning A*, 48(7), 1302–1317.

Barns, S. (2021). Out of the loop? On the radical and the routine in urban big data. *Urban Studies*, 58(15), 3203–3210.

Bear, C., & Holloway, L. (2019). Beyond resistance: Geographies of divergent more-thanhuman conduct in robotic milking, *Geoforum*, 104, 212–221.

Bissell, D. (2018). Automation interrupted: How autonomous vehicle accidents transform the material politics of automation, *Political Geography*, 65, 57–66.

Bissell, D., & Del Casino, V.J. (2017). Whither labor geography and the rise of the robots? *Social & Cultural Geography*, 18(3), 435–442.

Blunt, A., & Dowling, R.M. (2006). *Home*. Routledge, London and New York.

Blunt, A., & Sheringham, O. (2019). Home-city geographies: Urban dwelling and mobility, *Progress in Human Geography*, 43(5), 815–834.

Bradley, A., & Cerella, A. (2019). *Droneland: towards a domestic drone theory*. Available at: https://blogs.prio.org/SecurityDialogue/2019/07/droneland-towards-adomestic-drone-theory/ [Accessed 19/01/2023].

Brickell, K. (2012). 'Mapping' and 'doing' critical geographies of home, *Progress in Human Geography*, 36(2), 225–244.

Brickell, K. (2020). *Home SOS: Gender, Violence and Survival in Crisis Ordinary Cambodia*. Wiley, Oxford, UK.

Bridges, L. (2021). Infrastructural obfuscation: unpacking the carceral logics of the Ring surveillant assemblage, *Information, Communication & Society*, 24(6), 830–849.

Bridges, L. (2021a). Amazon's Ring is the largest civilian surveillance network the US has ever seen. *The Guardian*. Available at: https://www.theguardian.com/commentisfree/2021/may/18/amazon-ring-largest-civilian-surveillance-network-us [Accessed 19/01/2023].

Browne, S. (2012). Race and surveillance. In Ball, K., Haggerty, K., & Lyon, D. (Eds.), *Routledge Handbook of Surveillance Studies*. Routledge, London, pp. 72–79.

Buolamwini, J., & Gebru, T. (2018). Gender shades: Intersectional accuracy disparities in commercial gender classification, *Proceedings of Machine Learning Research*, 81, 1–15.

Cambridge Dictionary (n.d.) Definition: Disruptive Technology. Available at: https://dictionary.cambridge.org/dictionary/english/disruptive-technology [Accessed 19/01/2023].

Carter, S., & Woodyer, T. (2020). Introduction: Domesticating geopolitics, *Geopolitics*, 25(5), 1045–1049.

Coletta, C., & Kitchin, R. (2017). Algorhythmic governance: Regulating the 'heartbeat' of a city using the Internet of Things, *Big Data & Society*, 1–16, DOI:10.1177/2053951717742418.

Coley, R., & Lockwood, D. (2015). As above, so below: Triangulating drone culture, *Culture Machine*, 16, 1–19.

Comparethemarket.com (2020). *Life more automated report*. Available at: https://www.comparethemarket.com/globalassets/simples-lab/new-simples-lab-march2020/001_20_CTM_Automated_Report_doc_v10_ebf086b2-9f19-4cdd-ba67-92e10208d2cb.pdf [Accessed 19/01/2023].

Crampton, J. (2016). Assemblage of the vertical: Commercial drones and algorithmic life, *Geographica Helvetica*, 71, 137–146.

Crang, M., & Graham, S. (2007). Sentient Cities: Ambient Intelligence and the politics of urban space, *Information, Communication & Society*, 10, 789–817.

Cugurullo, F. (2020). Urban Artificial Intelligence: From automation to autonomy in the smart city, *Frontiers in Sustainable Cities*, 2(38), 1–14.

Cugurullo, F. (2021). *Frankenstein Urbanism: Eco, Smart and Autonomous Cities, Artificial Intelligence and the End of the City*. Routledge, London and New York.

Davies, O. (2019). Theorizing the advent of weaponized drones as techniques of domestic paramilitary policing, *Security Dialogue*, 50(4), 344–360.

Del Casino, V., House-Peters, L., Crampton, J., & Gerhardt, H. (2020). The social life of robots: The politics of algorithms, governance, and sovereignty, *Antipode*, 52(3), 605–618.

Del Casino, V.J. (2016). Social geographies II: Robots, *Progress in Human Geography*, 40(6), 846–855.

Dixon, D.P. (2014). The way of the flesh: Life, geopolitics and the weight of the future, *Gender, Place & Culture*, 21(2), 136–151.

Dixon, D.P., & Marston, S.A. (2011). Introduction: Feminist engagements with geopolitics, *Gender, Place & Culture*, 18(4), 445–453.

Dodge, M., & Kitchin, R. (2009). Software, objects, and home space, *Environment and Planning A*, 41, 1344–1365.

Duffy, J.P., Cunliffe, A.M., DeBell, L., Sandbrook, C., Wich, S.A., Shutler, J.D., Myers-Smith, I.H., Varela, M.R., & Anderson, K. (2018). Location, location, location: Considerations when using lightweight drones in challenging environments, *Remote Sensing in Ecology and Conservation*, 4, 7–19.

Dyck, I. (2005). Feminist geography, the 'everyday', and local–global relations: hidden spaces of place-making, *The Canadian Geographer*, 49(3), 233–243.

Elwood, S. (2021). Digital geographies, feminist relationality, Black and queer code studies: Thriving otherwise, *Progress in Human Geography*, 45(2), 209–228.

Fish, A., & Richardson, M. (2021). Drone power: Conservation, humanitarianism, policing and war, *Theory, Culture & Society*, 39(3), 1–24.

Garrett, B., & McCosker, A. (2017). Non-human sensing: New methodologies for the drone assemblage, in Gómez Cruz, E., Sumartojo, S., & Pink, S. (Eds.), *Refiguring Techniques in Digital Visual Research*, Palgrave Macmillan, New York, 13–23.

Gibbs, S. (2021). Amazon launches home robot Astro and giant Alexa display. *The Guardian*. Available at: https://www.theguardian.com/technology/2021/sep/28/amazon-launches-home-robot-astro-and-giant-alexa-display [Accessed 19/01/2023]

Graham, S., & Hewitt, L. (2012). Getting off the ground: On the politics of urban verticality, *Progress in Human Geography*, 37(1), 72–92.

Gregory, D. (2011a). From a view to a kill: Drones and late modern war, *Theory, Culture & Society*, 28(7), 188–215.

Gregory, D. (2011b). The everywhere war, *The Geographical Journal*, 177(3), 238–250.

Hall Kindervater, K. (2017). The technological rationality of the drone strike, *Critical Studies on Security*, 5(1), 28–44.

Harris, E., Brickell, K., & Nowicki, M. (2020). Door locks, wall stickers, fireplaces: Assemblage theory and home (un)making in Lewisham's temporary accommodation, *Antipode*, 52(5), 1286–1309.

Heilweil, R. (2020). *Amazon's surveillance cameras fly now – which is unsettling*. Recode. Available at: https://www.vox.com/recode/2020/9/24/21454991/amazon-ring-drone-always-home-flying-camera-surveillance-privacy [Accessed 19/01/2023].

Holland Michel, A. (2019). *Counter-drone systems, 2nd edition*. Center for the Study of the drone. Available at: https://dronecenter.bard.edu/files/2019/12/CSD-CUAS-2nd-Edition-Web.pdf [Accessed 19/01/2023].

Huws, U. (2019). The hassle of housework: Digitalisation and the commodification of domestic labour, *Feminist Review*, 123(1), 8–23.

Hyndman, J. (2003). Beyond either/or: A feminist analysis of September 11th, *ACME: An International E-Journal for Critical Geographies*, 2(1), 1–13.

Hyndman, J. (2007). Feminist geopolitics revisited: Body counts in Iraq, *The Professional Geographer*, 59(1), 35–46.

Hyndman, J. (2019). Unsettling feminist geopolitics: Forging feminist political geographies of violence and displacement, *Gender, Place & Culture*, 26(1), 3–29.

Jablonowski, M. (2015). Drone it yourself! On the decentring of 'drone stories', *Culture Machine*, 16, 1–15.

Jackman, A. (2019). Consumer drone evolutions: Trends, spaces, temporalities, threats, *Defense & Security Analysis*, 35(4), 362–383.

Jackman, A. (2021). Visualizations of the small military drone: Normalization through 'naturalization', *Critical Military Studies*, DOI: 10.1080/23337486.2020.1846955.

Jackman, A., & Brickell, K. (2021). 'Everyday droning': Towards a feminist geopolitics of the drone-home, *Progress in Human Geography*, 1–23. DOI: 10.1177/0309132521101874 5.

Jackman, A., & Jablonowski, M. (2021). Investments in the imaginary: Commercial drone speculations and relations, *Global Discourse*, 11(1-2), 1–24, DOI: 10.1332/204378920X16067521422126.

Jensen, O.B. (2020). Thinking with the drone – visual lessons in aerial and volumetric thinking, *Visual Studies*, 35(5), 417–428.

Kaplan, C. (2020). Atmospheric politics: Protest drones and the ambiguity of airspace, *Digital War*, 1, 50–57.

Kaplan, C., Kirk, G., & Lea, T. (2020). *Editors' Letter. Everyday Militarisms: Hidden in Plain Sight/Site*. Society & Space [Online]. Available at: https://www.societyand space.org/articles/editors-letter-everyday-militarisms-hidden-in-plain-sight-site [Accessed 19/01/2023].

Kaplan, C., & Miller, A. (2019). Drones as "Atmospheric Policing": From US border enforcement to the LAPD, *Public Culture*, 31(3), 419–445.

Katz, C. (2001). Vagabond capitalism and the necessity of social reproduction, *Antipode*, 33(4), 709–728.

King, H. (2015). *Watch animals destroy drones*. CNN Business [Online]. Available at: https://money.cnn.com/2015/08/14/technology/animals-destroy-drones/ (Accessed 13/06/2021).

Kinsley, S. (2012). Futures in the making: Practices to anticipate 'Ubiquitous Computing', *Environment and Planning A*, 44(7), 1554–1569.

Kitchin, R. (2015). *Data-Driven, Networked Urbanism*. Available at: https://papers. ssrn.com/sol3/papers.cfm?abstract_id=2641802 [Accessed 19/01/2023].

Klauser, F. (2021a). Policing with the drone: Towards an aerial geopolitics of security, *Security Dialogue*, 1–15, DOI: 10.1177/0967010621992661

Klauser, F. (2021b). Police drones and the air: Towards a volumetric geopolitics of security, *Swiss Political Science Review*, 27(1), 158–169.

Lally, N. (2021). "It makes almost no difference which algorithm you use": On the modularity of predictive policing, *Urban Geography*, DOI: 10.1080/02723 638.2021.1949142.

Leszczynski, A. (2016). Speculative futures: Cities, data, and governance beyond smart urbanism, *Environment and Planning A*, 48(9), 1691–1708.

Leszczynski, A. (2020). Glitchy vignettes of platform urbanism, *Environment and Planning D: Society and Space*, 38(2), 189–208.

Lin, W. (2021). Automated infrastructure: COVID-19 and the shifting geographies of supply chain capitalism, *Progress in Human Geography*, 1–21, DOI: 10.1177/ 03091325211038718.

Lupton, D., Pink, S., & Horst, H. (2021). Living in, with and beyond the 'smart home': Introduction to the special issue, *Convergence: The International Journal of Research into New Media Technologies*, 27(5), 1–8.

Luque-Ayala, A., & Marvin, S. (2015). Developing a critical understanding of smart urbanism? *Urban Studies*, 52(12), 2105–2116.

Lynch, C.R. (2021). Critical geographies of social robotics, *Digital Geography and Society*, 2, 100010, 1–3, DOI: 10.1016/j.diggeo.2021.100010.

Lynch, C.R., & Del Casino, V.J. (2020). Smart spaces, information processing, and the question of intelligence, *Annals of the American Association of Geographers*, 110(2), 382–390.

Lyon, D. (2007). Surveillance, security and social sorting, *International Criminal Justice Review*, 17(3), 161–170.

Maalsen, S., & Sadowski, J. (2019). The smart home on FIRE: Amplifying and accelerating domestic surveillance, *Surveillance & Society*, 17(1/2), 118–124.

Macrorie, R., Marvin, S., & While, A. (2021). Robotics and automation in the city: A research agenda, *Urban Geography*, 42(2), 197–217.

Martins, B.O., Lavallee, C., & Silkoset, A. (2021). Drone use for COVID-19 related problems: Techno-solutionism and its societal implications, *Global Policy*, doi:10.1111/1758-5899.13007.

Massaro, V., & Williams, J. (2013). Feminist geopolitics, *Geography Compass*, 7(8), 567–577.

Mattern, S. (2021). *A City Is Not a Computer: Other Urban Intelligences*. Princeton University Press, Princeton, USA.

McCullough, M. (2013). *Ambient Commons: Attention in the Age of Embodied Information*. MIT Press, Cambridge, USA.

McLean, J., Maalsen, S., & Prebble, S. (2019). A feminist perspective on digital geographies: activism, affect and emotion, and gendered human-technology relations in Australia, *Gender, Place & Culture*, 26(5), 740–761.

McNally, D. (2017). Intersections and dialectics: Critical reconstructions in social reproduction theory. In Bhattacharya, T. (Eds.), *Social Reproduction Theory: Remapping Class, Recentering Oppression*. Pluto Press: London, UK, pp. 94–111.

Meehan, K., Shaw, I.G.R., & Marston, S.A. (2013). Political geographies of the object, *Political Geography*, 33, 1–10.

Mirzoeff, N. (2020). Artificial vision, white space and racial surveillance capitalism, *AI & Society*, 1–11, DOI: 10.1007/s00146-020-01095-8.

Monahan, T. (2011). Surveillance as cultural practice, *The Sociological Quarterly*, 52(4), 495–508.

Mulero-Pázmány, M., Jenni-Eiermann, S., Strebel, S., Sattler, T., Negro, J.J., & Tablado, Z. (2017). Unmanned aircraft systems as a new source of disturbance for wildlife: A systematic review, *PLoS ONE*, 12(6), 1–14.

Oliver, C., Ragavan, S., Turnbull, S., Chowdhury, A., Borden, A., Fry, T., Gutgutia, S., & Srivastava, S. (2021). Introduction to the urban ecologies open collection: A call for contributions on methods, ethics, and design in geographical research with urban animals, *Geo: Geography and Environment*, 1–7.

Palumbo, J. (2021). *Are we ready for our smart home devices to become truly "smart"*. CNN. Available at: https://edition.cnn.com/style/article/future-smart-home-ambient-technology/index.html [Accessed 19/01/2023].

Parks, L. (2016). Drones, vertical mediation, and the targeted class, *Feminist Studies*, 42(1), 227–235.

Pauschinger, D., & Klauser, F. (2020). Aerial politics of visibility: Actors, spaces, and drivers of professional drone usage in Switzerland, *Surveillance & Society*, 18(4), 443–466.

Phan, T. (2019). Amazon Echo and the aesthetics of whiteness, *Catalyst: Feminism, Theory, Technoscience*, 5(1), 1–38.

Phan, T., & Wark, S. (2021). Racial formations as data formations, *Big Data & Society*, 1–5. DOI:10.1177/20539517211046377.

Pink, S., & Sumartojo, S. (2018). The lit world: Living with everyday urban automation, *Social & Cultural Geography*, 19(7), 833–852.

Richardson, M. (2018). Drone capitalism, *Transformations*, 31, 79–98.

Richardson, M. (2020). Drone cultures: Encounters with everyday militarisms, *Continuum*, 34(6), 858–869.

Ring (2020). *Introducing Ring Always Home Cam: An Innovative New Approach to Always Being Home*. Available at: https://blog.ring.com/products-innovation/introducing-ring-always-home-cam-an-innovative-new-approach-to-always-being-home/ [Accessed 19/01/2023].

Ring (n.d.) *Ring doorbell*. Available at: https://en-uk.ring.com/pages/doorbells [Accessed 19/01/2023].

Rothstein, A. (2015). *Drone. Object Lessons*. Bloomsbury Publishing Inc., USA.

Russell, L. (2012). *Digital dualism and The Glitch Feminist Manifesto*. The Society Pages. Available at: https://thesocietypages.org/cyborgology/2012/12/10/digital-dualism-and-the-glitch-feminism-manifesto/ [Accessed 19/01/2023].

Sadowski, J., Strengers, Y., & Kennedy, J. (2021). More work for Big Mother: Revaluing care and control in smart homes, *Environment and Planning A: Economy and Space*, 1–16, DOI: 10.1177/0308518X211022366.

Samsung Newsroom (2021). *Samsung Introduces Latest Innovations for a Better Normal at CES 2021*. Available at: https://news.samsung.com/us/samsung-ces-2021-latest-innovations-for-a-better-normal/ [Accessed 19/01/2023].

Schnepf, J.D. (2019). Unsettling aerial surveillance: Surveillance studies after standing rock, *Surveillance & Society*, 17(5), 747–751.

Sharp, J. (2020). Materials, forensics and feminist geopolitics, *Progress in Human Geography*, 1–13, DOI: 10.1177/03091325209 05653.

Shaw, I.G.R. (2016a). *Predator Empire: Drone warfare and full spectrum dominance*. University of Minnesota Press, USA.

Shaw, I.G.R. (2016b). The Urbanization of drone warfare: Policing surplus populations in the dronepolis, *Geographica Helvetica*, 71, 19–28.

Shaw, I.G.R. (2017a). The great war of enclosure: Securing the skies, *Antipode*, 49(4), 883–906.

Shaw, I.G.R. (2017b). Robot Wars: US Empire and geopolitics in the robotic age, *Security Dialogue*, 48(5), 451–470.

Sinanan, J., & Horst, H.A. (2021). Gendered and generational dynamics of domestic automations, *Convergence: The International Journal of Research into New Media Technologies*, 27(5), 1–12.

Stewart, B. (2020). One Ring to rule them all: Surveillance 'smart' tech won't make Canadian cities safer. *The Conversation*. Available at: https://theconversation.com/one-ring-to-rule-them-all-surveillance-smart-tech-wont-make-canadian-cities-safer-129747 [Accessed 19/01/2023]

Sumartojo, S., Lundberg, R., Tian, L., Carreno-Medrano, P., Kulić, D., & Mintrom, M. (2021). Imagining public space robots of the near-future, *Geoforum*, 124, 99–109.

Sunflower Labs (n.d.) *FAQ*. Available at: https://www.sunflower-labs.com/faq [Accessed 19/01/2023].

Tarrant, A., & Marie Hall, S. (2020). Everyday geographies of family: Feminist approaches and interdisciplinary conversations, *Gender, Place & Culture*, 27(5), 613–623.

Thomasen, K. (2018). Beyond airspace safety: A feminist perspective on drone privacy regulation, *Canadian Journal of Law and Technology*, 16(2), 307–338.

Thomasen, K. (2020). Robots, Regulation, and the Changing Nature of Public Space, *Ottawa Law Review*, 51(2). Available at: https://papers.ssrn.com/sol3/papers.cfm?abstract_id=3589896 [Accessed 19/01/2023].

Tibken, S. (2021). *Samsung's CES 2021 robots will clean your house and pour you a glass of wine*. CNET. Available at: https://www.cnet.com/home/smart-home/samsung-ces-2021-robots-will-clean-your-house-and-pour-you-a-glass-of-wine/ [Accessed 19/01/2023].

Valdez, A.-M., Cook, M., & Potter, S. (2018). Roadmaps to utopia: Tales of the smart city, *Urban Studies*, 55(15), 3385–3403.

Vasani, S. (2021). *How to sign up for an invite for the Ring Always Home Cam, Amazon's new security drone.* The Verge. Available at: https://www.theverge.com/2021/9/28/22698424/amazon-ring-always-home-cam-drone-preorder-invite-sign-up-how-to [Accessed 19/01/2023].

Vasudevan, P., & Smith, S. (2020). The domestic geopolitics of racial capitalism, *Environment and Planning C: Politics and Space*, 38(7–8), 1160–1179.

Walker, M., Winders, J., & Boamah, E.F. (2021). Locating artificial intelligence: A research agenda, *Space and Polity*, 25(2), 202–219.

Wall, T. (2013). Unmanning the police manhunt: Vertical security as pacification, *Socialist Studies*, 9, 32–56.

Wall, T. (2016). Ordinary emergency: Drones, police, and geographies of legal terror, *Antipode*, 48(4), 1122–1139.

Wall, T. and Monahan, T., 2011. Surveillance and violence from afar: The politics of drones and liminal security-scapes. *Theoretical Criminology*, 15, 239–254.

West, S.M., Whittaker, M., & Crawford, K. (2019). *Discriminating systems: Gender, race and power in AI.* AI Now Institute. Available at: https://ainowinstitute.org/discriminatingsystems.pdf [Accessed 19/01/2023].

While, A.H., Marvin, S., & Kovacic, M. (2021). Urban robotic experimentation: San Francisco, Tokyo and Dubai, *Urban Studies*, 58(4), 769–786.

Wilcox, L. (2017). Embodying algorithmic war: Gender, race, and the posthuman in drone warfare, *Security Dialogue*, 48(1), 11–28.

Williams, A.J. (2011). Enabling persistent presence? Performing the embodied geopolitics of the unmanned aerial vehicle assemblage, *Political Geography*, 30, 381–390.

Williams, J., & Massaro, V. (2013). Feminist geopolitics: Unpacking (in)security, animating social change, *Geopolitics*, 18(4), 751–758.

Yeo, S.J.I., & Lin, W. (2019). Autonomous vehicles, human agency and the potential of urban life, *Geography Compass*, 14(e12531), 1–12.

Yigitcanlar, T., & Cugurullo, F. (2020). The sustainability of Artificial Intelligence: An urbanistic viewpoint from the lens of smart and sustainable cities, *Sustainability 2020*, 12(8548), 1–24.

Zuboff, S. (2019). *The Age of Surveillance Capitalism: The Fight for a Human Future at the New Frontier of Power.* New York, USA, Public Affairs.

9

EXPLORING TEMPORAL PLEATS AND FOLDS

The role of urban AI and robotics in reinvigorating the cyborg city

Miguel Valdez, Matthew Cook and Stephen Potter

Introduction

Recent developments in AI and machine learning have made it possible to deploy robots in cities. Initial experiments already demonstrate considerable transformative potential as urban robots deliver technological capabilities and capacities beyond human abilities and existing infrastructural possibilities (While et al., 2021), automating and augmenting complex urban tasks that are unattractive, repetitive or labour intensive as well as those that are highly complex or dangerous (Macrorie et al., 2021). Such urban developments call for increased attention to the ways in which they become embedded in contingent configurations that include not only robots but also humans, institutions, infrastructures and the myriad of entities and encounters that constitute the urban (Macrorie et al., 2021; While et al., 2021). Drawing on case study research focused on grocery delivery robots in an urban setting, this chapter examines the cyborg urbanisms which emerge from the intensification of robotic and human interactions in unscripted, unpredictable urban contexts. As such, it contributes to a body of research on the highly contingent, spatially uneven and socially selective processes of robotic urban experimentation (While et al., 2021; Macrorie et al., 2021; Sumartojo and Lugli, 2021).

In 2020, the COVID-19 pandemic rendered simple tasks such as visiting the supermarket to shop for groceries unsafe due to the high risk of contagion. In Milton Keynes (a city located in South East England), the *Starship* robot grocery delivery service, became a safe way to complete this task, one which at the time was potentially too dangerous for humans to complete. Such disruptive events reveal aspects of urban life that would otherwise

DOI: 10.4324/9781003365877-11

remain invisible, with breakdowns bringing fleeting visibility to the complex practices and technologies that continuously bring urban life into being (Graham, 2010). In this instance, the impacts of COVID-19 and disruption to everyday life draw attention to renewed intensities of cyborg urbanism arising from robot–human interactions in certain urban contexts, with advances in AI and robotics reaching a threshold, anticipated by the founders of cybernetics, with the potential to transform urban life.

The case study of the Starship delivery robot service in the COVID-19 pandemic set out below interrogates the cybernetic, or rather cybernetic and organic (or cyborg) (re)configurations developing around urban robotics. It suggests that the presence of autonomous robots and their integration into the urban fabric has the potential to make cities more adaptable and better able to respond to unexpected shocks, as prefigured by early proponents of cyborg urbanism. However, it also suggests the presence of AI-driven robots is not by itself sufficient to produce such cyborg urbanisms. It requires an intensity of human–robot interactions through place-based processes of interfacing, learning and (re)configuration, with the moment of crisis potentially spurring the intensities required to transition to new ways of living with AI in the city.

New intensities of cyborg urbanism

Recent developments in urban robotics can be seen as renewed intensities of ways of thinking about humans and machines first developed in the context of the Second World War and further developed in the aftermath of the cold war. The foundations of cybernetics, established as scientists used feedback loops to chart missile trajectories, were later extended to systems with the ability to sense their environment and respond to changes to achieve and maintain a desired state (Wiener, 1954; Bowker, 1993). The notion of the cyborg, a cybernetically augmented organism with the ability to adapt to unpredictable and potentially dangerous environments, emerged in the context of the cold war and the space race (Clynes and Kline, 1960). As the cold war started to wind down, the notion of the cyborg was repurposed as a metaphor to draw attention to the increasingly blurred boundaries separating humans and machines (Haraway, 1991). Here, its application in urban contexts is of particular interest (Gandy, 2005). The notion of the cyborg became not so much a metaphor for understanding human–machine entanglements in urban contexts, but a diagram for prefiguring urban spaces as data flows to be sensed, visualized, modelled and scientifically optimized in real time (Marvin and Luque-Ayala, 2017).

Early attempts to bring cyborg urbanisms into practice were abandoned in the mid-1970s as the computing techniques imported from military operations proved ineffective in the urban domain (Marvin and Luque-Ayala,

2017), but recent advances in AI have renewed potential to transform cities and give rise to cyborg configurations. In the absence of AI, robots are comparable to the clockwork automata of the seventeenth century; incapable of making decisions of their own, their actions were entirely dictated by sequences fixed by humans beforehand (Wiener, 1948). Urban AIs are designed for learning, dealing with complex situations, making decisions on the basis of incomplete information, handling uncertainty and responding to changing situations in real time in pursuit of predetermined goals (Cugurullo, 2020), thus introducing a cybernetic dimension to the city. Consequently, aspects of urban life that were previously automated (i.e., following predetermined sequences, automaton-like) can now be adaptive and autonomous. Such transitions from the *automated* to the *autonomous* city (Cugurullo, 2020, 2021) are crucial but not sufficient to give rise to cyborg configurations in the city. When cybernetic machines are deployed in urban environments, which are unscripted, contingent and organic, the boundaries between cybernetic and organic systems are blurred. The interactions of autonomous robots and humans become entangled in the complex environment and systems that define urban life; there is increased potential for cities to behave as self-regulating, self-reconfiguring human–machine systems. In other words, cities may become cyborgs.

The cyborg, as an entity first envisioned in the context of the cold war, is defined by its ability to use cybernetic and organic elements to adapt to unpredictable, potentially hostile environments and maintain equilibrium and autonomous control (Clynes and Kline, 1960; Tomas, 1995). Here, we argue that developments of cyborg configurations at an urban level are not the result of linear advancements up a ladder of progress, but better understood as variations in intensity which, under certain conditions, may cross nonlinear critical thresholds. We draw on a topological, folded conception of history (Rosol, 2021; De Landa, 2000; Bingham and Thrift, 2000), where distant events, theories or practices can unexpectedly appear very near as time is folded like patterns on a folded handkerchief. The case study presented in this chapter suggests that unexpected shocks, such as the one caused by the COVID pandemic, create folds or connections linking the present time to the tensions and uncertainties of the wartime conditions that gave rise to the cyborg. Such tensions, in turn, provide the spark needed to intensify human–robot interactions and cross a boundary that goes beyond the autonomous city and into cyborg urbanisms.

Cyborg cities are defined by human–robot interaction in complex, unpredictable contexts. The cyber- prefix has been associated with various forms of virtuality (e.g., the *cyberspace*) but the idea of the cyborg is closely associated with situated knowledges, corporeal experiences of space and the underlying materialities of machines and humans (Haraway, 1991; Gandy, 2005). In this chapter, cyborg cities are investigated as places where humans and machines interface with each other, undergo processes of joint learning and distributed cognition as machines learn to be in the city and cities learn to live with the machines and, ultimately, we investigate cyborg cities in terms of the (re)configurations that take place as robots and humans become enmeshed in rapidly changing configurations.

To this end, the case study traces the introduction of Starship robots in MK starting in 2018 and the cybernetically enhanced response to the COVID pandemic in 2020 and 2021, particularly during the first lockdown in the UK.

Case study: humans and robots in complex times

Milton Keynes (MK) is a new town in England with a population of approximately 250,000 residents and located some 100 kilometres north of London. Starship robots were launched there in 2018 (Figure 9.1). Starship robots can transport up to 10 kilograms in a lockable cargo compartment, have a top speed of 6 km/h and can navigate urban environments autonomously,

FIGURE 9.1   A robot using MK's Redway network of cycle paths to navigate the city autonomously and deliver groceries to users of the Starship service from supermarkets or local businesses in their area.

Source: authors' original.

making them suitable for on-demand last-mile delivery services. The Starship service is organized around local hubs where the robots are loaded, recharged and cleaned when they return from a delivery.

Like so many other cities across the world, during the pandemic, MK was faced with a major disruption of key aspects of urban life including transport and food provision (Boons et al., 2021). The British population was instructed to stay home, non-essential shops and services were ordered to close and those at the highest risk of severe complications from COVID-19 were advised to follow shielding measures. Uncertainty regarding the duration of the stay-at-home orders and the capacity of supply chains to overcome the disruptions caused by the pandemic provided a rationale for consumers to build up their stocks of groceries and household supplies, engaging in what can be described as panic buying (O'Connell et al., 2021). Customers visiting supermarkets risked contagion, experienced long queues and found empty shelves. Online grocery delivery services were also affected by the disruption. Delivery drivers worked extended hours and supermarkets implemented virtual queueing systems but still struggled to cope with the sudden growth in demand (BBC News, 2021; DEFRA, 2020). Consequently, customers attempting to place an order would often face waiting times of several weeks before receiving their groceries (Hobbs, 2020). In contrast, Starship continued operations in MK during the pandemic with very little disruption. Although the service had not been specifically designed for that purpose, a robot-based service which avoided face-to-face contact proved to be well suited for delivering groceries to those housebound, shielding or self-isolating.

Analysis

Data collection supported by the Open University's Coronavirus rapid response fund focused on interviews with volunteers and representatives of community organizations supporting vulnerable populations during the crisis, as well as representatives from vulnerable groups. Researchers also engaged in socially distanced participant observation through various stages of the pandemic, paying attention to the interactions of robots, pedestrians, vehicles, pets and several other unpredictable elements that constitute the urban. The research also draws on a documentary corpus including newspaper articles, trade literature, policy documents and transcripts from policy debates in the United Kingdom, with some of the selected documents debating the introduction of robots in the urban realm and others debating their role in the response to the pandemic.

Data were analysed under themes emerging from iterative engagement between data and matters of concern identified in the developing agenda for research on urban AI and robotics (Macrorie et al., 2021; While et al., 2021; Yigitcanlar and Cugurullo, 2020; Fourcade and Johns, 2020; Hasse, 2019).

Theme selection was informed by a relational sensitivity to the urban geographies of robotic and autonomous systems and as such attention was centred on the place-based interactions of humans, robots and urban configurations. Specifically, the remainder of the case study interrogates the situated interactions of robots and humans and their joint response to a crisis in terms of the following themes: *Encounters and interfaces, Learning machines and distributed cognition* and *(Re)configurations*. A discussion of the ultimate effects and outcomes of the resulting (re)configurations is then presented as a conclusion to the case study.

Encounters and interfaces

Urban robots must negotiate complex environments, balancing the demands of their assigned tasks with the rights of other users of the public realm (While et al., 2021). Consequently, cities where robots are deployed become places for meaningful encounters which are contingent and take place in contexts where neither humans nor robots can know precisely what will happen next. Such encounters give rise to unscripted forms of human–machine interfacing that make urban robots parts of 'emergent assemblages more than stable entities' (Bissell and Del Casino, 2017: 439; quoted in Sumartojo and Lugli, 2021). Here, the word 'interface' is used in a broad sense, referring to any point where two entities meet and interact, as human–robot interactions are not exclusively or even predominantly directed by the on-screen interfaces of the computer or mobile phone applications through which robots might be controlled. Humans and robots may interface with each other physically, for instance, as well as affectively, developing trust and understanding which allow them to effectively share an urban environment – or failing to do so (Sumartojo and Lugli, 2021). With each encounter between humans and robots, meanings about automation and technology are (re)created (Yeo and Lin, 2020).

In the case of MK, the nature of those encounters was inflected by the suburban population density and by the extensive network of segregated pedestrian footpaths of the new town, which were relatively safe and easy for AIs to navigate (CMK Town Council, 2018). The impact of physical context on human–robot interfacing may be best understood by contrast with studies regarding the use of delivery robots in more dense urban centres. Low-density footpaths such as those available in MK make it possible for people to make their way around robots when they stop, as they often do when faced with an unexpected situation. However, if a robot were to stop in a crowded pavement in London or a sidewalk in New York, it would cause considerable aggravation and risk for pedestrians (Salvini et al., 2021). Classical mapping and navigation algorithms are considered insufficient for safe operation of robots around pedestrians in dense urban settings, which are likely to require consideration of the sometimes random and sometimes linear flows of pedestrians (Du et al., 2019). This is important so that robots can learn to either "go with the flow" or "get out of the way," as well as understand the social and psychological constraints on pedestrian behaviour and existing cultural conventions of behaviour in public space (Bera et al., 2017; Woo et al., 2020).

The current generation of urban robots has a limited ability to interface with humans when faced with an unscripted encounter – they can adjust their routes around them as if they were obstacles to be avoided but they cannot engage with them in a more meaningful way as they lack understanding of their psychology or the conventions of human space. However, this does not prevent the formation of impactful (even if one-sided) affective interfaces. The low density of MK, which is comparable to that of suburban areas of larger cities, made it possible for pedestrians to adapt to the behaviour of the robots, which can be seen as non-threatening, helpful, friendly and endearing even as they occasionally struggled to complete their assigned task (Sumartojo et al., 2021). As the wide footpaths of MK make it easy for robots and pedestrians to coexist, Starship notes that 70% of pedestrians do not pay any attention to the robots, with most of the rest of street-goers reacting positively to them (Jennings and Figliozzi, 2019). Consequently, the robots were rapidly accepted by users in MK and they were considered part of its everyday life, as even non-users would often see them making their way along pavements or footpaths and kids would try to pet them or feed them (Hamilton, 2021).

Having briefly discussed how humans and robots can interface through computer and mobile phone applications and also through social or parasocial interfaces, physical interfaces also merit brief discussion. Urban robots are also material artefacts and in the case of grocery deliveries users are required to physically interface with them – that is, to unlock the hatch, reach in, unload the robot and close the hatch. Although such a basic physical interface may seem simple and self-explanatory it can also constitute a barrier for some potential users, as may also be the case regarding digital interfaces. Such exclusions, which became more impactful in the context of the pandemic, will be further discussed later in this chapter.

Learning machines and distributed cognition

AI is strongly associated with machine learning. Deployments of urban AI have predominantly followed experimental logics designed to facilitate learning by the robots themselves, which are increasingly driven by neural networks as necessary for engaging with an uncertain environment that cannot be possibly apprehended in formal rules (Stilgoe, 2018). Cognition is the defining characteristic of AI. Specifically, to be considered as such an artificial intelligence must have the ability to learn, acquire information from its environment, make sense of it and make decisions under uncertain, unpredictable conditions without human supervision (Cugurullo, 2020; Yigitcanlar and Cugurullo, 2020). Robots such as the Starship fleet are intelligent enough to make decisions and act without supervision in complex urban environments, but only within very specific domains – determining and executing complex routes and optimizing the operations of a robot fleet. As such, when the robots are considered in isolation, they can be classified as possessing *artificial narrow intelligence*, the AI level that current technologies can provide (Yigitcanlar and Cugurullo, 2020). However, the case study suggests that the social–robotic symbiosis has learning capabilities that greatly exceed those of robots alone. Organizations and collectives also learn, including collectives that include human and non-human, artificially intelligent actors. Social and collective learning must therefore be analysed as co-productive of one another (Fourcade and Johns, 2020; Hasse, 2019).

In a narrow sense, the autonomous operation of the Starship robots relies on machine learning through neural networks (Pärnamaa, 2018) which allows them to navigate their surroundings, detect real-time changes (including the change of traffic lights as well as the movement of pedestrians and cars) and adapt to major changes in their environment (e.g., road closures or new constructions). Computations that need a rapid response are performed onboard, while those that are less time-sensitive are offloaded to servers in the cloud (Kosonen, 2020). Starship's neural networks learn from data collected in the course of everyday operations as each individual robot encounters and processes new situations. However, the learning process becomes collective as robots pool their knowledge to create a unified 3D map of a given area, which they use to identify and navigate the shortest and safest path between their hub and their destinations. Collective artificial intelligence is also used to orchestrate fleet operations – deciding which robot should do which delivery based on predictions about the expected demand, the availability of robots and the expected battery state after each journey (Kosonen, 2020). The presence of a collective AI became crucial during the pandemic as, supported by rapid social learning, it facilitated a rapid reconfiguration to be discussed in the following section. New additions to the fleet could be readily connected to the servers storing the aggregated navigational knowledge of the collective intelligence and could be readily handled by the AI system orchestrating fleet operations.

(Re)configurations

The notion of cyborg urbanism draws attention to the intensification of dependence and coevolution between urban societies and urban technological networks. Deployments of urban robots are predominantly driven by experimental logics specifically designed to investigate alternate sociotechnical futures and disrupt sociotechnical configurations (While et al., 2021). The introduction of robots in MK was explicitly experimental, as is often the case in cities where robots are deployed to prefigure alternate sociotechnical futures and disrupt sociotechnical configurations (ibid). When Starship delivery services were first envisioned, the legal status of unaccompanied autonomous robots in urban environments was unclear owing to a lack of regulations and legal precedent (Ackerman, 2015). The company sought to cultivate connections with industry bodies, becoming embedded within the autonomous and connected vehicle community in the UK as well as with innovation-friendly local authorities (Pinsent Masons, 2021), leading to the deployment of Starship robots in MK in 2018. Local authorities in MK were willing to work with a new technology which they acknowledged was not yet fully proven because they considered that it had the potential to support their economic goals (reinforcing the position of MK as a smart test-bed and its connection to technology industries and capitals) and they also had transformative aspirations – they considered that the introduction of robots would support their environmental goals by reducing car dependency, with users ordering robot deliveries instead of driving to the shops (Milton Keynes Council, 2018).

The various aspirations driving the acceptance of urban robots by local authorities in MK illustrate how such experiments can potentially transform urban life, but may also sustain existing configurations and reaffirm the dominance of existing interests deliberately or accidentally. Although urban robots can transform the city, they can also be used to give it continuity by repairing or optimizing urban activities (Yeo and Lin, 2020; Macrorie et al., 2021). That is illustrated by the role played by Starship robots during the global pandemic, when they functioned as automated infrastructure. Such deployments of urban AI are often associated with a logic that seeks to minimize disruption, increase efficiency and optimize network capacity. The cybernetic nature of such developments is applied to manage urban flows and processes with minimal human agency (Macrorie et al., 2021).

Even before the pandemic, the introduction of robots sought to reconfigure the links between grocery deliveries, transport and human labour, although the pandemic altered the rationale for the reconfiguration. Before the pandemic, the rationale was mainly economic. In terms of speed and carbon footprint, the robots' performance is comparable to that of bicycle couriers but they are expected to cost 10–15 times less than other last-mile delivery alternatives when deployed at scale (Ackerman, 2015; London Assembly, 2017). COVID-19 made it so that it was desirable to reduce the role of humans not only for economic reasons but also to avoid face-to-face contact and reduce the risk of contagion.

Company executives state that the number of orders doubled virtually overnight, and the fleet was working non-stop 14 hours a day (Shirbon, 2020), but the service remained able to offer same-day deliveries. A decision was made to expand the coverage and capacity of the service as quickly as possible, so that the number of robots available for deliveries in Milton Keynes doubled from 30 at the beginning of the pandemic in March 2020 to 70 by April and 100 by July of the same year. The 300% increase in capacity achieved during the first weeks of the lockdown in MK demonstrated that the mix of cybernetic and organic characteristics of the robotic autonomous system can facilitate very rapid reconfigurations. Such a rapid transformation would have been difficult or downright unfeasible for car-based and human-based services on account of the cost and difficulty of acquiring new vehicles in the middle of a pandemic which was severely affecting supply chains in addition to the difficulties in recruiting and training staff on a short notice. The Starship programme in MK was partially attributable to a fortuitous contingency: outside of MK, Starship robots were predominantly deployed in campus settings that acted as innovation precincts (Dowling and McGuirk, 2022). As universities closed due to the pandemic, robots became available and could be redeployed to MK. However, as the preceding section revealed, the characteristics of urban AI also played a crucial role in making such rapid reconfigurations possible.

Outcomes: towards the cyborg city

The preceding sections of the case study interrogate the processes, relations and affects through which a robotic system transformed the urban fabric and was transformed by it. Here, we investigate the effects (some temporary, some lasting and some unevenly distributed) that the robotic system had as it contributed to the response to the crisis, as well as the effect that the moment of crisis had on the system. As discussed in the introduction to this case study, factors including supply-chain disruptions, panic buying and the increased risk of contagion associated with grocery shopping during the early days of the pandemic greatly increased the demand for robot deliveries in MK. Consequently, the size of the Starship fleet increased through accelerated (re)configuration and learning processes. Before the crisis began, the Starship fleet in MK had 30 robots and had completed 100,000 deliveries in two years of operation. Six months into the pandemic, the fleet was expanded to 100 robots, and, one year into the pandemic, 1.5 million deliveries had been completed. The expansion reflected the framing of robot deliveries as one of the most reliable ways to protect vulnerable populations and enable social distancing during the COVID-19 pandemic (Starship, 2021). The disruption to online grocery deliveries caused by COVID-19 was particularly problematic for vulnerable individuals including older adults, people with underlying health conditions or those less able to move (Hobbs, 2020), who often rely on home deliveries to remain independent (Jesus et al., 2021). Individuals with disabilities and those in high-risk groups were often unable to secure deliveries despite attempts by supermarkets to allocate additional priority slots (Gleason et al., 2020). Consequently, 55% of disabled adults surveyed by the Office for National Statistics reported difficulties accessing groceries, medication and essentials and approximately 8% of the adults in the UK advised to self-isolate experience food insecurity directly attributable to isolation (Loopstra, 2020; Office for National Statistics, 2020) – this included vulnerable people who were not considered vulnerable enough to receive government or community support, as well as people who officially qualified for assistance but struggled to secure it (Eskytė et al., 2020).

Even before the crisis, local authorities in MK had anticipated that robots would be useful for providing deliveries to households that suffered from reduced personal mobility (Milton Keynes Council, 2018), a view supported by commercial partners (Co-op, 2020), investors (Lienert and Lee, 2020) and disability support groups (Disability Horizons, 2020). However, the benefits provided by the robots were not evenly distributed. The emergency exacerbated and gave relief to the potential role of urban robots in either challenging or inadvertently reinforcing inequality. This suggests that the emerging cyborg city is at risk of reproducing or reinforcing various forms of inequality, fragmentation, splintering and injustice as noted by urbanists and geographers who have investigated smart and cybernetic cities (e.g., Odendaal, 2021; Clark, 2020; Martin et al., 2018; Krivý, 2018). Such inequalities were present to some degree in MK according to interviews with local community organizations and support groups. Spatial inequalities were present because the robots were only available in selected areas of MK, with a tendency to cover more affluent areas and neglect those that were more marginalized.

Additionally, many members of vulnerable or marginalized groups, such as those subsisting on a disability allowance, would not be able to pay the delivery fee on a regular basis. Other vulnerable individuals who would have liked to rely on the robots during the pandemic were unable to use them because they were not able to use the mobile phone application, as was the case, for example, for less tech-savvy older adults or for the visually impaired. Vulnerable populations are often less connected to the Internet and less able to use online resources, particularly if they are older, have lower incomes or live alone (Gleason et al., 2020; Eskytė et al., 2020). The robots are also unsuitable for some users with physical and mobility impairments. For instance, wheelchair users found it difficult to reach and unload the robot.

The limitations discussed above indicate that robots are not suitable as sole responders to crisis events. In addition to their limitations and the inequalities that their use may introduce, artificially intelligent robots are likely to introduce new vulnerabilities. Urban robots, like other urban systems that rely on networked computation, are subject to malfunction as well as to forms of vandalism, disruption and criminal exploitation that risk making city infrastructures insecure and brittle (Kitchin and Dodge, 2019). However, even if the robots could not single-handedly address the crisis, they usefully complemented MK's response to it and increased its ability to cope. Resourceful communities can better respond to disaster events as they have more tools to come up with solutions (Zona et al., 2020; MacKinnon and Derickson, 2013), and, in the case of MK, a fleet of intelligent robots became a valuable resource with distinct benefits and limitations best understood in the context of a multi-faceted response. Various initiatives and responses by governmental, commercial and community organizations demonstrated distinct capabilities, strengths and weaknesses and served (or failed to serve) distinct groups at various points through the crisis. Although the safety network provided by robots was not equally available to everyone who would have needed it, it had the distinct advantage of being able to adapt and respond to an unexpected situation in real time, thus providing a crucial safety net during the early weeks of the pandemic when many vulnerable individuals experienced food insecurity.

In contrast, national and local authorities were not well suited to take rapid action when faced with an unprecedented situation. Weeks after the beginning of the lockdown, local authorities were still waiting for guidance from the national government and did not have access to the full lists of people identified as extremely vulnerable in their area. Community and volunteer organizations were also largely caught by surprise by the rapidly changing situation. Interviews with MK-based volunteers confirm that some organizations were able to respond in a matter of days but for others, it was a matter of weeks before they could adapt to the new situation and provide safe and effective support to those who needed it. Volunteer and community organizations benefited from their pre-existing knowledge of vulnerable individuals and were able to reach and support people that robots could not reach, but they could not easily identify and reach people who had not considered themselves vulnerable before the pandemic. People with manageable health conditions (e.g., immune deficiencies, asthma) who were able to live independently under ordinary circumstances unexpectedly found themselves vulnerable, housebound and unfamiliar with the support networks that could have helped them, but many of them were able to rely on the autonomous robot delivery system.

It must be noted that the rapid growth of the robot fleet was sparked by the crisis but outlasted it. The increased demand for on-demand grocery deliveries persisted after the end of the crisis, with the company planning to expand the total fleet across the UK to 500 robots across seven towns and cities by the end of 2022. Although some users declared that they tried the robots because they were simply attracted by the novelty of the service and many others first tried the robot in the context of the crisis, in the end, the service became habitual for a number of users who appreciated the convenience. Here, robots begin to demonstrate transformative potential by eroding car dependency in the city (a fact the company advertised during the fuel shortages of 2021). The company estimates that approximately 70% of its deliveries replace a car journey, so by the end of 2021 robots in MK had replaced approximately 280,000 journeys and avoided emissions equivalent to 500,000 miles.

Conclusions

In this chapter we have examined the renewed intensity of robot–human interactions in unpredictable urban contexts through the lens of cyborg urbanism. To this end, we have presented a case study tracing the contingent (re)configurations of robots, humans, institutions and infrastructures in the context of the COVID-19 pandemic and the ensuing lockdown. Thus, the case study draws attention to two salient aspects of the cyborg. First, the case study reveals that autonomous robots became part of urban configurations better able to adapt and respond to unpredictable and potentially hostile conditions. Second, it highlights how such benefits were not attributable to the robots alone but emerged from the symbiosis between humans and robots. The presence of AI-driven robots was not in itself sufficient to produce such urban cyborg configurations. Just as Frankenstein's monster was brought to life by a lightning bolt, the cyborg appears to gain renewed intensity when times of crisis provide a galvanizing spark. Here, the emergence of the cyborg city is seen not as a linear trajectory but as a non-linear fluctuation of intensities, a folded or crumpled time, with crises linking the present to the times of war and uncertainty in which cyborgs were originally conceived. Artificial intelligence is progressing linearly or perhaps even exponentially but even the relatively narrow AI powering the Starship robots proved to be enough to give rise to cyborg configurations as the crisis encouraged a symbiosis and intensified the encounters between humans and robots and the shared processes of learning, with the disruption to everyday life making reconfiguration necessary and spurring the intensities required to transition to new ways of living with AI in the city.

Although the case study discussed in this chapter is centred on the response to the COVID-19 pandemic, other urban crises may be expected and thus robots can be expected to play ever-increasing roles in crisis responses (Yigitcanlar et al., 2020). For instance, global climate change is causing increasingly unpredictable extreme weather events including, for example, floods, blizzards, storms and heat waves (Figure 9.2). In consequence, cities need a large array of options for coping with the unexpected (Roe, 2020). Starship robots were able to continue in operation during the major weather disruption caused by Storm Emma in 2018 (Pärnamaa, 2018; Morris et al., 2018) and were also advertised as a petrol-saving alternative to a shopping trip in response to the petrol shortages of 2021.

FIGURE 9.2   Starship robots have been tested in challenging weather conditions including rain, snow and ice.

Source: authors' original.

As robots were collectively learning how to become urban, an unexpected shock tested their ability to apply what they had learnt to deal with a suddenly changed world. The resulting urban (re)configuration can be seen as confirmation of a familiar pattern, as the relationship between disruption, shock and innovation is well-known in the literature (e.g., Van de Ven et al., 2000; Bessant et al., 2015). However, what is unexpected is the speed of the response. Robots adapted to the crisis in a matter of days or even hours, drawing attention to the cybernetic principles of real-time adaption to unpredictable environments (Tomas, 1995; Wiener, 1948). Here, real-time adaption depended on the mutual *attunement* of artificial intelligences and urban processes. Robots were able to support the city during a crisis because they were already embedded in its infrastructures, institutions and practices. In the case of MK, the robots' ability to respond and adapt in real time was only possible because the robots were already part of the urban system, thus increasing their cybernetic capabilities. When COVID-19 threatened to disrupt key urban functions in MK, the autonomous robot system could readily repair some urban flows because it was already embedded in them and trained to self-organize and maintain efficient operations in changing circumstances. Also, importantly, local authorities, users and other members of the extended constellations needed to sustain the system were already familiar with it. In the case of MK, the embeddedness required to make robots effective in times of crisis was only possible because the autonomous robot system was not designed or framed as a disaster-response mechanism. The robots were part of a useful everyday infrastructure, and they were also considered part of the unique culture of the city and seen as members of a human–robot community that proved to be surprisingly adaptable when faced with unprecedented times.

However, as the case study reveals, the deployment of urban robots has transformative potentials that go well beyond the cybernetic optimization and maintenance of urban flows in times of crisis. Emergent configurations and contingent encounters of humans, robots, spaces, infrastructures and institutions (re)configure the city as 'new technologies become enrolled into complex, contingent and subtle blendings of human actors and technical artifacts' (Graham, 1998: 167, quoted in Yeo and Lin, 2020). When the collective intelligence of Starship's "hive mind" and the institutions around it had to reframe their knowledges to cope with a world that changed seemingly overnight, the disruption proved to be revelatory of broader issues about how robots learn to be in cities and about the boundaries and interfaces between cybernetic and human networks in the city, thus bringing into sharp relief the easily neglected processes through which urban robotics sustains some aspects of urban life and challenges others.

References

Ackerman, E. (2015). *Startup Developing Autonomous Delivery Robots That Travel on Sidewalks*. Available at: https://spectrum.ieee.org/automaton/robotics/industrial-robots/starship-technologies-autonomous-ground-delivery-robots [Accessed 19/01/2023].

BBC News. (2021). *Supermarket websites struggle amid new lockdown*. Available at: https://www.bbc.co.uk/news/business-55540485 [Accessed 19/01/2023].

Bera, A., Randhavane, T., Prinja, R., & Manocha, D. (2017). Sociosense: Robot navigation amongst pedestrians with social and psychological constraints. *2017 IEEE/RSJ International Conference on Intelligent Robots and Systems (IROS)*, 7018–7025.

Bessant, J., Rush, H., & Trifilova, A. (2015). Crisis-driven innovation: The case of humanitarian innovation. *International Journal of Innovation Management*, 19(6), 1540014.

Bingham, N., & Thrift, N. (2000). The geography of Bruno Latour and Michel Serres. In M. Crang & N.J. Thrift (Eds.), *Thinking space*, Routledge, London, 281–301.

Bissell, D., & Del Casino, V. J. (2017). Whither labor geography and the rise of the robots? *Social & Cultural Geography*, 18(3), 435–442.

Boons, F., Doherty, B., Köhler, J., Papachristos, G., & Wells, P. (2021). Disrupting transitions: Qualitatively modelling the impact of Covid-19 on UK food and mobility provision. *Environmental Innovation and Societal Transitions*, 40, 1–19.

Bowker, G. (1993). How to be universal: Some cybernetic strategies, 1943–70. *Social Studies of Science*, 23(1), 107–127.

Clark, J. (2020). *Uneven innovation: The work of smart cities*. Columbia University Press, New York.

Clynes, M. E., & Kline, N. S. (1960). Cyborgs and space. *Astronautics*, 14(9), 26–27.

CMK Town Council. (2018). *Have you seen a Starship?* Available at: http://cmktown council.gov.uk/cmk-news/have-you-seen-a-starship/ [Accessed 19/01/2023].

Co-op. (2020). *Rise of the robots as Co-op and Starship roll-out autonomous delivery expansion*. Available at: https://www.co-operative.coop/media/news-releases/rise-of-the-robots-as-co-op-and-starship-roll-out-autonomous-delivery [Accessed 19/01/2023].

Cugurullo, F. (2020). Urban Artificial Intelligence: From automation to autonomy in the smart city. *Frontiers in Sustainable Cities*, 2(38), 1–14.

Cugurullo, F. (2021). *Frankenstein Urbanism: Eco, smart and autonomous cities, artificial intelligence and the end of the city*. Routledge, London.

De Landa, M. (2000). *A thousand years of nonlinear history*. Swerve Editions, New York.

Department for Environment, Food and Rural Affairs. (2020). *New measures on night time deliveries to supermarkets to support coronavirus response*. Available at: https://www.gov.uk/government/news/new-measures-on-night-time-deliveries-to-supermarkets-to-support-coronavirus-response [Accessed 19/01/2023].

Disability Horizons. (2020). *Coronavirus shopping safely: how to get your food if you're disabled*. Available at: https://disabilityhorizons.com/2020/04/coronavirus-uk-how-to-get-your-food-shopping-if-youre-disabled-people/ [Accessed 19/01/2023].

Dowling, R. & McGuirk, P. (2022). Autonomous vehicle experiments and the city. *Urban Geography*, 43(3), 409–426.

Du, Y., Hetherington, N., Oon, C. L., Chan, W., Quintero, C. P., Croft, E., & Loos, H. M. (2019). Group surfing: A pedestrian-based approach to sidewalk robot navigation. *2019 International Conference on Robotics and Automation (ICRA)*, IEEE, 6518–6524.

Eskytė, I., Lawson, A., Orchard, M., & Andrews, E. (2020). Out on the streets–crisis, opportunity and disabled people in the era of Covid-19: Reflections from the UK. *Alter*, 14(4), 329–336.

Fourcade, M., & Johns, F. (2020). Loops, ladders and links: The recursivity of social and machine learning. *Theory and Society*, 49(5), 803–832.

Gandy, M. (2005). Cyborg urbanization: Complexity and monstrosity in the contemporary city. *International Journal of Urban and Regional Research*, 29(1), 26–49.

Gleason, C., Valencia, S., Kirabo, L., Wu, J., Guo, A., Carter, E., Bigham, J., Bennett, C., Pavel, A. (2020). Disability and the COVID-19 pandemic: Using Twitter to understand accessibility during rapid societal transition. *The 22nd International ACM SIGACCESS Conference on Computers and Accessibility*, 1–14.

Graham, S. (1998). The end of geography or the explosion of place? Conceptualizing space, place and information technology. *Progress in Human Geography*, 22(2), 165–185.

Graham, S. (2010). *Disrupted cities: When infrastructure fails*. New York: Routledge.

Hamilton, I. A. (2021). *Food delivery company Starship Technologies has enjoyed explosive growth during the pandemic. It doesn't mind that kids are feeding its robots bananas*. Available at: https://www.businessinsider.com/starship-technologies-finds-kids-feeding-its-robots-bananas-2021-1?r=US&IR=T [Accessed 19/01/2023].

Haraway, D. (1991). *Simians, cyborgs, and women*. Routledge, New York.

Hasse, C. (2019). Posthuman learning: AI from novice to expert? *AI & Society*, 34(2), 355–364.

Hobbs, J. (2020). Food supply chains during the COVID-19 pandemic. *Journal of Agricultural Economics/Revue canadienne d'agroeconomie*, 68(2), 171–176.

Jennings, D., & Figliozzi, M. (2019). Study of sidewalk autonomous delivery robots and their potential impacts on freight efficiency and travel. *Transportation Research Record*, 2673(6), 317–326.

Jesus, T., Bhattacharjya, S., Papadimitriou, C., Bogdanova, Y., Bentley, J., Arango-Lasprilla, J. C., & Kamalakannan, S. (2021). Lockdown-Related Disparities Experienced by People with Disabilities during the First Wave of the COVID-19 Pandemic: Scoping Review with Thematic Analysis. *International Journal of Environmental Research and Public Health*, 18(12), 6178.

Kitchin, R., & Dodge, M. (2019). The (in) security of smart cities: Vulnerabilities, risks, mitigation, and prevention. *Journal of Urban Technology*, 26(2), 47–65.

Kosonen, P. (2020, December 3). *Autonomous robots out in the wild – a software engineering challenge*. Available at: https://medium.com/starshiptechnologies/running-autonomous-robots-on-city-streets-is-very-much-a-software-engineering-challenge-66927869090a [Accessed 19/01/2023].

Krivý, M. (2018). Towards a critique of cybernetic urbanism: The smart city and the society of control. *Planning Theory*, 17(1), 8–30.

Lienert, P., & Lee, J. (2020). *Automated delivery cashes in on pandemic-driven demand. Reuters*. Available at: https://www.reuters.com/article/us-health-coronavirus-delivery-robots-fo-idUKKBN22U1F8 [Accessed 19/01/2023].

London Assembly. (2017). *Transport Committee – Transcript of Agenda Item 6 – Future Transport*. Available at: https://www.london.gov.uk/about-us/londonassembly/meetings/documents/s66365/Appendix%201%20-%20transcript%20of%20item%206.pdf [Accessed 19/01/2023].

Loopstra, R. (2020). *Vulnerability to food insecurity since the COVID-19 lockdown – Preliminary report*. Available at: https://foodfoundation.org.uk/wp-content/uploads/2020/04/Report_COVID19FoodInsecurity-final.pdf [Accessed 19/01/2023].

MacKinnon, D., & Derickson, K. D. (2013). From resilience to resourcefulness: A critique of resilience policy and activism. *Progress in Human Geography*, 37(2), 253–270.

Macrorie, R., Marvin, S., & While, A. (2021). Robotics and automation in the city: A research agenda. *Urban Geography*, 42(2), 197–217.

Martin, C. J., Evans, J., & Karvonen, A. (2018). Smart and sustainable? Five tensions in the visions and practices of the smart-sustainable city in Europe and North America. *Technological Forecasting and Social Change*, 133, 269–278.

Marvin, S., & Luque-Ayala, A. (2017). Urban operating systems: Diagramming the city. *International Journal of Urban and Regional Research*, 41(1), 84–103.

Milton Keynes Council. (2018). *Minutes of the meeting of the cabinet held on 6 March 2018*, made available by MKC democratic services. Milton Keynes: MKC.

Morris, S., Weaver, M., & Khomami, N. (2018). Beast from the East meets storm Emma, causing UK's worst weather in years. *The Guardian*.

O'Connell, M., Paula, A. D. & Smith, K. (2021). Preparing for a pandemic: Spending dynamics and panic buying during the COVID-19 first wave. *Fiscal Studies*, 42(2), 249–264.

Odendaal, N. (2021). Everyday urbanisms and the importance of place: Exploring the elements of the emancipatory smart city. *Urban Studies*, 58(3), 639–654.

Office for National Statistics. (2020). *Coronavirus and the social impacts on disabled people in Great Britain*. Available at: https://www.ons.gov.uk/peoplepopulation andcommunity/healthandsocialcare/disability/articles/coronavirusandthesocialim pactsondisabledpeopleingreatbritain/may2020 [Accessed 19/01/2023].

Pärnamaa, T. (2018). *How Neural Networks Power Robots at Starship*. Available at: https://medium.com/starshiptechnologies/how-neural-networks-power-robots-at-starship-3262cd317ec0 [Accessed 19/01/2023].

Pinsent Masons. (2021). *Case Study – Paving the way for autonomous last-mile delivery*. Available at: https://www.pinsentmasons.com/thinking/case-studies/paving-the-way-for-autonomous-last-mile-delivery [Accessed 19/01/2023].

Roe, E. (2020). Control, manage or cope? A politics for risks, uncertainties and unknown-unknowns. In E. Roe (Ed.), *The politics of uncertainty*, Routledge, London, 73–84.

Rosol, C. (2021). Time Depth: Jean Epstein, Michel Serres and operational model time. In G. Dürbeck, & P. Hüpkes (Eds.), *Narratives of scale in the Anthropocene*, Taylor & Francis, New York, 55–72.

Salvini, P., Paez-Granados, D., & Billard, A. (2021). Safety concerns emerging from robots navigating in crowded pedestrian areas. *International Journal of Social Robotics*, 14, 441–462.

Shirbon, E. (2020). *These robots are delivering groceries to UK doorsteps in the pandemic*. Available at: https://www.weforum.org/agenda/2020/04/robots-united-kingdom-uk-coronavirus-covid19-ai [Accessed 19/01/2023].

Starship. (2021). *Starship Technologies Advances Adoption of Autonomous Delivery as Demand Quadruples in The Last Year*. Available at: https://www.starship.xyz/ press_releases/starship-technologies-advances-adoption-of-autonomous-delivery-as-demand-quadruples-in-the-last-year/ [Accessed 19/01/2023].

Stilgoe, J. (2018). Machine learning, social learning and the governance of self-driving cars. *Social Studies of Science*, 48(1), 25–56.

Sumartojo, S., & Lugli, D. (2021). Lively robots: robotic technologies COVID-19. *Social & Cultural Geography*. doi:10.1080/14649365.2021.1921245.

Sumartojo, S., Lundberg, R., Tian, L., Carreno-Medrano, P., Kulić, D., & Mintrom, M. (2021). Imagining public space robots of the near-future. *Geoforum*, 124, 99–109.

Tomas, D. (1995). Feedback and cybernetics: Reimaging the body in the age of the cyborg. *Body & Society*, 1(3–4), 21–43.

Van de Ven, A. H., Angle, H. L., & Poole, M. S. (Eds.). (2000). *Research on the management of innovation: The Minnesota studies*. Oxford University Press, Oxford.

While, A., Marvin, S., & Kovacic, M. (2021). Urban robotic experimentation: San Francisco, Tokyo and Dubai. *Urban Studies*, 58(4), 769–786.

Wiener, N. (1948). *Cybernetics, or control and communication in the animal and machine*. MIT Press, Cambridge, MA.

Wiener, N. (1954). *The human use of human beings: Cybernetics and society.* Houghton Mifflin, Boston.

Woo, J., Whittington, J., & Arkin, R. (2020). Urban robotics: Achieving autonomy in design and regulation of robots and cities. *Connecticut Law Review*, 52, 319.

Yeo, S. J., & Lin, W. (2020). Autonomous vehicles, human agency and the potential of urban life. *Geography Compass*, 14(10), e12531.

Yigitcanlar, T., & Cugurullo, F. (2020). The sustainability of artificial intelligence: An urbanistic viewpoint from the lens of smart and sustainable cities. *Sustainability*, 12(20), 8548.

Yigitcanlar, T., Butler, L., Windle, E., Desouza, K. C., Mehmood, R., & Corchado, J. M. (2020). Can building "artificially intelligent cities" safeguard humanity from natural disasters, pandemics, and other catastrophes? An urban scholar's perspective. *Sensors*, 20(10), 2988.

Zona, A., Kammouh, O., & Cimellaro, G. P. (2020). Resourcefulness quantification approach for resilient communities and countries. *International Journal of Disaster Risk Reduction*, 46, 101509.

10

ROBOTS IN AI URBANISM

Shanti Sumartojo

Introduction

In this chapter, I consider how robotic technologies come together with AI urbanism, the proposition that artificial intelligence is agential and even autonomous in shaping how our cities work and, in turn, how we can inhabit them. Taking up the theme of the book, I concur that we need to move past existing discourses of 'smart urbanism' to consider how AI-driven technologies actually articulate. This means locating AI in our cities, identifying where it is at work and how it touches the lives of people and the possibilities it opens up for researching the urban experiential world. It also means exploring how digital platforms such as robots are exercising new forms of agency, and autonomously organizing urban rhythms and networks. I argue that we need new analytical approaches to understand this, and to complicate the promise and problems of the implementation of AI in urban settings.

To advance these approaches, I reflect on how robots materialize the AI algorithmic networks and logics that are permeating our cities but also consider the everyday compromises, glitches and frictions that may occur as this shift takes hold – or how robots can reveal the roles and presence of AI-driven technologies in the ways that everyday life emerges. I treat robots as physical machines animated by computational processes that can sense and act apparently autonomously in their physical and material surroundings, and that are now part of our everyday lives for a range of purposes. However, and as I will discuss, as an example of how AI materializes, the spatial effects of these machines can exceed and escape what their designers intend. It is precisely because of their physical and material presence, and the contingencies that this presence highlights, that they provide a useful example to think about AI urbanism.

DOI: 10.4324/9781003365877-12

In the first half of the chapter, I explain how I understand robots, how this connects to ideas in AI urbanism and two foundational concepts that my own explorations of robots are in constant dialogue with *emergence* and *atmospheres*. This sets up the second half of the chapter, where I build an argument that robots can confound and extend our understandings of AI infrastructures with their agential capacities and "thingy" qualities. Here, I explore some of the ways that robots both operate *in* and are exemplars *of* AI urbanism and show how robots and AI urbanism might come together. To do so, I propose three principles for thinking about the integration of robots into our cities. These seek to move beyond the fantasy of seamless, auto-mated life that promoters of smart cities would have us believe, and instead adopt a more critical, but hopefully productive, perspective. These principles are: robotic contexts, robotic relationalities and robotic messiness.

Defining and conceptualizing robots

The term 'robot' has been stretched to include many different types of digital autonomous technologies. Often driven by algorithms that make decisions and accumulate knowledge about the world as they act, 'bots' now chat with us online, scan legal documents for any mistakes and examine financial trans-actions for anomalies that could signal fraud. Robots are, as Del Casino et al. (2020: 611) argue, 'increasingly becoming woven into and thus helping to create, our complex, continuously evolving, and contingent socio-spatial realities.' In this chapter, however, I am interested in robots defined as machines that have a material presence in the world and operate in ways that people can directly observe or otherwise sense. This allows me to consider their material and spatial effects, and focus my arguments on the physical world where they touch peoples' lives. Lynch (2021: 2) proposes that social robots, machines that are specifically designed for human interaction, help to produce distinctive spatialities because they can 'produce new kinds of spa-tial data at the embodied scale and perspective of the robot situated in a spatial environment.' He prompts us to reconsider spatiality by adopting the perspective of an individual robot and by considering the data it creates and uses to move through its surroundings. This zooms in from the datafied over-view often produced by AI-driven technologies, such as the analysis of multi-ple data points collected at the city level that are aimed at quantifying a particular activity, like urban traffic patterns or energy consumption rates at the metropolitan scale. Instead, the treatment of robots as individual machines in space highlights their physicality and contextualizes them in their sur-roundings, even if they are part of larger connected networks. It also demon-strates how their agential capacities can be exercised not only in the digital realm, for example through sensing and sharing information about their sur-roundings with other robots, but also through their physical, mechanical actions in their immediate material worlds. Indeed, as Bratton (2021: 1308) reminds us, AI needs to be considered through how it touches the world – rather than treating it an abstract, immaterial concept, he argues that researchers should understand AI's 'synthetic sensing and intelligence…as a distributed function of the material world.'

Having said that, an important recent approach to robots at the urban scale calls for a 'whole city' approach (Macrorie et al., 2019: 2) that recognizes and explores their possibility as a 'mode of urban restructuring.' This work orders robotic potential in a matrix that identifies the span of application from individual to collective on one axis and their control by centralized and private entities on the other. It shows the significance of not only the scale where robotic and other automated technologies are at play but also the importance of where their control is located, arguing that the capacities and the politics of robots are enmeshed. This 'whole city' scale aligns with work in AI urbanism that considers how AI is shaping the management and development of cities through, for example, sensing and analysing routine behaviours through algorithmic processes of predictive analytics, with important implications for how the city develops (Barns, 2021). These perspectives come together in developments in the Internet of Robotic Things (IoRT),

> a new concept that significantly leverages AI. The premise is that intelligent technology can be used to monitor and then manipulate events by combining robots' sensor data and IoT device data to decide on a calculated course of action that could control objects in the physical world.
>
> *(Jadhav et al., 2021: 64)*

IoRT takes AI-based processes of sensing, analysing and predicting a step further by materializing these processes in the physical interventions of robots in their immediate surroundings, whilst remaining connected to much bigger global networks. A current example is Automated Guided Vehicles, sensor-driven robots used in industrial warehouses to tirelessly and efficiently move things around on demand, without the direct intervention of people. Whilst the IoRT is not yet operational at a city-wide scale, it demonstrates the potential for a form of AI urbanism where mechanical objects participate directly and autonomously in the production of their immediate urban contexts. It is also an example of how the city-wide perspective of urbanism knots together and is articulated in the specific urban spatial settings where robots might be and where people might encounter them.

Accordingly, the emerging example of the IoRT shows how, in addition to attending to robots as networked devices, we also need to treat them as individual actants in their spatial contexts. It shows that alongside research on robots' city-wide implications and effects, we need to consider the specific and immediate contexts in which they operate and particular encounters with them. In doing so, we must consider robots' interactions with people, other organisms and things that share robots' material settings. Finally, we need to ask how we envision the limits of robotic capabilities, perspectives that are informed by personal and cultural imaginaries, but that can be confounded in actual encounters with robots. As I discuss next, two concepts have helped me to frame this thinking, both of which concern the spatialities that robots help to produce in the urban settings we share with them.

Emergence and atmosphere

The principles I develop below have emerged in dialogue with two concepts that help to focus AI urbanism on the complex encounters of everyday urban life where it can be located and apprehended. These encounters could include people, animals, materials or processes; they could occur in particular domestic or public settings and include other machines, networks or systems. This complexity requires concepts that can bridge between the programmed computational processes that drive AI-based technologies and the inherent unpredictability and messiness of the worlds where they operate.

The first is *emergence*. This concept highlights the ongoing, unfinished and uncertain qualities of the world, pulling against logics of predictability and perfectability that are important for robotics and other technologies. As design anthropologist Ton Otto (2018: no page) posits: 'The present is continuously moving, evolving from a past present and continuing into a new one; in short the present is always emerging.' By treating the experiential world as always in process, as continuously moving, a concept of emergence allows us to ask how robots constantly *become* part of how we make sense of and understand the city, both in the present and into the future. A concept of emergence helps us tap into technological possibilities, anticipatory imaginaries and forms of knowledge that are expressed in terms of our feelings, such as hope or anxiety, about the future. It invites speculation and imagination, both of which have long histories in how people envision technology and assess its capacities when it finally arrives. In terms of AI urbanism, emergence foregrounds two things: that it is always unfolding, with uncertain effects on the world; and that imaginative and affective perspectives on the city are crucial in identifying where AI actually articulates for urban inhabitants. In this context, emergence is a concept related closely to processual accounts of the production of spatiality that geographers have been developing for decades (see Sumartojo et al., 2022).

The second, related concept that I suggest is useful for thinking with AI urbanism is *atmosphere*. Elsewhere, I have described this as a quality of a specific configuration of sensation, temporality, movement, memory, our material and immaterial surroundings and other people, with qualities that affect how places and events feel and what they mean to people who participate in them.

(Sumartojo and Pink, 2019: 6)

Atmospheres are located in and help to compose our experiential worlds, by drawing together our surroundings with how we sense and feel about them. Applied to AI urbanism, this concept helps us locate the effects of AI in experience, from the inside how it feels to be immersed in a world where AI is at work, rather than identifying it from the outside via its discrete platforms, systems or computational processes. The implication is that AI becomes meaningful and agential in terms of how we are able to notice it and ascribe meaning to it, even if it also remains diffuse – that is, we are able to name AI processes as being at the world in composing how our worlds come into being and how they feel. These meanings can then attach to other aspects of our lives where AI is at work in the background, such as the prediction and direction of traffic flow that we experience as a frustrating or pleasing part of our everyday commutes or school drop-offs.

Accordingly, a concept of atmospheres reminds us that it is not AI *itself* that is significant, at least not from the perspective of the experiential world, but rather the specific and apprehendable ways it configures into peoples' lives and the effects it has as a result. Atmospheres help us perceive and grapple with this because they do not centre AI, even if it is the object of research inquiry. Instead, AI can be treated as only one aspect of how a city might feel to its inhabitants, even if it is driving key processes that collectively compose our cities. Put differently, a concept of atmospheres draws AI into complex and changing understandings of and feelings about urban life – we can see how AI configures with other things and the distinctive experiences that emerge as a result.

It is particularly useful when thinking about robots because their material and physical presence contributes to affective perceptions and narrative possibilities in urban settings, as Cook and Valdez (2021) discuss in their study of Milton Keynes. Robots' physical actions in their environments mean that they can be directly observed and identified as contributing to the distinctive atmospheres of the places we share with them. Bringing atmospheres together with emergence builds a picture of the experiential world that is dynamic, unpredictable and therefore always resistant to attempts to control or predict it, even if this appears in minor ways. These concepts ground my research approach to robots, by always locating them in the messy and dynamic experiential worlds of people. This is important because, as I argued above, AI urbanism is something that we need to understand from the perspective of the people (and other organisms and things) that live in its sway. If robots are indeed becoming an important part of how AI structures and produces the city spaces where most of us live, then we need concepts that can approach AI from the perspective of the experiential world, rather than interpreting the experiential world from the starting point of AI's computational logics. In the remainder of this chapter, I develop a set of ideas specifically to help frame robots through the conceptual pairing of emergence and atmospheres explained in this section. In doing so, I argue that we must attend to robotic contexts and relationalities, and the messiness of these, in order to understand the effects of robots on the worlds we share with them.

Robotic contexts

Robots introduce new and distinct materialities, spatialities and feelings as they act in our cities. However, often their development and design envision them as somehow independent of the worlds they operate in. Perspectives that put the robot at the centre of technical assessments of success or failure cannot adequately account for their contexts, or how those contexts shape the value of robot behaviours (Tian et al., 2021). Instead, we need a *situated* approach to how robots configure and configure into the experience of the city, one that treats them as part of everything else that is going on or 'always-with' the city and its inhabitants. This has value for the framings of AI urbanism because it shows how it plays out in the material world, and the complexities and contingencies that we need to consider to generate a rigorous account of it.

Accordingly, we need to attend to how AI urbanism articulates in normal life, and at smaller scales than the whole city: individual people, homes, public buildings, and urban precincts, for example.

While conceptual and structural perspectives are important, most of us actually experience digital and automated infrastructural technologies in our mundane, everyday routines. AI urbanism is located with people and in urban sites where research can reveal implications for much bigger infrastructures. That is, we need to account for how AI actually plays out in the everyday flows of the city, how people make sense of and experience these, and what sorts of everyday encounters manifest it.

A useful precedent is the body of work on 'datafication,' a term that implies that 'aspects of life can be rendered into digital data which can subsequently be analysed and used to understand, predict and guide interventions in society' (Sumartojo et al., 2016). Studies seek out the locations of data in people's lives and activities and grapple with its effects by tracing its imprints at the individual level. This approach has enabled the development of the concept of the 'datafied self' (Lupton, 2016) where invisible and somewhat abstract data is attached to the body through the self-tracking of weight, menstrual cycles, specific forms of exercise and more. While self-tracking has been shown to shape people's feelings and understandings of their bodies, it can also contribute to how spatiality is experienced. In one study (Sumartojo et al., 2016: 34), self-tracking was the 'vehicle by which to investigate the relationships between space and data' by asking people how it felt to measure their bodies in particular ways as they rode their bicycles on their regular commutes. In this way, data was shown to be entangled with spatiality, physical sensation and the affective lulls and spikes of bodily movement. Like self-tracking and datafication, robots are a technology that can demonstrate how AI is present in people's lives, the effects it can have on how we understand our own bodies, sensation and feelings, and points where intervention into algorithmic logics may be possible.

It follows that, because these contexts are spatial, we need ways to understand this spatiality from the perspective of the technology itself, as Lynch (2021) proposes. This helps us understand how the embedded logics of automated technologies play out when they enter an emerging and atmospheric world. In collaborative research with colleagues in Engineering and Policy Studies, I have helped to develop a framework to understand how robots order and act spatially, and the particular physical and material affordances that underpin this. We were particularly interested in how robots might shape the feel of public space because we felt that this had implications for both understanding and designing robots for public applications that had not been fully considered by roboticists, policymakers or other researchers. We thus developed a tripartite way of thinking the spatial logics of robots that held implications for their deployment in shared city spaces (Sumartojo et al., 2020).

First, we argued that robots treat their spatial surroundings as implicitly able to be predicted if only they can gather and process enough data. A major challenge for roboticists is therefore to perfect robots' sensing abilities of their surroundings because this is seen to improve spatial predictability and enhance robotic efficiency in carrying out pre-determined tasks. Treating the world as a 'taskscape' (Ingold, 1993) in this way makes sense when robots are based in warehouses with highly controlled ways of moving around and repetitive tasks that can be optimized for efficiency. However, the logic of predictability is much more problematic in the complex and contingent spaces where AI urbanism plays out. In urban settings where things are in motion and events are constantly unfolding, models that rely on a logic of predictability reinforce the unrealistic fantasy of perfectability – that is, no amount of data can completely predict what will happen next at any given moment, so robotic capability will always be limited. This point resonates with work on AI urbanism that interrogates the operation and application of AI in 'real life' cities, rather than in controlled or predictable settings. For example, Cugurullo (2020: 5) argues that researchers need to study 'what novel manifestations of intelligence are permeating the built environment and how cities are responding to them'; while Barns (2021) questions how Big Data interventions, such as the creation of 'digital twins,' might aim to recreate routine urban patterns and the implications for possible urban futures. The use of AI in urban settings, environments which are almost by definition dynamic and unpredictable, foregrounds the tensions, compromises and hegemonies that scholars of AI urbanism also consider.

This can be seen in the computational logics by which robots apprehend the world. In addition to predictability, we proposed that robots partition the world, in the sense that their programming drives actions that are made up of multiple discrete movements and decisions stacked together. For example, what appears to be a complex manual movement by a robot, such as picking up a cup, is actually composed of multiple smaller decisions, such as how much grip pressure to exert, which fingers to use and which side up the cup should face down. At multiple points, processes of sensing, assessing, deciding and acting are in play. This partitioning understands that the world is divided into 'discrete units of apprehension, assessment and decision-making' (Sumartojo et al., 2020: 6). As such, it cannot account for the ongoing flow of experience or deal very well with situations it has not encountered before (although new research on robots that learn as they go is well underway). Robots rely on this logic of partitioning because these individualized moments are where decision and action are located. The obvious problem is that this contradicts how people and other lifeforms might understand and act in the world – robots' flattening of spacetime into partitionable units can rub uncomfortably against other richer and more complex ontologies.

The third aspect of our proposition for robotic spatial logics was that robots apprehend and exist in an inescapably datafied world. They can connect to forms of information networked with other devices and enlivened by the algorithmic flows of AI urbanism. They can share how they sense their own surroundings and act on data accumulated from multiple sources. Developments such as the IoRT exemplify the dispersed sensing and physical actions that robots are becoming capable of. Again, this is quite distinct from human ways of apprehending and acting in the world – we may have access to large amounts of information, but we do not process or act on it in the same ways as robots. This last point brings robots directly into the discussion of AI urbanism because it situates them in the networks of data, control and prediction that also animate AI in our cities.

Bringing these logics together, we proposed that robotic autonomy is contingent on the machine's dynamic and complex environments, those of a world-in-process, rather than predetermined in the lab or by the programmer. This draws inspiration from Louise Amoore's concept of *cloud ethics* (2020), which similarly attributes accountability in AI to the ongoing writing that takes place when an algorithm is set loose in the world – that is, the effects of robots on the world expand far beyond what their programmers and designers can envision.

Robotic relationalities

The first principle hints at how robotic autonomy emerges as its computational processes play out in relation to its context. This connects to a notion of robotic liveliness that my colleagues and I developed in the context of the COVID-19 pandemic. We argued that we must understand the capacity of robots to exercise agency within the multivalent contexts where they are located, and that 'their "autonomy" is always conditional on human-machine relations, in the particular contexts of their actions' (Sumartojo and Lugli, 2021: 8). In doing so, we differentiated robotic liveliness from the leaky and fleshy liveliness of human bodies, qualities that have been particularly evident during the pandemic. Finally, building on Bennett's (2010) notion of vibrant matter, we argued for thinking about robots as always 'unfinished' because of the excessive 'thing-force,' that can never be fully proscribed. This also taps into the ongoing potential offered by affective flows that shape how people make sense of and feel about things (see Anderson, 2014).

This liveliness is valuable for thinking about the role of robots in AI urbanism because it moves away from computational or mechanical versions of technology, where a device might be thought of as self-contained and 'complete' when it enters the world, and instead locates them in *relation* to their environments and the people in them. By invoking a comparison with porous organic bodies, it invites us to think about robots as immersed in their surroundings and always relational. This means that I am interested in AI urbanism at the moment of encounter, at the point when we come into contact with it and feel its effects, rather than at the level of system, network or platform. I am also interested in the ongoing impacts of these encounters, even when they have passed, and how they shape our understandings of ourselves, the urban contexts that many of us inhabit and the technologies that are entangled with our lives into the future. Cook and Valdez (2021: 183) make a similar point when they identify how robots were enrolled in cultivating 'smart atmospheres' in Milton Keynes to curate narratives and thereby open possibilities for thinking about possible urban futures. Relationality connects directly to the concept of emergence because it highlights how robots are dynamic in relation to their environments, with their meaning subject to ongoing sensemaking by the people who encounter them. This opens a route to a critical understanding of AI that treats it as *always-with* people and other technologies and in an ongoing world.

Researching with robots can also show us how AI comes together with human activities and intentions – how it is, in some sense, always-with people, its agential capacities never quite meeting the aspiration of perfect automation or independent intelligence. Indeed, research with many different types of everyday automation (Pink et al., 2022) shows that automated technologies and people are always working together, rather than technology operating in isolation from people. Relatedly, studies in human–robot interaction (HRI) that seek to predetermine the best robotic behaviours when working with people, now includes a specific focus on human–robot collaboration.

This recognizes that robots that share spaces and tasks with people – from domestic vacuum machines to delivery warehouses logistics – must be conceptualized and designed as collaborators, helpers or partners to humans, where mistakes and corrections alongside people are part of their activities. This is borne out by research that shows how often robotic technologies in everyday settings do not operate 'perfectly,' but instead struggle to cope with the unpredictability of their surroundings. Recent accounts of robot vacuum cleaners, for example, point out how people rearrange objects or furniture to assist the robot or move it around manually when it becomes "confused" by textile patterns (Vincent, 2021).

It also includes other organisms, things and structures. For example, work on the use of robots in the dairy industry has shown how animals, mud, waste and farmers all combine to shape the value and efficacy of robotic milking machines. Cows become understood as recalcitrant or mischievous when they refuse the robotic overtures or damage the machines by rubbing against them (Bear and Holloway, 2019). New robots now contribute to the ongoing automation of dairy production by scrubbing away faeces and other waste materials. Such robotic examples demonstrate where AI is actually located and the forms of encounter where we can apprehend and study it.

An implication is that researchers need to consider what is happening in encounters with robots that may not be immediately visible (or measurable), but that may be felt or imagined. As I have argued, how we imagine robots is very important for how we experience and make sense of them, what we expect them to be able to do and whether their actions are acceptable (Sumartojo et al., 2021). Indeed, dynamic feelings such as wariness, concern, optimism or acceptance – feelings that directly relate to the impact of robots on the spaces they share with people – are also subject to what people already understand about these technologies and what they anticipate. This adds up to a contingent understanding of what people think robots might or could do that emerges as they encounter and reflect on robots. In terms of AI urbanism, this complicates somewhat the notion that AI is 'operating the city in an autonomous manner' (Cugurullo, 2020: 1) because it always situates technology in relation to the people and environments in which it operates, and locates it where it touches and in how it shapes the city, including the lives of the people who encounter its effects.

Robotic messiness

The scale of the encounter also reveals how robotic logics come together with the unpredictability and messiness of everyday life, the frictions immanent in this, and how this is managed. We found that people are actually quite tolerant of what programmers or designers might consider robot 'mistakes,' and in fact find ways to accommodate or work around these behaviours (Tian et al., 2021). The limits and capacities of robots to perform certain tasks, rather than being fixed qualities determined in advance of their deployment, are instead affordances that become part of how people come to understand them. That is, robots are not perceived as 'working' or 'failing' but rather as having capacities that emerge within their contexts and that advance or retard people's goals. People who encounter robots regularly, at work or at home, come to understand these capacities within those specific settings and can anticipate when the robot will need help or what tasks it will not be able to reliably perform. They find ways to work within the robot's limits.

This accommodation is not specific to robots but instead reflects the everyday improvisation and problem-solving that we engage in in our everyday lives. As other studies of technology have shown, 'good enough' is a condition that emerges from the capacities and affordances of the things around us and has to be worked out in our everyday contexts (Lupton et al., 2021). Indeed, robots help to highlight our habitual improvisations precisely because they carry narratives of optimization and efficiency that rub uncomfortably against the unpredictability and uncertainty – indeed, the emergence – of everyday life.

This pushes back against some research into peoples' perceptions of robots within engineering and design fields, for example, which is often focused on the robot itself. Instead, our research identified an 'assemblage of factors' that people incorporate into their understandings of robot abilities, including 'existing capabilities, the setting, the participants' pre-existing understanding of robots and their views on what would be a useful task for the robot to be able to do' (Tian et al., 2021: 4). This assemblage of factors does not only include people. AI urbanism takes in many different technologies, ones that do not always synchronize properly and that sometimes even pull against each other. Automated asynchronicity has always been a feature of the urban experience, such as when train timetables are misaligned or lighting in office buildings turns off unexpectedly because workers are not making movements big enough for the sensors to detect. Indeed, any new technology emerges into a world of already existing technology, and AI urbanism needs to account for this messy complexity and the potential frictions, overlaps, enhancements or discontinuities that may arise as a result.

Conclusions

The framework of robotic contexts, relationalities and messiness that I have sketched in this chapter can be used in urban studies to foreground and explore the contingency of actual automated processes, rather than remaining focused on the optimized efficiency which is so often the goal in smart city visions. This implies a shift to the everyday places and situations where people might encounter them. Indeed, robots are rapidly developing and are set to become much more commonplace in our everyday lives, entering into worlds already full of different technologies which we are accustomed to using or interacting with. This sense of promise has long characterized narratives about robots – that they are on the brink of revolutionizing how we work, live and relate to each other. They are intriguing characters in the AI-powered cities developing around us, immediate physical manifestations of incredibly complex global networks. Shaped by decades of creative speculation about their forms, functions and internal worlds, they are not neutral technologies. Rather, they are freighted with cultural baggage that shapes how we understand them, even if we have not actually encountered them. They are easy to identify as containers for and examples of artificial intelligence, even if most of us have no idea how this actually works and must rely on our imaginations to make sense of them.

However, even if we do not understand precisely how AI works, this may be less important than thinking about how it articulates in our lives, how we relate to its manifestations, such as robots, and what happens when these struggle to cope with the messiness of the world. So-called 'explainable AI' holds out the promise that if we understand technologies better, we can more completely grapple with their implications and effects, particularly the ways in which they arrive at specific predictions and perhaps hold them to account. However, such an approach is problematic for several reasons. It centres the technology, rather than people, in the worlds that we share, and insists that people engage with technology on its terms, rather than on the terms in which it might make sense in their lives. After all, most of us do not understand how smartphones work, but we still value them immensely for the connections, pleasure, access and utility they offer. It also assumes that the world is *able to be predicted* if only we could understand this process well enough. In a manner similar to the robotic spatial logic I discussed above, this is a fantasy that fails to account for the ways that our lives are always ongoing and in a state of emergence.

Like any other technology, robots are subject to malfunctions that are likely to be a significant part of how we get to know them – such as the robotic vacuum cleaner that must be manually redirected when it gets stuck in a corner. Robots tap into promises of efficiency and optimized value, based on prediction, that reflect a way of understanding the city – and seeking to control it – that holds open the fantasy of perfectability. Such visions do not necessarily align with the messy realities of everyday life, where things do not work as planned, where we improvise to do the things that we want as best we can, and where our desires and aims are not completely predetermined, but actually emerge along with the many things, technologies, people and more that we encounter every day.

AI urbanism proposes that beyond being just 'smart,' algorithmically powered platforms are also exercising new forms of agency and autonomously organizing urban rhythms and networks (Cugurullo, 2020). This means that we need new analytical approaches to understand this emerging urban phenomenon. As the principles I discussed above show, robots are a useful manifestation of AI urbanism to think with – they highlight how, when AI meets the world, it can have unexpected and unanticipated effects, and that this is part of the complex, ongoing and emergent nature of how people experiential that world.

References

Amoore, L. (2020). *Cloud Ethics: Algorithms and the Attributes of Ourselves and Others*. Duke University Press.

Anderson, B. (2014). *Encountering Affect: Capacities, Apparatuses, Conditions*. Routledge.

Barns, S. (2021). Out of the loop? On the radical and the routine in urban big data. *Urban Studies*, 58 (15), 3203–3210.

Bear, C., & Holloway, L. (2019). Beyond resistance: Geographies of divergent more-than-human conduct in robotic milking. *Geoforum*, 104, 212–221.

Bennett, J. (2010). *Vibrant Matter: a political ecology of things*. Duke University Press.

Bratton, B. (2021). AI urbanism: A design framework for governance, program, and platform cognition. *AI & Society*, 36 (4), 1307–1312.

Cook, M. & Valdez, A.M. (2021). Exploring smart city atmospheres: The case of Milton Keynes. *Geoforum*, 127, 180–188.

Cugurullo, F. (2020). Urban Artificial Intelligence: From *Automation* to *Autonomy* in the Smart City. *Frontiers in Sustainable Cities*, 2, 1–14.

Ingold, T. (1993). The temporality of the landscape, *World Archaeology*, 25 (2), 152–174.

Del Casino, V., House-Peters, L., Crampton, J. & Gerhardt, H. (2020). The social life of robots: The politics of algorithms, governance, and sovereignty. *Antipode*, 52 (3), 605–618.

Lupton, D. (2016). *The Quantified Self*. Wiley.

Lupton, D., Pink, S. & Horst, H. (2021). Living in, with and beyond the 'smart home': Introduction to the special issue. *Convergence*, 27 (5), 1147–1154.

Lynch, C. (2021). geographies of social robotics. *Digital Geography and Society*, 2, DOI: 10.1016/j.diggeo.2021.100010.

Macrorie, R., Marvin, S. & While, A. (2019). Robotics and automation in the city: a research agenda. *Urban Geography*, DOI:10.1080/02723638.2019.1698868.

Otto, T. (2018). Emergence. *Keywords for Ethnography and Design*. Society for Cultural Anthropology. Available at: https://culanth.org/fieldsights/emergence#:~:-text=The%20present%20is%20continuously%20moving,the%20present%20is%20always%20emerging. [Accessed 19/01/2023].

Pink, S., Berg, M., Lupton, D. & Ruckenstein, M. (2022). *Everyday Automation: Experiencing and Anticipating Emerging Technologies*. Routledge.

Sumartojo, S., Lundberg, R., Kulić, D., Tian, L., Carreno-Medrano, P., Mintrom, M., Lugli, D. & Allen, A. (2022). The robotic production of spatiality: Predictability, partitioning, and datafication. *Transactions of the Institute of British Geographers*. DOI:10.1111/tran.12574.

Sumartojo, S., Kulić, D., Tian, L., Mintrom, M., Carreno-Medrano, P. & Allen, A. (2020). Robotic logics of public space, *Mediapolis*. Available at: https://www.medi apolisjournal.com/2020/08/robotic-logics-of-public-space/. [Accessed 19/01/2023].

Sumartojo, S., & Lugli, D. (2021). Lively robots: Robotic technologies in COVID-19. *Social and Cultural Geography*. DOI: 10.1080/14649365.2021.1921245.

Sumartojo, S., Lundgren, R., Tian, L., Carreno-Medrano, P., Kulić, D. & Mintrom, M. (2021). Imagining Public Space Robots of the Near-Future. *Geoforum*, 124, 99–109.

Sumartojo, S. & Pink, S. (2019). *Atmospheres and the Experiential World: Theory and Methods*. Routledge.

Sumartojo, S., Pink, S., Lupton, D. & Heyes LaBond, C. (2016). 'The affective intensities of datafied space', *Emotion, Space and Society*, 21, 33–40.

Tian, L., Carreno-Medrano, P., Allen, A., Sumartojo, S., Mintrom, M., Coronado, E., Venture, G., Croft, E. & Kulic, D. (2021). Redesigning Human-Robot Interaction in Response to Robot Failures: a Participatory Design Methodology. *Extended Abstracts of the 2021 CHI Conference on Human Factors in Computing Systems*, pp. 1–8.

Jadhav, V., Gandhi, V. & Rathod, P. (2021). Internet of Robotic Things. *International Research Journal of Innovations in Engineering and Technology*, 5(12), 64.

Vincent, J. (2021). Need to trap a Roomba? You don't need anything more sophisticated than a rug. *The Verge*. Available at: https://www.theverge.com/tldr/2021/9/22/2268 7449/roomba-rug-dark-pattern-cliff-edge-why-problem. [Accessed 19/01/2023].

11

AIRPORT ROBOTS

Automation, everyday life and the futures of urbanism

Weiqiang Lin and Si Jie Ivin Yeo

Introduction

An industry that has long led technological advances in such sophisticated acts as navigation, surveillance and flow management (Amoore, 2006; Budd and Adey, 2009; Garrett and Anderson, 2018; Lin, 2017), aviation has recently begun to turn to robots and digital technologies to automate its most basic processes. From cleaning to baggage handling to information services, a new generation of machines – armed with prosthetics, sensors and artificial intelligence (AI) – now preside over a variety of tasks once thought too menial and low-value to be taken over by robots. Yet, this is precisely the trajectory of many modern airports, which have transformed themselves from spaces of aeromobile utility (Pascoe, 2001), into high-tech infrastructures responsible for the efficient sorting and transportation of people and goods (Lin, 2018; Wilts, 2020). Since the COVID-19 pandemic, the appeal of robots for (safe and physically distanced) airport facilitation has only increased (Sumartojo and Lugli, 2021). If airports were once envisioned as *non-places* of transit and hypermobility (Augé, 1995), they seem today one step closer to that a-social reality.

Yet, learning about robotic and digital installations in airports is not just an exercise in understanding how the aviation industry is changing; it also has significant implications for how scholars think about operations in other infrastructural spaces and, more broadly, technologically enabled urban environments. Instructively, Hirsh (2016) argues that aviation prototypes should be thought of as synecdochical of wider processes in the city, a part-whole, but also intricately interwoven, relationship he calls 'airport urbanism.'

DOI: 10.4324/9781003365877-13

For him, the airport speaks not simply of its own self-contained affordances, but reflects 'social and material conditions of global mobility' that require 'an expanded spatial and typological conception of the infrastructure of international aviation' (Hirsh, 2016: 11). Seen thus, the airport offers a perspective that connects itself with wider urban trends and proclivities. It serves as a node and window onto the changing configurations of informational flows in the contemporary city, as well as the politics of lives and livelihoods, as everyday spaces and tasks become increasingly rid of human interventions (Cugurullo, 2020).

This chapter is exactly interested in these extrapolative questions about everyday living in the city, using technological transformations in airports as a springboard for inquiry. Indeed, the conditions enabled by recent robotic and digital affordances in these gleaming artefacts of flight give not-a-few clues of the (worrying) urban features and futures that cities are quickly emulating and gravitating towards – smarter, more digitally reliant and ecologically self-contained (see Cugurullo, 2021; Macrorie et al., 2021; While et al., 2021). To reflect on these urban transformations, we consider the quality-of-life issues that the humble automatic cleaning machines at Singapore's Changi Airport (Figure 11.1) portend for a wide range of airport – and, by extension, urban – actors, as life gradually gets usurped by the pre-programmed logics and assumptions of these artificially intelligent devices. Following a review of literature on everyday living, we explore three interconnected threads of these effects in the rest of the chapter. These span airport robots' contentious relationship with labour, their influence over consumerist expectations and their propensity in the management of life.

FIGURE 11.1   A cleaning robot at Singapore's Changi Airport.

Source: authors' original.

Everyday living

The notion of *everydayness* has been variously employed in geography, sociology and urban studies, amongst other disciplines, to direct attention to the significance of ordinary places, mundane routines and prosaic practices of social life (Highmore, 2002). Referencing the city in particular, some geographers have sought to highlight the value and role of the ordinary in the production and reproduction of urban identities and socio-spatial relations, evincing how everyday sites like the home, transport infrastructures, childcare centres and even urban slums can have an impact on people's senses of being (Blunt, 2005; Datta, 2016; Holloway and Hubbard, 2001; Jarvis, 2010). Other scholars have demonstrated how everyday life is a product of a rhythmic temporal structure that is underpinned by the modality of repetitive practice (Jarvis, 2005; Kwan, 2002; Schwanen et al., 2008). The everyday thus serves as one of the most foundational concepts in the social sciences in understanding not merely the temporal structuring of social activities but also the spaces through which reality is made sense of.

Notwithstanding its seeming continuity, everyday life is not without structure. Henri Lefebvre's (1991) Marxist engagement with the everyday is instructive here, postulating that processes of modern life are commonly a product of capital and situated within highly particular urban spaces (Goonewardena et al., 2008). The implications of the capitalist transformation of urban space are, furthermore, critically uneven. Not only do some cities and urban regions become richer at the expense of others (Harvey, 1978; Massey, 1995), at the level of the individual, the experience of everyday life too is marked by power relations and socio-spatial inequalities (Valentine, 2008; Wilson, 2017). Here, the everyday ceases to be a site of quotidian subsistence and becomes one where strong and stubborn boundaries are inscribed, reproduced and reinforced. In turn, these lines of difference are instrumental for engendering bifurcated regimes of citizenship and labour classes, whose difference is normalized by social markers such as race, gender and migrancy (McDowell et al., 2007). Framed as such, an attention to the everyday then yields sobering insights into the workings of power relations in a city, making it anything but mundane or a-political.

If capital were seen as key to the production of everyday life in the early twentieth century, then the same could be said of the present. This time, however, the catalyst is not some means of production that is dependent on social differentiation, but robots that change (and displace) the place of humans in socio-economic relations. As disruptive technologies, robots and automation not only introduce a new agency to those relations but also alter lifestyles by making everyday tasks more remote, more abstract, faster and more adept. Indeed, these 'robotics and automation systems' are able to 'distinctly rework, augment, and extend the capabilities and capacities of infrastructure networks' in modern industrialization processes (Macrorie et al., 2021: 202), rendering 'old' ways of doing things seemingly inefficient and unsophisticated.

The smart city is perhaps where the creep of robotics and automation into everyday life has been most salient and conspicuous. Recent advancements in artificial intelligence and machine learning have spurred authorities around the world to initiate urban experiments with self-driving cars, service robots and autonomous infrastructural platforms, amongst others, in a range of urban processes and practices that are traditionally seen as the domain of human instruction and design (Cugurullo, 2021; Kitchin, 2020; Lynch, 2021). In particular, burgeoning research has been curious about the question of 'how the high-frequency, real-time city actually functions' (Batty, 2018: 5) and with what effects on urban life. According to these broad-based findings, not only are artificially intelligent urban technologies in smart cities taking over the role of providing everyday urban services and maintaining urban infrastructure from humans, but they are also increasingly involved in urban governance and planning. Especially, the everyday operations of the city are becoming 'autonomous' (Cugurullo, 2020) and AI can be seen in this equation as part of an emerging class of urban actors that 'routinely intervene, autonomously, to shape behavioural outcomes' (Barns, 2021: 3204).

Yet, this does not mean that humans then become invalid in these processes. People react to capital's attempts to outbid them, sometimes resisting these disruptions, but at other times cooperating and going along with them to allow life to evolve (Yeo, 2022). While labour scholars concentrate on the moments when technological changes spark discontent, labour resistance and class action (Silver, 2003), there are times when such (re)combinations of human and nonhuman agencies result in new conditions of cooperation and acquiescence. Pink and Sumartojo (2018), for instance, have alluded to how everyday interactions with technology could stir not quite outright opposition to, but new engagements with the latter to restore a sense of familiarity. Elsewhere, Bissell (2021: 378) has argued that human encounters with automation can contribute to activating particular dispositions and subjectivities among technology's users, for better or worse treating the non-humans in their midst as objects to assimilate and grow used to.

These structures and dynamics are highly relevant for thinking about the way Changi Airport, and by extension, Singapore as a whole, subscribes to specific technological projects and futures. Indeed, despite its fringe location in the far eastern corner of the city-state, the airport is only one – if perhaps the premier icon – of Singapore's many urban technological experiments. Other recent high-profile technological projects in urban Singapore include the building of a digital district, the deployment of robots to police streets, as well as the use of AI in healthcare, and these broadly consolidate under the banner of the Smart Nation initiative which was launched by the Singapore government in 2014 to digitally transform the everyday lives of urban dwellers in the city-state. Just as in the case of the adoption of robots in Changi Airport, the wider national push towards digitalization in Singapore not merely reflects but also prefigures the centrality of smart and digital technologies in enacting the technocratically biased vision of urban futures (Kong and Woods, 2018). It is in view of these resonances wrapped up in the airport, and more specifically its automatic cleaning machines, that we now turn to three groups of actors – workers, consumers and managers – to unpack lessons about new urbanisms in Singapore and beyond.

Workers

Whilst automation has long been introduced as a back-end feature in and of airport infrastructure, it was in recent years that it took on more front-house service delivery functions. For airport administrators and urban elites alike, such innovations have mostly been welcome, if not celebrated, for their ability to enhance productivity and reduce costs. McKinsey (2015), for example, predicts that automation can be put to replace as many as 45 per cent of the activities that individuals are paid to perform, which, in the United States, roughly amounts to $2 trillion in annual wages; it also expects that the adoption of AI will create $400 billion efficiency gains per year for the global travel industry (McKinsey, 2018). Economic studies and think-tank reports have been rife with projections that the rate of job replacement could rise to as high as 50 per cent in the next two decades (Dengler and Matthes, 2018).

The vantage point for on-ground, frontline airport workers is however not the same. Automation has arguably spelt a re-negotiation of the relationship between labour and employer, as the intrusion of machines resets the pace and expectation of work. At best, this has meant a need for further skills upgrading for workers (Richardson and Bissell, 2019); at worst, it has accentuated the precarity of work, as airport robots threaten to reduce labour needs through substitution (McNeill, 2015; Oppenheimer, 2019; West, 2018). Put simply, automation is not just some new-fangled gimmick that airports and cities are introducing in order to appear 'high-tech' and futuristic; more often than not, it transforms the tenor of work that pitches humans in competition with machines (Bissell and Del Casino, 2017).

In subtler ways, automation buffets workers, too, through deepening, rather than overcoming, existing fault lines of difference and unequal distribution of labour within society. An enduring issue is the question of race (Pulido, 2017; Strauss, 2020), which airport robots have further naturalized. Besides the use of multi-ethnic stickers to represent different – but highly particular – nationalities of cleaners, the aliases given to Changi's automated cleaning robots are revealing of the racialized and gendered dimensions of low-paid airport workers in Singapore and the attendant ways in which automation reproduces those differences. It is by no coincidence that when 11 units of these autonomous floor cleaning robots were first introduced in Terminals 3 and 4 in 2017, they were consigned with names that are skewed feminine and reflective of the nationalities of those who typically perform such low-wage work in Singapore's airport landscape – namely, Chinese, Indonesian and Indian migrant workers:

> Cute names are also given to these robotic helpers, to give them personas. In Chinese, there are Liang Liang and Jing Jing, as "Liang Jing Jing" (亮晶晶) in Mandarin means clean and shiny.
>
> *(Changi Airport Group, 2019)*

> In Malay, the names are Bersih, which means clean and Putih, which means white. Last but not least, in Tamil, the names are Minnal, which means very clean and Palich Palich, which means lightning.[1]
>
> *(Changi Airport Group, 2019)*

Somewhat demeaningly, the Facilities Management team of the Changi Airport Group emphasized that the discursive labelling exercise of these robots enhances the 'passenger experience' at the airport and counts it as a strategy to elicit public acceptance on grounds of 'recognisability' and familiarity with the quintessential cleaner at Changi:

> By "dressing" the machines in the same uniform as the cleaners, it has helped [autonomous cleaning equipment] to gain quicker and better acceptance with the cleaners. These robotic helpers are also easily recognisable by passengers, who are delighted by them.
>
> *(Changi Airport Group, 2019)*

These cleaning machines are thus personified carefully with very specific subject personas, in order to mimic the existing profile of service workers.

Experiments with automation technologies in everyday labour practices such as Changi's cleaning robots have several socio-cultural implications for on-ground workers. First, these experiments, especially if deemed successful, increase the prospect of labour replacement of an existing army of (already-cost-effective) foreign workers currently employed in the everyday maintenance of airports. Since these cleaning machines are ostensibly more efficient, easier to manage and cost less, the substitution of human labour with robots is a viable and more economical option for many airport managers. This consequently heightens the precarity of work and livelihood for this group of employees who are so often hired on a contract basis, in deference to abler technologies/agencies, to allow for easy termination of their service (Islam, 2018; Pierce et al., 2019). Second, the selective racialization (and gendering) of these automatons reinscribes and extends existing power geometries onto non-human counterparts, othering them and normalizing their place in the airport. By conflating race, gender and certain kinds of work (e.g. cleaning), it disenfranchises labour that ascribes to and performs these identities, relegating them to the diminished status and social position of non-humans. Put succinctly, the attribution of feminine-leaning and racialized qualities to robots that are designed for low-wage and often devalued jobs reifies the abjection and colonization of these subjects (MacKereth, 2019).

What, then, might this mean for work in the city if and when cleaning robots are deployed in the wider urban landscape? For one, and quite intuitively, people whose livelihoods are in the maintenance sector will likely be displaced from their jobs and, in large part, these individuals are working-class migrants and/or low-skilled elderly people. As Graham and Thrift (2007) note, modern urban societies are kept running because of all the maintenance and repair that goes into their making (McNeill, 2005) and this work has generally been performed by the city's vulnerable and marginalized labouring classes (Tripathy and Carrière, 2020). The progressive introduction of cleaning robots in the city will therefore see an inversely proportional relationship to the employment of working-class migrants and/or low-skilled elderly people servicing the urban. On another, more intimate level, cleaning robots will be implicated in everyday gendered relations since they are 'dictated by the need of the economic system to maintain in the domestic sphere a high level of value production, undertaken mostly by women' (Fortunati et al., 2015: 231). In this vein, not only will urban robotic machines rework questions of inequality and difference in the organization and governance of the public and private domains of the city, but, more crucially, they may potentially change the everydayness of work and how we come to understand work cultures and practices in cities around the world.

Users

Labour may seem to shoulder an inordinate proportion of the impacts of automation, but the inroads that these technologies make with respect to everyday life go much further than the arena of work. Notably, it is impossible to extricate the beneficiaries of everyday services from the values and cultures that automation subtly promotes through its use. To return to airport robots, Changi's automated cleaning machines do not just affect the conditions of employment for cleaning workers; they also instil, among passengers and the airport's visitors, particular affinities and expectations by their very (roving) existence. Indeed, the cleaning robots have outward-facing personas as well, both in the way they are (re)presented by airport managers and by dint of their presence as relatable autonomous equipment.

Consider first the manner in which these cleaning machines debuted to the public in 2017. Coinciding with the opening of futuristic Terminal 4, the robots were part of the airport's open house displays in August of that year and were introduced as floor-scrubbing equipment that 'can clean floor [sic] faster and cover a wider surface area' (exhibition description) than, presumably, regular labour. Adorned with bright colours, flashing lights and human voices, these robots are not only an intrigue to airport users (taking pictures of/with them, dodging them, testing their sensors by standing in front of them); they are also frequently showcased in promotional materials and the local media, which often tout their obstruction-detecting capabilities and endearing personalities:

> these "cleaning aunties" (colloquial and affectionate term for older women) are able to detect objects in front of them, and will stop when an obstruction is detected; just make sure you don't get in the way of them doing their jobs!
>
> *(DiscoverSG, 2017)*

> These robotic helpers are... easily recognisable by passengers, who are delighted by them.
>
> *(Changi Airport Group, 2019)*

During the pandemic, these same robots were vested with a new narrative of being in battle with COVID-19 and were celebrated for their role in keeping the airport's inhabitants safe:

> Autonomous cleaning robots complement the crew of cleaners by doing the heavy lifting and cleaning large surface areas like floors and carpets, while cleaners can focus on the difficult-to-reach areas like corners and handlebars.
>
> *(Changi Airport Group, 2021)*

Recent prototypes even came with interactive features to tickle passengers' imagination, in an otherwise spartan airport emptied of its usual traffic:

> Guests can also interact with the robots by either scanning a QR code or by pressing the "lionsheart" button... on the robots. The QR code will direct guests to a webpage where they can ask the robot a list of questions, including how it is feeling, or even make a request for the robot to sing or rap. Press the "lionsheart" button... and the robots will respond by giggling or saying 'ouch'!
>
> *(Changi Airport Group, 2020)*

Taking these theatrics into account, the cleaning robots thus do more than clean but are the poster child for what a modern, efficient and, now, epidemiologically safe airport should be.

Robots like Changi's cleaning machines signal the rise of a new breed of automation that does not just passively mediate human encounters with space (see Pink and Sumartojo, 2018; Popescu, 2017; Sheller, 2007). Rather, these contemporary technologies tend to be flexible and adaptive and come with almost an agency to engage, enthral and enchant those they serve. The power of such interactivity should not be underestimated, as they are able to condition a state of comfort and ease with users that render automation all but post-political and unquestionable. Indeed, automation has lately assumed a more "friendly" demeanour and actively appeals to human senses, emotions and affects to induce buy-ins. A phenomenon that has become more ubiquitous since the COVID-19 pandemic, this softer approach is especially germane to new prototypes such as life-like robots, cognitive artificial intelligence and interactive platforms that have been designed to interpellate users through personalization, care and even humour (see Macrorie et al., 2021; Richardson, 2021; Tay et al., 2016). Put succinctly, through new capabilities in adjusting to and mimicking humans, automation has augmented its influence over what people need and desire in everyday life.

This model has profound implications for future urbanisms beyond the airport. Not only is automation already more prevalently applied to a wide range of urban services, from tax collection to security provision, to transport planning; it is increasingly infiltrating urban dwellers' psyche as to what is deemed an acceptable threshold for automation. Consider the manner in which health has been incorporated into urban landscapes through user-friendly devices and apps. From "lively" (i.e. sickness-immune) robots that sanitize and clean streets on behalf of humans, to data-tracking algorithms through which people 'come to know their bodies and their capacity for speed, fitness or physical achievement' when they exercise (Sumartojo and Lugli, 2021: 4), automation is on the cusp of becoming unthinkingly accepted as an essential fixture of 'healthful' urban life, without so much regard for its ramifications on labour and data privacy. Equally intrusively, what Hildebrand and Sodero (2021) term 'pandemic drones' has recently emerged as a new, 'viral' form of urban surveillance and policing undertaken in the name of care. Citing how drones have been deployed during the COVID-19 pandemic to monitor street movements, provide real-time reminders and (audible) exhortations and call out errant behaviours, Hildebrand and Sodero's (2021) work shows the lengths to which automation can go to change the tenors of everyday urban life and its mobilities (see also McGuirk et al., 2021). Through such multi-sensorial interpellations and engagements, automation has clearly taken root not just in the airport, but the city too.

Thinking about automation in terms of its impact on everyday users/life accentuates the insidiousness of machine encroachment through acceptance and reframes any attempts at 'creative' adaptation within the expected bounds of technology's control (cf. Lynch, 2020). What this discussion has highlighted is an urgency to interrogate how robots and AI are setting new expectations and standards for urban living, so much so that what used to be taboo in the past, is now welcome and embraced by dint of machines' engaging demeanours. This is not to say that change is always bad, but the politics entrained by these subtle manoeuvres ought not to be neglected. Doing so would not only be tantamount to surrendering the conditions of life to technology but also to absolving another social group – urban managers – of their responsibility to the work of serving the people.

Managers

The affordances of robots and artificial intelligence may be observed not just in the way they mediate the experience of users but also in how they shape managerial practices and responsibilities. Many robots are now coded to routinely carry out mundane tasks based on demand rather than following a fixed schedule; some more advanced ones can even be programmed to independently respond to everyday environmental stimuli. At Changi Airport, cleaning robots are designed to work *autonomously*, without requiring any additional instruction or prompt from airport cleaning supervisors. In deferring, amongst others, the decision of cleaning – when, where and perhaps even how to clean – to autonomous robots, questions of responsibility and ethics as well as the labour of managing are implicitly reframed and reconfigured from previously involving only human actors to a wider range of more-than-human agencies and powers including machines and algorithms.

While it may be too early to draw a final conclusion, we are now arguably already witnessing the early hints of how automation might reduce, simplify and absolve responsibilities in managerial roles. This encompasses a wide range of domains, including decision-making, policing, disciplining and problem-solving, pushing the potential of automation and artificial intelligence beyond the managerial rank with respect to information processing and decision-making. Cushman and Wakefield, a global leader in commercial real estate, for example, has thus commented on the self-governing nature of Changi's cleaning robots:

> Odour and movement sensors will soon be able to "talk" to robot cleaners to activate a work order to clean areas that are littered and soiled, or once the number of people using the area crosses a certain threshold.
>
> *(Cushman & Wakefield, 2019)*

At the same time, it is important to recognize that alongside the physical cleaning machines, there is a whole collection of immaterial data that contributes to the shaping of a culture hinged on artificial intelligence and cybernetics:

> With the huge amount of data collected, cleaning companies are able to analyse the data to deduce cleaning patterns, plan resources to match demand, measure cleaner productivity and manage customer feedback.
> *(Cushman & Wakefield, 2019)*

In their current experimental stages, therefore, automated cleaning robots are enabled to process information and, correspondingly, with machine learning, adapt to make decisions for humans. And even if decisions are not made and problems are not solved entirely by robots, they can now be seen to exert a powerful mediating force on processes that used to be understood as ontologically human.

In this light, cleaning robots, and the data they generate in their work, draw into being a socio-technical configuration of humans and their non-human counterparts that encourages the reduction of rationality to machine language and logics. Algorithmic code, data analytics and real-time automated calculative processes, in particular, allow for decisions to be made through a series of pre-programmed intelligences and assumptions (Macrorie et al., 2021). Ironically, these reductive techniques are framed as more efficient than human determination, especially in socio-cultural contexts organized around neoliberalist productivity and the ideal of the protestant ethic. For airport managers, this means that what were deemed as menial and banal problems can now be devolved upon these self-governing robots that are trained with machine learning to solve and troubleshoot, freeing up time and space for them to engage with supposedly more important tasks and work. In this sense, the introduction of and reliance on urban robots such as cleaning machines could very well shift the job scope of an airport administrator from one of managing the everyday to that of only digital cases and files in bits and bytes.

A related and equally important point is the potential to foster a culture of binary thinking in managerial work, underpinned by the rules and grammar of programming language. The pervasive adoption of machines in management has the potential to reduce the way airport managers approach complex and multifaceted problems in their work. By foreclosing alternative pathways and conditioning the number of possible outputs, artificial intelligence and robotic technologies thus have serious consequences for the way everyday problems are addressed by managers and those in authority (see Amoore, 2020; Kitchin, 2021).

On a broader level, these affordances have ramifications for how cities and the everyday maintenance of urban spaces are organized. Robots and artificial intelligence further entrench the praxis of neoliberalism and aid the retreat of the state in the provision of services. Insofar as there is an assumption for autonomous robots to deliver services to the general public, and perhaps imagined to do so in a more efficient manner than by humans, urban officials and elites are also relieved from the roles for which they are employed and paid. By the same token, urban inhabitants would now have to rely on these same robots to access services – such as the maintenance and repair of electricity and water resources – that they otherwise would get from urban authorities.

This sleight of hand effectively replaces managerial responsibilities with a culture of self-service and prosumption (Ritzer and Jurgenson, 2010). It has the tendency to construct what Cugurullo (2021) terms 'Frankenstein urbanism,' which sees human decision-makers retreat in favour of a city reductively (perhaps also simplistically) managed and experienced through artificial and contrived logics based on digits and data (Barns, 2021). Such a future no doubt raises urgent questions about the ethics of deferring managerial functions to the sorting and profiling capabilities of algorithms while sounding a cautionary note on the decline of the living, innovative and compassionate city urban dwellers have taken for granted.

Conclusions

This chapter has used the example of airport robots to unpack the changing relationships that humans have with their environs and with each other, as automation encroaches on more and more aspects of everyday life. In particular, we have focused on the humble automatic cleaning machines at Singapore's Changi Airport and synecdochically deployed them as a foil to think through how nondescript machines can meaningfully alter the (everyday) lives and livelihoods of (airport) workers, users and managers. As Hirsh (2016) posits in his thesis on airport urbanism, these lessons must not be seen as relevant only to the confines of high-tech airports or air travel, but be recognized for their analogous value for cities and their daily functions. Indeed, automation today oversees an increasing range of urban activities – like cleaning, monitoring, patrolling and responding – that were once thought too menial, too uneconomical for machines to be built for. Here, automation has transformed workers, users and managers of cities-at-large too, rendering them, in their own ways, dependents of machines and (re)new(ed) personas of their former selves.

The intrusion of robots in urban everyday life is not to be dismissed as a natural or inevitable progression of modern urbanity. It elicits weighty questions that could impinge on quality-of-life issues in the city. Not only are machines poised to change the nature of urban jobs and replace some vocations by becoming faster and more efficient than humans; they also have the capacity to influence perceptions and expectations of citizens, as well as empower those in positions of governance to abdicate their managerial responsibilities through 'good enough' robotic decisions and algorithmic calculations (Amoore, 2020: 67). What is more, this turn towards technological solutions has only accelerated since the start of the COVID-19 pandemic. While previously unimaginable, the protracted crisis has seen city governments (and airports) turn to robots for basic tasks such as infrastructural maintenance, good deliveries, biometric surveillance, clinical care and the control of movement (Chen et al., 2020; Lew et al., 2020), which not only denotes a further infiltration of automation but also a further surrendering of intimate parts of everyday life to robots. The danger of this, of course, is that such drastic stopgaps – with all their implications on privacy, justice and power – become difficult to reverse in the future. As urban life gradually reconfigures to a new normative state, it may be that machines, not humans, become the focal point of care (Batty, 2018).

Notwithstanding, it is important to acknowledge that urban dwellers are not passive onlookers amid these high-tech experimentations. Indeed, automated futures can produce contradictions and crises, and therefore possibilities for challenge and change. As While et al. (2021: 769; our emphasis) argue, 'there are technical, trust and safety challenges in bringing robots into *dynamic* urban environments alongside humans.' This suggests that the coexistence between humans and robots is a fraught one and cannot be simply reduced to a scenario where the former are automatically inclined to cede their place to the latter (Yeo and Lin, 2020). In this respect, there is an urgency to seek out what these new equilibria are – ones in which workers and users can subsist alongside the managers, technologists and designers in more politically neutral terms (Bissell, 2021; Lynch, 2020). If the stakes of robotic airport/urban futures are high, it would precisely be because of the way everyday citizens (are able to) make good of these futures.

Note

1 While some of these robots sport masculine features, the names reflect either gender-neutral/unisex expressions in their language (Liang Liang, Putih and Palich) or feminine ideas such as Jing Jing (crystal), Bersih (spotless) and Minnal (brilliance).

References

Amoore, L. (2006). Biometric borders: Governing mobilities in the war on terror. *Political Geography*, 25(3), 336–351.

Amoore, L. (2020). *Cloud Ethics*. Duke University Press, Durham.

Augé, M. (1995). *Non-places: An Introduction to Supermodernity*. Verso Books, London.

Barns, S. (2021). Out of the loop? On the radical and the routine in urban big data. *Urban Studies*, 58(15), 3203–3210.

Batty, M. (2018). Artificial intelligence and smart cities. *Environment and Planning B: Urban Analytics and City*, 45(1), 3–6.

Bissell, D. (2021). Encountering automation: Redefining bodies through stories of technological change. *Environment and Planning D: Society and Space*, 39(2), 366–384.

Bissell, D., & Del Casino, V.J. (2017). Whither labour geography and the rise of robots? *Social & Cultural Geography*, 18(3), 435–442.

Blunt, A. (2005). Cultural geography: Cultural geographies of home. *Progress in Human Geography*, 29(4), 505–515.

Budd, L., & Adey, P. (2009). The software-simulated airworld: Anticipatory code and affective aeromobilities. *Environment and Planning A*, 41(6), 1366–1385.

Changi Airport Group (2019). *Keeping Changi Spick and Span*. Available at: https://www.changiairport.com/corporate/media-centre/changijourneys/the-changi-experience/keeping-changi-spick-and-span.html/ [Accessed 19/01/2023].

Changi Airport Group (2020). *How Robots are Revolutionalising the Guest Experience at Jewel*. Available at: https://www.changiairport.com/corporate/media-centre/changijourneys/the-changi-experience/how-robots-are-revolutionalising-the-guest-experience-at-Jewel.html/ [Accessed 19/01/2023].

Changi Airport Group (2021). *The Science of a Deep Clean*. Available at: https://www.changiairport.com/corporate/media-centre/changijourneys/the-airport-never-sleeps/deepclean.html/ [Accessed 19/01/2023].

Chen, B., Marvin, S., & While, A. (2020). Containing COVID-19 in China: AI and the robotic restructuring of future cities. *Dialogues in Human Geography*, 10(2), 238–241.

Cushman & Wakefield (2019). *Future Proofing the Cleaning Industry in Singapore*. Available at: https://www.cushmanwakefield.com/en/singapore/insights/blog/future-proofing-the-cleaning-industry-in-singapore/ [Accessed 19/01/2023].

Cugurullo, F. (2020). Urban artificial intelligence: From automation to autonomy in the smart city. *Frontiers in Sustainable Cities*, 2, 38.

Cugurullo, F. (2021). *Frankenstein Urbanism: Eco, Smart and Autonomous Cities, Artificial Intelligence and the End of the City*. Routledge, London.

Datta, A. (2016). The intimate city: Violence, gender and ordinary life in Delhi slums. *Urban Geography*, 37(3), 323–342.

Dengler, K., & Matthes, B. (2018). The impacts of digital transformation on the labour market: Substitution potentials of occupations in Germany. *Technological Forecasting and Social Change*, 137, 304–316.

DiscoverSG (2017). *Changi Airport Ramps Up Automation At Its New Terminal 4*. Available: https://discoversg.com/2017/07/26/changi-airport-terminal-4/ [Accessed 19/01/2023].

Fortunati, L., Esposito, A., & Lugano, G. (2015). Introduction to the special issue 'Beyond Industrial Robotics: Social Robots Entering Public and Domestic Spheres'. *The Information Society*, 31(3), 229–236.

Garrett, B., & Anderson, K. (2018). Drone methodologies: Taking flight in human and physical geography. *Transactions of the Institute of British Geographers*, 43(3), 341–359.

Goonewardena, K., Kipfer, S., Milgrom, R., & Schmid, C. (2008). *Space, Difference, Everyday Life: Reading Henri Lefebvre*. Routledge, New York.

Graham, S., & Thrift, N. (2007). Out of order: Understanding repair and mainte-nance. *Theory, Culture & Society*, 24(3), 1–25.

Harvey, D. (1978). The urban process under capitalism: A framework for analysis. *International Journal of Urban and Regional Research*, 2(1–3), 101–131.

Highmore, B. (2002). *Everyday Life and Cultural Theory: An Introduction.* Routledge, London.

Hildebrand, J., & Sodero, S. (2021). Pandemic drones. *Transfers*, 11(1), 148–158.

Hirsh, M. (2016). *Airport Urbanism: Infrastructure and Mobility in Asia.* University of Minnesota Press, Minneapolis.

Holloway, L., & Hubbard, P. (2001). *People and Place: The Extraordinary Geographies of Everyday Life.* Prentice Hall, London.

Islam, I. (2018). Automation and the future of employment: Implications for India. *South Asian Journal of Human Resources Management*, 5(2), 234–243.

Jarvis, H. (2005). Moving to London time: Household co-ordination and the infra-structure of everyday life. *Time & Society*, 14(1), 133–154.

Jarvis, H. (2010). Geography and everyday life. In Warf, B. (Eds.) *Encyclopedia of Geography*. SAGE, Thousand Oaks.

Kitchin, R. (2020). Civil liberties *or* public health, or civil liberties *and* public health? Using surveillance technologies to tackle the spread of COVID-19. *Space and Polity*, 24(3), 362–381.

Kitchin, R. (2021). *Data Lives: How Data Are Made and Shape Our World.* Bristol University Press, Bristol.

Kong, L., & Woods, O. (2018). The ideological alignment of smart urbanism in Singapore: Critical reflections on a political paradox. *Urban Studies*, 55(4), 679–701.

Kwan, M.P. (2002). Time, information technologies, and the geographies of everyday life. *Urban Geography*, 23(5), 471–482.

Lefebvre, H. (1991 [1947]). *Critique of Everyday Life*, vol. 1 (trans. John Moore). Verso, London.

Lew, A. A., Cheer, J. M., Haywood, M., Brouder, P., & Salazar, N. B. (2020). Visions of travel and tourism after the global COVID-19 transformation of 2020. *Tourism Geographies*, 22(3), 455–466.

Lin, W. (2017). Sky watching: Vertical surveillance in civil aviation. *Environment and planning D: Society and Space*, 35(3), 399–417.

Lin, W. (2018). Catering for flight: Rethinking aeromobility as logistics. *Environment and Planning D: Society and Space*, 36(4), 683–700.

Lynch, C.R. (2020). Unruly digital subjects: Social entanglements, identity, and the politics of technological expertise. *Digital Geography and Society*, 1, DOI: 10.1016/j.diggeo.2020.100001.

Lynch, C.R. (2021). Critical geographies of social robotics. *Digital Geography and Society*, 2, DOI: 10.1016/j.diggeo.2021.100010.

Mackereth, K. (2019). Mechanical maids and family androids: Racialised post-care imaginaries in Humans (2015–), Sleep Dealer (2008) and Her (2013). *Feminist Review*, 123(1), 24–39.

Macrorie, R., Marvin, S., & While, A. (2021). Robotics and automation in the city: A research agenda. *Urban Geography*, 42(2), 197–217.

Massey, D. (1995). *Spatial Divisions of Labour: Social Structures and the Geography of Production.* Macmillan Education UK, London.

McDowell, L., Batnitzky, A., & Dyer, S. (2007). Division, segmentation, and interpellation: The embodied labors of migrant workers in a greater London hotel. *Economic Geography*, 83(1), 1–25.

McGuirk, P., Dowling, R., Maalsen, S., & Baker, T. (2021). Urban governance innovation and COVID-19. *Geographical Research*, 59(2), 188–195.

McKinsey (2015). *Four Fundamentals of Workplace Automation*. Available: https://www.mckinsey.com/business-functions/mckinsey-digital/our-insights/four-funda mentals-of-workplace-automation/ [Accessed 19/01/2023].

McKinsey (2018). *Notes from the AI frontier: Applications and Value of Deep Learning*. Available: https://www.mckinsey.com/featured-insights/artificial-intelligence/notes-from-the-ai-frontier-applications-and-value-of-deep-learning/ [Accessed 19/01/2023].

McNeill, D. (2005). Skyscraper geography. *Progress in Human Geography*, 29(1), 41–55.

McNeill, D. (2015). Global firms and smart technologies: IBM and the reduction of cities. *Transactions of the Institute of British Geographers*, 40(4), 562–574.

Oppenheimer, A. (2019). *The Robots are Coming! The Future of Jobs in the Age of Automation*. Vintage Books, New York.

Pascoe, D. (2001). *Airspaces*. Reaktion Books, London.

Pierce, J., Lawhon, M., & McCreary, T. (2019). From precarious work to obsolete labour? Implications of technological disemployment for geographical scholarship. *Geografiska Annaler: Series B, Human Geography*, 101(2), 84–101.

Pink, S., & Sumartojo, S. (2018). The lit world: Living with everyday urban automation. *Social & Cultural Geography*, 19(7), 833–852.

Popescu, G. (2017). Biometric technologies and the automation of identity and space. In Warf, B. (Eds.) *Handbook on Geographies of Technology*. Edward Elgar Publishing, Cheltenham, 459–470.

Pulido, L. (2017). Geographies of race and ethnicity II: Environmental racism, racial capitalism and state-sanctioned violence. *Progress in Human Geography*, 41(4), 524–533.

Richardson, L. (2021). Coordinating office space: Digital technologies and the platformization of work. *Environment and Planning D: Society and Space*, 39(2), 347–365.

Richardson, L., & Bissell, D. (2019). Geographies of digital skill. *Geoforum*, 99, 278–286.

Ritzer, G., & Jurgenson, N. (2010). Production, consumption, prosumption: The nature of capitalism in the age of the digital 'prosumer'. *Journal of Consumer Culture*, 10(1), 13–36.

Schwanen, T., Dijst, M., & Kwan, M.P. (2008). ICTS and the decoupling of everyday activities, space and time: Introduction. *Tijdschrift voor Economische en Sociale Geografie*, 99(5), 519–527.

Sheller, M. (2007). Bodies, cybercars and the mundane incorporation of automated mobilities. *Social & Cultural Geography*, 8(2), 175–197.

Silver, B.J. (2003). *Forces of Labor: Workers' Movements and Globalization Since 1870*. Cambridge University Press, Cambridge.

Strauss, K. (2020). Labour geography II: Being, knowledge and agency. *Progress in Human Geography*, 44(1), 150–159.

Sumartojo, S., & Lugli, D. (2021). Lively robots: Robotic technologies in COVID-19. *Social & Cultural Geography*, 23(9), 1220–1237.

Tay, B. T., Low, S. C., Ko, K. H., & Park, T. (2016). Types of humor that robots can play. *Computers in Human Behavior*, 60, 19–28.

Tripathy, P., & Carrière, D. (2020). Filtering density and doing the maintenance work. *Urban Geography*, 41(10), 1326–1334.

Valentine, G. (2008). Living with difference: Reflections on geographies of encounter. *Progress in Human Geography*, 32(3), 323–337.

West, D. M. (2018). *The Future of Work: Robots, AI, and Automation*. Brookings Institution Press, Washington, DC.

While, A. H., Marvin, S., & Kovacic, M. (2021). Urban robotic experimentation: San Francisco, Tokyo and Dubai. *Urban Studies*, 58(4), 769–786.

Wilson, H.F. (2017). On geography and encounter: Bodies, borders, and difference. *Progress in Human Geography*, 41(4), 451–471.

Wilts, A. (2020). Living in a fly-over world: On moving in a heterogeneous navigational culture. *Cultural Geographies*, 27(1), 23–36.

Yeo, S. J. I. (2022). Smart urban living in Singapore? Thinking through everyday geographies. *Urban Geography*, 1–20. DOI: 10.1080/02723638.2021.2016258.

Yeo, S. J. I., & Lin, W. (2020). Autonomous vehicles, human agency and the potential of urban life. *Geography Compass*, 14(10), e12531.

PART III

City brains and urban platforms

12

AMBIENT COMMONS?

Valuing urban public spaces in an era of AI-enabled ambient computing

Sarah Barns

Introduction

> It is invisible, everywhere computing that does not live on a personal device
> of any sort, but is in the woodwork everywhere.
>
> *(Weiser, 1991)*

The fabric of urban spaces is increasingly embedded with automated, intelligence-gathering agents, seamlessly integrated within the myriad physical surfaces and social interactions that make up urban life. Through practices of navigating, driving, shopping, regulating, partying, policing and building, urban life is increasingly expressive of a range of objects, practices and business models integrated with digital automation. In automated cities, public agencies are now learning to govern, plan and manage complex urban settings through virtual simulations, such as digital twins, built using real-world data (Cugurullo, 2021; Luque-Ayala and Marvin, 2020). Companies from start-ups, scale-ups and global technology firms seek to generate new data-driven business models via software platforms that integrate physical sensors with data-servicing platforms (Barns, 2020; Maedche et al., 2019). Virtual assistants and automated software agents allow citizens to interact and navigate known and unknown spaces with ease.

In this context, local government agencies (LGAs) face complex challenges to do with how they manage the extension of automated urban–digital interactions in public spaces. The boundaries between public and private spaces are proving harder and harder to discern, as are the governing rules used to manage civic spaces and their use by automated devices and agents. As has

DOI: 10.4324/9781003365877-15

been widely observed in the rise of urban platforms, the rules and mechanisms governing how sensors, devices, virtual assistants and data platforms operate and inter-relate – the code-based ecosystems structuring digital and material spaces of interaction – are often highly opaque (Barns, 2021; Wachsmuth, 2018; Mackenzie, 2018; van Dijck, 2020: 2). This, in turn, has made them challenging to regulate (Belli and Zingales, 2020; Boeing et al., 2021; Domurath, 2018). Growing attention towards how digital platforms scale has also underscored how increasingly dependent many public agencies are on the operations of privatized data and digital ecosystems and the automated services they enable (Barns, 2020; Cugurullo, 2020; Stehlin et al., 2020; van Dijck, 2020). Likewise, hybridized spaces of urban–digital interaction – 'code/spaces' (Kitchin and Dodge, 2011) operating within everyday urban settings like retail malls, high streets, urban parks and railway centres – informs new protocols and standards determining how digitally informed urban interactions and behaviours are governed, from compliance under European data privacy protections (GDPR) to the emerging governance of curbsides by platform-based ride services (International Transport Forum, 2017).

Over the past decade, LGAs have been active in facilitating smart-city programs, encouraging the introduction of intelligent agents into urban services such as lighting, waste management and parking monitoring (Batty, 2018; D'Amico et al., 2020). In this capacity, authorities have worked in partnership with technology agencies to support integrated autonomous services into the infrastructures and services delivered by government (Karvonen et al., 2019; Kitchin et al., 2015; Söderström et al., 2014). However, the growing sophistication of urban digital platforms and the range of autonomous, ambient devices that support them also raise new challenges around data access and use, raising critical governance challenges. For example, a digital platform like Airbnb offers a practical accommodation service but does so in ways underpinned by opaque data-harvesting practices that can undermine the regulatory capacities of local authorities (Boeing et al., 2021). This points to the proliferation of 'digital divides' existing not at the level of digital access per se, but access to the data analytics and governance protocols governing how data is being used, exploited and adapted by digital platforms. As van Djick has argued (2020: 2), 'the platform mechanisms underpinning the ecosystem are largely opaque and out of sight for users and governments. Platformization is overwhelmingly driven by commercial interests which often take precedence over societal values.'

Such developments point to major current weaknesses in how the value of civic spaces is being upheld in the context of widespread digital automation. In this chapter, I discuss some of the challenges posed by the presence of automated agents in public spaces, examining the growing co-option of public spaces to the wider adoption of urban AI, in ways that undermine the public values associated with shared, civic spaces. As I outline, relatively limited definitions of urban data as a shared or public resource make it vulnerable to co-option as a private resource and limit the capacity of citizens to engage constructively with local authorities and technology providers in dialogue around the appropriate use of urban data within private platform ecosystems. Such challenges, I suggest, also point to the need for a more robust defence of the civic value of urban data. In conclusion, I suggest the idea of an *ambient commons* as a potentially useful framing device, which can support a more robust debate around the exploitation of shared civic spaces by private technology platforms.

The data provocations of urban digital platforms

Widespread attention towards digital platforms today recognizes the power of data-driven platform ecosystems to coordinate and disrupt different sectors by instituting a range of multi-sided, market-based interactions and transactions. The urban manifestations of these platforms, considered through the lens of *platform urbanism*, extend interest in the spatial implications of digital platforms away from specific technologies, interfaces, sensors and devices, and instead address the different organizational and relational practices they institute, including standardized approaches to data sharing policies, protocols and business models (Barns, 2020; Helmond, 2015; Krisch, 2022; Pollio, 2020; Söderström and Mermet, 2020; van Dijck, 2020). By instituting governing protocols around data sharing and use across platform ecosystems, digital platforms reconstitute existing urban relations, institutions and transactions through integrations of code, commerce and corporeality. This implicates multiple intersecting (digitized) relations and socio-spatial conditions and relationships, often in ways that entrench dependencies upon platforms and, in turn, data accumulation (Barns, 2020; Langley and Leyshon, 2017; Sadowski, 2019).

Data governance protocols and modes of data exploitation are central to the capacity of platform ecosystems to co-ordinate and intermediate relationships, achieved through their proprietary opacity (Mackenzie, 2018), which places limits on how proprietary algorithms are able to be regulated and governed under relevant data use legislation (Zarsky, 2017). Through the rise of urban platforms, the data ecosystems that underpin platforms are in turn becoming increasingly powerful in determining and shaping decisions made by urban actors. In the case of Uber, the coordinated uptake of the app by drivers and riders alike allows not only for the delivery of on-demand transport services but also facilitates the coordination of a vast array of data ecosystems, from spatial data to real-time user data. Today, this platform ecosystem has evolved to become an extensive network of application programming interfaces (APIs), machine-learning algorithms and code-based micro-services (MSA), which act to coordinate data points that originate within, but also extend beyond, Uber's platform ecosystem (Barns, 2019; Domurath, 2018; Pardeshi, n.d.; Stehlin et al., 2020; Vorwerk, 2019). Embedded within a platform ecosystem of this nature are myriad machine learning applications, including deep learning neural networks, which themselves act as generative teaching networks (GTNs) that facilitate the production of huge volumes of training data. In turn, these accelerate the predictive analytics that allows a user to know when its rider will arrive – a key incentive for the use of a ride-sharing platform like Uber's over alternate modes of transport. While Uber may feel like a simple mobile app to its users, it is also a powerful instrument coordinating a vast array of human and digital agents. It is designed to always be actively learning from urban behaviour and in so doing, is also increasing the generation of urban data and interactions at scale in ways that "train," and thereby reconstitute, everyday behaviours, continuously and autonomously. And it is but one of the millions of actively learning, actively informing intelligent interfaces that are part of the fabric of city life today (Cugurullo, 2020).

As is increasingly recognized, these systemic conditions for data accumulation and exploitation by private platforms raise challenges for governance and regulation. For example, the Airbnb platform produced radical shortages in long-term rentals in major cities, in turn provoking a significant regulatory backlash by local authorities in many cities (Ferreri and Sanyal, 2018; Gurran and Phibbs, 2017; Wachsmuth, 2018). But because Airbnb, as a private platform, could control how data could be shared across diverse informational points within and beyond its platform, for many years city authorities experienced significant challenges in accessing the information needed to enforce emerging regulation – despite the rapid increase in users across these cities (Boeing et al., 2021; Ferreri and Sanyal, 2018; Wachsmuth, 2018). In the case of New York, Airbnb's refusal to make key data points available to local policymakers necessitated novel data hacking techniques by researchers and generated protracted lawsuits (Wachsmuth and Weisler, 2018). As noted by Boeing et al. (2021), for close to a decade key information such as the identity of hosts, the addresses of their listings and their volume of activity required the cooperation from Airbnb or third-party firms such as Host Compliance, until regulatory pressure ultimately forced the company to create a new data sharing portal (Martineau, 2019).

While data-sharing practices at Airbnb have improved in recent years, the advance of algorithmic practices of price regulation and fixing raises new challenges. A proprietary machine learning (ML) application called 'Aerosolve' is responsible for determining the appropriate price of hosts' listings, with minimal transparency over its price-setting. It is widely believed these prices are set artificially low, so as to maximize the appeal of the Airbnb platform to renters, thereby undermining the commercial attractiveness of its competitors. However, there is no way for external authorities to determine whether this is the case without access to the Aerosolve algorithm. In this way, the opacity of Airbnb's data ecosystem continues to advance the goals of the platform often at the expense of other service providers, despite advances in (raw) data sharing in recent years. In this example, the data was made available in relation to basic host data, but not the more complex, data-rich area of algorithmic pricing, which remains a 'black box' operating with limited independent scrutiny (Boeing et al., 2021; Pasquale, 2015). These require large volumes of training data to be replicated, but also generate new volumes of training data, thus accelerating the information or data gap.

Governing ambient computing in urban spaces: new provocations and challenges

The practices and problematics of digital platforms like Uber and Airbnb are well known, however less visible are the proliferation of intelligent agents with everyday spaces of the city – the civic squares and main streets, public precincts championed as being vital to the health and wellbeing of communities – and the challenges they pose around their data accumulation. The practices of data accumulation evidenced by urban platforms are central to their 'intelligence-generating' capabilities – i.e., to the rise of urban AI. Public spaces are now becoming key sites for AI-driven ambient computing devices which monitor localized activity and environmental conditions for different purposes. Examples include Internet of Things (IoT) sensors embedded in smart lighting poles, neural networks utilized within digital out of home (DOOH) advertising and air quality monitors monitoring localized air quality ratings and pollution levels. Many such *ambient* computing devices have been introduced in the context of smart city programs sponsored or facilitated by local governance authorities, often for the purpose of monitoring environmental conditions, reducing resource use and, in the case of outdoor advertising, revenue-raising by local authorities in partnership with advertising companies. However, the growing dependences and integrations of these AI-driven ambient computing services within wider private data ecosystems also means these devices can support the accumulation of vast amounts of urban data for a variety of different uses.

As is increasingly clear, the uses of this data may not accord with the original intention behind its collection – facilitating what Koops (2021) describes as *function creep*. Smart light poles, for example, can be used not only for lighting but also for security monitoring, while digital advertising screens can also be used to harvest activity and sentiment data about passers-by, not limited only to the display of digital advertising. Agents and services that proliferate widely, for example virtual assistants that enable a user to navigate the range of ride sharing services offered through the Uber app to navigate a city, benefit from accessing and harvesting a large volume of urban activity data as training data, which is in turn used to enhance the sophistication of its service to users. As stated in a 2021 technology report, 'while the lamp posts of yesteryear provided only illumination, modern-day lamp post can serve as multi-functional smart-city nodes, capable of monitoring everything from crime to parking to weather' (Gehl, 2011: no page).

This form of distributed, relational, invisible connectivity has been described as *ambient computing*, denoting conditions in which agents, people, services, infrastructures, habitats and robots negotiate and respond to each other constantly (Svítek et al., 2020). As one 2016 O'Reilly report enthused in relation to the rise of ambient computing, 'we've entered the Age of Ambient Computing, a convergence of cheap sensors, wireless connectivity, increasingly powerful microchips, and advanced analytics that is redefining the nature of public and private spaces' (Barlow, 2016: no page). It's worth noting that this concept of ambient intelligence in relation to new forms of computing is not new. Crang and Graham (2007: 794), for example, wrote in 2007 about the rise of ambient intelligence as 'the "coding" of people, places and objects – that is processes of identification and then the layering and cross-referring of these identifications through software algorithms.' More recently, critical attention towards ambient computing has also addressed its mode of operation as that of surveillance infrastructure. Devices emblematic of ambient computing in the home, such as Google's Nest, Amazon's Alexa and Microsoft's Cortana, focus attention towards the encroachment of privatized data surveillance devices into domestic spaces, as these devices operate by constantly producing and harvesting data from their local environments (Wood and Monahan, 2019; Neville, 2020; Sadowski, 2019).

Perhaps what is most distinctive about the emergence of ambient computing within public precincts is the complex amalgams of public and private data this depends upon, through widespread data-harvesting practices. Just as domestic devices such as Alexa will actively harvest domestic data as part of its operations, so ambient outdoor devices will be harvesting large volumes of contextual data. In the case of outdoor public spaces, this involves a range of subjects who may be unaware of their data being collected in this way, and who do not see themselves as giving permission for their image, activity or transactions to be collected by autonomous agents that are co-present in a space with them. Likewise, while smart city programs may be framed by local authorities as supporting their capacity to improve the efficient management and operations of their cities, data practices adopted by ambient computing devices in public settings also creates new dependencies on private actors and private data ecosystems for the provision of basic urban services (Cugurullo, 2020; Kitchin et al., 2019; Sadowski, 2021). In the following section I explore in more detail some of the data governance challenges being posed by the presence of ambient computing in public spaces, linked to broader discussions about the rise of automated, artificial intelligence operating in cities.

Here, I am interested specifically in addressing how forms of ambient computing – and the data ecosystems that constitute its many devices, algorithms and services – implicate the 'life between buildings,' the civic spaces and the public realm of cities. These are complex, data-rich spaces that at once offer great commercial appeal to platforms and their algorithmic services, but are also spaces and places valued for the public value to the city. They are spaces where people enter freely, as strangers, and do so under the expectation of anonymity. What, then, is at risk in the co-optation of these spaces as data rich environs in a world of ambient computing and platform ecosystems?

Reframing the data values of civic spaces in an era of ambient computing

Twentieth-century urbanists from Jane Jacobs to Claus Oldenberg, William Whyte and Jan Gehl have famously championed the value of the *in-between* places of the public realm for their contribution to the wellbeing of a community and its capacity to tolerate difference, support inclusion, and offer a range of accessible services (Gehl, 2011; Jacobs, 1965; Oldenburg, 1989). Such spaces are valued as public spaces not because they are always publicly owned, or contain no private sector uses, but because they are understood to play a key role in the wider public or civic value of cities. Public spaces are highly unstable social formations which are contested and always in the-making (Amin, 2006; Mitchell, 2017). Nevertheless, public spaces are championed by urbanists as being vital to cities because they are places where social interaction, community building, and political dissent can take place, and because they contribute to the flourishing of individuals, communities, cities and societies (Low, 2023). There is an expectation, in the words of Amin (2006: 241), that 'the free and conducive mingling of strangers in streets, squares, parks, and other shared spaces fosters a culture of civility and civic responsibility.' Part of the value – including civic value – of public spaces is the capacity for citizens to address others, and be addressed by others, as strangers (Iveson, 2017).

Such spaces are necessarily complex assemblages of interaction across ecology, economy and civic culture. As such, they are rich sites for the harvesting of large volumes of data. Forms of data generated in shared, civic spaces are highly diverse and may include a mix of open data, shared data, transaction data and personally identifiable data. Nevertheless, data collection by intelligent devices operating in public spaces is likely not subject to conditions of transparency in terms of how it is used and for what purpose (Iveson, 2017). For this reason, many smart city projects have provoked concerns around privacy protection (Artyushina, 2020; Baibarac-Duignan and de Lange, 2021; De Lange, 2019; Sadowski, 2019). Algorithmic processes of data integration operating within larger private data ecosystems raise challenges around how the value of these spaces, and the forms of data generated within them, is being utilized. Key questions emerge: Who gets to own and exploit the data flows existing within these ambient environments? Who controls or gets to inform algorithmic modes of data governance that takes place? And, who might be responsible and accountable for decisions around data use? (van Dijck, 2020).

A smart light pole, for example, may collect data that can be used to monitor the activities of citizens, despite its intended use primarily as a lighting infrastructure. In the city of Sydney, the installation of new digital advertising kiosks across the city footprint in 2022 saw the implementation of new data-harvesting capabilities within the digital panels, allowing their function to extend beyond purely display advertising to include data aggregation and data on-selling to advertisers. Data collected by the private operator in this case, QMS, allows for the linking of urban activity data with other sources such as Visa transaction data, demographic data and GPS data for enhanced targeting of consumers and on-selling of consumer data to advertisers (Coyne, 2022). How this data is harvested, integrated and used by QMS may further enhance its capacity to sell advertising, however, there is no capacity for the uses of this data to be subject to any kind of regulatory or public transparency. Under Australian privacy provisions, there is no capacity for citizens to elect to opt out of the data harvesting taking place via the new digital kiosks or request it be ported to a different provider (OAIC, 2018).

As a 2021 European review of smart-city programs found, many such uses of digital sensors and data-harvesting devices in public spaces, achieved under the rubric of smart-city programs, face challenges around compliance with General Data Protection Regulation (GDPR) established under the European Union Data Protection Directive of 1995 (van Zeeland et al., 2021). The GDPR upholds a set of pillars around privacy protection that relate to the uses of personal data, including purpose specification, data minimization, automated decisions and data portability (Artyushina, 2020; Zarsky, 2017). Personal data, defined as any information that directly or indirectly relates to an identified or identifiable individual, 'must be collected for a "specific, explicit, and legitimate" purpose and cannot be further "processed" in a way which is "incompatible" with the original purpose' (Artyushina, 2020: 4). Data minimization means keeping data collection to the bare minimum required for data collectors' operations. The notion of automated decisions grants European citizens the right to opt out of automated decision-making, while data portability provides European data subjects the right to transfer their information to another service provider or to require the data controller to delete certain information about them (Zarsky, 2017).

The 2021 review of GDPR compliance in European smart cities identified particular risks to enforcement of its provisions around data privacy, including (a) the multitude and complexity of fundamental rights at stake in smart cities; (b) the difficulty of assessing cumulative effects arising from multiple projects; (c) a lack of transparency and limited citizen engagement in smart city development; and (d) the involvement of private companies (van Zeeland et al., 2021). A major issue the report addressed was the capacity for authorities to assess the impact of technology on personal data protection in a context in which both public and private actors are present (van Zeeland et al., 2021). Likewise, the algorithmic processing of large volumes of urban data by autonomous agents in city spaces provides ample opportunities for it to be used beyond the specific purpose for which it is collected – again contravening GDPR provisions.

As Zarsky (2017) has argued, much of the GDPR failed to properly address the surge in Big Data practices, and this is nowhere more evident than in the use of algorithmic forms of data harvesting and collection within urban public spaces. The 2021 European review found many smart city projects do not provide sufficient argumentation or documentation to support the (extent of the) processing of personal data implemented in the project, as required under the GDPR, nor undertake requisite Data Protection Impact Assessments (DPIA). Issues included a lack of understanding of the applicability of GDPR to smart city projects and a lack of resourcing of internal capability within local authorities for ongoing risk assessments around the potential privacy risks associated with the use of smart city technology (van Zeeland et al., 2021).

While there are clear privacy issues attached to the way automated, intelligent agents are accessing large volumes of data in public spaces, many of the issues addressed here relate primarily to the use and exploitation of personal data. Another challenging area concerns the ways in which urban data is being valued as a private resource. There is currently no clear definition of how urban data operates as a rich and complex data environment, beyond definitions of personal or private data, open data and commercial data. Interestingly, the failed Sidewalk Toronto initiative, a public–private partnership between the public developer Waterfront Toronto and Google sister company Sidewalk Labs, offered one of the most detailed considerations of urban data as a unique category of data harvesting which is of significant value to technology companies. While the program was highly controversial and ultimately failed to go ahead, work undertaken within the partnership by Sidewalk Labs did offer a useful outline of how technology company like Google values the data generated within the 'life between buildings' that makes up the public realm.

Under the proposed, ultimately doomed Sidewalk Toronto proposal, a set of governance conditions were established that would allow a technology operator to collect and monetize large volumes of urban data for commercial use via an independent *data trust*. As Artyushina (2020) outlines, the data trust concept was underpinned by a set of novel definitions around different kinds of data, which was transparent in outlining the value being generated through widespread data harvesting in public spaces. The term *urban data* was coined by Sidewalk to denote the anonymized information being collected 'in public and semi-private spaces such as streets, restaurants, and halls of buildings' (Artyushina, 2020: 8). Unlike 'conventional data,' which refers to all types of personally identifiable data, urban data was to be considered a public asset, enclosed within the framework of an Urban Data Trust, unlike conventional data which should remain a private asset of the company and its partners. The definition of urban data was later updated to refer to data 'gathered in the city's physical environment, including the public realm, publicly accessible spaces, and even some private buildings' (Artyushina, 2020: 8). This definition categorized urban data into four categories: personal information, deidentified data, aggregate data and non-personal data all to be managed within the Trust. The Trust itself was not a public or open data platform but rather an entity designed to allow citizens to 'take shares in the profits derived from their own data,' and companies monetizing this urban data would be required to submit self-assessment forms and 'urban data agreements' to 'govern the collection, disclosure, storage, security, analysis, use and destruction of urban data' (Artyushina, 2020: 10; Sidewalk Labs, 2019: 421).

There were a number of major controversies provoked by the data governance models established under Sidewalk Toronto, which ultimately is now useful as a case study of how to lose public trust in smart cities (Artyushina, 2020; Austin and Lie, 2021; Mann et al., 2020). Critical to the widespread public backlash was the lack of any capacity by citizens to opt out of their personal data being collected for commercial purposes by technology companies (Artyushina, 2020). And yet, arguably many of these data-gathering practices are already being undertaken in many public spaces around the world – they just lack formal rules and protocols around their use, including citizen input into their design. What the data governance framework put forward here also underscored was the ways in which many private companies are *already* actively using urban public spaces to establish and entrench data-driven business models, often without explicit permission from citizens or local authorities. Under the Data Trust model, the commercial uses of this urban data were at least made explicit, with provisions around how citizens could "take shares in its profit" through an attempt to distribute some of the private benefits of what is ultimately public activity.

Where to from here? Reviving the concept of ambient commons

As I have discussed in this chapter, the co-optation of public spaces by ambient computing devices raises a number of challenges around how urban data is being harvested and integrated within private platform ecosystems. While there has been a great deal of attention on the privacy implications of digital platforms and smart city technology, there has, to date, been less attention placed on the appropriate regulatory framework to effectively govern how these devices exploit and capitalize on the rich data surrounds that the public realm offers. As identified, the application of GDPR within smart city technologies is undermined by a relatively limited understanding of the multi-functional applications of ambient computing and the data ecosystems that underpin it, particularly at the municipal level.

Cities can be expected to respond proactively to these challenges in the coming years. A number of European cities, including the City of Barcelona, London, Amsterdam and UN-Habitat, have launched a Global Observatory of Urban Artificial Intelligence (UN-Habitat, 2022), which advocates for the application of digital rights to the implementation of AI initiatives at the municipal scale. This partnership includes the establishment of an AI register in Helsinki and Amsterdam, which is designed to enable citizens to locate the use algorithms being used within the operations of municipal government, and for what purposes, in a transparent way. Such developments point to a growing role for local authorities working in partnership with wider, multilateral organizations at different scales, adopting and adapting new experimental approaches to urban data governance.

In this context, it is worth considering how urban data might represent a unique domain of data custodianship for local authorities, which extends beyond private, personal data and open or commercial data, in ways that can reflect the broader civic values underpinning public spaces. Here, the term *ambient commons* coined by McCullough (2013), may prove useful. Recognizing the immanence of ambient computing within the material fabric of everyday urban interactions, the concept of the ambient commons could be used to elevate the need for 'commons-based' approaches that addresses more directly how urban AI operates in shared spaces (Calzada and Almirall, 2019). Signalling the shared, public realm of the city as a form of urban commons – an ambient commons – would consider the use of distributed sensors, algorithms and agents not just discrete intervention, as in the chatbot telling a passenger where to turn left on the highway, or a predictive algorithm informing a surveillance operation, or a lighting sensor switching on lighting as someone passes by, but as a recursive series of data-driven interventions taking place within spaces and places valued for their public, civic value.

The city to have most strongly advocated for a 'data commons' approach to urban data governance is the City of Barcelona, which in 2016 introduced sweeping new changes to data governance models in order to build a more proactive approach to the management of the city's data. The project has attracted global attention as a leading program of digital sovereignty in cities (Calzada, 2018; Charnock et al., 2021; Kitchin et al., 2019). In this instance, the City aspired to build its own data governance capacities, after a decade of smart-city policies had allowed data intelligence to be owned and controlled by suppliers of technology services to the city, most notably Cisco (Monge et al., 2022). As well as significant new investment in internal data management tools and processes, the reforms introduced a suite of new 'ethical digital standards' by the City, and negotiation of significant new data sharing policies, requiring contractors and other agencies which are licenced to operate in the city to share certain data on agreed terms. These digital reforms reflected the success of a citizen-led movement and saw Barcelona emerge as one of the leading cities to advocate for a data rights agenda on behalf of its citizens (Calzada and Almirall, 2019; Calzada, 2018; Charnock et al., 2021). As outlined by the City of Barcelona in the *Government Measure on Ethical and Responsible Data Management*:

> The public and private perception of data has to change from that of an asset that offers a competitive advantage to one of a social "infrastructure" that must be public in order to ensure common well-being, and which is exchanged on a quid pro quo basis.
>
> *(City of Barcelona, 2018: 7)*

Here, the model of data governance was described through the lens of the *quid pro quo* in which access to vibrant urban spaces and the data this constitutes is offered in exchange for certain urban services and data access by digital providers and platforms. The reforms, which are ongoing in the City, point to new opportunities for local authorities to co-ordinate different data sources generated in urban settings, including, for example, arrangements around 'Government to Citizen' or G2C data sharing, and Government-to-Business (G2B) data alliances. These initiatives depart from the more widespread open data approach, in which the city manages citizen data on behalf of citizens without consultation (Monge et al., 2022). Instead, theuse of encryption and 'privacy by design' technologies are being piloted to allow citizens to effectively 'triage' who could utilize their personal data, whether government or private sector usage. While not all of what Barcelona set out to achieve was successful, the reforms represent important new data governance precedents and highlight potential areas of intervention by cities to more proactively defend the value of urban data. By developing new licensing and procurement policies, the City demonstrated where there are opportunities for city authorities to negotiate improved data access and sharing on behalf of citizens, including new layers of permission.

Conclusion

As ambient computing devices, screens, agents and algorithms proliferate, public spaces are increasingly sites for the accumulation and harvesting of vast amounts of urban data, with uses, integrations and applications that remain unclear and unknown to the majority of people who uses those spaces. As is increasingly clear, the uses of this data may not accord with the original intention behind its collection, for example as a smart light pole, an air quality monitoring device or indeed a public information kiosk. Lack of transparency around the potential applications and uses of ambient computing devices in public spaces not only represents a privacy risk to citizens but also represents a co-optation of the value of thriving, public, civic spaces by private data ecosystems, with potential forms of value exchange between public and private uses highly limited in their conceptualization and formal use. As I have discussed, the concept of an *ambient commons* which upholds and maintains the shared value of public spaces and the rich forms of data generated in these domains, provides a way to think about what is unique about the many different kinds of data generated by citizens acting freely together, as strangers, in public. Hopefully, the coming years will see growing attention towards the appropriate mechanisms, standards and protocols needed to govern the operation of intelligent, ambient devices in public spaces. Such activities will likely be experimental in nature, such as the use of the AI registers in selected European cities, but are nevertheless critical, as more and more ambient computing devices, operating within large-scale platform ecosystems, operate, modulate and intermediate life in public spaces.

References

Amin, A. (2006). Collective culture and urban public space. In *Inclusive cities: Challenges of urban diversity.* Workshop papers produced by the Woodrow Wilson International the Center for Scholars, the Development Bank of Southern Africa and the CCCB. Available at: https://www.publicspace.org/multimedia/-/post/collective-culture-and-urban-public-space [Accessed 19/01/2023].

Artyushina, A. (2020). Is civic data governance the key to democratic smart cities? The role of the urban data trust in Sidewalk Toronto. *Telematics and Informatics, 55,* 101456. DOI:10.1016/j.tele.2020.101456.

Austin, D., & Lie, D. (2021). Data trusts and the governance of smart environments: Lessons from the failure of Sidewalk Labs' Urban Data Trust. *Surveillance and Society, 19*(2), 255–261.

Baibarac-Duignan, C. & de Lange, M. (2021). Controversing the datafied smart city: Conceptualising a 'making-controversial' approach to civic engagement. *Big Data & Society.* DOI: 10.1177/20539517211025557.

Barlow, M. (2016). *Ambient Computing.* O'Reilly Media, Sebastopol, CA.

Barns, S. (2019). Joining the Dots: Platform intermediation and the recombinatory governance of Uber's ecosystem. In J. Stehlin, K. Ward, A. McMeekin, J. Kasmire, & M. Hodson (Eds.), *Urban Platforms and the Future City: Transformations in Infrastructure, Governance, Knowledge, and Everyday Life.* Routledge.

Barns, S. (2020). *Platform Urbanism: Negotiating Platform Ecosystems in Connected Cities.* Palgrave Macmillan.

Barns, S. (2021). Out of the loop? On the radical and the routine in urban big data. *Urban Studies, 58*(15), 3203–3210.

Batty, M. (2018). Artificial intelligence and smart cities. *Environment and Planning B: Urban Analytics and City Science, 45*(1), 3–6.

Belli, L., & Zingales, N. (2020). Platform value(s): A multidimensional framework for online responsibility. *Computer Law & Security Review*, 36, 105364. DOI: 10.1016/j.clsr.2019.105364.

Boeing, G., Besbris, M., Wachsmuth, D., & Wegmann, J. (2021). Tilted platforms: Rental housing technology and the rise of urban big data oligopolies. *Urban Transformations*, 3(1), 6. DOI: 10.1186/s42854-021-00024-2.

Calzada, I. (2018). (Smart) Citizens from Data Providers to Decision-Makers? The Case Study of Barcelona. *Sustainability*, 12 September 2018.

Calzada, I., & Almirall, E. (2019). Barcelona's Grassroots-Led Urban Experimentation: Deciphering the 'Data Commons' Policy Scheme. *Conference Data for Policy 2019*. DOI:10.5281/zenodo.2604618.

Charnock, G., March, H., & Ribera-Fumaz, R. (2021). From smart to rebel city? Worlding, provincialising and the Barcelona Model. *Urban Studies*, 58(3), 581–600.

City of Barcelona. (2018). *Government Measure on Ethical Data Management*. Available at: https://www.barcelona.cat/digitalstandards/en/data-management/0.1/summary [Accessed 19/01/2023].

Coyne, B. (2022). QMS makes full play for marketing budgets. *Mi3*. Available at: https://www.mi-3.com.au/07-09-2022/qms-makes-play-full-funnel-marketing-budgets-tv-and-digital-budgets-city-sydney-targeted [Accessed 19/01/2023].

Crang, M., & Graham, S. (2007). Sentient Cities: Ambient intelligence and the politics of urban space. *Information, Communication & Society*, 10(6), 789–817.

Cugurullo, F. (2020). Urban artificial intelligence: From automation to autonomy in the smart city. *Frontiers in Sustainable Cities*, 2, 38.

Cugurullo, F. (2021). *Frankenstein Urbanism: Eco, Smart and Autonomous Cities, Artificial Intelligence and the End of the City*. Routledge.

D'Amico, G., L'Abbate, P., Liao, W., Yigitcanlar, T., & Ioppolo, G. (2020). Understanding sensor cities: Insights from technology giant company driven smart urbanism practices. *Sensors*, 20(16). DOI: 10.3390/s20164391.

De Lange, M. (2019). The right to the datafied city: Interfacing the urban data commons. In Cardullo, P., Di Feliciantonio, C., & Kitchin, R. (Eds.), *The Right to the Smart City*. Emerald Group Publishing.

Domurath, I. (2018). Platforms as contract partners: Uber and beyond. *Maastricht Journal of European and Comparative Law*, 25(5), 565–581.

Ferreri, M., & Sanyal, R. (2018). Platform economies and urban planning: Airbnb and regulated deregulation in London. *Urban Studies*, 55(15), 3353–3368.

Gehl, J. (2011). *The Life Between Buildings: Using Public Space. Second Edition. Originally published 1971*. Island Press.

Gurran, N., & Phibbs, P. (2017). When tourists move in: How should urban planners respond to airbnb? *Journal of the American Planning Association*, 83(1), 80–92.

Helmond, A. (2015). The platformization of the web: Making web data platform ready. *Social Media+Society*,1(2),2056305115603080.DOI:10.1177/2056305115603080.

International Transport Forum (2017). The Shared-Use City: Managing the Curb. Available at: https://www.itf-oecd.org/sites/default/files/docs/shared-use-city-managing-curb_3.pdf [Accessed 19/01/2023].

Iveson, K. (2017). 'Making space public' through occupation: The Aboriginal Tent Embassy, Canberra. *Environment and Planning A: Economy and Space*, 49(3), 537–554.

Jacobs, J. (1965). *The Death and Life of Great American Cities*. Random House.

Karvonen, A., Cugurullo, F., & Caprotti, F. (2019). *Inside Smart Cities: Place, Politics and Urban Innovation*. Routledge.

Kitchin, R., Cardullo, P., & Di Feliciantonio, C. (2019). Citizenship, justice and the right to the smart city. In Cardullo, P., Di Feliciantonio, C., & Kitchin, R. (Eds.), *The Right to the Smart City*. Emerald Group Publishing.

Kitchin, R., & Dodge, M. (2011). *Code/Space: Software and Everyday life*. MIT Press.

Kitchin, R., Lauriault, T., & McArdle, G. (2015). Smart cities and the politics of urban data. In S. Marvin, A. Luque-Ayala, & F. McFarlane (Eds.), *Smart Urbanism: Utopian Vision or False Dawn?* Routledge.

Koops, B. J. (2021). The concept of function creep. *Law, Innovation and Technology*, 13(1), 29–56.

Krisch, A. (2022). From smart to platform urbanism to platform municipalism planning ideas for platforms in Toronto and Vienna. In Struver, A. and Bauriedl (Eds.) *Platformization of Urban Life: Towards a Techno-capitalist Transformation of European Cities*.

Langley, P., & Leyshon, A. (2017). Platform capitalism: The intermediation and capitalization of digital economic circulation. *Finance and Society*, 2(1), 11–31.

Low, S. (2023). *Why Public Space Matters*. Oxford University Press.

Luque-Ayala, A., & Marvin, S. (2020). *Urban Operating Systems: Producing the Computational City*. MIT Press.

Mackenzie, A. (2018). From API to AI: platforms and their opacities. *Information, Communication & Society*, 1–18. DOI: 10.1080/1369118X.2018.1476569.

Maedche, A., Legner, C., Benlian, A., Berger, B., Gimpel, H., Hess, T., ... Söllner, M. (2019). AI-based digital assistants. *Business & Information Systems Engineering*, 61(4), 535–544.

Mann, M., Mitchell, P., Anastasiu, I., & Foth, M. (2020). #BlockSidewalk to Barcelona: Technological sovereignty and the social license to operate smart cities. *Journal of the Association for Information Science and Technology*, 71(9), 1103–1115.

Martineau, P. (2019, May 24). Airbnb and New York City Reach a Truce on Home-Sharing Data. *Wired*. Available at: https://www.wired.com/story/airbnb-new-york-city-reach-truce-on-home-sharing-data/ [Accessed 19/01/2023].

McCullough, M. (2013). *Ambient Commons: Attention in the age of embodied information*. MIT Press.

Mitchell, D. (2017). People's Park again: On the end and ends of public space. *Environment and Planning A: Economy and Space*, 49(3), 503–518.

Monge, F., Barns, S., Kattel, R., & Bria, F. (2022). A new data deal: The case of Barcelona. *UCL Institute for Innovation and Public Purpose Working Paper*, 2. Available at: https://www.ucl.ac.uk/bartlett/public-purpose/sites/bartlett_public_purpose/files/new_data_deal_Carcelona_fernando_Carns_kattel_and_Cria.pdf [Accessed 19/01/2023].

Neville, S. J. (2020). Eavesmining: A critical audit of the Amazon Echo and Alexa Conditions of Use. *Surveillance and Society*, 18(3), 343–356.

OAIC. (2018). *Australian entities and the EU General Data Protection Regulation (GDPR)*. Office of the Australian Information Commissioner. Available at: https://www.oaic.gov.au/privacy/guidance-and-advice/australian-entities-and-the-eu-general-data-protection-regulation [Accessed 19/01/2023].

Oldenburg, R. (1989). *The Great Good Place: Cafes, Coffee Shops, Community Centers, Beauty Parlors, General Stores, Bars, Hangouts, and How They Get You Through the Day*. Paragon House.

Pardeshi, H. (n.d.). *Making sense of Uber engineering*. Available at: https://flexiple.com/developers/making-sense-of-ubers-engineering/ [Accessed 19/01/2023].

Pasquale, F. (2015). *The Black Box Society: The secret algorithms that control money and information.* Harvard University Press.

Pollio, A. (2020). Uber, airports, and labour at the infrastructural interfaces of platform urbanism. *Geoforum, 118,* 47–55.

Sadowski, J. (2019). When data is capital: Datafication, accumulation, and extraction. *Big Data and Society.* DOI: 10.1177/2053951718820549.

Sadowski, J. (2021). Who owns the future city? Phases of technological urbanism and shifts in sovereignty. *Urban Studies, 58*(8), 1732–1744.

Sidewalk Labs. (2019). *Master Innovation and Development Plan (MIDP).* Available at: https://www.sidewalktoronto.ca/midp/ [Accessed 19/01/2023].

Söderström, O., & Mermet, A. C. (2020). When Airbnb sits in the control room: Platform urbanism as actually existing smart urbanism in Reykjavík. *Frontiers in Sustainable Cities, 2,* 15.

Söderström, O., Paasche, T., & Klauser, F. (2014). Smart cities as corporate storytelling. *City, 18*(3), 307–320.

Stehlin, J., Hodson, M., & McMeekin, A. (2020). Platform mobilities and the production of urban space: Toward a typology of platformization trajectories. *Environment and Planning A: Economy and Space, 52*(7), 1250–1268.

Svítek, M., Skobelev, P., & Kozhevnikov, S. (2020). Smart City 5.0 as an urban ecosystem of smart services. In T. Borangiu, D. Trentesaux, P. Leitão, A. Giret Boggino, & V. Botti (Eds.), *Service Oriented, Holonic and Multi-agent Manufacturing Systems for Industry of the Future* (pp. 426–438). Springer International Publishing.

UN-Habitat (2022). *AI in Cities: Risks, Applications and Governance.* UN-Habitat. Available at: https://unhabitat.org/ai-cities-risks-applications-and-governance [Accessed 19/01/2023].

van Dijck, J. (2020). Governing digital societies: Private platforms, public values. *Computer Law & Security Review, 36,* 105377. DOI: 10.1016/j.clsr.2019.105377.

van Zeeland, I., Breuer, J., Pierson, J., & Wauters, E. (2021). Identifying GDPR enforcement problems and requirements in Smart Cities. *WO-SBO 'Smart City Privacy: Enhancing Collaborative Transparency in the Regulatory Ecosystem. Deliverable 1.6.* Available at: https://researchportal.vub.be/en/publications/identifying-gdpr-enforcement-problems-and-requirements-in-smart-c [Accessed 19/01/2023].

Vorwerk, M. (2019). Data Science at Scale: A Conversation with Uber's Fran Bell. *Uber Engineering.*

Wachsmuth, D. (2018). Airbnb and the rent gap: Gentrification through the sharing economy. *Environment and Planning A: Economy and Space, 50*(6), 1147–1170.

Wachsmuth, D., & Weisler, A. (2018). Airbnb and the rent gap: Gentrification through the sharing economy. *Environment and Planning A: Economy and Space, 50*(6), 1147–1170.

Weiser, M. (1991). The computer for the 21st century. *Scientific American, 265*(3), 94–104.

Wood, D. M., & Monahan, T. (2019). Platform surveillance. *Surveillance & Society, 17*(1/2), 1–6.

Zarsky, T. (2017). Incompatible: The GDPR in the age of big data. *Seton Hall Law Review, 47*(4), 995–1020.

13

ENCOUNTERING LIMITS IN COOPERATIVE PLATFORMS

The more-than-technical labour of urban AI

Adam Moore and David Bissell

Introduction

We are collectively witness to the rise of large-scale urban AIs. With increasing influence, they are being introduced into multiple domains of urban life, from traffic flows to logistics, and from surveillance to climate control. Much of the existing work on AIs in geography and urban studies is exploring their enrolment into processes of urban governance. For instance, Batty (2018) prompts us to consider how AI can enhance processes of urban planning, analysis and design. In Batty's view, we would do well to explore both the possibilities and limitations of AI in how we might understand cities, automate aspects of their governance, and plan them in the future. With more obvious concern for the risks posed by urban AI, Barns (2021) draws our attention to the implications of the abstractions at work in Big Data and the AI that make use of them to make urban life and processes visible in novel ways. Following the logic of how such systems operate, Barns (ibid) challenges us to think carefully about the implications of how routine urban behaviours are abstracted and then replicated within Big Data and AI simulations. Furthermore, our capacity to intervene in urban politics will become more limited owing to the black boxing of such autonomous computation. These shared concerns emphasize the need for further research to scrutinize the 'conditions, assumptions, training data and applications that allow autonomous urban intelligence to be created' (Barns, 2021: 3208).

Yet despite the emergence of both celebratory and critical accounts of urban AI, what urban AI actually is in the first place is and, crucially, how we come to know it are a matter of heated debate. Though AI has become such a ubiquitous concept both within and outside the academy, Cugurullo (2020)

DOI: 10.4324/9781003365877-16

draws our attention to the spatial, temporal and ontological variability of this seemingly straightforward object of analysis, encouraging us to widen our appreciation of the sites in which AIs operate in cities, as well as their evolution in time. Cugurullo reminds us how, just as human intelligence is complex and variable, appraisals of artificial intelligence, and the subsequent representations we adopt, must be sensitive to the variegated qualities of specific AIs, rather than merely judging whether or not a system is intelligent.

Furthermore, in appreciating its specificity, urban AI should not be framed as a sudden revolution in cities (Cugurullo, 2020). Rather, such technologies need to be situated within broader technological shifts relating to automation, for example, and understood through a range of ideological, political and economic interests that relate to such shifts. As technologies, AIs are a product of specific social and cultural contexts and so we need to be attuned to the possibilities for AIs to exacerbate conservative, damaging and dangerous forms of governance (Cugurullo, 2020).

One specific site where AIs are becoming woven into the socio-technical landscape of cities is digital platforms. By performing an intermediary role, different digital platforms enrol different urban entities, publics and collectives (Acquier et al., 2017) and range across spectrums of visibility and access (Srnicek, 2017). Urban theorists have become particularly concerned about the operation of "hyper-lean" capitalist platforms involved in the on-demand provision of transportation, goods and services (through platforms such as Uber, Deliveroo and Airtasker, respectively). From a social justice perspective, workers are at the mercy of the AI algorithms that underpin these platforms, often with detrimental effects (Richardson, 2020). Scholars have drawn critical attention to the logic of profit extraction that these "hyperlean" platforms enact – profit extraction that is also premised on not recognizing workers as employees (Scholz, 2017).

The novelty and general impenetrability of hyperlean digital platforms – in terms of both their complexity and private ownership (Fields and Raymond, 2021; Fields and Rogers, 2021) – has prompted useful, necessary and, at times, unsettling questions about politics of enablement and constraint, how and where to imagine progressive intervention, and frameworks for understanding accountability in such socio-technical systems (Bissell, 2018). A wider research context examining urban robotics and automation (Macrorie et al., 2021), as well as the displacement of political agency to platforms (Hoffmann, 2019), further informs these debates. Collectively, this urban platform scholarship provides a sobering reminder of how the intermediation capacities of platforms – rapid scalability, automation of accounting, extraction and mobilization of capital and data (Kornberger et al., 2017; Lobel, 2016) – can be used for achieving dizzying extremes of profit-making, the hollowing-out of the variegated ways labour agency may be expressed, and control over market niches (Kenney and Zysman, 2016; Langley and Leyshon, 2017).

While this critical attention on hyperlean platforms is timely and necessary, there are possibilities for doing platforms and AI differently. One way of doing digital platforms differently is through the nascent movement of *platform cooperativism*, a vision and roadmap for developing and deploying platforms cooperatively run and owned by those who depend upon them. Open-source and labour-governed approaches to digital platforms – *platform cooperatives* (Scholz and Schneider, 2017) – have been posed as one way of countering the hegemony of privately owned, data-hungry and hyper-capitalist platforms, and a socially just antidote to the dominance of platform capitalism (ibid; Srnicek, 2017). An imaginary for possible resistance, platform cooperativism leverages the concerns of platform labour when it articulates a bundle of economic, socio-cultural and legislative measures for achieving better conditions for gig workers and those similarly dependent for work on platform technologies and their immanent AI systems (Pazaitis et al., 2017; Morgan and Kuch, 2015). Governed by the labour that relies on them for work, platform cooperatives might offer a counterbalance to the extractive and recondite processes of automated intermediation through which privately owned and operated platforms have precaratised platform labour in the gig economy.

However, despite the promise of platform cooperatives, there have been no deep dives into the world of actually existing cooperatively run platforms, their AI, and the communities assembled around them. Research to date provides useful but nonetheless unavoidably sparse cross-case description and comparison of platform cooperatives (Lampinen et al., 2018) or conceptual engagement but in the absence of empirics (Sandoval, 2020; Chatterton and Pusey, 2020).[1] Similarly, while research addressing platform-mediated labour (i.e., gig work) has been necessarily developed across multiple fields (Gregory and Maldonado, 2020; Bissell et al., 2021; Veen et al., 2020), research examining the work of building, governing and caring for digital platforms and their various applications of AI is needed. A subset of this must be the participation in and access to open-source software communities, especially given the purported benefits for workers to secure greater technological sovereignty over the platforms they use and rely on for work. While the examination of processes and norms of access, contribution and governance in open-source communities has been sustained across multiple disciplines (de Laat, 2007), including the experiences of various requirements and barriers to participation (Boehm, 2019; Carillo et al., 2017), these are not specifically related to cooperative platforms. Further work must examine how software users, who are comparatively unskilled in software engineering, take part in open-source communities, with what difficulties, and how they are able to shape conditions and possibilities for work alongside digital platforms.

This returns us to the key epistemological question of how we come to know and understand urban AIs. Existing research on AI technologies emphasize the importance of sensitivity to the epistemological subtleties of urban AI. For instance, there is acknowledgement that the burgeoning ubiquity of AI in everyday life tests the limits of our capacities to know how and when AI is at play (Batty 2018; Barns, 2021; Cugurullo, 2020). In response to the issue of AI and their interpretability, Arrieta et al. (2020: 108, 82) have highlighted the 'compelling need for a proper understanding of the potentiality and caveats opened up by Explainable Artificial Intelligence (XAI) techniques of AI' and outlined a methodology for 'responsible AI,' a way for organizations to commit through practice to 'fairness, model explainability and accountability' of the AI systems they apply and manage. Similarly, Gunning et al. (2019) have emphasized the link between knowability and explainability of AI technologies, and the degree to which understanding, trust and management of these AI systems is meaningful for the communities applying and impacted by them. However, though these researchers have indicated the ways that the knowability of AI can and should be enhanced, there is little research undertaken on how knowability of AI technologies is *navigated* as a practical challenge for users.

Our chapter contributes to the complimentary research agendas on the knowability of urban AI and the possibilities for digital platform cooperatives: we consider the various work practices involved in managing and navigating the vagaries and obfuscations which accompany the creation and application of urban AI and thereby deepen understandings of how digital platform cooperatives function and change. However, examining how the knowability of AI is managed and navigated means attuning to how such practices are situationally specific. McLean (2020) provides the useful term 'more-than-real' to describe how we live alongside and with such emergent technologies. For McLean, this entanglement is variegated, a matter of intensity and degree: 'we are patently not all using digital technologies in the same ways, in the same spaces, at the same times' (2020: 59). Ultimately, this points to the need for empirical sensitivity to difference when tracing the practical, affective and material presences of digital things in our everyday lives. Guided by such methodological concerns and the current limitations in understandings of the AI, labour and communities of digital platform cooperatives, we pursue the research question:

In what ways are limits to knowing urban AI systems navigated and managed through the work of platform labour, and with what implications?

To address this question, we draw attention to the essential more-than-technical work that goes on behind the scenes of a cooperative platform. We provide further methodological details on our chapter's data in the following section. Through explanation and analysis of the data we present in this chapter, we show how, first, the fragility of the technical components of cooperatively run platforms necessitates attention and care from the communities assembled around them. Second, this work of holding the platform together extends beyond software engineering to include work we term here as *more-than-technical*. Third, this more-than-technical work involves navigating absences and limits to knowing, and a reckoning with different forms of unknowability. Fourth, the multiple labours required to hold a digital platform together, including the doubts and limits to knowing encompassed within, suggest an expanded and embodied notion of AI. We suggest that it is useful to conceptualize platform AI as an emergent phenomenon of people and machines at work together. In this way, the AI observed in platforms can be understood as a relational, networked effect of both machinic and labour intelligences that is defined as much by the possibilities as the impossibilities of their spatio-temporal contexts. Methodologically, this evidences the instrumental importance of sustained and situated attentions to cooperative platforms through ethnographic methods and suggests an agenda for further research in digital geographies of platform AI.

Case study and methods

For this chapter, we draw from ethnographic research examining a cooperatively run, open-source digital platform. Data was produced through Adam's PhD research that seeks to examine the socio-technical relationships within and between the digital and the community of a platform cooperative, with particular attention given to the various forms of work involved in developing, maintaining and repairing the software. The research was conducted between 2018 and 2020 and involved repeat interviews with people in the community situated in various roles and in different sites; participant observation of in-person and online meetings and longer days of working; and archival analysis of both text and AV media publicly accessible through the community's Slack workspace, GitHub repository and separate *wiki style* forums used for promoting and recording the discussion of specific topics relevant to the community's work on the platform. This chapter, like the wider PhD research project it draws upon, understands the efforts of those involved in the community of this platform as an example of what is possible when altering the intermediation capacities of digital data infrastructures in the hope of doing digital platforms differently. For the purpose of ensuring anonymity for participants, the name of the platform and the community which use, develop and care for it, are not included here. Instead, throughout the chapter, our use of terms such as 'the platform' and 'the community' act as replacements.

The platform is an e-commerce site for food producers to sell their goods directly to consumers. The organization which developed the platform hopes to facilitate the formation of more sustainable and ethical food networks, with shorter supply chains and periodic order cycles reflective of seasonal variations in food production. From a user perspective, the platform functions as follows: food producers or food hubs respond to orders and provide necessary inputs of data concerning stock, cycles and delivery options via a dashboard interface while consumers – whether individuals or buying groups – interact with the platform's shopfront to view, order and pay for these items. The AI of the platform is certainly more humble and less technically complex in comparison to more prominent articulations of AI – systems exhibiting impressive and extensive capacities for sensing and ordering the contexts into which they are placed. Nonetheless, the platform draws together, organizes and produces information for those who interact with it. Layered automated processes in the platform's software, otherwise done by people or not at all, provide a digital data infrastructure for achieving the vision of the community. More than just automating tasks, the platform brings capacities for knowing which would otherwise not be possible.

A core team of dedicated people in the community work on the platform software and associated organizational procedures to ensure that it functions as smoothly as possible. The work going on in the community can be usefully thought of as *holding the platform together*: a shorthand articulation of the efforts going on out of the view of users, and thus *behind the scenes*, that keep the digital platform functional in the contexts it is deployed. The drafting and iteration of new builds or patches, the review and testing of this code, and coordination of the overlapping processes therein: these all take place alongside an array of non-technical or, more aptly put, "more-than-technical" work being carried out: the guiding of users through installation troubles; clear and timely reporting of bugs; and ironing out of misunderstandings about specific features or even the overall capacity of the software itself. These seemingly adjacent, peripheral acts feed into and support the operation of the platform as a digital data infrastructure. It is this work that our chapter is concerned with.

Resulting from the interaction and jostle of practices and digital materialities, the technology of the platform can be understood as a socio-technical achievement (cf. Swanton, 2013). Any apparent semblance of "givenness" is somewhat of an illusion which does not acknowledge the platform's fragilities and the ongoing work to soothe or overcome them through acts of maintenance and repair. Given how geographers have been particularly interested in practices of repair and maintenance (Graham and Thrift, 2007), it might be tempting to narrowly focus on the acts of fixing the code of the platform itself (cf. Graham, 2005). Yet doing so would risk obscuring the complex socio-technical relationships – the *technics* (Kinsley, 2014) – formed through acts of repair in computing and software contexts. It is important that we push this notion of holding platforms together further so that it encompasses more than acts of *technical* repair to software. In part, we are guided by ethnographies of repair literature (Strebel et al., 2018; Martínez and

Laviolette, 2019) and examples of work that specifically attend to relationships of care in the work of sustaining digital objects (Jackson, 2014, 2019). These provide useful inspiration for, and practical examples of, research that traces the myriad ways socio-technical arrangements are made, remade and tinkered with through relations of repair.

Narrating fragile encounters

In the following, we provide three vignettes of important moments witnessed by Adam during fieldwork. These assist in piecing together a richer understanding of the forms of work holding a digital platform together. The vignettes of this chapter help to conceptualize platform technologies and their AI as an emergent phenomenon of people and machines at work together. Methodologically, this sustained and situated attention to cooperative platforms evidences the possibilities that ethnographic fieldwork presents for digital geographical research of platforms and urban AI.

Vignette one: anticipating

Early during fieldwork, Adam joined the Australian instance of the platform's community as they conducted an in-person working day with a cooperative of farmers considering incorporating the platform's software into their core business practices. What follows are a selection of Adam's notes of the discussions from this day and then our reflections on them:

> To varying degree, many of the farmers used or had used software solutions as part of their work. Some were long standing spreadsheet advocates, although admitting – like the rest of us mere mortals – they didn't exactly know how Excel works. One was even making some progress via software solutions toward successfully integrating accounting, order management, and payment gateways. However, others described using multiple whiteboards, scrawled with orders and notes detailing arrangements for delivery or pick up of produce, amended constantly, always at risk of being mistakenly erased of information. Despite difference in experience and preference, all expressed interest in using the platform to automate tasks otherwise performed manually.

Reflecting on this event, Adam remembers having very little clue, substantially, as to what was being said. Knowing nothing of what it is to be a small-scale farmer, and next-to-nothing about how digital platforms function under the hood (so to speak), it was to be constantly on the back foot. Yet the reason everyone was there was to identify and, where possible, bridge such gaps in skill and knowledge.

Interestingly, this was all taking place well before many of these farmers had even begun to properly trial the software. As was later explained to Adam repeatedly by interview participants, this was part of the preliminary *soft* work of aligning practices and understandings of users with the capacities of the platform. Overtly, the work observed spruiked the possibilities of the platform. However, more subtly, it functioned as means to form shared and mutually beneficial understandings of the practicalities and possibilities of such a user–software relationship. It was a meeting in the middle, a mix of backgrounds and knowledges, all focused towards articulating a functional join of needs with capacities: approaching a clear articulation of what the platform would actually be able to do for them.

We understand this work as actively *preparing for the unknowns* of developing and operating a platform. The more-than-technical work performed in the community of the platform, just as much as any of the technical work performed, involves anticipatory efforts to mitigate, and possibly even eliminate, potential issues in the future. The attempts to anticipate and stave off risks before they may possibly (or ever arise) take place through the education of incoming users. This includes aligning values and expectations, and ensuring users understand the (in)capacities of the platform software.

Vignette two: grappling

Midway through fieldwork, Adam attended an in-person working day for those in the Australian instance of the platform's community. A significant part of the day involved progressing through a list of concerns or "pain points" associated with the work of supporting and communicating with users. What follows are a selection of Adam's notes of these discussions and then our reflections on them:

> As people shared experiences, it became clear there was a general feeling of frustration with slippages in communication when working with users of the platform. Many of those present were finding it difficult to convey the possibilities of the software to users; they were, as one put it, "struggling to explain what it is...what it does". Further, it was lamented that many users were struggling to find uses for it on their own without assistance. As others elaborated, this meant that those working for the platform could not "align expectation with realities, deliver on what users want and hope for".

The work meeting discussions described above extended beyond the limits of this vignette. These were carried out with the apparent intention of reviewing and improving the community's processes, practices and sensibilities towards doing this work of managing misunderstandings or difficulties associated with the software. Here, we summarize through narration some of these other matters discussed.

Communicating the benefit to users of the various software updates that were being released was said to be another significant issue. Providing users with a view of all the small improvements made to the general function of the software was argued by many present as being just as important as the larger updates. As one person emphatically explained, without this communication of progress going on behind the scenes then users' awareness of the project's momentum would be restricted. Linked to this communication of change, it was reported that some updates had disrupted users' work practices and rhythms. For those doing support work, this resulted in managing the frustrations of users in addition to assisting them with technical workarounds and troubleshooting. It was reflected upon by those doing this support work that there were also emotional dimensions: people seemed to appreciate their frustrations being heard just as much as receiving technical assistance. Cumulatively, those present noted how this was restorative of both user confidence in the platform as well as its functionality for them. However, the cost of this assistance remained a concern and it was then debated as to what could be practically done to alleviate the burden on the platform community. Ultimately, as was tentatively noted, this need for a human guide could actually be something of a design flaw in the software: 'software should lead the user down this path.'

Upon reflection, it would seem that, in essence, this work navigates and guides others around or across gaps and limits in individual or networked knowledges of the platform itself. Such acts as relaying the small, quality of life changes made through updates to the software, listening to the experiences behind a user's frustrations or assisting a user to develop their own technical understandings and digital skills, all contribute towards a broader aim of bringing the user and platform together. In this event of the community reflecting on this work, Adam was witness to various admissions: of difficulty in explanation of the software, of uncomfortable reflection on the slippages and gaps between understandings, and of the always constant anticipation of the unexpected.

We understand these observations as indicative of the experience of what it is to deal with, work with and depend upon an obscured digital infrastructure: one whose workings are often impenetrable but nonetheless felt as becoming increasingly essential and ubiquitous. The challenges of this work emphasize the importance of providing intimate, person-to-person forms of assistance. Doing so affords the community a way to encourage familiarization, build capacities and support positive emotional dispositions of users towards their use of the software. This suggests the importance of fostering and managing links between user and software for the purpose of conveying that the software project is alive and evolving – that things are happening even if they may not feel like it. Many users do not have an in-depth understanding of software which might otherwise make them more sensitive to such progress. Therefore, doing so was also seen as means to soften unintentional but nonetheless exclusionary barriers to technical understanding. In this way, working with digital infrastructures can be both mundane and weird. Whether during work performed on the software as someone in the platform's community or work as a user of the platform, such fractures and stoppages in function are weird reminders amidst the mundane of the embodied limits to knowing every present when working with digital things.

Vignette three: accepting

Here, we jump forward to late 2019 as Adam is attending an online meeting of the platform's community, including members from Australia and elsewhere in the world where the platform also operates. What follows are Adam's notes of this meeting interspersed with our reflections on them:

> I try my best to fade into the background, just another talking and nodding head on a Zoom call. The purpose of this meeting is to provide a general overview of any recent developments across the platform project, whether at local or global level. It's what often gets referred to as a "global check in". Discussion roamed across various agenda items: an update on the drafting of a framework for legal status as a cooperative in France; reflections on an outreach event with farmers in the UK; before settling on one agenda item in particular, the drafting of a "launch pad curriculum and networking events". This programme would connect new and more established users of the platform on the vendor side of platform so they may share reflections, knowledge and practical tips.

The discussions following this update on the "launchpad" programme pursued the uncomfortable but necessary question of 'how much support do we, and should we, provide?' Practically, this programme would go some way towards addressing this question: by establishing channels for vendor-side users of the platforms to assist each other, they would be less reliant on the assistance from those centrally placed within the community of the platform. Adam's notes reflect how in this meeting it was generally felt that, though this programme would help alleviate strain on the community, there was only so much assistance they could provide. As emphasized during subsequent interviews conducted by Adam with participants, this was not an expression of wanting to cut costs and to leave those using the software without assistance.

As one participant noted, this need for capacity building was reflective of the open-source ethic of the entire project itself, that it functions via its user base having a degree of self-reliance:

> It's not just as simple as – Are we spending too much time helping other people with their deployments? I think the bigger question is – How much help should we actually allow for within our pipe? Let's set an expectation. This is open-source software! We are really happy to help answer a few questions, but you need to have someone there that can tinker, set things up for yourself, have a play with it…We [must] set expectations right at the start so that people know they can get some help but we're not spending all of our day helping someone get set up. That's not how open source works.

Together, the observation of such meeting discussions and reflections from interview participants provide an important insight. They show that, behind the scenes of a digital platform cooperative, limits to the care enacted through technical and more-than-technical work are debated and decided on. The conversations witnessed illustrated how the community engages with, debates and acknowledges in practical terms that there is only so much that their work of buffering against the unknown can do. Determining the extent to which this care may be expressed, through the technical and more-than-technical work essential to the platform, involves accepting that there are practical limits of this care work itself and that these must be adhered to so as to avoid deterioration of the project itself. What is at stake, then, is doing *too much* in anticipation of risks, of possible issues, and thus being distracted from the necessary work of properly organizing the efforts of the platform community. In this way, these limits help to protect the possibilities for the platform, keeping free the necessary attentions and labour to continue developing and improving its codebase.

Instead of abandonment, such a "launch pad" programme is an experimentation of how an open-source software project can best enable new or experienced users to support themselves and each other when experiencing problems. This affirms something of the value but also the risk of open-source methods for platform cooperatives: they will be a community-driven endeavour, borne and dependent on that community. It was an uncomfortable but necessary discussion concerning the need, at certain times, to not care, to care less, or to care in a particular way. By virtue of the extensiveness of the things that are unknowable, a line somewhere, somehow, sometimes, must be drawn. The extent of the care expressed through the technical and more-than-technical work of support is defined against the knowledge that there are limits to how effective such efforts can ever be.

Discussion

An at-times messy, vibrant and constantly shifting affair of limits to skills, knowledge and finances, the community of this platform is comprised of brilliant and passionate people perfecting or reinventing their practices and sensibilities of digital materiality in the pursuit of their ideals for better, fairer food systems. There are problems, of varying scale, and some of these are intractable. However, understanding *how* such challenges are navigated is essential for supporting open-source, cooperative platforms to thrive and multiply. Our final section articulates four implications of the vignettes for understandings of digital platform cooperatives and their AI.

Cooperative platforms are fragile and require care

First, the fragility of technical components in cooperatively run platforms necessitates attention and care from the communities assembled around them. Such an observation grinds up against political economy accounts of hyper-lean platforms that focus on how software is wielded by and does the bidding of the powerful companies that own them. This belies the pre-sumed *efficacy* of code, the capacity of AI to modulate both consumption practices and platform workers. Shifting attention to a cooperative plat-form changes the political and ethical stakes in debates concerning plat-forms. These three vignettes demonstrate how the efficacy of a digital platform is by no means assured. When the code stumbles and breaks down, when users and platform workers find it difficult at times to know what they are doing, the very operation and potential of these platforms feel fragile.

These fragilities can be felt ambiguously: they are situated, context-de-pendent and open to interpretation. In research on hyper-lean platforms, software breakdowns, frictions and glitches are framed as indicative of the power of capitalist platforms creaking at the seams and thus celebrated as offering potential for more socially just interventions and insights (Leszczynski, 2020). Contrastingly, for cooperative platforms, such "glitch politics" are far less emancipatory. Instead, they are a constant reminder of their fragility as digital infrastructures and projects for difference. While no software is without issues, untended they accrete into "technical debts" and become a source of concern and further work for those involved in the devel-opment and maintenance of platforms. We must consider how breakdowns, frictions and glitches within and around software can be hugely detrimental to the viability and longevity of cooperative platforms, and re-evaluate the practices, materialities and attachments to work of mitigation performed in response.

Caring for cooperative platforms involves more-than-technical work

Second, holding platforms together ranges beyond software engineering to include more-than-technical work. The vignettes illustrate, respectively: how shared understandings are established; how processes for digital support, maintenance and care are reflected on; and how limits to this care are openly discussed despite possible associated discomfort. Certainly, software engineering work is essential to the maintenance and ongoing function of the cooperative platform discussed in this chapter. Patient debugging, prompt rectification of crashed servers and dutiful updates of external dependencies: it all culminates to extend, maintain and repair the technical systems underpinning the platform and make it what it is. However, guiding users through installation troubles; clear and timely reporting of bugs; and ironing out misunderstandings about specific features or even the overall capacity of the software itself: such more-than-technical work is vital for managing the fragilities of platform AI. Thus, the work of holding the platform together ranges beyond software engineering to include the more-than-technical work that takes place alongside software engineering work. These seemingly adjacent, peripheral acts feed into and support the platform, its AI and community, thereby evidencing the significance of more-than-technical work – how it *holds the platform together* across various sites and durations.

More-than-technical work must reckon with unknowability

Third, this more-than-technical work involves navigating absences and limits to knowing, and thus a reckoning with different forms of unknowability. This is not suggested in spirit of futility or defeatism. Instead, we contend that a serious engagement with the question of 'what it means to struggle with limits' (Rose et al., 2021: 3) is required in order to better understand the socio-technical relations formed through working practices, materialities and attachments in platform cooperatives. This is an opportunity for digital geography to 'consider more closely the limits of existence within which all such claims about hope, power, and capacity are made' (Rose et al., 2021: 3). The vignettes show how this more-than-technical work seeks to orient and shape the emotional dispositions, technical capacities and epistemic framings embodied by users when engaging with the platform, with the overall intention being to establish and secure the socio-technical environments in which the software can function at its best. Therefore, attention to technical work, like software engineering of AI applications, must be paired with the frequently overlooked more-than-technical work that involves negotiating, anticipating and reconciling risks and differences (cf. Richardson and Bissell, 2019). Encounters and exchanges in more-than-technical work involve reckoning with different forms of unknowability (Rose et al., 2021). Essential for geographies of digital platforms and AI is a fuller appreciation of the limits to knowability as they play out for both researchers, undertaking research into the operations of platforms, and for those who work on them, for them and alongside them.

Managing limits to knowing suggests an expanding and embodied understanding of AI

Fourth, how the work required to hold a platform together requires managing feelings of doubt and encounters with limits to knowing, suggests an expanded, distributed and embodied notion of AI. As we have shown, it is beneficial for understandings of platform AI that an attention to the technical labour of software engineering be paired with the often overlooked more-than-technical labour involving negotiation, anticipation and reconciliation with and of limits to knowing. Drawing on geographical work detailing how digital skills extend beyond the merely technical (Richardson and Bissell, 2019), we can see how these more-than-technical dimensions of labour are profoundly embodied and social, involving different kinds of interpersonal encounters and exchanges between differently positioned people. Expanding debates on what constitutes intelligence in socio-technical understandings of urban AI (cf. Lynch and Del Casino, 2020), we argue that a crucial but overlooked dimension of AI in digital platforms involves the bodily intelligences of reckoning with limits of knowability. The various capacities of *knowing*, and their immanent limits that define *knowability*, are distributed both across technical systems of platform AI and the work directed towards them, both technical and more-than-technical. Thus, doubt – a struggle with limits to knowing – pervades software and interactions with it (cf. Amoore 2019, 2020). As Amoore (2019, 2020) explains, there are limitations to what such platform AIs can make sense of determined by its design, its feed of data, and even how it is able to explain itself to those at work alongside it – whether in the sense of how it comes to an answer or a complication with its code. This highlights to us the ethical importance of doubt when working with algorithms (Amoore, 2020); specifically, how doubt, an encounter with limits to knowing, shapes platform AI. Attending to these encounters and exchanges with doubts, the struggles with limits to knowing, is crucial for understanding how platforms – and by extension, urban AI – evolve.

Conclusion

The work of holding platforms together involves navigating the limits of knowability and clearly illustrates the haunting fragility of platform cooperatives. Attending to the fragility of platform cooperatives importantly reveals a range of work going on to keep their AI functional that is largely obscured by current debates that are focused on hyper-lean platforms. Examining the work involved in navigating the limits to the knowability of AI helps to deepen our understandings of how digital platform cooperatives function and change. Attempting to develop a digital platform, one owned and governed by the community that rely on it as an infrastructure for whatever purposes, is made exceptionally precarious in the absence of the power and relative stability that accompany hyper-lean platforms that are underpinned by seemingly limitless venture capital investment and monetization of extracted data. Counter to the celebratory framing of glitches within capitalist platforms (Leszczynski, 2020), fragilities of cooperative platforms are felt anxiously by us and the participants. Therefore, attention to the contextual specifics of such complications is required, one that encompasses the associated doubts and work of overcoming these doubts – the technical and more-than-technical work that perceives and contends with the multiple forms of unknowability. We understand the labour directed towards such fragilities as defining whether they become impediments or possibilities.

Despite how a geographical approach foregrounds the spatiality of emergent digital technologies like platform AI, by providing a 'critical understanding of how AI is shaped by and itself shaping human geographies and spatial practices at all scales,' geography's engagement with AI is argued by some to be relatively nascent (Walker et al., 2021: 215). Partly in response, we have sought to show what an ethnographic, geographical attention to the more-than-technical work of platform labour can provide to understandings of platform AI. This extends work detailing the obscured, ignored and mundane data practices in research and everyday contexts (Bates et al., 2016; Hoffmann, 2018; Bellanova, 2017; Pink et al., 2017).[2]

In this example of an actually existing platform cooperative, we can see how platform labour interfaces with the platform AI according to various proximities. More intuitively, this occurs at the code-face through technical work, but it also happens through the more-than-technical efforts and processes that keep the platform cared for, ensure necessary practical understandings among its userbase and toy with uncomfortable hypotheticals concerning limits to organizational responsibility for the user–platform relationships. This attention to work has also allowed a tracing of various doubts surrounding the AI of this cooperative platform and thereby an extension of Amoore's (2019, 2020) articulation of the importance of an ethics of doubt concerning work with AI algorithms. We have shown how threaded throughout such practices is the concern and intention to navigate and reckon with the limits to knowability that shape how the AI of the platform lands, so to speak, within the contexts, it is introduced into. Therefore, this chapter is a call for a shift in focus in the study of platforms and their AIs. Examining the labour of platform AI is an opportunity to understand what platform cooperatives can mean for hope and difference in the pursuit of a digital that should be, but is not (yet?), ours. It is no longer enough to simply drive more wedges further into the machine. Instead, we must find ways to support and sustain efforts to apply these technologies in the pursuit of more socially just digital futures.

Notes

1 This is a comment on the virtues of cross-case study analysis compared with sustained single case study analysis, as per Gerring (2011) and Yin (2013).
2 Research on the mobility of digital data has shown their journey to be far from smooth, instead made to happen through actions that overcome frictions and stoppages or bring about periods of immobility (Bates et al., 2016). Similar work has drawn attention to the inseparability of data from the practices, tools, people that make them and the economic and political contexts they emerge and move through (Hoffman, 2018). Regardless of their application – whether for surveillance, research, consumption and everything in between – there is need to interrogate seemingly mundane practices of collection, storage, processing that data goes through (Bellanova, 2017). Attention to mundane data practices shows how devices are fit into everyday routines and 'how digital data become meaningful in mundane contexts of everyday life' (Pink et al., 2017: 1).

References

Acquier, A., Daudigeos, T., & Pinkse, J. (2017). Promises and paradoxes of the sharing economy: An organizing framework. *Technological Forecasting and Social Change*, 125, 1–10.

Amoore, L. (2019). Doubt and the algorithm: On the partial accounts of machine learning. *Theory, Culture & Society*, 36(6), 147–169.

Amoore, L. (2020). *Cloud ethics*. Duke University Press.

Arrieta, A. B., Díaz-Rodríguez, N., Del Ser, J., Bennetot, A., Tabik, S., Barbado, A., … Herrera, F. (2020). Explainable Artificial Intelligence (XAI): Concepts, taxonomies, opportunities and challenges toward responsible AI. *Information Fusion*, 58, 82–115.

Barns, S. (2021). Out of the loop? On the radical and the routine in urban big data. *Urban Studies*, DOI: 10.1177/00420980211014026.

Bates, J., Lin, Y. W., & Goodale, P. (2016). Data journeys: Capturing the socio-material constitution of data objects and flows. *Big Data & Society*, 3(2), 1–12.

Batty, M. (2018). Artificial intelligence and smart cities. *Environment and Planning B*, 15, 3–6.

Bellanova, R. (2017). Digital, politics, and algorithms: Governing digital data through the lens of data protection. *European Journal of Social Theory*, 20(3), 329–347.

Bissell, D. (2018). Automation interrupted: How autonomous vehicle accidents transform the material politics of automation. *Political Geography*, 65, 57–66.

Bissell, D., Rose, M., & Harrison, P. (Eds.). (2021). *Negative Geographies: Exploring the Politics of Limits*. University of Nebraska Press.

Boehm, M. (2019). The emergence of governance norms in volunteer-driven open source communities. *Journal of Open Law, Technology & Society*, 9, 3–40.

Carillo, K., Huff, S., & Chawner, B. (2017). What makes a good contributor? Understanding contributor behavior within large Free/Open Source Software projects–A socialization perspective. *The Journal of Strategic Information Systems*, 26(4), 322–359.

Chatterton, P., & Pusey, A. (2020). Beyond capitalist enclosure, commodification and alienation: Postcapitalist praxis as commons, social production and useful doing. *Progress in Human Geography*, 44(1), 27–48.

Cugurullo, F. (2020). Urban artificial intelligence: From automation to autonomy in the smart city. *Frontiers in Sustainable Cities*, 2, 38.

de Laat, B. (2007). Governance of open source software: State of the art. *Journal of Management & Governance*, 11(2), 165–177.

Fields, D., & Raymond, E. L. (2021). Racialized geographies of housing financialization. *Progress in Human Geography*, 45(6), 1625–1645.

Fields, D. & Rogers, D. (2021). Towards a critical housing studies research agenda on platform real estate. *Housing, Theory and Society*, 38(1), 72–94.

Gerring, J. (2011). The case study: What it is and what it does. In Goodin, E.D. (Ed.) *The Oxford Handbook of Political Science*, Oxford University Press, Oxford.

Graham, S., & Thrift, N. (2007). Out of order: Understanding repair and maintenance. *Theory, Culture & Society*, 24(3), 1–25.

Graham, S. D. (2005). Software-sorted geographies. *Progress in Human Geography*, 29(5), 562–580.

Gregory, K., & Maldonado, M. P. (2020). Delivering Edinburgh: Uncovering the digital geography of platform labour in the city. *Information, Communication & Society*, 23(8), 1187–1202.

Gunning, D., Stefik, M., Choi, J., Miller, T., Stumpf, S., & Yang, G. Z. (2019). XAI—Explainable artificial intelligence. *Science Robotics*, 4(37), 1–6

Hoffmann, A. L. (2018). Making data valuable: Political, economic, and conceptual bases of big data. *Philosophy & Technology*, 31(2), 209–212.

Hoffmann, J. (2019). Mediated democracy–Linking digital technology to political agency. *Internet Policy Review*, 8(2), 1–18.

Jackson, S. J. (2014). Rethinking Repair. In Gillespie, T., Boczkowski, P. J., & Foot, K. A. (Eds.). (2014). *Media technologies: Essays on communication, materiality, and society*. MIT Press.

Jackson, S. J. (2019). Repair as transition: Time, materiality, and hope. In Strebel, I., Bovet, A., & Sormani, P. (Eds.). *Repair Work Ethnographies*. Singapore: Palgrave Macmillan.

Kenney, M., & Zysman, J. (2016). The rise of the platform economy. *Issues in Science and Technology*, 32(3), 61.

Kinsley, S. (2014). The matter of 'virtual' geographies. *Progress in Human Geography*, 38(3), 364–384.

Kornberger, M., Pflueger, D., & Mouritsen, J. (2017). Evaluative infrastructures: Accounting for platform organization. *Accounting, Organizations and Society*, 60, 79–95.

Lampinen, A., McGregor, M., Comber, R., & Brown, B. (2018). Member-owned alternatives: Exploring participatory forms of organising with cooperatives. *Proceedings of the ACM on Human-Computer Interaction*, 2(CSCW), 1–19.

Langley, P., & Leyshon, A. (2017). Platform capitalism: The intermediation and capitalization of digital economic circulation. *Finance and Society*, 3(1), 11–31.

Leszczynski, A. (2020). Glitchy vignettes of platform urbanism. *Environment and Planning D: Society and Space*, 38(2), 189–208.

Lobel, O. (2016). The law of the platform. *Minnesota Law Review*, 101(1), 87–166.

Lynch, C. R., & Del Casino Jr, V. J. (2020). Smart spaces, information processing, and the question of intelligence. *Annals of the American Association of Geographers*, 110(2), 382–390.

Macrorie, R., Marvin, S., & While, A. (2021). Robotics and automation in the city: A research agenda. *Urban Geography*, 42(2), 197–217.

Martínez, F., & Laviolette, P. (Eds.). (2019). *Repair, brokenness, breakthrough: Ethnographic responses*. Berghahn Books.

McLean, J. (2020). *Changing digital geographies*. Palgrave Macmillan.

Morgan, B., & Kuch, D. (2015). Radical transactionalism: Legal consciousness, diverse economies, and the sharing economy. *Journal of Law and Society*, 42(4), 556–587.

Pazaitis, A., Kostakis, V., & Bauwens, M. (2017). Digital economy and the rise of open cooperativism: The case of the Enspiral Network. *Transfer: European Review of Labour and Research*, 23(2), 177–192.

Pink, S., Sumartojo, S., Lupton, D., & Heyes La Bond, C. (2017). Mundane data: The routines, contingencies and accomplishments of digital living. *Big Data & Society*, 4(1).

Richardson, L. (2020). Platforms, markets, and contingent calculation: The flexible arrangement of the delivered meal. *Antipode*, 52(3), 619–636.

Richardson, L., & Bissell, D. (2019). Geographies of digital skill. *Geoforum*, 99, 278–286.

Rose, M., Bissell, D., & Harrison, P. (2021). Negative geographies. in Bissell, D., Rose, M., & Harrison, P. (Eds.). *Negative geographies: Exploring the politics of limits*. University of Nebraska Press.

Sandoval, M. (2020). Entrepreneurial activism? Platform cooperativism between subversion and co-optation. *Critical Sociology*, 46(6), 801–817.

Scholz, T. (2017). *Uberworked and underpaid: How workers are disrupting the digital economy*. John Wiley & Sons.

Scholz, T., & Schneider, N. (Eds.). (2017). *Ours to hack and to own: The rise of platform cooperativism, a new vision for the future of work and a fairer internet*. OR Books.

Srnicek, N. (2017). *Platform capitalism*. John Wiley & Sons.

Strebel, I., Bovet, A., & Sormani, P. (Eds.). (2018). *Repair work ethnographies: Revisiting breakdown, relocating materiality*. Springer.

Swanton, D. (2013). The steel plant as assemblage. *Geoforum*, 44, 282–291.

Veen, A., Barratt, T., & Goods, C. (2020). Platform-capital's 'app-etite' for control: A labour process analysis of food-delivery work in Australia. *Work, Employment and Society*, 34(3), 388–406.

Walker, M., Winders, J., & Boamah, E. F. (2021). Locating artificial intelligence: A research agenda. *Space and Polity*, 25(2), 202–219.

Yin, R. K. (2013). Validity and generalization in future case study evaluations. *Evaluation*, 19(3), 321–332.

14

PERFORMED IMAGINARIES OF THE AI-CONTROLLED CITY

Conducting urban AI experimentation in China

Bei Chen

Introduction

Visions of an unprecedented new era marked by artificial intelligence (AI)-enabled disruptive changes are emerging as dominant imaginaries seeping into the collective consciousness of various national geographies. A bourgeoning body of literature – mainly in the field of sociology and science and technology studies (STS) – has broadly captured the way the emergent national AI imaginaries are fabricated, performed and deployed in the structures and functioning of a particular nation's societal processes and strategies (Schiølin, 2020; Bareis and Katzenbach, 2021). As demonstrated by the existing studies, the social imaginaries around AI are context-specific, morphing into different representations in differing communities (Pfotenhauer and Jasanoff, 2017). More importantly, the represented imaginaries of their (im)material forms are *performative* in the sense that they work to bring the imagined future into present actions by, for instance, mobilizing resources, attracting investment and endowing meanings with AI-labelled social practices (Borup et al., 2006; Jasanoff and Kim, 2015).

Interestingly, a majority of scholars interested in the interactive relations of AI, place, present and future are primarily focused on the nation state as a central locus for producing and enacting AI imaginaries. There are some exceptions of works examining cities as sites wherein AI imaginaries are formed and deployed. For example, Hodson and McMeekin (2021) interrogate the corporate actors and political cultures behind the aborted Sidewalk Toronto project, representation of a particular urban spatiality's imaginaries of building a digitally controlled infrastructural integration whereby the futuristic social order is arranged through robots, self-driving vehicles, affordable housing and smart neighbourhoods. However, the existing urban

DOI: 10.4324/9781003365877-17

future studies as such are overly absorbed in the city by itself, with little work addressing the relations between urban and state scales wherein AI imaginaries are produced and operated.

Largely drawing on the overlapped concepts of *expectations* (Borup et al., 2006) and *sociotechnical imaginaries* (Jasanoff, 2015), AI imaginaries in this chapter can be understood as a specific community's shared understanding, and potential adoption, of a desirable social order that will be maintained, or significantly supported, by AI technological innovations and societal applications. Based on this conceptualization, my argument is that a given society's adoption of the imagined AI-embedded order arrangement goes with, not a static condition, but a dynamic process wherein both the state and city alongside other loci entail normative and institutional power to enable the imaginaries to make sense and gain political legitimacy. In this sense, it is worth scrutinizing how power is exercised to rationalize a society's AI imaginaries into its socioeconomic and political practices, and how these are materialized through urban experiments.

This chapter is committed to interrogating, firstly, the relational power operating at the state and urban scales that affords performative AI imaginaries and secondly, the imaginaries' performative role in making material and discursive effects on a given society's trajectories. For this purpose, this research will ground AI imaginaries in China and adopt a case study approach to scrutinizing one of the world's most ambitious urban AI experimentations in Xiong'an New Area, hereinafter Xiong'an. Claimed as the model ushering in a new era of China's urbanization, the experimental AI practices in Xiong'an can be understood as a radical exemplar of China's emerging AI imaginaries spatially performed onto a bounded mega-urban space.

Conceptually, this study is situated within the field of *urban experimentation* (Evans et al., 2016; While et al., 2020) and STS studies, in particular, and informed by the body of literature on *sociotechnical imaginaries, expectations, coproduction* and *performativity* (Jasanoff 2004, 2015; Konrad et al., 2016). Empirically, my research proceeds at two levels.

Firstly, an analysis of China's policy and strategy documents was conducted to identify the deeper mechanism generating China's specific AI imaginaries.

Secondly, empirical fieldwork was carried out in Xiong'an to critically examine the place-specific material representations that perform imagined AI futures. This chapter has four sections. The second section identifies the main dimensions of China's particular AI imaginaries that steer its socio-political futures, while also examining the power that affords its performance at the state level. The third section focuses on Xiong'an as an urban AI testbed and analyses how the imaginaries are performed in that context-specific urban geography. Last, I conclude this chapter with a summary of the key implications drawn from my empirical research to deepen the debate about the political culture of urban AI experimentation.

Discoursing on AI futures: state imaginaries of improved economy and governance

This section examines the deeper mechanism underlying China's state AI imaginaries and their performativity that is enacted on the spatial scales. Empirically, by referring to a large body of national AI strategy and policy documents, I will critically examine four dimensions characterizing China's imagined AI futures. The narratives constructing these dimensions of AI's social purposes largely concur with the political and economic interests of the country's main stakeholders, while also resonating with the ideologies constitutive of its collective identity. The discursive formation henceforth provides a strong rationale for the imaginaries' performance working at the blurred boundaries of ideal and materiality, visions and actualities.

Firstly, like many other nations framed by the 'Fourth Industrial Revolution' (Schwab, 2016) discourse, AI as an emerging technology is hailed by the Chinese state as a new primary driver for advancing unprecedented economic growth. As articulated in its main national AI strategy document, *the Next-generation Artificial Intelligence Development Plan* (NAIDP), AI is defined as a 'key generic technology' that enables breakthroughs of a cohort of new technologies and industries, especially bioscience, autonomous and unmanned control system, and brain-inspired computing (see State Council, 2017: no page). Based on this stance on AI, the country's overarching vision of 'a major world centre for AI innovation' is directly translated to a futuristic 'intelligence economy, which is quantified by a ballooning 'AI industry market worth 10 trillion yuan (US$1.4 trillion) by 2030 (see State Council, 2017: no page).

At the heart of this linear linkage between advancement in AI innovation and an economically powerful country lies what Lee (2018: 84) terms China's distinctive 'techno-utilitarian' political culture. It means a toolkit of policies will be used to incentivize massive social investment in emerging high-technologies in the hope of securing a high return. Consequently, the envisioned AI-enabled social prosperity actuates policy mechanisms for rewarding AI research and adoption, including tax breaks, generous loans, talent pipeline management, as well as a package of national funds (Ding, 2018). In the realm of social activities, the given imaginaries are performed through experimentation of AI's integration with almost all socioeconomic fronts – ranging from AI finance to intelligent courts, from manufacturing robots to smart city initiatives (Roberts et al., 2021). Furthermore, the experiment of converging AI with any new technologies – 5G, robotics, cloud computing, digital twin, etc. – performs the vision of 'a fusion of technologies that is blurring the lines between the physical, digital, and biological spheres' (Schwab, 2016: 4). In the name of industrial upgrades and economic restructuring, the performativity as such creates a normativity of AI's sublimity and totality, which essentially preinstalls a societal lock-in pathway dependent on AI (Bareis and Katzenbach, 2021).

The second dimension characterizing China's imaginaries of AI potentials is its use for social governance. From the government's narratives, an AI-enabled intelligent society means affordance of an AI ubiquitous environment that ensures personal security and precision-targeted public service. More importantly, the AI-embedded social infrastructure is envisioned to anticipate and nip social problems in the bud via capturing, combining and calculating urban events and human behaviours, as depicted in NAIDP (State Council, 2017: 3):

> AI technologies can accurately sense, forecast, and provide early warning for major trends of infrastructures and social security operations; [...]; can actively make decisions and responses; will significantly improve the capability and level of social governance, and play an irreplaceable role in effectively maintaining social stability.

This vision suggests that AI as an instrumental tool is enlisted into Chinese leadership's power apparatus for the aim of maintaining a safe, stable and harmonious society, which is deemed as an important indicator of good governance. As Jeffreys and Sigley (2009) observe, social governance through the given ideological view is likened to social re-engineering. It sees society as a complicated system conditioned by objective laws, which can be discovered in light of sufficient data across time and space and then used to remodel societal behaviours. This political ideal shares many similarities with the promise that, if fed enormous volumes of data in a high-performance computing system, AI can automatically recognize patterns and then come out with predictive judgement or real-time solutions.

When it comes to performing the imaginaries on the ground, a batch of AI-empowered platforms for urban governance – typically represented by city brains, digital twins and the COVID Health Code – are promoted nationwide (Cugurullo, 2020; Chen et al., 2020). Irrespective of the names, what is central to these urban management platforms is an attempt to advance a data-driven and algorithmic governance regime (Curran and Smart, 2021; Cugurullo, 2021). It deems the urban space as 'a calculative machine,' wherein mathematical modelling tools for computing spatiotemporal event-based datasets become engines of producing knowledge and the way of governing the urban decision-making process (Luque-Ayala and Marvin, 2020: 129–148). Under the urban computational logic, the platforms by themselves become rationales for normalizing the approach of collecting and aggregating data that cut across diverse city systems. Take the city brain as an example. Arguably, it may well be understood as an AI-enabled computer vision system in cloud, which is promised to connect with, and process on a real-time basis the citywide interoperable data generated through surveillance cameras for biometric/image recognition systems, multiple urban service apps, government sectors' key databases, etc. Initiated by Alibaba, the city brain project was first trialled in Hangzhou's transportation sector for easing traffic congestion (Caprotti and Liu, 2022). The governing model has been then replicated to a wide range of urban domains and also exported to many other cities that may opt for Alibaba or other technology companies – such as Huawei, Baidu, Tencent and JD.com – as a "city brain vendor."

Thirdly, similar to other countries, AI is narratively constructed as a strategic technology around the discourse of international competition. Against the backdrop of the US defending its dominance in the world's geopolitical landscape and China being a strong challenger, AI is envisioned as a game-changer that enables the country to leapfrog its competitor and further become a new force for change in the international order (Hine and Floridi, 2022). This vision of AI's transformative power in geopolitics creates a sense of national security imperative, while also shifting the focus of China-US competition from economic areas to an escalated high-tech war. In response to the US growing hawkish stance, China's AI imaginaries are imbued with ideologies of patriotism. In particular, the Communist Party of China (CPC)-driven 'national rejuvenation' (NR) rhetoric largely attributes modern China to its honour and disgrace to the country's capability of indigenous innovation or technological self-reliance – a political legacy handed down from Chairman Mao amid external threats during the Cold War era. By evoking the collective memory of the so-called 'Century of Humiliation' (1840s–1940s) and the hope of a powerful global AI leader, the intertwined AI and NR imaginaries produce a strong effect on the national identity, which allows them to find a foothold not only in the political, academic and business spheres but the societal values. Consequently, through the lens of media, when the urban space is deployed with an AI-based system, a "transparent citizen" may care more about life convenience and national technologies' leading edge, and less about data tracking and surveillance.

The fourth dimension featuring China's AI imaginaries is the CPC-led, multi-stakeholder participated AI application initiative, which takes the city as a large-scale testbed. As Bareis and Katzenbach (2021: 1) observe, the 2017 NAIDP – as a 'peculiar hybrid of policy and discourse'– enables strong performative politics in urban spaces. The publicly performed AI imaginaries are embodied by AI conferences and labs hosted by different cities, creation of new AI spaces (Shanghai's AIsland, Xiong'an, Hangzhou's AI Town, Chongqing's Cloud Valley, etc.), use of driverless vehicles and robots in real-life scenes, deployment of facial biometric identification systems and introduction of AI-controlled urban governance platforms, to name but a few. Notwithstanding the urbanscape of multi-sited AI implementation, the key actors at the forefront of the AI practices are indeed China's most politically and economically influential cities, in particular, Beijing, Shanghai, Shenzhen and Hangzhou (Marvin et al., 2022). One of the main reasons for this is that, due to an unequal spatial development, these cities possess a better ICT infrastructure to feed massive data into the envisioned AI ubiquitous intelligent environment. More importantly, home to headquarters of the nation's top-line technology giants and AI unicorns, they harness a huge political, financial and human resource advantage to afford AI-enabled infrastructural facilities citywide.

It is worth pointing out that, in the context of China's 'recentralization of state power' (Wu, 2017: 1134) in post-neoliberalism, the urban AI experimentation is, on the one hand, tightly framed in the CPC-led political agendas and, on the other hand, largely entrepreneurial and market-oriented. From Beijing leaders' perspective, they recognize that the decentralized neoliberal city through the fast-growing private tech sector becomes a dominant market agent and core actor of commercializing new digital technologies. The central government henceforth rolls out a series of carrot-and-stick measures to align the urban entrepreneurial stakeholders to its national AI strategic visions. As many writers point out, the ambitious AI strategy of NAIDP serves not so much as an authoritarian controlled how-to, but rather as a do-it-yourself guidance and promise to relevant actors, in particular, local governments, private high-tech companies and AI venture market (Ding 2020; Carter and Crumpler 2019). In a similar vein, Lee (2018) indicates that active entrepreneurial engagement in AI development is more about a response to the market rather than the state's demand. Consequently, the urban space lends itself to an actually sociotechnical experimental field for performing the national AI imaginaries through multilateral interest alignment and coalition.

To sum up, the dimensions of China's emerging AI imaginaries help unpack the nation-specific power dynamics that mobilize collective expectations of an AI-enabled future society. As Konrad et al. (2016: 15) argue, the future – as an object of public imaginaries – is 'mobilized in the present as promises or expectations in policy documents or in legislation.' China's state-level AI strategy and policy documents can be seen as a hybrid of AI industrial policies, national discourses and promises to main stakeholders, which play a significant role in justifying AI-related actions ranging from resource allocation to actual effects on materiality and normativity on a national scale. In this sense, the city may well be treated as a bounded geographical space with its visions, infrastructural systems and governance approaches embodying the performativity of state-scale AI imaginaries to varying degrees. In the meantime, the future-oriented AI representations through urban practices are constitutive of the national imaginaries that are coming into being. For the aim of reflexively analysing the mode of AI imaginaries' intervention in the future pathways, in the next section, I will investigate the way in which the state's AI imaginaries are being transferred to and performed in the social structures of the urban space.

Performing AI imaginaries in the city: an experimental case in Xiong'an

Seen in terms of performative imaginaries, AI from the above analysis implies a process of ideal construct whereby national AI strategies, regulatory policies and political rhetoric materialize the context-specific imaginaries through 'reiterative and citational practice by which discourse produces the effects that it names' (Butler, 1993: 13). With reference to my empirical work in Xiong'an, I will explore how the norms, ideologies and socioeconomic policies around AI morph into specific forms of materiality in a bounded urban space. Two key questions will be addressed in this section. Firstly, *in what forms do the AI imaginaries become materially embedded in urban structures in Xiong'an?* Secondly, *how does the performativity of AI imaginaries animate the spatial power dynamics that render the materiality of AI in Xiong'an?* The study is based on my fieldwork conducted between October 2020 and December 2021, including multiple visits to Xiong'an and 11 semi-structured interviews with policy-makers, AI and robotic companies' senior executives, technology reporters and academics based in Beijing and Xiong'an. It is important to note that due to confidentiality agreements with multiple-level government agencies, this study's participants involved in planning and building Xiong'an – a national new area billed as 'President Xi's dream city' (Wong 2019) – are not always able to speak frankly, which may affect my findings at this stage of the research.

From entangled state imaginaries to urban vision

By all accounts, Xiong'an is a centrally top-down project that is embedded in two of Chinese state's intertwined grand imaginaries: 1) the AI imaginaries, which position the new space as a model performing urban China's socioeconomic transition towards an AI innovation and low-carbon economy; 2) the megacity-regional imaginaries, which serve politics of upscaling spatial power to upper tiers of regional governance in the post-neoliberalism context of a recentralized trend (Wu, 2017). Seen from the megacity Beijing's view, Xiong'an is envisioned as a spatial fix (Harvey, 2001) for the capital city to relieve its growth pressure and redirect key socioeconomic functions into an AI-enabled urban extension.

Entangled and multiple socio-political and economic dynamics motivate the central government's expectation of building a new paradigm of a high-tech socialist modern city, which is intelligent, low-carbon and innovative

(Xinhua, 2017). The Xiong'an project was publicly announced in April 2017, three months before the State Council's release of the NAIDP. Symbolically ushering in a new urban era, Xiong'an is built up from scratch by merging areas of three hinterland counties – Xiong'xian, Rong'cheng and An'xin – in Hebei province. The new space is located about 100 kilometres south of Beijing, which puts it at the heart of a triangle shaped by three major cities in northern China: Beijing (Jing), Tianjin (Jin) and Shijiazhuang, the capital city of Hebei province (Ji). The unique geographic location performs the party-state's imaginaries of creating a spatial vehicle to rescale power towards the governance of a vast unequally developed region covering Jing, Jin and Ji, and also to take over some of Beijing's non-capital functions.

In line with the discourses constructing China's AI imaginaries analysed in the previous sections, the AI expectations of Xiong'an focus on urban infra-structures that manifest convergence of AI with other emerging technologies, including 5G, unmanned driving, Big Data, the IoT, ultra-high-voltage (UHV) power transmission, renewable energy and digital twins, to name but a few. Politically, the envisioned intelligent urban paradigm emphasizes the superior-ity of CPC's governance model that drafts AI into its power apparatus to mate-rialize party-led unity, social stability, vast economic growth and environmental liveability. As Naughton (2020) notes, effective top-down control, environ-mental agenda and indigenous technological innovation have become the key theme dominating China's government-led urban development under the helm of Xi's administration. Motivated by the hybrid socio-political and economic interests, the context-specific urban imaginaries of an 'intelligent, innovative, and low carbon' (see Hebei Government, 2018: no page) are performed in Xiong'an via tangled discursive and material practices, embodied by urban masterplan documents and materiality of AI-powered cyber-physical interac-tive infrastructures. Underpinned by the urban computational logics, the material representation of the intelligent eco-city – examined below – points to an emerging urban governance regime in what Luque-Ayala and Simon Marvin (2020) metaphorically term as *Urban OS*, which epistemologically governs a particular way of seeing the city as a ubiquitous computing system.

Reconfiguring cyber-physical infrastructures

From the outset, Xiong'an was framed in the national discourse as the future city where physical and 'digital twin' spaces will be planned and built 'in a synchronised fashion' (Hebei Government, 2018: no page). Given the princi-ple that all infrastructural projects will be constructed in strict accordance with a masterplan system called '1+4+26' (see Table 14.1), the city planning blueprint plays a strong performative role in materializing the urban visions that are projected onto buildings and infrastructures in the name of AI. As shown in two key documents, 'Master Plan' (Hebei Government, 2018) and

TABLE 14.1 The blueprint of Xiong'an city planning

"1+4+26" System	*Date*	*Plans*
1 Guideline	April 2018	Guideline for Planning the Hebei Xiong'an New Area
4 Overall Plans	Dec 2018	Master Plan for Hebei Xiong'an New Area (2018 – 2035) (hereinafter 'Master Plan')
	Jan 2019	Governance and Protection Plan for Baiyang Lake Ecological Environment (2018–2035)
	Jan 2020	Controllability Plan for Initial Area of Xiong'an (hereinafter 'Controllability Plan')
	Jan 2020	Controllability Detailed Plan for Startup Area of Xiong'an
26 Specialized Plans	2019	Plans covering areas such as government service, transportation, energy, housing and natural disaster response

Source: author's original.

'Controllability Plan' (Hebei Government, 2020), the urban designers have a preconceived idea of building a city whose physical realities and corresponding AI-powered virtual simulations form an interactive, symbiotic relationship. With a belief in Gelernter's (1993) *Mirror Worlds*, the city's virtual model of its physical representations is envisioned to simulate the fixed assets (buildings, roads, plants) and dynamic behaviours (human mobility, electricity provision, transportation service, etc.) in the real-world environment, and furthermore, to extend its computational capabilities to the urban circulatory systems and events by means of cyber-physical interactive feedback, high-performance computing and real-time data analysis.

As one urban researcher involved in the masterplan says, the materialization of the digital twin city of Xiong'an is a 'large-scaled urban experimentation,' which enables 'the convergence of multi-layered AI-powered new technologies' and a 'ubiquitous network aggregating real-time data' about traffic, energy provisions and ecological environment (Interview, October 2021). In his opinion, the "mirror worlds" can describe, supervise and optimize the performance of a physical urban system's overall operations during its whole life cycle. Sharing a strikingly similar view with a majority of this study's participants (officials, academics and AI engineers), the urban researcher deems the digital twin space as a 'scientific viewing tool' (Gelernter, 1993: 38) accessible to city managers whereby they possess a top-sight vantage point to look at the wholeness the way a biologist sees, zooms and anatomizes a living organism.

Sort of like one single map with multiple interconnected points, the digital twin city integrates all urban data into the visualized map and renders spatio-temporal information about the city's operation of both its whole situation and partially minute details. Henceforth urban managers can address wicked problems from a holistic perspective. It is a way of "system of systems" governance or what President Xi demands to treat the whole city as one chess game (Interview, October 2021).

This belief in a centrally controlled, AI-empowered cybernetic governmentality leads to an AI urban experimentation framed in a narrative trope that the city of Xiong'an is extended to 'three cities (spaces) in symbiosis,' namely, one city built on the ground, one city underground and the other in the cloud (Mei, 2020). The 'underground city' is embodied by infrastructures of a 300-kilometre-long integrated utility tunnel network, which is deployed in different segments across Xiong'an. Figuratively described as the city's "artery," the two-level tunnel is layered with a wide array of new digital technologies under the AI umbrella (Figure 14.1). The second level is designed for accommodating unmanned transport systems for logistics and buses, and

FIGURE 14.1 A section of a utility tunnel network under construction in Xiong'an.

Source: author's original.

the first level is for integrated utility pipelines that provide the city with gas, electricity, water and telecommunication. The massive data flows collected from the sensor-embedded tunnel are operated in a feedback loop to the monitoring centre connected to the metaphorical "city on the cloud" or the envisioned digital twin space in its primary stage.

In actual urban experimentation, the 'digital twin' vision is translated to a large-scale digital infrastructure architecture that consists of what is normally called 'one centre plus four platforms.' Rhetorically working as the city's brain, the 'one centre' refers to the materiality of urban computing infrastructure that takes the form of a multi-storeyed building, called Xiong'an Urban Computing (Supercomputing Cloud) Centre. With a floor area exceeding 39,800 square metres, the centre hosts tens of thousands of computer servers. Functioning as an urban-scale computing system, the city's brain is designed to underpin the database of the imagined digital twin city by way of delivering computing, cloud storage and data analytic services for other data infrastructures, especially the four urban platforms, namely, block data platform, IoT integration platform, video network platform and City Information Modelling (CIM) platform.

Dubbed as 'city's nerves,' the four platforms work together to perform visions of collecting and aggregating different types of all urban heterogeneous data, whereby sensing and remotely controlling the urban environment and its functional process that ranges from infrastructural operation to building maintenance, from safety risk prediction to air quality assessment, and from bus scheduling to energy provisions. Specifically, the CIM platform is described as a prototype for future digital twin city modelling, which comes as a result of stacking technologies of AI, Geographic Information System (GIS), Building Information Modelling (BIM) and the IoT. Under national narratives, continuous iteration of the packed technologies will ultimately push the current form of urban spatial modelling towards the imagined digital twin city. Yet, none of my participants can offer a realistic timeframe for materializing the cyber-physical interactive vision. They acknowledge that 'there are a number of technical and socio-political limits to how much the CIM can truly mirror the physical city on a real-time basis' (Interview, November 2021). As Cureton and Dunn (2021: 269) point out, either CIM or digital twin city emphasizes massive data collected from sensors, which overlook the 'actual intricacies of urban life' ranging from human interactions to uncertainties that are indigenous to cities. The worship of algorithm simulation and computational prediction ignores the complexity and unpredictability of urban life.

As an exemplar testbed for an eco-city, the green urbanization vision in Xiong'an is performed through energy consumption of anything but fossil fuels. According to the 'Master Plan' (Hebei Government, 2018), the new city is designed to run on 100% clean power and green electricity – meaning generation from wind, solar and nuclear power – will take up roughly 52% of its overall energy use. Yet Xiong'an by itself cannot achieve self-sufficiency in affording locally generated electricity from renewables, which is a type of modernization-driven sustainability that lends itself to become 'a tool to produce profit' (Cugurullo, 2016: 2428). The lion's share will be imported from outside through ultra-high-voltage (UHV) transmission networks, one of the seven "new infrastructure" categories under China's massive stimulus measures. Under this circumstance, the UHV power grid is heavily deployed in Xiong'an and its neighbouring cities and provinces with abundant wind and solar power resources.

What is more, the city's green electricity vision is awash with labels of intelligent technologies. Futuristic buzzwords – such as AI algorithm-enabled active distribution network, robotic grid inspection and integrated solar PV systems that combine energy storage with electric vehicle charging – are repeatedly cited in media and policy documents as intelligent, green power solutions for Xiong'an. More recently, the city's first intelligent grid project, Jucun Smart Integrated Substation, was put into operation. It connects the UHV line between Xiong'an and Zhangbei, providing electricity to more than 70,000 residents in Rongdong district. The substation is reportedly layered with multiple technologies, such as digital twin, AI, intelligent robotics, 5G and Beidou Navigation Satellite System, thus achieving integrated functions of remotely monitoring physical facilities and using robots to inspect the substation.

Conclusion

This chapter has explored the mechanisms through which the state imaginaries of a global AI leader are morphed into context-specific visions of an intelligent eco-city, represented by the materiality of massive infrastructures that are layered with multiple information technologies under the umbrella of AI. This suggests that there are two distinct, yet interrelated, avenues through which AI imaginaries are produced and rigidified into norms, social institutions and urban governance models.

The first is at the state level. The AI policies mingled with the ruling party's rhetoric and socio-political agendas discursively construct China's particular AI imaginaries, which hold promise for massive economic growth, an intelligent governance model and a prospective path to global power. Endowed with political legitimacy as such, the AI imaginaries are enabled to function as a key sociotechnical institution that structures AI's normative rules, capital investment and range of social adoptions. Secondly, at the urban level, given its spatial heterogeneity of discursive and material elements, the city provides a fertile ground for performing the AI imaginaries 'associated with active exercises of state power' (Jasanoff and Kim, 2009: 123). In the process of urban experimental practices, an assemblage of city visions, values, rules and materiality that defines our socio-political futures is performed into being.

As demonstrated by the case of Xiong'an, the AI imaginaries work in a performative fashion to construct the materiality of multi-technology layered urban infrastructures, which are embodied by facilities and buildings such as urban computing centres, integrated utility tunnels and UHV power grids. The ongoing urban experimentation is, on the one hand, seen as a typical exemplar of China's national AI imaginaries that are spatially projected onto a real-life city context. On the other hand, by way of visually representing abstract visions in material infrastructures, the urban experimental practice breaks down public perceptive boundaries between "what is" and "what might be." In this sense, imaginaries about an alternative future pathway are rendered as "what the future is like" rather than "might be like." As van Lente and Rip (1998: 216) write, 'what starts as an option can be labelled a technical promise, and may subsequently function as a requirement to be achieved.' Holding a similar view, this chapter shows that the urban AI experimentation lends itself to a particular form of performative act that significantly contributes to the way the national AI imaginaries come into being. What's more important, the performativity generates a material lock-in pathway that is highly dependent on intelligence incarnation in the reconfiguration of cyber-physical urban infrastructures.

Positioned with a crucial national strategy, the Xiong'an urban AI experiment can now only be seen in an embryonic form given that a large number of infrastructure projects are yet to be implemented. Therefore, it might be premature to jump to conclusions about the city's future at this stage of research. Yet, key issues have emerged from the above critical analysis of how, and why, the state-produced AI imaginaries are translated, performed and represented in a bounded space through urban experimentation that is of significant societal and research concern. The wider implications of this analysis of an emblematic attempt to construct AI-enabled urban imaginaries may orientate further urban studies towards understanding AI imaginaries' role, both materially and discursively, in embedding a certain pathway dependency into cultural norms and social functioning.

Firstly, the spatial scales of the state and city arguably become two main interactive loci producing and performing China's emerging national AI imaginaries which establish a pathway for the development of the Chinese society. In the context of the Chinese party-state's powerful outreach to AI sectors, the state underwrites the risks of AI imaginaries' public performance, including potential big investment loss, and ethical and security challenges. The political legitimacy bestowed upon the performative imaginaries weakens the agency of other stakeholders – in particular, high-tech companies, subnational governments and academia – in terms of critically assessing AI's applied performance and potentials for social use. This might cause a danger of leading the country into an AI tech bubble behind the fast-growing AI start-ups and wide-ranging social applications. In addition, due to the politics of spatial inequality, the state-endorsed AI opportunities are largely skewed towards a few cities and interest groups. Xiong'an is a case in point. Therefore, it is highly questionable that the envisioned 'Xiong'an model' can be replicated nationwide due to the huge amount of political and financial investment thrown onto the mega-city project. As one of my participants said, 'China cannot have a second Pudong. And in a similar way, the Xiong'an model is hardly replicated due to the spatial political privilege that defies other cities.' (Interview, December 2021).

Secondly, while the computing centre in Xiong'an is depicted as a "city's brain," a close reading of media and official documents may lead to observations that ascribing human organisms to the urban infrastructure system through metaphors and technical hypes is shaping the national AI imaginaries. As examined in the previous section, the urban informational infrastructures are metaphorically constituted by "brains" (computing centre), "nerves" (IoT and video networking), "artery" (integrated underground tunnel pipes) and "digital twins" (CIM platforms). What lies underneath the metaphors is the specific action-guiding vision that the hybridity of urban infrastructures – seen as discrete micro-ecologies of the urban system – can be integrated into one AI-enabled centrally controlled cybernetic system. However, in actually existing urban experimental practices, my participants acknowledged that numerous sociotechnical factors, ranging from political institutions to technical and financial limitations, make it hard to integrate the infrastructures into one totality. A case in point is the intelligent electricity system, which is built on an energy system separately developed by the State Grid Corporation and not yet integrated into the envisioned unitary urban system of 'one centre plus four platforms.' In addition, observations of technical exaggerations linked to the metaphorical cybernetics emerge from my fieldwork. Few participants in this study agreed that Xiong'an or any other city in China are truly "intelligent" because of the urban platforms consisting of a city brain or CIM. 'What we are doing now is technology stacking, which is not yet AI. We are creating concepts and metaphors for packaging our urban demonstrative projects, which is an understandable market act,' says one participant (Interview, December 2021).

As I have demonstrated in this chapter, AI imaginaries are griping the collective consciousness of urban China's geography. The society's process of accepting the imagined AI-enabled social orders goes with a process of performing that imagined future. This foregrounds the importance of paying due attention to AI imaginaries' performativity that is expressed in various forms with both discursive and material dimensions. In this study, I critically analysed the power of AI imaginaries' public performance represented by national AI strategies, city planning blueprints, and physical material and digital infrastructures. My findings strongly point to the imaginaries' performative power in not only representing projections of an alternative AI-enable future but also generating certain material social lock-ins. What is more important is how the imaginaries' performativity, epistemologically, blurs the boundary between visions and actualities, and "what is" and "what might be" in the AI-controlled city.

Acknowledgements

I would like to thank my supervisors, Simon Marvin and Aidan While, for their support and enlightening discussions throughout the development of this chapter.

References

Bareis, J., & Katzenbach, C. (2021). Talking AI into being: The narratives and imaginaries of national AI strategies and their performative politics. *Science, Technology, & Human Values*, 47(5), 855–881.

Borup, M., Brown, N., Konrad, K., & Van Lente, H. (2006). The sociology of expectations in science and technology. *Technology Analysis and Strategic Management*, 18(3/4), 285–298.

Butler, J. (1993). *Bodies that matter: On the discursive limits of "sex"*. Routledge, New York.

Caprotti, F., & Liu, D. (2022). Platform urbanism and the Chinese smart city: The co-production and territorialisation of Hangzhou city brain. *GeoJournal*, 87(3), 1559–1573.

Carter, W., & Crumpler, W. (2019). *Smart money on Chinese advances in AI*. Centre for Strategic & International Studies, Washington.

Chen, B., Marvin, S., & While, A. (2020). Containing COVID-19 in China: AI and the robotic restructuring of future cities. *Dialogues in Human Geography*, 10(2), 238–241.

Cugurullo, F. (2016). Urban eco-modernisation and the policy context of new eco-city projects: Where Masdar City fails and why. *Urban Studies*, 53(11), 2417–2433.

Cugurullo, F. (2020). Urban artificial intelligence: From automation to autonomy in the smart city. *Frontiers in Sustainable Cities*, 2, 1–14.

Cugurullo, F. (2021). *Frankenstein urbanism: eco, smart and autonomous cities, artificial intelligence and the end of the city*. Routledge, London.

Cureton, P., & Dunn, N. (2021). Digital twins of cities and evasive futures. In Aurigi, A. and Odendaal, N. (Eds.) *Shaping Smart for Better Cities: Rethinking and Shaping Relationships between Urban Space and Digital Technologies*, Academic Press, 267–282.

Curran, D., & Smart, A. (2021). Data-driven governance, smart urbanism and risk-class inequalities: Security and social credit in China. *Urban Studies*, 58(3), 487–506.

Ding, J. (2018). *Deciphering China's AI dream*. Future of Humanity Institute, Oxford.

Ding, J. (2020). Promoting nationally, acting locally: China's next generation AI approach. In Chun, A., Ding, J., Creemers, R., Gal, D., Han, E., Liu, Y. L., & Lewis, D. (Eds.) *The AI Powered State: China's approach to public sector innovation*. Nesta.

Evans, J., Karvonen, A., & Raven, R. (Eds.). (2016). *The experimental city*. Routledge, Abingdon.

Gelernter, D. (1993). *Mirror worlds: Or the day software puts the universe in a shoebox… How it will happen and what it will mean*. Oxford University Press, Oxford.

Harvey, D. (2001). Globalization and the "Spatial Fix". *Geographische Revue*, 2, 23–30.

Hebei Government. (2018). *Guideline for Planning of Hebei Xiong'an New Area* [河北雄安新区规划纲要]. Available at: http://www.xiongan.gov.cn/2018-04/21/c_129855813.htm [Accessed 19/01/2023].

Hebei Government. (2020). *Controllability Plan for Initial Area of Xiong'an* [河北雄安新区起步区控制性规划]. Available at: http://xiongxian.gov.cn/content-621-54391.html [Accessed 19/01/2023.]

Hine, E., & Floridi, L. (2022). Artificial intelligence with American values and Chinese characteristics: a comparative analysis of American and Chinese governmental AI policies. *AI & Society*. DOI: 10.1007/s00146-022-01499-8.

Hodson, M., & McMeekin, A. (2021). Global technology companies and the politics of urban socio-technical imaginaries in the digital age: Processual proxies, Trojan horses and global beachheads. *EPA: Economy and Space*, 53(6), 1–21.

Jasanoff, S. (Ed.). (2004). *States of knowledge: The co-production of science and the social order*. Routledge, London.

Jasanoff, S. (2015). Future imperfect: Science, technology, and the imaginations of modernity. In Jasanoff, S. and Kim, S-H. (Eds.) *Dreamscapes of Modernity: Sociotechnical Imaginaries and the Fabrication of Power*. University of Chicago Press, Chicago, 1–47.

Jasanoff, S., & Kim, S-H. (2009). Containing the atom: Sociotechnical imaginaries and nuclear power in the United States and South Korea. *Minerva*, 47(2), 119–146.

Jasanoff, S., & Kim, S-H. (Eds.) (2015). *Dreamscapes of modernity: Sociotechnical imaginaries and the fabrications of power*. University of Chicago Press, Chicago.

Jeffreys, E., & Sigley, G. (2009). Governmentality, governance and China. In Jeffreys, E. (Ed.) *China's Governmentalities: Governing Change, Changing Government*. Routledge, London, 1–23.

Konrad, K., Van Lente, H., Groves, C., & Selin, C. (2016). Performing and governing the future in science and technology. In Miller, C., Felt, U., Fouché, R., & Smith-Doerr, L. (Eds.) *The Handbook of Science and Technology Studies*, MIT Press, Cambridge, 465–493.

Lee, K-F. (2018). *AI superpowers: China, Silicon Valley, and the new world order*. Houghton Mifflin Harcourt, Boston.

Luque-Ayala, A., & Marvin, S. (2020). *Urban operating systems: Producing the computational city*. MIT Press, Cambridge.

Marvin, S., While, A., Chen, B., & Kovacic, M. (2022). Urban AI in China: Social control or hyper-capitalist development in the post-smart city? *Frontiers in Sustainable Cities*, 4, 1–11.

Mei, J. (2020). Xiong'an, China's shining city, emerges. *China Daily*. Available at: https://global.chinadaily.com.cn/a/202011/30/WS5fc42885a31024ad0ba98336.html [Accessed 19/01/2023].

Naughton, B. (2020). Xi Jinping's economic policy and Chinese urbanization. In Huang, Y. Q. (Ed.) *Chinese Cities in the 21st Century*. Springer International Publishing, Gewerbestrasse (Switzerland), 35–60.

Pfotenhauer, S., & Jasanoff, S. (2017). Panacea or diagnosis? Imaginaries of innovation and the MIT model in three political cultures. *Social Studies of Science*, 47(6), 783–810.

Roberts, H., Cowls, J., Morley, J., Taddeo, M., Wang, V. & Floridi, L. (2021). The Chinese approach to artificial intelligence: an analysis of policy, ethics, and regulation. *AI & Society*, 36(1), 59–77.

Schiølin, K. (2020). Revolutionary dreams: Future essentialism and the sociotechnical imaginary of the fourth industrial revolution in Denmark. *Social Studies of Science*, 50(4), 542–566.

Schwab, K. (2016). The fourth industrial revolution. What it means and how to respond. In: Rose, G. (Ed.) *The Fourth Industrial Revolution: A Davos Reader.* Foreign Affairs, New York.

State Council, People's Republic of China. (2017). *New-generation of Artificial Intelligence Development Plan* [新一代人工智能发展规划]. Available at: http://www.gov.cn/zhengce/content/2017-07/20/content_5211996.htm [Accessed 19/01/2023].

Van Lente, H., & Rip, A. (1998). Expectations in technological developments: An example of prospective structures to be filled in by agency. In Disco, C. and van der Meulen, B. (Eds.) *Getting new technologies together: Studies in making sociotechnical order.* Walter de Gruyter, Berlin, 203–231.

While, A., Marvin, S., & Kovacic, M. (2020). Urban robotic experimentation: San Francisco, Tokyo and Dubai. *Urban Studies.* 58(4), 769–786.

Wong, F. (2019). Xiong'an New Area: President Xi's dream city. *China Briefing.* Available at: https://www.china-briefing.com/news/xiongan-new-area-beijing-tianjin-hebei/ [Accessed 19/01/2023].

Wu, F. L. (2017). China's emergent city-region governance: A new form of state spatial selectivity through state-orchestrated rescaling. *International Journal of Urban and Regional Research*, 40(6), 1134–1151.

Xinhua. (2017). Xiongan New Area to be built as AI city. *Xinhuanet.* Available at: http://www.xinhuanet.com//english/2017-11/08/c_136737900.htm [Accessed 19/01/2023].

15

OPTIMIZING THE IMMEASURABLE

On the techno-ethical limits of predictive policing

Aaron Shapiro

Introduction

Brutality against people of colour, gender and sexual minorities, the unhoused, political dissidents and the mentally ill is as old as professional law enforcement, but police violence is now more visible than ever. Bystander cellphone videos showing sworn officers using verbal assaults, excessive force, strangleholds, sound canons, Tasers, rubber bullets and live rounds – often against unarmed civilians – circulate widely on social media channels before getting picked up and redistributed by major news outlets. The murder of George Floyd in May 2020, captured on video, catalyzed what may have been the largest protests in US history (Buchanan et al., 2020). The politics and stakes of police reform in the United States appear to be changing as a result.

Several municipalities responded to the unrest by slashing police budgets and redirecting funds towards public safety, education and mental health programs (Levin, 2021). Some city governments seized the sentiment to reevaluate unpopular contracts with police technology providers and, particularly, vendors of *predictive policing* software. Predictive policing describes a range of statistical, machine learning and artificial intelligence (AI) techniques for forecasting the locations, times and/or perpetrators of criminal activity (Kaufmann et al., 2019; Lally, 2021). While proponents insist that predictive policing can increase accountability and improve police outcomes, critics argue that the technology is fundamentally flawed: it amplifies discrimination and uneven enforcement, concentrates surveillance in racial-minority communities and makes police agencies less accountable to the publics they

DOI: 10.4324/9781003365877-18

serve (American Civil Liberties Union, 2016; Angwin et al., 2016; Dencik et al., 2018; Ensign et al., 2017; Harcourt, 2006; Richardson et al., 2019).

Following the 2020 protests, some city governments opted to discontinue predictive policing programs. The Santa Cruz, CA, police department – one of the first to adopt the technology – banned algorithmic policing outright (Sturgill, 2020). But Santa Cruz may be an exception proving the rule of predictive policing's enduring appeal, as many of the largest police departments in the United States have doubled down on crime prediction tools. For example, the Los Angeles Police Department (LAPD) cancelled its contract with predictive policing vendor PredPol in April 2020 (Haskins, 2020), but a guidebook authored by LAPD Chief Michael Moore published the same month indicated that the agency planned to develop crime prediction software in-house, including real-time mapping programs that closely resemble commercial predictive policing platforms (Bhuiyan, 2021; Hvistendahl, 2021). The New York Police Department (NYPD), the largest in the United States, also uses crime prediction systems developed internally (Brennan Center for Justice, 2021). The Chicago Police Department (CPD) decommissioned a controversial offender-based prediction system in 2020 but renewed its contract with ShotSpotter, a third-party platform that integrates gunshot detection and crime prediction software (Byrne, 2021; Gorner and Sweeney, 2020).

In this chapter, I examine the politics of predictive policing to highlight the techno-ethical limits of AI-driven urban governance initiatives (Amoore, 2020; Amrute, 2019). I use 'techno-ethical' here to specify a relationship between the 'technicity' of crime prediction algorithms (Simondon, 2017; cf. Bucher, 2018: 14–16), the redistribution of decision-making between human and nonhuman agents in policing (Hayles, 2017) and the ethical appeals that legitimate technological intervention. Attending to the relationship between technicity and ethical discourse reveals predictive policing to be a failed *managerial reform* in the institution of policing. Police reform, as I use the term, designates efforts to negotiate incommensurable mandates for modern police forces: to distribute public safety benefits and to produce criminality through law enforcement (Jefferson, 2020; Muhammad, 2010). While members of marginalized communities experience police agencies as penetrating and intrusive, the very legitimacy of liberal government hinges on police agencies' restraint of force (De Lint, 2000; Dubber and Valverde, 2006, 2008; Foucault, 2007). Predictive policing responds to a crisis in police legitimacy by promising to tilt the balance back from the former to the latter. But as a reform, it does not alter or upend the police institution's contradictory mandates.

My argument proceeds in the next section by discussing the rationales motivating police agencies to adopt predictive policing. I then move on to discuss findings from ethnographic research conducted with the product team at HunchLab, a predictive policing platform developed by Philadelphia-based geospatial analytics company Azavea. I show how statistical indeterminacies within the predictive apparatus confound the technicity of AI and machine-learning decision-making systems. I conclude the chapter by arguing that these indeterminacies arise from policing's contradictory mandates to distribute both public safety benefits and sanctioned violence. In other words, the problem with predictive policing is not the predictions but the policing.

Predictive policing for reform

Predictive policing exemplifies broader changes in urban governance stemming from the integration of AI into the management of metabolic urban processes, such as energy consumption, mobility and crime (Batty, 2018; Cugurullo, 2020). Statistical crime forecasting often appears alongside other 'urban dashboard' features, such as traffic, weather, property prices, demographics, employment statistics and so on (McArdle and Kitchin, 2016). This suggests an ontological flattening of urban social and physical dynamics, such that domains as disparate as waste management, education and policing can be measured and managed using the same command and control tools (Söderström et al., 2014; White, 2016: 4). Policing, like other urban services and infrastructures, becomes "smarter" with AI.

But there is also something exceptional about predictive policing. The logic of crime prediction starts with four conceits that, while resonant with the *cognitive turn* in urban governance (Bratton, 2021), require precise assumptions about the nature of crime and criminality – that crime can be measured objectively; that AI and machine learning algorithms can detect patterns in crime data that elude human interpreters; that those patterns are predictive of future crime outcomes; and that police agencies can leverage crime predictions to increase the efficiency by which they manage patrol resources (Hälterlein, 2021; Kaufmann et al., 2019).

Predictive policing also involves a more complex entanglement of algorithms and institutions than the physical flows of energy or transit. This is because when put into practice, algorithmic crime prediction does not intervene in crime *per se* but in the geographies of police patrols. This point is crucial. The object of predictive policing is not the criminal but the beat cop, the constable on patrol, whose discretion – the authority to determine which actors and activities threaten the social order – is a perennial problem in policing institutions (Dubber and Valverde, 2006, 2008). How should officers' autonomy be managed? Since the establishment of the first modern police forces, law enforcement agencies have struggled to regulate where, when and how police officers patrol (De Lint, 2000). Predictive policing addresses this issue anew by augmenting police patrol routes with complex and granular analytics that direct officers to algorithmically sorted, block-sized grid cells for surveillance and patrol. The autonomy of artificial intelligence thus interacts with and conditions the police's on-the-ground autonomy (Brayne and Christin, 2021; Cugurullo, 2020). And it is precisely this algorithmic augmentation that makes predictive policing attractive to police departments – not forecasting crime so much as using algorithms to manage a mobile workforce of flawed and corruptible police officers (Benbouzid, 2019; Burrington, 2015).

A managerial perspective on predictive policing has two advantages. First, it frames AI and machine learning algorithms as integrated into the 'heterogeneous sociomaterial assemblages' of the police patrol (Introna, 2016: 20). The algorithm is not some immutable outside force acting on patrol officers, but a *technique* incorporated into routine institutional decision structures. Second, predictive policing's managerial function invites reflection on negotiations between (i) the technicity of machine learning algorithms, (ii) the distribution of agency across human and nonhuman components of police assemblages and (iii) the discursive constructs that legitimize predictive policing as an ethical technology. I deal with (i) and (ii) in the next section. In the remainder of this section, I unpack (iii): the discourse that justifies investment in predictive policing.

Early proponents of predictive policing likened crime prediction algorithms to logistical forecasting methods used by companies like Walmart or Amazon to manage inventory and consumer demand (Beck and McCue, 2009). In this framing, the problems of law enforcement were essentially problems of efficiency, and policing could be recast as a logistical dilemma (Reeves and Packer, 2013): where and how police officers patrolled the city became 'analogous to identifying the likely demand for Pop-Tarts' (Burrington, 2015: no page). This framing was driven in large part by a budgetary crisis. As austerity measures following the 2008 global financial crisis slashed public funding (Peck, 2012), law enforcement agencies struggled with limited personnel. Police leaders insisted that they needed new tools to 'do more with less' – to 'increase the effective use of police resources [and] make every agency more efficient, regardless of the availability of resources' (Beck and McCue, 2009: 1).

The discourse shifted, however, following a series of high-profile police murders of unarmed African American men and women. As critical legal scholar Andrew Guthrie Ferguson (2017: 29) writes, the widespread adoption of Big Data policing 'grew out of crisis and a need to turn the page on scandals that revealed systemic problems with policing tactics.' Police agencies were no longer struggling with tight budgets; now it was their reputations and legitimacy on the line. What was needed was not efficient policing but police reforms, and predictive policing again surfaced as the answer. According to sociologist Forrest Stuart, some of the most popular proposed solutions to the over-policing and over-incarceration of Black and brown communities have involved new technologies. There is a sense that if we could just design a good enough computer program, we could deploy police more fairly and reduce, or perhaps even eliminate, unwarranted disparities in criminal justice.

(quoted in Hvistendahl, 2021)

Predictive policing would help police departments foster 'new practices for racial equity' (Siegel, 2018: no page) and make law enforcement 'fairer,' more accountable and less biased (e.g., Corbett-Davies et al., 2017).

Behind this 'interpretative flexibility' (Pinch and Bijker, 1984) are two techno-ethical appeals. The first is to *crime prevention* (Benbouzid, 2015). Proponents argue that predictive policing improves policing outcomes because its objective is not *more* policing but *better* policing. For example, former NYPD and LAPD commissioner and leading advocate of predictive policing Bill Bratton (2014, 2018) refers to crime prediction as an algorithmic return to Sir Robert Peel's (1829: no page) tenet that 'the basic mission for which the police exist is to prevent crime and disorder.' In fact, the term 'predictive policing' first appeared in a 2009 unpublished manuscript, co-authored by Bratton, describing 'any policing strategy or tactic that develops and uses information and advanced analysis to inform forward-thinking crime prevention' (Uchida, 2014: 3781). Throughout the 2000s, a host of tech startups emerged to bring Bratton's vision to reality, and these vendors, too, would invoke prevention as a rationale and objective for predictive policing (PredPol, 2020; cf. Benbouzid, 2015; Hälterlein, 2021). With price tags comparable to or less than the cost of hiring full-time crime analysts, agencies eagerly pursued contracts with these vendors while publicly touting their benefits.

The second appeal is to *standardization*. As Brayne and Christin (2021) argue, predictive policing promises not only to increase the efficiency by which patrol resources are allocated but to rationalize and systematize those allocations, coupling decisions about where, when and how officers patrol to algorithmically generated routes, cycles and tactics. This latter appeal resonates especially with the reformer's view of policing as a fundamentally effective if flawed institution in which misconduct and brutality are individual rather than systemic problems. If police bias and corruption are caused by "a few bad apples," then what is needed is better quality assurance and tighter adherence to protocol and procedure.

Together, these appeals connect predictive policing to a longer history of technology-driven police reforms (Chan, 2001; Kelling and Moore, 1988; Manning, 2008)[1]. While patrol technologies like the squad car, two-way radio and mobile data terminal may have increased the police's logistical and informatic control over urban territories (Reeves and Packer, 2013), the same tools also subject officers in the field to managerial exposure and scrutiny. The history of police technologies is a history of supervisory control. 'With each new [patrol] technology,' writes police historian Willem De Lint (2000: 70), 'a fuller and more penetrating gaze has been envisioned, both of the police into the polity and of police supervision on police officer mobilization. [New] technologies structure the decision making of individual officers on patrol to organizationally vetted formats.' Predictive policing likewise structures police officers' decision-making to managerial imperatives, only now by empowering an algorithm to prescribe where, when and, sometimes, how to patrol. What is new then are the complex and relatively poorly understood interactions between human and machinic autonomies. Exactly how predictive policing augments officer decision-making and the new sociotechnical problems that arise from this interaction, are the subjects of the next section.

Case study: HunchLab

In order to understand the technicity of predictive policing algorithms, I conducted ethnographic research with the product team at HunchLab between October 2015 and May 2016. HunchLab was a predictive policing platform developed by Philadelphia-based geospatial software company Azavea. During the course of my study, I participated in business meetings, sat in on planning sessions, gave feedback on webinars, met with potential clients, travelled on-site visits and attended all-staff events at the company. The purpose was to understand how software developers, rather than police officers, framed policing as a problem for which AI presents as a viable solution. How do the producers of predictive policing systems understand the institution and practices of law enforcement, and how does that understanding inform the design of algorithmic interventions? Although Azavea would later sell HunchLab to technology vendor ShotSpotter (Cheetham, 2019), findings from the research remain relevant: HunchLab's core prediction algorithms are now integrated into ShotSpotter's Connect platform, which is currently used by several police departments, including Chicago's.

At the time of my research, HunchLab had cultivated a reputation for technical sophistication and commitment to police reform. The latter was buttressed by Azavea's corporate governance. Most of HunchLab's competitors were brought to market by large corporations (IBM, Microsoft, Motorola, Hitachi, LexisNexis and so on), often as a component of comprehensive smart city dashboards. Other products were sold by companies like PredPol which were backed by venture capital or by firms started with seed funding from the CIA, such as Palantir. Azavea, by contrast, was not beholden to shareholders, investors or covert government funding schemes. Instead, it adhered to a strict set of criteria for corporate social responsibility, environmental sustainability and transparency – all of which earned the company a certification as a 'social benefit' company or B Corp. With HunchLab, Azavea tried to translate those commitments into software to improve community–police relationships (HunchLab, 2017).

HunchLab's reputation for technical sophistication stemmed from the software team's data-sourcing practices and its models' theoretical agnosticism. First, unlike competitors, HunchLab prided itself on using a variety of data sets to train the crime prediction algorithm. Leading predictive policing vendor PredPol, by contrast, trains its algorithm on only three data points: time, location and type of crime. According to PredPol representatives, the parsimony of their modelling 'eliminates the possibility for privacy or civil rights violations' (PredPol, 2021: no page). HunchLab argued the opposite: using more diverse data sources added context and minimized the likelihood that *dirty data* – crime data skewed by police corruption and discrimination – would influence the algorithm's outputs (Richardson et al., 2019). HunchLab's programmers, therefore, trained its predictions on a variety of publicly available information sources. These included crime data but also weather, school schedules, housing density, concert and professional sports calendars, moon cycles, calls-for-service, geospatial location data for urban features and more.

The second reason that HunchLab was considered to be so sophisticated was its methodological agnosticism. HunchLab drew on a range of criminological theories and crime-forecasting approaches to define its variables. These included near-repeat victimization (NRV) and risk-terrain modelling (RTM), both developed by academic criminologists (Benbouzid, 2015). By representing NRV, RTM and other forecasting methods as variables in the same equations, HunchLab was able to produce a powerful 'meta-model' using machine learning techniques that customized crime-prediction formulae to client's data. For example, for any given crime, the model might specify that spatial variables (RTM) accounted for 30% of predictive power, temporal variables (NRV) made up 45% and environmental conditions, such as windspeed and temperature, accounted for the last 25%. So, while diverse data sources revealed unexpected correlations (between, say, moon phase and risk of aggravated assault), the meta-model's methodological agnosticism allowed the machine learning techniques to mix-and-match crime prediction approaches without theoretical justification.

Prediction, performance and performativity

HunchLab's prediction algorithm proved extraordinarily robust when it came to accuracy measures. Because the modelling process tweaked weights for each crime in each jurisdiction, models for the same crime types would differ across cities; and because HunchLab's clients uploaded new data daily or even between shifts, the weighting for each crime type would change over time. For example, LOCATION might be the variable that best predicts THEFT FROM AUTOMOBILES in Detroit, but in Philadelphia, it might be TIME OF DAY. Both models would adjust automatically with new crime data. When team members evaluated the predictions against ground-truth data (where and when crimes actually occurred), the predictions were highly accurate – sometimes as close as 92–97% correct, depending on the crime.

The HunchLab product team advertised these accuracy metrics to prospective clients. For example, on a site visit to the headquarters of the St. Louis County Police Department (SLCPD) in Clayton, Missouri, HunchLab product manager Jeremy Heffner explained to the department's crime analysis team how to run accuracy measurements:

> You're basically just picking grid cells at random and asking the computer to predict for recent data whether a cell will have a crime occur [in it] within a time window, and then calculating the percentage of the times that it picks the right one. With you guys, I ran the numbers last night, it comes to 93-95%, depending on the crime.
>
> *(Fieldnotes, 2 December 2015)*

By withholding ground truth from the past 90 days and then comparing HunchLab's crime predictions against that information, the HunchLab team could provide evidence of their models' precision. But team members were also careful to explain that measuring accuracy is only possible *before* a police department starts using HunchLab. When agencies start allocating resources based on algorithmic predictions, the patrols affect what happens in 'high-risk' areas, and this changes the ground truth data. When you can no longer compare predictions to crime outcomes represented in the ground truth data (or, as Heffner put it, 'calculating the percentage of the times that it picks the right one'), accuracy measurements become impossible.

Heffner explained the problem as a tension between two countervailing statistical effects: detection and deterrence. Detection refers to the increased likelihood that a police officer *observes* a crime take place because of the prediction, and deterrence refers to the increased likelihood that the officer *prevents* a crime. Both are problems of measurement. Detection skews towards observer bias (since the prediction may put officers on high alert), whereas deterrence skews towards confirmation bias (since the absence of a crime confirms expectations of patrol efficacy). These probabilities 'work in opposite directions,' Heffner explained during my fieldwork, 'so it's very hard to have a clean measurement of accuracy once you start using the output.' To put an even finer point on it: if a crime does *not* occur according to the prediction, one cannot know if the outcome was 'caused' by the officer or if the prediction was just plain wrong.

The 'detection–deterrence paradox' maps onto a distinction that sociologist Adrian Mackenzie (2015) draws between the *performance* and *performativity* of machine learning algorithms. Whereas performance metrics estimate the alignment between a statistical model and the world it represents (i.e., accuracy), performativity describes the effects that predictions have on the world represented in the model (Mackenzie, 2015: 441). Detection and deterrence are performative effects: by acting on crime predictions, police officers alter the world represented in the algorithmic model. This was a concept that the HunchLab team grasped and even embraced. The task of predictive policing, accordingly, could no longer be about optimizing predictive accuracy. It was figuring out ways to better *measure and manage performative effects* – to 'fold the performativity of models back into the modelling process' (Mackenzie, 2015: 443) puts it – in order to 'change [officers'] behavior,' as Heffner once put it during my ethnographic research.

With policing, "folding" the performativity of predictions back into the modelling process can work if the desired outcomes are observable behaviours or actions. If clients want the predictions to lead to increased crime detection and arrests, then this outcome can be modelled because arrests are observable in the crime data. But if the desired outcome is crime prevention – as in Peel's (1829: no page) final tenet that the ultimate 'test of police efficiency' must be 'the absence of crime and disorder, not the visible evidence of police action in dealing with it' – then HunchLab faced a conundrum. A crime that does not happen cannot be measured (as in the truism that 'you can't prove a negative'), but predictive policing's techno-ethical appeal was precisely to optimize for that immeasurable outcome.

The result is an indeterminacy which is not unique to predictive policing, but which has rarely been acknowledged as a feature of its technicity (Simondon, 2017). As Parisi (2019: 93) writes, 'indeterminacy is central to the epistemological possibilities of algorithmic thinking.' When automated procedures like crime predictions become indicators of variation (which is precisely how HunchLab's crime models work), then 'automation itself – the computational procedure – becomes open to the indeterminacy of its own function' (Dixon-Román and Paris, 2020: 120). This exposure is just as unstable in predictive policing as any other domain of artificial intelligence. What makes predictive policing unique is that its indeterminate effects arise not only from the epistemological possibilities of algorithmic thinking but from the institution of policing itself – an institution that has historically organized around the racialized *production* of crime and criminality, not its absence (Jefferson, 2020; Muhammad, 2010). If crime prevention and deterrence are central to predictive policing's ethical appeal, then they also confound its technical apparatus.

Scaffolding indeterminacies

As Heffner and his colleagues saw it, the challenge was to figure out ways to work with statistical indeterminacy. One strategy was to promote an experimentalist stance towards predictive policing. 'If you're just trying to maximize predictive accuracy and you're not doing any interventions,' Heffner explained to potential clients during a webinar, 'then, absolutely, selecting [the highest risk locations] every time would be what we'd do. But that's not the case here. You're going to act on [predictions] and so you're going to start to skew things, displace crime, and so forth' (Azavea, 2014). 'Prescriptive' (rather than predictive) analysis was the name the HunchLab team gave to this set of problems – not just forecasting crime but modelling how responses to predictions can themselves be modelled and optimized given the limited information available to officers and analysts (Bertsimas and Kallus, 2020).

For example, over the course of my study, HunchLab was in the process of rolling out a new set of platform tools called Advisor. These tools were designed for clients to experiment with police patrol tactics – that is, recommendations for what police officers actually *do* once they arrive at a predicted crime location. On the surface, Advisor seemed to automate the methodology of a randomized control trial. Departments could use the tool to test tactical responses to patterns spotted in the crime data and then evaluate outcomes by comparing results to a control group. Only, instead of a control group, the system would compare crime outcomes to the algorithm's crime predictions.

Advisor had several components. One, called Field Test, was for evaluating tactical efficacy in response to specific crimes. For instance, Field Test might monitor the rate of HOME BURGLARIES while a department tested HIGH VISIBILITY PATROL. Another variation, Adaptive Tactics, worked similarly but involved ongoing data collection on a range of tactical responses. Police departments created a list of actions that the system would recommend. The recommendations start as randomized assignments, with zero confidence in their efficacy, but over time accumulate enough data to weight them inferentially. In essence, Adaptive Tactics "learnt" through measurement which police responses were best suited to different types of crime.

While the HunchLab team spoke of Advisor as data-driven and empirical, this was not quite accurate. By substituting the algorithmic predictions for experimental control groups, Advisor abandoned some of the core tenets of scientific rigour by scaffolding experimentalism upon statistically indeterminate inferences. When Field Test or Adaptive Tactics evaluated tactical efficacy, the software compared crime outcomes against HunchLab's predictions of 'what likely would have happened [in a predicted crime location] had you not been doing the field test' (Azavea, 2015: no page). So, for example, if police tested PLAIN CLOTHES SURVEILLANCE in an area where the algorithm predicted ARMED ROBBERY, and no such robbery occurred, Advisor would feed itself an algorithmic reward and "learn" from the test. But because accuracy is impossible to measure after deployment, there is no way to verify whether the tactic actually prevented the crime: the prediction could simply have been incorrect. And considering the faith that police are likely to place in the algorithm's forecasts, such epistemological loose ends can accumulate as distortions.

I observed how this might play out during a ride-along with an officer of the SLCPD in December 2015. Although the algorithm directed where the officer should go, it did nothing to prevent him from drawing on intuition or using discretion once we arrived. At one point, the officer spotted a rental car on the perimeter of an area forecast to be at high risk for LARCENY. The driver had done nothing wrong, but the officer explained to me that rental cars can be a sign of suspicious activity. When the car turned at an intersection without signalling, the officer used the offence as a pretence for a traffic stop. After smelling marijuana in the car, the traffic stop turned into a warrant check, vehicle search, call for back-up and eventually a citation for drug possession. Although none of this had anything to do with larceny, our presence may or may not have deterred its occasion.

We can imagine how such a scenario can snowball into more significant distortions, even with a crime as minor as a traffic violation. A US Department of Justice (DOJ) investigation into the SLCPD found that the agency engages in a disproportionately high number of traffic stops leading to arrests of racial minority drivers, and that it does so without taking measures to prevent racial profiling. As the report states,

> While consistent with Missouri data collection law, the traffic stop analysis procedures employed by the SLCPD are inconsistent across the agency and lack the sophistication necessary for appropriate analysis of stop data. This results in a missed opportunity to fully understand if bias-based profiling is occurring.
>
> *(Norton et al., 2015: 7)*

Given the public forum in which the DOJ made these recommendations, the SLCPD was effectively compelled to comply (by public pressure alone, if not legal action). And yet, four years after findings from the DOJ investigation were published, racial-minority drivers continued to be disproportionately targeted in police stops. One study conducted in 2018 found that Black drivers in St. Louis County were more than twice as likely to be pulled over by police than other racial groups (Ballentine, 2019). Was this trend in "driving-while-Black" stops the SCLPD's response to the DOJ's recommendations? Perhaps a mission to gather more data, more consistently, on the tactic? Or was it simply a failure to comply with reform directives?

We are unlikely to answer these questions absent another investigation. But with the SLCPD using a system like HunchLab, it is not unreasonable to imagine them using Advisor as a solution to the data problem – a way to gather more and better data about the racial impact of traffic stops. After all, the aura of objectivity that a tool like Adaptive Tactics connotes would likely satisfy the DOJ's data collection recommendations. How would Advisor optimize traffic stops? The system would evaluate traffic stop data against crime predictions to infer evidence of deterrence. Say the algorithm incorrectly forecasts LARCENY near an intersection where a traffic stop takes place – like the situation I encountered on the SLCPD ride-along. Because the prediction is incorrect, the crime will never occur. But because it is impossible to know whether it is incorrect, the system will read the outcome as evidence of the traffic stop's efficacy and issue an algorithmic reward to reinforce the machine learning process. The data cycle would then proceed despite the fact that the record of deterrence is an artefact of error.

To put it another way, by sacrificing rigour and falsifiability for quick-and-dirty evidence-gathering, Advisor could actually make it *more difficult* for civil rights activists and legal monitors to prove disparate impact and, by extension, that the police were engaged in racial profiling. Conversely, if we consider the alternative – that the St. Louis County Police simply refused to comply with DOJ recommendations by continuing to stop Black motorists at higher rates – then it is equally unlikely that HunchLab will ever do much to 'reform' policing. Either way, little changes.

Conclusions: distributions of safety and harm

From the start, predictive policing has been supported by claims that the algorithm enhances control, certainty and exactitude. Early on, this meant learning from the logistics of Amazon and Walmart to help cash-strapped departments 'prevent, deter, thwart, mitigate, and respond to crime more effectively' (Beck and McCue, 2009: 3). Far from backing down from these claims, advocates extended the argument to present predictive policing as a techno-ethical reform, a way to standardize patrol policing and rein in officer discretion. Even if crime predictions falsely flag Black people and communities at higher rates than whites, data scientist Eric Siegel (2018) suggests, the information is not necessarily incorrect or inaccurate; it is just decontextualized. The algorithm is identifying racial disparities in enforcement and sentencing, and if we used the analytics to *quantify inequality*, then we could actually do something about it.

The HunchLab case illustrates that Siegel's optimism – and the techno-ethical gambit of predictive policing in general – is no straightforward proposition. When crime predictions are put into practice, it is not the difference between precision or imprecision that matters but *indeterminacy* – the inability to know whether crime predictions prevent crime or not. Most optimistically, we could read that indeterminacy as HunchLab did, as an opportunity to intervene in patrol geographies to make policing more equitable. In a sort of double negation, the *unknown-unknowns* of crime forecasting could be an opportunity to interrupt patterned discrimination, shuffle the biased geographies of police patrols and challenge assumptions about what constitutes evidence (cf. Chun, 2018). Although prediction is nominally about representing and anticipating future events, it works by capturing distributions of the present. And like forecasts of global warming's effects, we could use those indeterminant predictions to intervene, to divorce police patrols from the status quo of today and improve the 'ground truth' of tomorrow.

In the end, however, this optimism is overwhelmed by the inertia of policing's institutional practices, including the wide berth that officers are given to determine which persons and activities constitute a threat to the social order. Most critiques of predictive policing, for example, tend to ignore the fact that existing best practices, such as 'hotspot policing,' are themselves crude algorithms of criminalization. The HunchLab team was not wrong to frame their project as a corrective to this and other strategies that allow individual police officers to determine who or what should be criminalized. The goal for Heffner and his colleagues at HunchLab was to rationalize, systematize and optimize that autonomy, to introduce accountability for officer discretion, by coupling patrol circulations to managerial accountability and distributing public safety benefits more equitably. But with indeterminacy so thoroughly baked into the analytics, evaluating those redistributions became impossible without falling back on unfalsifiable claims.

In his study of the Chicago Police Department's predictive policing efforts, critical geographer Brian Jordan Jefferson (2017: 2, original emphasis) argues that the structure of the crime prediction apparatus 'ensures that negatively racialized fractions of surplus labor and the places they inhabit are only representable to state authorities and the public as *objects of policing and punishment*.' The HunchLab team may have tried to expand this narrow legibility, but ultimately the product is a reform: it poses no fundamental challenge to urban policing as an institution. Every fibre of the social, technical and institutional assemblage of policing is organized around positive outcomes. *Letting-alone, letting-be, respecting* – these outcomes are statistically inscrutable within the data structures and formats available to police institutions. Is it possible to upend this illegibility and truly disrupt entrenched police abuses and violence? What would it look like to view HunchLab's indeterminate interventions with an eye towards remediating disinvestment in Black and Brown communities, as Siegel suggests? Imagining such a scenario is difficult because the ambiguities and indeterminacies that plague predictive policing are effects not only of the algorithm but of policing itself.

In October 2018, Azavea sold HunchLab to ShotSpotter, a police tech firm specializing in gunshot detection. Robert Cheetham, Azavea's founder and CEO, authored a blog post explaining that the decision to sell was an ethical one, that he could no longer justify the incongruities between his company's commitments to social justice and the larger project of predictive policing:

> Over the past several years, an array of incidents has publicly documented violence, civil rights violations, and abuse of power by police officers across the United States. Law enforcement agencies have rightfully come under increasing scrutiny… 'Predictive policing' tools (license plate readers, facial recognition software, etc.) have been used in some communities to engage in pervasive surveillance of citizens, something that I believe is wrong. We're a B Corporation with a mission to not only advance the state of the art but also apply it for positive civic, social, and environmental impact. Developing a tool that would support surveillance or violate civil rights was not something I viewed as aligned with our mission.
>
> *(Cheetham, 2019: no page)*

What Cheetham sensed here – and what ultimately led him to abandon a project he oversaw personally for over a decade – is not new. It is the same set of contradictory mandates that have confounded policing since the earliest commissioned forces: the 'delicate balancing of respectful protection and intrusive penetration' (De Lint, 2000: 55). Every modern police force has been 'subject to intense scrutiny in its scripting and delivery of authority and restraint, penetration and protection' (De Lint, ibid). Police agencies adopt new technologies to manage these tensions, to tilt the balance back through better management, but the risk is always that the same technologies make the police's ability to criminalize more efficient.

In the end, not even HunchLab, arguably the industry's greatest champion of predictive policing's reformist, techno-ethical appeal, could resolve these contradictions. On the one hand, is the police's mandate to distribute public safety benefits as a collective good – an idea that traces back to early theorists of the modern state. On the other is the view from marginalized communities who for generations have experienced police officers' presence as an occupying force. In the first view, patrols act to safeguard the public from criminality, so the task is simply to optimize for the equitable distribution of police protection. In the latter view, entire neighbourhoods are criminalized as targets of observation, intervention and intrusion. For these communities, police departments are neither protecting nor serving; they are concentrating the law's uneven gaze in areas already isolated by unjust policies, disinvestment and renewal programs, so the optimization of policing is nothing but a recalibration of harm. That these incommensurable mandates cannot be reconciled is not the fault of the AI *per se*. But neither can an algorithm or a digital platform offer any sort of meaningful resolution. Improving public safety benefits for all communities – enacting more equitable geographies of risk and safety – will likely require grappling with, reorganizing and even dismantling the sociotechnical and institutional apparatus of urban policing.

Note

1 Though for dissenting conclusions on this history of police technology, see Williams and Murphy (1990) and, especially, Muhammad (2010).

References

American Civil Liberties Union (2016). *Predictive Policing Today: A Shared Statement of Civil Rights Concerns*. Available at: https://www.aclu.org/other/statement-con cern-about-predictive-policing-aclu-and-16-civil-rights-privacy-racial-justice [Accessed 19/01/2023].

Amoore, L. (2020). *Cloud Ethics: Algorithms and the Attributes of Ourselves and Others*. Duke University Press.

Amrute, S. (2019). Of techno-ethics and techno-affects. *Feminist Review* 123(1): 56–73.

Angwin, J., Larson, J., Mattu, S., & Kirchner, L. (2016). Machine bias. *Propublica*. Available at: https://www.propublica.org/article/machine-bias-risk-assessments-in-criminal-sentencing. [Accessed 19/01/2023].

Azavea (2014). *Beyond the Box: Towards Prescriptive Analysis in Policing*. Available at: http://www.youtube.com/playlist?list=PL0avZRN-1JNmpWCHou4ydBvjyFg 2wvfEY (accessed 27 June 2019). [Accessed 19/01/2023].

Azavea (2015). *HunchLab Advisor: Know What Works*. Available at: https://www.youtube.com/watch?v=hHDJfHPYTsU [Accessed 19/01/2023].

Ballentine, S. (2019). Black Missouri drivers 91% more likely to be stopped, state attorney general finds. *PBS News Hour*. Available at: https://www.pbs.org/news hour/nation/black-missouri-drivers-91-more-likely-to-be-stopped-state-attorney-general-finds [Accessed 19/01/2023].

Batty, M. (2018). Artificial intelligence and smart cities. *Environment & Planning B*. 15: 3–6.

Beck, C. & McCue, C. (2009). Predictive policing: What can we learn from Wal-mart and Amazon about fighting crime in a recession? *Police Chief*. Available at: http://acmcst373ethics.weebly.com/uploads/2/9/6/2/29626713/police-chief-magazine.pdf (accessed 27 June 2019). [Accessed 19/01/2023].

Benbouzid, B. (2015). From situational crime prevention to predictive policing. *Champ pénal/Penal field* 7. Available at: http://champpenal.revues.org/9066 [Accessed 19/01/2023].

Benbouzid, B. (2019). To predict and to manage: Predictive policing in the United States. *Big Data & Society* 6(1). DOI: 10.1177/2053951719861703.

Bertsimas, D. & Kallus, N. (2020). From predictive to prescriptive analytics. *Management Science* 66(3): 1025–1044.

Bhuiyan, J. (2021). LAPD ended predictive policing programs amid public outcry; a new effort shares many of their flaws. *The Guardian*. Available at: https://www.theguardian.com/us-news/2021/nov/07/lapd-predictive-policing-surveillance-reform [Accessed 19/01/2023].

Bratton, B. (2021). AI urbanism: A design framework for governance, program, and platform cognition. *AI & Society* 36: 1307–1312.

Bratton, W. (2014). *Manhattan Institute: Bill Bratton on the Future of Policing*. Available at: https://www.youtube.com/watch?v=X_xjqOp7y0w [Accessed 19/01/2023].

Bratton, W. (2018). Cops count, police matter: Preventing crime and disorder in the 21st century. Available at: https://www.heritage.org/sites/default/files/2018-03/HL1286.pdf [Accessed 19/01/2023].

Brayne, S. & Christin, A. (2021). Technologies of crime prediction: The reception of algorithms in policing and criminal courts. *Social Problems* 68(3): 608–624.

Brennan Center for Justice (2021). *NYPD Predictive Policing Documents*. Available at: https://www.brennancenter.org/our-work/research-reports/nypd-predictive-policing-documents [Accessed 19/01/2023].

Buchanan, L., Bui, Q., & Patel, J.K. (2020). Black Lives Matter may be the largest movement in U.S. history. *The New York Times*. Available at: https://www.nytimes.com/interactive/2020/07/03/us/george-floyd-protests-crowd-size.html [Accessed 19/01/2023].

Bucher, T. (2018) *If … Then: Algorithmic Power and Politics*. Oxford University Press, Oxford.

Burrington, I. (2015). What Amazon taught the cops. *The Nation*. Available at: https://www.thenation.com/article/what-amazon-taught-cops/. [Accessed 19/01/2023].

Byrne, J. (2021). Chicago Police Superintendent defends ShotSpotter gunshot detection system, says it's saved lives. *Chicago Tribune*. Available at: https://www.chicagotribune.com/news/breaking/ct-chicago-police-shotspotter-20211004-eou5dh76x5d67ejbrk73fuhae4-story.html [Accessed 19/01/2023].

Chan, J. (2001). The technological game: how information technology is transforming police practice. *Criminal Justice* 1(2): 139–159.

Cheetham, R. (2019). *Why We Sold HunchLab*. Available at: https://www.azavea.com/blog/2019/01/23/why-we-sold-hunchlab/ [Accessed 19/01/2023].

Chun, W.H.K. (2018). *Ways of Knowing (Cities) Networks*. Available at: http://c4sr.columbia.edu/knowing-cities/schedule.html. [Accessed 19/01/2023].

Corbett-Davies, S., Goel, S., & González-Bailon, S. (2017). Even imperfect algorithms can improve the criminal justice system. *The New York Times*. Available at: https://www.nytimes.com/2017/12/20/upshot/algorithms-bail-criminal-justice-system.html [Accessed 19/01/2023].

Cugurullo, F. (2020). Urban artificial intelligence: From automation to autonomy in the smart city. *Frontiers in Sustainable Cities*, 2, 38.

De Lint, W. (2000). Autonomy, regulation and the police beat. *Social & Legal Studies* 9(1): 55–83.

Dencik, L., Hintz, A., & Carey, Z. (2018). Prediction, pre-emption and limits to dissent: Social media and big data uses for policing protests in the United Kingdom. *New Media & Society* 20(4): 1433–1450.

Dixon-Román, E. & Paris, L. (2020). Data capitalism and the counter futures of ethics in artificial intelligence. *Communication and the Public* 5(3–4): 116–121.

Dubber, M.D. & Valverde, M. (2006). Introduction: Perspectives on the power and science of police. In Dubber, M. D., & Valverde, M. (Eds.), *The new police science: the police power in domestic and international governance*. Stanford University Press, pp. 1–16.

Dubber, M.D. & Valverde, M. (2008). Introduction: Policing the Rechtsstaat. In Dubber, M. D., & Valverde, M. (Eds.), *Police and the liberal state*. Stanford University Press, pp. 1–14.

Ensign, D., Friedler, S.A., & Neville, S. (2017). Runaway feedback loops in predictive policing. *Fairness, Accountability, and Transparency in Machine Learning.* arXiv. org. Available at: http://arxiv.org/abs/1706.09847

Ferguson, A.G. (2017). *The Rise of Big Data Policing: Surveillance, Race, and the Future of Law Enforcement.* NYU Press, New York.

Foucault, M. (2007). *Security, Territory, Population: Lectures at the College de France, 1977–78* (tran. G. Burchell). Palgrave Macmillan, New York.

Gorner, J. & Sweeney, A. (2020). For years Chicago police rated the risk of tens of thousands being caught up in violence. That controversial effort has quietly been ended. *Chicago Tribune.* Available at: https://www.chicagotribune.com/news/criminal-justice/ct-chicago-police-strategic-subject-list-ended-20200125-spn4kjmrxrh4tmktdjckhtox4i-story.html [Accessed 19/01/2023].

Hälterlein, J. (2021). Epistemologies of predictive policing: Mathematical social science, social physics and machine learning. *Big Data & Society* 8(1). DOI: 10.1177/20539517211003118.

Harcourt, B.E. (2006) *Against Prediction: Profiling, Policing, and Punishing in an Actuarial Age.* University of Chicago Press, Chicago.

Haskins, C. (2020). The Los Angeles Police Department says it is dumping a controversial predictive policing tool. *Buzzfeed News.* Available at: https://www.buzzfeednews.com/article/carolinehaskins1/los-angeles-police-department-dumping-predpol-predictive [Accessed 19/01/2023].

Hayles, K. (2017). *Unthought: The Power of the Cognitive Nonconscious.* University of Chicago Press, Chicago.

HunchLab (2017). *A Citizen's Guide to HunchLab.* Azavea, Philadelphia, PA. Available at: http://robertbrauneis.net/algorithms/HunchLabACitizensGuide.pdf. [Accessed 19/01/2023].

Hvistendahl, M. (2021). How the LAPD and Palantir use data to justify racist policing. *The Intercept.* Available at: https://theintercept.com/2021/01/30/lapd-palantir-data-driven-policing/ [Accessed 19/01/2023].

Introna, L.D. (2016). Algorithms, governance, and governmentality: On governing academic writing. *Science, Technology, & Human Values* 41(1): 17–49.

Jefferson, B.J. (2017). Digitize and punish: Computerized crime mapping and racialized carceral power in Chicago. *Environment and Planning D: Society and Space* 35(5): 775–796.

Jefferson, B.J. (2020). *Digitize and Punish: Racial Criminalization in the Digital Age.* University of Minnesota Press, Minneapolis.

Kaufmann, M., Egbert, S., & Leese, M. (2019). Predictive policing and the politics of patterns. *The British Journal of Criminology* 59(3): 674–692.

Kelling, G.L. & Moore, M.H. (1988). The evolving strategy of policing. *Perspectives on Policing* 4: 1–16.

Lally, N. (2021). 'It makes almost no difference which algorithm you use': on the modularity of predictive policing. *Urban Geography.* DOI:10.1080/02723638.2021.1949142.

Levin, S. (2021). These US cities defunded police: 'We're transferring money to the community'. *The Guardian.* Available at: https://www.theguardian.com/us-news/2021/mar/07/us-cities-defund-police-transferring-money-community [Accessed 19/01/2023].

Mackenzie, A. (2015). The production of prediction: What does machine learning want? *European Journal of Cultural Studies* 18(4–5): 429–445.

Manning, P.K. (2008). *The Technology of Policing: Crime Mapping, Information Technology, and the Rationality of Crime Control.* New York University Press, New York.

McArdle, G. & Kitchin, R. (2016). *The Dublin Dashboard: Design and development of a real-time analytical urban dashboard.* In *First International Conference on Smart Data and Smart Cities; ISPRS Annals Photogrammetry, Remote Sensing and Spatial Information Sciences,* III-4/W1, 7–9 September 2016, Split, Croatia.

Muhammad, K.G. (2010). *The Condemnation of Blackness: Race, Crime, and the Making of Modern Urban America.* Harvard University Press, Cambridge.

Norton, B., Hamilton, E.E., & Braziel, R. (2015) *Collaborative Reform Initiative: An Assessment of the St. Louis County Police Department.* National Police Foundation, Community-Oriented Policing Services. Available at: https://www.policefoundation. org/publication/collaborative-reform-initiative-an-assessment-of-the-st-louis-county-police-department/ [Accessed 19/01/2023].

Parisi, L. (2019) Critical computation: Digital automata and general artificial thinking. *Theory, Culture & Society* 36(2): 89–121.

Peck, J. (2012) Austerity urbanism. *City* 16(6): 626–655.

Peel, R. (1829). Principles of law enforcement. Available at: https://www.durham.police.uk/About-Us/Documents/Peels_Principles_Of_Law_Enforcement.pdf. [Accessed 19/01/2023].

Pinch, T. J. & Bijker, W. E. (1984). The social construction of facts and artefacts: or how the sociology of science and the sociology of technology might benefit each other. *Social Studies of Science* 14: 399–441.

PredPol (2020). Crime prevention with predictive policing. Available at: https://www.predpol.com/crime-prevention-with-predpol/ [Accessed 19/01/2023].

PredPol (2021). The three pillars of data-driven policing. Available at: https://web.archive.org/web/20210318163824/https:/predpol.com/law-enforcement/. [Accessed 19/01/2023].

Reeves, J. & Packer, J. (2013). Police media: The governance of territory, speed, and communication. *Communication and Critical/Cultural Studies* 10(4): 359–384.

Richardson, R., Schultz, J., & Crawford, K. (2019). Dirty data, bad predictions: How civil rights violations impact police data, predictive policing systems, and justice. *NYUL Review Online,* 94, 15.

Siegel, E. (2018) How to fight bias with predictive policing. *Scientific American.* Available at: https://blogs.scientificamerican.com/voices/how-to-fight-bias-with-predictive-policing/. [Accessed 19/01/2023].

Simondon, G. (2017) *On the Mode of Existence of Technical Objects.* University of Minnesota Press.

Söderström, O., Paasche, T., & Klauser, F. (2014). Smart cities as corporate storytelling. *City* 18(3): 307–320.

Sturgill, K. (2020). Santa Cruz becomes the first U.S. city to ban predictive policing. *Los Angeles Times.* Available at: https://www.latimes.com/california/story/2020-06-26/santa-cruz-becomes-first-u-s-city-to-ban-predictive-policing [Accessed 19/01/2023].

Uchida, C.D. (2014). Predictive policing. In Bruinsma, G and Weisburd, D (eds) *Encyclopedia of Criminology and Criminal Justice.* Springer, New York pp. 3871–3880.

White, J.M. (2016). Anticipatory logics of the smart city's global imaginary. *Urban Geography* 37(4): 572–589.

Williams, H. & Murphy, P.V. (1990). The evolving strategy of police: A minority view. *Perspectives on Policing* 13: 1–16.

16

CHINESE ARTIFICIAL INTELLIGENCE GOVERNANCE PLATFORMS 2.0

The belt and road edition

Alan Smart, Yawei Zhao and Dean Curran

Introduction

Mainstream smart city studies are often predominantly Eurocentric, neglecting important developments in Chinese smart urbanism. Most discussion of it is in specialist accounts of Chinese smart cities (e.g., Cowley et al., 2019), rather than being included in broader surveys of smart urbanism. Literature reviews generally retain the assumption that cutting-edge developments are taking place in the West, with the rest at best following.[1] Curran and Smart (2021) argue that China's immense data pools, enabled by heavy mobile shopping and the use of digital money, facilitate the training of increasingly competitive artificial intelligence (AI). Combined with the widespread implementation of smart city strategies, these trends raise the possibility that the dominant urban governance platforms of the future will be controlled by Alibaba or Huawei, rather than IBM, Google or Amazon. While there are valid concerns that Western corporate claims for smart cities consistently promise more than they deliver (Cugurullo, 2018; Green, 2019; Sadowski and Pasquale, 2015), the greater fear with Chinese smart urbanism is that they deliver more than they promise in terms of state surveillance and social control.

Federico Cugurullo (2021) argues that the increasing role of AI in urban governance reflects a crucial shift from the smart city to what he calls the *autonomous city*. In addition, however, the wide-ranging potential impacts, even existential threats (Russell, 2019), of AI means that the politics of smart urbanism push beyond neoliberal corporate influence and depoliticization to include global geopolitical issues. Chinese urban governance platforms that are used to train cutting-edge AI systems create potential challenges to

DOI: 10.4324/9781003365877-19

American hegemony (Allison, 2017). Therefore, we need to incorporate a geopolitical perspective into the study of the use of AI-enhanced governance: something that has previously been largely neglected, particularly in studies of smart urbanism, which are now only a part of broader developments in digitally based regional governance. AI is facilitating a shift from *automation* to *autonomy* in the management of cities and other political groupings (Cugurullo, 2020). This chapter will venture some initial considerations of how geopolitics is influencing the development of Chinese AI, with a particular focus on the Digital Silk Road (DSR), the digital component of China's Belt and Road Initiative.

Politics is currently threatening the rise of Chinese AI governance platforms, not because Chinese urban governance platforms are becoming less successful, but because of global competition between 'Sinosphere' and 'Anglosphere' (The Economist, 2019a) and domestic backlash against the dominance and abuses of Chinese tech giants. Unlike in the West, Chinese techlash is being led by the central government rather than citizens and NGOs, is less constrained by the limitations of antitrust law and appears to be having a much greater impact than in the West. After a review of developments in Big-Data-lead urban governance in China, the chapter will concentrate on these two political developments and the risk that they will result in competing 'walled data gardens' with sharply different political economic foundations (The Economist, 2019b: no page). Ironically, the controls needed to strengthen the Anglosphere walled garden may result in Western AI and governance platforms becoming more like its Chinese state capitalist rivals, while Chinese systems become even more state-controlled and less private sector driven.

The other important change is the shift of Big-Data-based governance from the urban scale to the regional and transnational scale through what is called the *Digital Silk Road*. This is an increasingly important part of China's Belt and Road Initiative. This initiative is often misinterpreted as simply an infrastructure and logistics program. Bruno Maçães (2019: 78) says that instead the 'Belt and Road is China's global development policy' because a 'policy of economic development – if it is to chart a sustainable course – must take the form of a global policy.' The fundamental problem the initiative was meant to address was 'China's dependence on a global system it could not shape or control' (Maçães, 2019: 20). The DSR is a set of standards, linkages and logistics management platforms that offers an alternative to the neoliberal, American dominated infrastructure of global trade and development management. DSR AI platforms include ones for urban governance but also stretch over much larger spaces.

Geopolitics has also made primary research on AI in China very difficult for Westerners, particularly for Canadians during the conflict over the extradition of Huawei Chief Financial Officer Meng Wanzhou. While drawing on our prior field research related to technologies of urban governance in China, we have had to rely on non-academic financial and technologically oriented periodicals. For rapidly changing fields like the study of the consequences of AI, the only alternative to primary research that is reasonably up to date is such periodicals because peer-reviewed articles are far behind by the time they come out. We have, however, surveyed relevant academic publications, which are more timely in scientific than social science fields.

The chapter first considers the emerging phenomenon of city-brain-style urban governance platforms whose rapid development in China is underappreciated in mainstream smart studies research. Then we turn to geopolitical conflicts that may undermine the rise of Chinese AI leadership. The following section considers the DSR as a response that may foreshadow the emergence of two divergent systems of AI governance, one centred on America and the other on China, with geopolitics becoming more important for both alternatives.

Alibaba's City Brain and other AI urban governance platforms

China is in some ways at the cutting edge of smart city developments (Manson, 2021). This developing lead in what Cugurullo (2021) considers to be the next stage for smart cities, *autonomous transurbanism*, is a new phenomenon for Chinese urban planning. Before, Chinese urban planning tended to follow, or adapt, trends elsewhere, first from the Soviet Union and later from the West and Asian market economies like Singapore. While smart city ideas originated in the West, the rapid development of AI platforms such as Alibaba's ET City Brain makes it likely that core technologies for smart urbanism and other implementations of AI for governance will originate from China (Lee, 2018). Increasing restrictions on facial recognition in the West are an example of policy advantages for Chinese technology, if not for Chinese citizens. These developments indicate the need to "provincialize" smart city research, rather than continuing with mainstream urban studies' assumptions that the global South either follows the paths set by the West or else falls farther behind (Smart and Curran, 2022). For data-driven urban governance, there is a new probability that China will be setting the path, making efforts in Western countries seem comparatively lacking in ambition: "provincial." This probability, however, is predicated on the assumption that American attempts to counter Chinese technical advantages do not succeed in undermining developments in Chinese AI and other core technologies for Big-Data-based governance (The Economist, 2022).

China's influence on future urbanism is partly due to the sheer extent of contemporary Chinese urbanization. Over 600 million people have moved from rural areas to China's cities since 1980. Between 2000 and 2020 China's urban population (including those without urban household registration) increased from 670 million to 902 million, 63.9% of the total population

(Chan, 2021). The massive extent of new urban habitats required for this urban transition allows rapid deployment of new smart technologies on remarkable scales. Social fixed investments increased by 30.1% in 2009 alone, in response to the global financial crisis, which China avoided through capital and other controls. This investment led to the rapid development of infrastructure (Wu et al., 2018).

Compared with the construction of traditional infrastructures in the wake of the 2008 global financial crisis, the new wave of investment is more directed towards the construction of digital infrastructures, characterized by 5G networks, AI and the Internet of Things. Infrastructural spending in turn facilitated the development of information and communication technologies, digital cities and other precursors of smart cities. In this wave, city brain AI platforms (the first of which was Alibaba's) have been promoted as indispensable to urban life and governance in ways similar to the more traditional electricity and water infrastructures.[2] *City brain* has been successfully marketed to local governments (Caprotti and Liu, 2020; Zheng, 2021). For instance, Haikou (the capital city of Hannan Province) spent 455 million RMB on the platform in 2018 (Yuntoutiao, 2018). Besides Hangzhou where Alibaba is based, the platform has been purchased by 22 cities in and outside of China (Alibaba Clouder, 2019). Infrastructure spending is now being sustained by the economic impact, and public health needs, of the COVID-19 pandemic. China's emerging competitiveness in urban AI is also facilitated by regulatory practices that make Big Data analysis much more accessible for training AI by corporations, although restrictions have recently begun to increase.

AI technology and Alibaba Cloud enable real-time analysis of the city. ET City Brain has the ability to automatically deploy public resources to amend defects in urban operations, such as traffic jams or infringements of traffic laws. Implementation of Alibaba's ET City Brain is possible because of the project's connection to governmental databases and authority. Combined with China's vast number of highly capable video cameras (now the largest array in the world), the system can index all video footage to be searched quickly when needed. If the police give ET City Brain a picture of a vehicle or pedestrian, the AI can return exact matches detailing where and when that vehicle or pedestrian has been in the city since the project began. While much of the key technology for smart cities is still the product of Western corporations like IBM, increasingly the cutting edge also involves Chinese corporations such as Alibaba, Tencent, Yitu and Huawei. Alibaba specializes in e-commerce, retail, digital payment and cloud technology (revenues 2020 US$109 billion). Tencent (revenues 2020 US$70 billion) focuses on online and mobile games, fintech and value-added services, and it is also a social networking giant owning WeChat (a messaging application). Yitu is a research and innovation company that integrates state-of-the-art AI technologies with industrial applications. Huawei is a telecommunications solutions provider that manufactures smartphones, smartwatches, laptops and telecom equipment (revenues 2020 US$137 billion). The centrality of Big Data to machine learning forms of AI gives China a considerable advantage, not only because of the size of the population but also because of the much greater adoption of mobile phone shopping. In 2016, Chinese mobile payment transactions were worth US$5.5 trillion, almost 50 times more than in the USA (Wildau and Hook, 2017).

More recently, a variety of different companies have started to develop their own 'city brains,' and the term seems to have become a more generic one.[3] In view of the overarching 'Digital China' strategy, *city brain* has grown into an urban management and governance concept more than a product owned by Alibaba. Tencent, for example, has Super Brain whose target market is governments and private companies. In 2019, Changsha (the capital of Hunan Province) purchased the platform for 520 million RMB (Xinlang Keji, 2019). Other tech giants like Baidu and Huawei have their own "brains" too. In Beijing, the government of the Haidan district is cooperating with Baidu to develop a city brain. It has sought to identify empty flats by studying power consumption. Huawei has also cooperated with Heshui, a small county in northwest Gansu, to build a system to track empty flats (Chen, 2021). In another example of the emerging functionality of city brains, Xi'an is using its city brain to track through data analytics the migration of individuals from the countryside (Basu, 2021).

This is not to suggest that Alibaba is slipping behind. Its sister company created the app that classified citizens' COVID-19 disease risk by colour code, while also sending their health and travel data to police (Andersen, 2020). The system was updated to a 3.0 version in June 2020 (Caprotti and Liu, 2020). Rather it is a testament to the massive growth of the city brain industry in China as the potential for automating city management based on Big Data collection and algorithms continues to grow. As one analyst recently said in the *South China Morning Post* (while requesting anonymity): 'Almost every city mayor and county magistrate wants a city brain or something like it these days' (Chen, 2021: no page). The emphasis on city brains may reflect a greater desire for top-down control of smart cities in China, rather than a more distributed response through automated sensors. These technologies developed by Chinese companies, however, are not just being applied to Chinese cities. In Malaysia, the government is collaborating with Yitu, to enable Kuala Lumpur's police force to use facial-recognition technology to work alongside Alibaba's ET City Brain platform. Likewise, Chinese companies have bid to fit every one of Singapore's 110,000 lampposts with facial-recognition cameras (Andersen, 2020).

To understand Chinese cities we cannot stop at considering the objectives and practices of private corporations, but need to incorporate the powerful state-party regime, which has been shown to generate very different forms of urban growth machines. The entrepreneurial urbanism of city leaders in China is constrained not simply by the pursuit of profit, but by their entrepreneurial competition for career development in a centralized personnel management system. This system requires, at minimum, compliance with state priorities and targets such as smart city plans, but rewards moderately innovative approaches to meeting these targets (Chien and Woodworth, 2018). Party-state personnel review and growth targets create a strong impetus for rapid growth.

Cugurullo (2021: 190) argues that

> in the context of capitalist political economies, there will then be countries where only a minority of economically powerful cities will enjoy superior urban AIs, and cities within which solely an urban elite will have access to the best and most expensive artificial intelligences on the market.

While this argument probably applies well to small-scale AIs, such as autonomous vehicles and robots, we doubt its applicability to urban governance AI. Wealthy citizens of democratic countries greatly value their privacy, which constrains the collection of data necessary for effective AI development and urban management. The middle class and the wealthy may resist the algorithms and data collection while poorer people are more subject to them (Eubanks, 2018) and authoritarian countries may be more capable of deploying them. The situation is rather similar to social media, where ordinary people get cutting-edge technology for free because the users, and their data, are the product.

The network effects of rapid deployment of urban AI, and its attendant data generation, are likely to put China into a lead in this field if tech wars between China and the West do not hobble it. Hobbling is looking more like a serious objective of Washington. It may also be under threat from its own government. State promotion of AI comes with greater oversight, and China is finding it difficult to attract foreign experts in this field or even retain its own AI researchers: about one-third of top AI talent is from China, but only a tenth of it works there (The Economist, 2022). Possessing an important platform in its networking technology, embattled Huawei has also developed smart city projects. On its website, Huawei (2022) claims to have constructed more than 160 Smart Cities in over 100 countries and regions. Given its increasing pressure from the United States and reliance on Beijing, Huawei could be a more trusted partner of Beijing for digital urban governance. All of these developments are dependent on emerging patterns of geopolitics and domestic decisions about the control of AI and platforms.

The impact of Washington's and Beijing's attacks on Chinese tech platforms

The future of Chinese Big-Data-driven AI, despite its key advantages, is currently threatened by both Washington and Beijing. Chinese tech corporations, particularly Huawei, have been under sustained pressure from

Washington since at least 2016, pressure that has not yet lightened under President Biden, but the attack on them from Beijing is newer and less expected.

Initially, Washington's efforts to maintain its technological supremacy, first through technology export controls and later by sanctions and diplomatic efforts to prevent the adoption of Chinese technology that might pose security threats, prompted Beijing's support for their own tech giants. For example, it adopted Big Data strategies at a high level from 2014 on. In 2020 the Chinese Communist Party's Central Committee and State Council added *data* to land, labour, capital and technology as a new factor of production, a remarkable step within a Marxist theoretical system (Gorman, 2021). The giant companies Baidu (search and self-driving cars), Alibaba (e-commerce and digital money) and Tencent (gaming, social media and digital money) were supported as national champions in the technological global competition. Huawei was particularly protected because of its blacklisting by Western countries.

In the last year, however, a continued desire to foster a technological revolution based on Big Data and AI has contended with concern about the risks posed by the tech giants. The first major sign of a backlash against them was the 2021 suspension of a $37 billion Initial Public Offering by Ant Financial (an affiliate that had originally been a subsidiary of Alibaba) just days before the launch and subsequent public criticism of Alibaba. This state-initiated techlash has spread to most of the largest consumer-facing technology companies. In August 2021, it was announced that regulations over tech businesses would be strengthened. Indices of their stock prices dropped by over 40% since February 2021, reducing value by about US$1 trillion (The Economist, 2021a). The new regulatory regime appears to be directed at reining in the corporations and making them more dependent on state supervision and support, while starting to put in place greater consumer protection, particularly against the unrestricted use of personal data, one of the core advantages for Chinese AI platforms (The Economist, 2021b). There is also a desire by the State to reduce the dominance of a few tech giants and foster a less oligopolistic industry through more open models 'where payments and shopping activity are no longer restricted to one platform, allowing merchants to regain some control over the prices of their wares' (The Economist, 2021b: 49). Beijing appears to want a technology sector less focused on frivolities such as social media, games and shopping,[4] and more based on "deep tech" to help it surpass the West in economic power (Doshi, 2021).[5]

Beijing's desire to steer the tech industry into global leadership in basic science collides with efforts from Washington to contain the security threats it perceives in China's technological and economic rise. While cracking down on the tech giants, China continues to strenuously encourage second-tier and smaller technology companies, as well as any companies blacklisted by the

West. A good example of how these conflicts work out is SenseTime, one of China's brightest hopes for world-leading AI, valued at $28 billion in a Hong Kong initial public offering in December 2021. SenseTime is one of the four most hyped AI companies in China, together with its peers Megvii (image recognition), Yitu and CloudWalk (facial recognition):

> All four have grown rapidly with Beijing's backing... But all four companies have also suffered concerns over the use of their technology and have been hit by sanctions from the US for allegedly aiding human rights abuses in the western region of Xinjiang... Since then, the companies have had to tread a careful path to maintain good relations with their most visible and most important customer: the Chinese government.
>
> *(Ruehl et al., 2021: no page)*

Companies like SenseTime are seen by Washington and others not only as enabling the oppression of Xinjiang's Uighurs but also as contributing to AI that can be used for military purposes and create security risks for the USA (Allen, 2019). In October 2019, concerns over Xinjiang prompted the US Commerce Department to ban American firms from selling software and hardware to 20 Chinese public security agencies and blacklisted 8 companies whose products 'facilitate the Orwellian surveillance in Xinjiang' (The Economist, 2019c: 66). These companies specialize in voice recognition, digital forensics, chipmaking, as well as facial recognition and visual surveillance.

SenseTime, one of the eight, has become a key player in smart city technology, with its software deployed in 119 cities, although a small minority of them are outside China. Its systems are being used in one Chinese city 'to detect people not wearing seat belts in cars, with a claimed precision rate of 94 per cent. It can also spot drivers who are using mobile phones with 86 to 96 per cent accuracy' (Ruehl et al., 2021: no page). In Shenzhen, its traffic management system

> logged traffic violations by people on mopeds. Police tracked down 50,000 such incidents, and the drop in monthly abuses by mopeds dropped by more than half in just a couple of months. The number of drivers choosing to wear a helmet, meanwhile, rose from under half to 94 per cent.
>
> *(Ruehl et al., 2021: no page)*

Washington's efforts to punish Chinese AI firms and otherwise contain the growing Chinese competitiveness in high technology may have serious unintended consequences. Beijing's desire to become more independent in core technologies has been reinforced, so that the result may end up being greater competition and less capacity to influence China. In addition, Chinese tech companies are becoming more reliant on Beijing's favour, resulting in an intensification of state capitalism.[6] Finally, the closing of the Western markets encourages efforts to create new regional spheres of technological influence, with an emerging battle of standards and platforms.

The Digital Silk Road and segregating the operating systems of the future global economy

If the Belt and Road Initiative is a bid to construct an alternative global system through infrastructure and coordinating standards (Maçães, 2019), China's DSR is the technological roadmap to making this new operating system digitally sophisticated and competitive. As with all platforms, it will create powerful lock-in (path dependency) network effects that will bind together nations, localities and organizations that buy into the system in core areas of their operations. As Easterling (2014) demonstrates, some of the most radical changes to the world are quietly being inscribed through infrastructural technologies, rather than through law or diplomacy. The DSR consists of a massive effort to build the physical components of digital infrastructure and to 'enhance the interoperability of digital ecosystems in such developing states … Its main drivers are Chinese technology companies that increasingly provide telecommunication and e-commerce services across the globe' (Erie and Streinz, 2021: 1). As of yet, unlike the EU and the United States, 'China has not leveraged legal instruments to directly influence other countries' data governance regimes. Yet, through the DSR, Chinese companies are increasingly supplying the digital infrastructure that forms an integral part of any data governance regime. Developing countries that exhibit growing demand for such infrastructures, may find the prospect of "data sovereignty" particularly appealing' (Erie and Streinz, 2021: 2).

Data, or cyber, sovereignty requires that data are subject to the laws and governance structures within the nation where it is collected, and is opposed to transnational rules that override national regulation. This goal is part of Beijing's project of 'building an international "community of common destiny", meant to counter the US-led top-down model and to widen global interdependence at the same time' (Hong and Goodnight, 2020: 17). Few countries have the capacity to replace corporate clouds and other elements of transnational data management, so China's promises seem attractive to the predominantly poorer postcolonial countries being recruited for the BRI, including the DSR that is tying this vast archipelago of infrastructure. Since digital infrastructure in 'developing countries is often embryonic, the impact of Chinese firms' activities in these markets might be more consequential than their presence in Western post-industrial societies' (Erie and Streinz, 2021: 3). The DSR has largely been led by China's private or quasi-private (e.g., Huawei) tech companies. Through investments in digital infrastructure, 'Chinese firms have exported surveillance technologies to over 63 countries worldwide, and with them a coalescing model of authoritarian governance in the digital arena' (Gorman, 2021: no page). In the long run, DSR is likely to operate as a regional base for China to project its norms, systems and models to the wider world while helping Chinese tech companies to take up the remaining markets of digital and telecommunication infrastructure (Hemmings, 2020).

With too many dimensions of the DSR to consider here, we will restrict ourselves to two platforms, one urban and another that is regional with aspirations to be global. The first is selected because it shows the implications of moving beyond urban AI governance platforms to consider operations at a transnational level, while the second is a rapidly expanding and little-recognized urban AI platform. In 2016, Jack Ma (then Executive Chairman of Alibaba Group) proposed the Electronic World Trade Platform (eWTP) to accommodate the expanding digital economy and evade global trade rules created by the United States and its allies (Ouyang et al., 2017a). The eWTP was first adopted as a policy recommendation at the Group of 20 Leaders Summit in Hangzhou, during which the platform was conceived as

> a market-driven, private sector-led, multi-stakeholder initiative for public-private dialogue and partnership to share best practice, incubate new e-trade rules, foster a more integraed, inclusive and effective policy and business environment for the development of ecommerce and digital economy in Internet Age.
>
> *(ibid: 40)*

The eWTP facilitates the creation of electronic commerce hubs by businesses through which small and medium enterprises will be 'able to export globally, with low or no taxes, fast logistics, and an efficient customs process' (ibid: 40). In 2017, the first overseas e-hub for the eWTP was established in Malaysia along with a digital free-trade zone (Gao, 2017). eWTP will then link each e-Hub and virtual free-trade zone with each other (Vila Seoane, 2020). Alibaba aims to establish through the eWTP an inclusive global ecosystem for sellers and buyers. The ambition is to 'spark fundamental changes in the way international trade is conducted by lowering costs, reducing and streamlining intermediaries, improving access to information and financing, and shortening global supply chain' (Ouyang et al., 2017b: 40). Alibaba's 'business strategy is quite different from other well-known e-commerce companies, such as Amazon … which primarily act as broker-dealers rather than operators of entire eco-systems' (Wang and Yu, 2022: 5). It claims to help the entrepreneur to overcome some of the informational and cost-related barriers to trade (Johnston, 2021).

Countries where the eWTP has advanced are all recipients of broader BRI projects, such as Malaysia, Thailand and Rwanda, but also Belgium. Enabled by the BRI, the eWTP 'claims to foster a more inclusive form of globalization. The eWTP proposes to achieve such an objective through the benefits of e-commerce, particularly for three types of identities: SMEs, young people, and women' (Vila Seoane, 2020: 74). Alibaba's Cloud is at the heart of this system, as it is for ET City Brain, and the acquisition of rich data globally will provide the corporation with multiple opportunities to profit from being at the centre of trade flows in the BRI targets throughout the Eurasian and African regions. COVID-19 has highlighted the importance of the eWTP and similar initiatives, particularly in emphasizing the developing countries and small and medium enterprises that have been hurt the most. While e-commerce within countries expanded dramatically with the pandemic, global trade flows have shrunk significantly, while delivery times have increased considerably. One reason for the shrinkage in world trade flows 'is that digitization of the global trading system remains limited' (Johnston, 2021: 67). In early 2020, eWTP played a leading role in the international distribution from China of donated and commercial personal protective equipment. Alibaba worked with Belgium customs to digitize customs clearance procedures. The goal of the eWTP hub at Liège Airport was to begin operations in 2021, but COVID-19 served to fast-forward eWTP in Europe. The hubs in Malaysia and Ethiopia also played key roles in the pandemic distribution efforts (Johnston, 2021).

There has been a trend recently to merge smart city projects with safe city endeavours: 'a technological fix to the governance of safety in the smart city' (Datta, 2020: 1320). "Safe cities" have been promoted heavily by Huawei along the DSR. While safe cities differ in orientation from smart cities, they overlap substantially. A common approach involves the 'coupling of Video surveillance and Cloud Storage; which entails large-scale video networking across urban nodes or the entire urban fabric' (Allam, 2019: 98). Huawei, along with ZTE, are strong supporters of the DSR. They are also

> the main drivers behind China's export of surveillance technology. China is supplying surveillance technology to 63 countries, 36 of which are BRI members. Huawei is the lead supplier of such technology in the world, providing surveillance equipment to over 50 countries worldwide.
>
> *(Erie and Streinz, 2021: 36)*

There has been growing concern over the safe city program specifically and, more generally, on the export of surveillance technology, which has been seen as a way to export authoritarianism (Bjeloš, 2021). Seventy-one per cent of Huawei's 'Safe City' agreements are in countries with an average rating between 2009 and 2018 of *partly free* (44 per cent) or *not free* (27 per cent) by Freedom House (Hillman and McCalpin, 2019). Chinese "safe" and "smart" city systems are said to carry a 'plethora of potential security and human rights threats. ... authoritarian governments may use the capacity to monitor individual people on a real-time basis to impose a digital form of totalitarianism.' In addition, there are worries about Chinese access to sensitive data and the possibility of a "kill switch" to shut down core infrastructure in case of a trade or other dispute (Kynge et al., 2021).[7] In Serbia, the 2019 launch of a safe city project has fostered concerns among civil society groups that 'Huawei cameras will enable the ruling regime .. control over every citizen and all aspects of life' (Bjeloš, 2021: 143).

Erie and Streinz (2021: 46) argue that safe cities 'are particularly attractive to Pakistan given its concerns for public order.' Since 2015, a number of sub-national police authorities were established (e.g., the Punjab Safe Cities Authority) to build safe cities. Originally designed for police use and traffic control, safe city tech has since been used by the Pakistani military and intelligence services. The

> union of Pakistani law and security enforcement with Chinese digital infrastructure shows both the benefits and pitfalls of mutual access. Whereas the technology may strengthen the police powers of local and national authorities, it may do so in ways that may exceed the relevant laws.
>
> *(Erie and Streinz, 2021: 46)*

Lindsay Gorman (2021: no page) says that

> Chinese technology giants are at the center of a large-scale effort to vacuum up global data, leveraging opportunities through the Digital Silk Road. Using investments in internet infrastructure and information and communications technology, Chinese firms have exported surveillance technologies to over 63 countries worldwide, and with them a coalescing model of authoritarian governance in the digital arena.
>
> *(Gorman, 2021)*

There has been a backlash in the West against the export of surveillance equipment that might contain "back doors," with Huawei in particular widely blacklisted (Kynge et al., 2021). The integration of the DSR with the BRI, combined with political opposition in the West to Chinese AI systems is heightening the likelihood of a "great divergence" between forms of AI platforms and smart urbanism in the Sinosphere and Anglosphere. There are clear indications that 'China intends the digital Silk Road to be the main stage on which the BRI plays out in future: The question is whether the West will let it' (The Economist, 2020: 11).

Conclusion

The dynamism, political support and lack of legal and political constraints for the development of Big-Data- and AI-based city governance suggest that smart cities research needs to take more seriously the futures that Chinese smart cities and AI platforms are contributing to, both in China and beyond. These developments are not just having economic and technological impacts. Given the extent to which Chinese state capitalism fuses the actions of corporations with strategies of the state, AI leadership for China not only generates the potential for economic power but also that of political power. This chapter has explored one important aspect of this, considering how the basic standards of the new digital economy are shaped by Chinese projects such as the DSR. The shift to regional, rather than simply urban, data-driven governance, is a key part of the current transformations of Chinese AI platforms.

The divergence between Chinese and Western trajectories for smart cities and AI platforms, driven by American sanctions and new controls from Beijing, raises the prospect of a global digital system bifurcated between starkly different standards and technology. These prospects require a fundamental rethinking of our understanding of smart and AI urbanism, with a greater integration of geopolitical considerations, rather than an exclusive emphasis on neoliberal agendas. The trend towards major confrontations between illiberal regimes (most importantly, Russia and Turkey in addition to China) over major geopolitical issues, such as those concerning Ukraine and Taiwan, poses considerable dangers of cybersecurity which the rapid advancement of AI intensifies, particularly with underprepared infrastructure and utilities.

The rapid development of AI governance platforms in China raises not only geopolitical issues but also existential ones. The "AI arms race" between China and the United States of America is likely to encourage greater risk-taking, which may heighten the danger of an AI "intelligence explosion" (Russell, 2019). In this global geopolitical context, the metaphor of "letting the genie out of the bottle" seems even more apt than that of Frankenstein (Cugurullo, 2021). There is a great need for global cooperation on effective ethical rules for AI experimentation, but the current confrontational contexts make agreements unlikely, with all sides seeing standard setting as a key part of their competitive advantage. The risks posed by a contemporary version of Thucydides's Trap where competition between a hegemon and a rising challenger resulted in tragedy for all (Allison, 2017) are particularly frightening when such competition between China and America might make the release of an intelligence explosion inevitable.

Notes

1 For useful exceptions, see Cugurullo (2021) and Miller et al. (2021).
2 We observed this after we sampled and analyzed the discourse on the city brain produced by Alibaba.

3 While generic reference to city brains other than Alibaba's is now common in China, it is beginning to be seen in other contexts. Cugurullo (2020: 4) describes city brains as a key part of platform urbanism and 'the most elusive manifestation of AI in the built environment,' although still minimal in its actual control of urban functions beyond transportation.

4 The Chinese newspaper *Economic Information Daily* has described games and social media as "spiritual opium" and its mention specifically of Tencent resulted in the company adding restrictions on use of its games within hours, which that day cut $60 billion off its value (Goh and Shen, 2021). This echoes the conservative attack on the "sugar-coated bullets" of Western consumer goods during the early Economic Reform era of the 1980s.

5 China's willingness to subject the digital economy to greater control, is likewise seen in its recent crackdown on crypto mining (see McMorrow, 2021).

6 There is a broader trend in this direction for the economy as a whole. 'The number of private owners with direct investments from the state almost tripled between 2000 and 2019, and the number of private owners indirectly connected to the state via investments from private owners with state connections increased 50-fold' (Bai et al., 2020: 2).

7 China's willingness to use economic tools to quash policies opposing their interests is well shown in Lithuania: 'Beijing recalled its ambassador from Vilnius—the first time it has done so with a country in the European Union—limited trade with Lithuania, and suspended rail freight services between the two countries' (Gramer, 2021: no page).

References

Alibaba Clouder. (2019, October 28). City Brain now in 23 cities in Asia. *Alibaba Cloud*. Available at: https://www.alibabacloud.com/blog/city-brain-now-in-23-cities-in-asia_595479 [Accessed 19/01/2023].

Allam, Z. (2019). The emergence of anti-privacy and control at the nexus between the concepts of safe city and smart city. *Smart Cities*, 2(1), 96–105.

Allen, G. C. (2019). *Understanding China's AI strategy: Clues to Chinese strategic thinking on artificial intelligence and national security*. Center for a New American Security. Available at: https://www.cnas.org/publications/reports/understanding-chinas-ai-strategy [Accessed 19/01/2023].

Allison, G. (2017). *Destined for war: Can America and China escape Thucydides's trap?* Houghton Mifflin Harcourt, Boston.

Andersen, R. (2020, July 30). China's Artificial Intelligence surveillance state goes global. *The Atlantic*. Available at: https://www.theatlantic.com/magazine/archive/2020/09/china-ai-surveillance/614197/ [Accessed 19/01/2023].

Bai, C.E., Hsieh, C.T., Hsieh, M.S., & Wang, X. (2020). The rise of state-connected private owners in China. *NBER Working Paper* No. 28170.

Basu, M. (2021). Three innovative data projects from China. *GovInsider*. Available at: https://govinsider.asia/security/three-innovative-data-projects-china/ [Accessed 19/01/2023].

Bjeloš, M. (2021). The sum of all fears–Chinese AI surveillance in Serbia. In Armakolas, I., Chrzová, B., Čermák, P., & Grabovac, A. (Eds.) *Western Balkans at the crossroads: Ways forward in analyzing external actors' influence*. The Prague Security Studies Institute, Prague, 141–152.

Caprotti, F., & Liu, D. (2020). Platform urbanism and the Chinese smart city: The co-production and territorialisation of Hangzhou City Brain. *GeoJournal*, 87, 1559–1573.

Chan, K.W. (2021). What the 2020 Chinese Census tells us about progress in hukou reform. *China Brief*, 21(15), 11–17.

Chen, S. (2021). Across China, AI 'city brains' are changing how the government runs. *South China Morning Post*. Available at: https://www.scmp.com/news/china/science/article/3136661/across-china-ai-city-brains-are-changing-how-government-runs [Accessed 19/01/2023].

Chien, S. S., & Woodworth, M. D. (2018). China's urban speed machine: The politics of speed and time in a period of rapid urban growth. *International Journal of Urban and Regional Research*, 42(4), 723–737.

Cowley, R., Caprotti, F., Ferretti, M., & Zhong, C. (2019). Ordinary Chinese smart cities: The case of Wuhan. In Karvonen, A., Cugurullo, F., & Caprotti, F. (Eds.) *Inside smart cities: place, politics and urban innovation*. Routledge, Oxon, 45–64.

Cugurullo, F. (2018). Exposing smart cities and eco-cities: Frankenstein urbanism and the sustainability challenges of the experimental city. *Environment and Planning A: Economy and Space*, 50(1), 73–92.

Cugurullo, F. (2020). Urban artificial intelligence: From automation to autonomy in the smart city. *Frontiers in Sustainable Cities*, 2, 1–14.

Cugurullo, F. (2021). *Frankenstein urbanism: Eco, smart and autonomous cities, artificial intelligence and the end of the city*. Routledge, London.

Curran, D., & Smart, A. (2021). Data-driven governance, smart urbanism and risk-class inequalities: Security and social credit in China. *Urban Studies*, 58(3), 487–506.

Datta, A. (2020). The "smart safe city": gendered time, speed, and violence in the margins of India's urban age. *Annals of the American Association of Geographers*, 110(5), 1318–1334.

Doshi, R. (2021). *The long game: China's grand strategy to displace American order*. Oxford University Press, New York.

Easterling, K. (2014). *Extrastatecraft: The power of infrastructure space*. Verso Books, Brooklyn.

Erie, M. S., & Streinz, T. (2021). The Beijing Effect: China's digital silk road as transnational data governance. *New York University Journal of International Law and Politics*, 54, 1.

Eubanks, V. (2018). *Automating inequality: How high-tech tools profile, police, and punish the poor*. St. Martin's Press, New York.

Gao, (2017). Forward II. In Ouyang, C., Pan, Y., Sheng, Z., Feng, J., Cheng, X., Xue, Y., Hao, J., Cui, H., & Su, R. (Eds) *Inclusive growth and E-commerce: China's experience*. AliResearch. Available at: https://i.aliresearch.com/img/20170630/20170630151728.pdf [Accessed 19/01/2023].

Goh, B. & Shen, S. (2021). Tencent vows fresh gaming curbs after 'spiritual opium' attack zaps $60 billion. *Reuters*. Available at: https://www.reuters.com/technology/tencent-falls-after-china-media-calls-online-gaming-spiritual-opium-2021-08-03/ [Accessed 19/01/2023].

Gorman, L. (2021). China's data ambitions: strategy, emerging technologies, and implications for democracies. *National Bureau of Asian Research*. Available at: https://www.nbr.org/publication/chinas-data-ambitions-strategy-emerging-technologies-and-implications-for-democracies/ [Accessed 19/01/2023].

Gramer, R. (2021). Pressured by China, Lithuania won't back down over Taiwan. *Foreign Policy*. Available at: https://foreignpolicy.com/2021/09/07/lithuania-taiwan-china-dispute-geopolitics-europe-landsbergis/ [Accessed 19/01/2023].

Green, B. (2019). *The smart enough city: putting technology in its place to reclaim our urban future*. MIT Press, Cambridge.

Hemmings, J. (2020). Reconstructing order: the geopolitical risks in China's Digital Silk Road. *Asia Policy*, 15(1), 5–21.

Hillman, J.E. & McCalpin, M. (2019, November 4). Watching Huawei's 'safe cities'. *Center for Strategic and International Studies*. Available at: https://www.csis.org/analysis/watching-huaweis-safe-cities [Accessed 19/01/2023].

Hong, Y., & Goodnight, G. T. (2020). How to think about cyber sovereignty: The case of China. *Chinese Journal of Communication*, 13(1), 8–26.

Huawei (2022). *Smart City Solutions*. Available at: https://e.huawei.com/uk/solutions/industries/government/smart-city [Accessed 19/01/2023].

Johnston, L.A. (2021). World trade, E-commerce, and COVID-19. *China Review*, 21(2), 65–86.

Keji, Xinlang. (2019). Tencent Cloud wan the bid to build Changsha's city super brain for 520 million. *Sina*. Available at: https://tech.sina.com.cn/i/2019-07-02/doc-ihytcerm0759157.shtml [Accessed 19/01/2023].

Kynge, J., Hopkins, V., Warrell, H., & Hille, K. (2021, June 9). Exporting Chinese surveillance: The security risks of 'smart cities'. *The Financial Times*. Available: https://www.ft.com/content/76fdac7c-7076-47a4-bcb0-7e75af0aadab [Accessed 19/01/2023].

Lee, K.F. (2018). *AI superpowers: China, silicon valley, and the new world order*. Houghton Mifflin Harcourt, New York.

Maçães, B. (2019). *Belt and road: A Chinese world order*. Oxford University Press, Oxford.

Manson, K. (2021). US has already lost AI fight to China, says ex-Pentagon software chief. *The Financial Times*. Available at: https://www.ft.com/content/f939db9a-40af-4bd1-b67d-10492535f8e0 [Accessed 19/01/2023].

McMorrow, R. (2021, October 4). Beijing vs bitcoin – China cracks down on crypto. *The Financial Times*. Available at: https://www.ft.com/content/286b6586-50d3-456e-a89b-ac7d2b509f39 [Accessed 19/01/2023].

Miller, B., Ward, K., Burns, R., Fast, V., & Levenda, A. (2021). Worlding and provincialising smart cities: From individual case studies to a global comparative research agenda. *Urban Studies*, 58(3), 655–673.

Ouyang, C., Cheng, X., & Xue, Y. (2017a). BRICS E-commerce Development Report 2017. *AliResearch*. Available at: https://i.aliresearch.com/img/20170904/20170904154721.pdf [Accessed 19/01/2023].

Ouyang, C., Pan, Y., Sheng, Z., Feng, J., Cheng, X., Xue, Y., Hao, J., Cui, H., & Su, R. (2017b). Inclusive Growth and E-commerce: China's Experience. *AliResearch*. Available at: https://i.aliresearch.com/img/20170630/20170630151728.pdf [Accessed 19/01/2023].

Ruehl, M., Riordan, P., & Olcott, E. (2021). Can SenseTime become a Chinese AI champion? *The Financial Times*. Available at: https://www.ft.com/content/c735e0f3-5704-47b5-a76f-7a02d53a1525 [Accessed 19/01/2023].

Russell, S. (2019). *Human compatible: Artificial intelligence and the problem of control*. Penguin, London.

Sadowski, J., & Pasquale, F. A. (2015). The spectrum of control: A social theory of the smart city. *First Monday*, 20(7). Available at: https://digitalcommons.law. umaryland.edu/cgi/viewcontent.cgi?article=2545&context=fac_pubs [Accessed 19/01/2023].

Smart, A., & Curran, D. (2022). Prospects and social impact of big data-driven urban governance in China: Provincializing smart city research. In Wu, W. & Gao, Q. (Eds.) *China urbanizing: Impacts and transitions*. University of Pennsylvania Press, Philadelphia, 205–227.

The Economist. (2019a). Anglosphere v Sinosphere. *The Economist*, 19.

The Economist. (2019b). Splinternet of things. *The Economist*, 17–18.

The Economist. (2019c). One in the AI. *The Economist*, 68–69.

The Economist. (2020). China's Belt and Road. *The Economist*, 3–12.

The Economist. (2021a). China's attack on tech. *The Economist*, 7.

The Economist. (2021b). What tech does Xi want? *The Economist* 51–53.

The Economist. (2022). In search of mastery. *The Economist* 63–65.

Vila Seoane, M. F. (2020). Alibaba's discourse for the digital Silk Road: the electronic World Trade Platform and 'inclusive globalization'. *Chinese Journal of Communication*, 13(1), 68–83.

Wang, H., & Yu, H. (2022). Aspiring rule-makers: Chinese business actors in global governance. *Journal of Chinese Governance*, 7(1), 137–157.

Wildau, G., & Hook, L. (2017). China mobile payments dwarf those in US as fintech booms, research shows. *The Financial Times*. Available at: https://www.ft.com/content/00585722-ef42-11e6-930f-061b01e23655 [Accessed 19/01/2023].

Wu, Y., Zhang, W., Shen, J., Mo, Z., & Peng, Y. 2018. Smart city with Chinese characteristics against the background of big data: Idea, action and risk. *Journal of Cleaner Production*, 173, 60–66.

Yuntoutiao. (2018). AliCloud wan the bid to build Haikou's City Brain for 455 million. Available at: https://www.sohu.com/a/259302569_465914 [Accessed 19/01/2023].

Zheng, H. (2021). A group of smart people explain City Brain. *Hangzhou Daily*, 1.

PART IV

Urban software agents and algorithms

17

PERCEPTIONS OF INTELLIGENCE IN URBAN AI AND THE CONTINGENT LOGICS OF REAL ESTATE ESTIMATE ALGORITHMS

Casey R. Lynch and Vincent J. Del Casino Jr.

Introduction

Building on the extensive literatures on "smart" spaces (Bian, 2021), Big Data (Kitchin, 2014), algorithms (Amoore, 2020), platforms (Barns, 2020) and other manifestations of digitality (Ash et al., 2018), geographers have turned their attention to the question of artificial intelligence (AI). In the case of urban governance, Cugurullo (2020) has explored the emergence of autonomous vehicles, robots and city brains, arguing that cities are being constituted as autonomous agents through the production of urban AI. A special issue of *Space and Polity* also traces 'AI's evolving spatialities,' with contributions focusing on AI in warfare (Walker et al., 2021), the capitalist space economy (Alvarez Leon, 2021), labour (Attoh et al., 2021; Samers, 2021) and emotional relations (Lynch, 2021).

While this literature raises important questions about emerging AI applications and their impacts on space and place, there continues to be little explicit discussion regarding what constitutes (artificial) intelligence, how AI is qualitatively or quantitatively different from previous innovations in digital technology and the multiple forms it might take (Lynch and Del Casino, 2020). The lack of a definition of intelligence, despite invocations of AI, is not unique to geography, but reflective of broader debates across computer science, philosophy, psychology and other fields. Despite the lack of operational precision, the geographic AI literature does appear to have a common focus on the *autonomy* of AI agents, from autonomous cities and autonomous vehicles to software agents automating decision-making processes in housing, insurance, transportation and policing sectors. This focus raises the question of whether *autonomy* might constitute intelligence, an implication in this literature, and if so, how autonomy might be measured or evaluated.

DOI: 10.4324/9781003365877-21

This literature also draws common distinctions between embodied forms of AI (autonomous vehicles, drones, robots, etc.) and supposedly disembodied AI, often described as *autonomous software agents* (Russell and Norvig, 2016). In this distinction, an embodied AI may appear to have a discrete and confined existence in that it might have the ability to navigate and engage in the material world without assistance. As such, embodied AI may be more easily observed and measured compared to software agents located in networked computer systems and without material actuators. In other words, the autonomy of software agents might be more difficult to observe and define, or perceived to operate in a different way. As such, the binary distinction between embodied and disembodied AI may be a helpful heuristic for evaluating the differential capacities of digital systems and the diverse ways they exist in and interact with the world.

Yet, geographers have also challenged the purported immateriality of algorithms. As Cugurullo (2020: 9) explains, 'although their actions are immaterial, their consequences are tangible.' Others have traced how algorithms form part of broader assemblages and are thus best understood through the extensive networks of software, hardware, interfaces, people and institutions through which they operate (Del Casino, 2016). In line with this approach, Rose (2017) argues that a focus on the agency of specific machines may distract from the more entangled, co-constituted forms of (post)human agency by positing that human agency is always positioned as a remainder or resistance to machines. Following Rose, we both build on and challenge geographies of AI that focus on the autonomy of AI agents and their differentially embodied or disembodied existences, arguing instead for the need to recognize all intelligence as fundamentally relational. A relational understanding of (artificial) intelligence approaches autonomy as always relative, contingent and partial. It also calls into question neat distinctions between embodied and disembodied agents, at the same time that it calls attention to the complex im/material and spatial relations in which different agents are enmeshed.

In developing a relational theory of intelligence, in the next section, we build on De Togni et al.'s (2021: 7) work 'examining how "intelligence", in its different dimensions, is being manifested and co-constituted through the human-technology interface, in ways that are re-materializing the boundaries of the human and the machine identities in affective, embodied, and relational ways.' We also expand on Han's (2017: 85) insistence that intelligence be understood as 'systems immanent,' reflecting that 'a given system defines as given intelligence.' To do so, we draw on roboticist Rodney Brooks (1999) and others who re-theorize intelligence and shift focus to *perceptions of intelligence*. Brooks moves away from an ontological understanding of intelligence as a trait or capacity of a given agent and argues, instead arguing that intelligence is the contingent projection of an observer. Brooks did not aim to build robots *with* intelligence but robots that would be *perceived as* intelligent by the humans with whom they interact. In this move, Brooks shifts attention away from the computational *capacities* of a given agent and towards the relationship between the agent and the complex contexts in which it is deployed. Adapting Brooks' thinking to examine a broader range of AI agents beyond robots, we thus question how particular digital systems might be *perceived* to be intelligent in the contexts in which they are enmeshed.

To ground this theoretical discussion, we offer a brief analysis of the AI software agents used to estimate real estate values in the second section below. We trace how perceptions of such algorithms as intelligent are contingent upon the values and assumptions of deregulated, capitalist housing markets and ongoing histories of racial and other discrimination in the housing sector. We show how shifting attention to *perceptions* of intelligence prompts new questions about the ways subjects are differentially positioned in relation to such systems, the dark history of measuring and evaluating intelligence, and – following Mattern (2021) – the possibilities for multiple urban intelligences. We conclude the chapter by outlining how and in what ways geographers can move forward to think more critically about the relations amongst different forms of intelligence in a robotic age.

Intelligence as relational and contingent

In an evaluation of AI in healthcare contexts, De Togni et al. (2021) resist a narrow definition of intelligence by taking an inductive approach to examine the multiple forms of AI emerging in healthcare and the contingent relations among bodies and machines that make those AI applications possible. They trace physical, interpretative and emotional intelligences through AI systems for robotic surgery, diagnostics, care and companionship. Contrasting a focus on autonomy in the literature, De Togni et al. (2021: 6) argue that '[u]nderstanding what "intelligence" might mean beyond the conceptual human-machine division allows further understanding of how AI functions as an "augmenting" technology that is moving beyond human bodily, cognitive, and spatial constraints.' This concern with augmentation as opposed to autonomy expands analysis from the capacities of specific systems, to a concern with the ways these systems combine with others in practice to produce particular outcomes. Significantly, De Togni et al.'s account of healthcare AI also eschews distinctions of AI systems as either embodied or disembodied. They highlight examples of embodied robots, the relationship between surgeons and robotic bodies and the disembodied realm of diagnostics. It is not that the question of embodiment is unimportant, but embodiment is just one of multiple factors determining the different manifestations of intelligence. Their distinction between physical and interpretative intelligence, for instance, contains within it distinct materializations of AI.

This understanding of intelligence as an emergent property of relations among agents within a given context is also reflected in Byung-Chul Han's description of intelligence as *system-immanent*. In critiquing the forms of control exercised through Big Data analytics, Han (2017: 85) explains that

> Intelligence means *choosing-between (inter-legere)*. It is not entirely free in so far as it is caught in a *between*, which depends on the system in operation. Intelligence has no access to *outside*, because it makes a choice between options in a system. Therefore, intelligence does not really exercise *free choice*: it can only *select* among the offerings the system affords. Intelligence follows the logic of a system. It is system-immanent. A given system defines a given intelligence.

Like De Togni et al., Han shifts attention from the capacities of specific computational engines towards their applications within broader constraints and expectations for performance. AI systems are intelligent only to the extent that they articulate with the logics of a system. For example, an autonomous vehicle will be considered intelligent if it is able to navigate roadways while obeying the rules and norms of such a space. These rules and norms may vary by city, state or country as well as context, such as evacuation or emergency scenarios or when encountering a funeral procession. The vehicle's supposed "intelligence" emerges only in relation to these specific contexts and their ability to navigate them appropriately (see also Bissell, 2018). In contrast, Han poses the *idiot* as a figure that takes leave of the given system, abandoning its logic and prescriptions.

While Han's description of intelligence is helpful for thinking about the situatedness and constraints of all intelligence, his binary logic of intelligence or the idiot fails to imagine the possibility for a broader array of competing systemic logics and thus the possibility to imagine a multiplicity of intelligences emergent in the interstices of contemporary digital capitalism. This calls into question how the logics of a given system change over time or may be open to contestation. It also fails to consider how different subjects may become differentially entangled in AI systems. Could the AI system, for example, become idiotic? This may happen when so-called outside parameters become normalized, albeit sometimes temporarily, in robotic systems (see Wolf et al., 2017).

What this all suggests is that an AI may be *perceived* as intelligent or not depending on the context of the encounter and the relation between a given subject and the AI in question, but that perceptions of intelligence and the ontological status of intelligence are two separate questions. This distinction is often demonstrated through a now classic thought experiment known as the Chinese Room. Philosopher John Searle (1980) imagines a scene in which an individual is locked inside a room. This person is fed texts written in

Chinese and is given a set of instructions for how to respond to those texts. Without ever learning or understanding Chinese, the person is eventually able to use the instructions so well that they produce responses that convince those outside the room that they were written by a fluent Chinese speaker. The individual may become highly efficient at producing texts in Chinese, but that does not mean that they know or understand the language. Natale (2021) further argues that the history of AI has often focused on producing machines that are perceived as intelligent, utilizing various forms of banal deception that make use of human psychology and the context of encounters to give the appearance of intelligence even if based on fairly simple computational systems.

Within AI research, many roboticists have focused on *perceptions of intelligence* instead of intelligence itself since at least the early 1990s. This shift occurred as part of MIT Roboticist Rodney Brooks' (1999) retheorization of intelligence in the process of designing robots capable of navigating and interacting in dynamic real-world contexts. Brooks rejected previous approaches to robotics which focused on reducing the complexity of the world to predetermined Internal World Models that are encoded in a robot. Previous generations of robots had to be given a complete picture of their world and would then reconcile sensor data with this model to determine how to respond in a given situation. Brooks' behaviour-based or bottom-up approach did away with these centralized computational engines, replacing them with a series of competing behaviours constituted of direct links between sensing and action. In effect, Brooks did away with the site where intelligence had traditionally been located in AI. In the process, he was able to design robots whose behaviours were perceived as intelligent by observers.

Brooks concludes that intelligence has less to do with the complexity of a centralized computational engine and more to do with the interactions of an agent within a context and the perceptions and expectations of others within that system. This has led roboticists to develop a number of methodologies and standardized indexes for measuring and evaluating perceptions of intelligence and other attributes in robots. The widely used Godspeed Questionnaire, for instance, measures perceptions of intelligence and safety, along with anthropomorphism, animism and likeability. Regarding intelligence, the questionnaire asks respondents to rate a robot on a scale of 1–5 on traits like incompetent/competent, ignorant/knowledgeable, irresponsibile/responsible, unintelligent/intelligent and foolish/sensible (Bartneck et al., 2009). Increasingly, researchers in human–robot interaction (HRI) are interested in perceptions of distinct forms of intelligence, like social intelligence, and developing new tools to evaluate these (Barchard et al., 2020). Such moves further point to an understanding of intelligence as multiple, relational and contingent upon context. They also call attention to the myriad ways human intelligence has been measured and evaluated in ways that reinforce hierarchies of difference (Gillborn, 2016; Silverberg, 2008; Stephens and Cryle, 2017). Shifting attention to perceptions of intelligence can help critical scholars better reflect on these problematic practices and better challenge their underlying logics as they come to inform discourses around AI.

Reflecting on the concern with autonomy as a marker of intelligence in the recent geographic literature, we might instead ask how specific AI systems are perceived as autonomous. Reporting and scholarship have highlighted how many nominally AI systems work to hide the human labour involved (Newlands, 2021; O'Brien, 2019; Tubaro et al., 2020). Rather than trace the replacement of humans with autonomous agents, it might be more appropriate to instead trace the multiple re-organizations of bodies and machines and affective relations among them (Lynch et al., 2022). We might therefore ask when and where an AI is perceived as autonomous, to what extent, by whom and for what purposes. Further, by focusing on the multiple forms of human–AI interaction, we might better trace the complex im/materialities of AI, troubling neat distinctions between embodied and disembodied AI. In so doing, we might follow Bissell (2018: 64), who argues that '[p]opular accounts of automation and its impacts...tend to ride roughshod over a much more intricately-patterned material world, where transformations might be happening, but according to specific and situated compositions, events and political rationalities.' Even supposedly disembodied AIs, after all, necessarily interact with humans, be it through a digital interface, manual data entry or through its material effects (say an automated bank transfer). Access to these interfaces is not always open to all or easily visible, obscuring the ways AI differentially materializes for different subjects. Therefore, while Brooks' theory is specific to robots and concerned with direct, embodied forms of interaction, in the following section we trace how this focus on perceptions of intelligence and the relational contexts in which agents are entangled can help us question the emergence of other forms of urban AI.

Perceptions of intelligence in real estate estimate algorithms

Real estate estimate algorithms and iBuyer programs

Several proprietary algorithms exist for estimating the value of individual homes, regardless of whether that home is currently listed for sale. This includes Zillow's Zestimate and Redfin's Estimate, both active in the United States. As Zillow (2022: no page)'s website explains:

> Zillow publishes Zestimate home valuations for 104 million homes across the country, and uses state of the art statistical and machine learning models that can examine hundreds of data points for each individual home. To calculate a Zestimate, Zillow uses a sophisticated neural network-based

model that incorporates data from county and tax assessor records and direct feeds from hundreds of multiple listing services and brokerages. The Zestimate also incorporates: Home characteristics including square footage, location or the number of bathrooms; On-market data such as listing price, description, comparable homes in the area and days on the market; Off-market data — tax assessments, prior sales and other publicly available records; Market trends, including seasonal changes in demand.

In a similar way, Redfin's (2022: no page) estimate is based on 'more than 500 data points about the market, the neighborhood, and the home itself' with the company publishing estimates for 92 million homes in the United States. While both Zillow and Redfin explicitly state that their estimates are not official appraisals, they effectively aim to automate the work of human appraisers. While official appraisals are still required for many real estate transactions, in other cases (such as when a buyer agrees to forgo an appraisal in a competitive market or in some cases of refinancing, a mortgage) these estimates may be accepted as truth and guide decision-making. Beyond such moments, these estimates increasingly influence how individual homeowners think about the value of their home, anticipate an acceptable sales price, decide when to sell or refinance or make other significant decisions. In most cases, these estimates are the most accessible data available to both buyers and sellers about the current state of the housing market. While there may be cases where either buyer or seller sees a specific estimate as unreasonable or not in line with the broader market, these algorithms may be deemed intelligent to the extent that they seem to reflect market trends, even if they almost certainly play a role in shaping those very trends through the estimates they publish.

Yet, in addition to potentially automating the work of a real estate appraiser, these algorithms increasingly form part of larger assemblages automating further aspects of the home buying and selling process. The emerging 'iBuyer' industry involves tech companies buying and selling homes for a profit aided by algorithms to help them determine fair market prices and evaluate potential investment returns (Strachan, 2021a). These firms include Zillow, but also others like OpenDoor and RocketHomes. These companies entice sellers by offering a faster and smoother process compared to traditional sales, where deals may fall through, houses may sit on the market for months or sales may be delayed by appraisals, inspections and renegotiations. After purchasing a home, these iBuyers may make minor cosmetic updates before reselling but are generally not involved in major renovations and upgrades like traditional house flippers. By buying and selling houses at scale, especially in some of the most in-demand markets, and charging sellers a fee, these companies extract a profit. As Strachan (2021a: no page) reports: 'In May and June [2021] in Phoenix [Arizona], iBuyers snagged a median appreciation of 11.5% on the resale–equating to $39,000–after holding the homes for even just a few days.' More speculatively, as some advocates push for blockchain-based property records to reduce transaction costs and time involved in home sales (Dewan and Singh, 2020), one could imagine the algorithms discussed here being used to more fluidly facilitate automated buying and selling of homes to profit from small differences between purchase and sales price. In these cases, the perceived ability of estimate algorithms to identify markets and properties for profitable iBuyer acquisitions may lead many to see such systems as artificially intelligent.

While this industry is still in its infancy, the limitations of this "intelligence" are already beginning to show. Just a few months after announcing a major expansion of its iBuyer program, Zillow Offers, Zillow announced in November 2021 that it was disbanding the program. CEO Rich Barton explained, 'We've determined the unpredictability in forecasting home prices far exceeds what we anticipated and continuing to scale Zillow Offers would result in too much earnings and balance-sheet volatility' (quoted in Strachan, 2021b: no page). Further reporting revealed that the company had adjusted their algorithm to make more aggressive offers amid a highly competitive market, though at a moment when the market began to plateau. The adjustment led the algorithm to purchase homes for prices above what they could resell them for. The higher offers also led to 'higher-than-anticipated conversion rates' and subsequently more homes being purchased (9,700 in Q3 of 2021, compared to 3,800 in Q2) (Clark, 2021: no page). Essentially the automated pricing and purchasing of homes was not able to adjust to the nuances of a cooling housing market, in the end creating significant financial strain on the company which laid off 25% of its workforce as a result. Despite this, other iBuyers like OpenDoor are continuing to expand their operations to new markets.

Questioning perceptions of intelligence

What if rather than discussing whether or not these real estate estimate algorithms and the systems in which they become enrolled are "intelligent" we instead ask: *Under what conditions and from whose perspective might these systems be perceived as intelligent in particular contexts? What logic undergirds such perceptions? And what work do such claims to intelligence do in the world?* In the case of real estate estimate algorithms and iBuyer programs, these questions shift our focus to the underlying logics of the housing market that are necessarily encoded into the algorithms but that also determine how the algorithms' performance will be perceived and evaluated. Thus, we can explore how the perception of these systems as intelligent is contingent upon the logics of deregulated, capitalist housing markets, the social and cultural values of homeownership, and ongoing histories of racial discrimination in housing (Bonds, 2019; Howell and Korver-Glenn, 2018; Rugh and Massey, 2010), as well as the work and practices of homeowners, appraisers, real estate agents, developers, mortgage brokers and others involved in (re)producing the housing market (Benites-Gambirazio, 2020; Besbris, 2016).

We might start by asking whose perceptions of intelligence matter in the case of an iBuyer program. While it is certainly important that prospective sellers perceive the system as intelligent in that it appears to make an acceptable offer on a home, it is perhaps most important that the system be perceived as intelligent by the company's executives or managers. These individuals will almost certainly evaluate this intelligence (as evidenced by the failure of Zillow Offers) based on the algorithm's ability to autonomously make offers, purchase properties and re-sell properties that create a profit for the company. In this sense, perceptions of the algorithm's intelligence are already dependent upon a particular approach to the housing market in which housing is understood not as shelter or as a human need, but as a speculative asset to be bought and sold to extract a profit. Perceptions of the algorithm's intelligence by those responsible for evaluating it are already constrained by these logics.

Yet, to the extent that the algorithm is designed to be interested in the current and projected future value of a home, it also necessarily incorporates within it the logics by which homes have traditionally been valued in US housing markets. This includes the long history of racial segregation in housing, produced and supported by practices of redlining, restrictive covenants, Homeowner Associations and discrimination in lending, among other practices. This also includes less visible biases, such as when a Black woman in Indianapolis, Indiana ordered two appraisals on her house in 2021. The first came back for $125,000. Then, when a white man pretended to be the homeowner, another appraisal came back at $259,000 (Sheridan, 2021). Howell and Korver-Glenn (2018) highlight the multiple ways racism influences the appraising industry, while Korver-Glenn (2018) has further explored how racism is compounded across the multiple stages of the home buying/selling process. In the United States and other contexts, the dynamics of capitalist housing markets are inextricably entangled with the dynamics of racial inequality as questions of 'availability, affordability, and desirability are intertwined with racialized conceptualizations of space' (Fluri et al., 2020: 1).

Unsurprisingly, the data and algorithms used to estimate and project value are the product of longstanding and ongoing systems of oppression. If the algorithm is perceived as intelligent by company executives for its ability to produce and exploit trends in the market, this intelligence also undergirds and reproduces ongoing racism in the housing sector. Its perceived objectivity masks the underlying racism, further exacerbating the problematic way value is assigned to homes. While it might be perceived as intelligent by company executives, it may come to be perceived as the continuation of racism in housing by people of colour who see their own properties and neighbourhoods undervalued and/or targeted for investment due to historical undervaluations. Claims about the purported intelligence of such systems work discursively to naturalize and obscure these inequalities, as the "truth" of a home's value is increasingly abstracted from the social conditions that unequally reproduce the housing market.

Others' perceptions of these systems may be very different and informed by different logics and values from those of real estate investors. For instance, following the collapse of Zillow Offers, local news in Orlando, Florida – where the company had purchased 994 properties in the past year – highlighted the case of a house listed for sale at $285,000 that Zillow's algorithm purchased for $430,000 and re-listed for $510,000 without making any major renovations (WFTV Channel 9, 2021). Media interviews highlighted how the neighbours' perception of this scenario diverged from the company's. Neighbours seem to perceive this valuation as divorced from reality, as their perceptions are more closely tied to their own knowledge of the property, its history, current state, the renovations or lack of renovations carried out and their own sense of value. One neighbour explained '[it] is kind of disgusting, for them to buy a property at a price that they did not really do anything in the way to increase the value of the home' (WFTV Channel 9, 2021: no page). In this sense, the algorithm is not perceived as intelligent, but as a brazen, calculated – and ultimately failed – attempt at real estate speculation. Likewise, these systems may be perceived differently by those currently searching for a home as they become locked in a bidding war with an algorithm acting on behalf of large financial interests rather than another person in need of housing. These individuals do not see whether or not the algorithm was successful at extracting a profit but rather experience its effect on local real estate prices and their access to housing. Their differential positioning in relation to the system and their different interactions with it inform their perceptions of the system.

The shift to studying perceptions of intelligence also calls attention to the broader assemblages within which autonomous software agents are articulated, the different materializations of those assemblages, and the different ways actors encounter or come to interact with those assemblages. Homebuyers, sellers, neighbours, real estate agents, appraisers, company executives and others are all differentially positioned in relation to such systems and will all likely perceive the behaviour of that system differently. For a seller who benefits from a flaw in the iBuyer's algorithm to get an extra $20,000 for their house by interacting with the system's user interface, the algorithm may not seem intelligent but likely does not matter for their interests. For someone looking to buy a home, they may be using Zillow's website to search for properties (perhaps also generating data to help Zillow determine relative interest in specific homes or neighbourhoods), touring and evaluating homes with a real estate agent, determining their budget with the help of a mortgage broker and then encountering an iBuyer algorithm when they are outbid on a property. For iBuyer executives, they interact with the algorithm through their balance sheets as properties are bought and sold. They may perceive these as intelligent when they work (that is when they are successful at buying properties that can be resold for a profit). This perception of intelligence may lead these executives to afford the algorithms a certain amount of autonomy. Yet, this perception can shift dramatically when the market shifts and the algorithm either fails to adjust or lags in its adjustment. The executives encounter this through balance-sheet volatility that forces them to lay off 25% of their workforce.

Finally, by focusing on perceptions of intelligence, we call attention not only to the differently situated subjects that interact with an AI, but also to the broader spatiality of those encounters. Despite attempts to develop universal algorithms for real estate estimates, housing markets are highly spatially dependent and responsive to minute shifts in the local context. The ability of an estimate algorithm or iBuyer program to successfully mediate an encounter, or rather to perform intelligence in a particular moment, is dependent on this context. Changes to zoning, infrastructure planning and development, municipal service provision, local businesses and numerous other aspects of a city drive changes to real estate valuations in ways that are likely not captured immediately by such algorithms, in addition to the multiple possible quirks of specific urban spaces that are not easily made visible in the data but may influence valuation. To put it differently, the complex dynamism of cities and the algorithms' articulation with that dynamism plays a key role in differential perceptions of the systems' intelligence. More speculatively, it is likely that the assumptions around housing valuations that are programmed into the algorithm may be more appropriate and thus function better in specific contexts than anything that we might actually think of as acting with "real intelligence."

Conclusion: multiple urban (artificial) intelligences

Rather than debating the intelligence or not of such autonomous software agents, we instead ask when they might be perceived as intelligent, by whom and under what conditions. This forces us to question the logics encoded in these systems, the assemblages they form, and how different actors encounter these systems and experience their effects. A tech executive's perception of a system will differ greatly from that of a homebuyer, a real estate agent or a resident of a gentrifying neighbourhood, even as those very subjects become enrolled in the broader assemblages that make the system possible. Housing markets are remarkably complex, continually evolving and the product of numerous contingent social relationships and interactions. Estimate algorithms and iBuyer programs represent attempts to predict and control this complexity. While they may have some success in doing so in specific scenarios, the inherent uncertainty and ambiguity of the housing market as a social process are likely to escape those attempts (Birhane, 2021), even as they may be successful at extracting profit for certain companies in certain contexts.

Focusing on perceptions of intelligence also calls attention to the moments when specific AI systems fail to work as expected, produce unexpected results or fail to adapt to changing conditions. These moments when AI systems are suddenly perceived as unintelligent, or less intelligent than expected, constitute moments when algorithms 'give accounts of themselves' (Amoore, 2020: 110) and thus become intelligible in new ways to those interacting with them. Leszczynski (2020) describes these as *glitches*, which open opportunities to contest or rethink our relationships with those algorithms. Rather than an autonomous city in which human agency can only be understood as a remainder or resistance against technology, subjects are differentially situated in relation to those systems and their agency is co-constituted through their active engagements with the systems (Rose, 2017). While several scholars have highlighted the possibilities for AI to develop their own logics or new systems of intelligence, becoming increasingly autonomous from human actors (Bostrom, 2014; Cugurullo, 2021), the relational understanding of intelligence put forward in this chapter cautions us to approach all notions of autonomy (human or machine) as always partial and contingent. AI may be able to carry out increasingly complex functions without direct human supervision or intervention, but AI cannot be extricated from its entanglement in the human (or perhaps posthuman) relations in which it is entangled.

Thinking in this way calls attention to the distinction between cognition and consciousness (Lynch and Del Casino, 2020). Whereas AI may be able to 'make a choice between options in a system' (Han, 2017: 85) and may be able to inflect the very logics of the system, consciousness (no matter how limited, contradictory and poorly understood) affords humans the ability to reflect on the system in operation, challenge it, subvert it and imagine other possibilities. In conceiving of a multiplicity of urban intelligences, Mattern (2021) explores the networked relations among humans, spaces and technologies that organize in the pursuit of distinct goals. Mattern (2021) compares and contrasts the goals of order, control, rationalization and optimization inherent in conceptions of the city-as-computer to the variety of other logics and goals through which cities might be conceived and the distinct socio-technical apparatuses that might constitute intelligence in those contexts. Contrasting iBuyer programs, how might digital systems be re-imagined to promote housing justice, and how might we view those systems as intelligent or not based on the goals we set for them and the values with which we imbue them? This is not to re-assert some absolute human agency or intelligence as over and above the agency of emergent AI systems but rather to recognize human and technological agencies as inextricably entangled and co-constituted. AI may radically reshape the forms and capacities of technological agency. Yet, rather than replacing or displacing the opportunities for human agency in totality or in some sense of teleological absolutism, such developments rearticulate the relations through which human agency may be exercised. Focusing on perceptions of AI systems and the relational and contingent performance of intelligence within specific encounters offers one way of exploring how these human–technology relations are evolving, but are never fully determined at the moment in which the algorithm is created or in the form it eventually takes out there in the world.

References

Alvarez Leon, L. (2021). AI and the capitalist space economy. *Space and Polity*, 25(2), 220–236.

Amoore, L. (2020). *Cloud Ethics: Algorithms and the Attributes of Ourselves and Others*. Duke University Press.

Ash, J., Kitchin, R., & Leszczynski, A. (2018). Digital turn, digital geographies? *Progress in Human Geography*, 42(1), 25–43.

Attoh, K., Cullen, D., & Wells, K. (2021). Between 'automated geography' and 'geographies of automation': three parables for thinking dialectically. *Space and Polity*, 25(2), 167–183.

Barchard, K. A., Lapping-Carr, L., Westfall, R. S., Fink-Armold, A., Banisetty, S. B., & Feil-Seifer, D. (2020). Measuring the perceived social intelligence of robots. *ACM Transactions on Human-Robot Interaction (THRI)*, 9(4), 1–29.

Barns, S. (2020). *Platform Urbanism: Negotiating Platform Ecosystems in Connected Cities*. Springer Nature, Singapore.

Bartneck, C., Kulić, D., Croft, E., & Zoghbi, S. (2009). Measurement instruments for the anthropomorphism, animacy, likeability, perceived intelligence, and perceived safety of robots. *International Journal of Social Robotics*, 1(1), 71–81.

Benites-Gambirazio, E. (2020). Working as a real estate agent. Bringing the clients in line with the market. *Journal of Cultural Economy*, 13(2), 153–168.

Besbris, M. (2016). Romancing the home: Emotions and the interactional creation of demand in the housing market. *Socio-Economic Review*, 14(3), 461–482.

Bian, L. (Ed.) (2021). *Smart Spaces and Places*. Routledge, Abingdon and New York.

Birhane, A. (2021). The impossibility of automating ambiguity. *Artificial Life*, 27(1), 44–61.

Bissell, D. (2018). Automation interrupted: how autonomous vehicle accidents transform the material politics of automation. *Political Geography*, 65(1), 57–66.

Bonds, A. (2019). Race and ethnicity I: Property, race, and the carceral state. *Progress in Human Geography*, 43(3), 574–583.

Bostrom, N. (2014). *Superintelligence: Paths, Dangers, Strategies*. Oxford University Press, Oxford.

Brooks, R. A. (1999). *Cambrian Intelligence: The Early History of the New AI*. The MIT Press, Boston.

Clark, P. (2021). Zillow shuts home-flipping business after racking up losses. *Los Angeles Times*. Available at: https://www.latimes.com/business/story/2021-11-02/zillow-shuts-home-flipping-business-after-losses-ibuyers-home-sales   [Accessed 19/01/2023].

Cugurullo, F. (2020). Urban artificial intelligence: From automation to autonomy in the smart city. *Frontiers in Sustainable Cities*, 2, 1–14.

Cugurullo, F. (2021). *Frankenstein Urbanism: Eco, Smart, and Autonomous Cities, Artificial Intelligence and the End of the City*. Routledge, Abingdon and New York.

De Togni, G., Erikainen, S., Chan, S., & Cunningham-Burley, S. (2021). What makes AI 'intelligent' and 'caring'? Exploring affect and relationality across three sites of intelligence and care. *Social Science & Medicine*, 277, 113–874.

Del Casino, V. J. (2016). Social Geographies II: Robots. *Progress in Human Geography*, 40(6), 846–855.

Dewan, S., & Singh, L. (2020). Use of blockchain in designing smart city. *Smart and Sustainable Built Environment*, DOI:10.1108/sasbe-06-2019-0078.

Fluri, J. L., Hickcox, A., Frydenlund, S., & Zackary, R. (2020). Accessing racial privilege through property: Geographies of racial capitalism. *Geoforum*, 132, 238–246.

Gillborn, D. (2016). Softly, softly: Genetics, intelligence and the hidden racism of the new geneism. *Journal of Education Policy*, 31(4), 365–388.

Han, B.-C. (2017). *Psychopolitics: Neoliberalism and New Technologies of Power*. Verso, London.

Howell, J., & Korver-Glenn, E. (2018). Neighborhoods, race, and the twenty-first-century housing appraisal industry. *Sociology of Race and Ethnicity*, 4(4), 473–490.

Kitchin, R. (2014). *The Data Revolution: Big Data, Open Data, Data Infrastructures & their Consequences*. SAGE, London, Thousand Oaks, Delhi, Singapore.

Korver-Glenn, E. (2018). Compounding inequalities: How racial stereotypes and discrimination accumulate across the stages of housing exchange. *American Sociological Review*, 83(4), 627–656.

Leszczynski, A. (2020). Glitchy vignettes of platform urbanism. *Environment and Planning D: Society and Space*, 38(2), 189–208.

Lynch, C. R. (2021). Artificial emotional intelligence and the intimate politics of robotic sociality. *Space and Polity*, 25(2), 184–201.

Lynch, C. R. & Del Casino Jr., V. (2020). Smart spaces, information processing, and the question of intelligence. *Annals of the American Association of Geographers*, 110(2), 382–390.

Lynch, C. R., Bissell, D., House-Peters, L. A., & Del Casino Jr, V. (2022). Robotics, affective displacement, and the autonomation of care. *Annals of the American Association of Geographers*, 112(3), 684–691.

Mattern, S. (2021). *A City is Not a Computer: Other Urban Intelligences*. Princeton University Press, Princeton, NJ.

Natale, S. (2021). *Deceitful media: Artificial intelligence and social life after the Turing test*. Oxford University Press, USA.

Newlands, G. (2021). Lifting the curtain: Strategic visibility of human labour in AI-as-a-Service. *Big Data & Society*, 8(1), DOI: 20539517211016026.

O'Brien, H. (2019, June 5). Ghosts in the machines: the invisible human labour that lurks behind technology. *New Statesman*. Available at: https://www.newstatesman.com/culture/observations/2019/06/ghosts-machines-invisible-human-labour-lurks-behind-technology [Accessed 19/01/2023].

Redfin (2022). *About the Redfin Estimate.* Available at: https://www.redfin.com/redfin-estimate [Accessed 19/01/2023].

Rose, G. (2017). Posthuman agency in the digitally mediated city: Exteriorization, individuation, reinvention. *Annals of the American Association of Geographers,* 107(4), 779–793.

Rugh, J. S., & Massey, D. S. (2010). Racial segregation and the American foreclosure crisis. *American Sociological Review,* 75(5), 629–651.

Russell, S. J., & Norvig, P. (2016). *Artificial Intelligence: A Modern Approach.* Pearson, Hoboken, NJ.

Samers, M. (2021). Futurological fodder: on communicating the relationship between artificial intelligence, robotics, and employment. *Space and Polity,* 25(2), 237–256.

Searle, J. R. (1980). Minds, brains, and programs. *Behavioral and Brain Sciences,* 3(3), 417–424.

Sheridan, J. (2021). A black woman says she had to hide her race to get a fair home appraisal. *National Public Radio.* Available at: https://www.npr.org/2021/05/21/998536881/a-black-woman-says-she-had-to-hide-her-race-to-get-a-fair-home-appraisal [Accessed 19/01/2023].

Silverberg, C. (2008). *IQ testing and tracking: The history of scientific racism in the American public schools: 1890–1924.* Unpublished dissertation. University of Nevada, Reno.

Stephens, E., & Cryle, P. (2017). Eugenics and the normal body: The role of visual images and intelligence testing in framing the treatment of people with disabilities in the early twentieth century. *Continuum,* 31(3), 365–376.

Strachan, M. (2021a). Zillow, other tech firms are in an 'arms race' to buy up American homes. *Vice.* Available at: https://www.vice.com/en/article/93ymxz/zillow-other-tech-firms-are-in-an-arms-race-to-buy-up-american-homes [Accessed 19/01/2023].

Strachan, M. (2021b). Zillow is killing its home-buyer service, cutting 25 percent of workforce. *Vice.* Available at: https://www.vice.com/en/article/4awy5m/zillow-is-killing-its-home-buyer-service-cutting-25-percent-of-workforce? [Accessed 19/01/2023].

Tubaro, P., Casilli, A. A., & Coville, M. (2020). The trainer, the verifier, the imitator: Three ways in which human platform workers support artificial intelligence. *Big Data & Society,* 7(1), DOI: 2053951720919776.

Walker, M., Winders, J., & Frimpong Boamah, E. (2021). Locating artificial intelligence: A research agenda. *Space and Polity,* 25(2), 202–219.

Wolf, M. J., Miller, K. W., & Grodzinsky, F. S. (2017). Why we should have seen that coming: Comments on Microsoft's Tay "Experiment," and wider implications. *The ORBIT Journal* 1(2), 1–12.

Zillow (2022). *How much is my home worth?* Available at: https://www.zillow.com/how-much-is-my-home-worth/ [Accessed 19/01/2023].

18

CARING IS CONNECTING

AI digital assistants and the surveillance of elderly and disabled family members in the home

Miriam E. Sweeney

Introduction

'More peace of mind as your loved ones need more care.' This tagline appears in large, bolded letters on Amazon's (2022: no page) website advertising their service, Alexa Together. Described as a 'new way to provide support for your loved ones, keeping you together even when you're apart,' this 'caregiving service' requires a subscription and an Amazon Echo device to facilitate the remote support of elderly and disabled family members, including control of household devices and increased surveillance opportunities (Amazon, ibid). AI digital assistants, like Amazon Alexa (the assistant that runs on Amazon's Echo devices), increasingly serve as the central interface to smart home applications and, by association, often connect people up to a suite of external social and governmental services, such as those advertised in Alexa Together that include policing, security and emergency health. Design and marketing strategies for AI digital assistants have emphasized the domestic role of these technologies as a way to facilitate user trust and acceptance of otherwise invasive forms of surveillance and access to personal and intimate data (e.g. health, biometric, spatial movements, consumption patterns, etc.).

Building on these ideas, I explore *caring* as a discursive frame that creates targeted opportunities for data extraction and further entangles the home (and family members) with the data assemblages that AI urbanism relies on for algorithmic decision-making. This chapter provides an overview of AI digital assistants as surveillant data-gathering devices and introduces basic concepts related to *digital domesticity* (Woods, 2018) that cast these technologies as ideal home management solutions. Using Alexa Together as one example, I consider how the frame of caregiving may be leveraged to

DOI: 10.4324/9781003365877-22

"smooth" people's concerns about privacy and data gathering, while justifying intensified surveillance for elder adults and disabled family members as a function of market segmentation. The framing of surveillant technologies as caregivers both reflects and reproduces the extractive logics of algorithmic culture that transform social relationships into opportunities for data gathering. I argue that a key feature of AI urbanism is the access to intimate and personal data in the home as a resource that can be commoditized and integrated into urban governance and planning. These concepts are critical for theorizing the role of AI digital assistants within broader autonomous processes of urban living and governance associated with AI urbanism.

AI digital assistants (data is the point)

Artificially intelligent (AI) digital assistants, like Amazon Alexa, act as voice-based interfaces to a variety of services, applications and information using personalized, conversational interaction with users. Digital assistants are often utilized via smart speakers (e.g. Amazon Echo or Google Home) but also may be accessed through mobile devices, search interfaces, applications and other Internet of Things (IoT) technologies. According to ReportLinker (2022: no page), 'the proliferation of virtual assistance is, in turn, driving the smart speaker market,' globally. The Asia-Pacific region experienced the most market growth in smart speakers in 2021, with Africa projected to be the next major growth region in the forecasted years (ReportLinker, 2022). In the United States, the public's enthusiasm for AI digital assistants has been steadily growing over the last decade, borne out by large jumps in consumer adoption rates. For instance, Edison Research found that 'smart-speaker adoption increased during the pandemic with about 94 million people in the U.S. estimated to own at least one smart speaker in 2021, up from 76 million in 2020' (Alcántara, 2021: no page). Additionally, 24% of Americans own an Amazon Echo device, reflecting Amazon's dominance in the smart speaker market at 53% of the market share (Alcántara, 2021; Amazon Echo & Alexa Stats, 2021).

AI digital assistants use advanced artificial intelligence combined with automatic speech recognition, natural language processing, text-to-speech and machine learning to extract and process data from conversational inquiries to meet users' informational and consumer needs and interact with a bevvy of smart home devices. AI digital assistants rely on a user's current and historical data (e.g. purchases, location, public records, demographics, preferences, biometrics and other existing information profiles) to create data models to answer complex questions, make recommendations and offer predictions to anticipate future needs and uses. None of these developments would have been possible without the growth of cost-effective and scaled-up information infrastructures such as cloud computing, server storage and data processing to handle the compiling and mining of massive data sets. In this sense, 'Big Data is both the driver of the development of these technologies, as well as the foundation of the consumer business model they support' (Sweeney, 2021: 152). Given this symbiotic relationship, it is fair to say that data extraction, not user service, is the critical function of AI digital assistants (and related smart technologies) and that user data is the prized commodity driving the push for integrative smart technologies.

Barns (2021) notes that the role of user routines in the production of Big Data is both quotidian and a hugely complicated computational problem for computer scientists and mathematicians to replicate. She notes: 'Where Lynch (1960) posited that each standard "image of the city" allows a city to become legible to its inhabitants, today it is also the case that routine behaviours [sic] allow activity to become legible computationally' (Barns, 2021: 2). Capturing the routine behaviours in the city has been previously conceptualized as a problem of tracking and quantifying city inhabitants' interactions with public spaces (e.g. city planning, transit systems). However, I argue that a key feature of AI urbanism is the unprecedented access to the *intimate* routines of domestic spaces (e.g. consumption patterns, spatial movements, social interactions, sexual activities, health and biometrics, information needs, environmental controls) and the capabilities to make these behaviours computationally legible as a resource that can be commoditized and integrated into urban governance and planning. In this sense, there is a shift from automating people's domestic routines to transducing the social, affective, economic, political and cultural aspects of everyday living, once harder to "see," into legible data that drives decision-making across an integrated and autonomous suite of data networks that govern daily life. In essence, we have moved from making the city legible to inhabitants to making inhabitants legible to the city, in this case, autonomous AI systems (see Cugurullo, 2020), even in their most private spaces and routines.

Quantification of behaviour is an important element of surveillance capitalism or the economic process of capturing and commodifying personal data for profit. Zuboff describes the 'extraction imperative' as the first economic imperative of surveillance capitalism, wherein 'raw material supplies must be produced at an ever-expanding scale (2019: 87).' The raw materials in question are user data which are transformed into commodities with market value. These, in turn, become 'behavioral prediction products' which are sold in a new type of market: the behavioral futures market' (2019: 8). In the context of AI urbanism, human experiences, activities, affect and social relationships are translated into a reserve of behavioural data controlled by technology companies, like Amazon, that design products for surveillance and data capture. These companies are the primary brokers of behavioural data and exert enormous political and economic control in all aspects of the Big Data landscape from data capture, storage, processes and services.

The current information landscape, presciently anticipated by Herbert Schiller (2020), is defined through information inequalities facilitated by privatization, deregulation, media consolidation and commodification of information. We might update Schiller's vision by specifying the specific role of Big Data within the information landscape, though the same market forces apply. In terms of AI urbanism, the relative market power and, in some cases, monopoly of the so-called "Big Four" tech companies (Apple, Amazon, Google and Facebook) leads to tremendous political influence and lobbying power. Market autonomy is actively fought for and upheld by tech companies to serve their own interests, consolidating and expanding the reach and control of the handful of powerful corporations that make AI digital assistants and other smart home technologies. For instance, Apple, Amazon, Google and Facebook spent more than $55 million lobbying the US government in 2021 on issues related to fighting antitrust reform (Birnbaum, 2022). The public advocacy group, Public Citizen, reported that 'Facebook and Amazon are now the two largest individual corporate lobbyists in Washington, with their political spending eclipsing that of telecommunications and arms companies in 2020' (Skelton, 2021: no page). Additionally, as governmental information and technology services and infrastructure in the United States are increasingly outsourced to these same companies, clear delineations between public/private infrastructure blur. The move to artificially intelligent city systems further entangles the agendas of private enterprise and city governance. Technology companies, like Amazon, are therefore poised as integral partners and benefactors of the *autonomous city* (see Cugurullo, 2021). Altogether, this paints a picture of a digital corporatocracy shaped by extreme power asymmetries in favour of corporate ownership and an important part of this involves the control of people's intimate data.

Nathan Ensmenger (2021) has noted that Amazon's business model is best described as a provision of services and infrastructure. He argues that this has been the case for the company all along, drawing fascinating parallels between Amazon and companies like Standard Oil and Sears Roebuck. However, as he notes, the innovative part of Amazon's business model as part of the digital economy is 'its integration of sophisticated computational technologies at every level of the firm, from customer-facing web interfaces to back-end databases to global positioning systems' (Ensmenger, 2021: 33). Amazon's move to promote services like Alexa Together, rather than just individual home devices like the Echo speakers, is a logical next step for expanding the information infrastructure that they have already invested in (e.g. Amazon Sidewalk, Amazon Web Services). Says Priya Abani, Amazon's director of AVS enablement: 'We basically envision a world where Alexa is everywhere' (Pierce, 2018: no page). These comments reflect the vision of total integration of AI digital assistants into daily life, across public and private domains.

This infrastructure depends on access points for Alexa. After all, an AI digital assistant can only be a seamless voice-controlled interface if it is in "hearing" range of spoken commands. Spatially speaking, this means that smart speakers are ideally positioned throughout the home where people are likely to spend the majority of their time. Market research supports this, showing that 71% of owners of smart speakers are likely to have more than one, and particularly desire access to their features in public living areas, bedrooms and kitchens (Clark, 2019). This creates multiple access points for people using these technologies and extends opportunities for 'data gathering between users and corporations' (Woods, 2018: 344). In this environment, consolidation of access points and interoperability become highly desired as a way to provide a simplified and unified user experience. Recent research from Parks Associates indicates that smart speakers with AI digital assistants have emerged as the leading default control interface for the smart home, with Amazon Echo/Alexa as the most popular device (Kung, 2021). Parks Associates' research analysts note that 'integration and partnerships will be critical for the smart home to cross into mass-market adoption' (Kung, 2021: no page). This means that the smart home landscape is essentially restructuring itself from a collection of individual applications to part of an integrated infrastructure that connects the home to an amalgam of external corporate and governmental data networks that function as the backbone of Big Data that undergird the autonomous city.

In this connected data environment, there are no discrete delineations between individual smart applications and the data networks they share. Linking together different applications creates a multiplicity of terms-of-service agreements and a tangled mess of data sharing across linked devices. For instance, linking Amazon Alexa with smart applications like security systems, music streaming, e-book libraries, appliances and telephony creates a web of data sharing between a variety of companies, institutions and services. Consolidating this web of shared data as a means to streamline and extend the commodification and control of user data is the central aim of tech companies. More user data translates directly into opportunities for personalization and advertising, which forms the basis of the economy driving the Internet.

Permissive corporate data-sharing practices along with the consolidated ownership of media, technology and telecommunications companies make tracing the flow of consumer data nearly impossible from a public auditing standpoint (Whittaker, 2018). Average people are not able to trace all of the ways their data is used out in the world or even clearly "see" what their data profiles consist of, much less who owns them. So, on the one hand, tech companies are able to get ever more intimate snapshots of people's daily routines, habits, personalities, relationships, identities and proclivities, but, on the other hand, these data profiles remain largely out of reach and control of the people they digitally represent. Legally, there are very few consumer protections for data in the United States, though the GDPR in Europe has made some positive headway in data privacy and protection. In the United States, federal and state governmental agencies are legally able to compel access to the trove of user of data under federal policies, like the USA PATRIOT ACT, which vastly lower the bar for access to personal and private data. This landscape creates a culture of compliance wherein technology and telecommunication companies end up handing over user data to federal, state and local law enforcement authorities (Nicas, 2021). Though it is not a requirement to do so, major tech companies like Apple and Google have taken to proactively publishing transparency reports to reveal how many requests they have received for customer data in a set time period. Of these, Amazon remains the most vague in their transparency reports offering the minimum information and has been accused of 'deliberately misleading' customers by 'actively refusing to clarify how many customers, and which customers, are affected by the data demands it receives' (Whittaker, 2018: no page). More recent audits report that the majority of requests for user data from tech companies by government authorities are, in fact, fulfilled by the tech companies in question (Nicas, 2021).

The public is largely unaware of, or unable to intervene in, how their personal data circulates through these systems that hold great influence over all aspects of their lives including banking, credit, housing, education, health care, policing, citizenship, information sharing, social networking, insurance and criminal justice. In all of these scenarios, people may experience data harms or be subject to algorithmic governance in ways they cannot fully "see" or trace. Data harms are defined by Joanna Redden, Jessica Brand and Vanesa Terzieva (2020: no page) as 'the adverse effects caused by uses of data that may impair, injure, or set back a person, entity or society's interests.' Data harms include but are not limited to, outcomes that violate privacy, reproduce social inequalities such as racist stereotypes (Noble, 2018), contribute to discriminatory hiring practices (O'Neil, 2016), put people into increased contact with law enforcement or carceral systems (Benjamin, 2019) and interfere with people's access to social services (Eubanks, 2018). While data harms have important implications for everyone, those who are part of communities that have been historically oppressed, marginalized or otherwise socially excluded disproportionally experience more data harms and with more severe outcomes. The irony, of course, is that as surveillance and algorithmic governance intensify for the public at large, there remains a dearth of accountability, transparency and regulatory structures for the companies and government agencies who are responsible for collecting and using this data.

AI digital assistants in the home

The home as a site of technological innovation and control has a long history, though it is often occluded or dismissed because of the associations with domesticity and home management as women's work (and thus invisible as a technological domain). Yet technology has always been integral in mediating homemaking, caretaking and domestic security. Many of the expectations, standards and blueprints for contemporary middle-class homemaking endure from the reorganization of society in the United States during the industrial revolution in the 19th century (Keister and Southgate, 2022). This time period was characterized by a strict gender division (the gender binary) that produced masculinity and femininity as essential and immutable identities that were spatially organized through a public/private dichotomy. This reorganization of society increased standards of housekeeping and caregiving as a function of expressing "true womanhood." The period of time between 1920 and 1940 ushered in 'an industrial revolution in the home' with the transition to new technologies for home management such as gas stoves, electric ranges, washing machines and vacuum cleaners that introduced automated processes to aid in the manual labour of housekeeping (Cowan, 1987: no page). Technological advances in the 1950s and 1960s fueled the mid-century imaginary of the home of the future, exemplified by Disney's Tomorrowland showcase, along with the 1960s Jetsons TV series. These examples reflect the twinned ideals of technological progress and cultural conservatism that characterized the Cold War era and persist in contemporary smart home design and imaginaries (Strengers and Kennedy, 2020).

As Heather notes, 'one way that technological advances are rhetorically negotiated is by threading stable components of the past into the present' (2018: 336). AI technologies such as smart security systems, robot vacuum cleaners, smart thermostats and IoT technologies extend this trajectory of home management, moving the home from an automated environment to an autonomous environment that enacts domestic care in new formations. Woods (2018: 337) aptly describes this phenomenon as *digital domesticity* wherein 'the technologies themselves become responsible for home-making' and care-taking, thereby simultaneously re-articulating femininity and domesticity in the process. Yolande Strengers and Jenny Kennedy (2020) describe smart home technologies like AI digital assistants as *smart wives*, using "wife" as both shorthand and a metaphor for a specific form of gendered labour within the heterosexual marriage institution that carries forward the ideologies and expectations of domesticity in modern homemaking.

Digital domesticity as a framework is helpful for understanding how caretaking roles are outsourced to AI digital assistants in the home, despite the increased surveillance they demand. As feminist care ethics scholars like Joan Tronto (1998) remind us, examining care work always necessitates accounting for the politics and power dynamics that shape which bodies are providing care labour, who are receiving care and where exploitation or abuse may occur as a part of that process. These questions gain new salience in the data environment of the smart home where the trade-off for receiving care involves relinquishing personal privacy and ceding access and control of intimate data to corporations and the state. Importantly for the context of AI urbanism, the movement from *automation* to *autonomy* in home management and caretaking parallels the shift Cugurullo (2020) articulates from traditional smart-city initiatives to emerging autonomous cities. Described by Cugurullo (2021: 166) as 'urban settlements managed and experienced by AIs which are capable of acting in an unsupervised manner,' *autonomous cities*, as a concept, embody algorithmic logics and data-driven decision-making put into large scale, coordinate action for urban governance. Cugurullo (2020: 38) argues that the movement from automation to autonomy is part of a 'long-standing process of technological development and a politico-economic agenda' that transfers the authority and decision-making of urban governance and planning to artificial intelligence. AI digital assistants are a powerful manifestation of this phenomenon and also form the anchor for consolidated data extraction in the home.

Caring is connecting

Amazon's advertising and marketing campaigns have heavily emphasized homemaking and caretaking as central affordances of the Alexa AI digital assistant since its launch. For example, one of the first advertisements features vignettes of Alexa "assisting" with numerous feminine-coded household tasks including pulling up recipes while cooking, compiling grocery lists, answering homework questions after school, teaching children proper etiquette and reading them to sleep with an audiobook. In these scenes, Alexa is explicitly positioned as a member of the household in feminized caretaking roles, alternatively cast as wife, mother, nanny, domestic servant, secretary or girlfriend, which Wood argues transforms Alexa into 'a whole-person caretaker' (2018: 340). As a child in the advertisements explains about Alexa and the Echo smart speaker device it runs on, 'it's really become part of the family' (Amazon Echo, 2016: no page).

These, and other advertisements, feature young or middle-aged, single, able-bodied adults getting ready for dates, cooking, asking about the weather and listening to music. Or, they feature young or middle-aged, heterosexual, able-bodied couples engaged in child-rearing and family activities. All appear to occupy middle or upper-middle-class status according to the depictions of housing and aesthetics (Phan, 2019). This communicates that these demographics are the imagined users and customer bases for the digital assistant. Depictions of disabled, elderly and non-independent adults are not represented in these advertisements. While parent-child caregiving has been central to the advertising of Alexa from the very beginning, new services, like Alexa Together focus on opportunities for supporting the caregiving of elderly family members. Thus, the introduction of services like Alexa Together (and also Alexa Kids) represents a new strategy of expansion through market segmentation to specific age and ability demographics within the household. Market segmentation is a common growth strategy for companies seeking to offer their existing products to a new market. In the case of Alexa Together, Amazon is targeting specific family members according to age, life stage and ability. Household members who fall into these particular demographics are identified by Amazon as requiring specialized care that can be ideally met via the intensified surveillance and connective affordances of Alexa Together.

Elderly and disabled people have been historically overlooked or ignored in the design of smart technologies. To date, the majority of AI digital assistant research has focused on able-bodied users and 'fails to account for the participants' actual motor, linguistic, and cognitive abilities' (Masina et al., 2020: 1). Given this, there are tremendous opportunities to rethink domestic smart technologies and consider the potentials for voice-interfaces and AI digital assistants as assistive devices similar to screen readers, spectacles, scooters and so on. Emerging research in this area has focused on the usefulness of voice assistants to physically disabled people (Mtshali and Khubisa, 2019) and to older adults with low technology use or proficiency (Pradhan et al., 2020). Of course, for all of these accessibility possibilities, voice technologies have a way to go before truly being considered inclusive: there are still many problematic examples of cultural language bias in voice technologies (Lawrence, 2021); research points to usability issues related to the syntax of voice commands and difficulties of pronunciation (Masina et al., 2020); and there are numerous speech recognition problems (Pradhan et al., 2018). However, beyond the technical and cultural challenges that need to be addressed to improve the usability of AI digital assistants for accessibility, inclusive design must also grapple with the power dynamics, inequalities and vulnerabilities that these technologies enable and reproduce through processes of surveillance, data extraction and data sharing. A closer look at Alexa Together can help raise some of these issues and identify areas where data harms such as privacy breaches may occur.

Described by Amazon (2022: no page) as 'a caregiving service that connects your Alexa app to their Echo devices,' Alexa Together emphasizes *connection* as a function of care in the advertising descriptions, blending the social and computational meanings of the term. While the social meaning of connection refers to the affective ties and social obligations shared between people, the computational meaning of connection suggests the tethering of digital devices to the Internet to send and receive information. The blending of these meanings is key not only to Amazon's marketing of Alexa as a digital caregiver but also for cementing the idea of data extraction as an integral part of modern social, and therefore informational, infrastructure. Informational infrastructure is thus both technical/material and cultural/ideological in nature.

Cultural ideas about *who* performs caretaking for elderly and disabled family members, and *where* caretaking takes place, are juxtaposed with the realities and constraints of modern living. For instance, multigenerational household dwelling is not the norm for white, middle-class families in the United States. People also may not live geographically near their families for a variety of reasons, with the availability of economic opportunities being one reason. At the same time, health care, at least in the United States, is largely privatized, tied to employment and otherwise expensive to the point of exclusion. Meanwhile, social services to support independent living or care assistance for elderly and disabled people have been critically defunded for decades. The promise of caregiving through the Alexa Together service ostensibly resolves these structural conflicts by offering individualized, technological solutions for caregiving that essentially replace anaemic public social services with private companies.

Alexa Together repackages previously available features and applications of Alexa, such as setting up customized alerts, with new services like 24/7 urgent response, circle of support and remote assist that extend the ability for family members, friends and health providers to monitor and communicate with an elderly or disabled person from a distance. The customized activity alerts for Alexa Together provide a real-time feed of 'what your loved one is doing with just a quick look at your phone' (Amazon, 2022: no page). Amazon's website advertises that this feature 'keeps you in the loop and keeps them independent' (Amazon, ibid). For remote assistance, the family member can use their phone 'for things like setting reminders, managing shopping lists, and managing certain settings for their Echo devices' and even 'drop in' on the loved one by initiating a call (Amazon, ibid). In case a family member is not available (because 'life can get in the way,' according to Amazon's marketing), the 'circle of support' feature can allow other people in the family and friends network to check on the loved one (Amazon, ibid).

Throughout the framing of the Alexa Together advertisements, the person being directly addressed and solicited, "you" is distinctly set apart from the family member in need of the service, often referred to in the third person "they" (e.g. "Give them a hand even from afar") or simply as the "loved one," with a formality reminiscent of a funeral service (Amazon, ibid). This subject/object dichotomy follows throughout the marketing and mirrors the surveillant dynamic of the services themselves, which are focused on allowing family members remote access to the elder or disabled family member. Whereas a phone call might enable a similar kind of connection with family members, Alexa Together offers an informational level of surveillance of the elderly or disabled person (receiving reports on the use of the Alexa device, for instance).

Though home medical assistance technologies are not new, the movement from an accessible telecommunication point to informationalized surveillance marks an important change in the role of these technologies. The care strategies for elderly or disabled family members have shifted from a paradigm of independent living facilitated by giving the elder/disabled person the ability to access medical services in times of emergency, to transferring control to external family members who can virtually "drop in" or monitor their loved one's datafied routines without them being aware. This extension of home medical devices from one-way communication devices to surveillant informational devices that depend on the collection of user data follows the trajectory of algorithmic culture that reduces people to their data profiles, valued for their perceived "objectivity" and predictive value. AI digital assistants provide the mechanism for data extraction to facilitate these goals and, in the process, expose the elderly or disabled person to heightened forms of surveillance in the home.

While Amazon claims that they are 'not in the business of selling your personal information to others' (Amazon, 2022: no page), they do share data with their own companies and third parties. The data captured through the Alexa Together service is tied into the third-party services that Amazon is partnering with that extend into public and health services. For instance, Alexa Together is connected to a 24/7 urgent response line that can be accessed via a voice request by saying *Alexa, call for help*. This feature connects the caller to 'trained agents who can request the dispatch of emergency responders—such as police, the fire department, or an ambulance—on your behalf' (Amazon, ibid). The Frequently Asked Questions (FAQs) explain that, since this is a private service, Alexa communication does not support 911 (a public emergency communication service) and cannot directly dispatch emergency services, instead the dispatcher can only request help from relevant agencies such as the police, fire department or ambulance. In other words, this privatized service acts as an infrastructural intermediary between the person in need and public services.

Amazon (ibid) asserts that 'as Alexa Together becomes even more advanced, you'll be able to do even more,' nodding to the culture of capital expansion and progress that undergirds the continued development of technologies to "do more," which usually indicates the parallel expansion into new forms and markets of data collection. Elderly and disabled people are already socially excluded in ways that structurally diminish (or fully deny) their autonomy, agency and authority. While there are existing models of caregiving that raise similar kinds of power imbalances, including retirement institutions and medical alert technologies, AI digital assistants potentially introduce new data harms, heightened by the integration with external applications and services. If data is the real commodity driving the expansion of AI digital assistants and smart home technologies, then we have to consider the true costs that our elderly and disabled family members may pay in terms of privacy, dignity, safety and autonomy in return for care.

Finally, the focus on surveilling family members in the home based on their age and ability creates an abundance of targeted data on populations who are often already hyper-surveilled in society (Eubanks, 2018). This ends up reproducing normative values about who is seen as "deserving" of bodily autonomy and independence and who is not. We are not all equally represented in the data streams that make up the reserves of Big Data. As in the over-policing of poor and minority neighbourhoods, hypervisibility often leads to disproportionate chances of being incorporated into institutions and systems of state control including policing, hospitals and asylums. Similarly, we might say that elderly and disabled people are at the frontline of digital home surveillance, raising questions about what it means to be incorporated into the Big Data networks that are increasingly shared between corporate and state institutions. Data harms in this context might violate personal privacy in ways that create unwanted or non-consented exposure to medical institutions, insurance companies, Medicaid, social security or other financial benefits. For instance, health data amassed from AI digital assistants could be used to track patterns of speech and assign diagnoses like Alzheimer's (Simon et al., 2022). Care outsourced to AI digital assistants might result in a reduction of human interaction and increase loneliness in elderly and disabled adults (Johnston, 2022). Altogether, many questions remain about the particular ways that the data from AI digital assistants is circulated and networked into social services, governance and city planning, and how this might impact elderly and disabled people, specifically.

Conclusion

Alexa Together offers just one vantage point from which we might explore issues of surveillance and AI digital assistants in the home within broader processes of AI urbanism. AI digital assistants function as powerful sites of data extraction within a vast apparatus of corporate and governmental data networks and political entities. The neoliberal context of deregulation and privatization that have enabled big tech companies, like Amazon, to consolidate market power and serve as a vital piece of information infrastructure, are some of the same political forces that have weakened social services, health access, affordable housing and financial safety nets for everyday people. In this landscape, elder care and support for disabled people has become more expensive, more tenuous and less accessible to those who require it. Alexa Together offers a technological solution to caregiving that obscures the fact that people are struggling to meet caregiving needs because the state has actively divested in the social, political and financial systems that would otherwise ensure that care work is accessible, sustainable and equitable to its citizenry. It is in this framework that we must situate AI digital assistants as surveillant devices and consider the larger political–economic factors that AI urbanism relies up on, at its core: ever-increasing levels of surveillance and data extraction that make people's intimate routines legible to the urban AI systems as a raw resource.

References

Alcántara, A.-M. (2021, May 10). Smart Speakers Go Beyond Waiting to Be Asked. *The Wall Street Journal*. Available at: https://www.wsj.com/articles/smart-speakers-go-beyond-waiting-to-be-asked-11620640802#:~:text=Smart%2Dspeaker%20 adoption%20continued%20to,to%20data%20from%20Edison%20Research. [Accessed 19/01/2023].

Amazon. (2022). *Alexa Together*. https://www.amazon.com/Alexa-Together/b?ie=UTF8 &node=21390531011&tag=googhydr-20&hvadid=512293179963&hvpos=&hve xid=&hvnetw=g&hvrand=8510020597883379033&hvpone=&hvptwo=&h vqmt=e&hvdev=c&hvdvcmdl=&hvlocint=&hvlocphy=9012579&hvtargid=k wd-1432099856796&ref=pd_sl_4wd9kixsf8_e [Accessed 19/01/2023].

Amazon Echo. (2016). *Introducing Amazon Echo*. Available at: https://www.youtube. com/watch?v=CYtb8RRj5r4 [Accessed 19/01/2023].

Amazon Echo & Alexa Stats. (2021). *Voicebot.Ai*. Available at: https://voicebot.ai/ amazon-echo-alexa-stats/ [Accessed 19/01/2023].

Barns, S. (2021). Out of the Loop? On the Radical and the Routine in Urban Big Data. *Urban Studies*, 58(15), 3203–3210.

Benjamin, R. (2019). *Race After Technology: Abolitionist Tools for the New Jim Code* (1st ed.). Polity.

Birnbaum, E. (2022). Tech spent big on lobbying last year. *Politico*. Available at: https://politi.co/33QmIWa [Accessed 19/01/2023].

Clark, E. (2019). Alexa, Are You Listening? How People Use Voice Assistants. *Clutch. co*. Available at: https://clutch.co/app-developers/resources/alexa-listening-how-people-use-voice-assistants [Accessed 19/01/2023].

Cowan, R. S. (1987). Less Work For Mother? *American Heritage*, 38(6). Available at: https://www.americanheritage.com/less-work-mother [Accessed 19/01/2023].

Cugurullo, F. (2020). Urban Artificial Intelligence: From Automation to Autonomy in the Smart City. *Frontiers in Sustainable Cities*, 2, 38.

Cugurullo, F. (2021). *Frankenstein Urbanism: Eco, Smart and Autonomous Cities, Artificial Intelligence and the End of the City*. Routledge.

Ensmenger, N. (2021). The Cloud is a Factory. In T. S. Mullaney, B. Peters, M. Hicks, & K. Philip (Eds.), *Your Computer Is on Fire*. MIT Press.

Eubanks, V. (2018). *Automating Inequality: How High-Tech Tools Profile, Police, and Punish the Poor*. St. Martin's Press.

Johnston, C. (2022). Ethical Design and Use of Robotic Care of the Elderly. *Journal of Bioethical Inquiry*, 19(1), 11–14.

Keister, L. A., & Southgate, D. (2022). *Inequality: A Contemporary Approach to Race, Class, and Gender* (2nd ed.). Cambridge University Press.

Kung, A. (2021). Today's Role of Smart Home and Voice Assistant Platforms. *Security Sales & Integration*. Available at: https://www.securitysales.com/automation/role-smart-home-voice-assistant-platforms/ [Accessed 19/01/2023].

Lawrence, H. (2021). Siri Disciplines. In T. S. Mullaney, B. Peters, M. Hicks, & K. Philip (Eds.), *Your Computer Is on Fire*. MIT Press.

Masina, F., Orso, V., Pluchino, P., Dainese, G., Volpato, S., Nelini, C., Mapelli, D., Spagnolli, A., & Gamberini, L. (2020). Investigating the Accessibility of Voice Assistants With Impaired Users: Mixed Methods Study. *Journal of Medical Internet Research*, 22(9), e18431.

Mtshali, P., & Khubisa, F. (2019). A Smart Home Appliance Control System for Physically Disabled People. *2019 Conference on Information Communications Technology and Society (ICTAS)*, 1–5.

Nicas, J. (2021). What Data About You Can the Government Get From Big Tech? *The New York Times*. Available at: https://www.nytimes.com/2021/06/14/technology/personal-data-apple-google-facebook.html [Accessed 19/01/2023].

Noble, S. (2018). *Algorithms of Oppression: How Search Engines Reinforce Racism* (1st ed.). NYU Press.

O'Neil, C. (2016). *Weapons of Math Destruction: How Big Data Increases Inequality and Threatens Democracy* (1st ed.). Crown.

Phan, T. (2019). Amazon echo and the aesthetics of whiteness. *Catalyst: Feminism, Theory, Technoscience*, 5(1), 1–38.

Pierce, D. (2018). Inside the Lab Where Amazon's Alexa Takes Over The World. *Wired*. Available at: https://www.wired.com/story/amazon-alexa-development-kit/ [Accessed 19/01/2023].

Pradhan, A., Lazar, A., & Findlater, L. (2020). Use of intelligent voice assistants by older adults with low technology use. *ACM Transactions on Computer-Human Interaction*, 27(4), 31:1–31:27.

Pradhan, A., Mehta, K., & Findlater, L. (2018). "Accessibility Came by Accident": Use of voice-controlled intelligent personal assistants by people with disabilities. *Proceedings of the 2018 CHI Conference on Human Factors in Computing Systems*, 1–13.

Redden, J., Brand, J., & Terzieva, V. (2020). Data Harm Record. *Data Justice Lab*. Available at: https://datajusticelab.org/data-harm-record/ [Accessed 19/01/2023].

ReportLinker. (2022). Smart Speakers Global Market Report 2022. *GlobeNewswire News Room*. Available at: https://www.globenewswire.com/news-release/2022/03/23/2408568/0/en/Smart-Speakers-Global-Market-Report-2022.html [Accessed 19/01/2023].

Schiller, H. (2020). Data Deprivation. In Karvonen, E., Melin, H., Nordenstreng, K., Puoskari, E., & Webster, F. (Eds.), *The Information Society Reader*, pp. 260–272. Routledge.

Simon, D. A., Evans, B. J., Shachar, C., & Cohen, I. G. (2022). Should Alexa Diagnose Alzheimer's?: Legal and Ethical Issues With At-home Consumer Devices. *Cell Reports Medicine*, 3(12), 100692.

Skelton, S. K. (2021). Big Tech eclipses telecoms and arms giants as biggest lobbying spenders. *ComputerWeekly.Com*. Available at: https://www.computerweekly.com/news/252498552/Big-Tech-eclipses-telecoms-and-arms-giants-as-biggest-lobbying-spenders [Accessed 19/01/2023].

Strengers, Y., & Kennedy, J. (2020). *The Smart Wife: Why Siri, Alexa, and Other Smart Home Devices Need a Feminist Reboot*. MIT Press.

Sweeney, M.E. (2021). Digital Assistants. In Agostinho, D., D'Ignazio, C., Ring, A., Thylstrup, N.B., & Veel, K. (Eds.), *Uncertain Archives*. MIT Press.

Tronto, J. C. (1998). An Ethic of Care. *Generations: Journal of the American Society on Aging*, 22(3), 15–20.

Whittaker, Z. (2018). *Echo is listening, but Amazon's not talking.* ZDNet. Available at: https://www.zdnet.com/article/amazon-the-least-transparent-tech-company/ [Accessed 19/01/2023].

Woods, H. S. (2018). Asking More of Siri and Alexa: Feminine Persona in Service of Surveillance Capitalism. *Critical Studies in Media Communication*, 35(4), 334–349.

Zuboff, S. (2019). *The Age of Surveillance Capitalism: The Fight for a Human Future at the New Frontier of Power* (1st ed.). Profile Books.

19

AI DOCTORS OR AI FOR DOCTORS?

Augmenting urban healthcare services through artificial intelligence

Zongtian Guo and Federico Cugurullo

Introduction

In China, artificial intelligence (AI) plays an important role in developing the national economy and it features prominently in the national development strategy (17th Central Committee of the Chinese Communist Party, 2016). Since 2013, China's central government has released a series of planning strategies and policies to promote the development of AI research and related industries (Cugurullo, 2021a; Roberts et al., 2021), such as *Made in China 2025*, the 2016 *Robotics Industry Development Plan* and the *Next Generation Artificial Intelligence Development Plan*. According to the final report of the 19th National Congress of the Chinese Communist Party (CCP), the CCP aims to turn China into an AI superpower by placing AI at the centre of the national economy and governance (18th Central Committee of the Chinese Communist Party, 2017). So far AI has been applied in a number of sectors, such as transportation, manufacturing and security, and the CCP's vision is reflected in several real-world examples including autonomous port terminals, industrial robots and facial recognition systems (Lee, 2018).

However, there is a significant gap between the technological aims of China's AI revolution and citizen well-being, especially in relation to aspects of governance such as healthcare and education where AI applications have been relatively scarce. In order to address this issue, all levels of government are now following the direction set by the CCP in an attempt to integrate AI technology into people's daily lives, and this is particularly evident in the healthcare sector. In recent years, the central government has released policies on Big Data healthcare (State Council of the People's Republic of China, 2016a), population health informatization (Hu et al., 2019) and Internet healthcare

DOI: 10.4324/9781003365877-23

(State Council of the People's Republic of China, 2016b), which have laid the foundation for the development of a novel sector: *AI healthcare*. For example, the Action Plan for Promoting Quality Development in the Health Industry (2019–2022) prioritizes the application of AI technology in urban and rural areas with weak medical resources and underdeveloped medical institutions (National Development and Reform Commission, 2019).

Zhang Wenhong, a prominent member of the CCP, points out that AI technologies play a key role in national public health services, particularly in response to epidemics (Xu, 2020). Since the COVID-19 pandemic, Chinese medical institutions and public health surveillance systems have utilized AI technology extensively in epidemiological investigations, medical diagnostics and treatment, and infection prevention, thereby narrowing the gap between China's AI vision and its actual implementation in the healthcare sector (Wang et al., 2022; Zhang et al., 2020). In the future, the CCP foresees that citizen health data from different medical institutions will be seamlessly integrated and consolidated into a national public health system. Through AI, the CCP expects to identify public health problems promptly (Zeng et al., 2021) and be able to assist so-called *grassroots doctors*[1] in disease diagnosis, treatment and patient data management, in an attempt to improve health practices in urban and rural areas that have been chronically under-resourced.

By drawing upon qualitative data collected in the field between 2021 and 2022, this chapter aims to critically examine two types of urban software agents that are prominent in the governance of urban health in China. Urban software agents can be broadly defined as the combination of urban AI and software agents. The concept of urban AI refers to the application of AI tech in urban areas, services and infrastructures (Cugurullo, 2020; Macrorie et al., 2019). Urban AIs are:

> artifacts operating in cities, which are capable of acquiring and making sense of information in the surrounding urban environment…They make decisions in an unsupervised manner, thus displaying a rudimentary form of thinking, and take actions which can potentially trigger radical changes in the city.
>
> *(Cugurullo, 2020: 3)*

Most urban AIs have a physical body through which they operate and act in urban spaces. For example, urban robotics has been widely employed in China during the COVID-19 pandemic. In Shanghai, hospitals have used robots to disinfect public environments and to deliver food to those who are quarantining in hotels (Chen et al., 2020). Conversely, a software agent does not have a physical body. It is a piece of pure software or, in other words, a computer program that exists and operates without continuous and direct human supervision (Huhns and Singh, 1998; Klügl, 2004). For example, a Chinese AI medical company called Airdoc developed a software capable of identifying 14 common retinal abnormalities, with an accuracy comparable to human retinal specialists (Lin et al., 2021). By measuring the size and shape of the lens in a patient's eye, the AI software can note changes in the retina, including discolouration, and it is now widely utilized in Chinese hospitals to assist clinicians in medical diagnostics.

In this chapter, we conceptually synthesize *urban AI* and *software agents* into *urban software agents* that can be defined as immaterial computer programs that manage and mediate urban services, by following goals set by human stakeholders. More specifically, we see urban software agents as a type of urban AI, in the sense that they are artificial intelligences which operate and act primarily in urban spaces. However, we distinguish them from other types of urban AI, such as autonomous cars and service robots, since they are virtual, i.e., non-physical entities which do not necessitate physical attributes. We divide this chapter into two main parts. In the next section, we analyse two urban software agents employed in China, specifically during the COVID-19 public health crisis. Subsequently, we provide an overview of urban software agents designed to practice medicine (i.e., AI doctors) and discuss their use in urban China. Overall, we offer a comparison between public and individual healthcare and shed light on how AI is infiltrating these practices, particularly in cities.

COVID-19 and AI-mediated epidemiological investigations

Particularly in China, COVID-19 has contributed to the formation of a variety of health-tracking applications whose key component is the *QR code* which is used to record the PCR test and vaccine status of citizens. On 11 February 2020, Hangzhou[2] introduced the first Chinese health QR code system, 'Hangzhou Health Code' (Wang, 2020). The local government devised a classification principle employing three colours (Red, Yellow and Green) to represent different exposure risks to COVID-19 among citizens (Mozur et al., 2020). Within a week, Hangzhou's health code approach and related classification principles were implemented in 11 additional cities within the province. Subsequently, on 15 February other provinces and cities quickly adopted similar health code systems based on Hangzhou's original QR code (Wang, 2020). Although the QR code remains a common denominator in the management of the COVID-19 crisis across different provinces, it is important to note that in China there is no unified or single national health code system. This is because, since 2020, numerous cities (megacities, in particular) have developed their own health code systems, such as Guangzhou's Suikang Code (穗康码),[3] Beijing's Health Kit (健康宝) and Shanghai's Suishen Code (随申码).

Closely related to health code systems, an epidemiological investigation is a crucial method for identifying COVID-19 infections and providing evidence of the spaces where the virus is circulating. The results of an epidemiological investigation also determine citizens' risk of exposure to COVID-19, thereby influencing their QR codes. According to the National Health Commission, when a Chinese city receives a report of one or more COVID-19 cases, its disease control and prevention agency is required to complete an initial epidemiological investigation within 24 hours. During a standard epidemiological investigation, an investigator group is supposed to immediately contact all confirmed cases to track their recent movements. Moreover, investigator groups must identify the source of infection (including infection modes, pathways and sources) as well as individuals who have been in close contact with infected individuals (The National Health Commission of the People's Republic of China, 2022). The guidelines require investigators to manually compile, compare, filter and analyse a huge quantity of data in a short period of time (The National Health Commission of the People's Republic of China, 2022). In addition, standard epidemiological investigations rely mostly on landlines and mobile phones to communicate with citizens who often hang up or refuse to respond.

In late 2021, the Omicron variant began to spread and epidemiological investigations became extremely time-consuming and labor-intensive. To address this issue, Chinese authorities turned to AI (Liu et al., 2022). Today, urban software agents are widely utilized in Chinese cities to reduce investigator labour and to accelerate epidemiological investigations. For example, Shenzhen Municipal Health Commission Calling and international technology company Tencent jointly implemented the 'Shenzhen's Epidemiological Investigation and Disposal System' (Shenzhen Disease Prevention and Control Center, 2022). Similarly, the Shanghai Municipal Health Commission and iFLYTEK, another Chinese technology company, developed the 'Smart Speech Robot' (Tang & Xuan, 2022). These examples integrate AI solutions, such as automated calls, voice recognition software, natural language processing and human–machine coupling (Xiao Ke, 2022). They are *urban* because they operate almost exclusively in Chinese cities and impact the health of urban residents and, in the remainder of the section, we provide a practical example of how this immaterial AI has been deployed to manage COVID-19 in urban China.

There are three interconnected steps. First, the urban software agent automatically notifies citizens suspected of having caught COVID by sending them a message, nudging them to answer the investigators' call. In Shenzen, for instance, people receive the following message:

The Shenzhen Municipal Health Commission is calling. Please answer the call. The virus is merciless, while our society is full of love. So let's combat COVID-19 together.

Shanghai's citizens receive a similar message:

> The investigator is calling, so please answer the phone and cooperate with the investigations. Thank you very much.

Second, the urban software agents include digital assistants to initiate contact with citizens on the telephone. In this case, while the digital assistant is communicating with citizens, inquiring about their health and movements, human investigators can monitor multiple conversations simultaneously to improve their efficiency. For instance, in Shanghai, iFLYTEK applied this AI solution during the 2022 outbreak and its digital assistants managed to call around 70,000 people in just three hours. Furthermore, the human investigators can intervene and join the conversation if required. At the end of the call, citizens receive an automated message with information on prevention measures or a questionnaire if the human investigator requires further information.

Third, by means of speech recognition software and natural language processing, the urban software agent identifies and extracts core information from the text of the telephone conversations. For example, if a citizen mentions that he or she took Line 5 of Shenzhen Metro, the system then displays all station names of Line 5 on a screen and the human investigator can select the specific stations mentioned by the citizen. Once the phone call ends, the system automatically generates a preliminary epidemiological report. The report displays relevant information about the citizen on a standardized template including a list of the places where he or she has been (including the time and duration of the stay), the trip mode and his or her close contacts.

Every time there is a local outbreak, the government's plan is to use the aforementioned AI technologies and solutions to identify infected individuals and their close contacts (Liu et al., 2022). In essence, AI becomes a tool to identify those people who are infected and who the government will eventually quarantine. It is also important to note that China employs authoritarian governance strategies to stop the spread of COVID-19, as the recent outbreak in Shanghai exemplifies (Gao & Zhang, 2021). AI is now extending Chinese authoritarianism, but its actions are not those of a fully autonomous societal actor. Table 19.1 provides an overview of the timeline of the Shanghai COVID-19 outbreak in the spring of 2022, including the primary control measures and responsible authorities. This table highlights how urban software agents were deployed to manage the COVID-19 pandemic while key decisions were ultimately made by human actors.

During the early events listed in Table 19.1, urban software agents were extensively used to collect epidemiological data that was shared with Shanghai's Leading Group. From a governance perspective, human stakeholders made the final decision, not AI. This is an observation that we want

TABLE 19.1 Timeline of the 2022 Shanghai COVID-19 outbreak

Time	Primary control measures	Responsible authorities
1 March 2022	• The first case of the 2022 Shanghai COVID-19 outbreak was identified. The urban area where the first case was discovered was immediately categorized as *middle-risk* by Shanghai's Leading Group[a] on COVID-19 Prevention and Control.	Shanghai's Leading Group
12 March 2022	• Shanghai's Leading Group on COVID-19 Prevention and Control required all citizens to provide proof of a negative PCR test (within 48 hours) when entering or exiting Shanghai. • Shanghai Municipal Education Commission decided to close all kindergartens, pre, primary, middle and high schools.	Shanghai's Leading Group Shanghai Municipal Education Commission
13 March 2022	• Shanghai's universities and colleges went into lockdown on the basis of the Leading Group's decision.	Shanghai's Leading Group
17 March 2022	• The Leading Group decided to enforce mass testing twice within 48 hours in the whole city.	Shanghai's Leading Group
28 March 2022	• The Leading Group decided that eastern Shanghai (Pudong) should be locked down for mass testing, and western Shanghai (Puxi) should be locked down for another four days.	Shanghai's Leading Group
2 April 2022	• Sun Chunlan[b] went to Shanghai for an inspection visit, and she called for resolute and swift actions to stop the virus.	CCP
4 April 2022	• The Leading Group decided to continue the lockdown and to extend it to the entire city.	Shanghai's Leading Group

Source: authors' original.

[a] A Leading Group is a task force created to solve a particular problem, by combining the expertise of multiple government offices. For example, during the COVID-19 pandemic, Shanghai established an ad hoc Leading Group including 54 civil servants from different government offices.

[b] She is a member of the Politburo of the Chinese Communist Party and second Vice Premier of the People's Republic of China.

to stress in light of the recent debates in governance studies and urban studies, in which scholars have been questioning the extent to which AI can actually make decisions (Bullock et al., 2022; Cugurullo, 2021b). In the case of the 2022 Shanghai outbreak detailed in Table 19.1, key decisions related to lockdowns and mass-testing strategies, for instance, were made by the Leading Group, i.e., *human* city managers, experts and policymakers. AI simply provided the data that informed those decisions. In a nutshell, the role of AI was to collect and then rapidly analyse and synthesize vast volumes of information, rather than developing and enforcing policies.

AI doctors

For a long time, China's medical system has been plagued by insufficient and unevenly distributed medical resources (Lv et al., 2019), medical inequity (Wang et al., 2019) and an internal brain drain, a phenomenon whereby educated medical professionals gravitate towards the largest Chinese cities (Zweig, 2006). China spends only 6.5% of its GDP on the national medical system, which is significantly less than the United States and most European Countries (National Health Commission of the People's Republic of China, 2022). To contextualize and better understand this figure, it is important to remember that China provides healthcare services to 18% of the world's population. In addition, in China the average rate of misdiagnosis is 30%, reaching 40% for severe cases, especially in places where medical facilities are underdeveloped (Gao et al., 2019). In this context, the Chinese government is pioneering AI solutions to improve the speed and accuracy of medical diagnoses. AI serves as an advanced tool that human doctors use to facilitate their existing practices. More specifically, we can observe two distinct yet related cases.

First, AI is transforming China's healthcare in the field of medical imaging, particularly in cities where the most advanced hospitals featuring AI technology are located. In *Guangdong Second Provincial General Hospital*, for instance, AI assists radiologists by analysing multiple X-ray images in a couple of seconds and by enhancing diagnosis accuracy. Second, in addition to the AI applications in Chinese hospitals, the combination of AI and healthcare appears in novel ways in the daily lives of many Chinese citizens on the street. A private company called *Ping An Good Doctor* (PAGD) has developed what are informally called "One-minute Clinics," based upon AI technologies (Figure 19.1). They are located in urban areas with high population densities to serve as many residents as possible. More specifically, PAGD's One-minute Clinics have been installed in shopping malls, community centres, university campuses and public spaces in over 50 Chinese cities (Ping An Good Doctor, 2018).

When a patient enters this one square metre space, an "AI doctor" begins to operate autonomously. This is essentially a software agent that PAGD has fed with data from more than 300 million consultations. Initially, this

FIGURE 19.1 A One-minute Clinic in Shenzhen.

Source: authors' original.

virtual doctor communicates with the patient, asking the individual to describe his or her symptoms or disease before writing a medical history and providing a preliminary diagnosis. During this process, the virtual doctor also asks the patient to use the examination equipment for basic tests (such as blood pressure) inside the box (Figure 19.2). Once the AI doctor has examined a patient's general condition and symptoms, the system immediately connects her or him with a human doctor who conducts a more detailed diagnosis and issues the appropriate prescription. According to PAGD, the AI doctor serves de facto as an assistant to the human doctor (Ping An Good Doctor, 2018).

Discussion: AI *for* doctors

The common denominator between the two cases examined above is that AI does not replace doctors but rather supports them. Whether it is software analysing X-ray images in a hospital or a digital agent providing a preliminary medical analysis in a pop-up clinic on the street, the final decision is in the hands of a human doctor. This shows that AI is not a fully autonomous

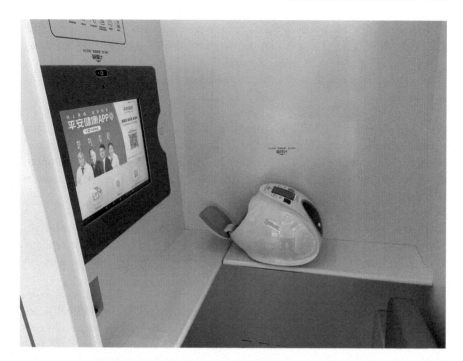

FIGURE 19.2   A blood-pressure monitor inside the same clinic.

Source: authors' original.

agent yet. Overall, in China, AI is expanding and improving existing urban health practices led by humans. It does not replace these practices or introduce new practices and thus, it would be inaccurate to introduce the notion of *AI doctors* given that, in practice, AI is working *for doctors* instead of superseding them. As an interviewee from a prominent Chinese AI medical imaging research institute noted, 'AI healthcare is currently at a very early stage. Artificial intelligence may be able to replace humans in the future, but not for several decades.'

In certain aspects of medicine, AI can outperform human doctors, but in terms of general intelligence, that is not the case. For instance, AI can exceed human limitations in terms of perception and provide doctors with a more-than-human visual understanding of a given disease. However, complex diseases, especially when they vary from person to person, necessitate the expertise and experience of human doctors. It is also important to note that human doctors themselves do not fully trust AI and believe it is their responsibility to be in charge and protect their patients from the harm that machines might accidentally cause. Fears and concerns abound when it comes to AI (see Cugurullo and Acheampong, 2023). In the words of a surgeon working in a public hospital,

The machine can improve the accuracy of a surgical operation, but the doctor should be able to judge and control the AI, otherwise something will go wrong. Also, if a doctor makes a mistake, only one patient gets affected. However, if an AI program makes an error, it will harm many patients.

The surgeon notes the fallibility of AI as well as its amplifying effects. It is interesting to see that while some patients do not fully agree with this statement, they seem to be afraid of completely losing healthcare's human dimension. According to a typical patient from Guangzhou with no expertise in medicine or AI:

AI will eventually replace human doctors because it can provide brilliant solutions for patients. However, I think it won't be a complete replacement. Human doctors and machines should figure out a way to collaborate.

Overall, our inquiry into China's use of urban software agents in healthcare reveals three interconnected implications for the study and understanding of urban AI. First is the question of autonomy. Urban software agents are generally portrayed in the literature as autonomous artificial intelligences, meaning that they can act and affect urban services without being directed or supervised by humans (Barns, 2021; Cugurullo, 2021b). Our case studies show that the autonomy of urban software agents is a complex and multifaceted attribute whose empirical and theoretical understanding requires considerable nuance. Being autonomous is not a black-and-white issue and the way AIs manifest their autonomy needs to be considered in relation to the specific context and scope. For example, while it is true that urban software agents support epidemiological investigations in urban China and the AI doctors that operate in pop-up clinics can indeed act in the absence of human supervision, their sphere of influence is actually very limited. They are autonomous only in relation to small and specific tasks, such as collecting information on who has been in close contact with someone with COVID-19 and performing a basic medical examination. However, when it comes to decision-making in delicate situations where the stakes are high, these digital agents manifest little or no autonomy. Instead, it is a human representative of the local government that orders a lockdown or a human doctor that confirms a final diagnosis.

A second interrelated implication concerns the meaning of intelligence in urban AI. Human geographers who specialize in AI have stressed that intelligence is a heterogeneous category comprising a variety of skills and capabilities that different AI technologies can in turn manifest (Lynch, 2021; Lynch and Del Casino Jr, 2020). Our case study research on urban software agents resonates with this conceptualization of intelligence and, more specifically, points to a twofold distinction: *narrow AI* and *general AI*. The bodiless urban AIs that we have discussed in this chapter present a very narrow type of intelligence, in the sense that their ability to understand and act is related to specific and small tasks, such as analysing X-ray images and understanding blood pressure readings. They do not manifest what in computer science literature is called 'artificial general intelligence' (AGI): 'the ability to achieve a variety of goals, and carry out a variety of tasks, in a variety of different contexts and environments' like humans do (Goertzel, 2014: 2). AGI, as our research shows, is still a long way from the current capabilities of urban software agents. Whether or not urban AI will ever be capable of developing AGI so that it might be applied in contexts going beyond discrete and narrowly defined tasks remains an open question, but it is worth remembering that this type of technology is still in its infancy and its capabilities are growing rapidly (Callaway, 2020).

Third, because of their narrow intelligence, the actions of the digital agents examined in this chapter are confined to small, but nonetheless influential, domains of urban governance and public policy. Therefore, despite their relatively limited intelligence and autonomy, we should not underestimate the impact of urban software agents, especially when their work legitimates governing actions. In this chapter, for instance, we have shown how in the urban governance of COVID-19, Chinese city managers and policymakers have made key decisions, such as enforcing lockdowns and mass testing, on the basis of information that was collected and interpreted by AI. As Kitchin, Lauriault and McArdle (2017: 10) remind us, it is often the case that 'data are cooked and utilized to perform political work.' In our case study, data have been produced by non-human intelligences in ways that many of us would not comprehend. Explainable Artificial Intelligence scholars warn us that AIs interpret information and generate knowledge, by following intricate cognitive and logical patterns that not even experts in computer science and engineering can fully understand (Langer et al., 2021). We, as citizens, should therefore be cautious in accepting a system of governance driven by an obscure epistemological process.

Conclusions

Our case studies of public and individual healthcare in Chinese cities have shown that, particularly since the COVID-19 crisis, AI in the shape of immaterial urban software agents has increasingly mediated existing health practices. In both cases, AI has not made human agents obsolete, nor has it replaced human-led practices. When AI infiltrates the governance of COVID-19 outbreaks in Chinese cities, or when it influences the healthcare services for individual citizens, what we observe is *augmentation* rather than replacement, by expanding current services and policies. More specifically, AI is adding novel processes of data collection, analysis and interpretation which produce information that is ultimately employed by human decision-makers to improve healthcare services.

We have shown that, in the context of urban health, AI is currently an advanced tool that human doctors and city managers use to facilitate their existing activities. AI is not an autonomous societal actor *yet* and, given the fast speed at which AI tech is now developing, we cannot exclude the possibility that this condition might change and alter the current equilibrium between human and artificial intelligences in urban governance. Future research should therefore monitor the potential autonomy of urban software agents under the assumption that being autonomous is an attribute that is fixed neither in time nor in space.

Finally, in this chapter, we have emphasized the sheer amount of personal data that AI is collecting and analysing in Chinese cities. In the context of our case studies, AI is collecting information that relates mostly, but not exclusively, to the health of citizens. Whether it happens through an AI-mediated epidemiological investigation or inside a pop-up clinic, the process of data collection is intensive and it captures a vast range of personal information, including the individual's location, her or his movements in cities and her or his network of friends and relatives. We conclude this chapter with a warning about a phenomenon called *function creep* (Greenfield, 2017; Koops, 2021). Data collected for a seemingly neutral and harmless function, like healthcare for example, can subsequently serve another function and become the foundation of something completely different such as a comprehensive surveillance state. It remains to be seen how urban software agents will evolve in the coming decades.

Notes

1 In China, grassroot doctors are general practitioners working in remote towns and villages.
2 Hangzhou is the capital of the Zhejiang province in Eastern China and home to the headquarters of prominent high-tech companies such as Alibaba and Tencent which are key players in the Chinese AI industry.
3 Guangzhou is the capital of the Guangdong province in the south of China.

References

17th Central Committee of the Chinese Communist Party. (2016). *The 13th Five Year Plan for Economic and Social Development of the People's Republic of China (2016)* 12th National People's Congress: Communist Party of China. (trans. Compilation and Translation Bureau) Available at: https://en.ndrc.gov.cn/policies/202105/P020210527785800103339.pdf [Accessed 19/01/2023].

18th Central Committee of the Chinese Communist Party. (2017). *Securea Decisive Victory in Buildinga Moderately Prosperous Society in All Respects and Strive fort he Great Success of Socialism with Chinese Characteristics for a New Era*. 19th National Congress of the Chinese Communist Party: Xi Jinping. Available at: https://www.mfa.gov.cn/ce/ceil/eng/zt/19thCPCNationalCongress/W02017112 0127269060039.pdf [Accessed 19/01/2023].

Barns, S. (2021). Out of the loop? On the radical and the routine in urban big data. *Urban Studies*, 58(15), 3203–3210.

Bullock, J., Chen, Y.-C., Himmelreich, J., Hudson, V.M., Korinek, A., Young, M., & Zhang, B. (2022). *The Oxford Handbook of AI Governance*. Oxford University Press, Oxford.

Callaway, E. (2020). 'It will change everything': DeepMind's AI makes gigantic leap in solving protein structures. *Nature*, 588(7837), 203–205.

Chen, B., Marvin, S., & While, A. (2020). Containing COVID-19 in China: AI and the robotic restructuring of future cities. *Dialogues in Human Geography*, 10(2), 238–241.

Greenfield, A. (2017). *Radical technologies: the design of everyday life*. Verso, London.

Cugurullo, F. (2020). Urban artificial intelligence: From automation to autonomy in the smart city. *Frontiers in Sustainable Cities*, 2, 38.

Cugurullo, F. (2021a). "One AI to rule them all": The Unification of Chinese Urban Governance Under Artificial Intelligence. *GREEN*, 1(1), 123–126.

Cugurullo, F. (2021b). *Frankenstein Urbanism: Eco, Smart and Autonomous Cities, Artificial Intelligence and the End of the City*. Routledge.

Cugurullo, F., & Acheampong, R. A. (2023). Fear of AI: an inquiry into the adoption of autonomous cars in spite of fear, and a theoretical framework for the study of artificial intelligence technology acceptance. *AI & Society*, 1–16. DOI: 10.1007/s00146-022-01598-6.

Gao, J., & Zhang, P. (2021). China's public health policies in response to COVID-19: From an "Authoritarian" perspective. *Frontiers in Public Health*, 2085.

Gao, P., Li, X., Zhao, Z., Zhang, N., Ma, K., & Li, L. (2019). Diagnostic errors in fatal medical malpractice cases in Shanghai, China: 1990–2015. *Diagnostic Pathology*, 14(1), 1–11.

Goertzel, B. (2014). Artificial General Intelligence: Concept, State of the Art, and Future Prospects. *Journal of Artificial General Intelligence*, 5(1), 1–48.

Hu, H., Xie, L., Chen, Q., Gao, X., Pi, Y., & Dai, T. (2019). Analysis and Measurement of China's Population Health Informatization Development Strategy. In *MEDINFO 2019: Health and Wellbeing e-Networks for All* (pp. 1388–1392). IOS Press.

Huhns, M. N., & Singh, M. P. (1998). *Readings in agents*. Morgan Kaufmann.

Koops, B. J. (2021). The concept of function creep. *Law, Innovation and Technology*, 13(1), 29–56.

Kitchin, R., Lauriault, T. P., & McArdle, G. (2017). Data and the city. In Kitchin, R., Lauriault, T. P., & McArdle, G. (Eds.), *Data and the City*. Routledge, London.

Klügl, F. (2004). Applications of software agents. *Künstliche Intell.*, 18(2), 5–10.

Langer, M., Oster, D., Speith, T., Hermanns, H., Kästner, L., Schmidt, E., … Baum, K. (2021). What do we want from Explainable Artificial Intelligence (XAI)?–A stakeholder perspective on XAI and a conceptual model guiding interdisciplinary XAI research. *Artificial Intelligence*, 296, 103473.

Lee, K. F. (2018). *AI Superpowers: China, Silicon Valley, and the new world order*. Houghton Mifflin, Boston and New York.

Lin, D., Xiong, J., Liu, C., Zhao, L., Li, Z., Yu, S., Wu, X., Ge, Z., Hu, X., & Wang, B. (2021). Application of Comprehensive Artificial intelligence Retinal Expert (CARE) system: a national real-world evidence study. *The Lancet Digital Health*, 3(8), e486–e495.

Liu, J., Liu, M., & Liang, W. (2022). The Dynamic COVID-Zero Strategy in China. *China CDC Weekly*, 4(4), 74–75.

Lv, Q., Jiang, Y., Qi, J., Zhang, Y., Zhang, X., Fang, L., Tu, L., Yang, M., Liao, Z., & Zhao, M. (2019). Using mobile apps for health management: A new health care mode in China. *JMIR mHealth and uHealth*, 7(6), e10299.

Lynch, C. R. (2021). Artificial emotional intelligence and the intimate politics of robotic sociality. *Space and Polity*, 25(2), 184–201.

Lynch, C. R., & Del Casino Jr, V. J. (2020). Smart spaces, information processing, and the question of intelligence. *Annals of the American Association of Geographers*, 110(2), 382–390.

Macrorie, R., Marvin, S., & While, A. (2019). Robotics and automation in the city: A research agenda. *Urban Geography*, 42(2), 197–217.

Mozur, P., Zhong, R., & Krolik, A. (2020). In coronavirus fight, China gives citizens a color code, with red flags. *The New York Times*, 1(3).

National Development and Reform Commission. (2019). Action Plan for Promoting Quality Development of Health Industry (2019–2022) Available at: http://www.gov.cn/xinwen/2019-09/30/5435160/files/4ab8512c9b3d40a49792fd633c32c337.pdf [Accessed 19/01/2023].

National Health Commission of the People's Republic of China. (2022). Statistical Bulletin for China's Health Care Development in 2021. Available at: http://www.gov.cn/xinwen/2022-07/12/content_5700670.htm [Accessed 19/01/2023].

Ping An Good Doctor. (2018). AI Technology Makes Ping An Good Doctor's 'One Minute Clinic' the Most Popular 'New Invention' at PharmChina. Available at: https://www.pagd.net/newsPage/newDetail/4-1-4 [Accessed 19/01/2023].

Roberts, H., Cowls, J., Morley, J., Taddeo, M., Wang, V., & Floridi, L. (2021). The Chinese approach to artificial intelligence: An analysis of policy, ethics, and regulation. *AI & Society*, 36(1), 59–77. https://doi.org/10.1007/s00146-020-00992-2.

Shenzhen Disease Prevention and Control Center. (2022). Eliminate "scam" suspicion! A secret trick to help Shenzhen's investigators track virus. Available at: https://mp.weixin.qq.com/s/Z2wO-yv9RuzpqkTe1Qe0Rg [Accessed 19/01/2023].

State Council of the People's Republic of China. (2016a). Guiding Opinions of the General Office of the State Council on Promoting and Regulating the Application and Development of Big Data in Health and Medical Care. Available at: http://lawinfochina.com/display.aspx?id=26003=law [Accessed 19/01/2023].

State Council of the People's Republic of China. (2016b). *Guiding Opinions of the State Council on Vigorously Advancing the "Internet Plus" Action*.

Tang, X., & Xuan, Z. (2022). 70,000 people Covid-19 tested in 3 hours! "Intelligent voice robots" participate in the fight against outbreak with high efficiency. *People's Daily Online*.

The National Health Commission of the People's Republic of China. (2022). *The prevention and control of 2019 Novel Coronavirus Pneumonia (9th Edition)*. Available at: http://www.gov.cn/xinwen/2022-06/28/5698168/files/9585944023424f45a4b4d522b5f5c034.pdf [Accessed 19/01/2023].

Wang, Z., Chen, Y., Pan, T., Liu, X., & Hu, H. (2019). The comparison of healthcare utilization inequity between URRBMI and NCMS in rural China. *International Journal for Equity in Health*, 18(1), 1–12.

Wang, H. (2020). Hangzhou Health Code: A local innovation in risk management and its extension. *Zhejiang Academic Journal*, 3.

Wang, T., Zhang, Y., Liu, C., & Zhou, Z. (2022). Artificial intelligence against the first wave of COVID-19: Evidence from China. *BMC Health Services Research*, 22(1), 1–14.

Xiao Ke. (2022). Digital Investigation Solutions for Outbreak | Through more efficient and intelligent outbreak control, we are able to achieve accurate outbreak prevention and control. *36Kr*. Available at: https://www.36dianping.com/dianping/5550640113 [Accessed 19/01/2023].

Xu, J. (2020). Data integration is key to integrating public health systems with artificial intelligence, *Southern Metropolis Daily*. Available at: https://www.sohu.com/a/407449086_161795 [Accessed 19/01/2023].

Zhang, X., Lin, H., Wang, J., Chengdong, X., Hu, M., Meng, B., Liu, D., Xu, M., Zhu, C., & Wang, G. (2020). Scientific and technical suggestions for the construction of digital public health emergency management system in China. *Geomatics and Information Science of Wuhan Universit*, 45(5), 633–639.

Zeng, D., Cao, Z., & Neill, D. B. (2021). Artificial intelligence–enabled public health surveillance—from local detection to global epidemic monitoring and control. In Xing, L., Giger, M. L., & Min, J. K. (Eds.), *Artificial Intelligence in Medicine* (pp. 437–453). Elsevier.

Zweig, D. (2006). Competing for talent: China's strategies to reverse the brain drain. *The International Labour Review*, 145, 65.

20

ALGORITHMS AND RACIAL DISCRIMINATION IN THE US HOUSING MARKET

Eva Rosen and Philip Garboden

Introduction

Tenant screening is an act of gatekeeping, where landlords accept certain tenants while excluding others (DeLuca et al., 2013; Desmond, 2016; Hartman and Robinson, 2003; Korver-Glenn, 2018; Rosen, 2014; Rosen and Garboden, 2022). This gatekeeping employs technologies that range enormously depending on a variety of contextual factors: a low-income homeowner looking for a roommate to help cover the mortgage might explicitly select a friend from church, while a corporate landlord might use an algorithm based on credit scores, criminal background and income. But regardless of the technology employed, all tenant screening comes down to essentially the same process: the gatekeeper leverages observable characteristics of the applicant to predict how he or she will behave in the unit and minimize the risk of financial loss. In other words, the goal of screening is to accurately estimate a tenant's latent risk profile, which is necessarily unobservable as it manifests exclusively in the future.[1]

Different gatekeepers prioritize different types of behaviour and use different sets of characteristics to develop their selection models, but a prediction problem nevertheless rests at the heart of all screening. It thus is not surprising that, as with other forms of prediction, tenant screening is increasingly given over to algorithmic rather than personal or heuristic technologies (Fields, 2022; Rosen et al., 2021; So, 2022). In this chapter, we ask: When and why do some landlords rely on screening software based on algorithms? What implications do algorithms and other computational methods of tenant screening have on housing access for poor renters? In what ways are they reflective of extant social relations of exclusion, distinction and

DOI: 10.4324/9781003365877-24

discrimination? What power do algorithms have – if any – to reduce or exacerbate such outcomes?

Of particular interest is the role that algorithmic screening plays in issues of housing discrimination, particularly against Black and Latino households, women and individuals receiving housing subsidies. Racial discrimination and segregation in the United States have remained remarkably durable over the last century (Logan and Stults, 2021), but the ways in which such social structures are maintained have evolved significantly away from overt racial bias to increasingly more covert processes based on automation and digital technologies. We argue that landlords' use of screening technology puts them in line with a larger set of processes that are becoming increasingly automated within the smart city (Cugurullo, 2020, 2021; Fields, 2022; Garboden et al., 2021; Goodspeed, 2015). Urban sociology has long documented a varied set of processes through which urbanites are sorted across space (Park and Burgess, 1925; Sampson, 2012; Zorbaugh, 1929) but in this chapter, we connect these processes to the use of algorithmic technology, raising questions for the study of automation and artificial intelligence (AI) within urban areas.

We find that algorithms play a key role in how landlords screen tenants, especially for landlords with large property portfolios who commonly use screening software tools that rely on algorithms to weigh various tenant characteristics, thereby purporting to estimate tenant risk profiles. Like all so-called automation, however, algorithms do not operate outside the realm of social relations: far from it. Landlords have a great deal of discretion in the degree to which they use this technology and how they interpret it. The inputs and thresholds of the algorithms themselves are, of course, tuned by humans (often by property owners themselves), who seek to align them with often idiosyncratic ideas of what constitutes a "good" tenant. Furthermore, we argue that like many prediction technologies, tenant screening algorithms do not succeed or fail purely on the accuracy of their predictions, but rather serve a function in and of themselves. Specifically, they represent a technology that, given current laws in the United States, is largely unassailable by fair housing testing and litigation, which is the main mechanism to enforce fair housing in the US context. By using an algorithm to make screening decisions, landlords can legally claim that their selections are free from both implicit and explicit bias and thereby protect themselves from lawsuits.

More than the algorithms themselves – which we do not observe here directly – we argue that the way landlords interpret, understand and use algorithms is key. In this chapter, we discuss a range of screening techniques, from those with explicit discriminatory intent (where proxies are used because landlords understand them to result in unequal outcomes that are profitable to their business model) to those where the discriminatory outcomes are unintentional and collateral to other objectives, and finally to instances in which algorithms are tweaked to help landlords privilege certain criteria over others, at times resulting in more inclusive and equitable screening decisions. We find that it is not the use of the algorithm in and of itself, but rather why the algorithm is used, how it is made and how it is tuned that matters when it comes to discriminatory outcomes. The algorithm remains nevertheless meaningful insofar as it obfuscates and legitimizes discrimination, providing it with a patina of fairness that more informal methods lack.

Background: automated technologies in the urban environment and implications for inequality

The use of screening algorithms such as those used by landlords in the housing market is a powerful manifestation of the broader trend of the emerging role that technology plays in managing cities. In the era of AI, smart cities integrate technologies across functional areas to solve social problems, applying digital technologies to connect and streamline existing problems like traffic, crime, poor access to public services and even access to political participation (Green & Franklin-Hodge, 2019). One such smart technology approach involves the collection of so-called Big Data which is then used to train predictive models on all manner of routine urban processes (Barns, 2021; Batty, 2018; Cugurullo, 2020; Garboden, 2019). These technologies generally aim to accomplish any of three possible goals: efficiency, prediction and fairness.

Digital technologies play an ever-increasing role in the realm of housing, creating an *automated landlord* (see Fields, 2022), where 'landlord tech' – including everything from selective advertising on online platforms such as Facebook, to tenant screening, to rent collection and eviction processes – is automated, initiated and, in some cases, carried out with technological assistance (Maalsen and Sadowski, 2019). Research shows how digital technologies are mobilized in the housing supply chain to simplify and make the tenant management process more efficient, with the goal of more accurately predicting who will make a good tenant, providing legal protection during the screening process (Rosen et al., 2021; So, 2022) and ultimately, as a means to realize the financialization of housing (Fields, 2022; Fields and Raymond, 2021).

In the world of landlording and tenant screening, automation is a fairly simple process. The majority of tenant screening tools provide the landlord with a series of data points pulled from large public and proprietary databases of credit scores, criminal histories, evictions and more. The actual predictive model used by the screening tool is often little more than comparing these data points to the landlord's screening criteria and rejecting any tenants who fail to qualify on any measure (So, 2022). Of course, as we will describe below, more sophisticated models are also utilized, whereby different criteria can be compensatory (e.g., a bad credit score can be compensated for by a housing voucher) or where security deposits can be raised, or insurance purchased, to mitigate the financial risks of a particular tenant (Rogal, 2006). The nominal goal of any of these tools is again, to reduce operating costs to the landlord by expediting screening (efficiency), to decrease risks of default and vandalism (prediction) and to avoid housing discrimination (fairness). Questions remain, however, as to whether such goals are achieved.

Automated screening techniques are often touted as a tool to reduce the sorts of inequality and discrimination that emerge from both landlords' implicit and explicit bias (Benjamin, 2019; Broussard 2018). An algorithm, this logic suggests, will focus only on legal inputs when making its determination and is thus unable to manifest unequal treatment on attributes it does not utilize in its model. Indeed, landlords increasingly rely on purportedly unbiased computer software to screen tenants for exactly this reason – following this process shields them from any legal claims of discrimination. By using technologies that are often invisible to the applicant, landlords can legitimize decisions that are ultimately not too different from low-tech discrimination. In this way, rather than preventing discrimination and dismantling inequality, automated technologies used by landlords exacerbate a pre-existing power dynamic between themselves and their tenants (Desmond, 2016; Fields, 2022; Garboden and Rosen, 2018, 2019; Reosti, 2020), making housing potentially less affordable, less available and of lower quality to tenants.

This chapter connects these tenant screening technologies to research in sociology, economics and science and technology studies examining how purportedly race-blind algorithms – used in employment, criminal justice and even self-driving cars – can actually punish the poor and reinforce racial inequality (Benjamin, 2019; Broussard, 2018; Eubanks, 2018; Noble, 2018). Benjamin delineates several pathways through which 'discriminatory design' in technology operates to reinforce and recreate racial inequality such as that which existed in the American Jim Crow South 'by explicitly amplifying racial hierarchies; by ignoring but thereby replicating social divisions; or by aiming to fix racial bias but ultimately doing quite the opposite' (Benjamin, 2019: 142). As she puts it, algorithms streamline discrimination 'making it easier to sift, sort, and *justify*' racial stratification (Benjamin, ibid). This body of literature demonstrates that despite some of their proponents' claims, algorithms often fail to prevent racism or dismantle racial inequality, and often even aid in the targeting and endangering of marginalized groups (Benjamin, 2019; Broussard, 2018; Eubanks, 2018; Fields and Raymond, 2021; McElroy, 2020).

We also connect this question to a literature in economics that examines the effects of a set of local initiatives and laws in the United States referred to as 'Ban the Box.' With the goal of reducing bias at the application stage, this type of legislation makes it illegal for employers to ask candidates about their criminal history on job applications. This body of research interrogates the question of what gatekeepers (such as employers) do when they lack certain information about applicants (such as criminal history) during the screening process – in this way, it provides an interesting corollary to landlords who use the screening process to try to predict who will make a good tenant. Findings show that when information on criminal records is removed, rather than reducing bias, employers fall back on and even amplify other knowable data points such as race, which may be correlated with criminal history. In this way, 'Ban the Box' initiatives appear to backfire: when employers cannot access an applicant's criminal history (when the algorithm is missing this information) they instead discriminate more broadly against demographic groups that are more likely to have a criminal record (Agan and Starr, 2018; Doleac and Hansen, 2020; Holzer et al., 2006; Wozniak, 2014). This body of work sheds light on the manner in which employers – and possibly those in other sectors such as landlords – operating in low-information environments, use observable signals in place of unobservable signals, with adverse outcomes for marginalized groups.

These questions have also been asked of algorithmic sentencing laws in criminal justice. Predictions from algorithms are used by another type of gatekeeper, judges, to make decisions about sentencing, where abdicating such decisions to a machine is thought to reduce bias. Yet, studies show that algorithms are no better at predicting recidivism than randomly selected everyday people are (Dressel and Farid, 2018) and, in fact, they may be worse.[2] More broadly, researchers argue that rather than replacing discriminatory discretion, supposedly predictive technologies simply displace such discretion to less visible places (Brayne and Christin, 2020) without reducing recidivism (Stevenson and Doleac, 2020). These algorithmic methods – much like those larger landlords use to screen tenants – tend to substitute illegal signifiers such as race, for legal sets of signifiers that are highly correlated with race and, therefore, produce the same discriminatory outcomes. In this way, researchers have increasingly argued that algorithmic technologies serve as a mechanism through which the financialization of housing is inextricably linked to racialized dispossession by providing it with a patina of objectivity (Fields and Raymond, 2021; McElroy, 2020).

Data and methods

Data for this chapter come from 157 in-depth interviews with landlords and property managers in four cities: Baltimore, Maryland MD, Cleveland OH, Dallas TX, and Washington DC (for detailed methodology see Garboden and Rosen, 2018; Rosen et al., 2021).[3] These cities provide a range of rental market characteristics: Baltimore and Cleveland are both declining rust belt cities with high levels of Black–white segregation, although Cleveland is substantially worse off economically; Dallas is a growing sunbelt city with a large Latino population; and Washington, DC is a high-priced housing market with substantial displacement pressure. We selected landlords from a stratified random sample of property listings to ensure heterogeneity with respect to housing subsidy acceptance and the type of neighbourhood in which they owned rental properties. We conducted semi-structured interviews designed to understand each landlord's business practices holistically including information on tenant screening. We coded data in MaxQDA and used analytic memoing to extract themes. We supplemented approximately one-third of interviews with direct ethnographic observation by shadowing landlords during their daily routines.

Findings

Historically, landlords have relied on their own intuition and information-gathering tools to screen tenants – such as looking up names on eviction court records or calling previous landlords. Today, the sharp increase in personal data collection has introduced far more computational methods for tenant screening (Fields, 2022; Garboden, 2019; Porton et al., 2021; Richards and King, 2014). Despite the broader trend towards automation, however, traditional practices remain very much in evidence in our research particularly for smaller landlords who lack professional experience and training. Some smaller landlords check credit scores, residential history or criminal background, but most of the time these records were interpreted through their own personal judgement, what they call *gut checks*. In our research, we found that the more units in a landlord's portfolio, the more likely they were to utilize formal algorithmic screening processes and the less likely they were to use informal ones (see also Rosen et al., 2021).

Informal screening techniques: gut checks and smell tests

Rather than using formal methods, smaller landlords are more likely to rely on informal information gathering during non-structured interactions and home visits. Because fair housing enforcement rarely targets these small "mom and pop" landlords, they have less incentive to engage in algorithmic approaches, which are costly if not employed at scale and, in their minds, not particularly reliable. Instead, they are more likely to rely on an array of informal screening techniques – including relying on gut feelings that come to them during non-structured interactions and home visits – that they use to identify applicants who are not only technically qualified but also exhibit some form of responsibility and self-efficacy (measured in highly subjective and idiosyncratic ways).

For example, before leasing out a unit, Gary, a small-time Baltimore landlord, visits and inspects applicants' current living spaces to gain information that he thinks will help him ascertain whether they will be good tenants. Gary automatically denies any tenant who refuses a home visit, taking it as a signal that there is something they do not want him to see. By checking information reported on rental applications and seeing things with his own eyes, he feels better able to predict how a tenant will behave in his property. Other landlords used more idiosyncratic methods such as evaluating tenants' parenting skills or using "smell tests" to see how well-groomed tenants' children are.

These cases illustrate the invasive screening processes that – in Gary's words – 'lower income people who can't afford more' have to go through to find homes, especially when renting from more amateur landlords with smaller portfolios. For these tenants, their flawed credit and volatile income make them subject to unannounced home visits and evaluations of their parenting ability. This set of practices is infused with a power dynamic that is distinctly patterned by race and gender with landlords largely basing their criteria on stereotypes of the Black underclass and Black motherhood (see Rosen et al., 2021). Given this visible bias that is apparent in these informal screening practices, many have looked to automated approaches to screening in the hopes of finding a better way.

Formal screening techniques

In contrast, larger landlords are much more likely to rely on formal checks and screening software algorithms. These technologies, designed by third-party companies such as CoreLogic and LeaseRunner, operate by accounting for legally observable traits such as income, credit, criminal background and eviction history. They use these data points to indicate to the landlord who they should or should not rent to either by rejecting any tenant who fails to meet particular thresholds or by producing a *rental score*. Landlords generally cannot see what data points contribute to the overall score, though some services provide more details than others, and they cannot manipulate the algorithm to weigh some traits more heavily than others. However, they can of course choose which software they subscribe to (although we did not find that landlords generally had knowledge of or familiarity with multiple types of screening software).

The technology is marketed as a way to improve screening outcomes for landlords, to help landlords estimate risk and better predict who will be a "good" tenant and pay on time – but they are also marketed as a way to improve equitable outcomes by reducing landlord bias and, therefore, discrimination. Larger professional landlords, particularly those with corporate ownership, subscribe to this software for these two reasons. First, they need some way to select a tenant who is likely to pay on time and not cause problems such as vandalism or nuisance ordinance violations – a prediction problem that corporate landlords believe screening software will help them solve more accurately and efficiently. Second, and perhaps more importantly, they use automated techniques because, if they pick the tenant that the software tells them to, they are protected from discrimination lawsuits in the United States.

To prove discrimination, it is legally insufficient in the United States simply to show that a screening process yields outcomes that are detrimental to a protected group (ethnic minorities, women, the elderly and so forth) (Bridges, 2008). So long as each criterion used during screening can be linked to a legitimate business purpose and the process does not explicitly take into account race, gender or other protected classes, it is extremely unlikely that a fair housing lawsuit would be decided against a landlord. In some cases, specific screening practices have been ruled as a violation of the Fair Housing Act because they have what is called a *disparate impact* on a protected group, but the bar for such claims is very high (Bourland, 2017; Schwemm and Bradford, 2016; Williams, 2017).[4] It requires the plaintiff to argue that the criteria employed do not accomplish a necessary business objective or that said objective could be satisfied in a less discriminatory manner. At the current moment, the typical algorithmic inputs – credit scores, rental histories, criminal background, income – have been largely deemed legitimate even though America's racist legacy means that disadvantaged minorities, on average, score lower on all of these measures (Oliver and Shapiro, 2010; Shapiro, 2004). Because algorithmic approaches clearly define the inputs used and are intentionally blind to other applicant characteristics, they are perfectly positioned to protect landlords from lawsuits.

Moreover, the primary vehicle for fair housing enforcement is auditing – the process of employing pairs of testers who are identical on paper but differ on one salient vector (race, gender, etc.) (Gaddis, 2018). If, after repeated tests, the matched pairs of applicants receive unequal outcomes (on average), it is strong evidence that discrimination is present. Of course, this is precisely the sort of test that algorithmic approaches are designed to pass. Indeed, when asked to reflect on these systems, property managers emphasized the importance of fairness to avoid running afoul of fair housing law. But this view of fairness means treating everyone exactly the same regardless of circumstance. Rochelle, a property manager of a large complex, provided an example: 'When you come in and I shake your hand, I've got to shake everybody's hand that comes through that door. [if] somebody else comes in and I don't shake their hand, then their friend [reports], "she didn't shake my hand…".' This can leave the company open to a lawsuit, especially if the two people differ in race or gender. Rochelle's point is that everything they do must appear the same for each tenant. Her company may not be able to automate a handshake, but their primary solution to fair housing audits by HUD and other enforcement entities is to rely on software to determine eligibility for tenants. Rochelle noted that the system she uses gives her a straight yes or no, never allowing for any uncertainty: 'It's not in between... If you don't qualify and you're short a dollar, you're still denied.'

This type of fairness, while nominally race-blind in *process* or *treatment*, is far from race-neutral in *outcome*. The goal of any screening is to use observable characteristics as proxies for future behaviour. But proxies such as credit history, residential history and criminal background – while legal – can be crude measures that serve as stand-ins for historical vectors of discrimination and are thus highly correlated with race. For example, labour market discrimination and mass incarceration can lead to Black applicants having poorer scores than equivalent white applicants (Harper et al., 2021). In some cases, landlords select these proxies with discriminatory intent – as when landlords in cities with income protection laws implement a credit check to avoid accepting housing vouchers (and by extension, the non-white tenants who most often use them) (Faber and Mercier, 2022). But more often, algorithmic discrimination is collateral rather than intentional, with landlords implementing "fairness" in ways that reinforce other sources of injustice. Thus, by relying on, in one landlord's words, 'normal screening techniques,' they are swapping fairness in *outcome* for fairness in *process*.

A "better" algorithm?

Roger, a landlord and property manager in DC, provides an interesting contrast case. Roger has made his own algorithm to favour the kinds of tenants he thinks are most profitable: those who receive a housing voucher. Housing voucher recipients are part of a large federal housing subsidy program, the Housing Choice Voucher Program (aka 'Section 8'), which subsidizes the difference between 30 % of the tenant's income and the cost of a modestly priced rental. It serves poor and low-income families (see Rosen, 2020). Roger's screening algorithm – which he sells to landlords – calculates a score for each applicant based on their rental history, how many times they have been in landlord–tenant court, eviction history, the number of bedrooms in their voucher, the tenant's portion of the rent and so on. Roger claims his scoring system 'allows real estate professionals and landlords to quickly make an informed decision with regards to renting to Section 8 and helps them to steer clear of fair housing violations.'

Roger knows that many landlords are afraid of voucher tenants who they worry will cause problems or trash the unit. But he thinks he can convince landlords to open up to the program because it is profitable. To do this, Roger has engineered his algorithm to discount a tenant's history of eviction because their payment portion is low. Since most of the rent will be coming from the housing authority, a tenant like this would be low risk to a landlord, even if they never paid their portion of the rent.

Roger's interest in overcoming voucher discrimination is less motivated by a desire for fairness than in helping landlords find a sustainable and profitable business model. The voucher program offers this, and the algorithm helps Roger sell it to them. This algorithm could potentially open up a lot of places for voucher tenants to find places to rent. But like Rochelle's case (as well as in the cases of the small-time amateur landlords) the technique is motivated by profit, not by equity.

Discussion

In this chapter, we further elucidate Benjamin's (2019) point that discriminatory design can be either explicit or, in the case of automation, often more implicit. Our findings show that landlords engage in two primary modes of screening: formal techniques with quantifiable metrics and informal techniques with highly personal evaluations, both of which can result in discrimination. While both formal and informal screening techniques can exist in either digital or analogue spaces, the former was far more likely to be accomplished with the help of digital technologies, particularly proprietary datasets and algorithmic approaches to tenant screening. Importantly, much of the landlord's motivation is grounded in two profit-minded goals: 1) minimizing risk and 2) avoiding fair housing litigation. We found that while smaller, less professionalized landlords were still likely to report making decisions regarding whom to accept based on a gut feeling or gut check, larger landlords were more likely to rely on formalized screening tools such as residential history, credit scores and criminal background reports. These "checks" were often conducted indirectly through software tools that are based on algorithms, which make suggestions to landlords about which tenants are riskier than others. These two screening modes have important implications when it comes to discriminatory outcomes for tenants and, importantly, the algorithmic approach does not appear to prevent such outcomes.

While the techniques used by smaller landlords are often overtly biased in both process and outcome, formal checks based on software offer the promise of being *un*biased, by only taking into account observable tenant traits that are legal to screen, such as credit score and eviction history. However, there are two problems with this technological solution. First, when tenant pools are fairly homogeneous (as they are in the low-end rental market where most tenants have shaky credit histories and previous encounters with eviction courts), predictive approaches run the risk of creating distinctions without differences. In other words, they tend not to be able to prevent the landlord from selecting a tenant who may be unable to pay rent. Indeed, small landlords explicitly cited this concern as a motivation for relying on gut-level decision-making instead.

Second, algorithms can only be unbiased with respect to the observable criteria used as inputs in the model. In other words, while overtly race-neutral *in process* – because they do not directly build race into the model – these metrics are nevertheless highly correlated with race due to the history of labour, credit and institutional exclusion in the United States and are, therefore, still biased *in outcome*. An algorithm used to predict the likelihood of a tenant paying rent assigns no value to determining *why* a tenant might be unable to pay rent, only *whether* that tenant has had financial trouble in the past. Even if the algorithm is explicitly prohibited from using race directly, its ability to use past experiences of the applicant – all of which will, at least in part, be a function of that applicant's lived experience, their intersectional identity (Crenshaw, 1989) – will produce predictions highly correlated with race, gender and other traits that are, therefore, biased in outcome. Thus, if the algorithm detects that Black tenants are more likely to experience labour market discrimination or incarceration, it will inevitably assess them as higher risk, even if the tenant's race was never explicitly entered into the equation.

As such, when our respondents describe algorithmic screening tools as "fair," they mean this only in the sense that they rule out explicit discrimination for which the company can be held liable, not that they are actually immune to racial bias. We see this in the way that landlords turn away tenants who have histories of eviction, a poor credit score or a criminal history, all of which are more common in communities of colour even after accounting for individual-level factors (Desmond, 2016; Hepburn et al., 2020; Pager, 2003; Pager and Shepherd, 2008; Western, 2007).

Our data thus reveal the complex tradeoffs involved in algorithmic approaches. Other work suggests that tenants with known marks on their residential history are likely to seek out landlords who avoid formal screening techniques in favour of those who are more likely to evaluate each applicant based on informal interactions (DeLuca and Jang-Trettien, 2020; Engel et al., 2022). While it is tempting to romanticize these personal evaluations as more humane, we find that the characteristics that amateur landlords use to evaluate their tenants generally align with racist narratives of "underclass" neighbourhoods and Black motherhood (see Rosen et al., 2021). Thus, while it appears to benefit tenants to have a heterogeneous landlord pool, the reality is that neither an appeal to algorithmic fairness nor a return to informality will solve the problem of who should receive housing. Indeed, is any method of screening "fair" if it results in certain groups being systematically denied housing?

Conclusion

As we see more and more autonomous technology governing the urban environment (Cugurullo, 2020, 2021), we must think critically about how it shapes experiences for those who live within it. Landlords are crucial gatekeepers to anyone who wants to rent a home in an urban area, and so the tools they use to select between applicants merit careful scrutiny. Indeed, more and more of the job is automated (Fields, 2022). And while these technological advances are often promised to be better, more efficient and more equitable solutions to housing problems (Rogal, 2006), our research raises questions about whether this is the case. In this chapter, we show how relying on algorithms to assess tenant risk does not improve equity in outcomes for tenants and often fails to provide accurate predictions.

Why? Is the problem the content of the algorithms, or is it the fact of using an algorithm at all? We argue that the answer is both. The kind of categorical exclusion enacted by the landlords in our sample who rely on automated screening software tools is based solely on income, credit score and eviction history. As such, they end up disadvantaging tenants of colour, due to a history of racism and discrimination in the United States (Rosen et al., 2021). Certainly, getting more data and adjusting for more contextual factors could indeed be better, particularly when compared to racist smell tests. But it seems unlikely that any amount of tweaking of the algorithm will disconnect it from the historic correlation between race and economic mobility (Connolly, 2016; Oliver and Shapiro, 2010; Shapiro, 2004).

Given the tradeoffs revealed by our findings, is it interesting to consider a hypothetical tenant screening algorithm that accurately predicts an applicant's ability to pay rent with only trivial residuals and is able to fully account for structural inequalities. It is possible, without too much appeal to dystopia, to imagine that AI technologies could combine with existing data systems to accurately predict tenant profitability. The second criterion of 'no reflection of structural inequalities' lives more in the realm of fantasy, but maybe it is at least possible to imagine a world without racial or gender bias. This raises the question of whether the goal of "perfect" tenant screening is even normatively desirable. The easy answer is yes – if landlords do not attempt to predict their tenants' ability to pay, they will admit tenants who cannot pay, and this will lead to highly undesirable outcomes for both parties. Thus, if current tenure arrangements remain in place, it is both necessary and desirable to improve landlords' ability to accurately screen tenants.

Market assumptions would lead us to believe that accurate prediction simply pushes an undesirable tenant into a lower, more affordable tranche of housing when they are rejected from a higher one. However, this naïve assumption ignores the way the housing market actually works. The vast majority of developed countries have a strong price floor on housing due to factors related to health, safety and housing financialization (Schwartz, 2021). This means that tenants who struggle to be accepted into housing are tasked not with finding housing they can afford (which does not exist at scale) or housing subsidies (which are not adequately available), but instead with finding a landlord who is willing to take on a high-risk tenant (DeLuca and Jang-Trettien, 2020). Some of these landlords may be dupes, but the majority are going to compensate for this risk either by charging higher rents or by providing an inferior home (Garboden and Rosen, 2018). In either case, the families suffer greatly for being high-risk.

It is thus necessary that we carefully consider both the structural forces that create higher risk (such as labour market discrimination, education and funding) but also the precision with which we can measure that risk. If we have poor precision, then we must ultimately treat individuals more or less the same despite different latent risk profiles. This ultimately represents a redistribution of material resources as those with low risk are overcharged (or under-included) and those with high risk are undercharged (or over-included). The degree to which people should be normatively responsible for their actions is a seemingly fruitless debate within moral philosophy (Mounk, 2017), but that does not mean that we should not conceptualize a family's predictive risk profile as a critical material asset, which algorithmic screening has the long-run potential to perfectly stratify. If redistribution of risk profile can be seen as normatively desirable (and we believe a case can be made), then more than a little fuzziness in our screening is perhaps desirable as well.

But here we should proceed with caution. The nature of urban landlording is one of exclusion and inclusion, and it is unlikely that landlords would respond to predictive imprecision simply by taking all comers. If we have learnt anything from the failures of Ban the Box legislation, it is that gatekeepers will always seek to establish a process of distinction (Agan and Starr, 2018; Doleac and Hansen, 2020; Holzer et al., 2006). When they are deprived of particular means to do so, they will not simply cease to discriminate, but will utilize other criteria with potentially worse collateral consequences. Thus, the only real solution to the exacerbation of risk profile inequality is for the state to intervene with affirmative and compensatory resources, to ensure that those who need housing, receive it. Any algorithm, by definition, creates winners and losers. We think that housing is not a commodity for which there should be losers.

Our data suggests that what little the state already does in this regard is somewhat effective. When the state ensures a family's ability to pay by providing them with a housing voucher, it greatly reduces the degree to which landlords' screening is sensitive to other factors; it directly obviates the need for income verification, and our data also suggest that some landlords put less weight on credit and rental history, opening up housing opportunities for disadvantaged renters (Garboden et al., 2018). While there is nothing new about our claim that affirmative policy intervention is necessary to redress structural injustices, we believe that it is an important reminder when considering a technological innovation within the urban environment, including nearly all examples of AI utilization, that exacerbates the consequences of those injustices.

Notes

1 This definition, while straightforward, is important as it eschews the colloquial understanding of screening as a reward for good behaviour (or a punishment for bad behaviour). While parents, church officials or even agents of the state may be motivated to concern themselves with the moral upbringing of others, a landlord ought to care only about future behaviour, using past behaviour simply as a predictive variable.

2 A ProPublica (2016) study finds that COMPAS algorithms predict Black defendants to recidivate at higher rates than they actually do, and predicts that white defendants do so at lower rates than in reality.

3 For each property we interviewed, the individual was responsible for making screening decisions, whether that was the landlord or the property manager.

4 See Bridges (2008) for the legal distinction between disparate treatment and disparate impact. See also Texas Dept. of Housing and Community Affairs v. Inclusive Communities Project, Inc., No. 13-1731, Supreme Court June 15, 2015, for a precedent setting case disparate impact without discriminatory intent.

References

Agan, A., & Starr, S. (2018). Ban the Box, Criminal Records, and Racial Discrimination: A Field Experiment. *The Quarterly Journal of Economics*, 133(1), 191–235.

Barns, S. (2021). Out of the Loop? On the Radical and the Routine in Urban Big Data. *Urban Studies*, 58(15), 3203–3210.

Batty, M. (2018). Artificial Intelligence and Smart Cities. *Environment and Planning B: Urban Analytics and City Science*, 45(1), 3–6.

Benjamin, R. (2019). *Race After Technology: Abolitionist Tools for the New Jim Code*. Polity Press.

Bourland, N. (2017). When Causation is too "Robust": Disparate Impact in the Crosshairs in De Reyes. *CUNY Law Review*. Available at: http://www.cunylawreview.org/nick-bourland/ [Accessed 19/01/2023].

Brayne, S., & Christin, A. (2020). Technologies of Crime Prediction: The Reception of Algorithms in Policing and Criminal Courts. *Social Problems*, 68(3), 608–624.

Bridges, K. (2008). Justifying Facial Discrimination by Government Defendants under the Fair Housing Act: Which Standard to Apply. *Missouri Law Review*, 73(19).

Broussard, M. (2018). *Artificial Unintelligence: How Computers Misunderstand the World*. MIT Press.

Connolly, N. D. B. (2016). *A World More Concrete: Real Estate and the Remaking of Jim Crow South Florida*. University of Chicago Press.

Crenshaw, K. (1989). Demarginalizing the Intersection of Race and Sex: A Black Feminist Critique of Antidiscrimination Doctrine, Feminist Theory and Antiracist Politics. *University of Chicago Legal Forum*, 1, 139–167.

Cugurullo, F. (2020). Urban artificial intelligence: From automation to autonomy in the smart city. *Frontiers in Sustainable Cities*, 2, 38.

Cugurullo, F. (2021). *Frankenstein Urbanism: Eco, Smart and Autonomous Cities, Artificial Intelligence and the End of the City*. Routledge.

DeLuca, S., Garboden, P. M., & Rosenblatt, P. (2013). Segregating Shelter: How Housing Policies Shape the Residential Locations of Low-Income Minority Families. *The Annals of the American Academy of Political and Social Science*, 647(1), 268–299.

DeLuca, S., & Jang-Trettien, C. (2020). "Not Just a Lateral Move": Residential Decisions and the Reproduction of Urban Inequality. *City & Community*, 19(3), 451–488.

Desmond, M. (2016). *Evicted: Poverty and Profit in the American City*. Crown.

Doleac, J. L., & Hansen, B. (2020). The Unintended Consequences of "Ban the Box": Statistical Discrimination and Employment Outcomes When Criminal Histories Are Hidden. *Journal of Labor Economics*, 38(2), 321–374.

Dressel, J., & Farid, H. (2018). The Accuracy, Fairness, and Limits of Predicting Recidivism. *Science Advances*, 4(1), DOI: 10.1126/sciadv.aao5580

Engel, R., Garboden, P., & Darrah-Okike, J. (2022). *"I Don't Fit the Stereotypes": Housing Choice Voucher Recipients in Hawai'i and the Navigation of a Voucher 'Identity.'* American Sociological Association Annual Meeting, Los Angeles, CA.

Eubanks, V. (2018). *Automating Inequality: How High-Tech Tools Profile, Police, and Punish the Poor*. St. Martin's Press.

Faber, J. W., & Mercier, M.-D. (2022). Multidimensional Discrimination in the Online Rental Housing Market: Implications for Families with Young Children. *Housing Policy Debate*. DOI: 10.1080/10511482.2021.2010118.

Fields, D. (2022). Automated Landlord: Digital Technologies and Post-crisis Financial Accumulation. *Environment and Planning A: Economy and Space*, 54(1).

Fields, D., & Raymond, E. L. (2021). Racialized Geographies of Housing Financialization. *Progress in Human Geography*, 45(6), 1625–1645.

Gaddis, M. (2018). *Audit Studies: Behind the Scenes with Theory, Method, and Nuance*. Springer.

Garboden, P., Rosen, E., DeLuca, S., & Edin, K. (2018). Taking Stock: What Drives Landlord Participation in the Housing Choice Voucher Program. *Housing Policy Debate*, 28(6), 979.

Garboden, P. M. (2019). Sources and Types of Big Data for Macroeconomic Forecasting. In P. Fuleky (Ed.), *Macroeconomic Forecasting in the Era of Big Data: Theory and Practice*. Springer.

Garboden, P. M., & Rosen, E. (2018). Talking to Landlords. *Cityscape: A Journal of Policy Development and Research*, 20(3).

Garboden, P. M., & Rosen, E. (2019). Serial Filing: How Landlords Use the Threat of Eviction. *City & Community*, 18(2), 638–661.

Garboden, P. M. E., Fan, C.-W., Budavári, T., Basu, A., Braverman, M., & Evans, J. D. (2021). Combinatorial Optimization for Urban Planning: Strategic Demolition of Abandoned Houses in Baltimore, MD. *Journal of Planning Education and Research*, DOI: 10.1177/0739456X211003642.

Goodspeed, R. (2015). Smart Cities: Moving beyond Urban Cybernetics to Tackle Wicked Problems. *Cambridge Journal of Regions, Economy and Society*, 8(1), 79–92.

Green, B., & Franklin-Hodge, J. (2019). *The Smart Enough City: Putting Technology in Its Place to Reclaim Our Urban Future* (1st ed.). The MIT Press.

Harper, A., Ginapp, C., Bardelli, T., Grimshaw, A., Justen, M., Mohamedali, A., Thomas, I., & Puglisi, L. (2021). Debt, Incarceration, and Re-entry: A Scoping Review. *American Journal of Criminal Justice*, 46(2), 250–278.

Hartman, C., & Robinson, D. (2003). Evictions: The Hidden Housing Problem. *Housing Policy Debate*, 14(4), 461–501.

Hepburn, P., Louis, R., & Desmond, M. (2020). Racial and Gender Disparities among Evicted Americans. *Sociological Science*, 7, 649–662.

Holzer, H. J., Raphael, S., & Stoll, M. A. (2006). Perceived Criminality, Criminal Background Checks, and the Racial Hiring Practices of Employers. *The Journal of Law and Economics*, 49(2), 451–480.

Korver-Glenn, E. (2018). Compounding Inequalities: How Racial Stereotypes and Discrimination Accumulate across the Stages of Housing Exchange. *American Sociological Review*, 83(4), 627–656.

Logan, J., & Stults, B. (2021). *Metropolitan Segregation: No Breakthrough in Sight*. Diversity and Disparities Project.

Maalsen, S., & Sadowski, J. (2019). The Smart Home on FIRE: Amplifying and Accelerating Domestic Surveillance. *Surveillance & Society*, 17(1/2), 118–124.

McElroy, E. (2020). Property as Technology. *City*, 24(1–2), 112–129.

Mounk, Y. (2017). *The Age of Responsibility: Luck, Choice, and the Welfare State*. Harvard University Press.

Noble, S. U. (2018). *Algorithms of Oppression: How Search Engines Reinforce Racism*. NYU Press.

Oliver, M., & Shapiro, T. (2010). *Black Wealth/White Wealth: A New Perspective on Racial Inequality* (2nd ed.). Routledge.

Pager, D. (2003). The Mark of a Criminal Record. *American Journal of Sociology*, 108(5), 937–975.

Pager, D., & Shepherd, H. (2008). The Sociology of Discrimination: Racial Discrimination in Employment, Housing, Credit, and Consumer Markets. *Annual Review of Sociology*, 34, 181–209.

Park, R. E., & Burgess, E. W. (1925). *The City: Suggestions for Investigation of Human Behavior in the Urban Environment*. University of Chicago Press.

Porton, A., Gromis, A., & Desmond, M. (2021). Inaccuracies in Eviction Records: Implications for Renters and Researchers. *Housing Policy Debate*, 31(3–5), 377–394.

ProPublica (2016). *How We Analyzed the COMPAS Recidivism Algorithm*. Available at: https://www.propublica.org/article/how-we-analyzed-the-compas-recidivism-algorithm [Accessed 19/01/2023].

Reosti, A. (2020). "We Go Totally Subjective": Discretion, Discrimination, and Tenant Screening in a Landlord's Market. *Law & Social Inquiry*, 45(3), 618–657.

Richards, N. M., & King, J. H. (2014). Big Data Ethics. *Wake Forest Law Review*, 49(2), 393–432.

Rogal, B. (2006). Screen Doors: Resident Screening Software Helps Managers Determine Which Residents Are Top Choice. *Journal of Property Management*, 71(4), 38–41.

Rosen, E. (2014). Rigging the Rules of the Game: How Landlords Geographically Sort Low-Income Renters. *City & Community*, 13(4), 310–340.

Rosen, E. (2020). *The Voucher Promise: "Section 8" and the Fate of an American Neighborhood*. Princeton University Press.

Rosen, E., & Garboden, P. M. (2022). Landlord Paternalism: Housing the Poor with a Velvet Glove. *Social Problems*, 69(2), 470–491.

Rosen, E., Garboden, P. M., & Cossyleon, J. E. (2021). Racial Discrimination in Housing: How Landlords use Algorithms and Home Visits to Screen Tenants. *American Sociological Review*, 86(5), 787–822.

Sampson, R. J. (2012). *Great American City: Chicago and the Enduring Neighborhood Effect*. Chicago University Press.

Schwartz, A. (2021). *Housing Policy in the United States*. Routledge.

Schwemm, R., & Bradford, C. (2016). Proving Disparate Impact in Fair Housing Cases After *Inclusive Communities*. *N.Y.U. Journal of Legislation & Public Policy*, 19(4), 685–770.

Shapiro, T. M. (2004). *The Hidden Cost of Being African American: How Wealth Perpetuates Inequality*. Oxford University Press.

So, W. (2022). Which Information Matters? Measuring Landlord Assessment of Tenant Screening Reports. *Housing Policy Debate*, DOI: 10.1080/10511482. 2022.2113815.

Stevenson, M. T., & Doleac, J. L. (2020). *Algorithmic Risk Assessment in the Hands of Humans*. *Social Science Research Network*. Available at: https://papers.ssrn. com/abstract=3513695 [Accessed 19/01/2023].

Western, B. (2007). *Punishment and Inequality in America*. Russell Sage Foundation.

Williams, C. (2017). Inclusive Communities and Robust Causality: The Constant Struggle to Balance Access to the Courts with Protection for Defendants. *Minnesota Law Review*, 102, 969.

Wozniak, A. (2014). Discrimination and the Effects of Drug Testing on Black Employment. *The Review of Economics and Statistics*, 97(3), 548–566.

Zorbaugh, H. W. (1929). *The Gold Coast and the Slum: A Sociological Study of Chicago's Near North Side*. Chicago University Press.

21

ARCHITECTURAL AI

Urban artificial intelligence in architecture and design

Davide Pisu and Silvio Carta

Introduction

This chapter investigates the impact of artificial intelligence (AI) on contemporary cities through the lens of architectural and urban design. It explores design computing approaches where computers characterize the production and management of design. These include AI, machine learning (ML) as a subset of AI and, in general terms, generative approaches to urban design where AI components are employed to create spatial configurations. We look at these systems as invisible forces that have significant consequences for both the built environment and people living in cities, providing examples and considerations of how intelligent systems and designers are reshaping cities today through a new form of agency. We present two intentionally polarized paradigms that underpin the idea of agency in the design process and the extent to which designers (or machines) are in control of the design process and final outcomes. These are the *digital demiurge*, where designers have full control of their project and, contra, the *black box*, where AI determines the final design outcome in an opaque and often inscrutable way.

The former paradigm (*digital demiurge*) suggests that designers oversee the entire project from conception to construction. This may happen directly through traditional Computer-Aided Design/Computer-Aided Manufacturing (CAD/CAM) tools or indirectly when designers build their own automated design tools and decide the rules that AI will follow (although they may defer some decisions to an AI). The latter paradigm (*black box*) suggests that designers may lose control of some parts of the design, especially when complex AI models are used, or when the design process hinges on "closed" software packages, like proprietary Application Programming Interfaces (APIs), libraries, etc.

DOI: 10.4324/9781003365877-25

The second section describes the *P versus NP* problem to frame the deterministic versus non-deterministic nature of design within the context of human-made design and artificial intelligence. It explores the tension between the two paradigms through a theoretical framework meant to clarify how design agency moves across the two extreme positions of the digital demiurge and the black box. The third section describes practical design approaches to architecture, urban design, urban analytics and space-making in order to provide real-life examples of the complex designer/machine relationships and the author's agency in the era of urban AI (cf. Carpo, 2011). The conclusion elaborates on the importance of looking at the gradient between the *digital demiurge* and *black box* paradigms with nuance and proposes a hybrid model of control and authorship between machines and humans, algorithms and designers.

Coordinates

Artificial intelligence and machine learning methods are being increasingly used by designers and planners as a powerful tool to analyse, manage and design cities. Designers have engaged with digital technologies and computational methods for a long time, as the pioneering work of John Gero, George Stiny, Lionel March, William J. Mitchell and Rivka Oxman, exemplifies. However, as artificial intelligence becomes increasingly present in a number of urban processes and systems and, more importantly, available to non-experts, its impact on the design of cities grows exponentially. Many authors have been exploring the importance of AI for urban development and planning, highlighting potentials and possible drawbacks (Barns, 2021; Batty, 2018; Cugurullo, 2020, 2021).

The relationship between designer and machine can be characterized by two extreme positions that hinge on the role of the designer within the automated (design) process. One position sees the designer as a central figure with complete control of the process, while the machine is considered primarily as a powerful yet passive tool. In the other, the machine can be understood as an autonomous agent that takes a substantial role in the design process where, due to the complexity of the operations involved, computers have a higher degree of autonomy in decision-making.

Such a polarized understanding of *designers VS machines* is not a novel idea in design. Following a cultural trajectory akin to that explored by Eco (1954) in Apocalypse Postponed, Bottazzi (2018: vii) eloquently illustrates the dichotomy between 'detractors and devotees' – which in Eco's book were referred to as 'Apocalyptic and Integrated Intellectuals,' respectively – with regard to the adoption of digital technologies in design:

> The former group stubbornly resists acknowledging that digital tools can be used generatively and therefore struggles to grasp the wider, often not

even spatial, issues at stake when designing with computers. [...] The latter group [...] attributes to computers such degree of novelty and internal coherence to self-validate any outcome.

(Bottazzi, 2018: vii)

The following section delves into these two paradigms from an architectural design viewpoint and discusses the idea of the designer as a creator in full control of the creative process, which we refer to as *digital demiurge* in reference to Plato's notion of an omnipotent, artisan-like creator. We position this in contrast to the paradigm of *black box*, where the machine produces its design outputs in inscrutable ways.

Digital demiurge and the black box

Within the context of computational design, AI can significantly extend designers' possibilities. With a fraction of the effort once needed to elaborate a single drawing, computation enables designers to produce accurate urban models, with greater precision than ever before. Similarly, with AI applications, one designer alone can do the work of ten, handling a level of complexity unmanageable by humans. With the aid of computational toolsets (including data analysis, algorithms and modelling), designers can create and manage complex projects in an effective and productive manner, limited only by computational capacity and speed. In the notational space of their design software (a two- or three-dimensional environment) and with the ability to manipulate code, designers have great creative capacity and can generate objects and spatial configurations regardless of their complexity, thus becoming *demiurges* that shape and manipulate the digital world.

This idea of the architect as a creative mind with great power seems to fit what, since the Renaissance, has been known as the *authorial paradigm*, according to which, the person who retains the credit of the creative act is considered to be the *author*. Arguably, the one who produces the algorithms and then assembles and adapts them to achieve a desired (design) goal should be considered the author of the design. However, the notion of automation (an inherent part of computational approaches) implies a certain degree of collaboration (Carpo, 2017). Algorithms are produced and distributed among designers who can use, manipulate and adapt them, in relation to specific design problems. Within this open and shared domain, designers are responsible for the systematic combination of different elements of their projects. In this scenario, designers cede some agency to algorithms, while remaining in an overall position of control. But what happens when the complexity of algorithms increases to a point where designers lose an overview of the design process? In this scenario, agency gravitates towards computers, thereby resulting in what is usually referred to as a *black box* situation.

With recent advancements in Neural Networks (NNs) research (see Chaillou, 2019; Huang and Zheng, 2018; Nauata et al., 2021), a design solution may depend on several variables, including the type of neural network (a complex system of nodes and links through which messages are propagated by AI), its architecture (the structure of the network), the type and quality of input data, the type of learning and the number of iterations used in the training. This complexity makes the design outcome extremely difficult for humans to predict and manage. Designers using computational methods are responsible for the selection and preparation of input data and are in charge of evaluating the results and outcomes. However, they have a limited understanding of the inner mechanisms of artificial intelligent systems. Designers need to trust the systems they are using to guide their design without necessarily having a deep understanding of how they work. Designers using algorithms are delegating their agency to systems that are difficult if not impossible to comprehend; that is to say, they are *pushing a design through a black box*.

We borrow the definition of black box in design from Durmus Ozturk (2020: 3): 'as a device, system, or object evaluated by an input and output that does not contain any internal knowledge.' This approach is characterized by a lack of transparency in the process where designers need to use their intuition to navigate the system (Durmus Ozturk, 2020). We can trace the origin of the term *black box* back to 1970 when John Christopher Jones in his seminal book on design methods, explained that

> the most valuable part of the design process is that which goes inside the designer's head and partially out of reach of his conscious control [...] The blackbox view of designing [suggests that] the human designer is capable of outputs in which he has confidence, and which often succeed, without his being able to say how these outputs were obtained.
>
> *(Jones 1970: 46)*

More specifically, there are two levels of trust in an autonomous system, or degrees of superficial understanding in the black box paradigm. The first is related to designers who may not necessarily have the skills or theoretical knowledge to master algorithmic models, especially in ML and AI. This problem is somehow compounded by the proliferation of ready-made AI tools, libraries and software packages that make it possible for anyone with basic/medium (design) software skills to use AI applications (cf. Carta, 2020). This phenomenon is even more evident when designers use proprietary software or libraries where source codes are not publicly available and, therefore, it is difficult to have a deep understanding of the mechanisms underpinning those programs.

The second cause of superficial understanding (and thus control) in autonomous systems is related to the mechanics of AI and neural networks. This factor has to do with the complexity that characterizes neural networks. In essence, a neural network works through a sequence of nodes and links organized in levels (which are called layers or perceptrons). Data (like an image of a cat, for example) passes through many different layers to be classified. This means that a category (or class) is suggested by the neural network as an output. The network provides a suggestion for the picture used as the input. For example, 'yes, it is a picture of a cat,' or 'no, this is not a cat' (Figure 21.1). As data passes through each layer, each piece of information is multiplied and added through a system of nodes (through layers) where complexity increases exponentially. Very soon, the manipulation of information becomes too complex for the human brain to grasp. We are able to control the input of a neural network and evaluate the accuracy of outputs (*before* and *after* the computation), but the complexity that characterizes the *in-between* layers is well beyond human reach.

This critical aspect is evident in most machine training experiments in architectural design where the large amount of data needed for training is obtained from generic datasets such as Lianjia.com, SUNCG, LIFULL HOME, Archimaps or DeZeen. Training is one of the first stages in setting up a neural network, where humans provide a large number of correct examples ('this is a cat' and 'this is not a cat') to the network which, in turn, "learns" to classify images. Even if, hypothetically, the black box could be opened and potentially even fully understood by designers, these operations may be simply uneconomical. Given the often frantic pace of work in architectural practices, urban designers and architects have little time or will to open the box and study it. This can lead to what can be termed a 'pragmatic' black box where designers employ AI instruments or packages without questioning their functioning as long as they are useful. In this case, agency shifts from the designer to an unquestioned automated system.

FIGURE 21.1 A simple neural network used to classify pictures into cats and no-cats. Photographs are fed into the neural network as inputs, and a binary decision (cat/no-cat) is produced as an outcome.

Source: authors' original.

With the emergence of more sophisticated and autonomous design tools, the designer-machine relation becomes increasingly complex as computational methods become more elaborated and precise and more powerful tools are developed. Our analysis can help understand these changes through a theoretical lens borrowed from the domain of computer science: the deterministic versus non-deterministic approach in a P versus NP problem which we elucidate in the next section. We propose the deterministic (P) in contrast to the non-deterministic (NP) positions as a proxy to analyse the digital demiurge versus black box paradigms and clarify the nuanced design agency within architectural AIs.

P versus NP problem

In computer science, *P* stands for polynomial time, while *NP* for non-deterministic polynomial time. The two terms refer to the time an algorithm takes to solve a given problem. There are problems that can be solved in a P time (more precisely, they belong to a P complexity class), which means that an algorithm can find the solution for the problem in an efficient and relatively fast way. Conversely, NP problems include those cases where an algorithm can find the solution, yet in a very long time, for example, in exponential time (as opposed to polynomial time). However, the solution to such NP problems can be easily verified. This means that, once one can see the solution, it is relatively easy to verify its correctness. To ascertain, however, whether a problem that is quickly solvable (i.e., solvable in polynomial time) is also quickly verifiable is not banal, to the point that the question of whether P = NP or P ≠ NP is considered one of the most challenging and important mathematical problems of the millennium and is listed as one of the six unsolved mathematical problems of the Clay Institute (Clay Mathematics Institute, 2022).

Within the design domain, NP problems correspond to design approaches where architects do not explore all possible options to find a solution, relying instead on intuition, experience and subjectivity. Once a possible solution is drawn, designers can easily and quickly verify whether it works or not. Note that the N in the acronym NP stands for 'non-deterministic,' indicating that the algorithm (or the designer) does not follow a particular rule in guessing the solution (Peres and Castelli, 2021). We are suggesting here that both the designer and the algorithmic process that they develop have agency over the resolution of a design problem. The NP approach (guessing and quickly verifying the efficacy of the solution) is countered by the P model, whereby the designer follows an established set of rules. An example of a P problem in architecture may be about finding the best angle for a facade panel to maximize solar gain and avoid overheating at the same time, so the building maintains an optimal balance between natural light quality and energy performance. Such a problem is easily solvable using computational power where computers can calculate all possible solutions providing numerical values (energy performance, angles of each panel, etc.) to support the final choice. Conversely, an NP problem could be about determining whether or not a particular museum building shape will be appreciated by visitors. This is a problem that a computer is not able to resolve easily as it involves questions that are difficult to encode as an algorithmic logic. However, any experienced architect would immediately be able to ascertain whether the suggested shape will work or not, simply by looking at it. This is when human experience and intuition come into play.

The difference between the two models underpins two different approaches to computation. The NP problem follows a *gut-feeling* approach (cf. Dawson, 2015), guessing the design solution on the basis of instinct, experience and perception (within an NP class), whilst the P problem usually follows an established method or model (or series of rules) to determine the solution (P class). The relevance of this paradigm is crucial. In the attempt to regulate automation in design and human–machine co-design, architects have developed a number of approaches which include shape grammars (Mitchell, 1990; Çağdaş, 1996; Lee et al., 2021) and self-organizing floor plans (Carta, 2020), among others. Overall, as Derix (2014) notes, there are two main approaches to automation in design. One is pursued by John Frazer and Paul Coates from the 1960s onwards where the focus is on self-organizing methods, autonomy of space and the translation of architectural skills and knowledge into computable techniques (Derix, 2014). The second focuses on the search for objectivity and extreme rationalization in the design process, where all nuances and complexities of human behaviours are reduced to computable and standardized factors (Derix, 2014). Interestingly, the work of Frazer and Coates was underpinned by a heuristic approach, where generative design approaches were developed to systematically and intelligently reproduce the architect's knowledge and skills. Derix (2014) suggests that this latter approach was a response to Organic architects (like Hans Scharoun and Rudolf Steiner, for instance) to systematize an empirical approach to space in architecture.

The framework N-NP problem and deterministic versus non-deterministic approaches to design problems are helpful to understand the two positions that architects have with respect to algorithms. From this perspective, architectural design can be seen as a practice ranging from intuition to rule-based models. From a design perspective, this idea can be extended to both digital and physical relationships. There is no fixed hierarchy among the designers and AIs: people do not entirely control software, while, in turn, people are not (entirely) controlled by software. The same applies to the built environment, which is not entirely controlled by people or software and does not always or entirely determine designers' choices or how software adapts to the designed environment. According to this perspective, the boundaries between the author and their instruments begin to fade.

One of the effects (or by-products) of the co-constitutive relationship between designer and software is *emergence*. The notion of emergence can be understood as 'collective phenomena or behaviors in complex adaptive systems that are not present in their individual parts' (Pines, 2014: no page) and is related to a large body of studies, including the work of Holland (2000), Johnson (2002) and Watts (2000), to name but a few. In spatial and urban terms, there are key approaches that are used by designers to produce and manage emergent properties in the practice of spatial production. Examples include Procedural Content Generation (PCG; cf. Salge et al., 2018) where well-established techniques and algorithms used in computer graphics, video production and visual effects are applied to the generation of contents (architectural elements) in an urban environment (cf. Kelly and McCabe, 2006 for an overview of commonly used methods). Such approaches may include the generation of spatial elements through well-known mathematical structures, including fractals (Barnsley, 2014; Mandelbrot and Frame, 1987), cellular automata (Wolfram, 1983), and the production of voxels (Xiao et al., 2020) and maxels (Bottazzi, 2018).

If the idea of the N-NP problem helps to frame the designer–algorithms relationship in terms of deterministic versus non-deterministic approaches, the notion of emergence can be used to explain the dynamics that underpin those approaches. The N-NP problem explains how and why architects use algorithms in their design: how they solve design challenges by means of rule-based models or heuristics, and the extent to which designers trust algorithms and rules to resolve parts of the design, thus devolving part of their agency. In turn, the notion of emergence is helpful to see how such devolution is often neither linear nor hierarchical, but in a state of continuous adaptation, a condition that we will explore empirically in the next section.

Autonomy at work: case studies

To clarify how algorithmic processes and AI work within computational design and how they have direct and indirect implications for the physical elements of the city, we analyse two case studies. First, we will discuss KPF Architects' One Vanderbilt in New York City (KPFui, 2018) where a number of algorithmic models (including multi-objective optimization) have been used to determine the Floor Area Ratio (FAR), orientation, pedestrian flow and overall shape of the building and annexed public spaces. Additionally, we will examine the work of Carta et al. (2022) where Convolutional Neural Networks (CNNs) were used to understand and predict the spatial configurations that characterize urban areas in resilient communities.

The projects were selected to provide examples of how AI is being applied in the Architecture Engineering and Construction (AEC) industry at two different scales: i) multi-purpose high-rise and complex buildings (One

Vanderbilt in New York City) which, due to their high complexity, influence the infrastructure, mobility and overall social use of the urban area surrounding the building; and ii) neighbourhood scale (AI for resilient communities), where AI methods are used to explore the social use of space in urban communities. The selected projects represent two of the main AI-mediated approaches to architecture and urban design: design optimization (the systematic change of a number of design variables to obtain a desired solution measured in terms of performance) and design inference, where a mathematical model is applied to discover new urban aspects (in this case, urban resilience).

In analysing and discussing these projects, we focus on two main aspects: i) the algorithmic strategies and the use of AI-based models to inform the design process in general, as well as the generation of architectural forms and spatial configuration specifically; and ii) the designer/computer relation along the entire design process. Furthermore, we intentionally emphasize the quantitative nature of some architectural processes over the appreciation of qualitative aspects. Most of the design methods included in these projects operate under the assumption that aspects of the built environment can be accurately measured and quantified. As such, they can then be optimized against measurable targets (the amount of energy used by a building, the length of walking paths for pedestrians, etc.). As these projects are instrumental to illustrate how AI is currently used in urban design, we admittedly exclude those aspects of the built environment that are inherently qualitative and relate to the subjectivity, indeterminacy and uncertainties that (also) characterize our cities (Sennett, 2012).

One Vanderbilt in New York City

One Vanderbilt is a complex 162,600 square metre multi-programme building in Midtown Manhattan designed by global architecture firm KPF and completed in 2020 (Figure 21.2). The project includes spaces for civic and cultural activities, mixed-use programmes, office spaces, transportation sections and retail areas that are strongly connected to the existing city fabric and infrastructure. The building is directly connected to Grand Central Terminal. The 427-metre-high main tower combines four interlocked and tapering sections that are shaped to respond to a number of criteria, including a formal and visual relationship with the nearby Chrysler Building and adjacent Grand Central. Corners of the main volumes have been cut to maximize the view from the street and to emphasize key pedestrians' perspectives.

As a part of this project, the computational section of KPF, KPFui (Urban Interface) developed an analytical tool that, through simulations, helped designers to encode several inputs and criteria from different stakeholders into the design process. This method involved a multi-objective optimization

FIGURE 21.2 Skyline of Manhattan with One Vanderbilt (the tallest building on the left) shown in its urban context.

Source: Raimund Koch. Courtesy of Kohn Pedersen Fox Associates.

approach where several objectives are included in the computation. Such objectives can be articulated in terms of the minimization or maximization of the performance values of the building; for example, minimization of solar heating or maximization of pedestrian flows. In particular, the designers focused on the maximization and quality of sky exposure, which can be defined as the quantity of sky visible by users of the building (both inside and outside the building envelope). The amount of sky that people can see is a component of a more general measure of ambient daylight access (KPF, 2021), which contributes to the overall environmental quality of the project. Once the parameters for optimization were determined, the designers employed an evolutionary solver based on a genetic algorithm and a simulated annealing algorithm (Figure 21.3). Both algorithms are based on real-life experience, one drawing from physics and metallurgy and the other from biology and genetics (Rutten, 2013). Evolutionary solvers are a powerful method to determine the best solution to a given problem. By best solution, we mean the (design) solution that is the closest to a pre-set value (a minimum or maximum value, for example). Possible solutions are generated by altering a set of parameters within given ranges and then evaluated using a fitness function, i.e., a mathematical function that compares solutions to a desired value and evaluates how close each design solution is to the optimum score.

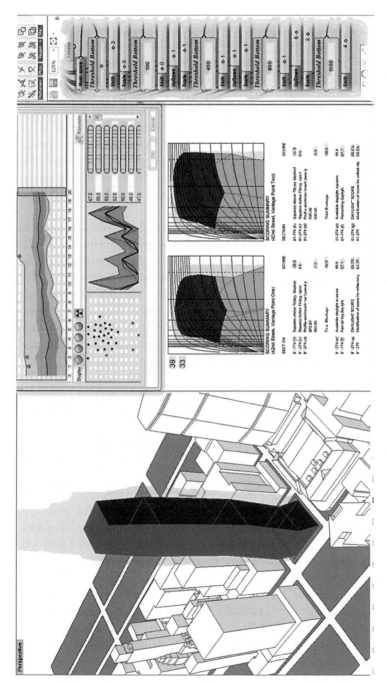

FIGURE 21.3   Interface used by the architects to visualize the results of the genetic algorithm (right-hand), its performance (centre) and the final building shape resulting from the computation (left).

Source: Courtesy of Kohn Pedersen Fox Associates.

Although an evolutionary solver is not strictly categorized as artificial intelligence since it is not able to learn and make decisions independently, it is a good example of how computational methods are applied to help designers with complex design tasks by identifying optimized solutions and devising better strategies to tackle complicated design challenges. The formal research which led to the final form of One Vanderbilt was made possible by advanced computational tools that allowed for the use and manipulation of complex algorithms. The designers are empowered by the machine and, in near real time, can explore infinite variations and weigh their impact on an array of significant metrics. They can do that after the design of the optimization criteria and the implementation in the form of a machine-readable system is decided at the start of the project. During the form-finding operation, agency is shared by the designer (who inputs and tests the machine) and computers (that retrieve the desired inputs).

The method developed by KPF for this project supported the designers to 'reconcile competing objectives and facilitate the design' of the building (KPF, 2021: no page). With this project, designers relied on a quantitative and analytical approach to find the best solution to complex design problems, for example, reducing the portion of sky that the new building would block, optimizing pedestrian circulation and maximizing street views and perspectives. Moreover, the KPFui team devised a robust method that allowed them to positively interact with the stakeholders involved in the design and approval process. According to the team:

> once the design for One Vanderbilt was made public, it became especially important to communicate its impact to the community board and the Landmarks Preservation Committee. Our models and data analysis were key to facilitating the conversation and the review process.
>
> *(KPF, 2021: no page)*

It is worth noting that an evolutionary solver can perhaps illustrate more easily (compared to a traditional neural network approach) the extent to which designers have active involvement in the human–machine collaboration within the design. The parameters to be optimized (minimized or maximized) are decided by the designers in consultation with stakeholders, including representatives of local communities, regulators and local governments. The fitness function (and, therefore, the desired values for each performative aspect of the project) is decided by designers on the basis of what is expected and needed for the building. The generative process which underpinned the evolutionary phase yielded multiple design solutions (options) which have been selected by the computer (through a function) which is instructed and monitored by the designers. In this example, it is easy to see how the computer has been given clear tasks under close observation. This approach clearly illustrates a case of P-class problems, where the domain of possible solutions can be easily and exhaustively computed by a machine through a finite number of logic steps. The designer instructs and oversees this process, expecting a defined output that will inform further design decisions.

AI for resilient communities

ML methods have been extensively and successfully used to simulate new configurations and explore possible design solutions in cities (e.g. Steinfeld, 2019; Wallish, 2019; Del Campo et al., 2021). However, so far these methods have not typically been used as quantitative tools for urban analysis and assessment, especially in net-zero and resilience design. With this project (Carta et al., 2022), we started exploring a new method to generate a tool that can help designers, local governments and policymakers automatically calculate the degree to which a specific neighbourhood is (and can be) resilient, on the basis of a given urban configuration (Figure 21.4).

The project explores the extent to which deep neural networks (specifically CNNs) can help designers quantitatively assess the level of resilience of urban areas and suggest how to improve it. Working from the assumption that the behaviour of people in a neighbourhood is heavily influenced by the spatial configuration and architectural forms of that neighbourhood, we used a combination of AI methods (primarily based on object detection) to assign a resilience score to each given area. We employed CNNs to extract spatial features that characterize resilient areas. In very simple terms, a CNN is able to extract features from images with gradual levels of abstraction through filters. The first filters provide low levels of distinction (e.g. main lines and boundaries dividing areas with colours in stark contrast). After multiple iterations, the neural network gradually raises the level of abstraction to recognize medium-level features (e.g. eyes and noses of human faces). Finally, the last set of filters is able to extract high-level features that imply a certain level of intelligibility such as facial expressions and emotions. Sequential levels of abstraction are generally referred to as layers and their depth determines the way in which the neural network learns.

In this project, we used a large set of satellite images to train the CNN to detect the presence of key urban typologies that have a high influence on resilience, including green and recreational areas, transportation buildings (e.g. train and bus stations) and key buildings like schools, museums and civic centres. Once trained, the model returns a resilience score for each urban area. We validated the model (via the method developed in Carta et al., 2022) using a linear equation that considers the distance of key typologies (schools, green areas, train stations, etc.) from the centre of the neighbourhood. We used a combination of data sources and software packages, including OpenStreetMap, QGIS and Rhinoceros Grasshopper, as shown in Figure 21.5.

FIGURE 21.4 Example of satellite images used for the training of the ML model. The neural network has been trained to detect key elements in the images and classify them into pre-determined groups, including buildings, infrastructure and green areas.

Source: authors' original.

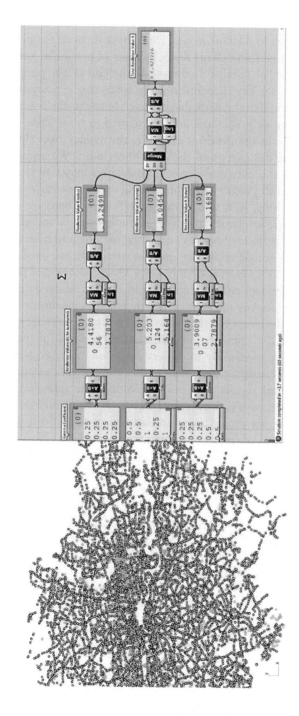

FIGURE 21.5 Data points representing the georeferenced position of key urban elements (bus stops, schools, train stations, etc.) from OpenStreetMap (left) are computed into a linear equation that returns an overall value of resilience (right).

Source: authors' original.

Experimentation with CNNs allows designers to partially influence a very complex system that is otherwise considered a black box. Feedback-loop mechanisms allowed us to adjust the way we trained them to the point that we could predict (to a certain extent) the behaviour of particular urban systems and produce a set of reliable analytics. At the end of the process, our tool was able to recognize key elements in urban areas (e.g. a primary school or a housing unit), establish the walkable distance between the centre of the area and each building or green area and calculate a general value of resilience for that area. As in the previous example, the agency over the design alternates between the designers and the algorithms used. We argue, therefore, that agency is in this case multileveled. First, there exists an element of design in both the overall project (including the theoretical premises for such work) and the algorithms, APIs and libraries employed. There are multiple designers with different levels of trust. For example, we, as architects and urban designers, used software libraries consisting of code and routines written by other designers for different purposes. In particular, we used a detection algorithm called YOLOv5 (You Only Look Once), developed primarily for object detection in videos and with moving objects. We adapted the library running YOLOv5 for our own purposes. We, therefore, asynchronously collaborated with other designers (of algorithms and software packages).

Second, we trusted the libraries and APIs that we used in this project to run calculations for us; specifically for object detection and classification of key urban elements. As designers, we made choices and selections during this process, sending partial results back to our model for refinement. This approach creates an iterative process where designers and machines cooperate. On a deeper level, we should mention that the computations were run both locally (on our local computers) and remotely (using graphical processing units (GPUs) within the Google Colab environment). We also used a number of software frameworks (e.g. PyTorch) and parallel computing platforms (e.g. CUDA) as a part of our ML process.

Finally, since our model has been published as a web app, we have extended its agency so that other designers can use it from their own computers without our intervention. Since our model is completed, at least at a prototype stage, the ML process works automatically and without the control, input or supervision of the original designers. Users of the app will make their own use of the model, changing settings, areas and scale of the selected urban context.

Conclusion: a different kind of agency

In the described case studies, we can see how AI can be employed as an integral part of the design process. Borrowing from algebraic concepts, Bernard Cache describes this process of parametrization (notations) through the notion of *objectiles* (Cache, 1995). The idea is depicted using the example of a single function (e.g. $f(x) = y$) that can contain infinite possible formal outcomes depending on the parameters chosen (Cache, 1995). The idea of an *objectile* is helpful to describe an open system: a model where a flexible basic structure is coupled with variables that can be filled with different values depending on the design strategy. This notion is purposely generic, and can be applied to many types of work. When an *objectile* is applied to a concrete design project, this becomes a *projectile* (Cache, 1995). Within the domain of digital and computational architecture, a projectile is expressed in the form of a series of algorithms created and combined by designers to address a specific design challenge. A case in point is One Vanderbilt where the project can be seen as the result of the collaboration between designers and machines. The building, in its infinite variations, remains under the control of the designers as *projectiles*. The designers, having evaluated the complex results from the computation, have the ability to select the most suitable options for a given project.

In Resilient Communities, several different *objectiles* were combined and applied, through reiterated tests and operations until the results were deemed satisfactory against a pre-determined set of design objectives. Here the process is more fluid and changes at every iteration, combining parts developed by different designers and machines. While in One Vanderbilt the design task consists of *finding* the best possible solution to a given design problem (projectile), the main task in Resilient Communities is to exist as an *objectile*, embodying different possible abstract configurations at once. In this case, architects and planners are still responsible for devising the design strategy and combining the different parts of the process together. However, to obtain more complex and performative formal results, designers must test their ideal spatial configuration against many AI-generated options. In such processes, design agency moves from the (human) designer who is in full control of certain phases to algorithmic processes where humans cede their control to automated routines and complex calculations, with a certain degree of serendipity. This complex relationship between humans and AI is summarized in Figure 21.6.

The figure illustrates how the process starts with *the designer* and *other designers and software developers* as the two main inputs of the architectural artificial intelligence (AAI). The input of the designer translates into data curation and the supervision of the entire process which, in turn, provides certain feedback to the designer who can then consider it for the next cycle in the process. This internal feedback loop of the designer–algorithmic system is coupled with input from other designers and developers producing the AAI that eventually produces the final design which is the ultimate outcome.

While it is certainly true that AI has the potential to produce a paradigm shift in design practices, this does not mean that AI tools will necessarily

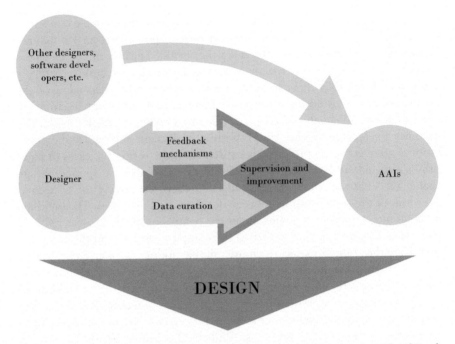

FIGURE 21.6 Co-creation scheme of design agency in *architectural artificial intelligence* (AAI) where architectural design is the product of the interaction of the designer with AAIs.

Source: authors' original.

reduce the need for designers or even free them from the burden of responsible work. Moreover, we do not expect AI to foster an inscrutable production of space without human supervision, at least not in the near future. While designers are constantly looking for ways to devote as much time as possible to the design activity to produce better designs (Fairs, 2021), they also need to change their way of thinking and approaching design problems, by studying, for example, algorithms and data structures to be able to 'justify every single design decision your computer has made on your behalf' (Rutten, 2021: 132).

Once developed, AAI tools must still be managed, questioned and combined with the work of other designers. A fundamental aspect of this collaborative paradigm is that the diversity of approaches, solutions and the cultural milieu of architectural and urban design remain preserved, as well as empowered, by AI tools. Rather than fitting already existing paradigms (and thus becoming a mannerism), AAIs can potentially produce their own expressions in new design schemes and discoveries. As illustrated by a recent exchange between Thom Mayne (Morphosis) and Wolf Prix (Coop Himmelb(l)au), two of the most prominent architects working in the digital architecture domain, the designs produced by AI are 'more engaging, compelling, useful than the one I did that was manipulated through my own single instinct' (Mayne and Prix 2020: no page).

What we define as AAI is currently at the centre of a fast-paced experimentation among design practices. In this sense, AAI is a relatively recent field of exploration in design studies which, as a consequence of its application of AI to design, strongly connects the traditionally complex fields of the architectural industry to computer science, formal methods and, to some extent, neuroscience and ethics. All these interdisciplinary components converge into a complex human–AI relationship. The nature of this relationship is constantly mutating. AAIs, framed as *digital demiurges* or as *black boxes*, correspond to two polarized paradigms. We suggest that the relationship that designers have with computers and, therefore, their agency over the production of urban space is amorphous and non-hierarchical. Today, design automation entails a profound collaborative paradigm and constant feedback between designers and AI, to the point that a design project can be considered a collective oeuvre.

References

Barns, S. (2021). Out of the loop? On the radical and the routine in urban big data. *Urban Studies*, 58(15), 3203–3210.

Barnsley, M. F. (2014). *Fractals everywhere*. Academic Press.

Batty, M. (2018). Artificial intelligence and smart cities. *Environment and Planning B: Urban Analytics and City Science*, 45, 3–6.

Blau, J. R. (1976). Toward A Scientific Architecture by Yona Friedman. The MIT Press, Cambridge, Massachusetts, 1975. pp. 169 (Translated by Cynthia Lang.). *International Journal of General System*, 3(1), 68–70.

Bottazzi, R. (2018). *Digital architecture beyond computers: Fragments of a cultural history of computational design*. Bloomsbury Publishing.

Cache, B. (1995). *Earth moves: the furnishing of territories*. MIT Press.

Cache, B., & Girard, C. (1999). Objectile: The pursuit of philosophy by other means? In Stephen, P. (Ed.). *Hypersurface Architecture II*, Vol. 69 (9/10),

Çağdaş, G. (1996). A shape grammar model for designing row-houses. *Design Studies*, 17(1), 35–51.

Carpo, M. (2011). *The alphabet and the algorithm*. MIT Press.

Carpo, M. (2017). *The second digital turn: design beyond intelligence*. MIT Press.

Carta, S. (2019). *Big data, code and the discrete city: Shaping public realms*. Routledge.

Carta, S. (2020). Machine learning and computational design. *Ubiquity*, 1–10. DOI: 10.1145/3401842

Carta, S. (2021). Self-Organizing Floor Plans. *Harvard Data Science Review HDSR*. DOI: 10.1162/99608f92.e5f9a0c7

Carta, S., St Loe, S., Turchi, T., & Simon, J. (2020). Self-organising floor plans in care homes. *Sustainability*, 12(11), 4393.

Carta, S., Turchi, T., & Pintacuda, L. (2022). Measuring Resilient Communities: an Analytical and Predictive Tool. In Jeroen van Ameijde, Nicole Gardner, Kyung

Hoon Hyun, Dan Luo, Urvi Sheth (Eds.), *POST-CARBON - Proceedings of the 27th CAADRIA Conference*, Sydney, 9–15 April 2022.

Chaillou, S. (2019). AI Architecture Towards a New Approach (2019). Available at: https://www.academia.edu/39599650/AI_Architecture_Towards_a_New_Approach. [Accessed 19/01/2023].

Clay Mathematics Institute (2022. *Millennium Problems.* Clay Mathematics Institute. Available at: https://www.claymath.org/millennium-problems. [Accessed 19/01/2023]

Cugurullo, F. (2020). Urban artificial intelligence: From automation to autonomy in the smart city. *Frontiers in Sustainable Cities, 2,* 38.

Cugurullo, F. (2021). *Frankenstein Urbanism: Eco, Smart and Autonomous Cities, Artificial Intelligence and the End of the City.* Routledge.

Dawson, J. (2015). Building to sustain body and soul. *JBU Journal of Biourbanism,* 1, 49.

Del Campo, M., Carlson, A., & Manninger, S. (2021). Towards hallucinating machines-designing with computational vision. *International Journal of Architectural Computing, 19*(1), 88–103.

Derix, C. (2014). The space of people in computation. In Derix, Å. & E. Christian and Izaki (Eds.), *Architectural Design.* Wiley.

Durmus Ozturk, S. (2020). Rethinking the black box in architecture design studio. *SAGE Open, 10*(2), DOI: 10.1177/2158244020927.

Fairs, M. (2021). Artificial intelligence "will empower designers" say Clippings co-founders. *DeZeen.* Available at: https://www.dezeen.com/2021/08/19/artificial-intelligence-empower-designers-clippings-co-founders/ [Accessed 19/01/2023].

Foth, M., Forlano, L., Satchell, C., & Gibbs, M. (2011). *From social butterfly to engaged citizen: Urban informatics, social media, ubiquitous computing, and mobile technology to support citizen engagement.* MIT Press.

Holland, J. H. (2000). *Emergence: From chaos to order.* OUP Oxford.

Huang, W., & Zheng, H. (2018). Architectural drawings recognition and generation through machine learning. In Anzalone, P., Del Signore, M., Wit, A.J., (Eds.) *Proceedings of the 38th Annual Conference of the Association for Computer Aided Design in Architecture (ACADIA).* Universidad Iberoamericana, Mexico City.

Johnson, S. (2002). *Emergence: The connected lives of ants, brains, cities, and software.* Simon and Schuster.

Jones, J. C. (1970). *Design methods: seeds of human futures.* Wiley Interscience.

Joyce, S. C., & Nazim, I. (2021). Limits to Applied ML in Planning and Architecture-Understanding and defining extents and capabilities. In Stojakovic, V and Tepavcevic, B (Eds.), *Towards a new, configurable architecture - Proceedings of the 39th eCAADe Conference* - Volume 1, University of Novi Sad, Novi Sad, Serbia, 8–10 September 2021, pp. 243–252.

Kelly, G., & McCabe, H. (2006). A survey of procedural techniques for city generation. *ITB Journal, 14*(3), 342–351.

Kitchin, R. (2014). *The data revolution: Big data, open data, data infrastructures and their consequences.* Sage.

Kitchin, R., Lauriault, T. P., & McArdle, G. (2018). *Data and the City.* Routledge, London.

KPF. (2021). *Case Study: One Vanderbilt. New York, NY.* Available at: https://ui.kpf.com/one-vanderbilt [Accessed 19/01/2023].

KPFui. (2018). *One-Vanderbilt.* Available at: https://www.kpf.com/projects/one-vanderbilt and https://ui.kpf.com/projects. [Accessed 19/01/2023].

Krizhevsky, A., Sutskever, I., & Hinton, G. E. (2012). Imagenet classification with deep convolutional neural networks. *Advances in Neural Information Processing Systems*, 25, 1–9.

Lee, J. H., Ostwald, M. J., & Gu, N. (2021). A statistical shape grammar approach to analysing and generating design instances of Murcutt's domestic architecture. *Environment and Planning B: Urban Analytics and City Science*, 48(4), 929–944.

Mackenzie, A. (2002). *Transductions: Bodies and machines at speed*. A&C Black.

Mandelbrot, B., & Frame, M. (1987). *Fractals//Encyclopedia of Physical Science and Technology*. Academic Press, Inc., San Diego CA, 579–593.

Marston, S. A., Jones III, J. P., & Woodward, K. (2005). Human geography without scale. *Transactions of the Institute of British Geographers*, 30(4), 416–432.

Mayne, T., & Prix, W. (2020). *DigitalFUTURES: FROM DECON TO AI: AI and Architectural Practice*. Available at: https://www.youtube.com/watch?v=OlvYzm WuMsU [Accessed 19/01/2023].

Mitchell, W. J. (1990). *The logic of architecture: Design, computation, and cognition*. MIT Press.

Nauata, N., Hosseini, S., Chang, K.-H., Chu, H., Cheng, C.-Y., & Furukawa, Y. (2021). House-GAN++: Generative Adversarial Layout Refinement Network towards Intelligent Computational Agent for Professional Architects. *Proceedings of the IEEE/CVF Conference on Computer Vision and Pattern Recognition*. Available at: https://openaccess.thecvf.com/content/CVPR2021/html/Nauata_House-GAN_Generative_Adversarial_Layout_Refinement_Network_towards_Intelligent_Computational_Agent_CVPR_2021_paper.html [Accessed 19/01/2023].

Negroponte, N. (1969). Toward a theory of architecture machines. *Journal of Architectural Education*, 23(2), 9–12.

Oxman, R., & Gu, N. (2015). Theories and models of parametric design thinking. In Martens, B., Wurzer, G., Grasl, T., Lorenz, W.E. & Schaffranek, R. (Eds.), *Real Time - Proceedings of the 33rd eCAADe Conference - Volume 2*, Vienna University of Technology, Vienna, Austria, 16–18 September 2015, pp. 477–482.

Peres, F., & Castelli, M. (2021). Combinatorial optimization problems and meta-heuristics: Review, challenges, design, and development. *Applied Sciences*, 11(14), 6449.

Pines, D. (2014). Emergence: A unifying theme for 21st century science. Medium. Available at: https://medium.com/sfi-30-foundations-frontiers/emergence-a-unifying-theme-for-21st-century-science-4324ac0f951e [Accessed 19/01/2023].

Rittel, H. W., & Webber, M. M. (1973). Dilemmas in a general theory of planning. *Policy sciences*, 4(2), 155–169.

Rutten, D. (2013). Galapagos: On the logic and limitations of generic solvers. *Architectural Design*, 83(2), 132–135.

Rutten, D. (2021). The inevitable and utter demise of the entire architectural profession. Available at: https://discourse.mcneel.com/t/unpublished-opinion-piece/118250. [Accessed 19/01/2023].

Salge, C., Green, M. C., Canaan, R., & Togelius, J. (2018). Generative design in minecraft (gdmc) settlement generation competition. *Proceedings of the 13th International Conference on the Foundations of Digital Games*. DOI: 10.1145/3235765.3235814.

Sennett, R. (2012). No one likes a city that's too smart. *The Guardian*.

Senseable City Lab. (2019). *AI Station. Senseable City Lab*. Available at: http://senseable.mit.edu/ai-station/app_wifi/ [Accessed 19/01/2023].

Steinfeld, K. (2019). GAN Loci. 392–403. In *ACADIA 19: UBIQUITY AND AUTONOMY*. Proceedings of the 39th Annual Conference of the Association for Computer Aided Design in Architecture (ACADIA) ISBN 978-0-578-59179-7. The University of Texas at Austin School of Architecture, Austin, Texas 21–26 October, 2019. pp. 392–403.

Wallish, S. (2019). *Counterfeiting daily: An exploration of the use of generative adversarial neural networks in the architectural design process*. Columbia University.

Wang, Z., Liang, Q., Duarte, F., Zhang, F., Charron, L., Johnsen, L., Cai, B., Ratti, C. (2019). Quantifying legibility of indoor spaces using Deep Convolutional Neural Networks: Case studies in train stations. *Building and Environment*, 160, DOI: 10.1016/j.buildenv.2019.04.035.

Watts, D. J. (2000). *Small worlds: The dynamics of networks between order and randomness*. Princeton University Press Princeton.

Wolfram, S. (1983). Cellular Automata, *Los Alamos Science*, 9, 2–21.

Xiao, K., Chen, C.-C., Guo, Z., Wang, X., & Yan, C. (2020). Research on Voxel-based Aggregation Design and its Fabrication. In D. Holzer, W. Nakapan, A. Globa, I. Koh (Eds.), *RE: Anthropocene, Design in the Age of Humans - Proceedings of the 25th CAADRIA Conference* - Volume 1, Chulalongkorn University, Bangkok, Thailand, 5–6 August 2020, pp. 13–22.

22

CONCLUSIONS

The present of urban AI and the future of cities

Federico Cugurullo, Federico Caprotti, Matthew Cook,
Andrew Karvonen, Pauline McGuirk and Simon Marvin

Introduction: urban AI across spaces and scales

The era of urban artificial intelligences has begun. It is already difficult to imagine urban futures without artificial intelligence (AI). As the previous chapters have empirically shown, AI is being strongly integrated into the nature, character and functioning of urban spaces. Cities, in particular, are increasingly absorbing large volumes of AI technology into their transport, government and economic portfolios, triggering urban transformations of rare impetus. The technology in question is new, but the type of techno-urban symbiosis that we are now witnessing runs deep in the history of the city. For example, the reverberations of the introduction of combustion engines into the urban environment at the end of the nineteenth century are still echoing (Hall, 2014). Likewise, when the digital revolution of the 1970s transformed society's fundamental dynamics, the changes wrought on urban systems continued this momentum of sociotechnical change (Castells, 2011; Graham and Marvin, 2002). In essence, urban history tells us that significant technological innovations carry substantial and long-standing urban changes with them. Today, in the belief that 'AI is the new electricity,' entrepreneurs and politicians from all over the world position AI as a great technological innovation (see Lee, 2018: 25). As urbanists, we expect such positioning to drive ongoing changes in the fabric of cities for many years to come.

This volume has clarified the urbanity of AI, revealing the urban as a space where multiple AIs become prominently visible, materially situated in the physical landscape and imbricated in everyday life. The contributors have identified several key reasons for the growth of AI in urban spaces, thereby shedding light on the drivers of the *urban AI phenomenon* which in recent

DOI: 10.4324/9781003365877-26

years has emerged in the urban studies, design and planning literatures (Cugurullo, 2020; Luusua et al., 2023; Sanchez et al., 2022; Ye et al., 2023; Yigitcanlar et al., 2023). In Chapter 2, for instance, Dowling, McGuirk and Sisson illustrate how AI is emplaced through urban experiments, particularly in cities as the loci of pressing socio-environmental challenges. Their focus on autonomous vehicles (AVs) links this specific type of urban AI experimentation to the challenges of urban transportation. Similarly, in Chapter 9, Valdez, Cook and Potter find a connection between tackling some of the biggest challenges in transportation, such as car-dependency and traffic congestion, and experiments in urban robotics. Seen in these terms, the connection between AI and the urban is consolidated because cities present numerous development challenges and are sites of potential solutions. This problem/solution interconnection and narrative at the basis of the diffusion of urban AI goes beyond transportation and is also observable in relation to pandemics (Chapter 19), the capacity to cope with climate change and environmental disasters (Chapter 21) and the issue of energy provision (Chapter 14). If, as Angelo and Wachsmuth (2020: 2201) remark, 'everyone thinks cities can save the planet,' now an increasingly common belief seems to be that AI can save cities and thus the planet.

There are also potent economic drivers at play in the urbanization of AI. Cities provide demand and thus a market for AI-supported mobility innovations: hence the proliferation of AV experiments in the city (see Chapters 2 and 3). In addition, as While notes in Chapter 7, city managers do not simply see an opportunity in AI to improve the management of complex and often unsustainable urban systems. They also recognize the economic power of being at the cutting-edge of urban innovation. In this sense, AI becomes entrained in boosting a city's reputation internationally, elevating it as a global pioneer in technology and sustainability (see also Chapter 9). Last but not least, there is the pragmatic issue of infrastructure. AI is inevitably sutured to the urban as the site of concentration of technologically advanced infrastructures. This is the case, for instance, with mega hospitals in Chinese cities which are characterized by state-of-the-art infrastructure (necessary for the functioning of delicate AI systems), as well as by high-population densities which generate enough demand for expensive AI technologies and guarantee sufficient return on investment (Chapter 19).

As the case studies examined in this volume show, the emergence of urban AI becomes visible at multiple urban scales. The works of Jackman (Chapter 8) and Sweeney (Chapter 18) reveal that urban AI is entering intimate domestic spaces, thereby affecting the everyday life of individuals and families. Urban AI is also animating single buildings (Chapter 21) and urban precincts such as airports (Chapter 11) in a way that affects both their metabolism and experience. Overall, as many chapters illustrate, urban AI operates most consequentially in the city at the scale of large urban systems. Multiple urban AIs are reshaping cities' transport systems and supply chains (Chapters 2, 3, 4, 5, 6, 9 and 13), the mechanisms through which public security is maintained in the city (Chapters 7 and 15), the provision of housing (Chapters 17 and 20), the delivery of health services in urban areas (Chapter 19) and the generation and distribution of energy across urban spaces (Chapter 14).

There are of course importance exceptions to consider. These include urban AIs whose agency and spatial impact exceed the scale of the city, overflowing into international geopolitical networks (Chapter 16) and global supply chains (Chapter 5). In this sense, our urbanistic perspective on AI is in line with the work of scholars such as Dauvergne (2020), Crawford (2021) and Van Wynsberghe (2021) who have fleshed out the international character of AI as a technology whose production, distribution, consumption and ultimately (un)sustainability transcend geographical boundaries. In addition, we need to remember that there are AIs that are not strictly urban and operate in rural areas (Guo and Li, 2018), under the sea (Blanchard and Flint, 2017) and in outer space (Campa et al., 2019), in realms that are beyond the analytical scope of this volume, but that may converge with urban AIs in the near future due to the pull of planetary urbanization and the increasing interdependence of the planet's socio-economic, environmental and digital systems (Brenner, 2014; Jain and Korzhenevych, 2022).

When it comes to the spaces of urban AIs, this volume's contributions also show how the blurring between *physical* and *digital* spaces is accelerating. The seeds of these processes were evident in early smart-city experiments from decades ago (Angelidou, 2014; Couclelis, 2004; Willis and Aurigi, 2017). However, urban AI both increases and changes the dynamics whereby physical and digital spaces collide, to the point of becoming almost inseparable from one another. In Chapter 5, for example, Cugurullo and Kassens-Noor stress that AI-driven vehicles are part of digital platforms without which they would not function. More specifically, Waymo's autonomous cars are part of the Alphabet platform (i.e. Google) while Zoox's vehicles are a component of Amazon's platform. Through such digital platforms, AVs both share and receive urban data that the AI behind the wheel needs to understand and navigate urban spaces. Similarly, Chapter 9 highlights the hybrid location of urban robots' intelligence which partly resides in servers and clouds where much of the computation takes place and where data is stored. In this sense, urban AI becomes a medium that incorporates physical and digital spaces into a seemingly homogeneous whole where what is material and what is aethereal coexist under the aegis of a single non-biological intelligence. This is particularly the case of city brains which, as Chen's study indicates in Chapter 14, are an assemblage of material and digital infrastructures including tangible utility pipelines through which essential resources such as water and electricity flow, and intangible digital twins that mirror and monitor the physical reality of cities.

In the next section, we turn from the multiple spaces and scales of urban AI to its impacts on the city and the ways in which the emergence of AI in cities is reshaping urban society, urban infrastructure, urban governance, urban planning and urban sustainability. Subsequently, we demonstrate how the city is influencing the evolution of AI, by moulding its physical manifestations in actually existing spaces and determining its very intelligence. The second half of the chapter is dedicated to unpacking the similarities that exist between this collection's case studies and well-known practices of smart urbanism. Here, we highlight connections with past and present smart-city initiatives, as well as points of departure indicating the formation of a novel AI urbanism. We conclude the volume by discussing the implications that the emergence of urban AI has for urban theory and the future of cities. Ours is a warning about the impending risks posed by multiple urban AIs and the obscure black boxes driving their operations, but also an invitation to politically engage as citizens with increasingly autonomous cities that might forever escape our understanding and thus our control.

How AI changes the city

AI is changing the city in multiple ways and through heterogenous impacts because, as we stress in Chapter 1, we are not addressing a single universal technology. An urbanistic perspective on AI means recognizing the existence of diverse urban artificial intelligences and acknowledging that these entail different urban repercussions. For example, tangible urban AIs such as AVs and urban robots have a physical volume, size and weight and therefore influence the shape of cities which need to adapt to their material presence. Autonomous cars and trucks, in particular, represent a bulky type of urban AI whose circulation in the city requires space in the shape of roads and traffic lanes. Chapter 5 delves into the production of urban space that the diffusion of AVs implies, emphasizing that the adoption of Shared Autonomous Vehicles (SAVs) would mitigate the pressure for *ex novo* road infrastructure. As Vitale Brovarone and Staricco remark in Chapter 6, the spatial impact of AVs does not depend simply on the technology per se, but also on how the technology in question is being employed. Both chapters make the case for SAVs as a more sustainable urban AI than privately owned AVs which are expected to decrease travel disutility, prompt people to commute long distances and lead to greater suburbanization (see also Cugurullo et al., 2021; Hawkins and Nurul Habib, 2019; Larson and Zhao, 2020; Silva et al., 2022). It follows that the spatial impact of urban AI is not predetermined nor is its sustainability.

Yet, this collection makes clear that urban AIs will unavoidably influence urban sustainability. Hopkins points out in Chapter 4 that autonomous trucks are reshaping the very supply chains that sustain cities' metabolism.

Similarly, While observes in Chapter 7 that urban robots are producing new mobilities, in a way that is not neutral for the social sustainability of the city. The presence of service robots operating on public streets, for example, implies a reformulation of pedestrian rights of way, and the diffusion of drones across cities is connected to the creation of new flight paths and corridors (see also Lockhart et al., 2021; Umlauf and Burchardt, 2022). These new spaces might not be evenly distributed and accessible, particularly when, for instance, private delivery companies such as Amazon compete for exclusive access to urban drone corridors in an attempt to establish a 'flying warehouse' above the city (Jeong et al., 2022: 1). From this perspective, the production of space triggered by urban AIs is intrinsically connected to the distribution of power in the city.

This volume exposes the depth of the changes driven by urban AI and the need to understand them before they become irreversible. Some of the most poignant examples include domestic drones which, as shown in Chapter 8, are contributing to the formation of an intimate state of surveillance in a way that, particularly in the West, is firmly fixed on well-known dynamics of *surveillance capitalism* (see Zuboff, 2019). Similarly, Chapters 7, 9 and 11 focus on how robots are changing urban ecosystems by adding a *more-than-human* element to them, which is agential in nature and thus has the capacity to alter fundamental urban dynamics. The impacts of robots are ambiguous, ranging from support of humans in times of crisis such as delivering food during COVID-19 restrictions when human-to-human contact was prohibited (Chapter 9), to the application of police tracking and subsequent use of weaponized robots to intervene at a distance (Chapter 7). More subtly, as Lin and Yeo note in Chapter 11, the deployment of robots is resulting in labour precarity as this type of urban AI provides urban managers with a cheaper and more compliant workforce. They also consider how urban robots are establishing new standards of urban living, particularly with regard to cleanliness and health, as well as a comprehensive system of surveillance that lurks behind the smiling face of a robot.

At first glance, the repercussions of urban AIs tend to become less visible when the focus shifts to AI-enabled digital platforms, city brains, urban software agents and algorithms. However, the implementation of these immaterial urban AIs actually entails profound urban changes and consequences which are explored in the second half of the volume. In Chapter 15, Shapiro focuses on AI-controlled platforms employed to foresee the spaces and times of criminal activities and identify those individuals who are likely to be offenders and victims (see also Lally, 2022). His chapter highlights how the predictive solutions of urban AIs lack precision and tend to reproduce injustice by discriminating against racial minorities and chronically deprived urban residents (Richardson et al., 2019). Similarly, in Chapters 14 and 16, the authors observe a potent logic of predictability in the use of city brains in the governance of urban transport, security and energy. Chen's research in particular reveals how city managers utilize a city brain as a *mirror world* (Gelernter, 1993). City brains produce digital twins of existing cities through which human policymakers can zoom in on specific urban systems and foresee their evolution, but there is a problematic discrepancy between the real city and its digital representation (Chapter 14).

The logic of predictability that the contributors identify in city brains and digital platforms is also revealed in urban software agents and algorithms. In Chapter 20, Rosen and Garboden note how screening algorithms are widely used in the housing market to identify "good" and "bad" tenants and to predict their future behaviour (see also Fields, 2022). However, as the authors remark, the way this type of urban AI operates is undermined by biases and stereotypes. It tends to exacerbate pre-existing biases and power-relations between landlords and tenants, resulting in discrimination against racial minorities, low-income people and women. Of course, there are also positive consequences to acknowledge, particularly in situations where urban AI is not set loose but rather controlled by human actors as a tool to improve well-established practices. For instance, Pisu and Carta's study shows how AI is aiding architects and urban designers in the design of buildings, districts and cities (Chapter 21). Similarly, Chapter 19 emphasizes the helpful role of urban software agents in the acceleration of epidemiological investigations.

Nonetheless, other chapters highlight how such aid comes at the expense of privacy. Guo and Cugurullo's research stresses that in the course of an epidemiological investigation, urban software agents obtain a lot of personal information on people's health, mobility and contacts, which serves as the foundation for a comprehensive system of surveillance (Chapter 19). These observations resonate with Sweeney's study of the *modus operandi* of AI digital assistants in domestic spaces (Chapter 18). With a focus on Amazon's Alexa, she examines the central role that this type of urban AI plays in housekeeping and caretaking, assisting in delicate and sensitive household tasks such as teaching children and reading to them at bedtime. In so doing, urban AI enters our homes and monitors our most intimate activities while extracting large volumes of personal data. In this sense, urban AIs can be seen as unlimited *extractive technologies* that use private information as raw material (Zuboff, 2019).

In addition to specific urban changes connected to the implementation of particular urban AIs, this volume identifies broader urban repercussions that transcend single case studies. These urban trends are driven by the integration of AI into the city and are symptomatic of the transformative force of AI as a new technology which has entered urban spaces and systems only in recent times. The novel nature of AI means that there is not a simple process of assimilation into the urban fabric. Rather most cities go through delicate processes of experimentation whereby different urban AIs are trialled. In these terms, as is emphasized particularly in Chapters 2 and 3, the emergence of urban AIs are connected to the development of urban experiments (see also Beukers and Bertolini, 2021; Cugurullo, 2018; Evans et al., 2016; While et al., 2021). Such urban AI experiments de facto alter the material and digital infrastructures of cities, to create spaces where urban AIs can be tested. They also influence governance by forging new partnerships between the private and public sectors to carry out urban experiments (Dowling and McGuirk, 2022; McCarroll and Cugurullo, 2022). Problematically, as Stilgoe and O'Donovan stress in Chapter 3, the governance of urban AI experiments can be undemocratic when they are driven by public–private consortiums that do not involve citizens.

Especially in relation to urban governance, this collection shows how large-scale urban AIs are changing the status quo by establishing unprecedented levels of connectivity across multiple urban domains. AI-driven digital platforms and city brains, in particular, have agency over a plethora of urban sectors ranging from energy provision to policing. Furthermore, as Greenfield (2018) reminds us, AIs "speak to each other," in the sense that they can be interconnected, thereby sharing information and functioning together as part of a larger technological assemblage. In other words, small-scale urban AIs such as AVs and robots do not operate in isolation but are instead connected to digital platforms. Urban governance is undergoing a process of homogenization whereby a single AI platform controls multiple urban systems as well as smaller urban AIs (Cugurullo, 2021a). The process is so pervasive that in some cases, as Smart, Zhao and Curran argue in Chapter 16, individuals cannot opt-out and have no choice but to live in cities and urban regions managed by city brains which, particularly in China, have become a pervasive tool of national governance.

The aforementioned AI-driven homogenization of urban governance in which multiple urban AIs coalesce into a single AI platform also has significant data implications. Several chapters shed light on the increasing dangers of *function creep*: 'the tendency of data initially collected for one purpose to be used for another often unintended or unanticipated purpose' (Brayne, 2017: 980; Koops, 2021). An emblematic case is that of public health data that Chinese urban software agents collect as part of epidemiological investigations (Chapter 19), which then feeds into the same governmental platforms that are employed to identify potential political dissidents and profile citizens in the age of the Social Credit System (Roberts et al., 2021). Indeed, as Barns observes in Chapter 12, urban AIs are frequently installed in public urban spaces where they can access large amounts of information that go well beyond their original purpose. In this sense, a potent repercussion of urban AI is an acute disturbance and transformation of what Kitchin and Moore-Cherry (2021) term *urban data ecosystems*.

How the city changes AI

Cities are far from passive recipients of new technologies. While AI is reconstituting the city, the city is actively constituting AI. This collection illuminates this mutual constitution and provides evidence of how the urban is reframing AI. First and foremost, several chapters highlight how urban AI experiments are shaped by their contexts. In Chapter 2, for example, Dowling, McGuirk and Sisson argue that in places where existing technology companies do not challenge car dependency, AV experiments evolve in a way that reinforces the dominance of the car. Such place-based AI experimentation reaffirms pre-existing logics, cultures and politico-economic interests (Acheampong and Cugurullo, 2019; Aoyama and Leon, 2021; Escandon-Barbosa et al., 2021), rarely being transformative and instead tending to reinforce the status quo.

In addition, the city dictates how certain urban AIs will be employed. Vitale Brovarone and Staricco argue in Chapter 6 that urban governance is key to the development of AVs, as it can make the difference between the implementation of AV services and the diffusion of private autonomous cars. They also reflect on the importance of democratic urban governance, since urban AI is a technology that, if left unchecked in the hands of private companies, is likely to generate negative socio-environmental effects by reproducing established patterns of private ownership and consumption. Similarly, Moore and Bissell consider in Chapter 13 how the role and purpose of urban AI is determined by its context. Their study examines local dynamics whereby a community comes to utilize and control an AI platform in a cooperative manner, as an alternative to private ownership and management. They reveal how the community debates and doubts about the digital platform and the underpinning AI, ultimately shaping its function and evolution. Urban AIs are thus not static entities but rather evolve in a relational manner as they engage with urban residents.

Urban communities and urban authorities may indeed seek to hinder the diffusion of AIs across the city. This is the case in San Francisco where, as While points out in Chapter 7, the municipal government banned street robots in 2017 in light of public concerns about surveillance and mobility. San Francisco's story resonates with Lefebvre's idea of *the right to the city* (see Attoh, 2011; Harvey, 2008). In this instance, the right in question was that of pedestrians to walk without robots' interference in public spaces. This is also a story of fears and concerns which are powerful determinants in the acceptance of novel AIs (Cugurullo and Acheampong, 2023; Kelly et al., 2022; Li and Huang, 2020). In 2022, San Francisco's Board of Supervisors authorized the weaponization of police robots and gave them the right to kill criminal suspects. Citizens responded by protesting against killer robots and convinced the local authorities to remove that right in less than a month (Blanchard, 2023). Ultimately, the emergence of AI can be held in check or pushed forward depending on whether a city's culture is rooted in a tradition of public resistance or faith in innovation. San Francisco belongs to the former category, while Chinese cities where privacy issues and new technologies are perceived differently, often fall in the latter category (cf. Chapter 19). Urban geography matters. Place and its culture plays a key role in the acceptance and fruition of urban AIs, exactly like it did in relation to early smart-city technologies (Karvonen et al., 2019; Miller et al., 2021).

The influence of place extends beyond matters of acceptance and modes of employment. Cities affect the very nature of urban AIs. As Sumartojo notes in Chapter 10, when an AI is set loose in an urban space, its actions and capabilities usually transcend what its creators had in mind. Her study on urban robots shows that urban AIs are not complete until they enter the real world. This is because urban AIs make mistakes and adapt to their surrounding urban environment and, is so doing, they change. In this sense, the urban experience defines what urban AIs are and what they do. Similarly, Valdez, Cook and Potter observe in Chapter 9 that the capabilities and actions of urban AIs are significantly influenced by the built environment and its inhabitants. Their research on delivery robots illustrates how urban AI can serve its function only if the interaction with urban residents works well. Human–AI relations in the urban context are thus central to the existence of urban AI. These relations can be facilitated through the design of the city, as in the case of Milton Keynes, a new town where robots have abundant space to circulate without impeding the mobility of other road users (Chapter 9). By the same token, urban design can hinder the relations between urban AIs and humans in contexts in which space is restricted and artificial and human intelligences have to compete for it (Gaio and Cugurullo, 2023).

Furthermore, the city has an influence on the intelligence of urban AI, in terms of how the quality of being intelligent is understood and perceived. Stilgoe and O'Donovan point out in Chapter 3 that urban consortia composed of private and public transport stakeholders make urban AIs such as AVs intelligent, at least superficially. They do so by conducting urban experiments to prove that AVs are indeed intelligent, designing and controlling these experiments so that they do not fail. Upon observing AV trials, the public's perception is that of intelligent machines capable of navigating complex urban spaces but, as the authors remark, this is precisely what the urban experiment has been predetermined to achieve. In these terms, the appearance of urban AI as an intelligent entity becomes a matter of public persuasion and, in turn, the city becomes the stage where the spectacle of artificial intelligence is performed.

Finally, the actual intelligence of urban AI, intended as the capacity to develop knowledge and use it to act spatially, is shaped by the urban context where it is present. Lynch and Del Casino in Chapter 17 find a strong connection between the logic followed by urban software agents and the logic underpinning the context in which these AIs operate. More specifically, they recognize in the operations of real-estate algorithms the capitalist logic of deregulated housing that is commonplace in many American cities, urging us to remember that the same logic is biased by 'racialized conceptualizations of space' (Fluri et al., 2020: 1). These findings resonate with Chapter 11 in which Lin and Yeo's work demonstrates that some urban cultures have negative effects on the manifestation of urban AI's intelligence, such as in the case of Singapore's airport where robots have been characterized in racist and sexist ways, mirroring the stereotypical image of low-wage workers. Overall, the collection highlights the agency of urban spaces and urban residents and its constitutive effect on the agency of urban AI. In this sense, Rosen and Garboden's findings from Chapter 20 are emblematic: landlords tune tenant-screening algorithms according to their interests and use them to reinforce their idiosyncrasies and to protect themselves from lawsuits. In the city, AI becomes both a shield and a weapon, in the hands of urban stakeholders, that can protect some interests while undermining others.

The legacy of smart urbanism

The emergence of urban AIs should not only be examined from a spatial perspective. It should also be situated temporally to see where this urban phenomenon is coming from and leading to. AI is, in relative terms, a novel technology. Some urban AIs such as city brains are very new technologies and are being invented and rolled out proximate to the time of this writing (Zhang et al., 2019). However, as we note in Chapter 1, urban AI has not emerged out of the blue, but rather it represents the most recent link in a long chain of techno-urban development, and its ancestry can be traced to smart urbanism (Cugurullo, 2021b). This link is particularly evident in Chapter 11 where Lin and Yeo describe how new urban AIs are being rolled out in Singapore as part of a long-standing smart-city programme, *Smart Singapore*, that was initiated in 2014. Most importantly, we need to critically examine the legacy of smart urbanism to shed light on how recurring urban issues and unsustainable dynamics of high-tech urban development and governance are being reproduced in the age of urban AI. It is of crucial importance to realize that the advent of AI is not a tabula rasa that eliminates all the problems that have been caused by smart cities, providing planners, policymakers and citizens with a fresh start. Quite the opposite: in the contemporary city, AI exacerbates past and present urban issues that, unless are fully comprehended and addressed, will come back with a vengeance and characterize the city of the future too.

A recurring problem that the contributors to this volume expose is the preponderant intrusion of private tech companies in the governance of cities. In Chapter 3, Stilgoe and O'Donovan emphasize the massive influence of technology companies in the governance of AVs, since they are the specialists supposed to enable the autonomy and intelligence of this type of urban AI. Similarly, Barns remarks in Chapter 12 that the owners of AI-mediated digital platforms also own the data that these AIs are collecting and often refuse to share it with city managers, thereby de facto governing a large portion of cities' data ecosystems singlehandedly. The delineation between private and public is increasingly blurred as governmental services and public infrastructures are outsourced to AI companies, as described by Sweeney in Chapter 18. In the not-so-distant past, the same issues were stressed by geographers and urbanists when major tech firms such as IBM and Cisco began to intervene in urban governance as part of early smart-city initiatives (Barns et al., 2017; McNeill, 2015; Vanolo, 2014). One crucial implication of such governance is that its mechanics remain opaque and impenetrable to city authorities. It reinforces power asymmetries by creating a condition in which AI companies know more about a city and its inhabitants than the government and the public do. In her chapter, Barns laments Airbnb's refusal to make its data available to city managers, despite the serious urban issues this digital platform leaves in its wake, including rental property shortages and gentrification-fueled residential evictions (Ferreri and Sanyal, 2018; Wachsmuth and Weisler, 2018).

These very mechanics are opaque to citizens. This volume provides evidence of the marginal role that citizens play in the implementation of urban AIs. Urban residents are largely removed from urban AI experiments, and when they do participate their role is often that of mere spectators (Chapters 3 and 14). Many people traverse urban environments while ignoring that public urban spaces are permeated by AIs sensing their presence and analysing their actions (Chapters 10 and 12). Most of the time, when individuals do engage with urban AIs, it is through uneven and obscure relations because artificial intelligence is capturing and processing private information in ways that are beyond the comprehension of human intelligence (Chapters 8, 11, 13, 16, 18, 19 and 21). These uneven and undemocratic dynamics resonate with one of the most long-standing and extensively discussed critiques of smart urbanism: that of the marginalized role of citizens in the smart city. For Gabrys (2014), people living in a smart city are simply data points, producing information that governments use to control them and private companies leverage to generate profits. Citizens are not involved in the governance of smart cities, apart from tokenistic forms of participation such as hackathons and citizen-science projects (Perng et al., 2018). Instead, they are governed in a paternalistic manner by authorities that profess to have a better understanding of a city's problems and priorities (Cardullo and Kitchin, 2019; Shelton and Lodato, 2019). As Cardullo, Di Feliciantonio, and Kitchin (2019) stress, the citizens' right to the smart city is largely missing, and this collection shows that this is still the case in the post-smart city mediated by AIs. The problem seems to be even more acute today, as one of the assumptions under-pinning urban governance in the age of AI is that *artificial* rather than *human* intelligences know better.

Furthermore, this volume finds a recurring syncretism between discourses about urban AI and *sustainability* discourses. In Chapter 4, for example, Hopkins' study indicates that the idea of sustainability is being instrumental-ized to push for the implementation and diffusion of urban AI. Her research reveals that AVs in particular are being hailed as a sustainable transport tech-nology on the grounds that they should be able to reduce car accidents and human fatalities. Similarly, in Chapters 14 and 15, Chen and Shapiro high-light that urban AI systems are wrapped in a logic of efficiency, as their pro-moters claim that the application of AI can improve a city's metabolic processes from environmental, social and economic points of view. These are the same discourses that smart-city researchers have repeatedly identified and critiqued. In the mid-2010s, there was a turn in smart-city discourses when *smart* started to be associated with *sustainable* (Bibri and Krogstie, 2017; Martin et al., 2018; Yigitcanlar et al., 2019). Today, *AI* is emerging as the new *sustainable*.

However, critical scholars noted that being *smart* does not necessarily mean being *sustainable* and today, we see a similar tension between AI and sustainability. In Chapter 2, Dowling, M⸦Guirk and Sisson's findings suggest that the scientific mission of urban AI experiments, supposed to benefit cities' sustainability, can conceal more pressing economic agendas. As their contri-bution shows, established companies such as Volvo, General Motors and Volkswagen run AV experiments to preserve their economic power in a rap-idly changing market, while new companies like NuTomony fight to become the new leaders with AI experiments as their weapon of choice. In this sense, the emergence of urban AI continues to be connected to the dynamics of *neoliberalism urbanism* that smart-city scholars have exposed for decades (Chakrabarty, 2019; Grossi and Pianezzi, 2017).

As previous studies on smart urbanism have reported, private tech compa-nies usually enter the field of urban governance to increase their market and accomplish their economic agendas, often to the detriment of non-monetiza-ble goals including social justice, environmental preservation and citizen wellbeing (Cugurullo, 2018; Macke et al., 2018; Mackinnon et al., 2022). This collection reveals how private tech companies (Amazon and Google, in particular) reinforce their influence in city governance to craft the city as the ideal market for their new AI products. However, we are hesitant to suggest that this is a neoliberal urbanism redux (Peck et al., 2013). This volume illustrates the cosmopolitan geography of urban AI compared to smart urbanism's largely Western-centric dynamics. In Asia, for example, hybrid tech giants such as Alibaba, Tencent, Huawei and Baidu combine elements of both private and public companies and their operations, so markedly prominent in the emergence of urban AI (Chapters 14, 16, 19), cannot be simply ascribed to Western neoliberalism.

In terms of the actual sustainability of urban AI, more empirical research is needed. However, this collection has already shown that the socio-environmental problems typical of smart cities continue to be present in the age of urban AI. A common denominator between smart technologies and AI technologies is that their production requires the extraction of critical raw materials (Crawford, 2021; Zhou et al., 2021). From an environmental sustainability perspective then, technology lingers as a double-edged sword. For example, AI technology can lower the carbon emissions of the city where it is applied in the shape of autonomous energy systems predicting and managing citizens' demand in an efficient manner, but it can also wreak ecological havoc in the places where it is produced and disposed of (Van Wynsberghe, 2021; Yigitcanlar and Cugurullo, 2020). Above all, what *efficiency* actually means in practice remains vague (Chapter 15). This is particularly evident with urban metabolic processes and experiences that cannot be easily measured and quantified. How AI can improve the efficiency of cities is highly debatable (Broussard, 2018). Even in relation to tangible urban issues such as ecosystem preservation and the provision of renewable energy, initial urban AI experiments are not maintaining their lofty environmental promises (Chapter 14). This is a worrying echo of the many broken environmental promises of smart-city experiments (Colding and Barthel, 2017; Cugurullo, 2021b; Koh et al., 2022; Rosol et al., 2017).

Finally, it is important to recognize that similar to smart technologies, urban AIs are prone to glitches, malfunctions and cyberattacks (Kitchin and Dodge, 2019; Leszczynski and Elwood, 2022). As Maalsen (2022: 456) reminds us, the digitalization of urban governance via smart urbanism has made cities 'programmable' but also 'ultimately hackable.' In the era of urban AI, cities continue to be susceptible to intentional and unintentional disruptions. The glitchy nature of urban AIs has been noted in this volume (Chapter 13). AI is a delicate technology requiring constant maintenance, monitoring and updates. Most problematically, it is a technology that is developing and growing exponentially. In the recent past, city managers and urban policymakers have struggled to keep up with the fast pace of smart urbanism's technological innovation, due to unwieldy planning and policy processes (Angelidou, 2017). As Vitale Brovarone and Staricco note in Chapter 6, today some city authorities are not even willing to fully commit to the transition to urban AI because they will not be around long enough to steer it through to completion. The emergence and repercussions of urban AI cover a temporal scale that is much longer than the timeframe of urban administrations. This was a huge challenge in smart-city initiatives and one which will undoubtably plague any city that is in the process of embracing urban AI.

The future of AI urbanism

In the age of urban AI, cities are undergoing intensive transformations that are changing their shape, metabolism and governance. There are connections with well-known practices of smart urbanism, but also departures with end points that are unpredictable. As we argued in Chapter 1, the proliferation of multiple urban AIs in the life, governance and planning of cities is producing a novel urbanism that we have termed *AI urbanism*. In this section, we draw upon the case studies examined in Parts I, II, III and IV to look at the distinctiveness of novel AI logics and manifestations in the urban context and inquire into the emergence of post-smart cities. We do so by operationalizing the three main axes of urban changes identified in the beginning of the volume, namely *function, presence* and *agency*.

First, several chapters showed that what urban AIs do in practice diverges from the function of traditional smart-city technologies. In Chapter 8, Jackman's study indicates that home-surveillance drones do not simply quantify urban phenomena by generating heatmaps that calculate and locate heat in a given urban space. They also give meaning to them by determining, for instance, whether the source of heat is coming from a potentially dangerous person who is not supposed to be there. Their functions, therefore, include a value judgement (in this case, the determination of someone's malevolence or goodness) that was absent in smart urbanism. Similarly, in Chapter 19, Guo and Cugurullo illustrate the actions of urban software agents that calculate as well as interpret, providing an account of the health of both entire cities and individual citizens. This distinction between *counting* and *accounting* is particularly evident in Chapter 20 where Rosen and Garboden point out that screening algorithms not only count people but also qualitatively evaluate them to distinguish between good and bad tenants. Likewise, in Chapter 21, Pisu and Carta reveal how, in the field of urban design, algorithms do not simply quantify urban spaces but also evaluate them and propose design solutions underpinned by assumptions of what constitutes good design. This distinction cuts across multiple urban domains and operations.

Second, this collection provides numerous empirical examples of the presence of urban AI as an overt sociotechnical phenomenon. Tangible cars driven by AI are trialled on public roads or in urban testbeds where the built environment is designed specifically to test AVs in a sheltered environment separated from everyday urban mobility (Chapters 2 and 3). Urban robots have a highly visible presence: we can see them and also be seen by them (Chapter 7). This type of urban AI needs space just like humans. When robots occupy urban spaces, they can hinder our movements, for example, as pedestrians unless the urban environment is spacious enough to accommodate both human and non-human mobilities (Chapter 9). As Sumartojo stresses in Chapter 10, their spatiality is embedded in the real world and this diverges from smart technologies, such as sensors and underground smart grids, that tend to be hidden from everyday life. Some urban AIs are a constant part of our daily life. Digital assistants animated by AI are present in our homes. They connect with a plethora of smart devices already present in domestic spaces, including smart speakers, smart TVs, cameras, thermostats and vacuum cleaners, making them their appendages whereby AI infiltrates our households and interacts with us (Chapter 18). This constant AI presence is something that we cannot ignore, particularly when urban software agents talk to us, inquiring about what we do, with whom and where (Chapter 19).

Third, this volume sheds light on the agency of urban AIs, examining their autonomy across several real-world examples. The question of autonomy is arguably one of the most complex aspects of urban AI and understanding its variegated nature requires nuance and a twofold perspective. On the one hand, the urban AIs discussed in this collection are *autonomous* rather than *automated*, in the sense that they do not follow prescribed routes or courses of action, acting instead in a non-repetitive manner and constantly changing their behaviour in space with little or no human supervision. AVs, for example, operate autonomously because a human driver is unnecessary and the machine is constantly adapting its route on a case-by-case basis (Chapters 3 and 5). Similarly, delivery robots are material artefacts that navigate complex urban spaces without guidance from a human supervisor (Chapter 9). Once in the field, police robots do not need to be instructed or prompted to act, potentially supplanting the role of public officers and urban managers (Chapter 7). Likewise, the inputs of urban planners, architects and urban designers are redirected and, at times, decreasing as some algorithms are capable of developing design solutions by themselves (Chapter 21).

On the other hand, the agency of urban AIs depends upon the actions of a number of people. During an urban experiment, for instance, marshals notify vulnerable road users that an AV is approaching (Chapter 3). On public roads, while there may be no human driver steering the wheel, for an AV to function autonomously a lot of *ghost work* is required, as Cugurullo and Kassens-Noor illustrate in Chapter 5. This work is usually carried out by underpaid workers whose main task is to clean and classify the data that AIs need to comprehend and navigate complex urban spaces (Gray and Suri, 2019). Furthermore, part of the computation that is necessary for an urban AI to make sense of the surrounding environment takes place elsewhere, such as in the case of urban robots whose computational capabilities rely on servers, clouds and digital platforms (Chapter 9). Thus, the autonomy of urban AIs has complex geographies that transcend the physical spaces where they are materially present.

It is also important to note that space constitutes a limitation on the autonomy of urban AIs, particularly in relation to their predictive capabilities. Urban AIs operate in real-life urban environments that are always *emerging*: they are constantly changing and far from being finite and finished spaces (Chapter 10). This spatial condition, characterized by an immanent indeterminacy, clashes with the logic of predictability underpinning AI which, de facto, is incapable of managing the uncertainty of urban futures, particularly over extended time periods (Luque-Ayala and Marvin, 2020). For this reason, urban AIs often operate together with human agents who employ their intuition (a quality that urban AI does not possess yet) to deal with uncertain scenarios (Chapter 19). Thus, urban AIs are only autonomous up to a point, and their sphere of influence is limited to what can be calculated since AI cannot predict what it cannot first calculate. When the urban future becomes incalculable and nebulous, it is necessary for humans to step in and exercise their autonomy together with that of machines in a relational manner.

However, this operational limitation does not necessarily mean that the impact of urban AIs is limited. In fact, most of the contributors portray urban situations in which the agency of urban AIs can have substantial consequences. Autonomous cars and trucks traverse chaotic urban spaces adjacent to other road users (Chapters 2, 3, 4 and 5). As Stilgoe's (2020) work demonstrates, in this complex context rich in uncertainty, an inaccurate sensor reading can be lethal for a pedestrian. Furthermore, even in the best-case scenario, accidents will not be completely eliminated and AVs will find themselves in the position of having to distribute inevitable harm (Awad et al., 2018). Comparatively, surveillance drones and police robots will not distribute inevitable harm: they will cause harm to individuals whom they perceive to be dangerous (Chapters 7 and 8). Similarly, urban software agents and algorithms will decide who is not a good tenant and does not have the right to occupy a place, and who is a suspicious citizen that deserves scrutiny by the police (Chapters 15 and 20). These are all ethical decisions freighted with life-changing repercussions that urban AI is catalyzing in post-smart cities where critical value judgements are no longer the exclusive domain of human stakeholders.

Urban AI and urban theory

The rise of urban AI is generating new dynamics in the governance, planning and everyday experience of cities. This collection provides empirical evidence of the presence of autonomous technologies that are populating the built environment and interacting with its inhabitants across multiple scales. These dynamics, characterized by urban AI's novel capacity to produce accounts of urban phenomena and shape their evolution without human supervision (in limited but nonetheless significant spheres of influence), are indicative of an urbanism that goes beyond the impacts of smart cities. We are witnessing the formation of *post*-smart cities in which an emerging AI urbanism is producing novel urban experiences, designs and forms of governance and potentially new urban spatialities that require new theorizations. In this section, we draw upon insights from this volume to develop a core set of theories and concepts that can help urban researchers and stakeholders make sense of the variegated relations between AI and the city.

First is the need to conceptualize the spatial dimensions of urban AIs. In Chapter 8, Jackman introduces the concept of *ambient AI* to illuminate the ubiquitous and yet seemingly invisible presence of urban AIs. Notwithstanding their often tangible materiality, the concept of ambience is helpful to highlight how some urban AIs, such as domestic robots and digital AI assistants, can disappear into the background of our lives, instead of imposing their presence upon us (Augusto and McCullagh, 2007; Payne and Macdonald, 2004). We often forget that urban AI is all around us, constantly observing and influencing what we do. On a related note, Sumartojo reflects in Chapter 10 on the notion and importance of *atmosphere*, paying attention to how urban AIs are perceived and felt in specific places and, in turn, how this perception changes the way a given place is experienced (Sumartojo and Pink, 2018). This is an important conceptual perspective that extends current AI studies, particularly in computer science, focusing on how AIs perceive space but not on how places perceive AIs (see, for example, Ke et al., 2020).

Second is the related question of how we should approach the ubiquity of urban AI as a pervasive ambient technology. For Barns, urban AIs should be understood as a form of *ambient commons* (Chapter 12). Drawing upon McCullough's (2013) theories, she proposes a commons-based approach to the regulation and application of urban AIs. The conceptual premise is to see public spaces and infrastructures as urban commons. In this sense, most urban AIs such as AVs, urban robots, city brains and AI digital platforms, should be seen as urban commons too, given that they are embedded in public spaces and infrastructures. This perspective provides a stepping stone to argue for the integration of hitherto missing principles of public and civil values in the deployment of urban AIs and for citizens to play an active role in AI urbanism. Furthermore, it complements contemporary AI studies in relation to the thorny issue of *alignment* (Dafoe et al., 2021; Gabriel, 2020; McDonald, 2022). Since urban AIs have become de facto materially *public* – surrounding and affecting urban residents – they should be aligned with the interests and needs of the public. Therefore, citizens should be regularly consulted on matters of urban AI and, as Moore and Bissell posit in Chapter 13, they also deserve the right to question it by exercising what Amoore (2019, 2020) refers to as an *ethics of doubt*.

Third is the question of how to effectively unpack the imaginaries and the trajectories of urban AI. Drawing upon Science and Technology Studies (STS) literature, Chen proposes, in Chapter 14, the concept of *sociotechnical imaginaries* as a useful framework to understand the lock-in pathways that make cities and societies dependent on new technologies (see Jasanoff and Kim, 2015). These imaginaries depict an idealized social and environmental order that AIs are supposed to enable (Sartori and Bocca, 2022). She considers how AI imaginaries embody a trajectory of urban development that some cities follow almost blindly without paying attention to what is behind these imaginaries and the lived conditions that they produce. These reflections are important because these imaginaries are shaped by local political contexts and, in the case of China for instance, they mirror the objectives of the Communist Party (Chapters 14, 16 and 19). On the ground, there are profound discrepancies between imagination and reality. For example, there is little or no evidence that urban AIs are supporting urban sustainability goals (Chapter 14). Thus, as urbanists and critical social scientists, we need to devise alternative signifiers to describe what urban AI represents and is actually doing on the ground. Some suggestions are provided in Chapter 5 in which urban AIs such as AVs are alternatively portrayed as *mobile data collectors*, *space-shapers* and *environmental drainers*, rather than idealized modes of sustainable transportation.

Fourth is the meaning of the concept of *intelligence* in urban AIs. In Chapter 17, Lynch and Del Casino use a relational perspective to study the intelligence of urban AIs and focus on the relations between a given urban AI and its urban context. They refer to the philosophy of Byung-Chul Han according to whom any intelligence depends on the system in which it functions (Han, 2017). From an urban perspective then, we can think of urban AIs as autonomous technologies that are incapable of exercising their intelligence outside of the urban context in which they are designed to operate. An AV, for example, can be intelligent only while it is traversing a flat public road. Similarly, a service robot designed to serve food can exercise its intelligence solely within specific contexts such as restaurants and cafes. Their sphere of influence is limited to their designated urban spaces. Moreover, as Guo and Cugurullo note in Chapter 19, there is an important conceptual distinction between *narrow* and *general* (urban) AIs, as most of the technologies discussed in this collection manifest intelligence exclusively in relation to single tasks, and the prospect of Artificial General Intelligence (AGI) seems to be far away from the contemporary urban landscape (Hirsch-Kreinsen, 2023).

Fifth, even if AGI is not around the corner, the presence of multiple urban AIs should make us reflect on our role as humans living in cities increasingly populated by non-biological intelligences. In Chapter 21, Pisu and Carta propose the figure of the *digital demiurge* intended as a human designer fully in charge of the production and design of urban spaces, who employs AI as a tool to craft the built environment. They stress the epistemological problems that arise when urban designers delegate their agency to an AI system whose mechanics are almost impossible to understand: the design would enter a *black box* and change through processes that lack transparency. The black-box conundrum of AI can be already seen in several domains (Carabantes, 2020). In addition to urban design, planning and architecture, we should carefully consider the black-box problem in relation to policy and governance. We need to question what happens when urban policies are developed by obscure AI systems and what the role of human policymakers should be in the age of large-scale urban AIs, such as city brains, that are currently applied to govern cities.

As Valdez, Cook and Potter suggest in Chapter 9, it is possible that a clear-cut conceptual distinction between human and artificial intelligences in the urban experience and governance of cities is too simplistic and thus unnecessary in the first place. They evoke the notion of the *cyborg city* to emphasize how contemporary organic (humans) and mechanical (robots) entities are converging as part of the same urban processes in a fluid manner (Gandy, 2005). Ultimately, what is clear in this collection is that with the emergence of multiple urban AIs, the composition of the population of cities is changing and so are their power-relations and governance. In this emerging urban order, characterized by a hybrid of humans and AIs, it is important to recognize that human stakeholders are no longer the sole intelligence influencing urban development. We propose *posthumanism* as a useful theoretical framework to interpret the decentering of human agents in the governance and life of cities, and capture the complexity of nonhierarchical networks of human and artificial intelligences (Hughes, 2018; Wolfe, 2010). Particularly, the rise of large-scale urban AIs, such as city brains and AI-driven urban platforms, indicates the formation of a *posthuman urban governance* which goes beyond the human in the sense that human agency constitutes only a portion of it: most actions and powers of governing come from intricate human–AI relations that are yet to be explored.

Conclusion: warnings and invitations

In the age of AI, the formation of a posthuman urban governance is a problematic prospect. However, by *problematic* we do not necessarily mean *catastrophic* or *apocalyptic*. On the one hand, this is a warning in the sense that hybrid urban experiences, power-relations and governance networks characterized by human stakeholders and urban AIs will be undoubtably difficult to manage and regulate. On the other hand, this is an invitation to examine what is actually happening on the ground and avoid what Floridi (2020, 2022) refers to as *sci-fi distractions* involving AGI and futuristic superintelligences that do not exist. These distractions have the tendency to shift our attention away from the real-world problems and opportunities generated by real-world AIs. In this spirit, a core aim and contribution of this collection has been to expose and interrogate, both empirically and theoretically, what happens in reality when existing AIs come into play in existing cities.

The findings of this volume clarify the complex processes of co-constitution and co-determination through which AI and the city co-evolve. They also have broader implications for AI studies and pertain to diverse disciplines such as computer science, philosophy, engineering, sociology and political science, which are collectively attempting to shed light on long-standing questions about the nature of non-biological intelligences and their regulation. This collection illuminates one of the most debated aspects of AI: its presumed capacity to think. Urban AIs do not think in the same way as humans and, therefore, it would be inappropriate to describe them as conscious entities. None of the urban AIs examined in this volume are capable of reflection and feeling emotions in a humanistic sense. Nonetheless, the same urban AIs are all capable of generating logics, rationalities and rule-sets that drive their actions and influence urban processes. Thus, it is important to acknowledge the fundamental difference between *thought* and *rationality*. Urban AI cannot think and, for example, reflect upon an ideal form of urban development, but it can produce a logical explanation that would make a certain form of urban development seem consistent with or based upon reason.

This volume's case studies provide multiple examples. Home-surveillance drones do not have the capacity to reflect on the nature of good and evil, but they can conclude that an intruder represents a dangerous individual (Chapter 8). Urban software agents cannot reflect on the social and economic implications of a pandemic lockdown, but they can reach the conclusion that a growing number of infected citizens justifies a limit to their mobility, to avoid a disease outbreak (Chapter 19). These findings are in line with recent debates about the intelligence of emerging generative AIs such as ChatGPT and Dall-E which can act and perform complex tasks in a rational manner, including the creation of new content, without actually grasping the implication and meaning of their actions (Floridi, 2023).

In addition, we draw on Flyvbjerg (1998) to stress that, especially in urban planning and governance, rationality is often shaped by power and discourses. In the context of this study, therefore, urban AI could seem intelligent, as in capable of rational thought and driven by reason, while in reality, this capacity might be simply a label imposed by powerful human stakeholders. During a trial, an autonomous car might appear to be intelligent because of the way it navigates a complex urban space, but this could be a performance scripted by a consortium of private and public actors (Chapter 3). Real-estate algorithms might give the impression of thinking, but it is more likely that they are simply reproducing preexisting power-relations in the housing market (Chapter 17). As Natale (2021) warns us, many AIs are purposely deceptive: they are built to appear intelligent and their alleged intelligence becomes a veil hiding speculations and inequalities. This is an important warning that resonates with past urban experiments in which labels such as *eco, smart, resilient* and *low-carbon* were hiding unecological urban spaces (Avery and Moser, 2023; Cugurullo, 2021b; De Jong et al., 2015; Xie et al., 2019). This is also an invitation to critically examine potential discrepancies between the labels attached to urban AIs and their actual performance.

Several case studies also show that the level of intelligence of urban AIs is decoupled from their capacity to draw conclusions and make decisions. While it would be ambiguous to say that urban AIs can think and incorrect to state that AVs, urban robots, city brains and urban software agents can reason like humans, this volume provides evidence of the decision-making capabilities of these technologies. Without following the same cognitive process as human road users, an AV can decide in a split second what route to take in a way that surpasses human speed (Chapter 4). Similarly, city brains can quickly reconfigure a city's flow of energy and vehicles by simultaneously making complex decisions about urban transport and energy systems (Chapters 14 and 16). However, even if their decision-making skill is faster than that of humans and tends to embrace more than one issue at the same time, it lacks ethical considerations precisely because of urban AI's inability to reason like a human stakeholder. Furthermore, the decisions made by urban AIs often lack nuance. For example, if a screening algorithm is assessing your profile, either you qualify as a tenant and you get the opportunity to rent a property, or you do not even if you are only missing a dollar (Chapter 20). This is of course problematic because real-life urban experiences and systems are characterized by shades of grey, rendering the binary logics by which urban AIs reach their conclusions too simplistic.

More problematically, the decisions that urban AIs make are at times not just simplistic but are also incorrect and biased. There is an epistemological discrepancy between how several urban AIs digitally represent reality and the actually existing cities. For instance, there are distortions between a digital twin created by a city brain and its material counterpart (Chapter 14). The decisions of urban AIs are frequently divorced from reality, as in the case of real-estate estimate algorithms that significantly overprice properties (Chapter 17). As Shapiro remarks in Chapter 15, such distortions can be exacerbated by the use of *dirty data* defined as 'data that is derived from or influenced by corrupt, biased, and unlawful practices, including data that has been intentionally manipulated' (Richardson et al., 2019: 18; see also Liang et al., 2022).

There is a need to be cautious about the decisions of urban AIs, not simply in relation to their impact on contemporary cities, but also in their influence on urban futures. This collection exposes the future-oriented nature of urban AIs' logics and actions. Urban AI can be both *predictive* and *prescriptive* (Chapter 15). In addition to predicting likely urban scenarios, it gives directives on what should be done to enable certain urban futures while preempting others. This is an invitation to carefully regulate urban AIs from an urbanistic perspective, with a double focus on present and future repercussions on urban living, governance and sustainability. Such regulatory efforts should go beyond current legislation and ethical frameworks about AI that, as Munn (2023) laments, are too abstract and general (also see Mökander et al., 2022; Roberts et al., 2022). This volume clearly shows that a single, universal AI does not exist. When AI becomes materially situated in the city, multiple heterogenous urban AIs emerge, ranging from autonomous cars to weaponized police robots and from home-surveillance drones to city brains. Their urban impact and role in cities must be highly regulated on a case-by-case basis. A task like this will not be easy because of how deregulated many cities are in the first place (particularly in environments where urban and digital spaces mesh) but, given the plethora of problems discussed so far, the need to regulate urban AIs is necessary and urgent (Boeing et al., 2021; Ferreri and Sanyal, 2018).

We stand at a critical juncture in the history of the city. Through this collection, we see how what Cugurullo (2020) terms the passage from *automation* to *autonomy* in urbanism is occurring across spaces and scales, with its effects already visible in numerous urban AI experiments. There are evident similarities with common smart-city initiatives, but also significant points of departure and challenges. In post-smart cities, traces of smart urbanism will remain and continue to influence urban processes. Looking back at its history, smart urbanism started as a niche in the late 1990s to quickly emerge as a global urban phenomenon that generated an explosion of smart-city projects (Joss et al., 2019). A similar escalation in AI urbanism has the potential to substantially shape the future of new and existing cities. What this volume has illustrated is likely only the beginning.

In many existing cities, urban AIs are becoming popular because they fill a void created by anaemic and underfunded public services. Citizens, for example, are lacking public child- and elder-care services and thus rely on Amazon's AI home assistants (Chapter 18). Similarly, dysfunctional public transport systems result in excruciating commutes, leading commuters to contemplate the idea of autonomous cars as an idealized alternative where they can sleep or work while traversing the city in a self-driving vehicle (Chapters 5 and 6). In some cases, these dreams culminate in fully *autonomous cities*, such as The Line in Saudi Arabia, where key urban services and operations are expected to be 'run not by *human* but by *artificial* intelligences' (Cugurullo, 2021b: 14; also see Allam and Takun, 2022). Rather than dreaming of autonomous urban futures enabled by AIs, we may be better served by focusing on addressing the deficiencies in urban services and experiences that fuel such dreams.

The risks embodied in autonomous cities are not those of sci-fi apocalyptic scenarios that pit humans against artificial superintelligences (Bostrom, 2017). Instead, they involve the amplification of the real-world problems discussed in this volume, such as the formation of comprehensive states of surveillance, issues of alignment, injustice and epistemological distortions between how AI sees the city and the actual urban experience. These risks created by technological innovations cannot be addressed by simply banning AI. Indeed, it is difficult to imagine an urban future in which AI will not be present in one form or another. Instead, they must be addressed by thinking carefully about the ways that we design and use urban AIs. At the end of the day, as this volume clarifies, many of the problems, risks and challenges of urban AIs are not intrinsic to the technologies per se but are an end result of how different urban AIs are deployed. This makes them social, political and, above all, urbanistic problems that we can fix or, at the very least mitigate, by improving the urban planning and governance processes whereby AI enters into our cities.

Conceptually, one way forward could be to reverse the fourth axis identified in Chapter 1 and rephrase the *discourse* that surrounds the passage from smart to AI urbanism, with a focus on the crucial issue of control. This is about abandoning the idea of fully autonomous urban AIs and autonomous cities where control over the course of urban development and living has been delegated to non-biological intelligences. This would follow the example of a city like San Francisco where the citizens fought politically for their own vision of the city of the future, resisting some forms of autonomous urban AI (Chapter 7). This also means striving to provide citizens with access to the obscure black boxes that animate the numerous urban AIs populating our urban public spaces and demand regular reality checks to verify the actual sustainability impact of urban AI imaginaries across time and space. These are all examples of urban political acts that urbanists have been advocating for a long time (Baviskar, 2020; Leitheiser et al., 2022; Swyngedouw, 2018). We have shown that AI changes the nature of cities as much as the city changes the nature of AI, and we need to remind ourselves that we are the city.

References

Acheampong, R. A., & Cugurullo, F. (2019). Capturing the behavioural determinants behind the adoption of autonomous vehicles: Conceptual frameworks and measurement models to predict public transport, sharing and ownership trends of self-driving cars. *Transportation Research Part F: Traffic Psychology and Behaviour*, 62, 349–375.

Allam, Z., & Takun, Y. R. (2022). Future smart and autonomous cities: an overview toward future trends. In Allam, Z., & Takun, Y. R. (Eds.). *Rethinking smart cities*. Edward Elgar Publishing.

Amoore, L. (2019). Doubt and the algorithm: On the partial accounts of machine learning. *Theory, Culture & Society*, 36(6), 147–169.

Amoore, L. (2020). *Cloud ethics: Algorithms and the attributes of ourselves and others*. Duke University Press.

Angelidou, M. (2014). Smart city policies: A spatial approach. *Cities*, 41, S3–S11.

Angelidou, M. (2017). Smart city planning and development shortcomings. *TeMA-Journal of Land Use, Mobility and Environment*, 10(1), 77–94.

Angelo, H., & Wachsmuth, D. (2020). Why does everyone think cities can save the planet?. *Urban Studies*, 57(11), 2201–2221.

Aoyama, Y., & Leon, L. F. A. (2021). Urban governance and autonomous vehicles. *Cities*, 119, 103410.

Attoh, K. A. (2011). What kind of right is the right to the city?. *Progress in human geography*, 35(5), 669–685.

Augusto, J. C., & McCullagh, P. (2007). Ambient intelligence: Concepts and applications. *Computer Science and Information Systems*, 4(1), 1–27.

Avery, E., & Moser, S. (2023). Prizes for Fantasy: The Role of the Urban Awards Industry in Validating Greenfield Eco-Cities. Available at SSRN 4086319.

Awad, E., Dsouza, S., Kim, R., Schulz, J., Henrich, J., Shariff, A., ... & Rahwan, I. (2018). The moral machine experiment. *Nature*, 563(7729), 59–64.

Barns, S., Cosgrave, E., Acuto, M., & Mcneill, D. (2017). Digital infrastructures and urban governance. *Urban Policy and Research*, 35(1), 20–31.

Baviskar, A. (2020). *Uncivil city: Ecology, equity and the commons in Delhi*. Sage Publications.

Beukers, E., & Bertolini, L. (2021). Learning for transitions: An experiential learning strategy for urban experiments. *Environmental Innovation and Societal Transitions*, 40, 395–407.

Bibri, S. E., & Krogstie, J. (2017). Smart sustainable cities of the future: An extensive interdisciplinary literature review. *Sustainable Cities and Society*, 31, 183–212.

Blanchard, A. (2023). Autonomous force beyond armed conflict. *Minds and Machines*.

Blanchard, J. M. F., & Flint, C. (2017). The geopolitics of China's maritime silk road initiative. *Geopolitics*, 22(2), 223–245.

Boeing, G., Besbris, M., Wachsmuth, D., & Wegmann, J. (2021). Tilted platforms: rental housing technology and the rise of urban big data oligopolies. *Urban Transformations*, 3(1), 1–10.

Bostrom, N. (2017). *Superintelligence*. Oxford University Press.

Brayne, S. (2017). Big data surveillance: The case of policing. *American Sociological Review*, 82(5), 977–1008.

Brenner, N. (2014). *Implosions/explosions: Towards a study of planetary urbanization*. Jovis.

Broussard, M. (2018). *Artificial unintelligence: How computers misunderstand the world*. MIT Press.

Campa, R., Szocik, K., & Braddock, M. (2019). Why space colonization will be fully automated. *Technological Forecasting and Social Change*, 143, 162–171.

Carabantes, M. (2020). Black-box artificial intelligence: an epistemological and critical analysis. *AI & Society*, 35(2), 309–317.

Cardullo, P., Di Feliciantonio, C., & Kitchin, R. (Eds.). (2019). *The right to the smart city*. Emerald Group Publishing.

Cardullo, P., & Kitchin, R. (2019). Being a 'citizen'in the smart city: Up and down the scaffold of smart citizen participation in Dublin, Ireland. *GeoJournal*, 84(1), 1–13.

Castells, M. (2011). *The rise of the network society*. John Wiley & Sons.

Chakrabarty, A. (2019). Smart mischief: an attempt to demystify the Smart Cities craze in India. *Environment and Urbanization*, 31(1), 193–208.

Colding, J., & Barthel, S. (2017). An urban ecology critique on the "Smart City" model. *Journal of Cleaner Production*, 164, 95–101.

Couclelis, H. (2004). The construction of the digital city. *Environment and Planning B: Planning and Design*, 31(1), 5–19.

Crawford, K. (2021). *Atlas of AI: Power, politics, and the planetary costs of artificial intelligence*. Yale University Press.

Cugurullo, F. (2018). Exposing smart cities and eco-cities: Frankenstein urbanism and the sustainability challenges of the experimental city. *Environment and Planning A: Economy and Space*, 50(1), 73–92.

Cugurullo, F. (2020). Urban artificial intelligence: From automation to autonomy in the smart city. *Frontiers in Sustainable Cities*, 2, 38.

Cugurullo, F. (2021a). "One AI to rule them all": The Unification of Chinese Urban Governance Under Artificial Intelligence. *GREEN*, 1(1), 123–126.

Cugurullo, F. (2021b). *Frankenstein urbanism: Eco, smart and autonomous cities, artificial intelligence and the end of the city*. Routledge.

Cugurullo, F., & Acheampong, R. A. (2023). Fear of AI: an inquiry into the adoption of autonomous cars in spite of fear, and a theoretical framework for the study of artificial intelligence technology acceptance. *AI & Society*, 1–16.

Cugurullo, F., Acheampong, R. A., Gueriau, M., & Dusparic, I. (2021). The transition to autonomous cars, the redesign of cities and the future of urban sustainability. *Urban Geography*, 42(6), 833–859.

Dafoe, A., Bachrach, Y., Hadfield, G., Horvitz, E., Larson, K., & Graepel, T. (2021). Cooperative AI: machines must learn to find common ground. *Nature*, 593(7857), 33–36.

Dauvergne, P. (2020). *AI in the wild: Sustainability in the age of artificial intelligence*. MIT Press.

De Jong, M., Joss, S., Schraven, D., Zhan, C., & Weijnen, M. (2015). Sustainable–smart–resilient–low carbon–eco–knowledge cities; making sense of a multitude of concepts promoting sustainable urbanization. *Journal of Cleaner production*, 109, 25–38.

Dowling, R., & McGuirk, P. (2022). Autonomous vehicle experiments and the city. *Urban Geography*, 43(3), 409–426.

Escandon-Barbosa, D., Salas-Paramo, J., Meneses-Franco, A. I., & Giraldo-Gonzalez, C. (2021). Adoption of new technologies in developing countries: The case of autonomous car between Vietnam and Colombia. *Technology in Society*, 66, 101674.

Evans, J., Karvonen, A., & Raven, R. (2016). *The experimental city*. Routledge.

Ferreri, M., & Sanyal, R. (2018). Platform economies and urban planning: Airbnb and regulated deregulation in London. *Urban Studies*, 55(15), 3353–3368.

Fields, D. (2022). Automated landlord: Digital technologies and post-crisis financial accumulation. *Environment and Planning A: Economy and Space*, 54(1).

Floridi, L. (2020). Artificial intelligence as a public service: Learning from Amsterdam and Helsinki. *Philosophy & Technology*, 33(4), 541–546.

Floridi, L. (2022). Ultraintelligent Machines, Singularity, and Other Sci-fi Distractions about AI. Lavoro, Diritti, Europa. Available at: https://www.lavorodirittieuropa.it/images/Ultraintelligent_Machines.pdf [Accessed 19/01/2023]

Floridi, L. (2023). AI as Agency without Intelligence: On ChatGPT, large language models, and other generative models. *Philosophy & Technology*, 36(1), 15.

Fluri, J. L., Hickcox, A., Frydenlund, S., & Zackary, R. (2020). Accessing racial privilege through property: Geographies of racial capitalism. *Geoforum*, 132, 238–246.

Flyvbjerg, B. (1998). *Rationality and power: Democracy in practice*. University of Chicago Press.

Gabriel, I. (2020). Artificial intelligence, values, and alignment. *Minds and Machines*, 30(3), 411–437.

Gabrys, J. (2014). Programming environments: Environmentality and citizen sensing in the smart city. *Environment and Planning D: Society and Space*, 32(1), 30–48.

Gaio, A., & Cugurullo, F. (2023). Cyclists and autonomous vehicles at odds: Can the transport oppression cycle be broken in the era of artificial intelligence? *AI & Society*, 38(3), 1223–1237.

Gandy, M. (2005). Cyborg urbanization: complexity and monstrosity in the contemporary city. *International Journal of Urban and Regional Research*, 29(1), 26–49.

Gelernter, D. (1993). *Mirror worlds: Or the day software puts the universe in a shoebox... How it will happen and what it will mean*. Oxford University Press.

Graham, S., & Marvin, S. (2002). *Splintering urbanism: networked infrastructures, technological mobilities and the urban condition*. Routledge.

Gray, M. L., & Suri, S. (2019). *Ghost work: How to stop Silicon Valley from building a new global underclass*. Eamon Dolan Books.

Greenfield, A. (2018). *Radical technologies: The design of everyday life*. Verso Books.

Grossi, G., & Pianezzi, D. (2017). Smart cities: Utopia or neoliberal ideology?. *Cities*, 69, 79–85.

Guo, J., & Li, B. (2018). The application of medical artificial intelligence technology in rural areas of developing countries. *Health Equity*, 2(1), 174–181.

Hall, P. (2014). *Cities of tomorrow: An intellectual history of urban planning and design since 1880*. John Wiley & Sons.

Han, B-C. (2017). *Psychopolitics: Neoliberalism and new technologies of power*. Verso.

Harvey, D. (2008). The right to the city. In LeGates, R. T., & Stout, F. (Eds.). *The city reader*. Routledge. 23–40.

Hawkins, J., & Nurul Habib, K. (2019). Integrated models of land use and transportation for the autonomous vehicle revolution. *Transport Reviews*, 39(1), 66–83.

Hirsch-Kreinsen, H. (2023). Artificial intelligence: a "promising technology". *AI & Society*, 1–12.

Hughes, J. (2018). Algorithms and posthuman governance. *Journal of Posthuman Studies*, 1(2), 166–184.

Jain, M., & Korzhenevych, A. (2022). The concept of planetary urbanization applied to India's rural to urban transformation. *Habitat International*, 129, 102671.

Jasanoff, S., & Kim, S. H. (2015). *Dreamscapes of modernity: Sociotechnical imaginaries and the fabrication of power*. University of Chicago Press.

Jeong, H. Y., Song, B. D., & Lee, S. (2022). Optimal scheduling and quantitative analysis for multi-flying warehouse scheduling problem: Amazon airborne fulfillment center. *Transportation Research Part C: Emerging Technologies*, 143, 103831.

Joss, S., Sengers, F., Schraven, D., Caprotti, F., & Dayot, Y. (2019). The smart city as global discourse: Storylines and critical junctures across 27 cities. *Journal of Urban Technology*, 26(1), 3–34.

Karvonen, A., Cugurullo, F., & Caprotti, F. (2019). *Inside smart cities*. Routledge.

Ke, R., Zhuang, Y., Pu, Z., & Wang, Y. (2020). A smart, efficient, and reliable parking surveillance system with edge artificial intelligence on IoT devices. *IEEE Transactions on Intelligent Transportation Systems*, 22(8), 4962–4974.

Kelly, S., Kaye, S. A., & Oviedo-Trespalacios, O. (2022). What factors contribute to acceptance of artificial intelligence? A Systematic Review. *Telematics and Informatics*, 101925.

Kitchin, R., & Dodge, M. (2019). The (in) security of smart cities: Vulnerabilities, risks, mitigation, and prevention. *Journal of Urban Technology*, 26(2), 47–65.

Kitchin, R., & Moore-Cherry, N. (2021). Fragmented governance, the urban data ecosystem and smart city-regions: The case of Metropolitan Boston. *Regional Studies*, 55(12), 1913–1923.

Koh, S. Y., Zhao, Y., & Shin, H. B. (2022). Moving the mountain and greening the sea: the micropolitics of speculative green urbanism at Forest City, Iskandar Malaysia. *Urban Geography*, 43(10), 1469–1495.

Koops, B. J. (2021). The concept of function creep. *Law, Innovation and Technology*, 13(1), 29–56.

Lally, N. (2022). 'It makes almost no difference which algorithm you use': on the modularity of predictive policing. *Urban Geography*, 43(9), 1437–1455.

Larson, W., & Zhao, W. (2020). Self-driving cars and the city: Effects on sprawl, energy consumption, and housing affordability. *Regional Science and Urban Economics*, 81, 103484.

Lee, K.F. (2018). *AI superpowers: China, Silicon Valley, and the new world order*. Houghton Mifflin.

Leitheiser, S., Trell, E. M., Horlings, I., & Franklin, A. (2022). Toward the commoning of governance. *Environment and Planning C: Politics and Space*, 40(3), 744–762.

Leszczynski, A., & Elwood, S. (2022). Glitch epistemologies for computational cities. *Dialogues in Human Geography*, 12(3), 361–378.

Li, J., & Huang, J. S. (2020). Dimensions of artificial intelligence anxiety based on the integrated fear acquisition theory. *Technology in Society*, 63, 101410.

Liang, W., Tadesse, G. A., Ho, D., Fei-Fei, L., Zaharia, M., Zhang, C., & Zou, J. (2022). Advances, challenges and opportunities in creating data for trustworthy AI. *Nature Machine Intelligence*, 4(8), 669–677.

Lockhart, A., While, A., Marvin, S., Kovacic, M., Odendaal, N., & Alexander, C. (2021). Making space for drones: The contested reregulation of airspace in Tanzania and Rwanda. *Transactions of the Institute of British Geographers*, 46(4), 850–865.

Luque-Ayala, A., & Marvin, S. (2020). *Urban operating systems: Producing the computational city*. MIT Press.

Luusua, A., Ylipulli, J., Foth, M., & Aurigi, A. (2023). Urban AI: understanding the emerging role of artificial intelligence in smart cities. *AI & Society*, 8, 1039–1044.

Maalsen, S. (2022). The hack: What it is and why it matters to urban studies. *Urban Studies*, 59(2), 453–465.

Macke, J., Casagrande, R. M., Sarate, J. A. R., & Silva, K. A. (2018). Smart city and quality of life: Citizens' perception in a Brazilian case study. *Journal of Cleaner Production*, 182, 717–726.

Mackinnon, D., Burns, R., & Fast, V. (Eds.). (2022). *Digital (in) justice in the Smart City*. University of Toronto Press.

Martin, C. J., Evans, J., & Karvonen, A. (2018). Smart and sustainable? Five tensions in the visions and practices of the smart-sustainable city in Europe and North America. *Technological Forecasting and Social Change*, 133, 269–278.

McCarroll, C., & Cugurullo, F. (2022). No city on the horizon: Autonomous cars, artificial intelligence, and the absence of urbanism. *Frontiers in Sustainable Cities*, 4, 184.

McCullough, M. (2013). *Ambient commons: Attention in the age of embodied information*. MIT Press.

McDonald, F. J. (2022). AI, alignment, and the categorical imperative. *AI and Ethics*, 1–8.

McNeill, D. (2015). Global firms and smart technologies: IBM and the reduction of cities. *Transactions of the Institute of British Geographers*, 40(4), 562–574.

Miller, B., Ward, K., Burns, R., Fast, V., & Levenda, A. (2021). Worlding and provincialising smart cities: From individual case studies to a global comparative research agenda. *Urban Studies*, 58(3), 655–673.

Mökander, J., Juneja, P., Watson, D. S., & Floridi, L. (2022). The US Algorithmic Accountability Act of 2022 vs. The EU Artificial Intelligence Act: what can they learn from each other?. *Minds and Machines*, 32, 751–758.

Munn, L. (2023). The uselessness of AI ethics. *AI and Ethics*, 1–9.

Natale, S. (2021). *Deceitful media: Artificial intelligence and social life after the Turing test*. Oxford University Press.

Payne, R., & Macdonald, B. (2004). Ambient technology—Now you see It, now you don't. *BT Technology Journal*, 22(3), 119–129.

Peck, J., Theodore, N., & Brenner, N. (2013). Neoliberal urbanism redux?. *International Journal of Urban and Regional Research*, 37(3), 1091–1099.

Perng, S. Y., Kitchin, R., & Mac Donncha, D. (2018). Hackathons, entrepreneurial life and the making of smart cities. *Geoforum*, 97, 189–197.

Richardson, R., Schultz, J., & Crawford, K. (2019). Dirty data, bad predictions: How civil rights violations impact police data, predictive policing systems, and justice. *NYUL Review Online*, 94, 15.

Roberts, H., Cowls, J., Hine, E., Morley, J., Wang, V., Taddeo, M., & Floridi, L. (2022). Governing artificial intelligence in China and the European Union: Comparing aims and promoting ethical outcomes. *The Information Society*, 1–19.

Roberts, H., Cowls, J., Morley, J., Taddeo, M., Wang, V., & Floridi, L. (2021). The Chinese approach to artificial intelligence: an analysis of policy, ethics, and regulation. *Ethics, Governance, and Policies in Artificial Intelligence*, 47–79.

Rosol, M., Béal, V., & Mössner, S. (2017). Greenest cities? The (post-) politics of new urban environmental regimes. *Environment and Planning A: Economy and Space*, 49(8), 1710–1718.

Sanchez, T. W., Shumway, H., Gordner, T., & Lim, T. (2022). The prospects of artificial intelligence in urban planning. *International Journal of Urban Sciences*, 1–16.

Sartori, L., & Bocca, G. (2022). Minding the gap (s): public perceptions of AI and socio-technical imaginaries. *AI & Society*, 1–16.

Shelton, T., & Lodato, T. (2019). Actually existing smart citizens: Expertise and (non) participation in the making of the smart city. *City*, 23(1), 35–52.

Silva, Ó., Cordera, R., González-González, E., & Nogués, S. (2022). Environmental impacts of autonomous vehicles: A review of the scientific literature. *Science of the Total Environment*, 154615.

Stilgoe, J. (2020). *Who's driving innovation. New technologies and the collaborative state*. Palgrave Macmillan.

Sumartojo, S., & Pink, S. (2018). *Atmospheres and the experiential world: Theory and methods*. Routledge.

Swyngedouw, E. (2018). *Promises of the political: Insurgent cities in a post-political environment*. MIT Press.

Umlauf, R., & Burchardt, M. (2022). Infrastructure-as-a-service: Empty skies, bad roads, and the rise of cargo drones. *Environment and Planning A: Economy and Space*, 54(8), 1489–1509.

Van Wynsberghe, A. (2021). Sustainable AI: AI for sustainability and the sustainability of AI. *AI and Ethics*, 1(3), 213–218.

Vanolo, A. (2014). Smartmentality: The smart city as disciplinary strategy. *Urban Studies*, 51(5), 883–898.

Wachsmuth, D., & Weisler, A. (2018). Airbnb and the rent gap: Gentrification through the sharing economy. *Environment and Planning A: Economy and Space*, 50(6), 1147–1170.

While, A. H., Marvin, S., & Kovacic, M. (2021). Urban robotic experimentation: San Francisco, Tokyo and Dubai. *Urban Studies*, 58(4), 769–786.

Willis, K., & Aurigi, A. (2017). *Digital and smart cities*. Routledge.

Wolfe, C. (2010). *What is posthumanism?* University of Minnesota Press.

Xie, L., Flynn, A., Tan-Mullins, M., & Cheshmehzangi, A. (2019). The making and remaking of ecological space in China: The political ecology of Chongming Eco-Island. *Political Geography*, 69, 89–102.

Ye, X., Newman, G., Lee, C., Van Zandt, S., & Jourdan, D. (2023). Toward Urban artificial intelligence for developing justice-oriented smart cities. *Journal of Planning Education and Research*, 43(1), 6–7.

Yigitcanlar, T., Agdas, D., & Degirmenci, K. (2023). Artificial intelligence in local governments: perceptions of city managers on prospects, constraints and choices. *AI & Society*, 38, 1135–1150.

Yigitcanlar, T., & Cugurullo, F. (2020). The sustainability of artificial intelligence: An urbanistic viewpoint from the lens of smart and sustainable cities. *Sustainability*, 12(20), 8548.

Yigitcanlar, T., Kamruzzaman, M., Foth, M., Sabatini-Marques, J., da Costa, E., & Ioppolo, G. (2019). Can cities become smart without being sustainable? A systematic review of the literature. *Sustainable Cities and Society*, 45, 348–365.

Zhang, J., Hua, X. S., Huang, J., Shen, X., Chen, J., Zhou, Q., ... & Zhao, Y. (2019). City brain: practice of large-scale artificial intelligence in the real world. *IET Smart Cities*, 1(1), 28–37.

Zhou, L., Fan, H., & Ulrich, T. (2021). Editorial for special issue "critical metals in hydrothermal ores: Resources, recovery, and challenges". *Minerals*, 11(3), 299.

Zuboff, S. (2019). *The age of surveillance capitalism: The fight for a human future at the new frontier of power*. Profile Books.

INDEX

Pages in *italics* refer to figures, pages in **bold** refer to tables, and pages followed by "n" refer to notes.